General Motors
Buick Regal
Chevrolet Lumina
Olds Cutlass Supreme
Pontiac Grand Prix
Automotive Repair Manual

by Robert Maddox
and John H Haynes
Member of the Guild of Motoring Writers

Models covered:
Buick Regal (1988 thru 2004)
Olds Cutlass Supreme (1988 thru 1997)
Pontiac Grand Prix (1988 thru 2007)
Chevrolet Lumina (1990 thru 1994)

(38010-3M21-2)
(1671)

ABCDE
FGHIJ
KLMNO
PQRS 3

Haynes Publishing Group
Sparkford Nr Yeovil
Somerset BA22 7JJ England

Haynes North America, Inc
861 Lawrence Drive
Newbury Park
California 91320 USA

Acknowledgements

Wiring diagrams provided exclusively for Haynes North America, Inc. by Valley Forge Technical Communications. Technical writers who contributed to this project include Tim Imhoff, Larry Warren and Brian Styve.

A book in the Haynes Automotive Repair Manual Series

Printed in the U.S.A.

ISBN-13: 978-1-56392-726-3
ISBN-10: 1-56392-726-8

Library of Congress Contol Number 2008929368

Contents

About this manual   0-5
Introduction to the Chevrolet Lumina, Oldsmobile Cutlass,
    Buick Regal and Pontiac Grand Prix   0-5
Vehicle identification numbers   0-6
Buying parts   0-7
Maintenance techniques, tools and working facilities   0-7
Booster battery (jump) starting   0-15
Jacking and towing   0-16
Automotive chemicals and lubricants   0-17
Conversion factors   0-18
Fraction/decimal/millimeter equivalents   0-19
Safety first!   0-20
Troubleshooting   0-21

Chapter 1
Tune-up and routine maintenance   **1-1**

Chapter 2 Part A
2.2 liter four-cylinder engine   **2A-1**

Chapter 2 Part B
2.5 liter four-cylinder engine   **2B-1**

Chapter 2 Part C
2.3 liter four-cylinder (Quad-4) engine   **2C-1**

Chapter 2 Part D
2.8L, 3.1L and 3100 V6 engines   **2D-1**

Chapter 2 Part E
3.4 liter V6 engine   **2E-1**

Chapter 2 Part F
3800 V6 engine   **2F-1**

Chapter 2 Part G
V8 engine   **2G-1**

Chapter 2 Part H
General engine overhaul procedures   **2H-1**

Chapter 3
Cooling, heating and air conditioning systems   **3-1**

Chapter 4
Fuel and exhaust systems   **4-1**

Chapter 5
Engine electrical systems   **5-1**

Chapter 6
Emissions and engine control systems   **6-1**

Chapter 7 Part A
Manual transaxle   **7A-1**

Chapter 7 Part B
Automatic transaxle   **7B-1**

Chapter 8
Clutch and driveaxles   **8-1**

Chapter 9
Brakes   **9-1**

Chapter 10
Suspension and steering systems   **10-1**

Chapter 11
Body   **11-1**

Chapter 12
Chassis electrical system and wiring diagrams   **12-1**

Index   **IND-1**

Haynes author, photographer and mechanic with 1990 Oldsmobile Cutlass

About this manual

Its purpose

The purpose of this manual is to help you get the best value from your vehicle. It can do so in several ways. It can help you decide what work must be done, even if you choose to have it done by a dealer service department or a repair shop; it provides information and procedures for routine maintenance and servicing; and it offers diagnostic and repair procedures to follow when trouble occurs.

We hope you use the manual to tackle the work yourself. For many simpler jobs, doing it yourself may be quicker than arranging an appointment to get the vehicle into a shop and making the trips to leave it and pick it up. More importantly, a lot of money can be saved by avoiding the expense the shop must pass on to you to cover its labor and overhead costs. An added benefit is the sense of satisfaction and accomplishment that you feel after doing the job yourself.

Using the manual

The manual is divided into Chapters. Each Chapter is divided into numbered Sections, which are headed in bold type between horizontal lines. Each Section consists of consecutively numbered paragraphs.

At the beginning of each numbered Section you will be referred to any illustrations which apply to the procedures in that Section. The reference numbers used in illustration captions pinpoint the pertinent Section and the Step within that Section. That is, illustration 3.2 means the illustration refers to Section 3 and Step (or paragraph) 2 within that Section.

Procedures, once described in the text, are not normally repeated. When it's necessary to refer to another Chapter, the reference will be given as Chapter and Section number. Cross references given without use of the word "Chapter" apply to Sections and/or paragraphs in the same Chapter. For example, "see Section 8" means in the same Chapter.

References to the left or right side of the vehicle assume you are sitting in the driver's seat, facing forward.

Even though we have prepared this manual with extreme care, neither the publisher nor the author can accept responsibility for any errors in, or omissions from, the information given.

NOTE

A **Note** provides information necessary to properly complete a procedure or information which will make the procedure easier to understand.

CAUTION

A **Caution** provides a special procedure or special steps which must be taken while completing the procedure where the Caution is found. Not heeding a Caution can result in damage to the assembly being worked on.

WARNING

A **Warning** provides a special procedure or special steps which must be taken while completing the procedure where the Warning is found. Not heeding a Warning can result in personal injury.

Introduction to the Chevrolet Lumina, Oldsmobile Cutlass, Buick Regal and Pontiac Grand Prix

These front-wheel drive full-size General Motors vehicles, sometimes referred to as the "W" body style or 10 series, are available in two and four-door sedan body styles.

Engines used in these vehicles include the 2.2 liter and 2.5 liter overhead valve (OHV) four-cylinder, the 2.3 liter overhead cam (OHC) Quad-4 cylinder, the 2.8 liter V6, the 3.1 liter and 3100 V6, the 3.4 liter double overhead cam V6, 3800 V6 and the 5.3L V8.

Throttle body injection (TBI) is used on the 2.5 liter four-cylinder engine. All other engines are equipped with multi-port fuel injection.

The engine drives the front wheels through either a manual or automatic transaxle via driveaxles equipped with Constant Velocity (CV) joints. The power assisted rack and pinion steering is mounted behind the engine.

The front suspension is composed of MacPherson struts, three point control arms and a stabilizer bar. The rear suspension is independent, with trailing arms, strut/shock absorber units, a transversely mounted leaf spring, and in some cases coil springs.

The brakes are disc at all four wheels on most models, although some are equipped with drums at the rear wheels. Power assist is standard equipment.

Vehicle identification numbers

Modifications are a continuing and unpublicized part of vehicle manufacturing. Since spare parts manuals and lists are compiled on a numerical basis, the individual vehicle numbers are essential to correctly identify the component required.

Vehicle Identification Number (VIN)

This very important identification number is stamped on a plate attached to the left side of the dashboard and is visible through the driver's side of the windshield (see illustration). The VIN also appears on the Vehicle Certificate of Title and Registration. It contains valuable information such as where and when the vehicle was manufactured, the model year and the body style.

Body identification plate

This metal plate is usually located on the top side of the radiator support or on the upper surface of the fan shroud. Like the VIN, it contains important information concerning the production of the vehicle as well as information about how the vehicle came equipped from the factory. It's especially useful for matching the color and type of paint during repair work.

Service parts identification label

This label is located in the trunk, usually either on the inside of the trunk lid or on the spare tire cover. It lists the VIN number, wheelbase, paint number, options and other information specific to the vehicle it's attached to. Always refer to this label when ordering parts.

Engine identification numbers

The engine code number on the 2.2 liter and 2.5 liter four-cylinder engine is stamped on a pad on the radiator side, at the rear of the block. The 2.3 liter OHC (Quad-4) engine VIN number is stamped into the rear of the block, near the starter motor. The Quad-4 engine also has a code label attached to the rear edge of the timing belt housing. On V6 engines, the code number is found on a pad on the rear of the block, just above the starter motor. On the 3800, the number is also stamped on a pad adjacent to the water pump. On 5.3L V8 models, the number is found on the left side at the rear of the engine.

Manual transaxle number

The Muncie transaxle has an adhesive-backed identification label attached to the rear of the case and an ID number stamped into the front. On the Getrag five-speed transaxle, the VIN is on a pad at the front (radiator) side of the case edge, near the bellhousing. If the transaxle label is missing or unreadable, use the Service parts identification label to determine which transaxle was installed at the factory.

Automatic transaxle number

The nameplate/ID number on the THM 125C/3T40 transaxle is attached to the upper surface of the case, near the rear (see illustration). On the 440-T4/4T60-E and 4T65-E transaxle, the transaxle VIN number is stamped into the right rear of the housing; a unit number label is attached above it.

Vehicle Emissions Control Information label

This label is found in the engine compartment. See Chapter 6 for more information on this label.

The Vehicle Identification Number (VIN) is on a plate attached to the top of the dashboard on the driver's side of the vehicle - it can be seen from outside the vehicle, looking through the windshield

On the THM 125 transaxle, the ID number is on a plate attached to the upper surface of the transmission case

Buying parts

Replacement parts are available from many sources, which generally fall into one of two categories - authorized dealer parts departments and independent retail auto parts stores. Our advice concerning these parts is as follows:

Retail auto parts stores: Good auto parts stores will stock frequently needed components which wear out relatively fast, such as clutch components, exhaust systems, brake parts, tune-up parts, etc. These stores often supply new or reconditioned parts on an exchange basis, which can save a considerable amount of money. Discount auto parts stores are often very good places to buy materials and parts needed for general vehicle maintenance such as oil, grease, filters, spark plugs, belts, touch-up paint, bulbs, etc. They also usually sell tools and general accessories, have convenient hours, charge lower prices and can often be found not far from home.

Authorized dealer parts department: This is the best source for parts which are unique to the vehicle and not generally available elsewhere (such as major engine parts, transmission parts, trim pieces, etc.).

Warranty information: If the vehicle is still covered under warranty, be sure that any replacement parts purchased - regardless of the source - do not invalidate the warranty!

To be sure of obtaining the correct parts, have engine and chassis numbers available and, if possible, take the old parts along for positive identification.

Maintenance techniques, tools and working facilities

Maintenance techniques

There are a number of techniques involved in maintenance and repair that will be referred to throughout this manual. Application of these techniques will enable the home mechanic to be more efficient, better organized and capable of performing the various tasks properly, which will ensure that the repair job is thorough and complete.

Fasteners

Fasteners are nuts, bolts, studs and screws used to hold two or more parts together. There are a few things to keep in mind when working with fasteners. Almost all of them use a locking device of some type, either a lockwasher, locknut, locking tab or thread adhesive. All threaded fasteners should be clean and straight, with undamaged threads and undamaged corners on the hex head where the wrench fits. Develop the habit of replacing all damaged nuts and bolts with new ones. Special locknuts with nylon or fiber inserts can only be used once. If they are removed, they lose their locking ability and must be replaced with new ones.

Rusted nuts and bolts should be treated with a penetrating fluid to ease removal and prevent breakage. Some mechanics use turpentine in a spout-type oil can, which works quite well. After applying the rust penetrant, let it work for a few minutes before trying to loosen the nut or bolt. Badly rusted fasteners may have to be chiseled or sawed off or removed with a special nut breaker, available at tool stores.

If a bolt or stud breaks off in an assembly, it can be drilled and removed with a special tool commonly available for this purpose. Most automotive machine shops can perform this task, as well as other repair procedures, such as the repair of threaded holes that have been stripped out.

Flat washers and lockwashers, when removed from an assembly, should always be replaced exactly as removed. Replace any damaged washers with new ones. Never use a lockwasher on any soft metal surface (such as aluminum), thin sheet metal or plastic.

Fastener sizes

For a number of reasons, automobile manufacturers are making wider and wider use of metric fasteners. Therefore, it is important to be able to tell the difference between standard (sometimes called U.S. or SAE) and metric hardware, since they cannot be interchanged.

All bolts, whether standard or metric, are sized according to diameter, thread pitch and length. For example, a standard 1/2 - 13 x 1 bolt is 1/2 inch in diameter, has 13 threads per inch and is 1 inch long. An M12 - 1.75 x 25 metric bolt is 12 mm in diameter, has a thread pitch of 1.75 mm (the distance between threads) and is 25 mm long. The two bolts are nearly identical, and easily confused, but they are not interchangeable.

In addition to the differences in diameter, thread pitch and length, metric and standard bolts can also be distinguished by examining the bolt heads. To begin with, the distance across the flats on a standard bolt head is measured in inches, while the same dimension on a metric bolt is sized in millimeters (the same is true for nuts). As a result, a standard wrench should not be used on a metric bolt and a metric wrench should not be used on a standard bolt. Also, most standard bolts have slashes radiating out from the center of the head to denote the grade or strength of the bolt, which is an indication of the amount of torque that can be applied to it. The greater the number of slashes, the greater the strength of the bolt. Grades 0 through 5 are commonly used on automobiles. Metric bolts have a property class (grade) number, rather than a slash, molded into their heads to indicate bolt strength. In this case, the higher the number, the stronger the bolt. Property class numbers 8.8, 9.8 and 10.9 are commonly used on automobiles.

Strength markings can also be used to distinguish standard hex nuts from metric hex nuts. Many standard nuts have dots stamped into one side, while metric nuts are marked with a number. The greater the number of dots, or the higher the number, the greater the strength of the nut.

Metric studs are also marked on their ends according to property class (grade). Larger studs are numbered (the same as metric bolts), while smaller studs carry a geometric code to denote grade.

It should be noted that many fasteners, especially Grades 0 through 2, have no distinguishing marks on them. When such is the case, the only way to determine whether it is standard or metric is to measure the thread pitch or compare it to a known fastener of the same size.

Standard fasteners are often referred to as SAE, as opposed to metric. However, it should be noted that SAE technically refers to a non-metric fine thread fastener only. Coarse thread non-metric fasteners are referred to as USS sizes.

Grade 1 or 2   Grade 5   Grade 8

Bolt strength marking (standard/SAE/USS; bottom - metric)

Grade	Identification	Grade	Identification
Hex Nut Grade 5	3 Dots	Hex Nut Property Class 9	Arabic 9
Hex Nut Grade 8	6 Dots	Hex Nut Property Class 10	Arabic 10

Standard hex nut strength markings

Metric hex nut strength markings

Class 10.9   Class 9.8   Class 8.8

Metric stud strength markings

Since fasteners of the same size (both standard and metric) may have different strength ratings, be sure to reinstall any bolts, studs or nuts removed from your vehicle in their original locations. Also, when replacing a fastener with a new one, make sure that the new one has a strength rating equal to or greater than the original.

Tightening sequences and procedures

Most threaded fasteners should be tightened to a specific torque value (torque is the twisting force applied to a threaded component such as a nut or bolt). Overtightening the fastener can weaken it and cause it to break, while undertightening can cause it to eventually come loose. Bolts, screws and studs, depending on the material they are made of and their thread diameters, have specific torque values, many of which are noted in the Specifications at the beginning of each Chapter. Be sure to follow the torque recommendations closely. For fasteners not assigned a specific torque, a general torque value chart is presented here as a guide. These torque values are for dry (unlubricated) fasteners threaded into steel or cast iron (not alumi-num). As was previously mentioned, the size and grade of a fastener determine the amount of torque that can safely be applied to it. The figures listed here are approximate for Grade 2 and Grade 3 fasteners. Higher grades can tolerate higher torque values.

Fasteners laid out in a pattern, such as cylinder head bolts, oil pan bolts, differential cover bolts, etc., must be loosened or tightened in sequence to avoid warping the component. This sequence will normally be shown in the appropriate Chapter. If a specific pattern is not given, the following procedures can be used to prevent warping.

Metric thread sizes	Ft-lbs	Nm
M-6	6 to 9	9 to 12
M-8	14 to 21	19 to 28
M-10	28 to 40	38 to 54
M-12	50 to 71	68 to 96
M-14	80 to 140	109 to 154
Pipe thread sizes		
1/8	5 to 8	7 to 10
1/4	12 to 18	17 to 24
3/8	22 to 33	30 to 44
1/2	25 to 35	34 to 47
U.S. thread sizes		
1/4 - 20	6 to 9	9 to 12
5/16 - 18	12 to 18	17 to 24
5/16 - 24	14 to 20	19 to 27
3/8 - 16	22 to 32	30 to 43
3/8 - 24	27 to 38	37 to 51
7/16 - 14	40 to 55	55 to 74
7/16 - 20	40 to 60	55 to 81
1/2 - 13	55 to 80	75 to 108

00-2 HAYNES

Standard (SAE and USS) bolt dimensions/grade marks

- G   Grade marks (bolt strength)
- L   Length (in inches)
- T   Thread pitch (number of threads per inch)
- D   Nominal diameter (in inches)

Metric bolt dimensions/grade marks

- P   Property class (bolt strength)
- L   Length (in millimeters)
- T   Thread pitch (distance between threads in millimeters)
- D   Diameter

Micrometer set

Dial indicator set

Initially, the bolts or nuts should be assembled finger-tight only. Next, they should be tightened one full turn each, in a criss-cross or diagonal pattern. After each one has been tightened one full turn, return to the first one and tighten them all one-half turn, following the same pattern. Finally, tighten each of them one-quarter turn at a time until each fastener has been tightened to the proper torque. To loosen and remove the fasteners, the procedure would be reversed.

Component disassembly

Component disassembly should be done with care and purpose to help ensure that the parts go back together properly. Always keep track of the sequence in which parts are removed. Make note of special characteristics or marks on parts that can be installed more than one way, such as a grooved thrust washer on a shaft. It is a good idea to lay the disassembled parts out on a clean surface in the order that they were removed. It may also be helpful to make sketches or take instant photos of components before removal.

When removing fasteners from a component, keep track of their locations. Sometimes threading a bolt back in a part, or putting the washers and nut back on a stud, can prevent mix-ups later. If nuts and bolts cannot be returned to their original locations, they should be kept in a compartmented box or a series of small boxes. A cupcake or muffin tin is ideal for this purpose, since each cavity can hold the bolts and nuts from a particular area (i.e. oil pan bolts, valve cover bolts, engine mount bolts, etc.). A pan of this type is especially helpful when working on assemblies with very small parts, such as the carburetor, alternator, valve train or interior dash and trim pieces. The cavities can be marked with paint or tape to identify the contents.

Whenever wiring looms, harnesses or connectors are separated, it is a good idea to identify the two halves with numbered pieces of masking tape so they can be easily reconnected.

Gasket sealing surfaces

Throughout any vehicle, gaskets are used to seal the mating surfaces between two parts and keep lubricants, fluids, vacuum or pressure contained in an assembly.

Many times these gaskets are coated with a liquid or paste-type gasket sealing compound before assembly. Age, heat and pressure can sometimes cause the two parts to stick together so tightly that they are very difficult to separate. Often, the assembly can be loosened by striking it with a soft-face hammer near the mating surfaces. A regular hammer can be used if a block of wood is placed between the hammer and the part. Do not hammer on cast parts or parts that could be easily damaged. With any particularly stubborn part, always recheck to make sure that every fastener has been removed.

Avoid using a screwdriver or bar to pry apart an assembly, as they can easily mar the gasket sealing surfaces of the parts, which must remain smooth. If prying is absolutely necessary, use an old broom handle, but keep in mind that extra clean up will be necessary if the wood splinters.

After the parts are separated, the old gasket must be carefully scraped off and the gasket surfaces cleaned. Stubborn gasket material can be soaked with rust penetrant or treated with a special chemical to soften it so it can be easily scraped off. A scraper can be fashioned from a piece of copper tubing by flattening and sharpening one end. Copper is recommended because it is usually softer than the surfaces to be scraped, which reduces the chance of gouging the part. Some gaskets can be removed with a wire brush, but regardless of the method used, the mating surfaces must be left clean and smooth. If for some reason the gasket surface is gouged, then a gasket sealer thick enough to fill scratches will have to be used during reassembly of the components. For most applications, a non-drying (or semi-drying) gasket sealer should be used.

Hose removal tips

Warning: *If the vehicle is equipped with air conditioning, do not disconnect any of the A/C hoses without first having the system depressurized by a dealer service department or a service station.*

Hose removal precautions closely parallel gasket removal precautions. Avoid scratching or gouging the surface that the hose mates against or the connection may leak. This is especially true for radiator hoses. Because of various chemical reactions, the rubber in hoses can bond itself to the metal spigot that the hose fits over. To remove a hose, first loosen the hose clamps that secure it to the spigot. Then, with slip-joint pliers, grab the hose at the clamp and rotate it around the spigot. Work it back and forth until it is completely free, then pull it off. Silicone or other lubricants will ease removal if they can be applied between the hose and the outside of the spigot. Apply the same lubricant to the inside of the hose and the outside of the spigot to simplify installation.

As a last resort (and if the hose is to be replaced with a new one anyway), the rubber can be slit with a knife and the hose peeled from the spigot. If this must be done, be careful that the metal connection is not damaged.

If a hose clamp is broken or damaged, do not reuse it. Wire-type clamps usually weaken with age, so it is a good idea to replace them with screw-type clamps whenever a hose is removed.

Tools

A selection of good tools is a basic requirement for anyone who plans to maintain and repair his or her own vehicle. For the owner who has few tools, the initial investment might seem high, but when compared to the spiraling costs of professional auto maintenance and repair, it is a wise one.

To help the owner decide which tools are needed to perform the tasks detailed in this manual, the following tool lists are offered: *Maintenance and minor repair, Repair/over-*

Dial caliper

Hand-operated vacuum pump

Timing light

Compression gauge with spark plug hole adapter

Damper/steering wheel puller

General purpose puller

Hydraulic lifter removal tool

haul and *Special.*

The newcomer to practical mechanics should start off with the *maintenance and minor repair* tool kit, which is adequate for the simpler jobs performed on a vehicle. Then, as confidence and experience grow, the owner can tackle more difficult tasks, buying additional tools as they are needed. Eventually the basic kit will be expanded into the *repair and overhaul* tool set. Over a period of time, the experienced do-it-yourselfer will assemble a tool set complete enough for most repair and overhaul procedures and will add tools from the special category when it is felt that the expense is justified by the frequency of use.

Maintenance and minor repair tool kit

The tools in this list should be considered the minimum required for performance of routine maintenance, servicing and minor repair work. We recommend the purchase of combination wrenches (box-end and open-

Valve spring compressor

Valve spring compressor

Ridge reamer

Piston ring groove cleaning tool

Ring removal/installation tool

end combined in one wrench). While more expensive than open end wrenches, they offer the advantages of both types of wrench.

> Combination wrench set (1/4-inch to
>   1 inch or 6 mm to 19 mm)
> Adjustable wrench, 8 inch
> Spark plug wrench with rubber insert
> Spark plug gap adjusting tool
> Feeler gauge set
> Brake bleeder wrench
> Standard screwdriver (5/16-inch x
>   6 inch)
> Phillips screwdriver (No. 2 x 6 inch)
> Combination pliers - 6 inch
> Hacksaw and assortment of blades
> Tire pressure gauge
> Grease gun
> Oil can
> Fine emery cloth
> Wire brush
> Battery post and cable cleaning tool
> Oil filter wrench
> Funnel (medium size)
> Safety goggles
> Jackstands (2)
> Drain pan

Note: *If basic tune-ups are going to be part of routine maintenance, it will be necessary to purchase a good quality stroboscopic timing*

light and combination tachometer/dwell meter. Although they are included in the list of special tools, it is mentioned here because they are absolutely necessary for tuning most vehicles properly.

Repair and overhaul tool set

These tools are essential for anyone who plans to perform major repairs and are in addition to those in the maintenance and minor repair tool kit. Included is a comprehensive set of sockets which, though expensive, are invaluable because of their versatility, especially when various extensions and drives are available. We recommend the 1/2-inch drive over the 3/8-inch drive. Although the larger drive is bulky and more expensive, it has the capacity of accepting a very wide range of large sockets. Ideally, however, the mechanic should have a 3/8-inch drive set and a 1/2-inch drive set.

> Socket set(s)
> Reversible ratchet
> Extension - 10 inch
> Universal joint
> Torque wrench (same size drive as
>   sockets)
> Ball peen hammer - 8 ounce
> Soft-face hammer (plastic/rubber)

Ring compressor

> Standard screwdriver (1/4-inch x 6 inch)
> Standard screwdriver (stubby -
>   5/16-inch)
> Phillips screwdriver (No. 3 x 8 inch)
> Phillips screwdriver (stubby - No. 2)
> Pliers - vise grip
> Pliers - lineman's
> Pliers - needle nose
> Pliers - snap-ring (internal and external)
> Cold chisel - 1/2-inch

Cylinder hone

Brake hold-down spring tool

Scribe
Scraper (made from flattened copper
    tubing)
Centerpunch
Pin punches (1/16, 1/8, 3/16-inch)
Steel rule/straightedge - 12 inch
Allen wrench set (1/8 to 3/8-inch or
    4 mm to 10 mm)
A selection of files

Wire brush (large)
Jackstands (second set)
Jack (scissor or hydraulic type)
Note: Another tool which is often useful is an
electric drill with a chuck capacity of 3/8-inch
and a set of good quality drill bits.

Special tools

    The tools in this list include those which
are not used regularly, are expensive to buy,
or which need to be used in accordance with
their manufacturer's instructions. Unless
these tools will be used frequently, it is not
very economical to purchase many of them. A
consideration would be to split the cost and
use between yourself and a friend or friends.
In addition, most of these tools can be
obtained from a tool rental shop on a temporary basis.
    This list primarily contains only those
tools and instruments widely available to the
public, and not those special tools produced
by the vehicle manufacturer for distribution to
dealer service departments. Occasionally, references to the manufacturer's special tools
are included in the text of this manual. Generally, an alternative method of doing the job
without the special tool is offered. However,

sometimes there is no alternative to their use.
Where this is the case, and the tool cannot be
purchased or borrowed, the work should be
turned over to the dealer service department
or an automotive repair shop.

Valve spring compressor
Piston ring groove cleaning tool
Piston ring compressor
Piston ring installation tool
Cylinder compression gauge
Cylinder ridge reamer
Cylinder surfacing hone
Cylinder bore gauge
Micrometers and/or dial calipers
Hydraulic lifter removal tool
Balljoint separator
Universal-type puller
Impact screwdriver
Dial indicator set
Stroboscopic timing light (inductive
    pick-up)
Hand operated vacuum/pressure pump
Tachometer/dwell meter
Universal electrical multimeter
Cable hoist
Brake spring removal and installation
    tools
Floor jack

Torque angle gauge

Clutch plate alignment tool

Tap and die set

Buying tools

For the do-it-yourselfer who is just starting to get involved in vehicle maintenance and repair, there are a number of options available when purchasing tools. If maintenance and minor repair is the extent of the work to be done, the purchase of individual tools is satisfactory. If, on the other hand, extensive work is planned, it would be a good idea to purchase a modest tool set from one of the large retail chain stores. A set can usually be bought at a substantial savings over the individual tool prices, and they often come with a tool box. As additional tools are needed, add-on sets, individual tools and a larger tool box can be purchased to expand the tool selection. Building a tool set gradually allows the cost of the tools to be spread over a longer period of time and gives the mechanic the freedom to choose only those tools that will actually be used.

Tool stores will often be the only source of some of the special tools that are needed, but regardless of where tools are bought, try to avoid cheap ones, especially when buying screwdrivers and sockets, because they won't last very long. The expense involved in replacing cheap tools will eventually be greater than the initial cost of quality tools.

Care and maintenance of tools

Good tools are expensive, so it makes sense to treat them with respect. Keep them clean and in usable condition and store them properly when not in use. Always wipe off any dirt, grease or metal chips before putting them away. Never leave tools lying around in the work area. Upon completion of a job, always check closely under the hood for tools that may have been left there so they won't get lost during a test drive.

Some tools, such as screwdrivers, pliers, wrenches and sockets, can be hung on a panel mounted on the garage or workshop wall, while others should be kept in a tool box or tray. Measuring instruments, gauges, meters, etc. must be carefully stored where they cannot be damaged by weather or impact from other tools.

When tools are used with care and stored properly, they will last a very long time. Even with the best of care, though, tools will wear out if used frequently. When a tool is damaged or worn out, replace it. Subsequent jobs will be safer and more enjoyable if you do.

How to repair damaged threads

Sometimes, the internal threads of a nut or bolt hole can become stripped, usually from overtightening. Stripping threads is an all-too-common occurrence, especially when working with aluminum parts, because aluminum is so soft that it easily strips out.

Usually, external or internal threads are only partially stripped. After they've been cleaned up with a tap or die, they'll still work. Sometimes, however, threads are badly damaged. When this happens, you've got three choices:

1) *Drill and tap the hole to the next suitable oversize and install a larger diameter bolt, screw or stud.*
2) *Drill and tap the hole to accept a threaded plug, then drill and tap the plug to the original screw size. You can also buy a plug already threaded to the original size. Then you simply drill a hole to the specified size, then run the threaded plug into the hole with a bolt and jam nut. Once the plug is fully seated, remove the jam nut and bolt.*
3) *The third method uses a patented thread repair kit like Heli-Coil or Slimsert. These easy-to-use kits are designed to repair damaged threads in straight-through holes and blind holes. Both are available as kits which can handle a variety of sizes and thread patterns. Drill the hole, then tap it with the special included tap. Install the Heli-Coil and the hole is back to its original diameter and thread pitch.*

Regardless of which method you use, be sure to proceed calmly and carefully. A little impatience or carelessness during one of these relatively simple procedures can ruin your whole day's work and cost you a bundle if you wreck an expensive part.

Working facilities

Not to be overlooked when discussing tools is the workshop. If anything more than routine maintenance is to be carried out, some sort of suitable work area is essential.

It is understood, and appreciated, that many home mechanics do not have a good workshop or garage available, and end up removing an engine or doing major repairs outside. It is recommended, however, that the overhaul or repair be completed under the cover of a roof.

A clean, flat workbench or table of comfortable working height is an absolute necessity. The workbench should be equipped with a vise that has a jaw opening of at least four inches.

As mentioned previously, some clean, dry storage space is also required for tools, as well as the lubricants, fluids, cleaning solvents, etc. which soon become necessary.

Sometimes waste oil and fluids, drained from the engine or cooling system during normal maintenance or repairs, present a disposal problem. To avoid pouring them on the ground or into a sewage system, pour the used fluids into large containers, seal them with caps and take them to an authorized disposal site or recycling center. Plastic jugs, such as old antifreeze containers, are ideal for this purpose.

Always keep a supply of old newspapers and clean rags available. Old towels are excellent for mopping up spills. Many mechanics use rolls of paper towels for most work because they are readily available and disposable. To help keep the area under the vehicle clean, a large cardboard box can be cut open and flattened to protect the garage or shop floor.

Whenever working over a painted surface, such as when leaning over a fender to service something under the hood, always cover it with an old blanket or bedspread to protect the finish. Vinyl covered pads, made especially for this purpose, are available at auto parts stores.

Booster battery (jump) starting

Observe the following precautions when using a booster battery to start a vehicle:

a) *Before connecting the booster battery, make sure the ignition switch is in the Off position.*

b) *Turn off the lights, heater and other electrical loads.*

c) *Your eyes should be shielded. Safety goggles are a good idea.*

d) *Make sure the booster battery is the same voltage as the dead one in the vehicle.*

e) *The two vehicles MUST NOT TOUCH each other.*

f) *Make sure the transmission is in Neutral (manual transaxle) or Park (automatic transaxle).*

g) *If the booster battery is not a maintenance-free type, remove the vent caps and lay a cloth over the vent holes.*

Connect the red jumper cable to the positive (+) terminals of each battery.

Connect one end of the black cable to the negative (-) terminal of the booster battery. The other end of this cable should be connected to a good ground on the engine block **(see illustration)**. Make sure the cable will not come into contact with the fan, drivebelts or other moving parts of the engine.

Start the engine using the booster battery, then, with the engine running at idle speed, disconnect the jumper cables in the reverse order of connection.

Make the booster battery cable connections in the numerical order shown (note that the negative cable of the booster battery is NOT attached to the negative terminal of the dead battery)

Jacking and towing

Jacking

Warning: *The jack supplied with the vehicle should only be used for changing a tire or placing jackstands under the frame. Never work under the vehicle or start the engine while this jack is being used as the only means of support.*

The vehicle should be on level ground. Place the shift lever in Park, if you have an automatic, or Reverse if you have a manual transaxle. Block the wheel diagonally opposite the wheel being changed. Set the parking brake.

Remove the spare tire and jack from stowage. Remove the wheel cover and trim ring (if so equipped) with the tapered end of the lug nut wrench by inserting and twisting the handle and then prying against the back of the wheel cover. On aluminum wheels, tap the back side of the wheel hub cover after removing the wheel (do not attempt to pull off the wheel hub cover by hand). Loosen, but do not remove, the lug nuts (one-half turn is sufficient).

Place the scissors-type jack under the side of the vehicle and adjust the jack height until it fits between the notches in the vertical rocker panel flange nearest the wheel to be changed. There is a front and rear jacking point on each side of the vehicle **(see illustration)**.

Turn the jack handle clockwise until the tire clears the ground. Remove the lug nuts and pull the wheel off. Replace it with the spare.

Install the lug nuts with the beveled edges facing in. Tighten them snugly. Don't attempt to tighten them completely until the vehicle is lowered or it could slip off the jack. Turn the jack handle counterclockwise to lower the vehicle. Remove the jack and tighten the lug nuts in a diagonal pattern.

Install the cover (and trim ring, if used) and be sure it's snapped into place all the way around.

Stow the tire, jack and wrench. Unblock the wheels.

Towing

As a general rule, the vehicle should be towed with the front (drive) wheels off the ground. If they can't be raised, place them on a dolly. The ignition key must be in the ACC position, since the steering lock mechanism isn't strong enough to hold the front wheels straight while towing.

On 1990 and earlier models, vehicles equipped with an automatic transaxle can be towed from the front only with all four wheels on the ground, provided that speeds don't exceed 30 mph and the distance is not over 50 miles. Before towing, check the transmission fluid level (see Chapter 1). If the level is below the HOT line on the dipstick, add fluid or use a towing dolly.

When towing a vehicle equipped with a manual transaxle with all four wheels on the ground, be sure to place the shift lever in neutral and release the parking brake.

Equipment specifically designed for towing should be used. It should be attached to the main structural members of the vehicle, not the bumpers or brackets.

Safety is a major consideration when towing and all applicable state and local laws must be obeyed. A safety chain system must be used at all times.

On 1991 and later models, the manufacturer does not recommend towing except with a towing dolly under the front wheels. In an emergency the vehicle can be towed a short distance with a cable or chain attached to one of the towing eyelets located under the front or rear bumpers following the precautions above. The driver must remain in the vehicle to operate the steering and brakes (remember that power steering and power brakes will not work with the engine off).

Jacking points

GRAND PRIX

8 inches   5.5 inches

Automotive chemicals and lubricants

A number of automotive chemicals and lubricants are available for use during vehicle maintenance and repair. They include a wide variety of products ranging from cleaning solvents and degreasers to lubricants and protective sprays for rubber, plastic and vinyl.

Cleaners

Carburetor cleaner and choke cleaner is a strong solvent for gum, varnish and carbon. Most carburetor cleaners leave a dry-type lubricant film which will not harden or gum up. Because of this film it is not recommended for use on electrical components.

Brake system cleaner is used to remove brake dust, grease and brake fluid from the brake system, where clean surfaces are absolutely necessary. It leaves no residue and often eliminates brake squeal caused by contaminants.

Electrical cleaner removes oxidation, corrosion and carbon deposits from electrical contacts, restoring full current flow. It can also be used to clean spark plugs, carburetor jets, voltage regulators and other parts where an oil-free surface is desired.

Demoisturants remove water and moisture from electrical components such as alternators, voltage regulators, electrical connectors and fuse blocks. They are non-conductive and non-corrosive.

Degreasers are heavy-duty solvents used to remove grease from the outside of the engine and from chassis components. They can be sprayed or brushed on and, depending on the type, are rinsed off either with water or solvent.

Lubricants

Motor oil is the lubricant formulated for use in engines. It normally contains a wide variety of additives to prevent corrosion and reduce foaming and wear. Motor oil comes in various weights (viscosity ratings) from 0 to 50. The recommended weight of the oil depends on the season, temperature and the demands on the engine. Light oil is used in cold climates and under light load conditions. Heavy oil is used in hot climates and where high loads are encountered. Multi-viscosity oils are designed to have characteristics of both light and heavy oils and are available in a number of weights from 0W-20 to 20W-50.

Gear oil is designed to be used in differentials, manual transmissions and other areas where high-temperature lubrication is required.

Chassis and wheel bearing grease is a heavy grease used where increased loads and friction are encountered, such as for wheel bearings, balljoints, tie-rod ends and universal joints.

High-temperature wheel bearing grease is designed to withstand the extreme temperatures encountered by wheel bearings in disc brake equipped vehicles. It usually contains molybdenum disulfide (moly), which is a dry-type lubricant.

White grease is a heavy grease for metal-to-metal applications where water is a problem. White grease stays soft under both low and high temperatures (usually from -100 to +190-degrees F), and will not wash off or dilute in the presence of water.

Assembly lube is a special extreme pressure lubricant, usually containing moly, used to lubricate high-load parts (such as main and rod bearings and cam lobes) for initial start-up of a new engine. The assembly lube lubricates the parts without being squeezed out or washed away until the engine oiling system begins to function.

Silicone lubricants are used to protect rubber, plastic, vinyl and nylon parts.

Graphite lubricants are used where oils cannot be used due to contamination problems, such as in locks. The dry graphite will lubricate metal parts while remaining uncontaminated by dirt, water, oil or acids. It is electrically conductive and will not foul electrical contacts in locks such as the ignition switch.

Moly penetrants loosen and lubricate frozen, rusted and corroded fasteners and prevent future rusting or freezing.

Heat-sink grease is a special electrically non-conductive grease that is used for mounting electronic ignition modules where it is essential that heat is transferred away from the module.

Sealants

RTV sealant is one of the most widely used gasket compounds. Made from silicone, RTV is air curing, it seals, bonds, waterproofs, fills surface irregularities, remains flexible, doesn't shrink, is relatively easy to remove, and is used as a supplementary sealer with almost all low and medium temperature gaskets.

Anaerobic sealant is much like RTV in that it can be used either to seal gaskets or to form gaskets by itself. It remains flexible, is solvent resistant and fills surface imperfections. The difference between an anaerobic sealant and an RTV-type sealant is in the curing. RTV cures when exposed to air, while an anaerobic sealant cures only in the absence of air. This means that an anaerobic sealant cures only after the assembly of parts, sealing them together.

Thread and pipe sealant is used for sealing hydraulic and pneumatic fittings and vacuum lines. It is usually made from a Teflon compound, and comes in a spray, a paint-on liquid and as a wrap-around tape.

Chemicals

Anti-seize compound prevents seizing, galling, cold welding, rust and corrosion in fasteners. High-temperature ant-seize, usually made with copper and graphite lubricants, is used for exhaust system and exhaust manifold bolts.

Anaerobic locking compounds are used to keep fasteners from vibrating or working loose and cure only after installation, in the absence of air. Medium strength locking compound is used for small nuts, bolts and screws that may be removed later. High-strength locking compound is for large nuts, bolts and studs which aren't removed on a regular basis.

Oil additives range from viscosity index improvers to chemical treatments that claim to reduce internal engine friction. It should be noted that most oil manufacturers caution against using additives with their oils.

Gas additives perform several functions, depending on their chemical makeup. They usually contain solvents that help dissolve gum and varnish that build up on carburetor, fuel injection and intake parts. They also serve to break down carbon deposits that form on the inside surfaces of the combustion chambers. Some additives contain upper cylinder lubricants for valves and piston rings, and others contain chemicals to remove condensation from the gas tank.

Miscellaneous

Brake fluid is specially formulated hydraulic fluid that can withstand the heat and pressure encountered in brake systems. Care must be taken so this fluid does not come in contact with painted surfaces or plastics. An opened container should always be resealed to prevent contamination by water or dirt.

Weatherstrip adhesive is used to bond weatherstripping around doors, windows and trunk lids. It is sometimes used to attach trim pieces.

Undercoating is a petroleum-based, tar-like substance that is designed to protect metal surfaces on the underside of the vehicle from corrosion. It also acts as a sound-deadening agent by insulating the bottom of the vehicle.

Waxes and polishes are used to help protect painted and plated surfaces from the weather. Different types of paint may require the use of different types of wax and polish. Some polishes utilize a chemical or abrasive cleaner to help remove the top layer of oxidized (dull) paint on older vehicles. In recent years many non-wax polishes that contain a wide variety of chemicals such as polymers and silicones have been introduced. These non-wax polishes are usually easier to apply and last longer than conventional waxes and polishes.

Conversion factors

Length (distance)

Inches (in)	X	25.4	= Millimeters (mm)	X 0.0394	= Inches (in)
Feet (ft)	X	0.305	= Meters (m)	X 3.281	= Feet (ft)
Miles	X	1.609	= Kilometers (km)	X 0.621	= Miles

Volume (capacity)

Cubic inches (cu in; in^3)	X	16.387	= Cubic centimeters (cc; cm^3)	X 0.061	= Cubic inches (cu in; in^3)
Imperial pints (Imp pt)	X	0.568	= Liters (l)	X 1.76	= Imperial pints (Imp pt)
Imperial quarts (Imp qt)	X	1.137	= Liters (l)	X 0.88	= Imperial quarts (Imp qt)
Imperial quarts (Imp qt)	X	1.201	= US quarts (US qt)	X 0.833	= Imperial quarts (Imp qt)
US quarts (US qt)	X	0.946	= Liters (l)	X 1.057	= US quarts (US qt)
Imperial gallons (Imp gal)	X	4.546	= Liters (l)	X 0.22	= Imperial gallons (Imp gal)
Imperial gallons (Imp gal)	X	1.201	= US gallons (US gal)	X 0.833	= Imperial gallons (Imp gal)
US gallons (US gal)	X	3.785	= Liters (l)	X 0.264	= US gallons (US gal)

Mass (weight)

Ounces (oz)	X	28.35	= Grams (g)	X 0.035	= Ounces (oz)
Pounds (lb)	X	0.454	= Kilograms (kg)	X 2.205	= Pounds (lb)

Force

Ounces-force (ozf; oz)	X	0.278	= Newtons (N)	X 3.6	= Ounces-force (ozf; oz)
Pounds-force (lbf; lb)	X	4.448	= Newtons (N)	X 0.225	= Pounds-force (lbf; lb)
Newtons (N)	X	0.1	= Kilograms-force (kgf; kg)	X 9.81	= Newtons (N)

Pressure

Pounds-force per square inch (psi; lbf/in^2; lb/in^2)	X	0.070	= Kilograms-force per square centimeter (kgf/cm^2; kg/cm^2)	X 14.223	= Pounds-force per square inch (psi; lbf/in^2; lb/in^2)
Pounds-force per square inch (psi; lbf/in^2; lb/in^2)	X	0.068	= Atmospheres (atm)	X 14.696	= Pounds-force per square inch (psi; lbf/in^2; lb/in^2)
Pounds-force per square inch (psi; lbf/in^2; lb/in^2)	X	0.069	= Bars	X 14.5	= Pounds-force per square inch (psi; lbf/in^2; lb/in^2)
Pounds-force per square inch (psi; lbf/in^2; lb/in^2)	X	6.895	= Kilopascals (kPa)	X 0.145	= Pounds-force per square inch (psi; lbf/in^2; lb/in^2)
Kilopascals (kPa)	X	0.01	= Kilograms-force per square centimeter (kgf/cm^2; kg/cm^2)	X 98.1	= Kilopascals (kPa)

Torque (moment of force)

Pounds-force inches (lbf in; lb in)	X	1.152	= Kilograms-force centimeter (kgf cm; kg cm)	X 0.868	= Pounds-force inches (lbf in; lb in)
Pounds-force inches (lbf in; lb in)	X	0.113	= Newton meters (Nm)	X 8.85	= Pounds-force inches (lbf in; lb in)
Pounds-force inches (lbf in; lb in)	X	0.083	= Pounds-force feet (lbf ft; lb ft)	X 12	= Pounds-force inches (lbf in; lb in)
Pounds-force feet (lbf ft; lb ft)	X	0.138	= Kilograms-force meters (kgf m; kg m)	X 7.233	= Pounds-force feet (lbf ft; lb ft)
Pounds-force feet (lbf ft; lb ft)	X	1.356	= Newton meters (Nm)	X 0.738	= Pounds-force feet (lbf ft; lb ft)
Newton meters (Nm)	X	0.102	= Kilograms-force meters (kgf m; kg m)	X 9.804	= Newton meters (Nm)

Vacuum

Inches mercury (in. Hg)	X	3.377	= Kilopascals (kPa)	X 0.2961	= Inches mercury
Inches mercury (in. Hg)	X	25.4	= Millimeters mercury (mm Hg)	X 0.0394	= Inches mercury

Power

Horsepower (hp)	X	745.7	= Watts (W)	X 0.0013	= Horsepower (hp)

Velocity (speed)

Miles per hour (miles/hr; mph)	X	1.609	= Kilometers per hour (km/hr; kph)	X 0.621	= Miles per hour (miles/hr; mph)

Fuel consumption*

Miles per gallon, Imperial (mpg)	X	0.354	= Kilometers per liter (km/l)	X 2.825	= Miles per gallon, Imperial (mpg)
Miles per gallon, US (mpg)	X	0.425	= Kilometers per liter (km/l)	X 2.352	= Miles per gallon, US (mpg)

Temperature

Degrees Fahrenheit = (°C x 1.8) + 32

Degrees Celsius (Degrees Centigrade; °C) = (°F - 32) x 0.56

*It is common practice to convert from miles per gallon (mpg) to liters/100 kilometers (l/100km), where mpg (Imperial) x l/100 km = 282 and mpg (US) x l/100 km = 235

DECIMALS to MILLIMETERS

Decimal	mm	Decimal	mm
0.001	0.0254	0.500	12.7000
0.002	0.0508	0.510	12.9540
0.003	0.0762	0.520	13.2080
0.004	0.1016	0.530	13.4620
0.005	0.1270	0.540	13.7160
0.006	0.1524	0.550	13.9700
0.007	0.1778	0.560	14.2240
0.008	0.2032	0.570	14.4780
0.009	0.2286	0.580	14.7320
		0.590	14.9860
0.010	0.2540		
0.020	0.5080		
0.030	0.7620		
0.040	1.0160	0.600	15.2400
0.050	1.2700	0.610	15.4940
0.060	1.5240	0.620	15.7480
0.070	1.7780	0.630	16.0020
0.080	2.0320	0.640	16.2560
0.090	2.2860	0.650	16.5100
		0.660	16.7640
0.100	2.5400	0.670	17.0180
0.110	2.7940	0.680	17.2720
0.120	3.0480	0.690	17.5260
0.130	3.3020		
0.140	3.5560		
0.150	3.8100		
0.160	4.0640	0.700	17.7800
0.170	4.3180	0.710	18.0340
0.180	4.5720	0.720	18.2880
0.190	4.8260	0.730	18.5420
		0.740	18.7960
0.200	5.0800	0.750	19.0500
0.210	5.3340	0.760	19.3040
0.220	5.5880	0.770	19.5580
0.230	5.8420	0.780	19.8120
0.240	6.0960	0.790	20.0660
0.250	6.3500		
0.260	6.6040		
0.270	6.8580	0.800	20.3200
0.280	7.1120	0.810	20.5740
0.290	7.3660	0.820	21.8280
		0.830	21.0820
0.300	7.6200	0.840	21.3360
0.310	7.8740	0.850	21.5900
0.320	8.1280	0.860	21.8440
0.330	8.3820	0.870	22.0980
0.340	8.6360	0.880	22.3520
0.350	8.8900	0.890	22.6060
0.360	9.1440		
0.370	9.3980		
0.380	9.6520		
0.390	9.9060		
		0.900	22.8600
0.400	10.1600	0.910	23.1140
0.410	10.4140	0.920	23.3680
0.420	10.6680	0.930	23.6220
0.430	10.9220	0.940	23.8760
0.440	11.1760	0.950	24.1300
0.450	11.4300	0.960	24.3840
0.460	11.6840	0.970	24.6380
0.470	11.9380	0.980	24.8920
0.480	12.1920	0.990	25.1460
0.490	12.4460	1.000	25.4000

FRACTIONS to DECIMALS to MILLIMETERS

Fraction	Decimal	mm	Fraction	Decimal	mm
1/64	0.0156	0.3969	33/64	0.5156	13.0969
1/32	0.0312	0.7938	17/32	0.5312	13.4938
3/64	0.0469	1.1906	35/64	0.5469	13.8906
1/16	0.0625	1.5875	9/16	0.5625	14.2875
5/64	0.0781	1.9844	37/64	0.5781	14.6844
3/32	0.0938	2.3812	19/32	0.5938	15.0812
7/64	0.1094	2.7781	39/64	0.6094	15.4781
1/8	0.1250	3.1750	5/8	0.6250	15.8750
9/64	0.1406	3.5719	41/64	0.6406	16.2719
5/32	0.1562	3.9688	21/32	0.6562	16.6688
11/64	0.1719	4.3656	43/64	0.6719	17.0656
3/16	0.1875	4.7625	11/16	0.6875	17.4625
13/64	0.2031	5.1594	45/64	0.7031	17.8594
7/32	0.2188	5.5562	23/32	0.7188	18.2562
15/64	0.2344	5.9531	47/64	0.7344	18.6531
1/4	0.2500	6.3500	3/4	0.7500	19.0500
17/64	0.2656	6.7469	49/64	0.7656	19.4469
9/32	0.2812	7.1438	25/32	0.7812	19.8438
19/64	0.2969	7.5406	51/64	0.7969	20.2406
5/16	0.3125	7.9375	13/16	0.8125	20.6375
21/64	0.3281	8.3344	53/64	0.8281	21.0344
11/32	0.3438	8.7312	27/32	0.8438	21.4312
23/64	0.3594	9.1281	55/64	0.8594	21.8281
3/8	0.3750	9.5250	7/8	0.8750	22.2250
25/64	0.3906	9.9219	57/64	0.8906	22.6219
13/32	0.4062	10.3188	29/32	0.9062	23.0188
27/64	0.4219	10.7156	59/64	0.9219	23.4156
7/16	0.4375	11.1125	15/16	0.9375	23.8125
29/64	0.4531	11.5094	61/64	0.9531	24.2094
15/32	0.4688	11.9062	31/32	0.9688	24.6062
31/64	0.4844	12.3031	63/64	0.9844	25.0031
1/2	0.5000	12.7000	1	1.0000	25.4000

Safety first!

Regardless of how enthusiastic you may be about getting on with the job at hand, take the time to ensure that your safety is not jeopardized. A moment's lack of attention can result in an accident, as can failure to observe certain simple safety precautions. The possibility of an accident will always exist, and the following points should not be considered a comprehensive list of all dangers. Rather, they are intended to make you aware of the risks and to encourage a safety conscious approach to all work you carry out on your vehicle.

Essential DOs and DON'Ts

DON'T rely on a jack when working under the vehicle. Always use approved jackstands to support the weight of the vehicle and place them under the recommended lift or support points.

DON'T attempt to loosen extremely tight fasteners (i.e. wheel lug nuts) while the vehicle is on a jack - it may fall.

DON'T start the engine without first making sure that the transmission is in Neutral (or Park where applicable) and the parking brake is set.

DON'T remove the radiator cap from a hot cooling system - let it cool or cover it with a cloth and release the pressure gradually.

DON'T attempt to drain the engine oil until you are sure it has cooled to the point that it will not burn you.

DON'T touch any part of the engine or exhaust system until it has cooled sufficiently to avoid burns.

DON'T siphon toxic liquids such as gasoline, antifreeze and brake fluid by mouth, or allow them to remain on your skin.

DON'T inhale brake lining dust - it is potentially hazardous (see *Asbestos* below).

DON'T allow spilled oil or grease to remain on the floor - wipe it up before someone slips on it.

DON'T use loose fitting wrenches or other tools which may slip and cause injury.

DON'T push on wrenches when loosening or tightening nuts or bolts. Always try to pull the wrench toward you. If the situation calls for pushing the wrench away, push with an open hand to avoid scraped knuckles if the wrench should slip.

DON'T attempt to lift a heavy component alone - get someone to help you.

DON'T *rush or take unsafe shortcuts to finish a job.*

DON'T allow children or animals in or around the vehicle while you are working on it.

DO wear eye protection when using power tools such as a drill, sander, bench grinder, etc. and when working under a vehicle.

DO keep loose clothing and long hair well out of the way of moving parts.

DO make sure that any hoist used has a safe working load rating adequate for the job.

DO get someone to check on you periodically when working alone on a vehicle.

DO carry out work in a logical sequence and make sure that everything is correctly assembled and tightened.

DO keep chemicals and fluids tightly capped and out of the reach of children and pets.

DO remember that your vehicle's safety affects that of yourself and others. If in doubt on any point, get professional advice.

Steering, suspension and brakes

These systems are essential to driving safety, so make sure you have a qualified shop or individual check your work. Also, compressed suspension springs can cause injury if released suddenly - be sure to use a spring compressor.

Airbags

Airbags are explosive devices that can **CAUSE** injury if they deploy while you're working on the vehicle. Follow the manufacturer's instructions to disable the airbag whenever you're working in the vicinity of airbag components.

Asbestos

Certain friction, insulating, sealing, and other products - such as brake linings, brake bands, clutch linings, torque converters, gaskets, etc. - may contain asbestos or other hazardous friction material. Extreme care must be taken to avoid inhalation of dust from such products, since it is hazardous to health. If in doubt, assume that they do contain asbestos.

Fire

Remember at all times that gasoline is highly flammable. Never smoke or have any kind of open flame around when working on a vehicle. But the risk does not end there. A spark caused by an electrical short circuit, by two metal surfaces contacting each other, or even by static electricity built up in your body under certain conditions, can ignite gasoline vapors, which in a confined space are highly explosive. Do not, under any circumstances, use gasoline for cleaning parts. Use an approved safety solvent.

Always disconnect the battery ground (-) cable at the battery before working on any part of the fuel system or electrical system. Never risk spilling fuel on a hot engine or exhaust component. It is strongly recommended that a fire extinguisher suitable for use on fuel and electrical fires be kept handy in the garage or workshop at all times. Never try to extinguish a fuel or electrical fire with water.

Fumes

Certain fumes are highly toxic and can quickly cause unconsciousness and even death if inhaled to any extent. Gasoline vapor falls into this category, as do the vapors from some cleaning solvents. Any draining or pouring of such volatile fluids should be done in a well ventilated area.

When using cleaning fluids and solvents, read the instructions on the container carefully. Never use materials from unmarked containers.

Never run the engine in an enclosed space, such as a garage. Exhaust fumes contain carbon monoxide, which is extremely poisonous. If you need to run the engine, always do so in the open air, or at least have the rear of the vehicle outside the work area.

The battery

Never create a spark or allow a bare light bulb near a battery. They normally give off a certain amount of hydrogen gas, which is highly explosive.

Always disconnect the battery ground (-) cable at the battery before working on the fuel or electrical systems.

If possible, loosen the filler caps or cover when charging the battery from an external source (this does not apply to sealed or maintenance-free batteries). Do not charge at an excessive rate or the battery may burst.

Take care when adding water to a non maintenance-free battery and when carrying a battery. The electrolyte, even when diluted, is very corrosive and should not be allowed to contact clothing or skin.

Always wear eye protection when cleaning the battery to prevent the caustic deposits from entering your eyes.

Household current

When using an electric power tool, inspection light, etc., which operates on household current, always make sure that the tool is correctly connected to its plug and that, where necessary, it is properly grounded. Do not use such items in damp conditions and, again, do not create a spark or apply excessive heat in the vicinity of fuel or fuel vapor.

Secondary ignition system voltage

A severe electric shock can result from touching certain parts of the ignition system (such as the spark plug wires) when the engine is running or being cranked, particularly if components are damp or the insulation is defective. In the case of an electronic ignition system, the secondary system voltage is much higher and could prove fatal.

Hydrofluoric acid

This extremely corrosive acid is formed when certain types of synthetic rubber, found in some O-rings, oil seals, fuel hoses, etc. are exposed to temperatures above 750-degrees F (400-degrees C). The rubber changes into a charred or sticky substance containing the acid. *Once formed, the acid remains dangerous for years. If it gets onto the skin, it may be necessary to amputate the limb concerned.*

When dealing with a vehicle which has suffered a fire, or with components salvaged from such a vehicle, wear protective gloves and discard them after use.

Troubleshooting

Contents

Symptom	Section
Engine and performance	
Engine backfires	15
Engine diesels (continues to run) after switching off	18
Engine hard to start when cold	3
Engine hard to start when hot	4
Engine lacks power	14
Engine lopes while idling or idles erratically	8
Engine misses at idle speed	9
Engine misses throughout driving speed range	10
Engine rotates but will not start	2
Engine runs with oil pressure light on	17
Engine stalls	13
Engine starts but stops immediately	6
Engine stumbles on acceleration	11
Engine surges while holding accelerator steady	12
Engine will not rotate when attempting to start	1
Oil puddle under engine	7
Pinging or knocking engine sounds during acceleration or uphill	16
Starter motor noisy or excessively rough in engagement	5
Engine electrical system	
Battery will not hold a charge	19
Voltage warning light fails to come on when key is turned on	21
Voltage warning light fails to go out	20
Fuel system	
Excessive fuel consumption	22
Fuel leakage and/or fuel odor	23
Cooling system	
Coolant loss	28
External coolant leakage	26
Internal coolant leakage	27
Overcooling	25
Overheating	24
Poor coolant circulation	29
Clutch	
Clutch pedal stays on floor	38
Clutch slips (engine speed increases with no increase in vehicle speed)	35
Fluid in area of master cylinder dust cover and on pedal	31
Fluid on release cylinder	32
Grabbing (chattering) as clutch is engaged	36
High pedal effort	39
Noise in clutch area	37
Pedal feels spongy when depressed	33
Pedal travels to floor - no pressure or very little resistance	30
Unable to select gears	34
Manual transaxle	
Leaks lubricant	45
Noisy in all gears	43
Noisy in Neutral with engine running	41
Noisy in one particular gear	42
Slips out of gear	44
Vibration	40
Automatic transaxle	
Engine will start in gears other than Park or Neutral	50
Fluid leakage	46
General shift mechanism problems	48
Transaxle fluid brown or has a burned smell	47
Transaxle slips, shifts roughly, is noisy or has no drive in forward or reverse gears	51
Transaxle will not downshift with accelerator pedal pressed to the floor	49
Driveaxles	
Clicking noise in turns	52
Knock or clunk when accelerating after coasting	53
Shudder or vibration during acceleration	54
Brakes	
Brake pedal feels spongy when depressed	62
Brake pedal travels to the floor with little resistance	63
Brake roughness or chatter (pedal pulsates)	57
Dragging brakes	60
Excessive brake pedal travel	59
Excessive pedal effort required to stop vehicle	58
Grabbing or uneven braking action	61
Noise (high-pitched squeal when the brakes are applied)	56
Parking brake does not hold	64
Vehicle pulls to one side during braking	55
Suspension and steering systems	
Abnormal or excessive tire wear	66
Abnormal noise at the front end	71
Cupped tires	76
Erratic steering when braking	73
Excessive pitching and/or rolling around corners or during braking	74
Excessive play or looseness in steering system	80
Excessive tire wear on inside edge	78
Excessive tire wear on outside edge	77
Hard steering	69
Steering wheel does not return to center position correctly	70
Rattling or clicking noise in rack and pinion	81
Shimmy, shake or vibration	68
Suspension bottoms	75
Tire tread worn in one place	79
Vehicle pulls to one side	65
Wander or poor steering stability	72
Wheel makes a "thumping" noise	67

This section provides an easy reference guide to the more common problems which may occur during the operation of your vehicle. Various symptoms and their possible causes are grouped under headings denoting components or systems, such as Engine, Cooling system, etc. They also refer to the Chapter and/or Section that deals with the problem.

Remember that successful troubleshooting isn't a mysterious "black art" practiced only by professional mechanics. It's simply the result of knowledge combined with an intelligent, systematic approach to a problem. Always use a process of elimination, starting with the simplest solution and working through to the most complex - and never overlook the obvious. Anyone can run the gas tank dry or leave the lights on overnight, so don't assume that you're exempt from such oversights.

Finally, always establish a clear idea why a problem has occurred and take steps to ensure that it doesn't happen again. If the electrical system fails because of a poor connection, check all other connections in the system to make sure they don't fail as well. If a particular fuse continues to blow, find out why - don't just go on replacing fuses. Remember, failure of a small component can often be indicative of potential failure or incorrect functioning of a more important component or system.

Engine and performance

1 Engine will not rotate when attempting to start

1   Battery terminal connections loose or corroded (Chapter 1).
2   Battery discharged or faulty (Chapter 1).
3   Automatic transaxle not completely engaged in Park (Chapter 7) or clutch not completely depressed (Chapter 8). Also, the neutral start switch (automatic transaxle) or starter/clutch interlock switch (manual transaxle) could be faulty (Chapter 7 or 8).
4   Broken, loose or disconnected wiring in the starting circuit (Chapters 5 and 12).
5   Starter motor pinion jammed in flywheel ring gear (Chapter 5).
6   Starter solenoid faulty (Chapter 5).
7   Starter motor faulty (Chapter 5).
8   Ignition switch faulty (Chapter 12).
9   Starter pinion or flywheel teeth worn or broken (Chapter 5).

2 Engine rotates but will not start

1   Fuel tank empty.
2   Battery discharged (engine rotates slowly) (Chapter 5).
3   Battery terminal connections loose or corroded (Chapter 1).
4   Leaking fuel injector(s), fuel pump, pressure regulator, etc. (Chapter 4).
5   Fuel not reaching fuel injection system (Chapter 4).
6   Ignition components damp or damaged (Chapter 5).
7   Worn, faulty or incorrectly gapped spark plugs (Chapter 1).
8   Broken, loose or disconnected wiring in the starting circuit (Chapter 5).
9   Broken, loose or disconnected wires at the ignition coil(s) or faulty coil(s) (Chapter 5).

3 Engine hard to start when cold

1   Battery discharged or low (Chapter 1).
2   Fuel system malfunctioning (Chapter 4).
3   Injector(s) leaking (Chapter 4).

4 Engine hard to start when hot

1   Air filter clogged (Chapter 1).
2   Fuel not reaching the fuel injection system (Chapter 4).
3   Corroded battery connections, especially ground (Chapter 1).

5 Starter motor noisy or excessively rough in engagement

1   Pinion or flywheel gear teeth worn or broken (Chapter 5).
2   Starter motor mounting bolts loose or missing (Chapter 5).

6 Engine starts but stops immediately

1   Loose or faulty electrical connections at coil pack or alternator (Chapter 5).
2   Insufficient fuel reaching the fuel injectors (Chapter 4).
3   Vacuum leak at the gasket between the intake manifold/plenum and throttle body (Chapters 1 and 4).

7 Oil puddle under engine

1   Oil pan gasket and/or oil pan drain bolt seal leaking (Chapters 1 and 2).
2   Oil pressure sending unit leaking (Chapter 2).
3   Rocker arm cover gaskets leaking (Chapter 2).
4   Engine oil seals leaking (Chapter 2).
5   Timing cover sealant or sealing flange leaking (Chapter 2).

8 Engine lopes while idling or idles erratically

1   Vacuum leaks (Chapter 4).
2   Leaking EGR valve or plugged PCV valve (Chapters 1 and 6).
3   Air filter clogged (Chapter 1).
4   Fuel pump not delivering sufficient fuel to the fuel injection system (Chapter 4).
5   Leaking head gasket (Chapter 2).
6   Timing chain and/or gears worn (Chapter 2).
7   Camshaft lobes worn (Chapter 2).

9 Engine misses at idle speed

1   Spark plugs worn or not gapped properly (Chapter 1).
2   Faulty spark plug wires (Chapter 1).
3   Vacuum leaks (Chapters 1 and 4).
4   Ignition system malfunctioning (Chapter 5).
5   Uneven or low compression (Chapter 2).

10 Engine misses throughout driving speed range

1   Fuel filter clogged and/or impurities in the fuel system (Chapters 1 and 4).
2   Low fuel output at the injector (Chapter 4).
3   Faulty or incorrectly gapped spark plugs (Chapter 1).
4   Leaking spark plug wires (Chapter 1).
5   Other fault in the ignition system (Chapter 5).
6   Faulty emission system components (Chapter 6).
7   Low or uneven cylinder compression pressures (Chapter 2).
8   Weak or faulty ignition system (Chapter 5).
9   Vacuum leak in fuel injection system, intake manifold or vacuum hoses (Chapter 4).

11 Engine stumbles on acceleration

1   Spark plugs fouled (Chapter 1).
2   Fuel injection system needs adjustment or repair (Chapter 4).
3   Fuel filter clogged (Chapter 1).
4   Faulty spark plug wires (Chapter 1).
5   Intake manifold air leak (Chapter 4).

12 Engine surges while holding accelerator steady

1   Intake air leak (Chapter 4).
2   Fuel pump faulty (Chapter 4).
3   Loose fuel injector harness connections (Chapter 4).
4   Defective ECM (Chapter 6).

13 Engine stalls

1   Fuel filter clogged and/or water and

impurities in the fuel system (Chapters 1 and 4).
2 Ignition components damp or damaged (Chapter 5).
3 Faulty emissions system components (Chapter 6).
4 Faulty or incorrectly gapped spark plugs (Chapter 1).
5 Faulty spark plug wires (Chapter 1).
6 Vacuum leak in the fuel injection system, intake manifold or vacuum hoses (Chapter 4).

14 Engine lacks power

1 Faulty or incorrectly gapped spark plugs (Chapter 1).
2 Fuel injection system out of adjustment or malfunctioning (Chapter 4).
3 Faulty coil(s) (Chapter 5).
4 Brakes binding (Chapter 1).
5 Automatic transaxle fluid level incorrect (Chapter 1).
6 Clutch slipping (Chapter 8).
7 Fuel filter clogged and/or impurities in the fuel system (Chapter 1).
8 Emission control system not functioning properly (Chapter 6).
9 Low or uneven cylinder compression pressures (Chapter 2).

15 Engine backfires

1 Emissions system not functioning properly (Chapter 6).
2 Spark plug wires not routed correctly (Chapter 1).
3 Faulty secondary ignition system (Chapter 5).
4 Fuel injection system in need of adjustment or worn excessively (Chapter 4).
5 Vacuum leak at fuel injectors, intake manifold or vacuum hoses (Chapter 4).
6 Valves sticking (Chapter 2).

16 Pinging or knocking engine sounds during acceleration or uphill

1 Incorrect grade of fuel.
2 Excessive carbon build-up in combustion chambers.
3 Fuel injection system in need of repair (Chapter 4).
4 Improper or damaged spark plugs or wires (Chapter 1).
5 Worn or damaged ignition components (Chapter 5).
6 Faulty emissions system (Chapter 6).
7 Vacuum leak (Chapter 4).

17 Engine runs with oil pressure light on

1 Low oil level (Chapter 1).

2 Short in wiring circuit (Chapter 12).
3 Faulty oil pressure sender (Chapter 2).
4 Worn engine bearings and/or oil pump (Chapter 2).

18 Engine diesels (continues to run) after switching off

1 Excessive engine operating temperature (Chapter 3).
2 Excessive carbon build-up in combustion chambers (Chapter 2).
3 Fuel injection system malfunctioning (Chapter 4).
4 Ignition system malfunctioning (Chapter 5).

Engine electrical system

19 Battery will not hold a charge

1 Alternator drivebelt defective or not adjusted properly (Chapter 1).
2 Battery terminals loose or corroded (Chapter 1).
3 Alternator not charging properly (Chapter 5).
4 Loose, broken or faulty wiring in the charging circuit (Chapter 5).
5 Short in vehicle wiring (Chapters 5 and 12).
6 Internally defective battery (Chapters 1 and 5).

20 Voltage warning light fails to go out

1 Faulty alternator or charging circuit (Chapter 5).
2 Alternator drivebelt defective or out of adjustment (Chapter 1).
3 Alternator voltage regulator inoperative (Chapter 5).

21 Voltage warning light fails to come on when key is turned on

1 Warning light bulb defective (Chapter 12).
2 Fault in the printed circuit, dash wiring or bulb holder (Chapter 12).

Fuel system

22 Excessive fuel consumption

1 Dirty or clogged air filter element (Chapter 1).
2 Fuel leak (usually accompanied by a fuel

odor) (see the next Section).
3 Emissions system not functioning properly (Chapter 6).
4 Fuel injection internal parts excessively worn or damaged (Chapter 4).
5 Low tire pressure or incorrect tire size (Chapter 1).
6 Clutch (Chapter 8) or automatic transaxle (Chapter 7) slipping (normally you will also hear excessive engine revving during acceleration).

23 Fuel leakage and/or fuel odor

1 Leak in a fuel feed or vent line (Chapter 4).
2 Tank overfilled.
3 Evaporative canister filter clogged (Chapters 1 and 6).
4 Fuel injector internal parts excessively worn (Chapter 4).

Cooling system

24 Overheating

1 Insufficient coolant in system (Chapter 1).
2 Water pump drivebelt defective or out of adjustment (Chapter 1).
3 Radiator core blocked or grille restricted (Chapter 3).
4 Thermostat faulty (Chapter 3).
5 Electric cooling fan blades broken or cracked (Chapter 3).
6 Radiator cap not maintaining proper pressure (Chapter 3).

25 Overcooling

Faulty thermostat (Chapter 3).

26 External coolant leakage

1 Deteriorated/damaged hoses or loose clamps (Chapters 1 and 3).
2 Water pump seal defective (Chapters 1 and 3).
3 Leakage from radiator core or header tank (Chapter 3).
4 Engine drain or water jacket core plugs leaking (Chapter 2).

27 Internal coolant leakage

1 Leaking cylinder head gasket (Chapter 2).
2 Cracked cylinder bore or cylinder head (Chapter 2).

28 Coolant loss

1   Too much coolant in system (Chapter 1).
2   Coolant boiling away because of over-heating (Chapter 3).
3   Internal or external leakage (Chapter 3).
4   Faulty radiator cap (Chapter 3).

29 Poor coolant circulation

1   Inoperative water pump (Chapter 3).
2   Restriction in cooling system (Chapters 1 and 3).
3   Water pump drivebelt defective or out of adjustment (Chapter 1).
4   Thermostat sticking (Chapter 3).

Clutch

30 Pedal travels to floor - no pressure or very little resistance

1   Master or release cylinder faulty (Chapter 8).
2   Hose/pipe burst or leaking (Chapter 8).
3   Connections leaking (Chapter 8).
4   No fluid in reservoir (Chapter 8).
5   If fluid is present in master cylinder dust cover, rear master cylinder seal has failed (Chapter 8).
6   If fluid level in reservoir rises as pedal is depressed, master cylinder center valve seal is faulty (Chapter 8).
7   Broken release bearing or fork (Chapter 8).

31 Fluid in area of master cylinder dust cover and on pedal

Rear seal failure in master cylinder (Chapter 8).

32 Fluid on release cylinder

Release cylinder seal faulty (Chapter 8).

33 Pedal feels spongy when depressed

Air in system (Chapter 8).

34 Unable to select gears

1   Faulty transaxle (Chapter 7).
2   Faulty clutch disc (Chapter 8).
3   Fork and bearing not assembled properly (Chapter 8).
4   Faulty pressure plate (Chapter 8).
5   Pressure plate-to-flywheel bolts loose (Chapter 8).

35 Clutch slips (engine speed increases with no increase in vehicle speed)

1   Clutch plate worn (Chapter 8).
2   Clutch plate is oil soaked by leaking rear main seal (Chapter 8).
3   Clutch plate not seated. It may take 30 or 40 normal starts for a new one to seat.
4   Warped pressure plate or flywheel (Chapter 8).
5   Weak diaphragm spring (Chapter 8).
6   Clutch plate overheated. Allow to cool.

36 Grabbing (chattering) as clutch is engaged

1   Oil soaked, burned or glazed linings (Chapter 8).
2   Worn or loose engine or transaxle mounts (Chapters 2 and 7).
3   Worn splines on clutch plate hub (Chapter 8).
4   Warped pressure plate or flywheel (Chapter 8).

37 Noise in clutch area

1   Fork shaft improperly installed (Chapter 8).
2   Faulty release bearing (Chapter 8).

38 Clutch pedal stays on floor

1   Fork shaft binding in housing (Chapter 8).
2   Broken release bearing or fork (Chapter 8).

39 High pedal effort

1   Fork shaft binding in housing (Chapter 8).
2   Pressure plate faulty (Chapter 8).

Manual transaxle

40 Vibration

1   Rough wheel bearing (Chapter 10).
2   Damaged driveaxle (Chapter 8).
3   Out-of-round tires (Chapter 1).
4   Tire out-of-balance (Chapter 10).
5   Worn or damaged CV joint (Chapter 8).

41 Noisy in Neutral with engine running

Damaged clutch release bearing (Chapter 8).

42 Noisy in one particular gear

1   Damaged or worn constant mesh gears (Chapter 7).
2   Damaged or worn synchronizers (Chapter 7).

43 Noisy in all gears

1   Insufficient lubricant (Chapter 1).
2   Damaged or worn bearings (Chapter 7).
3   Worn or damaged input gear shaft and/or output gear shaft (Chapter 7).

44 Slips out of gear

1   Worn or improperly adjusted linkage (Chapter 7).
2   Transaxle loose on engine (Chapter 7).
3   Shift linkage does not work freely, binds (Chapter 7).
4   Input shaft bearing retainer broken or loose (Chapter 7).
5   Dirt between clutch cover and engine housing (Chapter 7).
6   Worn shift fork (Chapter 7).

45 Leaks lubricant

1   Excessive amount of lubricant in transaxle (Chapter 1).
2   Loose or broken input shaft bearing retainer (Chapter 7).
3   Input shaft bearing retainer O-ring and/or lip seal damaged (Chapter 7).

Automatic transaxle

Note: *Due to the complexity of the automatic transaxle, it's difficult for the home mechanic to properly diagnose and service this component. For problems other than the following, the vehicle should be taken to a dealer service department or a transmission shop.*

46 Fluid leakage

1   Automatic transmission fluid is a deep red color. Fluid leaks should not be confused with engine oil, which can easily be blown by air flow to the transaxle.
2   To pinpoint a leak, first remove all built-up dirt and grime from the transaxle housing with degreasing agents and/or steam cleaning. Drive the vehicle at low speeds so air flow will not blow the leak far from its source. Raise the vehicle and determine where the leak is coming from. Common areas of leakage are:

a) *Pan (Chapters 1 and 7)*
b) *Filler pipe (Chapter 7)*
c) *Transaxle oil lines (Chapter 7)*
d) *Speedometer gear or sensor (Chapter 7)*
e) *Modulator*

47   Transaxle fluid brown or has a burned smell

Transaxle overheated. Change fluid (Chapter 1).

48   General shift mechanism problems

1   Chapter 7 Part B deals with checking and adjusting the shift linkage on automatic transaxles. Common problems which may be attributed to poorly adjusted linkage are:

a) *Engine starting in gears other than Park or Neutral.*
b) *Indicator on shifter pointing to a gear other than the one actually being used.*
c) *Vehicle moves when in Park.*

2   Refer to Chapter 7 Part B for the shift linkage adjustment procedure.

49   Transaxle will not downshift with accelerator pedal pressed to the floor

Throttle valve (TV) cable out of adjustment (Chapter 7).

50   Engine will start in gears other than Park or Neutral

Starter safety switch malfunctioning (Chapter 7).

51   Transaxle slips, shifts roughly, is noisy or has no drive in forward or reverse gears

There are many probable causes for the above problems, but the home mechanic should be concerned with only one possibility - fluid level. Before taking the vehicle to a repair shop, check the level and condition of the fluid as described in Chapter 1.

Correct the fluid level as necessary or change the fluid and filter if needed. If the problem persists, have a professional diagnose the probable cause.

Driveaxles

52   Clicking noise in turns

Worn or damaged outer CV joint. Check for cut or damaged boots (Chapter 1). Repair as necessary (Chapter 8).

53   Knock or clunk when accelerating after coasting

Worn or damaged outer CV joint. Check for cut or damaged boots (Chapter 1). Repair as necessary (Chapter 8).

54   Shudder or vibration during acceleration

1   Excessive inner CV joint angle. Check and correct as necessary (Chapter 8).
2   Worn or damaged CV joints. Repair or replace as necessary (Chapter 8).
3   Sticking inboard joint assembly. Correct or replace as necessary (Chapter 8).

Brakes

Note: *Before assuming that a brake problem exists, make sure . . .*

a) *The tires are in good condition and properly inflated (Chapter 1).*
b) *The front end alignment is correct (Chapter 10).*
c) *The vehicle isn't loaded with weight in an unequal manner.*

55   Vehicle pulls to one side during braking

1   Incorrect tire pressures (Chapter 1).
2   Front end out of line (have the front end aligned).
3   Unmatched tires on same axle.
4   Restricted brake lines or hoses (Chapter 9).
5   Malfunctioning brake assembly (Chapter 9).
6   Loose suspension parts (Chapter 10).
7   Loose brake calipers (Chapter 9).

56   Noise (high-pitched squeal when the brakes are applied)

Front disc brake pads worn out. The noise comes from the wear sensor rubbing against the disc. Replace pads with new ones immediately (Chapter 9).

57   Brake roughness or chatter (pedal pulsates)

1   Excessive front brake disc lateral runout (Chapter 9).
2   Parallelism not within specifications (Chapter 9).
3   Uneven pad wear caused by caliper not sliding due to improper clearance or dirt (Chapter 9).
4   Defective brake disc (Chapter 9).

58   Excessive pedal effort required to stop vehicle

1   Malfunctioning power brake booster (Chapter 9).
2   Partial system failure (Chapter 9).
3   Excessively worn pads (Chapter 9).
4   One or more caliper pistons or wheel cylinders seized or sticking (Chapter 9).
5   Brake pads contaminated with oil or grease (Chapter 9).
6   New pads installed and not yet seated. It will take a while for the new material to seat.

59   Excessive brake pedal travel

1   Partial brake system failure (Chapter 9).
2   Insufficient fluid in master cylinder (Chapters 1 and 9).
3   Air trapped in system (Chapters 1 and 9).

60   Dragging brakes

1   Master cylinder pistons not returning correctly (Chapter 9).
2   Restricted brakes lines or hoses (Chapters 1 and 9).
3   Incorrect parking brake adjustment (Chapter 9).

61   Grabbing or uneven braking action

1   Malfunction of proportioner valves (Chapter 9).
2   Malfunction of power brake booster unit (Chapter 9).
3   Binding brake pedal mechanism (Chapter 9).

62   Brake pedal feels spongy when depressed

1   Air in hydraulic lines (Chapter 9).
2   Master cylinder mounting bolts loose (Chapter 9).
3   Master cylinder defective (Chapter 9).

63   Brake pedal travels to the floor with little resistance

Little or no fluid in the master cylinder reservoir caused by leaking caliper or wheel cylinder pistons, loose, damaged or disconnected brake lines (Chapter 9).

64   Parking brake does not hold

Check the parking brake (Chapter 9).

Suspension and steering systems

Note: Before attempting to diagnose the suspension and steering systems, perform the following preliminary checks:

a) *Check the tire pressures and look for uneven wear.*
b) *Check the steering universal joints or coupling from the column to the steering gear for loose fasteners and wear.*
c) *Check the front and rear suspension and the steering gear assembly for loose and damaged parts.*
d) *Look for out-of-round or out-of-balance tires, bent rims and loose and/or rough wheel bearings.*

65   Vehicle pulls to one side

1   Mismatched or uneven tires (Chapter 10).
2   Broken or sagging springs (Chapter 10).
3   Front wheel alignment incorrect (Chapter 10).
4   Front brakes dragging (Chapter 9).

66   Abnormal or excessive tire wear

1   Front wheel alignment incorrect (Chapter 10).
2   Sagging or broken springs (Chapter 10).
3   Tire out-of-balance (Chapter 10).
4   Worn shock absorber (Chapter 10).
5   Overloaded vehicle.
6   Tires not rotated regularly.

67   Wheel makes a "thumping" noise

1   Blister or bump on tire (Chapter 1).
2   Improper shock absorber action (Chapter 10).

68   Shimmy, shake or vibration

1   Tire or wheel out-of-balance or out-of-round (Chapter 10).
2   Loose or worn wheel bearings (Chapter 10).
3   Worn tie-rod ends (Chapter 10).
4   Worn balljoints (Chapter 10).
5   Excessive wheel runout (Chapter 10).
6   Blister or bump on tire (Chapter 1).

69   Hard steering

1   Lack of lubrication at balljoints, tie-rod ends and steering gear assembly (Chapter 10).
2   Front wheel alignment incorrect (Chapter 10).
3   Low tire pressure (Chapter 1).

70   Steering wheel does not return to center position correctly

1   Lack of lubrication at balljoints and tie-rod ends (Chapter 10).
2   Binding in steering column (Chapter 10).
3   Defective rack-and-pinion assembly (Chapter 10).
4   Front wheel alignment problem (Chapter 10).

71   Abnormal noise at the front end

1   Lack of lubrication at balljoints and tie-rod ends (Chapter 1).
2   Loose upper strut mount (Chapter 10).
3   Worn tie-rod ends (Chapter 10).
4   Loose stabilizer bar (Chapter 10).
5   Loose wheel lug nuts (Chapter 1).
6   Loose suspension bolts (Chapter 10).

72   Wander or poor steering stability

1   Mismatched or uneven tires (Chapter 10).
2   Lack of lubrication at balljoints or tie-rod ends (Chapters 1 and 10).
3   Worn shock absorbers (Chapter 10).
4   Loose stabilizer bar (Chapter 10).
5   Broken or sagging springs (Chapter 10).
6   Front wheel alignment incorrect (Chapter 10).
7   Worn steering gear clamp bushings (Chapter 10).

73   Erratic steering when braking

1   Wheel bearings worn (Chapters 8 and 10).
2   Broken or sagging springs (Chapter 10).
3   Leaking wheel cylinder or caliper (Chapter 9).
4   Warped brake discs (rotors) (Chapter 9).
5   Worn steering gear clamp bushings (Chapter 10).

74   Excessive pitching and/or rolling around corners or during braking

1   Loose stabilizer bar (Chapter 10).
2   Worn shock absorbers or mounts (Chapter 10).
3   Broken or sagging springs (Chapter 10).
4   Overloaded vehicle.

75   Suspension bottoms

1   Overloaded vehicle.
2   Worn shock absorbers (Chapter 10).

3   Incorrect, broken or sagging springs (Chapter 10).

76   Cupped tires

1   Front wheel alignment incorrect (Chapter 10).
2   Worn shock absorbers (Chapter 10).
3   Wheel bearings worn (Chapters 8 and 10).
4   Excessive tire or wheel runout (Chapter 10).
5   Worn balljoints (Chapter 10).

77   Excessive tire wear on outside edge

1   Inflation pressures incorrect (Chapter 1).
2   Excessive speed in turns.
3   Front end alignment incorrect (excessive toe-in or positive camber). Have professionally aligned.
4   Suspension arm bent or twisted (Chapter 10).

78   Excessive tire wear on inside edge

1   Inflation pressures incorrect (Chapter 1).
2   Front end alignment incorrect (toe-out or excessive negative camber). Have professionally aligned.
3   Loose or damaged steering components (Chapter 10).

79   Tire tread worn in one place

1   Tires out-of-balance.
2   Damaged or buckled wheel. Inspect and replace if necessary.
3   Defective tire (Chapter 1).

80   Excessive play or looseness in steering system

1   Wheel bearings worn (Chapter 10).
2   Tie-rod end loose or worn (Chapter 10).
3   Steering gear loose (Chapter 10).

81   Rattling or clicking noise in rack and pinion

Steering gear clamps loose (Chapter 10).

Chapter 1   Tune-up and routine maintenance

Contents

	Section
Air filter and PCV filter replacement	20
Automatic transaxle fluid and filter change	28
Automatic transaxle fluid level check	6
Battery check and maintenance	8
Brake check	18
Chassis lubrication	36
Cooling system check	9
Cooling system servicing (draining, flushing and refilling)	30
Driveaxle boot check	13
Drivebelt and tensioner check and replacement	22
Engine oil and filter change	12
Evaporative emissions control system check	32
Exhaust system check	15
Fluid level checks	4
Fuel filter replacement	27
Fuel system check	19
Introduction	1
Maintenance schedule	2
Manual transaxle lubricant change	29
Manual transaxle lubricant level check	16

	Section
Positive Crankcase Ventilation (PCV) valve - check and replacement	31
Power steering fluid level check	7
Rotating the engine	34
Seat belt check	23
Seatback latch check	25
Spare tire and jack check	26
Spark plug replacement	33
Spark plug wire check and replacement	35
Starter safety switch check	24
Suspension and steering check	14
Throttle Body Injection (TBI) mounting nut/bolt torque check (2.5L engine only)	21
Throttle linkage check	37
Tire and tire pressure checks	5
Tire rotation	17
Tune-up general information	3
Underhood hose check and replacement	10
Windshield wiper blade inspection and replacement	11

Specifications

Recommended lubricants and fluids

Note: *Listed here are manufacturer recommendations at the time this manual was written. Manufacturers occasionally upgrade their fluid and lubricant specifications, so check with your local auto parts store for current recommendations.*

Engine oil
  Type .... API grade "certified for gasoline engines"
  Viscosity .... See accompanying chart
Automatic transaxle fluid
  1988 through 2005 .... Dexron ® III automatic transmission fluid (ATF)
  2006 and later .... Dexron ® VI automatic transmission fluid (ATF)
Manual transaxle lubricant .... See your owner's manual or consult a dealer service department
Engine coolant .... 50/50 mixture of water and the specified ethylene glycol-based (green color) antifreeze or "DEX-COOL", silicate-free (orange-color) coolant - DO NOT mix the two types (refer to Sections 4, 9 and 30)
Brake fluid .... Delco Supreme II or DOT 3 fluid
Clutch fluid .... Delco Supreme II or DOT 3 fluid
Power steering fluid .... GM power steering fluid or equivalent
Chassis grease .... SAE NLGI no. 2 chassis grease

Engine oil viscosity chart

For best fuel economy and cold starting, select the lowest SAE viscosity grade for the expected temperature range

Capacities

Engine oil (with filter change)	
2.5L four cylinder..	3.0 qts
3.4L V6..	5.0 qts
5.3L V8..	6.0 qts
All others	
1996 and earlier..	4.0 qts
1997 and later...	4.5 to 5.0 qts
Fuel tank	
2.2L four-cylinder	17.1 gals
All others	
1988 through 1990...	16 gals
1991 through 1996...	16.5 gals
1997 and later...	17 gals
Cooling system..	Depends on engine, transaxle and cooling system options. Consult your owner's manual for exact capacity
Automatic transaxle (fluid and filter change)	
3T40 transaxle	4.0 qts
All others	
1995 and earlier..	6.0 qts
1996 through 2001...	7.0 qts
2002 and later...	7.4 qts
Manual transaxle (approximate)...........................	2.1 qts

All capacities approximate. Add as necessary to bring to appropriate level.

Ignition system

Spark plug type and gap	
Four cylinder engines	
2.2L..	AC type R44LTSMA or equivalent @ 0.045 inch
2.3L..	AC type FR3L or equivalent @ 0.035 inch
2.5L..	AC type R43CTS6 or equivalent @ 0.060 inch
V6 engines	
1990 and earlier...	AC type R43LTSE or equivalent @ 0.045 inch
1991 through 1995	
3.1L...	AC type R44LTSM or equivalent @ 0.045 inch
3100...	AC type R44LTSM or equivalent @ 0.060 inch
3.4L...	AC type R42LTSM or equivalent @ 0.045 inch
3800...	AC type R44LTS6 or equivalent @ 0.060 inch
1996 and later	
3100 (1996 through 2003)............................	AC type 41-940 or equivalent @ 0.060 inch
3100 (2004 and later)...................................	AC type 41-101 or equivalent @ 0.060 inch
3.4L...	AC type 41-919 or equivalent @ 0.045 inch
3800...	AC type 41-921 or equivalent @ 0.060 inch
5.3L V8 engine...	AC type 41-985 or equivalent @ 0.040 inch
Firing order	
Four-cylinder engines..	1-3-4-2
3.1L, 3100 and 3.4L...	1-2-3-4-5-6
3800 engines...	1-6-5-4-3-2
5.3L V8 engine...	1-8-7-2-6-5-4-3

General

Radiator cap pressure rating	15 psi
Brake pad lining wear limit......................................	1/8 inch
Brake shoe lining wear limit.....................................	1/16 inch from rivets

Torque specifications

Ft-lbs (unless otherwise indicated)

Note: *One foot-pound of torque is equivalent to 12 inch-pounds of torque. Torque values below approximately 15 foot-pounds are expressed in inch-pounds, because most foot-pound torque wrenches are not accurate at these smaller values.*

Automatic transaxle oil pan bolts	
3T40	97 to 120 in-lbs
4T60-E and 4T65-E...	156 in-lbs
Engine oil drain plug...	15 to 20
Throttle body nuts/bolts...	144 in-lbs
Torque strut bolts...	50

2.2 Liter four-cylinder engine

2.5L engine

Front

2.3L engine

3800 V6 engine

1995 and earlier 2.8L, 3.1L and 3.4L V6 engines

1671H

FRONT OF VEHICLE

1994 and later 3100 V6 engine

24048-1-B HAYNES

FRONT OF VEHICLE

1996 3.4L V6 engine

24048-1-C HAYNES

5.3L V8 engine

Front of vehicle

24017-1-B HAYNES

Cylinder and coil terminal locations

Torque specifications (continued)

	Ft-lbs (unless otherwise indicated)
Spark plugs	
Four cylinder engines	
2.2L	132 in-lbs
2.3L and 2.5L	15
V6 engines	
2.8L and 3.1L	20
3100, 3.4L and 3800	15
5.3L V8 engine	11
Wheel lug nuts...	100

A typical V6 engine compartment

1	Brake fluid reservoir	6	Engine coolant reservoir
2	Windshield washer fluid reservoir	7	Engine oil dipstick
3	Battery	8	Radiator cap
4	Air cleaner housing	9	Radiator hose
5	Engine oil filler cap		

10	Engine compartment fuse block
11	Drivebelt routing decal
12	Power steering fluid reservoir
13	Serpentine drivebelt

1 Introduction

This Chapter is designed to help the home mechanic maintain the Chevrolet Lumina, Pontiac Grand Prix, Buick Regal and Oldsmobile Cutlass W-body models with the goals of maximum performance, economy, safety and reliability in mind.

Included is a master maintenance schedule, followed by procedures dealing specifically with each item on the schedule. Visual checks, adjustments, component replacement and other helpful items are included. Refer to the accompanying illustrations of the engine compartment and the underside of the vehicle for the locations of various components.

Servicing your vehicle in accordance with the mileage/time maintenance schedule and

the step-by-step procedures will result in a planned maintenance program that should produce a long and reliable service life. Keep in mind that it's a comprehensive plan, so maintaining some items but not others at the specified intervals will not produce the same results.

As you service your vehicle, you'll discover that many of the procedures can - and should - be grouped together because of the nature of the particular procedure you're performing or because of the close proximity of two otherwise unrelated components to one another.

For example, if the vehicle is raised, you should inspect the exhaust, suspension, steering and fuel systems while you're under the vehicle. When you're rotating the tires, it makes good sense to check the brakes since the

wheels are already removed. Finally, let's suppose you have to borrow or rent a torque wrench. Even if you only need it to tighten the spark plugs, you might as well check the torque of as many critical fasteners as time allows.

The first step in this maintenance program is to prepare yourself before the actual work begins. Read through all the procedures you're planning to do, then gather up all the parts and tools needed. If it looks like you might run into problems during a particular job, seek advice from a mechanic or an experienced do-it-yourselfer. **Caution:** *On models equipped with the Theftlock audio system, be sure the lockout feature is turned off before performing any procedure which requires disconnecting the battery (see the front of this manual).*

A typical Quad-4 engine compartment

1 Automatic transaxle fluid dipstick	6 Air cleaner housing
2 Brake fluid reservoir	7 Engine coolant reservoir
3 Power steering fluid reservoir	8 Engine oil filler cap/dipstick
4 Windshield washer fluid reservoir	9 Radiator cap
5 Battery	10 Engine compartment fuse block

Typical front underside components

1 Radiator drain plug (not visible)	4 Fuel lines	7 Steering gear
2 Front brake caliper	5 Automatic transaxle fluid pan	8 Tie-rod end
3 Lower control arm bushing	6 Engine oil drain plug	9 Driveaxle

Typical rear underside view – leaf-spring models

1 *Muffler*	2 *Fuel tank*	3 *Fuel filter*	4 *Rear disc brake caliper*

Typical rear underside view – coil spring/strut models

1 *Muffler*	3 *Fuel tank (under plastic shield)*
2 *Fuel filter*	4 *Coil-spring/strut unit*

2 Buick Regal, Chevrolet Lumina, Pontiac Grand Prix, Olds Cutlass Supreme Maintenance schedule

The following maintenance intervals are based on the assumption that the vehicle owner will be doing the maintenance or service work, as opposed to having a dealer service department do the work. Although the time/mileage intervals are loosely based on factory recommendations, most have been shortened to ensure, for example, that such items as lubricants and fluids are checked/changed at intervals that promote maximum engine/driveline service life. Also, subject to the preference of the individual owner interested in keeping his or her vehicle in peak condition at all times, and with the vehicle's ultimate resale in mind, many of the maintenance procedures may be performed more often than recommended in the following schedule. We encourage such owner initiative.

When the vehicle is new it should be serviced initially by a factory authorized dealer service department to protect the factory warranty. In many cases the initial maintenance check is done at no cost to the owner (check with your dealer service department for more information).

Every 250 miles or weekly, whichever comes first

Check the engine oil level (Section 4)
Check the engine coolant level (Section 4)
Check the windshield washer fluid level (Section 4)
Check the brake and clutch fluid levels (Section 4)
Check the tires and tire pressures (Section 5)

Every 3000 miles or 3 months, whichever comes first

All items listed above plus:
Check the automatic transmission fluid level (Section 6)
Check the power steering fluid level (Section 7)
Check the cooling system (Section 9)
Change the engine oil and filter (Section 12)

Every 7500 miles or 6 months, whichever comes first

All items listed above plus:
Check and service the battery (Section 8)
Inspect and replace, if necessary, all underhood hoses (Section 10)
Inspect and replace, if necessary, the windshield wiper blades (Section 11)
Check the driveaxle boots (Section 13)
Inspect the suspension and steering components (Section 14)
Inspect the exhaust system (Section 15)
Check the manual transaxle lubricant level (Section 16)
Rotate the tires (Section 17)
Check the brakes (Section 18)*
Lubricate the chassis (Section 36)
Check the throttle linkage (Section 37)

Every 15,000 miles or 12 months, whichever comes first

Inspect the fuel system (Section 19)
Replace the air filter and the PCV filter (Section 20)
Check the throttle body nut/bolt torque - 2.5L four cylinder engine only (Section 21)
Check the engine drivebelt(s) (Section 22)
Inspect the seat belts (Section 23)
Check the starter safety switch (Section 24)
Check the seat back latch (Section 25)
Check the spare tire and jack (Section 26)

Every 30,000 miles or 24 months, whichever comes first

All items listed above plus:
Replace the fuel filter (Section 27)***
Change the automatic transaxle fluid (Section 28)**
Change the manual transaxle lubricant (Section 29)***
Service the cooling system (drain, flush and refill) (green-colored ethylene glycol anti-freeze only) (Section 30)
Inspect and replace, if necessary, the PCV valve (Section 31)
Inspect the evaporative emissions control system (Section 32)
Replace the spark plugs (conventional [non-platinum] spark plugs) (Section 33)
Inspect the spark plug wires (Section 35)

Every 60,000 miles or 48 months, whichever comes first

Inspect and replace, if necessary the timing belt (3.4L V6 engines) (Chapter 2E). **Note:** *After 60,000 miles, the timing belt should be inspected every 15,000 miles.*

Every 100,000 miles or 5 years, whichever comes first

Replace the spark plugs (platinum-tipped spark plugs) (Section 33)
Service the cooling system (drain, flush and refill) (orange-colored "DEX-COOL" silicate-free coolant only) (Section 30)

* If the vehicle frequently tows a trailer, is operated primarily in stop-and-go conditions or its brakes receive severe usage for any other reason, check the brakes every 3000 miles or three months.

** If operated under one or more of the following conditions, change the automatic transaxle fluid every 15,000 miles:

In heavy city traffic where the outside temperature regularly reaches 90-degrees F (32-degrees C) or higher
In hilly or mountainous terrain
Frequent trailer pulling

***On later models these may not be required maintenance items. Consult your owner's manual.

4.2a The engine oil dipstick is clearly marked - "ENGINE OIL", as is the oil filler cap, which threads into the engine - on the Quad-4 shown here, the filler cap incorporates the dipstick

4.2b On most V6 applications, the oil filler cap (A) and dipstick (B) are near the front valve cover and clearly marked

3   Tune-up general information

The term tune-up is used in this manual to represent a combination of individual operations rather than one specific procedure.

If, from the time the vehicle is new, the routine maintenance schedule is followed closely and frequent checks are made of fluid levels and high wear items, as suggested throughout this manual, the engine will be kept in relatively good running condition and the need for additional work will be minimized.

More likely than not, however, there will be times when the engine is running poorly due to lack of regular maintenance. This is even more likely if a used vehicle, which has not received regular and frequent maintenance checks, is purchased. In such cases, an engine tune-up will be needed outside of the regular routine maintenance intervals.

The first step in any tune-up or diagnostic procedure to help correct a poor running engine is a cylinder compression check. A compression check (see Chapter 2, Part H) will help determine the condition of internal engine components and should be used as a guide for tune-up and repair procedures. If, for instance, a compression check indicates serious internal engine wear, a conventional tune-up won't improve the performance of the engine and would be a waste of time and money. Because of its importance, the compression check should be done by someone with the right equipment and the knowledge to use it properly.

The following procedures are those most often needed to bring a generally poor running engine back into a proper state of tune.

Minor tune-up

Check all engine related fluids (Section 4)
Clean, inspect and test the battery (Section 8)
Check and adjust the drivebelts (Section 22)
Replace the spark plugs (Section 33)
Inspect the spark plug wires (Section 34)
Check the PCV valve (Section 31)

Check the air and PCV filters (Section 20)
Check the cooling system (Section 9)
Check all underhood hoses (Section 10)

Major tune-up

All items listed under Minor tune-up plus . . .
Check the EGR system (Chapter 6)
Check the ignition system (Section 33 and Chapter 5)
Check the charging system (Chapter 5)
Check the fuel system (Section 19)
Replace the air and PCV filters (Section 20)
Replace the spark plug wires (Section 35)

4   Fluid level checks

Note: *The following are fluid level checks to be done on a 250 mile or weekly basis. Additional fluid level checks can be found in specific maintenance procedures, which follow. Regardless of intervals, be alert to fluid leaks under the vehicle, which would indicate a problem to be corrected immediately.*

1   Fluids are an essential part of the lubrication, cooling, brake and windshield washer systems. Because the fluids gradually become depleted and/or contaminated during normal operation of the vehicle, they must be periodically replenished. See *Recommended lubricants and fluids* at the beginning of this Chapter before adding fluid to any of the following components. **Note:** *The vehicle must be on level ground when fluid levels are checked.*

Engine oil

Refer to illustrations 4.2a, 4.2b and 4.4
2   The engine oil is checked with a dipstick **(see illustrations)**.
3   The oil level should be checked before the vehicle has been driven, or about 15 minutes after the engine has been shut off. If the oil is checked immediately after driving the vehicle, some of the oil will remain in the upper part of the engine, resulting in an inaccurate reading on the dipstick.
4   Pull the dipstick from the tube and wipe all the oil from the end with a clean rag or paper towel. Insert the clean dipstick all the way back into the tube and pull it out again. Note the oil at the end of the dipstick. Add oil as necessary to keep the level above the ADD mark in the cross-hatched area of the dipstick **(see illustration)**.
5   Do not overfill the engine by adding too much oil since this may result in oil fouled spark plugs, oil leaks or oil seal failures.
6   Oil is added to the engine after removing a twist-off cap located on the engine. On the Quad-4 engine, add the oil through the tube where the dipstick was removed. A funnel may help to reduce spills.
7   Checking the oil level is an important preventive maintenance step. A consistently low oil level indicates oil leakage through damaged seals, defective gaskets or past worn rings or valve guides. If the oil looks milky in color or has water droplets in it, the cylinder head gasket may be blown or the head or block may be cracked. The engine should be checked immediately. The condition

4.4 The oil level should be in the cross-hatched area - if it's below the ADD line, add enough oil to bring the level into the cross-hatched area

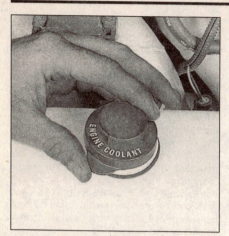

4.9 Coolant can be added to the reservoir after flipping the cap up

4.14 Flip the windshield washer fluid cap up to add fluid

4.18 Unscrew the reservoir cap and make sure the brake fluid level is up to the bottom of the slot in the neck

of the oil should also be checked. Whenever you check the oil level, slide your thumb and index finger up the dipstick before wiping off the oil. If you see small dirt or metal particles clinging to the dipstick, the oil should be changed (Section 12).

Engine coolant

Refer to illustration 4.9

Warning: *Do not allow antifreeze to come in contact with your skin or painted surfaces of the vehicle. Rinse off spills immediately with plenty of water. Antifreeze is highly toxic if ingested. Never leave antifreeze lying around in an open container or in puddles on the floor; children and pets are attracted by its sweet smell and may drink it. Check with local authorities about disposing of used antifreeze. Many communities have collection centers which will see that antifreeze is disposed of safely.* **Caution:** *Never mix green-colored ethylene glycol anti-freeze and orange-colored "DEX-COOL" silicate-free coolant because doing so will destroy the efficiency of the "DEX-COOL" coolant which is designed to last for 100,000 miles or five years.*

8   All vehicles covered by this manual are equipped with a pressurized coolant recovery system. A white plastic coolant reservoir located at the front of the engine compartment is connected by a hose to the radiator filler neck. As the engine warms up and the coolant expands, it escapes through a valve in the radiator cap and travels through the hose into the reservoir. As the engine cools, the coolant is automatically drawn back into the cooling system to maintain the correct level. Coolant recovery tanks on 1999 and later models are mounted at the right rear of the engine compartment.

9   The coolant level in the reservoir should be checked regularly. **Warning:** *Do not remove the radiator cap to check the coolant level when the engine is warm. The level in the reservoir varies with the temperature of the engine.* When the engine is cold, the coolant level should be at or slightly above the FULL COLD mark on the reservoir. Once the

engine has warmed up, the level should be at or near the FULL HOT mark. If it isn't, add coolant to the reservoir. To add coolant simply flip up the cap and add a 50/50 mixture of ethylene glycol based green-colored antifreeze or orange-colored "DEX-COOL" silicate-free coolant and water (see **Caution** above). The coolant and windshield washer reservoirs look similar, so be sure to add the correct fluids; the caps are clearly marked **(see illustration)**.

10   Drive the vehicle and recheck the coolant level. If only a small amount of coolant is required to bring the system up to the proper level, water can be used. However, repeated additions of water will dilute the antifreeze and water solution. In order to maintain the proper ratio of antifreeze and water, always top up the coolant level with the correct mixture. An empty plastic milk jug or bleach bottle makes an excellent container for mixing coolant. Do not use rust inhibitors or additives.

11   If the coolant level drops consistently, there may be a leak in the system. Inspect the radiator, hoses, filler cap, drain plugs and water pump (see Section 9). If no leaks are noted, have the radiator cap pressure tested by a service station.

12   If you have to remove the radiator cap, wait until the engine has cooled completely, then wrap a thick cloth around the cap and turn it to the first stop. If coolant or steam escapes, let the engine cool down longer, then remove the cap.

13   Check the condition of the coolant as well. It should be relatively clear. If it is brown or rust colored, the system should be drained, flushed and refilled. Even if the coolant appears to be normal, the corrosion inhibitors wear out, so it must be replaced at the specified intervals.

Windshield washer fluid

Refer to illustration 4.14

14   Fluid for the windshield washer system is located in a plastic reservoir in the engine compartment **(see illustration)**. In milder climates, plain water can be used in the reser-

voir, but it should be kept no more than two-thirds full to allow for expansion if the water freezes. In colder climates, use windshield washer system antifreeze, available at any auto parts store, to lower the freezing point of the fluid. Mix the antifreeze with water in accordance with the manufacturer's directions on the container. **Caution:** *Do not use cooling system antifreeze - it will damage the vehicle's paint.*

15   To help prevent icing in cold weather, warm the windshield with the defroster before using the washer.

Battery electrolyte

16   All vehicles covered by this manual are equipped with a battery which is permanently sealed (except for vent holes) and has no filler caps. Water does not have to be added to these batteries at any time; however, if a maintenance-type battery has been installed on the vehicle since it was new, remove all the cell caps on top of the battery (usually there are two caps that cover three cells each). If the electrolyte level is low, add distilled water until the level is above the plates. There is usually a split-ring indicator in each cell to help you judge when enough water has been added. Add water until the electrolyte level is just up to the bottom of the split ring indicator. Do not overfill the battery or it will spew out electrolyte when it is charging.

Brake and clutch fluid

Refer to illustration 4.18

17   The brake master cylinder is mounted on the front of the power booster unit in the engine compartment. The clutch master cylinder used with manual transaxles is mounted adjacent to it on the firewall. On early models equipped with ABS, apply the brake 40 times before checking the fluid level.

18   Unscrew the cap and make sure the fluid level is even with the bottom of the filler neck slot **(see illustration)**. On early models equipped with ABS, release the clips and lift the reservoir cover off.

5.2 Use a tire tread depth indicator to monitor tire wear - they are available at auto parts stores and service stations and cost very little

19   When adding fluid, pour it carefully into the reservoir to avoid spilling it on surrounding painted surfaces. Be sure the specified fluid is used, since mixing different types of brake fluid can cause damage to the system. See Recommended lubricants and fluids at the front of this Chapter or your owner's manual.

Warning: *Brake fluid can harm your eyes and damage painted surfaces, so use extreme caution when handling or pouring it. Do not use brake fluid that has been standing open or is more than one year old. Brake fluid absorbs moisture from the air. Excess moisture can cause a dangerous loss of braking effectiveness.*

20   At this time the fluid and master cylinder can be inspected for contamination. The system should be drained and refilled if deposits, dirt particles or water droplets are seen in the fluid.

21   After filling the reservoir to the proper level, make sure the cap is on tight to prevent fluid leakage.

22   The brake fluid level in the master cylinder will drop slightly as the pads at each wheel wear down during normal operation. If the master cylinder requires repeated replenishing to keep it at the proper level, this is an indication of leakage in the brake system, which should be corrected immediately. Check all brake lines and connections (see Section 18 for more information).

23   If, when checking the master cylinder fluid level, you discover one or both reservoirs empty or near empty, the brake system should be bled and checked for leaks (Chapter 9).

5   Tire and tire pressure checks

Refer to illustrations 5.2, 5.3, 5.4a, 5.4b and 5.8

1   Periodic inspection of the tires may spare you the inconvenience of being stranded with a flat tire. It can also provide you with vital information regarding possible problems in the steering and suspension systems before major damage occurs.

2   The original tires on this vehicle are equipped with 1/2-inch side bands that appear when tread depth reaches 1/16-inch, but they don't appear until the tires are worn out. Tread wear can be monitored with a simple, inexpensive device known as a tread depth indicator **(see illustration)**.

3   Note any abnormal tread wear **(see illustration)**. Tread pattern irregularities such as cupping, flat spots and more wear on one side than the other are indications of front end alignment and/or balance problems. If any of these conditions are noted, take the vehicle to a tire shop or service station to correct the problem.

4   Look closely for cuts, punctures and embedded nails or tacks. Sometimes a tire will hold air pressure for short time or leak down very slowly after a nail has embedded

INCORRECT TOE-IN OR EXTREME CAMBER

CUPPING

Cupping may be caused by:
- Underinflation and/or mechanical irregularities such as out-of-balance condition of wheel and/or tire, and bent or damaged wheel.
- Loose or worn steering tie-rod or steering idler arm.
- Loose, damaged or worn front suspension parts.

OVERINFLATION

FEATHERING DUE TO MISALIGNMENT

UNDERINFLATION

5.3 This chart will help you determine the condition of the tires, the probable cause(s) of abnormal wear and the corrective action necessary

5.4a If a tire loses air on a steady basis, check the valve core first to make sure it's snug (special inexpensive wrenches are commonly available at auto parts stores)

5.4b If the valve core is tight, raise the corner of the vehicle with the low tire and spray a soapy water solution onto the tread as the tire is turned slowly - leaks will cause small bubbles to appear

5.8 To extend the life of the tires, check the air pressure at least once a week with an accurate gauge (don't forget the spare!)

6.3a On earlier models the transaxle dipstick is clearly marked "TRANS FLUID" . . .

6.3b . . . while on later models the transaxle dipstick is indicated by a RED handle (arrow) - In either case the dipstick is located at the rear of the engine compartment between the engine and the firewall

itself in the tread. If a slow leak persists, check the valve stem core to make sure it's tight **(see illustration)**. Examine the tread for an object that may have embedded itself in the tire or for a "plug" that may have begun to leak (radial tire punctures are repaired with a plug that's installed in a puncture). If a puncture is suspected, it can be easily verified by spraying a solution of soapy water onto the suspected area **(see illustration)**. The soapy solution will bubble if there's a leak. Unless the puncture is unusually large, a tire shop or service station can usually repair the tire.

5 Carefully inspect the inner sidewall of each tire for evidence of brake fluid. If you see any, inspect the brakes immediately.

6 Correct air pressure adds miles to the lifespan of the tires, improves mileage and enhances overall ride quality. Tire pressure cannot be accurately estimated by looking at a tire, especially if it's a radial. A tire pressure gauge is essential. Keep an accurate gauge in the vehicle. The pressure gauges attached to the nozzles of air hoses at gas stations are often inaccurate.

7 Always check tire pressure when the

tires are cold. Cold, in this case, means the vehicle has not been driven over a mile in the three hours preceding a tire pressure check. A pressure rise of four to eight pounds is not uncommon once the tires are warm.

8 Unscrew the valve cap protruding from the wheel or hubcap and push the gauge firmly onto the valve stem **(see illustration)**. Note the reading on the gauge and compare the figure to the recommended tire pressure shown on the label attached to the inside of the glove compartment door. Be sure to reinstall the valve cap to keep dirt and moisture out of the valve stem mechanism. Check all four tires and, if necessary, add enough air to bring them up to the recommended pressure.

9 Don't forget to keep the spare tire inflated to the specified pressure (refer to your owner's manual or the tire sidewall).

6 Automatic transaxle fluid level check

Refer to illustrations 6.3a, 6.3b and 6.6

1 The automatic transaxle fluid level should

be carefully maintained. Low fluid level can lead to slipping or loss of drive, while overfilling can cause foaming and loss of fluid.

2 With the parking brake set, start the engine, then move the shift lever through all the gear ranges, ending in Park. The fluid level must be checked with the vehicle level and the engine running at idle. **Note:** *Incorrect fluid level readings will result if the vehicle has just been driven at high speeds for an extended period, in hot weather in city traffic, or if it has been pulling a trailer. If any of these conditions apply, wait until the fluid has cooled (about 30 minutes).*

3 With the transaxle at normal operating temperature, remove the dipstick from the filler tube. The dipstick is located at the rear of the engine compartment **(see illustration)**.

4 Carefully touch the fluid at the end of the dipstick to determine if the fluid is cool, warm or hot. Wipe the fluid from the dipstick with a clean rag and push it back into the filler tube until the cap seats.

6.6 The automatic transaxle fluid level must be maintained within the cross-hatched area on the dipstick

7.2 The power steering fluid reservoir is located near the front (drivebelt end) of the engine; turn the cap clockwise for removal (V6 engine shown)

7.6 The marks on the dipstick indicate the safe fluid level range

5 Pull the dipstick out again and note the fluid level.

6 If the fluid felt cool, the level should be about 1/8-to-3/8 inch below the "ADD 1 PT" mark (see illustration). If it felt warm, the level should be close to the "ADD 1 PT" mark. If the fluid was hot, the level should be within the cross-hatched area. If additional fluid is required, pour it directly into the tube using a funnel. It takes about one pint to raise the level from the ADD mark to the upper edge of the cross-hatched area with a hot transaxle, so add the fluid a little at a time and keep checking the level until it's correct.

7 The condition of the fluid should also be checked along with the level. If the fluid at the end of the dipstick is a dark reddish-brown color, or if the fluid has a burned smell, the fluid should be changed. If you're in doubt about the condition of the fluid, purchase some new fluid and compare the two for color and smell.

7   Power steering fluid level check

Refer to illustrations 7.2 and 7.6

1 Unlike manual steering, the power steering system relies on fluid which may, over a period of time, require replenishing.

2 The fluid reservoir for the power steering pump is located behind the radiator near the front (drivebelt end) of the engine (see illustration).

3 For the check, the front wheels should be pointed straight ahead and the engine should be off.

8.1 Tools and materials required for battery maintenance

1 *Face shield/safety goggles - When removing corrosion with a brush, the acidic particles can easily fly up into your eyes*

2 *Rubber gloves - Another safety item to consider when servicing the battery - remember that's acid inside the battery!*

3 *Battery terminal/cable cleaner - This wire brush cleaning tool will remove all traces of corrosion from the battery and cable*

4 *Treated felt washers - Placing one of these on each terminal, directly under the cable end, will help prevent corrosion (be sure to get the correct type for side-terminal batteries)*

5 *Baking soda - A solution of baking soda and water can be used to neutralize corrosion*

6 *Petroleum jelly - A layer of this on the battery terminal bolts will help prevent corrosion*

4 Use a clean rag to wipe off the reservoir cap and the area around the cap. This will help prevent any foreign matter from entering the reservoir during the check.

5 Twist off the cap and check the temperature of the fluid at the end of the dipstick with your finger.

6 Wipe off the fluid with a clean rag, reinsert it, then withdraw it and read the fluid level.

The level should be at the HOT mark if the fluid was hot to the touch (see illustration). It should be at the COLD mark if the fluid was cool to the touch. Note that on some models the marks (FULL HOT and COLD) are on opposite sides of the dipstick. At no time should the fluid level drop below the ADD mark.

7 If additional fluid is required, pour the specified type directly into the reservoir, using a funnel to prevent spills.

8 If the reservoir requires frequent fluid additions, all power steering hoses, hose connections, the power steering pump and the rack and pinion assembly should be carefully checked for leaks.

8   Battery check and maintenance

Refer to illustrations 8.1, 8.4, 8.5a, 8.5b, 8.5c and 8.5d

Warning: *Certain precautions must be followed when checking and servicing the battery. Hydrogen gas, which is highly flammable, is always present in the battery cells, so keep lighted tobacco and all other open flames and sparks away from the battery. The electrolyte inside the battery is actually dilute sulfuric acid, which will cause injury if splashed on your skin or in your eyes. It will also ruin clothes and painted surfaces. When removing the battery cables, always detach the negative cable first and hook it up last!* **Caution:** *On models equipped with the Theftlock audio system, be sure the lockout feature is turned off before performing any procedure which requires disconnecting the battery.*

1 Battery maintenance is an important procedure which will help ensure you aren't stranded because of a dead battery. Several tools are required for this procedure (see illustration).

2 A sealed battery is standard equipment on all vehicles covered by this manual. Although this type of battery has many advantages over the older, capped cell type, and never requires the addition of water, it should

8.4 Check the tightness of the battery cable terminal bolts

8.5a A tool like this one (available at auto parts stores) is used to clean the side terminal type battery contact area

8.5b Use the brush to finish the cleaning job

8.5c The result should be a clean, shiny terminal area

8.5d Some models are also equipped with a remote positive battery terminal - be sure to remove the cover and check for corrosion and a that the cable is securely fastened

still be routinely maintained according to the procedures which follow.

Check

3   The battery is located on the left side of the engine compartment. The exterior of the battery should be inspected periodically for damage such as a cracked case or cover.

4   Check the tightness of the battery cable terminals and connections **(see illustration)** to ensure good electrical connections and check the entire length of each cable for cracks and frayed conductors.

5   If corrosion (visible as white, fluffy deposits) is evident, remove the cables from the terminals, clean them with a battery brush and reinstall the cables **(see illustrations)**. Corrosion can be kept to a minimum by using special treated fiber washers available at auto parts stores or by applying a layer of petroleum jelly to the terminals and cables after they are assembled.

6   Make sure that the battery tray is in good condition and the hold-down clamp bolt is tight. If the battery is removed from the tray, make sure no parts remain in the bottom of the tray when the battery is reinstalled. When reinstalling the hold-down clamp bolt, do not overtighten it.

7   Information on removing and installing the battery can be found in Chapter 5. Information on jump starting can be found at the front of this manual. For more detailed battery checking procedures, refer to the *Haynes Automotive Electrical Manual*.

Cleaning

8   Corrosion on the hold-down components, battery case and surrounding areas can be removed with a solution of water and baking soda. Thoroughly rinse all cleaned areas with plain water.

9   Any metal parts of the vehicle damaged by corrosion should be covered with a zinc-based primer, then painted.

Charging

Warning: *When batteries are being charged, hydrogen gas, which is very explosive and flammable, is produced. Do not smoke or*

allow open flames near a charging or a recently charged battery. Wear eye protection when near the battery during charging. Also, make sure the charger is unplugged before connecting or disconnecting the battery from the charger.

10   Slow-rate charging is the best way to restore a battery that's discharged to the point where it will not start the engine. It's also a good way to maintain the battery charge in a vehicle that's only driven a few miles between starts. Maintaining the battery charge is particularly important in the winter when the battery must work harder to start the engine and electrical accessories that drain the battery are in greater use.

11   It's best to use a one or two-amp battery charger (sometimes called a "trickle" charger). They are the safest and put the least strain on the battery. They are also the least expensive. For a faster charge, you can use a higher amperage charger, but don't use one rated more than 1/10th the amp/hour rating of the battery. Rapid boost charges that claim to restore the power of the battery in one to two hours are hardest on the battery and can damage batteries not in good condition. This type of charging should only be used in emergency situations.

12   The average time necessary to charge a battery should be listed in the instructions that come with the charger. As a general rule, a trickle charger will charge a battery in 12 to 16 hours.

13   Remove all of the cell caps (if equipped) and cover the holes with a clean cloth to prevent spattering electrolyte. Disconnect the negative battery cable and hook the battery charger leads to the battery posts (positive to positive, negative to negative), then plug in the charger. Make sure it is set at 12 volts if it has a selector switch. **Caution:** *On models equipped with the Theftlock audio system, be sure the lockout feature is turned off before performing any procedure which requires disconnecting the battery.*

14   If you're using a charger with a rate higher than two amps, check the battery regularly during charging to make sure it doesn't overheat. If you're using a trickle charger, you can safely let the battery charge overnight after you've checked it regularly for the first couple of hours.

15   If the battery has removable cell caps, measure the specific gravity with a hydrome-

ter every hour during the last few hours of the charging cycle. Hydrometers are available inexpensively from auto parts stores - follow the instructions that come with the hydrometer. Consider the battery charged when there's no change in the specific gravity reading for two hours and the electrolyte in the cells is gassing (bubbling) freely. The specific gravity reading from each cell should be very close to the others. If not, the battery probably has a bad cell(s).

16   Some batteries with sealed tops have built-in hydrometers on the top that indicate the state of charge by the color displayed in the hydrometer window. Normally, a bright-colored hydrometer indicates a full charge and a dark hydrometer indicates the battery still needs charging. Check the battery manufacturer's instructions to be sure you know what the colors mean.

17   If the battery has a sealed top and no built-in hydrometer, you can hook up a digital voltmeter across the battery terminals to check the charge. A fully charged battery should read 12.5 volts or higher.

---

9   Cooling system check

Refer to illustration 9.4

Caution: *Never mix green-colored ethylene glycol anti-freeze and orange-colored "DEX-COOL" silicate-free coolant because doing so will destroy the efficiency of the "DEX-COOL" coolant which is designed to last for 100,000 miles or five years.*

1   Many major engine failures can be attributed to a faulty cooling system. If the vehicle is equipped with an automatic transaxle, the cooling system also cools the transaxle fluid and plays an important role in prolonging transaxle life.

2   The cooling system should be checked with the engine cold. Do this before the vehicle is driven for the day or after the engine has been shut off for at least three hours.

3   Remove the radiator cap by turning it to the left until it reaches a stop. If you hear any hissing sounds (indicating there is still pressure in the system), wait until it stops. Now press down on the cap with the palm of your hand and continue turning to the left until the cap can be removed. Thoroughly clean the cap, inside and out, with clean water. Also clean the filler neck on the radiator. All traces of corrosion should be removed. The coolant inside the radiator should be relatively transparent. If it is rust colored, the system should be drained and refilled (Section 30). If the coolant level is not up to the top, add additional antifreeze/coolant mixture (see Section 4).

4   Carefully check the large upper and lower radiator hoses along with any smaller diameter heater hoses which run from the engine to the firewall. Inspect each hose along its entire length, replacing any hose which is cracked, swollen or shows signs of deterioration. Cracks may become more apparent if the hose is squeezed **(see illustration)**.

5   Make sure all hose connections are tight.

Check for a chafed area that could fail prematurely.

Check for a soft area indicating the hose has deteriorated inside.

Overtightening the clamp on a hardened hose will damage the hose and cause a leak.

Check each hose for swelling and oil-soaked ends. Cracks and breaks can be located by squeezing the hos

9.4   Hoses, like drivebelts, have a habit of failing at the worst possible time - to prevent the inconvenience of a blown radiator or heater hose, inspect them carefully as shown here

---

A leak in the cooling system will usually show up as white or rust colored deposits on the areas adjoining the leak. If wire-type clamps are used at the ends of the hoses, it may be wise to replace them with more secure screw-type clamps.

6   Use compressed air or a soft brush to remove bugs, leaves, etc. from the front of the radiator or air conditioning condenser. Be careful not to damage the delicate cooling fins or cut yourself on them.

7   Every other inspection, or at the first indication of cooling system problems, have the cap and system pressure tested. If you don't have a pressure tester, most gas stations and repair shops will do this for a minimal charge.

10.1   Air conditioning hoses are easily identified by the metal tubes used at all bends (arrow) - DO NOT disconnect or accidentally damage the air conditioning hoses (the system is under high pressure)

---

10   Underhood hose check and replacement

General

Refer to illustration 10.1

Caution: *Replacement of air conditioning hoses must be left to a dealer service department or air conditioning shop that has the equipment to depressurize the system safely. Never remove air conditioning components or hoses* **(see illustration)** *until the system has been depressurized.*

1   High temperatures under the hood can cause the deterioration of the rubber and plastic hoses used for engine, accessory and emission systems operation. Periodic inspection should be made for cracks, loose clamps, material hardening and leaks. Information specific to the cooling system hoses can be found in Section 9.

2   Some, but not all, hoses are secured to the fittings with clamps. Where clamps are used, check to be sure they haven't lost their tension, allowing the hose to leak. If clamps aren't used, make sure the hose hasn't expanded and/or hardened where it slips over the fitting, allowing it to leak.

Vacuum hoses

3   It's quite common for vacuum hoses, especially those in the emissions system, to be color coded or identified by colored stripes molded into each hose. Various systems require hoses with different wall thicknesses, collapse resistance and temperature resistance. When replacing hoses, be sure the new ones are made of the same material.

4   Often the only effective way to check a hose is to remove it completely from the vehicle. If more than one hose is removed, be sure to label the hoses and fittings to ensure correct installation.

5   When checking vacuum hoses, be sure

11.5a On 1995 and earlier models, lift the release lever (arrow), then slide the blade assembly off the wiper arm

11.5b On 1996 and later models, press down the release tab, then slide the blade assembly down and out of the hook in the arm

11.7 The rubber element is retained to the blade by small clips - the metal backing of the rubber element can be compressed at one end with pliers, allowing the element to slide out of the clips

to include any plastic T-fittings in the check. Inspect the fittings for cracks and the hose where it fits over the fitting for distortion, which could cause leakage.

6   A small piece of vacuum hose (1/4-inch inside diameter) can be used as a stethoscope to detect vacuum leaks. Hold one end of the hose to your ear and probe around vacuum hoses and fittings, listening for the "hissing" sound characteristic of a vacuum leak. **Warning:** *When probing with the vacuum hose stethoscope, be careful not to allow your body or the hose to come into contact with moving engine components such as the drivebelt, cooling fan, etc.*

Fuel hose

Warning: *Gasoline is extremely flammable, so take extra precautions when you work on any part of the fuel system. Don't smoke or allow open flames or bare light bulbs near the work area, and don't work in a garage where a natural gas-type appliance (such as a water heater or a clothes dryer) with a pilot light is present. Since gasoline is carcinogenic, wear latex gloves when there's a possibility of being exposed to fuel, and, if you spill any fuel on your skin, rinse it off immediately with soap and water. Mop up any spills immediately and do not store fuel-soaked rags where they could ignite. When you perform any kind of work on the fuel system, wear safety glasses and have a Class B type fire extinguisher on hand.*

7   Check all rubber fuel lines for deterioration and chafing. Check especially for cracks in areas where the hose bends and just before fittings, such as where a hose attaches to the fuel filter and fuel injection unit.

8   High quality fuel line, usually identified by the word Fluroelastomer printed on the hose, should be used for fuel line replacement. Never, under any circumstances, use unreinforced vacuum line, clear plastic tubing or water hose for fuel lines.

9   Spring-type clamps are commonly used on fuel lines. These clamps often lose their tension over a period of time, and can be "sprung" during the removal process. As a result spring-type clamps be replaced with screw-type clamps whenever a hose is replaced.

Metal lines

10   Sections of steel tubing often used for fuel line between the fuel pump and fuel injection unit. Check carefully for cracks, kinks and flat spots in the line.

11   If a section of metal fuel line must be replaced, only seamless steel tubing should be used, since copper and aluminum tubing do not have the strength necessary to withstand normal engine vibration.

12   Check the metal brake lines where they enter the master cylinder and brake proportioning unit (if used) for cracks in the lines and loose fittings. Any sign of brake fluid leakage calls for an immediate thorough inspection of the brake system.

11 Windshield wiper blade inspection and replacement

Refer to illustrations 11.5a, 11.5b and 11.7

1   The windshield wiper and blade assembly should be inspected periodically for damage, loose components and cracked or worn blade elements.

2   Road film can build up on the wiper blades and affect their efficiency, so they should be washed regularly with a mild detergent solution.

3   The action of the wiping mechanism can loosen the bolts, nuts and fasteners, so they should be checked and tightened, as necessary, at the same time the wiper blades are checked.

4   If the wiper blade elements (sometimes called inserts) are cracked, worn or warped, they should be replaced with new ones.

5   On 1995 and earlier models remove the wiper blade assembly from the wiper arm by using a small screwdriver to lift the release lever while pulling on the blade to release it **(see illustration)**. On 1996 and later models lift the arm assembly away from the glass for clearance, press on the release lever, then slide the wiper blade assembly out of the hook in the end of the arm **(see illustration)**.

6   With the blade removed from the vehicle, you can remove the rubber element from the blade.

7   Using pliers, pinch the metal backing of the element **(see illustration)**, then slide the element out of the blade assembly.

8   Compare the new element with the old for length, design, etc.

9   Slide the new element into place. It will automatically lock at the correct location.

10   Reinstall the blade assembly on the arm, wet the windshield glass and test for proper operation.

12 Engine oil and filter change

Refer to illustrations 12.3, 12.9, 12.14 and 12.18

1   Frequent oil changes are the most important preventive maintenance procedures that can be done by the home mechanic. As engine oil ages, it becomes diluted and contaminated, which leads to premature engine wear.

2   Although some sources recommend oil filter changes every other oil change, we feel that the minimal cost of an oil filter and the relative ease with which it is installed dictate that a new filter be used every time the oil is changed.

3   Gather together all necessary tools and

12.3 These tools are required when changing the engine oil and filter

1   *Drain pan* - *It should be fairly shallow in depth, but wide to prevent spills*
2   *Rubber gloves* - *When removing the drain plug and filter, you will get oil on your hands (the gloves will prevent burns)*
3   *Breaker bar* - *Sometimes the oil drain plug is tight, and a long breaker bar is needed to loosen it*
4   *Socket* - *To be used with the breaker bar or a ratchet (must be the correct size to fit the drain plug - six-point preferred)*
5   *Filter wrench* - *This is a metal band-type wrench, which requires clearance around the filter to be effective*
6   *Filter wrench* - *This type fits on the bottom of the filter and can be turned with a ratchet or breaker bar (different-size wrenches are available for different types of filters)*

materials before beginning the procedure **(see illustration)**.
4   In addition, you should have plenty of clean rags and newspapers handy to mop up any spills. Access to the underside of the vehicle is greatly improved if the vehicle can be lifted on a hoist, driven onto ramps or supported by jackstands. **Warning:** *Do not work under a vehicle which is supported only by a bumper, hydraulic or scissors-type jack.*
5   If this is your first oil change, get under the vehicle and familiarize yourself with the locations of the oil drain plug and the oil filter. The engine and exhaust components will be warm during the actual work, so note how they are situated to avoid touching them when working under the vehicle.
6   Warm the engine to normal operating temperature. If the new oil or any tools are

12.9 The engine oil drain plug is located at the rear of the oil pan – it is usually very tight, so use a box-end wrench to avoid rounding off the hex

needed, use this warm-up time to gather everything necessary for the job. The correct type of oil for your application can be found in *Recommended lubricants and fluids* at the beginning of this Chapter.
7   With the engine oil warm (warm engine oil will drain better and more built-up sludge will be removed with the oil), raise and support the vehicle. Make sure it's safely supported.
8   Move all necessary tools, rags and newspapers under the vehicle. Position the drain pan under the drain plug. Keep in mind that the oil will initially flow from the pan with some force, so place the pan accordingly.
9   Being careful not to touch any of the hot exhaust components, remove the drain plug at the bottom of the oil pan **(see illustration)**. Depending on how hot the oil is, you may want to wear gloves while unscrewing the plug the final few turns.
10   Allow the old oil to drain into the pan. It may be necessary to move the pan farther under the engine as the oil flow slows to a trickle.
11   After all the oil has drained, wipe off the drain plug with a clean rag. Small metal particles may cling to the plug which would immediately contaminate the new oil.
12   Clean the area around the drain plug opening and reinstall the plug. Tighten the plug securely with the wrench. If a torque wrench is available, use it to tighten the plug.
13   Move the drain pan into position under the oil filter.
14   Use the filter wrench to loosen the oil filter **(see illustration)**. Chain or metal band filter wrenches may distort the filter canister, but this is of no concern as the filter will be discarded anyway.
15   Completely unscrew the old filter. Be careful - it's full of oil. Empty the oil inside the filter into the drain pan.
16   Compare the old filter with the new one to make sure they are the same type.
17   Use a clean rag to remove all oil, dirt and sludge from the area where the oil filter

12.14 The oil filter is usually on very tight as well and will require a special wrench for removal - DO NOT use the wrench to tighten the new filter!

mounts on the engine. Check the old filter to make sure the rubber gasket isn't stuck to the engine. If the gasket is stuck to the engine (use a flashlight if necessary), remove it.
18   Apply a light coat of oil to the rubber gasket on the new oil filter **(see illustration)**. Open a can of oil and partially fill the oil filter with fresh oil. Oil pressure will not build in the engine until the oil pump has filled the filter with oil, so partially filling it at this time will reduce the amount of time the engine runs with no oil pressure.
19   Attach the new filter to the engine, following the tightening directions printed on the filter canister or box. Most filter manufacturers recommend against using a filter wrench due to the possibility of overtightening and damage to the seal.
20   Remove all tools, rags, etc. from under the vehicle, being careful not to spill the oil in the drain pan, then lower the vehicle.
21   Move to the engine compartment and locate the oil filler cap.
22   Pour the fresh oil through the filler opening. A funnel can be used.
23   Pour three quarts of fresh oil into the engine. Wait a few minutes to allow the oil to

12.18 Lubricate the oil filter gasket with clean engine oil before installing the filter on the engine

13.2 Push on the driveaxle boots to check for cracks

16.2 The manual transaxle dipstick (arrow) is located adjacent to the brake master cylinder

16.3 Follow the manual transaxle lubricant checking procedure printed on the dipstick

drain into the pan, then check the level on the dipstick (see Section 4 if necessary). If the oil level is above the ADD mark, start the engine and allow the new oil to circulate.

24   Run the engine for only about a minute and then shut it off. Immediately look under the vehicle and check for leaks at the oil pan drain plug and around the oil filter. If either is leaking, tighten with a bit more force.

25   With the new oil circulated and the filter now completely full, recheck the level on the dipstick and add more oil as necessary.

26   During the first few trips after an oil change, make it a point to check frequently for leaks and proper oil level.

27   The old oil drained from the engine cannot be reused in its present state and should be disposed of. Oil reclamation centers, auto repair shops and gas stations will normally accept the oil, which can be refined and used again. After the oil has cooled it can be drained into a container (capped plastic jugs, topped bottles, milk cartons, etc.) for transport to a disposal site.

13   Driveaxle boot check

Refer to illustration 13.2

1   The driveaxle boots are very important because they prevent dirt, water and foreign material from entering and damaging the constant velocity (CV) joints.

2   Inspect the boots for tears and cracks as well as loose clamps **(see illustration)**. If there is any evidence of cracks or leaking lubricant, they must be replaced as described in Chapter 8.

14   Suspension and steering check

1   Raise the front of the vehicle periodically and visually check the suspension and steering components for wear.

2   Be alert for excessive play in the steering wheel before the front wheels react, excessive sway around corners, body move-

ment over rough roads and binding at some point as the steering wheel is turned. If you notice any of the above symptoms, the steering and suspension systems should be checked.

3   Support the vehicle on jackstands placed under the frame rails. Because of the work to be done, make sure the vehicle cannot fall off the stands.

4   Check the front wheel hub nuts and make sure they are securely locked in place.

5   Working under the vehicle, check for loose bolts, broken or disconnected parts and deteriorated rubber bushings on all suspension and steering components. Look for grease or fluid leaking from the steering assembly. Check the power steering hoses and connections for leaks.

6   Have an assistant turn the steering wheel from side-to-side and check the steering components for free movement, chafing and binding. If the steering doesn't react with the movement of the steering wheel, try to determine where the slack is located.

15   Exhaust system check

1   With the engine cold (at least three hours after the vehicle has been driven), check the complete exhaust system from the engine to the end of the tailpipe. Ideally, the inspection should be done with the vehicle on a hoist to permit unrestricted access. If a hoist is not available, raise the vehicle and support it securely on jackstands.

2   Check the exhaust pipes and connections for evidence of leaks, severe corrosion and damage. Make sure that all brackets and hangers are in good condition and tight.

3   At the same time, inspect the underside of the body for holes, corrosion, open seams, etc. which may allow exhaust gases to enter the interior. Seal all body openings with silicone or body putty.

4   Rattles and other noises can often be traced to the exhaust system, especially the

mounts and hangers. Try to move the pipes, muffler and catalytic converter. If the components can come in contact with the body or suspension parts, secure the exhaust system with new mounts.

5   Check the running condition of the engine by inspecting inside the end of the tailpipe. The exhaust deposits here are an indication of engine state-of-tune. If the pipe is black and sooty or coated with white deposits, the engine is in need of a tune-up, including a thorough fuel system inspection and adjustment.

16   Manual transaxle lubricant level check

Refer to illustrations 16.2 and 16.3

1   A dipstick is used for checking the lubricant level in the manual transaxles used on these models.

2   With the transaxle cold (cool to the touch) and the vehicle parked on a level surface, remove the dipstick from the filler tube located at the left rear side of the engine compartment, adjacent to the brake master cylinder **(see illustration)**.

3   The level must be even with or slightly above the FULL COLD mark on the dipstick **(see illustration)**. Make sure the level is at the FULL COLD mark because lubricant may appear on the end of the dipstick even when the transaxle is several pints low.

4   If the level is low, add the specified lubricant through the filler tube, using a funnel.

5   Insert the dipstick into the filler tube and seat it securely.

17   Tire rotation

Refer to illustration 17.2

1   The tires should be rotated at the specified intervals and whenever uneven wear is noticed.

LF   RF

LR   RR

RADIAL TIRE ROTATION

1-AJ HAYNES

17.2 Tire rotation diagram

18.5 Look through an opening in the front of the caliper to check the brake pads – the pad lining, which rubs against the disc, can also be inspected by looking from the bottom of the caliper

18.9 If the lining is bonded to the brake shoe, measure the lining thickness from the outer surface to the metal shoe, as shown here; if the lining is riveted to the shoe, measure from the lining outer surface to the rivet head

2   Front wheel drive vehicles require a special tire rotation pattern **(see illustration)**.
3   Refer to the information in Jacking and towing at the front of this manual for the proper procedures to follow when raising the vehicle and changing a tire. If the brakes are going to be checked, don't apply the parking brake as stated. Make sure the tires are blocked to prevent the vehicle from rolling as it's raised.
4   The entire vehicle should be raised at the same time. This can be done on a hoist or by jacking up each corner and then lowering the vehicle onto jackstands placed under the frame rails. Always use four jackstands and make sure the vehicle is safely supported.
5   After rotation, check and adjust the tire pressures as necessary and be sure to check the lug nut tightness.

18   Brake check

Refer to illustrations 18.5 and 18.9
Warning: *Brake system dust contains asbestos, which is hazardous to your health. DO NOT blow it out with compressed air or inhale it. DO NOT use gasoline or solvents to remove the dust. Use brake system cleaner or denatured alcohol only.*
Note: *For detailed photographs of the brake system, refer to Chapter 9.*
1   In addition to the specified intervals, the brakes should be inspected every time the wheels are removed or whenever a defect is suspected. Raise the vehicle and place it securely on jackstands. Remove the wheels (see Jacking and towing at the front of this manual, if necessary).

Disc brake pads

2   Disc brakes are used on the all four wheels of this vehicle. Extensive rotor damage can occur if the pads are not replaced when needed.
3   The disc brake pads have built-in wear indicators which make a high-pitched squealing or cricket-like warning sound when the pads are worn. **Caution:** *Expensive rotor damage*

can result if the pads are not replaced soon after the wear indicators start squealing.
4   The disc brake calipers, which contain the pads, are now visible. There is an outer pad and an inner pad in each caliper. All pads should be inspected.
5   Each caliper has one or two "windows" to inspect the pads **(see illustration)**. If the pad material has worn to about 1/8-inch thick or less, the pads should be replaced.
6   If you're unsure about the exact thickness of the remaining lining material, remove the pads for further inspection or replacement (refer to Chapter 9).
7   Before installing the wheels, check for leakage and/or damage at the brake hoses and connections. Replace the hose or fittings as necessary, referring to Chapter 9.
8   Check the condition of the brake rotor. Look for score marks, deep scratches and overheated areas (they will appear blue or discolored). If damage or wear is noted, the rotor can be removed and resurfaced by an automotive machine shop or replaced with a new one. Refer to Chapter 9 for more detailed inspection and repair procedures.

Drum brake shoes

9   Remove the brake drum and note the thickness of the lining material on brake shoes **(see illustration)**. If the material has worn away to within 1/16-inch of the recessed rivets or metal backing, the shoes should be replaced. If the linings look worn, but you are unable to determine their exact thickness, compare them with a new set at an auto parts store. The shoes should also be replaced if they are cracked, glazed (shiny surface) or contaminated with brake fluid.
10   Check to see that all the brake assembly springs are connected and in good condition.
11   Check the brake components for signs of fluid leakage. With your finger, carefully pry back the rubber cups on the wheel cylinder located at the top of the brake shoes. Any leakage is an indication that the wheel cylinders should be overhauled immediately (see Chapter 9). Also check the hoses and con-

nections for signs of leakage.
12   Clean the inside of the drum with brake system cleaner. Again, be careful not to breathe the dust.
13   Check the inside of the drum for cracks, scores, deep scratches and hard spots which will appear as small discolored areas. If imperfections cannot be removed with fine emery cloth, the drum must be taken to a machine shop for resurfacing.
14   After the inspection process, if all parts are found to be in good condition, reinstall the brake drum. Install the wheel and lower the vehicle to the ground, then tighten the lug nuts to the torque listed in this Chapter's Specifications.

Parking brake

15   The parking brake is operated by a foot pedal and locks the rear brake system. The easiest, and perhaps most obvious, method of periodically checking the operation of the parking brake assembly is to park the vehicle on a steep hill with the parking brake set and the transaxle in Neutral. If the parking brake cannot prevent the vehicle from rolling, it needs service (see Chapter 9).

19   Fuel system check

Warning: *Gasoline is extremely flammable, so take extra precautions when you work on any part of the fuel system. Don't smoke or allow open flames or bare light bulbs near the work area, and don't work in a garage where a natural gas-type appliance (such as a water heater or a clothes dryer) with a pilot light is present. Since gasoline is carcinogenic, wear latex gloves when there's a possibility of being exposed to fuel, and, if you spill any fuel on your skin, rinse it off immediately with soap and water. Mop up any spills immediately and do not store fuel-soaked rags where they could ignite. When you perform any kind of work on the fuel system, wear safety glasses and have a Class B type fire extinguisher on hand.*

20.2a Remove the wingnut . . .

20.2b . . . lift off the cover and spark arrestor (if equipped) . . .

20.2c . . . and pull the air filter element out of the housing

1   The fuel system is most easily checked with the vehicle raised on a hoist so the components underneath the vehicle are readily visible and accessible.

2   If the smell of gasoline is noticed while driving or after the vehicle has been in the sun, the system should be thoroughly inspected immediately.

3   Remove the gas tank cap and check for damage, corrosion and an unbroken sealing imprint on the gasket. Replace the cap with a new one if necessary.

4   With the vehicle raised, inspect the gas tank and filler neck for punctures, cracks and other damage. The connection between the filler neck and tank is especially critical. Sometimes a rubber filler neck will leak due to loose clamps or deteriorated rubber, problems a home mechanic can usually rectify. **Warning:** *Do not, under any circumstances, try to repair a fuel tank yourself (except rubber components). A welding torch or any open flame can easily cause the fuel vapors to explode if the proper precautions are not taken.*

5   Carefully check all rubber hoses and metal lines leading away from the fuel tank. Check for loose connections, deteriorated hoses, crimped lines and other damage. Follow the lines to the front of the vehicle, carefully inspecting them all the way. Repair or replace damaged sections as necessary.

20 Air filter and PCV filter replacement

1   At the specified intervals, the air filter should be replaced with a new one. The filter should be inspected between changes.

Air filter replacement

2.5 liter four-cylinder and 2.8 liter V6 engine

Refer to illustrations 20.2a, 20.2b and 20.2c

2   The air filter is located inside the air cleaner housing located at the front of the engine, near the battery. Remove the wing nut, lift off the cover and spark arrestor (if equipped), then lift the filter out **(see illustrations)**.

3.1 liter V6 engine

Turbocharged models

3   Detach the clips, remove the PCV breather from the valve cover and lift the air cleaner housing off, then remove the filter from the housing.

Non-turbocharged models

4   Remove the bolts, lift the upper air cleaner housing off, then lift the filter element out.

5.3L V8, 3.4 liter V6, 3800 V6, 3100 V6 and 2.3 liter four-cylinder (Quad-4) engines

Refer to illustrations 20.5a and 20.5b

5   The air cleaner housing is located on the left (driver's) side of the engine compartment. Loosen or remove the nuts or retainer clips, lift the top cover off and withdraw the filter **(see illustrations)**.

All models

6   While the filter housing cover is off, be careful not to drop anything down into the throttle body or air cleaner assembly.

7   Wipe out the inside of the air cleaner housing with a clean rag.

8   Except on TBI models with a PCV filter, place the new filter in the air cleaner housing. Make sure it seats properly in the bottom of the housing. Install the top plate or cover.

PCV filter replacement

Refer to illustrations 20.9 and 20.10

9   Some 2.5L models are equipped with a PCV filter. It is usually located in a holder in the side of the filter housing and can be removed after disconnecting the hose and removing the clip **(see illustration)**.

20.5a Remove the screws and separate the cover from the air cleaner housing . . .

20.5b . . . then lift up the cover and remove the filter element

20.9 Remove the clip and withdraw the PCV filter housing from the air cleaner

20.10 Pull the PCV filter element out of the holder

22.2 Small cracks in the underside of a serpentine belt are acceptable - lengthwise cracks, or missing pieces are cause for replacement

ACCEPTABLE

Cracks Running Across "V" Portions of Belt

1/2"

Missing Two or More Adjacent Ribs 1/2" or longer

UNACCEPTABLE

Cracks Running Parallel to "V" Portions of Belt

10   Pull the PCV filter out of the holder (**see illustration**).

11   Install the PCV filter in the holder and attach it to the air cleaner housing. Install the air filter.

21   Throttle Body Injection (TBI) mounting bolt torque check (2.5L engine only)

1   The TBI throttle body is attached to the top of the intake manifold by two bolts. They can sometimes work loose from vibration and temperature changes during normal engine operation and cause a vacuum leak.

2   If you suspect a vacuum leak exists at the bottom of the throttle body, use a rubber hose as a stethoscope. Start the engine and place one end of the hose next to your ear as you probe around the base of the throttle body with the other end. You will hear a hissing sound if a leak exists (be careful of hot and moving engine components).

3   Remove the air cleaner assembly (see Chapter 4).

4   Locate the throttle body mounting bolts. Decide what special tools or adapters will be necessary, if any, to tighten them.

5   Tighten the bolts securely and evenly. Do not overtighten them, as the manifold threads could strip.

6   If, after the bolts are properly tightened, a vacuum leak still exists, the throttle body must be removed and a new gasket installed. See Chapter 4 for more information.

7   After tightening the fasteners, reinstall the air cleaner and return all hoses to their original positions.

22   Drivebelt and tensioner check and replacement

Drivebelt

Refer to illustrations 22.2, 22.4, 22.5 and 22.9

1   A single serpentine drivebelt is located at the front of the engine and plays an important role in the overall operation of the engine and its components. Due to its function and material makeup, the belt is prone to wear and should be periodically inspected. The serpentine belt drives the alternator, power steering pump, water pump and air-conditioning compressor.

2   With the engine off, open the hood and use your fingers (and a flashlight, if necessary) , to move along the belt checking for cracks and separation of the belt plies. Also check for fraying and glazing, which gives the belt a shiny appearance (**see illustration**). Both sides of the belt should be inspected, which means you will have to twist the belt to check the underside.

3   Check the ribs on the underside of the belt. They should all be the same depth, with none of the surface uneven.

4   The tension of the belt is maintained by the tensioner assembly and isn't adjustable. Looking at the tension scale on the tensioner will give you some indication of how much life is left in the belt (**see illustration**). The belt should be checked at the mileage interval specified in the maintenance schedule at the front of this Chapter. If the belt shows noticeable damage or wear during these checks, it should be replaced.

5   To replace the belt on 3.1L and 3.8L engines, rotate the tensioner counter-clockwise to release belt tension (**see illustration**). **Note:** *If you are working on a supercharged model, the supercharger belt must be removed first (see Chapter 4, Section 20).* To replace the belt on 3.4L engines, rotate the tensioner clockwise to release belt tension. Note the routing of the belt before removing it. **Note:** *These models have a drivebelt routing decal on the engine to help during drivebelt installation. If the decal is missing, make a sketch.*

6   Access is very limited on 5.3L V8 engines. It's best to first remove the diagonal fender brace, then move the electrical power center assembly out of the way. Use a special thin drivebelt wrench to turn the tensioner clockwise and carefully remove it from the power steering pulley. Make notes of how the belt is routed and refer to the information

decal in the engine compartment.

7   Remove the belt from the auxiliary components and slowly release the tensioner.

8   Route the new belt over the various pulleys, again rotating the tensioner to allow the belt to be installed, then release the belt tensioner.

Tensioner

9   Remove the engine drivebelt as described above in Steps 5 through 7.

3.1L and 3.4l engines

Refer to illustration 22.10

10   On 3.lL and 3.4L engines, simply remove the tensioner retaining bolt (**see illustration**) and detach the tensioner assembly from the front of the engine. **Note:** *It may be necessary to detach and position the coolant recovery reservoir aside to allow access to the tensioner retaining bolt. Installation is the reverse of the removal procedure.*

3.8L engine

Warning: *If you're removing the tensioner from a 3.8L engine, wait until the engine has cooled completely before beginning the job.*

11   Drain the engine coolant (see Section 27).

12   Move a large container under the front of the engine to catch the coolant and remove the heater hose adapters with the heater hoses attached from the drivebelt tensioner assembly (not all models).

13   Detach the drivebelt tensioner retaining bolts and remove the tensioner assembly from the vehicle. Installation is the reverse of the removal procedure.

14   Refill the cooling system (see Section 27), start the engine and check for leaks.

5.3L V8 engine

15   Loosen the lug nuts on the right front wheel. Raise the vehicle and support it securely on jackstands.

16   Remove the right front wheel.

17   Remove the right inner splash shield.

18   Remove the power steering hose retainer bolt.

22.4   The drivebelt tensioner automatically keeps proper tension on the drivebelt, but does have limits - the indicator mark should remain in the nominal range, between the "INSTALL" and "REPLACE BELT" marks

22.5   On some models it will be necessary to insert a breaker bar into the notch on the tensioner arm, on other models it will be necessary to use a box end wrench on the pulley bolt to rotate the tensioner

19   Remove the bolts from the drivebelt tensioner and remove the tensioner.
20   Installation is the reverse of removal.

23   Seat belt check

1   Check the seat belts, buckles, latch plates and guide loops for obvious damage and signs of wear.
2   See if the seat belt reminder light comes on when the key is turned to the Run or Start position. A chime should also sound.
3   The seat belts are designed to lock up during a sudden stop or impact, yet allow free movement during normal driving. Make sure the retractors return the belt against your chest while driving and rewind the belt fully when the buckle is unlatched.
4   If any of the above checks reveal problems with the seat belt system, replace parts as necessary.

24   Starter safety switch check

Warning: *During the following checks there's a chance the vehicle could lunge forward, possibly causing damage or injuries. Allow*

plenty of room around the vehicle, apply the parking brake and hold down the regular brake pedal during the checks.
1   On automatic transaxle equipped vehicles, try to start the engine in each gear. The engine should crank only in Park or Neutral.
2   If equipped with a manual transaxle, place the shift lever in Neutral and push the clutch pedal down about halfway. The engine should crank only with the clutch pedal fully depressed.
3   Make sure the steering column lock allows the key to go into the Lock position only when the shift lever is in Park (automatic transaxle) or Reverse (manual transaxle).
4   The ignition key should come out only in the Lock position.

25   Seatback latch check

1   It's important to periodically check the seatback latch mechanism on two-door models to prevent the seatback from moving forward during a sudden stop or an accident.
2   Grasping the top of the seat, attempt to tilt it forward. It should tilt only when the latch on the rear of the seat is pulled up. Note that there is a certain amount of free play built into the latch mechanism.

3   When returned to the upright position, the seatback should latch securely.

26   Spare tire and jack check

1   Periodically checking the security and condition of the spare tire and jack will help to familiarize you with the procedures necessary for emergency tire replacement and also ensure that no components work loose during normal vehicle operation.
2   Following the instructions in your owner's manual or under Jacking and towing near the front of this manual, remove the spare tire and jack.
3   Using a reliable air pressure gauge, check the pressure in the spare tire. It should be kept at the pressure marked on the tire sidewall.
4   Make sure the jack operates freely and all components are undamaged.
5   When finished, make sure the wing nuts hold the jack and tire securely in place.

27   Fuel filter replacement

Refer to illustration 27.3
Warning: *Gasoline is extremely flammable, so take extra precautions when you work on any part of the fuel system. Don't smoke or allow open flames or bare light bulbs near the work area, and don't work in a garage where a natural gas-type appliance (such as a water heater or a clothes dryer) with a pilot light is present. Since gasoline is carcinogenic, wear latex gloves when there's a possibility of being exposed to fuel, and, if you spill any fuel on your skin, rinse it off immediately with soap and water. Mop up any spills immediately and do not store fuel-soaked rags where they could ignite. When you perform any kind of work on the fuel system, wear safety glasses and have a Class B type fire extinguisher on hand.*

22.10   Remove the retaining bolt (arrow) located at the center of the tensioner assembly

27.3 Use a back-up wrench on the fuel filter side of the fitting; use a flare-nut wrench to unscrew the outer nut

Note: *Later models are not equipped with serviceable fuel filters. The fuel filters on these vehicles are located in the fuel tank. After raising your vehicle, trace the fuel supply line from the fuel tank forward to find if it's equipped with an external fuel filter.*

1   Relieve the fuel system pressure (see Chapter 4).
2   Raise the vehicle and support it securely on jackstands.
3   Unscrew the fuel line-to-fuel filter fittings **(see illustration)**. Use a back-up wrench to keep from twisting the line.
4   If the car is equipped with plastic "quick-connect" fittings, squeeze the tabs on the fitting and pull it apart. If the car is equipped with metal quick-connect fittings, pull back the rubber boot and twist the fitting one-quarter turn to loosen any dirt, then, if compressed air is available, blow the dirt away from the connection. Use a special fuel line separator tool to disconnect the fitting. (See Chapter 4 for more information on the quick-connect fittings.)
5   Remove the filter from the clip.
6   Snap the new filter securely into the clip. Make sure the arrow on the filter points toward the engine.
7   Using new O-rings, reattach the fuel lines to the filter. Apply a few drops of clean engine oil to the O-rings to ease reassembly.

28 Automatic transaxle fluid and filter change

Refer to illustration 28.11
1   At the specified time intervals, the transaxle fluid should be drained and replaced. Since the fluid will remain hot long after driving, perform this procedure only after everything has cooled down completely.
2   Before beginning work, purchase the specified transaxle fluid (see Recommended lubricants and fluids at the front of this Chapter) and a new filter.
3   Other tools necessary for this job include jackstands to support the vehicle in a raised position, a drain pan capable of holding several

28.11 Automatic transaxle filter installation details

1   *Seal*
2   *Filter*
3   *Pan gasket*

quarts, newspapers and clean rags.
4   Raise and support the vehicle on jackstands.
5   With a drain pan in place, remove the front and side transaxle pan mounting bolts.
6   Loosen the rear pan bolts one turn.
7   Carefully pry the transaxle pan loose with a screwdriver, allowing the fluid to drain.
8   Remove the remaining bolts, pan and gasket. Carefully clean the gasket surface of the transaxle to remove all traces of the old gasket and sealant.
9   Drain the fluid from the transaxle pan, clean the pan with solvent and dry it with compressed air. Be careful not to lose the magnet.
10   Remove the filter from the mount inside the transaxle.
11   Install a new filter and seal **(see illustration)**.
12   Make sure the gasket surface on the transaxle pan is clean, then install a new gasket. Put the pan in place against the transaxle and install the bolts. **Note:** *If the bolts are equipped with captive crush washers, they should be replaced.* Working around the pan, tighten each bolt a little at a time until the final torque figure is reached.
13   Lower the vehicle and add the specified amount of automatic transmission fluid through the filler tube (see Section 6).
14   With the shift lever in Park and the parking brake set, run the engine at a fast idle, but don't race it.
15   Move the shift lever through each gear and back to Park. Check the fluid level when the engine is fully warmed up.
16   Check under the vehicle for leaks during the first few trips.

29 Manual transaxle lubricant change

Refer to illustration 29.3
1   Raise the vehicle and support it securely on jackstands.
2   Move a drain pan, rags, newspapers and wrenches under the transaxle.
3   Remove the transaxle drain plug and allow the lubricant to drain into the pan **(see illustration)**.

4   After the lubricant has drained completely, reinstall the plug and tighten it securely.
5   Remove the transaxle dipstick. Using a hand pump, syringe or funnel, fill the transaxle with the correct amount of specified lubricant.
6   Lower the vehicle. Check the lubricant level as described in Section 16. Add more lubricant as necessary.

30 Cooling system servicing (draining, flushing and refilling)

Warning: *Make sure the engine is completely cool before performing this procedure.*
Caution: *Never mix green-colored ethylene glycol anti-freeze and orange-colored "DEX-COOL" silicate-free coolant because doing so will destroy the efficiency of the "DEX-COOL" coolant which is designed to last for 100,000 miles or five years.*
1   Periodically, the cooling system should be drained, flushed and refilled to replenish the antifreeze mixture and prevent formation of rust and corrosion, which can impair the performance of the cooling system and cause engine damage.
2   At the same time the cooling system is serviced, all hoses and the radiator cap should be inspected and replaced if defective (see Section 9).

29.3 The manual transaxle drain plug (arrow) is located on the side of the case

31.1 The PCV valve (arrow) on most engines is located in the valve cover

31.5 The PCV valve on 1995 and later 3800 engines is located at the front of the intake manifold below the MAP sensor (arrow)

3   Since antifreeze is a corrosive and poisonous solution, be careful not to spill any of the coolant mixture on the vehicle's paint or your skin. If this happens, rinse it off immediately with plenty of clean water. Consult local authorities about the recycling of antifreeze before draining the cooling system. In many areas, reclamation centers have been set up to collect automobile oil and drained antifreeze/water mixtures, rather than allowing them to be added to the sewage system.

4   With the engine cold, remove the radiator cap.

5   On 2.5 liter four-cylinder engines, remove the thermostat.

6   On the 3800 V6, open the air bleed vents on the thermostat housing.

7   On the 3100 V6, open the air bleed vents on the thermostat housing and coolant pump.

8   On the 3.4L V6, open the air bleed vents on the thermostat housing and the heater coolant inlet pipe (near the brake master cylinder).

9   On the Quad-4 and on other V6 engines, open the vent plugs in the thermostat housing and (if equipped) bypass pipe.

10   If accessible, remove the engine block drains. **Note:** *On 3800 engines it will be necessary to remove the knock sensors from each side of the engine block to allow the block to drain.*

11   On the 3.4L engine, remove the inlet hose at the left side of the engine oil cooler.

12   Move a large container under the radiator to catch the coolant as it's drained.

13   Drain the radiator by removing (or opening) the plug at the bottom. If the plug is corroded and can't be turned easily, or if the radiator isn't equipped with a plug, disconnect the lower radiator hose to allow the coolant to drain. Be careful not to get antifreeze on your skin or in your eyes.

14   Disconnect the hose from the coolant reservoir and remove the reservoir. Flush it out with clean water.

15   Place a garden hose in the radiator filler neck and flush the system until the water runs clear at all drain points.

16   In severe cases of contamination or clogging of the radiator, remove it (see Chapter 3) and reverse flush it. This involves inserting the hose in the bottom radiator outlet to allow the water to run against the normal flow, draining through the top. A radiator repair shop should be consulted if further cleaning or repair is necessary.

17   When the coolant is regularly drained and the system refilled with the correct antifreeze/water mixture, there should be no need to use chemical cleaners or descalers.

18   To refill the system, reconnect all hoses and the coolant reservoir.

19   Reinstall (or close) the radiator drain plug, and reinstall the engine block drains.

20   On V6 and Quad-4 models, fill the radiator with the recommended mixture of antifreeze and water (see Section 4) to the base of the filler neck, tighten the vent plugs securely but leave the radiator cap off.

21   On 2.5 liter four-cylinder engines, fill the cooling system through the thermostat housing until the level reaches the base of the radiator filler neck and install the cap. Fill the thermostat housing to one half inch from the top and install the thermostat and cap.

22   On all models add more coolant to the reservoir until it reaches the lower mark.

23   On 3.4L, 3100 and 3800 V6 engines, install the radiator cap and close all the air bleeds.

24   On other V6 engines and on the Quad 4, start the engine and run it until normal operating temperature is reached. With the engine idling, add additional coolant to the radiator and the reservoir. Install the radiator and reservoir caps.

25   Keep a close watch on the coolant level and the cooling system hoses during the first few miles of driving. Tighten the hose clamps and/or add more coolant as necessary. The coolant level should be a little above the HOT mark on the reservoir with the engine at normal operating temperature.

26   On 3.4L, 3100 and 3800 V6 engines, after flushing the system add two engine coolant supplement sealant pellets when refilling.

31 Positive Crankcase Ventilation (PCV) valve check and replacement

Check

All engines (except 1995 and later 3800 engines)
Refer to illustration 31.1

1   On most of the engines covered by this manual the PCV valve is located in the valve cover **(see illustration)**. On 3.4L engines the PCV valve is located in the intake manifold just behind the throttle body assembly.

2   With the engine idling at normal operating temperature, pull the valve (with hose attached) out of the rubber grommet in the intake plenum or valve cover.

3   Place your finger over the end of the valve. If there is no vacuum at the valve, check for a plugged hose, manifold port, or the valve itself. Replace any plugged or deteriorated hoses.

4   Turn off the engine and shake the PCV valve, listening for a rattle. If the valve doesn't rattle, replace it with a new one.

3800 engine (1995 and later)
Refer to illustration 31.5

5   On 3800 engines the PCV valve is located in the intake manifold under the MAP sensor at the front (passenger side) of the engine **(see illustration)**.

6   To check the valve it must first be removed (see Step 12). Then shake the PCV valve, listening for a rattle. If the valve doesn't rattle, replace it with a new one.

Replacement

All engines (except 1995 and later 3800 engines)

7   To replace the valve, pull it out of the end of the hose, noting its installed position and direction.

8   When purchasing a replacement PCV

31.13 Disconnect the electrical connector and unclip the MAP sensor from the PCV valve access cover

31.14 Press down on the PCV valve access cover, rotate it counterclockwise then pull up to remove it (be sure to check the O-ring and replace it if necessary)

31.15 Remove the PCV valve and the O-ring from the intake manifold

valve, make sure it's for your particular vehicle, model year and engine size. Compare the old valve with the new one to make sure they are the same.

9   Push the valve into the end of the hose until it's seated.

10   Inspect the rubber grommet for damage and replace it with a new one if necessary.

11   Push the PCV valve and hose securely into position.

3800 engine (1995 and later)

Refer to illustration 31.13, 31.14 and 31.15

12   Detach the fuel injector cover (see Chapter 4).

13   Disconnect the electrical connector from the MAP sensor and unclip the MAP sensor from the PCV valve access cover **(see illustration)**.

14   Press downward on the PCV valve access cover and rotate it counterclockwise to remove it **(see illustration)**. On models with a supercharger, the PCV valve is under a plate at the top of the supercharger housing, near the throttle body. Remove the bolt and cover and take out the spring, the PCV valve and the O-ring. Use a new O-ring when replacing the PCV valve.

15   To replace the valve, pull the PCV valve and O-ring assembly from the intake manifold noting its installed position and direction **(see illustration)**.

16   When purchasing a replacement PCV valve, make sure it's for your particular vehicle, model year and engine size. Compare the old valve with the new one to make sure they are the same.

17   Installation of the valve is the reverse of removal.

32   Evaporative emissions control system check

1   The function of the evaporative emissions control system is to draw fuel vapors from the gas tank and fuel system, store them

in a charcoal canister and then burn them during normal engine operation.

2   The most common symptom of a fault in the evaporative emissions system is a strong fuel odor in the engine compartment. If a fuel odor is detected, inspect the charcoal canister, located at the front of the engine compartment. Check the canister and all hoses for damage and deterioration.

3   The evaporative emissions control system is explained in more detail in Chapter 6.

33   Spark plug replacement

Refer to illustrations 33.2, 33.5a, 33.5b, 33.6a, 33.6b, 33.6c, 33.6d, 33.8 and 33.10
Caution: *On engines equipped with aluminum cylinder heads such as the 5.3L, wait for the engine to cool completely before removing the spark plugs. Failure to do so can result in damage to the threads in the soft cylinder head material.*
Note: *On many V6 engines, it will be necessary to rotate the engine for access to the rear spark plugs, as outlined in Section 34.*

1   The spark plugs are located on the front (radiator) side of the engine on 2.2L and 2.5 liter four-cylinder models. The spark plugs on Quad-4 engines are located under a cover on the top of the engine, in the valley between the camshaft covers. On 3.4L V6 engines, the spark plugs are located in the valleys between the camshafts, three on each cylinder head. On other V6 engines and the 5.3L V8 engine, the plugs are located at the front and at the rear (firewall) side of the engine. With the exception of the 3.4L, 3800 V6 and 5.3L V8 engines, the engine must be rotated forward to gain access to rear spark plugs (see Section 34).
Note 1: *On 3.4L engines the upper intake manifold must be removed first to allow access to the right side (rear) spark plugs or plug wires. See Chapter 4 for the upper intake plenum removal procedure.*

Note 2: *On 1996 and later 3800 engines the acoustic engine cover must be removed first to access the right side (rear) spark plugs or plug wires (see Chapter 2F).*
2   In most cases, the tools necessary for spark plug replacement include a spark plug socket which fits onto a ratchet (spark plug sockets are padded inside to prevent damage to the porcelain insulators on the new plugs), various extensions and a gap gauge to check and adjust the gaps on the new plugs **(see illustration)**. A special plug wire removal tool is available for separating the wire boots from

33.2 Tools required for changing spark plugs

1   *Spark plug socket* - This will have special padding inside to protect the spark plug's porcelain insulator
2   *Torque wrench* - Although not mandatory, using this tool is the best way to ensure the plugs are tightened properly
3   *Ratchet* - Standard hand tool to fit the spark plug socket
4   *Extension* - Depending on model and accessories, you may need special extensions and universal joints to reach one or more of the plugs
5   *Spark plug gap gauge* - This gauge for checking the gap comes in a variety of styles. Make sure the gap for your engine is included

33.5a Spark plug manufacturers recommend using a wire-type gauge when checking the gap - if the wire does not slide between the electrodes with a slight drag, adjustment is required

33.5b To change the gap, bend the side electrode only, as indicated by the arrows, and be very careful not to crack or chip the porcelain insulator surrounding the center electrode

33.6a On Quad-4 engines, use a small screwdriver to detach the electrical connector

33.6b Remove the ignition cover bolts (arrows) (Quad-4 engine)

33.6c Lift the ignition cover straight up to detach the spark plug connectors

the spark plugs, and is a good idea on these models because the boots fit very tightly. On the 3800 V6 engine, a special tool is required to remove the spark plug heat shields from the right rear spark plugs. A torque wrench should be used to tighten the new plugs. Because the aluminum cylinder heads used on some of these models are easily damaged, allow the engine to cool before removing or installing the spark plugs.

3   The best approach when replacing the spark plugs is to purchase the new ones in advance, adjust them to the proper gap and replace the plugs one at a time. When buying the new spark plugs, be sure to obtain the correct plug type for your particular engine. The plug type can be found in the Specifications at the front of this Chapter and on the Emission Control Information label located under the hood. If these two sources list different plug types, consider the emission control label correct.

4   Allow the engine to cool completely before attempting to remove any of the plugs. While you are waiting for the engine to cool,

check the new plugs for defects and adjust the gaps.

5   Check the gap by inserting the proper thickness gauge between the electrodes at the tip of the plug **(see illustration)**. The gap between the electrodes should be the same as the one specified on the Emissions Control Information label. The wire should slide between the electrodes with a slight amount of drag. If the gap is incorrect, use the adjuster on the gauge body to bend the curved side electrode slightly until the proper gap is obtained **(see illustration)**. If the side electrode is not exactly over the center electrode, bend it with the adjuster until it is. Check for cracks in the porcelain insulator (if any are found, the plug should not be used).

6   On Quad-4 engines, unplug the electrical connector and remove the ignition cover for access to the spark plugs **(see illustrations)**. On all models, with the engine cool, remove the spark plug wire from one spark plug. Pull only on the boot at the end of the wire - do not pull on the wire **(see illustration)**. A plug wire removal tool should be used

if available.

7   If compressed air is available, use it to blow any dirt or foreign material away from the spark plug hole. The idea here is to eliminate the possibility of debris falling into the cylinder as the spark plug is removed.

33.6d A spark plug boot removal tool will be required to remove the tight-fitting boots used on the Quad-4

33.8 Various sockets will be required to remove the spark plug on these models, because of access - here on the Quad-4, a long extension is needed to reach down into the camshaft valley

33.10 A length of 3/16-inch ID rubber hose will save time and prevent damaged threads when installing the spark plugs

8   Place the spark plug socket over the plug and remove it from the engine by turning it in a counterclockwise direction **(see illustration)**.

9   Compare the spark plug to those shown in the accompanying photos to get an indication of the general running condition of the engine.

10   Thread one of the new plugs into the hole until you can no longer turn it with your fingers, then tighten it with a torque wrench (if available) or the ratchet. It might be a good idea to slip a short length of rubber hose over the end of the plug to use as a tool to thread it into place **(see illustration)**. The hose will grip the plug well enough to turn it, but will start to slip if the plug begins to cross-thread in the hole - this will prevent damaged threads and the accompanying repair costs.

11   Before pushing the spark plug wire onto the end of the plug, inspect it following the procedures outlined in Section 35.

12   Attach the plug wire to the new spark plug, again using a twisting motion on the boot until it's seated on the spark plug.

13   Repeat the procedure for the remaining spark plugs, replacing them one at a time to prevent mixing up the spark plug wires.

34   Rotating the engine

Refer to illustration 34.4 and 34.5

Note: *This procedure provides easier access to the spark plugs, particularly the rear bank on V6 models.*

1   Block the wheels, place the transaxle in neutral, and disconnect the negative battery cable. **Caution:** *On models equipped with the Theftlock audio system, be sure the lockout feature is turned off before performing any procedure which requires disconnecting the battery.*

2   Disconnect the air duct.

3   Without disconnecting any hoses, remove the coolant recovery bottle and set it aside.

4   Remove the torque strut to engine bracket bolts and swing the struts aside. Place the bolt back into passenger side bracket **(see illustration)**.

5   Using a pry bar in the passenger side bracket (2.5L four-cylinder and V6 engines) or exhaust manifold (2.2L four-cylinder), rotate the engine forward and secure it in this position. To secure the engine in the forward (rotated) position on earlier models it will

require placing a bolt through the slave hole on the driver's side torque strut and bracket. **(see Chapter 2B illustration 6.9)**. To secure the engine in the forward (rotated) position on later models it will require connecting a ratchet strap to the engine and to the frame or radiator core support **(see illustration)**.

6   Reverse the procedure when you have completed the task that required rotating the engine. Torque the strut to engine bracket bolts to 50 ft-lbs.

35   Spark plug wire check and replacement

Note 1: *These models are equipped with distributorless ignition systems. The spark plug wires are connected directly to the ignition coils.*

Note 2: *On many V6 engines (except 3.4L), it will be necessary to rotate the engine for access to the rear spark plugs or wires, as outlined in Section 34.*

Note 3: *Quad-4 engines are not equipped with spark plug wires.*

Note 4: *On 3.4L engines the upper intake manifold must be removed first to allow*

34.4 To reach the rear spark plugs, remove the strut bolts (arrows) and rotate the engine forward

34.5 Rotate the engine forward with a prybar and secure it in place

36.1 Materials required for chassis and body lubrication

1 **Engine oil** - Light engine oil in a can like this can be used for door and hood hinges
2 **Graphite spray** - Used to lubricate lock cylinders
3 **Grease** - Grease, in a variety of types and weights, is available for use in a grease gun. Check the Specification for your requirements
4 **Grease gun** - A common grease gun, shown here with a detachable hose and nozzle, is needed for chassis lubrication. After use, clean it thoroughly!

access to the right side (rear) spark plugs or plug wires. See Chapter 4 for the upper intake plenum removal procedure.

Note 5: On 1996 and later 3800 engines the acoustic engine cover must be removed first to access the right side (rear) spark plugs or plug wires (see Chapter 2F).

1 The spark plug wires should be checked at the recommended intervals and whenever new spark plugs are installed in the engine.
2 The wires should be inspected one at a time to prevent mixing up the order, which is essential for proper engine operation.
3 Disconnect the plug wire from the spark plug. To do this, grab the rubber boot, twist slightly and pull the wire off. Do not pull on the wire itself, only on the rubber boot.
4 Check inside the boot for corrosion, which will look like a white crusty powder. Push the wire and boot back onto the end of the spark plug. It should be a tight fit on the plug. If it isn't, remove the wire and use pliers to carefully crimp the metal connector inside the boot until it fits securely on the end of the spark plug.
5 Using a clean rag, wipe the entire length of the wire to remove any built-up dirt and grease. Once the wire is clean, check for burns, cracks and other damage. Do not bend the wire excessively or pull the wire lengthwise

- the conductor inside might break.
6 Disconnect the wire from the coil. Again, pull only on the rubber boot. Check for corrosion and a tight fit in the same manner as the spark plug end. Replace the wire at the coil.
7 Check the remaining spark plug wires one at a time, making sure they are securely fastened at the ignition coil and the spark plug when the check is complete.
8 If new spark plug wires are required, purchase a set for your specific engine model. Wire sets are available pre-cut, with the rubber boots already installed. Remove and replace the wires one at a time to avoid mix-ups in the firing order.

36 Chassis lubrication

Refer to illustrations 36.1, 36.3 and 36.10

1 Most suspension and steering joints are factory sealed and DO NOT require lubrication, although some model years do require the tie rod ends to be lubricated. Other various chassis components such as hood and door hinges, door locks, parking brake cable guides and transaxle shift linkage also require regularly scheduled lubrication. Specific materials and equipment are needed to perform

these tasks **(see illustration)**.
2 To determine whether your vehicle will require tie rod lubrication, raise it with a jack and place jackstands under the frame. Make sure it is safely supported by the stands. If the wheels are to be removed at this interval for tire rotation or brake inspection, loosen the lug nuts slightly while the vehicle is still on the ground.
3 Look under the vehicle for grease fittings or plugs on the steering components **(see illustration)**. They are normally found on the tie-rod ends. If there are plugs, remove them and install grease fittings, which will thread into the component. An automotive parts store will be able to supply the correct fittings. Straight, as well as angled, fittings are available. If no grease fittings are found proceed to Step 9.
4 Refer to Recommended lubricants and fluids at the front of this Chapter to obtain the necessary grease, etc.
5 Before beginning, force a little grease out of the nozzle to remove any dirt from the end of the gun. Wipe the nozzle clean with a rag.
6 With the grease gun and plenty of clean rags, crawl under the vehicle and begin lubricating the components.
7 Wipe the area around the grease fitting free of dirt, then squeeze the trigger on the grease gun to force grease into the component. Continue pumping grease into the fitting until it oozes out of the joint between the two components. If it escapes around the grease gun nozzle, the fitting is clogged or the nozzle is not completely seated on the fitting. Resecure the gun nozzle to the fitting and try again. If necessary, replace the fitting with a new one.
8 Wipe the excess grease from the components and the grease fitting. Repeat the procedure for the remaining fittings.
9 While under the vehicle clean and lubricate the parking brake cable guides and levers. This can be done by using a grease gun. **Note:** DO NOT lubricate the parking brake cables, as this will deteriorate the plastic coating used to prevent the cables from rusting.
10 Clean and lubricate the transaxle shift linkage with engine oil **(see illustration)**.

36.3 Typical tie rod end grease fitting (arrow)

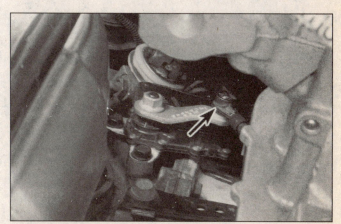

36.10 Lubricate the transaxle shift linkage (arrow) with clean engine oil

37.2 Check the throttle linkage for binding

11   Open the hood and smear a little chassis grease on the hood latch mechanism. Have an assistant pull the hood release lever from inside the vehicle as you lubricate the cable at the latch.

12   Lubricate all the hinges (door, hood, etc.) with engine oil to keep them in proper working order.

13   The key lock cylinders can be lubricated with spray graphite or silicone lubricant, which is available at auto parts stores.

14   Lubricate the door weatherstripping with silicone spray. This will reduce chafing and retard wear.

37 Throttle linkage check

Refer to illustration 37.2
Note: *Some later models are not equipped with mechanical throttle linkage. Throttle operation is done electrically.*

1   At the specified intervals the throttle link-age should be inspected for kinks, binding and misalignment.

2   Starting at the throttle body in the engine compartment, with the engine OFF, grasp the throttle lever and open it to the full throttle position **(see illustration)**. Quickly release your hand from the throttle lever and note the amount of time it takes the throttle lever to return to the idle position. If the lever returns quickly to the idle position the throttle linkage is in proper working order. If the lever returns slowly to the idle position, inspect the accel-erator cable or cruise control cable for kinks or signs of binding. Also check the cable retaining brackets for missing retaining clips. **Note:** *Never lubricate the accelerator or cruise control cable as this will destroy the protective plastic coating on the outside of the cable.* If signs of kinks or binding exist in the cable assembly, replace the cable as described in Chapter 4.

3   If there's no evidence of binding in the cable assembly, remove the cables from the throttle lever and repeat the test described in Step 2. If the throttle lever returns slowly to the idle position with the cables detached, the problem lies in the throttle body assembly. See Chapter 4 for further inspection of the throttle body assembly.

Chapter 2 Part A
2.2 liter four-cylinder engine

Contents

	Section
Camshaft and bearings - removal, inspection and installation	14
CHECK ENGINE light	See Chapter 6
Crankshaft front oil seal - replacement	11
Crankshaft pulley - removal and installation	10
Cylinder compression check	See Chapter 2H
Cylinder head - removal and installation	8
Drivebelt check, adjustment and replacement	See Chapter 1
Engine mounts - check and replacement	19
Engine oil and filter change	See Chapter 1
Engine overhaul - general information	See Chapter 2H
Engine - removal and installation	See Chapter 2H
Exhaust manifold - removal and installation	7
Flywheel/driveplate - removal and installation	17
General information	1
Hydraulic lifters - removal, inspection and installation	9
Intake manifold - removal and installation	6

	Section
Oil pan - removal and installation	15
Oil pump - removal and installation	16
Rear main oil seal - replacement	18
Repair operations possible with the engine in the vehicle	2
Rocker arms and pushrods - removal, inspection and installation	4
Spark plug replacement	See Chapter 1
Timing chain and sprockets - inspection, removal and installation	13
Timing chain cover - removal and installation	12
Top Dead Center (TDC) for number one piston - locating	See Chapter 2H
Valve cover - removal and installation	3
Valve springs, retainers and seals - replacement	5
Water pump - removal and installation	See Chapter 3

Specifications

General

Cylinder numbers (drivebelt end-to-transaxle end)	1-2-3-4
Firing order	1-3-4-2

Torque specifications

Ft-lbs (unless otherwise indicated)

Note: *One foot-pound (ft-lb) of torque is equivalent to 12 inch-pounds (in-lbs) of torque. Torque values below approximately 15 foot-pounds are expressed in inch-pounds, because most foot-pound torque wrenches are not accurate at these smaller values.*

Camshaft sprocket bolt	77
Crankshaft pulley-to-hub bolts	37
Crankshaft pulley center bolt	77
Cylinder head bolts	
Step 1	
Short bolts	43
Long bolts	46
Step 2	Rotate all bolts an additional 90-degrees
Exhaust manifold fasteners	115 in-lbs
Flywheel bolts	54
Driveplate bolts	52
Intake manifold fasteners	
Upper	22
Lower	24
Oil pan nuts	89 in-lbs
Oil pump mounting bolt	32
Valve cover bolts	89 in-lbs
Rocker arm nuts	22
Timing chain cover bolts	97 in-lbs
Timing chain tensioner bolts	18

0758H

2.2 litre four-cylinder engine

Cylinder and coil terminal location

1 General information

This Part of Chapter 2 is devoted to in-vehicle repair procedures for the 2.2 liter four-cylinder overhead valve engine. The 2.2L engine became available in 1993, in the Lumina model only. These engines have cast iron blocks and cast aluminum pistons. The aluminum cylinder head has replaceable valve seats and guides. Stamped steel rocker arms and tubular pushrods actuate the valves. To positively identify this engine, locate the vehicle identification number on the left front cor-

ner of the instrument panel. This plate is visible from outside the vehicle (**see illustration 1.1** in Chapter 2, Part B). The eighth character in the sequence is the engine designation:

4 = 2.2L four-cylinder, overhead valve engine

3.6 Valve cover bolt locations (arrows)

4.2 Loosen the nuts and pivot the rocker arms to one side if just the pushrods are being removed (otherwise, remove the nuts and lift off the pivot balls and rocker arms)

Information concerning engine removal and installation and engine overhaul can be found in Part H of this Chapter.

The following repair procedures are based on the assumption the engine is in the vehicle. If the engine has been removed from the vehicle and mounted on a stand, many of the steps outlined in this Part of Chapter 2 will not apply.

2   Repair operations possible with the engine in the vehicle

Many major repair operations can be accomplished without removing the engine from the vehicle.

Clean the engine compartment and the exterior of the engine with some type of degreaser before any work is done. It'll make the job easier and help keep dirt out of the internal areas of the engine.

Depending on the components involved, it may be helpful to remove the hood to improve access to the engine as repairs are performed (refer to Chapter 11 if necessary). Cover the fenders to prevent damage to the paint. Special pads are available, but an old bedspread or blanket will also work.

If vacuum, exhaust, oil or coolant leaks develop, indicating a need for gasket or seal replacement, the repairs can generally be made with the engine in the vehicle. The intake and exhaust manifold gaskets, timing chain cover gasket, oil pan gasket, crankshaft oil seals and cylinder head gasket are all accessible with the engine in place.

Exterior engine components, such as the intake and exhaust manifolds, the oil pan (and the oil pump), the water pump, the starter motor, the alternator and the fuel system components can be removed for repair with the engine in place.

Since the cylinder head can be removed without pulling the engine, valve component servicing can also be accomplished with the engine in the vehicle. Replacement of the tim-ing chain and sprockets is also possible with the engine in the vehicle.

In extreme cases caused by a lack of necessary equipment, repair or replacement of piston rings, pistons, connecting rods and rod bearings is possible with the engine in the vehicle. However, this practice is not recommended because of the cleaning and preparation work that must be done to the components involved.

3   Valve cover - removal and installation

Refer to illustration 3.6

Removal

1   Remove the air cleaner assembly, tagging each hose to be disconnected with a piece of numbered tape to simplify installation.
2   Remove the breather hose from the valve cover.
3   Remove the spark plug wires from the spark plugs and from the valve cover clips.
4   Detach the control cable bracket at the intake plenum and valve cover.
5   Disconnect the cables at the throttle body.
6   Remove the valve cover bolts **(see illustration)**.
7   Detach the valve cover from the head. **Note:** *If the cover is stuck to the cylinder head, use a block of wood and hammer to dislodge it. If that doesn't work, try to slip a flexible putty knife between the head and cover to break the gasket seal. Don't pry at the cover-to-head joint or damage to the sealing surfaces may occur (leading to oil leaks in the future).*

Installation

8   The mating surfaces of the cylinder head and valve cover must be perfectly clean when the cover is installed. Use a gasket scraper to remove all traces of sealant or old gasket, then clean the mating surfaces with lacquer thinner or acetone (if there's sealant or oil on the mating surfaces when the cover is installed, oil leaks may develop). The head and cover are made of aluminum, so be extra careful not to nick or gouge the mating surfaces with the scraper.
9   Clean the mounting bolt threads with a die if necessary to remove any corrosion and restore damaged threads. Make sure the threaded holes in the head are clean - run a tap into them if necessary to remove corrosion and restore damaged threads.
10   Apply a thin coat of RTV-type sealant to the sealing flange on the cover and install a new gasket.
11   Place the valve cover on the cylinder head and install the mounting bolts. Tighten the bolts a little at a time to the torque listed in this Chapter's Specifications. Work from the center out in a spiral pattern.
12   Complete the installation by reversing the removal procedure.

4   Rocker arms and pushrods - removal, inspection and installation

Refer to illustrations 4.2, 4.4a and 4.4b

Removal

1   Refer to Section 3 and detach the valve cover from the cylinder head.
2   Beginning at the front of the cylinder head, loosen the rocker arm nuts **(see illustration)**. **Note:** *If the pushrods are the only items being removed, rotate the rocker arms to one side so the pushrods can be lifted out.*
3   Remove the nuts, the rocker arms and the pivot balls and store them in marked containers (they must be reinstalled in their original locations).
4   Remove the pushrods and store them separately to make sure they don't get mixed up during installation **(see illustrations)**.

4.4a The pushrods can be lifted straight out

4.4b A perforated cardboard box can be used to store the pushrods to ensure they're reinstalled in their original locations - note the label indicating the front (drivebelt end) of the engine

5   If the pushrod guides must be removed for any reason, make sure they're marked so they can be reinstalled in their original locations.

Inspection

6   Check each rocker arm for wear, cracks and other damage, especially where the pushrods and valve stems contact the rocker arm faces.

7   Make sure the hole at the pushrod end of each rocker arm is open.

8   Check each rocker arm pivot area for wear, cracks and galling. If the rocker arms are worn or damaged, replace them with new ones and use new pivot balls as well.

9   Inspect the pushrods for cracks and excessive wear at the ends. Roll each pushrod across a piece of plate glass to see if it's bent (if it wobbles, it's bent).

Installation

10   Lubricate the lower ends of the pushrods with clean engine oil or moly-base grease and install them in their original locations. Make sure each pushrod seats completely in the lifter socket.

11   Apply moly-base grease to the ends of the valve stems and the upper ends of the pushrods before positioning the rocker arms and installing the nuts.

12   Set the rocker arms in place, then install the pivot balls and nuts. Apply moly-base grease to the pivot balls to prevent damage to the mating surfaces before engine oil pressure builds up. Tighten the nuts to the torque listed in this Chapter's Specifications.

5   Valve springs, retainers and seals - replacement

Refer to illustrations 5.4, 5.9 and 5.17
Note: Broken valve springs and defective valve stem seals can be replaced without

5.4 This is what the air hose adapter that threads into the spark plug hole looks like - they're commonly available at auto parts stores

removing the cylinder head. Two special tools and a compressed air source are normally required to perform this operation, so read through this Section carefully and rent or buy the tools before beginning the job. If compressed air isn't available, a length of nylon rope can be used to keep the valves from falling into the cylinder during this procedure.

1   Refer to Section 3 and remove the valve cover.

2   Remove the spark plug from the cylinder which has the defective component. If all of the valve stem seals are being replaced, all of the spark plugs should be removed.

3   Turn the crankshaft until the piston in the affected cylinder is at top dead center on the compression stroke (refer to Chapter 2, Part H, for instructions). If you're replacing all of the valve stem seals, begin with cylinder number one and work on the valves for one cylinder at a time. Move from cylinder-to-cylinder following the firing order sequence (see this Chapter's Specifications).

4   Thread an adapter into the spark plug hole (see illustration) and connect an air hose from a compressed air source to it. Most auto parts stores can supply the air hose adapter. Note: *Many cylinder compression gauges utilize a screw-in fitting that may work with your air hose quick-disconnect fitting.*

5   Remove the nut, pivot ball and rocker arm for the valve with the defective part and pull out the pushrod. If all of the valve stem seals are being replaced, all of the rocker arms and pushrods should be removed (refer to Section 4).

6   Apply compressed air to the cylinder. Warning: *The piston may be forced down by compressed air, causing the crankshaft to turn suddenly. If the wrench used when positioning the number one piston at TDC is still attached to the bolt in the crankshaft nose, it could cause damage or injury when the crankshaft moves.*

7   The valves should be held in place by the air pressure. If the valve faces or seats are in poor condition, leaks may prevent air pressure from retaining the valves - a "valve job" is necessary to correct this problem.

8   If you don't have access to compressed air, an alternative method can be used. Position the piston at a point just before TDC on the compression stroke, then feed a long piece of nylon rope through the spark plug hole until it fills the combustion chamber. Be sure to leave the end of the rope hanging out of the engine so it can be removed easily. Use a large ratchet and socket to rotate the crankshaft in the normal direction of rotation (clockwise) until slight resistance is felt.

5.9 Once the spring is compressed, remove the keepers with a magnet or needle-nose pliers

5.17 Keepers don't always stay in place, so apply a small dab of grease to each one, as shown here, before installation - it'll hold them in place on the valve stem as the spring is released

9   Stuff shop rags into the cylinder head holes above and below the valves to prevent parts and tools from falling into the engine, then use a valve spring compressor to compress the spring. Remove the keepers with small needle-nose pliers or a magnet **(see illustrations)**. **Note:** *A couple of different types of tools are available for compressing the valve springs with the head in place. One type utilizes the rocker arm stud and nut for leverage, while the other type grips the lower spring coils and presses on the retainer as the knob is turned. Both types work very well, although the lever type is usually less expensive.*

10   Remove the spring retainer and valve spring, then remove the valve guide seal. **Note:** *If air pressure fails to hold the valve in the closed position during this operation, the valve face or seat is probably damaged. If so, the cylinder head will have to be removed for additional repair operations.*

11   Wrap a rubber band or tape around the top of the valve stem so the valve won't fall into the combustion chamber, then release the air pressure. **Note:** *If a rope was used instead of air pressure, turn the crankshaft slightly in the direction opposite normal rotation.*

12   Inspect the valve stem for damage. Rotate the valve in the guide and check the end for eccentric movement, which would indicate the valve stem is bent.

13   Move the valve up-and-down in the guide and make sure it doesn't bind. If the valve stem binds, either the valve is bent or the guide is damaged. In either case, the head will have to be removed for repair.

14   Reapply air pressure to the cylinder to retain the valve in the closed position, then remove the tape or rubber band from the valve stem. If a rope was used instead of air pressure, rotate the crankshaft in the normal direction of rotation until slight resistance is felt.

15   Lubricate the valve stem with engine oil and install a new valve guide seal. **Note:** *Intake and exhaust valve seals are different.*

16   Install the spring in position over the valve.

17   Install the valve spring retainer. Com-

press the valve spring and carefully install the keepers in the groove. Apply a small dab of grease to the inside of each keeper to hold it in place if necessary **(see illustration)**. Remove the pressure from the spring tool and make sure the keepers are seated.

18   Disconnect the air hose and remove the adapter from the spark plug hole. If a rope was used in place of air pressure, pull it out of the cylinder.

19   Refer to Section 4 and install the rocker arm(s) and pushrod(s).

20   Install the spark plug(s) and hook up the wire(s).

21   Refer to Section 3 and install the valve cover.

22   Start and run the engine, then check for oil leaks and unusual sounds coming from the valve cover area.

6   Intake manifold - removal and installation

Refer to illustration 6.8
Note: *This procedure may be easier with the engine rotated forward (see Chapter 1).*

1   Relieve the fuel pressure (see Chapter 4), then disconnect the negative battery cable from the battery. **Caution:** *On models equipped with the Theftlock audio system, be sure the lockout feature is turned off before performing any procedure which requires disconnecting the battery.*

2   Remove the upper intake manifold assembly (see Chapter 4).

3   Raise the front of the vehicle and support it securely on jackstands. Drain the coolant (refer to Chapter 1).

4   If necessary for clearance, remove the power steering pump (if equipped) and tie it aside in an upright position (see Chapter 10).

5   Remove the heater hose and coolant line retaining nut near the bottom of the intake manifold.

6   Remove the mounting nuts from the intake manifold.

7   Separate the intake manifold and gasket from the engine. Scrape all traces of gasket material off the intake manifold and head gas-

6.8 Intake manifold bolt tightening sequence

ket mating surfaces. When scraping, be careful not to scratch or gouge the delicate aluminum gasket surfaces on the head and manifold. Clean the surfaces with a rag soaked in lacquer thinner or acetone.

8   Installation is the reverse of removal. Be sure to use a new gasket. Tighten the nuts/bolts to the torque listed in this Chapter's Specifications **(see illustration)**.

9   Add coolant, run the engine and check for leaks and proper operation.

7   Exhaust manifold - removal and installation

Refer to illustration 7.11
Caution: *Allow the engine to cool completely before beginning this procedure.*

1   Disconnect the negative cable from the battery. **Caution:** *On models equipped with the Theftlock audio system, be sure the lockout feature is turned off before performing any procedure which requires disconnecting the battery.*

2   Unplug the oxygen sensor lead.

3   Remove the air cleaner and air duct assembly.

4   Remove the air-inlet resonator from the upper tie bar.

5   Remove the lower air duct.

6   Disconnect the upper engine mounting torque strut from the engine.

7   Remove the nuts and bolts and discon-

7.11 The exhaust manifold bolt locations (arrows)

8.11a To avoid mixing up the head bolts, use the new gasket to transfer the bolt hole pattern to a piece of cardboard, then punch holes in the cardboard to accept the bolts

nect the engine strut bracket from the cylinder head.

8   Remove the drivebelt, the alternator and the alternator rear support bracket (see Chapters 1 and 5).

9   Remove the oil level dipstick and dipstick holder.

10   Raise the front of the vehicle, support it securely on jackstands and apply the parking brake. Block the rear wheels to keep the vehicle from rolling off the jackstands. Unbolt the exhaust pipe from the manifold. Lower the vehicle.

11   Remove the exhaust manifold-to-cylinder head nuts/bolts **(see illustration)**, pull the manifold off the engine and lift it out of the exhaust pipe flange. Remove and discard the gasket.

12   Scrape all traces of gasket material off the exhaust manifold and cylinder head mating surfaces. Be careful not to scratch or gouge the delicate aluminum cylinder head or exhaust leaks will develop. Wipe the surfaces clean with a rag soaked in lacquer thinner or acetone.

13   Clean all bolt and stud threads before installation. A wire brush can be used on the manifold mounting studs, while a tap works well when cleaning the cylinder head bolt holes.

14   If a new manifold is being installed, transfer the oxygen sensor from the old manifold to the new one.

15   Installation is the reverse of removal. Be sure to use a new gasket and tighten the nuts/bolts to the torque listed in this Chapter's Specifications. Work in a spiral pattern from the center out.

8   Cylinder head - removal and installation

Caution: *Allow the engine to cool completely before beginning this procedure.*
Note: *On vehicles with high mileage and dur-*

8.11b Loosen the cylinder head bolts in 1/4-turn increments to avoid warping the head

ing an engine overhaul, camshaft lobe height should be checked prior to cylinder head removal (see Chapter 2, Part H for instructions).

Removal

Refer to illustrations 8.11a and 8.11b

1   Relieve the fuel pressure (see Chapter 4). Disconnect the cable from the negative battery terminal. **Caution:** *On models equipped with the Theftlock audio system, be sure the lockout feature is turned off before performing any procedure which requires disconnecting the battery.*

2   Remove the alternator and brackets as described in Chapter 5.

3   Remove the intake manifold as described in Section 6.

4   Remove the exhaust manifold as described in Section 7.

5   Unbolt the drivebelt tensioner bracket.

6   Unbolt the power steering pump (if equipped) and set it aside without disconnecting the hoses (see Chapter 10).

7   Disconnect any remaining wires, hoses, fuel and vacuum lines from the cylinder head.

Be sure to label them to simplify reinstallation.

8   Disconnect the spark plug wires and remove the spark plugs. Be sure the plug wires are labeled to simplify reinstallation.

9   Remove the valve cover (see Section 3).

10   Remove the rocker arms and pushrods (see Section 4).

11   Using the new head gasket, outline the cylinders and bolt pattern on a piece of cardboard **(see illustration)**. Be sure to indicate the front of the engine for reference. Punch holes at the bolt locations. Loosen each of the cylinder head mounting bolts 1/4-turn at a time until they can be removed by hand **(see illustration)**. Store the bolts in the cardboard holder as they're removed - this will ensure they are reinstalled in their original locations, which is absolutely essential.

12   Lift the head off the engine. If it's stuck, don't attempt to pry it off - you could damage the sealing surfaces. Instead, use a hammer and block of wood to tap the head and break the gasket seal.

13   Place the head on a block of wood to prevent damage to the gasket surface.

14   Remove the cylinder head gasket.

8.17 A die should be used to remove corrosion and sealant from the head bolt threads prior to installation

8.21 Cylinder head bolt tightening sequence – note that the rear head bolts (long bolts) have a higher specified torque than the front bolts

10.4a Crankshaft pulley installation details

10.4b Have an assistant hold the ring gear with a large screwdriver as the pulley-to-crankshaft bolt is loosened/tightened

Installation

Refer to illustrations 8.17 and 8.21

15   If a new cylinder head is being installed, transfer all external parts from the old cylinder head to the new one.

16   If not already done, thoroughly clean the gasket surfaces on the cylinder head and the engine block. Do not gouge or otherwise damage the soft aluminum gasket surfaces.

17   To get the proper torque readings, the threads of the head bolts must be clean **(see illustration)**. This also applies to the threaded holes in the engine block. Run a tap through the holes to ensure they are clean.

18   Place the gasket in position over the engine block dowel pins. Note any marks like "THIS SIDE UP" and install the gasket accordingly.

19   Carefully lower the cylinder head onto the engine, over the dowel pins and the gasket.

20   Install the bolts finger tight. Don't tighten any of the bolts at this time.

21   Tighten each of the bolts in 1/4-turn increments in the recommended sequence

(see illustration). A special tool must be used on the head bolts. Note that the rear bolts have a different torque specification than the front bolts. Continue tightening in the recommended sequence until the torque (and angle of rotation) specified in this Chapter is reached. Mark each bolt with a felt-tip marker each time you tighten it to make sure none of the bolts have been left out of the sequence.

22   The remaining installation steps are the reverse of removal.

23   Be sure to refill the cooling system and change the oil and filter (see Chapter 1).

9 Hydraulic lifters - removal, inspection and installation

This procedure is essentially the same as for the 2.5L four-cylinder engine (see Chapter 2, Part B), except there's no pushrod cover to remove. You'll need a long magnetic tool, scribe or lifter removal tool, since you'll have to reach down into the cylinder block to remove the lifters.

10 Crankshaft pulley - removal and installation

Refer to illustrations 10.4a, 10.4b and 10.6

Removal

1   Remove the cable from the negative battery terminal. **Caution:** *On models equipped with the Theftlock audio system, be sure the lockout feature is turned off before performing any procedure which requires disconnecting the battery.*

2   Remove the drivebelt (see Chapter 1).

3   Raise the front of the vehicle and support it securely on jackstands. Remove the right front tire and the inner fender splash shield.

4   Remove the crankshaft pulley-to-crankshaft bolt **(see illustration)**. A breaker bar will probably be needed, since the bolt is very tight. If necessary, remove the lower bellhousing cover and insert a large screwdriver into the teeth of the flywheel/driveplate ring gear to prevent the crankshaft from turning **(see illustration)**.

10.6 Use a puller to remove the crankshaft pulley hub

12.5 Location of the timing chain cover mounting bolts (arrows)

5   Remove the three bolts that attach the pulley to the hub.
6   Using a puller, remove the crankshaft pulley or hub from the crankshaft **(see illustration)**.

Installation

7   Refer to Section 11 for the oil seal replacement procedure.
8   Apply a thin layer of clean multi-purpose grease to the seal contact surface of the hub.
9   Position the hub on the crankshaft and slide it through the seal until it bottoms against the crankshaft gear. Note that the slot (key-way) in the hub must be aligned with the Woodruff key in the end of the crankshaft. The pulley-to-crankshaft bolt can be used to press the hub into position.
10   Tighten the pulley-to-crankshaft bolt to the torque listed in this Chapter's Specifications.
11   The remaining installation steps are the reverse of removal.

11 Crankshaft front oil seal - replacement

1   Remove the crankshaft pulley (see Section 10).
2   Pry the old oil seal out with a seal removal tool or a screwdriver. Be very careful not to nick or otherwise damage the crankshaft in the process. Wrap the screwdriver tip with vinyl tape to protect the crankshaft.
3   Apply a thin coat of RTV-type sealant to the outer edge of the new seal. Lubricate the seal lip with moly-base grease or clean engine oil.
4   Place the seal squarely in position in the bore and drive it into place with special tool J-35468 (or equivalent).
5   If you don't have the special, carefully tap the seal into place with a large socket or piece of pipe and a hammer. The outer diameter of the socket or pipe should be the same

size as the seal outer diameter. Make sure the seal is seated completely in the bore.
6   Install the crankshaft pulley (see Section 10).
7   Reinstall the remaining parts in the reverse order of removal.
8   Start the engine and check for oil leaks at the seal.

12 Timing chain cover - removal and installation

Refer to illustration 12.5

1   Remove the crankshaft pulley (and hub, if equipped) as described in Section 10.
2   Remove the oil pan (see Section 15).
3   Remove the bolts holding the power steering pump and position it aside.
4   Remove the alternator bolts and position it aside.
5   Remove the drivebelt tensioner and bracket and the timing chain cover-to-block bolts, then detach the cover **(see illustration)**.
6   Using a scraper and degreaser, remove all old gasket material from the sealing surfaces of the timing chain cover, engine block and oil pan.
7   If necessary, replace the front oil seal by carefully prying it out of the cover with a large screwdriver. Don't distort the cover.
8   Install the new seal with the spring side toward the inside of the cover. Drive the seal into place using a seal installation tool or a large socket and hammer. A block of wood will also work.
9   Use a thin coat of RTV-type sealant to position a new gasket on the timing chain cover.
10   Place the cover in position over the dowel pins on the block.
11   Install the bolts that secure the cover to the block, then tighten all of them to the torque listed in this Chapter's Specifications. Follow a criss-cross pattern to avoid distorting the cover.

12   Install the oil pan (see Section 15).
13   Complete the installation by reversing the removal procedure.

13 Timing chain and sprockets - inspection, removal and installation

Refer to illustrations 13.9 and 13.18

Inspection

1   Disconnect the cable from the negative battery terminal. **Caution:** *On models equipped with the Theftlock audio system, be sure the lockout feature is turned off before performing any procedure which requires disconnecting the battery.*
2   Remove the crankshaft pulley (see Section 10).
3   Remove the timing chain cover (see Section 12).
4   Before removing the chain and sprockets, visually inspect the teeth on the sprockets for wear and the chain for excessive slack. Also check the condition of the timing chain tensioner.
5   If either or both sprockets show any signs of wear (edges on the teeth of the camshaft sprocket not "square," bright or blue areas on the teeth of either sprocket, chipping, pitting, etc.), they should be replaced with new ones. Wear in these areas is very common.
6   Failure to replace a worn timing chain may result in erratic engine performance, loss of power and lowered fuel mileage.
7   If any one component requires replacement, all related components, including the tensioner, should be replaced as well.
8   If the chain and sprockets must be replaced, proceed as follows.

Removal

9   Temporarily install the bolt in the end of the crankshaft. Turn the engine over using the

13.9 Align the camshaft and crankshaft sprocket marks as shown here

13.18 Compress the timing chain tensioner and insert a drill bit or nail into the hole to retain the tensioner in its retracted position

bolt until the marks on the camshaft and crankshaft line up **(see illustration)**. **Note:** *Do not attempt to remove the timing chain until this is done and do not turn the crankshaft or camshaft while the sprockets/chain are off.*

10   Remove the timing chain tensioner upper bolt. Loosen the timing chain tensioner Torx bolt as far as possible but don't remove it.

11   Remove the camshaft sprocket retaining bolt and detach the camshaft sprocket and timing chain. It may be necessary to tap the sprocket with a soft-face hammer to dislodge it.

12   If the crankshaft sprocket must be removed, it can be drawn off the crankshaft with a puller.

Installation

13   Lubricate the thrust side with moly-base grease and install the crankshaft sprocket (if removed) on the crankshaft using a special tool. Be sure the Woodruff key is aligned with the keyway as the sprocket is installed. If the special tool is unavailable, drive the sprocket into place using a section of pipe just large enough to fit over the nose of the crankshaft.

14   Slip the timing chain onto the camshaft sprocket.

15   With the timing marks aligned, slip the chain over the crankshaft sprocket. Align the dowel in the camshaft with the dowel hole in the camshaft sprocket and install the sprocket on the camshaft. Draw the camshaft sprocket into place with the retaining bolt and tighten it to the torque listed in this Chapter's Specifications. **Caution:** *Do not hammer or attempt to drive the camshaft sprocket into place - it could dislodge the welch plug at the rear of the engine.*

16   With the chain and both sprockets in place, check again to make sure the timing marks on the two sprockets are properly aligned **(see illustration 13.9)**. If not, remove the camshaft sprocket and move the chain until they are.

17   Lubricate the chain with clean engine oil.

18   The timing chain tensioner spring must be compressed using a special tool, prior to installation. Insert a nail or cotter pin into hole A **(see illustration)** to hold the spring in place during installation. Remove the nail or pin after installation.

19   Install the remaining components in the reverse order of removal.

14   Camshaft and bearings - removal, inspection and installation

Due to the fact the engine is mounted transversely in the vehicle, there isn't enough room to remove the camshaft with the engine in place. Therefore, the procedure is covered in Chapter 2, Part H.

15   Oil pan - removal and installation

1   Warm up the engine, then drain the oil and remove the oil filter (see Chapter 1).

2   Detach the cable from the negative battery terminal. **Caution:** *On models equipped with the Theftlock audio system, be sure the lockout feature is turned off before performing any procedure which requires disconnecting the battery.*

3   Remove the air cleaner and air-duct assembly.

4   Remove the drivebelt (see Chapter 1).

5   Disconnect the upper engine mounting strut from the engine bracket.

6   Install engine support fixture or, by other suitable means, ensure that the engine is properly supported.

7   Loosen the right front wheel lug nuts, then raise the vehicle and support it securely on jackstands.

8   Remove the right front wheel and tire.

9   Remove the right-side engine splash shield.

10   Remove the exhaust pipe and catalytic converter.

11   On air conditioned models, remove the air conditioner brace at the starter and compressor bracket.

12   Remove the starter and bracket (see Chapter 5).

13   Remove the lower bellhousing cover.

14   On air conditioned models, remove the air conditioner brace.

15   Remove the four right support bolts. Lower the support slightly to gain clearance for oil pan removal.

16   Remove the oil filter extension (automatic transaxle equipped models only).

17   Remove the bolts and nuts securing the oil pan to the engine block.

18   Tap on the pan with a soft-face hammer to break the gasket seal, then detach the oil pan from the engine.

19   Using a gasket scraper, remove all traces of old gasket and/or sealant from the engine block and oil pan. Make sure the threaded bolt holes in the block are clean. Wash the oil pan with solvent and dry it thoroughly.

20   Check the gasket flanges for distortion, particularly around the bolt holes. If necessary, place the pan on a block of wood and use a hammer to flatten and restore the gasket surfaces. Clean the mating surfaces with lacquer thinner or acetone.

21   Place a 2 mm diameter bead of RTV sealant on the oil pan-to-block sealing flanges and the oil pan-to-front cover surface.

22   Apply a thin coat of RTV sealant to the ends of the rear oil pan seal down to the ears. Press the oil pan seal into position.

23   Carefully place the oil pan against the block.

24   Install the bolts/nuts and tighten them in 1/4-turn increments to the torque listed in this Chapter's Specifications. Start with the bolts closest to the center of the pan and work out in a spiral pattern. Don't overtighten them or leakage may occur.

25   Reinstall components removed for

17.3 Most flywheels and driveplates have locating dowels (arrow) - if the one you're working on doesn't, make some marks to ensure correct installation

17.4 A large screwdriver wedged in the starter ring gear teeth or one of the holes in the driveplate can be used to keep the flywheel/driveplate from turning as the mounting bolts are removed

access to the oil pan.

26   Add oil and install a new filter, run the engine and check for oil leaks.

16 Oil pump - removal and installation

1   Remove the oil pan (see Section 15).

2   Place a large drain pan under the engine.

3   Unbolt the pump from the rear main bearing cap.

4   Lower the pump and extension shaft from the engine.

5   Before installation, prime the pump with engine oil. Pour oil into the pick-up while the pump extension shaft is turned.

6   Attach the pump, extension shaft and retainer to the main bearing cap. While aligning the pump with the dowel pins at the bottom of the main bearing cap, align the top end of the extension shaft with the lower end of the oil pump drive. When aligned properly, it should slip into place easily.

7   Install the pump mounting bolt and tighten it to the torque listed in this Chapter's Specifications.

8   Install the oil pan and add oil (see Section 15).

17 Flywheel/driveplate - removal and installation

Refer to illustrations 17.3 and 17.4

1   Raise the vehicle and support it securely on jackstands, then refer to Chapter 7 and remove the transaxle. If it's leaking, now would be a very good time to replace the front pump seal/O-ring (automatic transaxle only).

2   Remove the pressure plate and clutch disc (Chapter 8 - manual transaxle equipped vehicles). Now is a good time to check/replace

the clutch components and pilot bearing.

3   If there is no dowel pin, make some marks on the flywheel/driveplate and crankshaft to ensure correct alignment during reinstallation **(see illustration)**.

4   Remove the bolts that secure the flywheel/driveplate to the crankshaft **(see illustration)**. If the crankshaft turns, wedge a screwdriver through the openings in the driveplate (automatic transaxle) or against the flywheel ring gear teeth (manual transaxle). Since the flywheel is fairly heavy, be sure to support it while removing the last bolt.

5   Remove the flywheel/driveplate from the crankshaft.

6   Clean the flywheel to remove grease and oil. Inspect the friction surface for cracks, rivet grooves, burned areas and score marks. Light scoring can be removed with emery cloth. Check for cracked and broken ring gear teeth. Lay the flywheel on a flat surface and use a straightedge to check for warpage.

7   Clean and inspect the mating surfaces of the flywheel/driveplate and the crankshaft. If the crankshaft rear seal is leaking, replace it before reinstalling the flywheel/driveplate.

8   Position the flywheel/driveplate against the crankshaft. Be sure to align the dowel or marks made during removal. Before installing the bolts, apply thread locking compound to the threads.

9   Keep the flywheel/driveplate from turning as described above while you tighten the bolts to the torque listed in this Chapter's Specifications.

10   The remainder of installation is the reverse of the removal procedure.

18 Rear main oil seal - replacement

1   Remove the flywheel/driveplate (see Section 17).

2   Using a thin screwdriver or seal removal

tool, carefully remove the oil seal from the engine block. Be very careful not to damage the crankshaft surface while prying the seal out.

3   Clean the bore in the block and the seal contact surface on the crankshaft. Check the seal contact surface on the crankshaft for scratches and nicks that could damage the new seal lip and cause oil leaks - if the crankshaft is damaged, the only alternative is a new or different crankshaft. Inspect the seal bore for nicks and scratches. Carefully smooth it with a fine file if necessary, but don't nick the crankshaft in the process.

4   A special tool is recommended to install the new oil seal. Lubricate the oil seal lips. Slide the seal onto the mandril until the dust lip bottoms squarely against the collar of the tool. **Note:** *If the special tool isn't available, carefully work the seal lip over the crankshaft and tap it into place with a hammer and blunt punch.*

5   Align the dowel pin on the tool with the dowel pin hole in the crankshaft and attach the tool to the crankshaft by hand-tightening the bolts.

6   Turn the tool handle until the collar bottoms against the case, seating the seal.

7   Loosen the tool handle and remove the bolts. Remove the tool.

8   Check the seal and make sure it's seated squarely in the bore.

9   Install the flywheel/driveplate (see Section 17).

10   Install the transaxle.

19 Engine mounts - check and replacement

1   Engine mounts seldom require attention, but broken or deteriorated mounts should be replaced immediately or the added strain placed on the driveline components may cause damage or wear.

Check

2   During the check, the engine must be raised slightly to remove the weight from the mounts.

3   Raise the vehicle and support it securely on jackstands, then position a jack under the engine oil pan. Place a large block of wood between the jack head and the oil pan, then carefully raise the engine just enough to take the weight off the mounts. **Warning:** *DO NOT place any part of your body under the engine when it's supported only by a jack!*

4   Check the mounts to see if the rubber is cracked, hardened or separated from the metal plates. Sometimes the rubber will split right down the center.

5   Check for relative movement between the mount plates and the engine or frame (use a large screwdriver or prybar to attempt to move the mounts). If movement is noted, lower the engine and tighten the mount fasteners.

6   Rubber preservative should be applied to the mounts to slow deterioration.

Replacement

7   Disconnect the negative battery cable from the battery. **Caution:** *On models equipped with the Theftlock audio system, be sure the lockout feature is turned off before performing any procedure which requires disconnecting the battery.*

Lower mount

8   Remove the through-bolt from the engine bracket end of the upper mount strut and rotate the strut out of the way.

9   Raise the engine slightly with a jack or hoist. Remove the fasteners and detach the mount from the frame bracket.

10   Remove the mount-to-block bracket bolts/nuts and detach the mount.

Upper mount strut

11   Disconnect the negative battery cable from the battery and remove the bolts and nuts from the strut and the brace. **Caution:** *On models equipped with the Theftlock audio system, be sure the lockout feature is turned off before performing any procedure which requires disconnecting the battery.*

12   Installation is the reverse of removal. Use thread locking compound on the threads and be sure to tighten everything securely.

Chapter 2 Part B
2.5 liter four-cylinder engine

Contents

	Section
Camshaft and bearings - removal, inspection and installation	13
Crankshaft force balancer - removal and installation	16
Crankshaft front oil seal - replacement...........................	11
Crankshaft pulley - removal and installation.................................	10
Cylinder compression check......................... See Chapter 2H	
Cylinder head - removal and installation	8
Drivebelt check, adjustment and replacement................ See Chapter 1	
Driveplate - removal and installation	17
Engine mounts - check and replacement	19
Engine oil and filter change .... See Chapter 1	
Engine overhaul - general information......................... See Chapter 2H	
Engine - removal and installation .... See Chapter 2H	
Exhaust manifold - removal and installation.............................	7
General information	1
Hydraulic lifters - removal, inspection and installation..................	9
Intake manifold - removal and installation	6
Oil pan - removal and installation	14
Oil pump - removal and installation	15
Rear main oil seal - replacement..	18
Repair operations possible with the engine in the vehicle............	2
Rocker arms and pushrods - removal, inspection and installation	4
Spark plug replacement......................... See Chapter 1	
Timing cover, timing chain, sprockets and tensioner - removal, inspection and installation	12
Timing gears - inspection, removal and installation .... See Chapter 2H	
Top Dead Center (TDC) for number one piston - locating .... See Chapter 2H	
Valve cover - removal and installation	3
Valve springs, retainers and seals - replacement........................	5
Water pump - removal and installation .... See Chapter 3	

Specifications

General

Cylinder numbers (drivebelt end-to-transaxle end)	1-2-3-4
Firing order	1-3-4-2

Torque specifications

Ft-lbs (unless otherwise indicated)

Note: *One foot-pound (ft-lb) of torque is equivalent to 12 inch-pounds (in-lbs) of torque. Torque values below approximately 15 foot-pounds are expressed in inch-pounds, because most foot-pound torque wrenches are not accurate at these smaller values.*

Crankshaft pulley center bolt...	162
Cylinder head bolts **(see illustration 8.21)**	
First step	18
Second step	
All bolts except no. 9..	26
Bolt no. 9...	18
Fourth step (all bolts)	Rotate an additional 90-degrees (1/4 turn)
Force balancer assembly	
Step 1 - All bolts	107 in-lbs
Step 2	
Short bolts...	11 plus 75-degrees additional rotation
Long bolts	11 plus 90-degrees additional rotation

FRONT ↓

1
4
2
3

① ② ③ ④

2.5L engine

Cylinder and coil terminal location

Torque specifications (continued)   **Ft-lbs** (unless otherwise indicated)

Note: *One foot-pound of torque is equivalent to 12 inch-pounds of torque. Torque values below approximately 15 foot-pounds are expressed in inch-pounds, because most foot-pound torque wrenches are not accurate at these smaller values.*

Exhaust manifold fasteners

Inner bolts	37
Outer bolts	26
Driveplate bolts	55
Intake manifold fasteners	25
Oil pan bolts	89 in-lbs
Oil pan drain plug	25
Oil pump cover bolts	89 in-lbs
Valve cover bolts	80 in-lbs
Rocker arm bolts	20
Pushrod cover nuts	89 in-lbs

1   General information

Refer to illustration 1.1

This Part of Chapter 2 is devoted to in-vehicle repair procedures for the 2.5 liter four-cylinder, overhead valve engine. The 2.5L engine became available in 1990, in the Lumina model only. These engines have cast iron blocks and cast aluminum pistons. The cast iron cylinder head has valve guides that are cast integrally. Steel rocker arms and tubular pushrods actuate the valves. This engine is also equipped with a force balancer assembly. This unit is attached to the crankshaft and it dampens the engine vibration using two eccentrically weighted shafts and gears complemented by a concentric gear on the crankshaft. The engine is transversely mounted and can be recognized by the black steel valve cover with the oil fill cap in the left rear corner (as viewed from the front of the engine compartment). To positively identify this engine, locate the vehicle identification number on the left front corner of the instrument panel. This plate is visible from outside the vehicle **(see illustration)**. The eighth character in the sequence is the engine designation:

R = 2.5L four-cylinder, overhead valve engine

Information concerning engine removal and installation and engine overhaul can be found in Part H of this Chapter.

The following repair procedures are based on the assumption the engine is in the vehicle. If the engine has been removed from the vehicle and mounted on a stand, many of the steps outlined in this Part of Chapter 2 will not apply.

2   Repair operations possible with the engine in the vehicle

Many major repair operations can be accomplished without removing the engine from the vehicle.

Clean the engine compartment and the exterior of the engine with some type of degreaser before any work is done. It'll make the job easier and help keep dirt out of the internal areas of the engine.

1.1 The vehicle identification number is located on the left front corner of the instrument panel

Depending on the components involved, it may be helpful to remove the hood to improve access to the engine as repairs are performed (refer to Chapter 11 if necessary). Cover the fenders to prevent damage to the paint. Special pads are available, but an old bedspread or blanket will also work.

If vacuum, exhaust, oil or coolant leaks develop, indicating a need for gasket or seal replacement, the repairs can generally be made with the engine in the vehicle. The intake and exhaust manifold gaskets, timing cover gasket, oil pan gasket, crankshaft oil seals and cylinder head gasket are all accessible with the engine in place.

Exterior engine components, such as the intake and exhaust manifolds, the oil pan (and the oil pump), the water pump, the starter motor, the alternator and the fuel system components can be removed for repair with the engine in place.

Since the cylinder head can be removed without pulling the engine, valve component servicing can also be accomplished with the engine in the vehicle.

In extreme cases caused by a lack of necessary equipment, repair or replacement of piston rings, pistons, connecting rods and rod bearings is possible with the engine in the vehicle. However, this practice is not recommended because of the cleaning and preparation work that must be done to the components involved.

3   Valve cover - removal and installation

Removal

1   Remove the air cleaner assembly, tagging each hose to be disconnected with a piece of numbered tape to simplify installation.

2   Disconnect and remove the PCV valve (see Chapter 1).

3   Remove the EGR valve (see Chapter 6).

4   Remove the spark plug wires and the clips from the valve cover.

5   Remove the valve cover bolts.

6   Detach the valve cover from the cylinder head using special tools. The use of these tools will prevent distorting the valve cover, but if they are not available, carefully tap on the cover with a wood block and a hammer. Don't pry between the cover and the cylinder head, as this would bend the sealing flange, causing oil leaks.

Installation

7   The mating surfaces of the cylinder head and valve cover must be perfectly clean when the cover is installed. Use a gasket scraper to remove all traces of sealant or old gasket, then clean the mating surfaces with lacquer thinner or acetone (if there's sealant or oil on the mating surfaces when the cover is

4.2a Removing the rocker arm pivot bolt

4.2b Loosen the rocker arm bolt, rotate the rocker arm to one side and lift out the pushrod

installed, oil leaks may develop).

8   Clean the mounting bolt threads with a die if necessary to remove any corrosion and restore damaged threads. Make sure the threaded holes in the head are clean - run a tap into them if necessary to remove corrosion and restore damaged threads.

9   Apply a 3/16 inch bead of RTV-type sealant all the way around the sealing flange on the cover. Allow the sealant to dry or "set up" for approximately 1 minute.

10   Place the valve cover on the cylinder head and install the mounting bolts. Tighten the bolts a little at a time to the torque listed in this Chapter's Specifications.

11   Complete the installation by reversing the removal procedure.

4   Rocker arms and pushrods - removal, inspection and installation

Refer to illustrations 4.2a, 4.2b and 4.4

Removal

1   Refer to Section 3 and detach the valve cover from the cylinder head.

2   Beginning at the front of the cylinder head, loosen the rocker arm bolts **(see illustration)**. **Note:** *If the pushrods are the only items being removed, rotate the rocker arms to one side so the pushrods can be lifted out* **(see illustration)**.

3   Remove the bolts, the rocker arms and the pivot balls and store them in marked containers (they must be reinstalled in their original locations).

4   Remove the pushrods and store them separately to make sure they don't get mixed up during installation **(see illustration)**.

5   If the pushrod guides must be removed for any reason, make sure they're marked so they can be reinstalled in their original locations.

Inspection

6   Check each rocker arm for wear, cracks and other damage, especially where the pushrods and valve stems contact the rocker arm faces.

7   Make sure the hole at the pushrod end of each rocker arm is open.

8   Check each rocker arm pivot area for wear, cracks and galling.

If the rocker arms are worn or damaged, replace them with new ones and use new pivot balls as well.

9   Inspect the pushrods for cracks and excessive wear at the ends. Roll each pushrod across a piece of plate glass to see if it's bent (if it wobbles, it's bent).

Installation

10   Lubricate the lower ends of the pushrods with clean engine oil or moly-base grease and install them in their original locations. Make sure each pushrod seats completely in the lifter socket.

4.4 A perforated cardboard box can be used to store the pushrods to ensure they're reinstalled in their original locations - note the label indicating the front (drivebelt end) of the engine

11   Apply moly-base grease to the ends of the valve stems and the upper ends of the pushrods before positioning the rocker arms and installing the nuts.

12   Install the pivot balls onto the rocker arm bolts. Apply moly-base grease to the pivot balls to prevent damage to the mating surfaces before engine oil pressure builds up. Insert the bolt and pivot ball assemblies into their respective rocker arms, then install them to the cylinder head. Make sure the pushrods seat properly in the rocker arms. Tighten the bolts to the torque listed in this Chapter's Specifications.

13   Install the valve cover (see Section 3).

5   Valve springs, retainers and seals - replacement

Refer to illustrations 5.4, 5.9a, 5.9b and 5.17
Note: *Broken valve springs and defective valve stem seals can be replaced without removing the cylinder head. Two special tools and a compressed air source are normally required to perform this operation, so read through this Section carefully and rent or buy the tools before beginning the job. If compressed air isn't available, a length of nylon rope can be used to keep the valves from falling into the cylinder during this procedure.*

1   Refer to Section 3 and remove the valve cover.

2   Remove the spark plug from the cylinder which has the defective component. If all of the valve stem seals are being replaced, all of the spark plugs should be removed.

3   Turn the crankshaft until the piston in the affected cylinder is at top dead center on the compression stroke (refer to Chapter 2, Part H, for instructions). If you're replacing all of the valve stem seals, begin with cylinder number one and work on the valves for one cylinder at a time. Move from cylinder-to-cylinder following the firing order sequence (see this Chapter's Specifications).

5.4 This is what the air hose adapter that threads into the spark plug hole looks like - they're commonly available at auto parts stores

5.9a A lever-type valve spring compressor is used to compress the spring and remove the keepers to replace valve seals or springs with the head installed – note that a rocker arm bolt has been reinstalled to be used for leverage

5.9b Typical engine valves and related components – exploded view

1 Keepers
2 Retainer
3 Oil shield
4 O-ring oil seal
5 Umbrella seal
6 Spring and damper
7 Intake valve
8 Retainer/rotator
9 Exhaust valve

5.17 Keepers don't always stay in place, so apply a small dab of grease to each one as shown here before installation - it'll hold them in place on the valve stem as the spring is released

4   Thread an adapter into the spark plug hole (see illustration) and connect an air hose from a compressed air source to it. Most auto parts stores can supply the air hose adapter. Note: Many cylinder compression gauges utilize a screw-in fitting that may work with your air hose quick-disconnect fitting.

5   Remove the bolt, pivot ball and rocker arm for the valve with the defective part and pull out the pushrod. If all of the valve stem seals are being replaced, all of the rocker arms and pushrods should be removed (refer to Section 4).

6   Apply compressed air to the cylinder. Warning: The piston may be forced down by compressed air, causing the crankshaft to turn suddenly. If the wrench used when positioning the number one piston at TDC is still attached to the bolt in the crankshaft nose, it could cause damage or injury when the crankshaft moves.

7   The valves should be held in place by the air pressure. If the valve faces or seats are in poor condition, leaks may prevent air pressure from retaining the valves - a "valve job" is necessary to correct this problem.

8   If you don't have access to compressed air, an alternative method can be used. Position the piston at a point just before TDC on the compression stroke, then feed a long piece of nylon rope through the spark plug hole until it fills the combustion chamber. Be sure to leave the end of the rope hanging out of the engine so it can be removed easily. Use a large ratchet and socket to rotate the crankshaft in the normal direction of rotation (clockwise) until slight resistance is felt.

9   Stuff shop rags into the cylinder head holes above and below the valves to prevent parts and tools from falling into the engine, then use a valve spring compressor to compress the spring (see illustration). Remove the keepers with small needle-nose pliers or a magnet (see illustration). Note: A couple of different types of tools are available for compressing the valve springs with the head in place. One type, shown here, utilizes the rocker arm bolt for leverage, while the other type grips the lower spring coils and presses on the retainer as the knob is turned. Both types work very well, although the lever type is usually less expensive.

10   Remove the spring retainer and valve spring, then remove the valve guide seal.

Note: If air pressure fails to hold the valve in the closed position during this operation, the valve face or seat is probably damaged. If so, the cylinder head will have to be removed for additional repair operations.

11   Wrap a rubber band or tape around the top of the valve stem so the valve won't fall into the combustion chamber, then release the air pressure. Note: If a rope was used instead of air pressure, turn the crankshaft slightly in the direction opposite normal rotation.

12   Inspect the valve stem for damage. Rotate the valve in the guide and check the end for eccentric movement, which would indicate the valve stem is bent.

13   Move the valve up-and-down in the guide and make sure it doesn't bind. If the valve stem binds, either the valve is bent or the guide is damaged. In either case, the head will have to be removed for repair.

14   Reapply air pressure to the cylinder to retain the valve in the closed position, then remove the tape or rubber band from the valve stem. If a rope was used instead of air pressure, rotate the crankshaft in the normal direction of rotation until slight resistance is felt.

15   Lubricate the valve stem with engine oil

6.9 Pry the engine forward then insert the bolt through the slave hole on the torque rod and into the bracket

and install a new valve guide seal. **Note:** *Intake and exhaust valve seals are different.*

16   Install the spring in position over the valve.

17   Install the valve spring retainer. Compress the valve spring and carefully install the keepers in the groove. Apply a small dab of grease to the inside of each keeper to hold it in place if necessary **(see illustration).** Remove the pressure from the spring tool and make sure the keepers are seated.

18   Disconnect the air hose and remove the adapter from the spark plug hole. If a rope was used in place of air pressure, pull it out of the cylinder.

19   Refer to Section 4 and install the rocker arm(s) and pushrod(s).

20   Install the spark plug(s) and hook up the wire(s).

21   Refer to Section 3 and install the valve cover.

22   Start and run the engine, then check for oil leaks and unusual sounds coming from the valve cover area.

6   Intake manifold - removal and installation

Refer to illustrations 6.9, 6.10a and 6.10b

Removal

1   Relieve the fuel pressure (see Chapter 4), then disconnect the negative battery cable from the battery. **Caution:** *On models equipped with the Theftlock audio system, be sure the lock-out feature is turned off before performing any procedure which requires disconnecting the battery.*

2   Remove the TBI cover/air cleaner assembly (see Chapter 4).

3   Raise the front of the vehicle and support it securely on jackstands. Drain the coolant (refer to Chapter 1).

4   Label and disconnect any wires and vacuum hoses which will interfere with manifold removal.

5   Remove the throttle and TV cables and brackets (see Chapter 4).

6   Remove the TBI assembly and fuel lines (see Chapter 4).

7   Remove the power steering pump (if equipped) and tie it aside in an upright position (see Chapter 10).

8   Remove the heater hose.

9   Pry the engine forward to make extra room for intake manifold clearance. First remove the torque strut-to-engine bracket nut and bolt. Then use a prybar at the bracket and move the engine forward. Next, support the torque strut by installing a bolt through the slave hole and into the bracket **(see illustration).**

10   Remove the mounting fasteners from the intake manifold **(see illustrations).**

11   Separate the intake manifold and gasket from the engine. Scrape all traces of gasket material off the intake manifold and head gasket mating surfaces.

Installation

12   Installation is the reverse of removal. Be sure to use a new gasket. Tighten the nuts/bolts to the torque listed in this Chapter's Specifications, following the correct sequence **(see illustration 6.10a and 6.10b).**

13   Add coolant, run the engine and check for leaks and proper operation.

7   Exhaust manifold - removal and installation

Refer to illustration 7.11

Removal

1   Disconnect the negative cable from the battery. **Caution:** *On models equipped with the Theftlock audio system, be sure the lock-out feature is turned off before performing any procedure which requires disconnecting the battery.*

2   Unplug the electrical connector from the oxygen sensor.

3   Remove the drivebelt and the alternator (see Chapters 1 and 5).

4   Remove the torque rod.

5   Raise the front of the vehicle, support it securely on jackstands and apply the parking brake. Block the rear wheels to keep the vehicle from rolling off the jackstands. Unbolt the exhaust pipe from the manifold. Lower the vehicle.

6   Remove the oil level indicator tube.

7   Remove the exhaust manifold-to-cylinder head nuts/bolts, pull the manifold off the engine and lift it out of the exhaust pipe flange. Remove and discard the gasket.

8   Scrape all traces of gasket material off the exhaust manifold and cylinder head mating surfaces.

Installation

9   Clean all bolt and stud threads before installation. A wire brush can be used on the manifold mounting studs, while a tap works well when cleaning the cylinder head bolt holes.

6.10a On models through 1990, tighten the intake manifold mounting bolts a little at a time, in the order shown, until they are all at the torque listed in this Chapter's Specifications

6.10b Use this intake manifold bolt tightening sequence on 1991 and later models

7.11 Tightening sequence for the exhaust manifold mounting bolts

8.11 To avoid mixing up the head bolts, use the new gasket to transfer the bolt hole pattern to a piece of cardboard, then punch holes in the cardboard to accept the bolts

8.17 A die should be used to clean the head bolt threads prior to installation

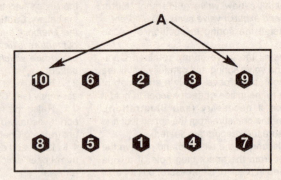

A - Apply sealing compound to threads on bolts 9 and 10

8.21 Cylinder head bolt tightening sequence

10   If a new manifold is being installed, transfer the oxygen sensor from the old manifold to the new one.

11   Installation is the reverse of removal. Be sure to use a new gasket and tighten the bolts, using the correct sequence, to the torque listed in this Chapter's Specifications **(see illustration)**.

8   Cylinder head - removal and installation

Caution: *Allow the engine to cool completely before loosening the cylinder head bolts.*
Note: *On vehicles with high mileage and during an engine overhaul, camshaft lobe height should be checked prior to cylinder head removal.*

Removal
Refer to illustration 8.11

1   Relieve the fuel pressure and remove the TBI cover (see Chapter 4). Disconnect the cable from the negative battery terminal. **Caution:** *On models equipped with the Theftlock audio system, be sure the lockout feature is*
turned off before performing any procedure which requires disconnecting the battery.

2   Remove the alternator and brackets as described in Chapter 5.

3   Remove the intake manifold as described in Section 6.

4   Remove the exhaust manifold as described in Section 7.

5   Detach the dipstick tube from the exhaust manifold.

6   Unbolt the power steering pump (if equipped) and set it aside without disconnecting the hoses (see Chapter 10).

7   Disconnect any remaining wires, hoses, fuel and vacuum lines from the cylinder head. Be sure to label them to simplify reinstallation.

8   Disconnect the spark plug wires and remove the spark plugs. Be sure the plug wires are labeled to simplify reinstallation.

9   Remove the valve cover (see Section 3).

10   Remove the rocker arms and pushrods (see Section 4).

11   Using the new head gasket, outline the cylinders and bolt pattern on a piece of cardboard **(see illustration)**. Be sure to indicate the front (radiator side) of the engine for reference. Punch holes at the bolt locations.
Loosen each of the cylinder head mounting bolts 1/4-turn at a time until they can be removed by hand. Store the bolts in the cardboard holder as they're removed - this will ensure they are reinstalled in their original locations, which is absolutely essential.

12   Lift the head off the engine. If it's stuck, don't attempt to pry it off - you could damage the sealing surfaces. Instead, use a hammer and block of wood to tap the head and break the gasket seal.

13   Place the head on a block of wood to prevent damage to the gasket surface.

14   Remove the cylinder head gasket.

Installation
Refer to illustrations 8.17 and 8.21

15   If a new cylinder head is being installed, transfer all external parts from the old cylinder head to the new one.

16   If not already done, thoroughly clean the gasket surfaces on the cylinder head and the engine block. Do not gouge or otherwise damage the gasket surfaces.

17   To get the proper torque readings, the threads of the head bolts must be clean **(see illustration)**. This also applies to the threaded

9.6 The pushrod cover is held in place with four nuts (arrows) (the exhaust manifold is removed for clarity)

9.7a Location of the pushrod cover stud locknuts (arrows) - manifold removed for clarity

9.7b Remove the lifter guide - if you're removing more than one guide, keep them in order to prevent mix-ups during installation

9.8 On engines that haven't become sticky with sludge and varnish, the lifters can usually be removed by hand

holes in the engine block. Run a tap through the holes to ensure they are clean.

18 Place the gasket in position over the engine block dowel pins. Note any marks like "THIS SIDE UP" and install the gasket accordingly.

19 Carefully lower the cylinder head onto the engine, over the dowel pins and the gasket.

20 Install the bolts finger tight. Don't tighten any of the bolts at this time.

21 Tighten each of the bolts in 1/4-turn increments in the recommended sequence **(see illustration)**, until the stage 1 torque listed in this Chapter's Specifications is reached. Mark each bolt with a felt-tip marker each time you tighten it to make sure none of the bolts have been left out of the sequence. Repeat the sequence, tightening the head bolts to the stage 2 torque listed in this Chapter's Specifications. Repeat the sequence again, tightening all the bolts the amount of angle listed in this Chapter's Specifications.

22 The remaining installation steps are the reverse of removal.

23 Be sure to refill the cooling system and change the oil and filter (see Chapter 1).

9 Hydraulic lifters - removal, inspection and installation

Removal

Refer to illustrations 9.6, 9.7a, 9.7b, 9.8 and 9.9

1 A noisy valve lifter can be isolated when the engine is idling. Place a length of hose or tubing near the position of each valve while listening at the other end. Or, remove the valve cover and, with the engine idling, place a finger on each of the valve spring retainers, one at a time. If a valve lifter is defective, it'll be evident from the shock felt at the retainer as the valve seats.

2 The most likely cause of a noisy valve

lifter is a piece of dirt trapped between the plunger and the lifter body.

3 Remove the valve cover (see Section 3).

4 Loosen both rocker arm bolts at the cylinder with the noisy lifter and rotate the rocker arms away from the pushrods.

5 Remove the pushrod guides and pushrods (see Section 4).

6 Remove the pushrod cover **(see illustration)**.

7 Remove the lifter guide retainer by unscrewing the locknuts on the pushrod cover studs. Remove the lifter guide **(see illustrations)**.

8 There are several ways to extract a lifter from its bore. A special removal tool is available, but isn't always necessary. On newer engines without a lot of varnish buildup, lifters can often be removed with a small magnet or even with your fingers **(see illustration)**. A scribe can also be used to pull the lifter out of the bore. **Caution:** *Don't use pliers of any type to remove a lifter unless you intend to*

9.9 If you're removing more than one lifter, keep them in order in a clearly labeled box

9.11a Check the pushrod seat (arrow) in the top of each lifter for wear

replace it with a new one - they will damage the precision machined and hardened surface of the lifter, rendering it useless.

9   Store the lifters in a clearly labeled box to insure their reinstallation in the same lifter bores **(see illustration)**.

Inspection
Refer to illustrations 9.11a and 9.11b

10   Clean the lifters with solvent and dry them thoroughly without mixing them up.

11   Check each lifter wall and pushrod seat for scuffing, score marks and uneven wear **(see illustration)**. Check the rollers carefully for wear and damage and make sure they turn freely without excessive play **(see illustration)**. If the lifter walls are damaged or worn (which isn't very likely), inspect the lifter bores in the engine block as well. If the pushrod seats are worn, check the pushrod ends.

12   Used roller lifters can be reinstalled with a new camshaft and the original camshaft can be used if new roller lifters are installed.

Installation
Refer to illustration 9.19

13   If the same lifters are being used, they must be installed in their original bores. Coat them with moly-base grease or engine assembly lube.

14   Lubricate the bearing surfaces of the lifter bores with engine oil.

15   Install the lifter(s) in the lifter bore(s). **Note:** *Make sure the oil orifice is facing toward the front of the engine.*

16   Install the lifter guide(s) and retainer(s) **(see illustrations 9.7a and 9.7b)**.

17   Install the pushrods, pushrod guides, rocker arms and rocker arm retaining bolts (see Section 4).

18   Tighten the rocker arm bolts to the torque listed in this Chapter's Specifications.

19   Clean the pushrod cover and its mating surface on the cylinder block. Apply a continuous 3/16 inch (5 mm) diameter bead of RTV sealant to the pushrod cover **(see illustration)**, then install the pushrod cover. Tighten the nuts to the torque listed in this Chapter's Specifications.

20   Install the valve cover (see Section 3).

21   The remainder of installation is the reverse of removal.

10   Crankshaft pulley - removal and installation

Refer to illustrations 10.9, 10.10 and 10.11

Removal

1   Remove the cable from the negative battery terminal. **Caution:** *On models equipped with the Theftlock audio system, be sure the lockout feature is turned off before performing any procedure which requires disconnecting the battery.*

2   Remove the torque strut bolt from the cylinder head bracket.

3   Remove the drivebelt (see Chapter 1).

4   With the parking brake applied and the shifter in Park (automatic), raise the front of the vehicle and support it securely on jackstands. Remove the right front wheel and the fender inner splash shield.

5   Disconnect the right side control arm from the steering knuckle (see Chapter 10).

6   If necessary, support the engine with a floor jack positioned under the oil pan. Place a wood block on the jack head to serve as a cushion.

7   If necessary, remove the two right side

9.11b The roller on roller lifters must turn freely - check for wear and excessive play as well

9.19 The valve cover is sealed with RTV – make sure the sealant is still tacky and the semi-circular cutout (arrow) is facing down

10.9 Remove the crankshaft hub bolt using a breaker bar and socket

10.10 Separate the pulley from the hub

frame attaching bolts and loosen, but do not remove, the bolts and nuts from the left side frame member.

8   If necessary, lower the engine slightly with the floorjack.

9   Remove the crankshaft hub bolt **(see illustration)**. A breaker bar will probably be needed, since the bolt is very tight. If necessary, remove the bellhousing cover and insert a large screwdriver into the teeth of the starter ring gear to prevent the crankshaft from turning.

10   Remove the pulley bolts and remove the crankshaft pulley from the crankshaft hub **(see illustration)**.

11   Using a puller, remove the crankshaft hub from the crankshaft **(see illustration)**.

Installation

12   Refer to Section 11 for the oil seal replacement procedure.

13   Apply a thin layer of multi-purpose grease to the seal contact surface of the hub.

14   Position the hub on the crankshaft and slide it through the seal until it bottoms against the crankshaft gear. Note that the slot (keyway) in the hub must be aligned with the Woodruff key in the end of the crankshaft. Install the pulley-to-crankshaft bolt.

15   Tighten the pulley-to-crankshaft bolt to the torque listed in this Chapter's Specifications.

16   The remaining installation steps are the reverse of removal.

11 Crankshaft front oil seal - replacement

1   Remove the crankshaft pulley (see Section 10).

2   Pry the old oil seal out with a seal removal tool or a screwdriver. Be very careful not to nick or otherwise damage the crankshaft in the process. Wrap the screwdriver tip with vinyl tape to protect the crankshaft.

3   Apply a thin coat of RTV-type sealant to

10.11 Use a puller to detach the hub from the crankshaft

the outer edge of the new seal. Lubricate the seal lip with moly-based grease or clean engine oil.

4   Place the seal squarely in position in the bore and drive it into place with special tool.

5   If you don't have the special tool, carefully tap the seal into place with a large socket (or piece of pipe) and a hammer. The outer diameter of the socket or pipe should be the same size as the seal outer diameter. Make sure the seal is seated completely in the bore.

6   Install the crankshaft pulley (see Section 10).

7   Reinstall the remaining parts in the reverse order of removal.

8   Start the engine and check for oil leaks at the seal.

12 Timing cover, timing chain, sprockets and tensioner - removal, inspection and installation

Note: *On models through 1990, timing gears are used. On 1991 and later models, a timing chain and sprockets are used. The timing gears cannot be removed in the vehicle on 1990 and earlier models. On 1991 and later*

models, the timing chain and sprockets can be removed in the vehicle.

Timing cover (all models)

Removal

1   Remove the crankshaft pulley as described in Section 10.

2   Remove the timing gear cover-to-block bolts, then detach the cover.

3   Using a scraper and degreaser, remove all old sealant from the sealing surfaces of the timing gear cover, engine block and oil pan.

Installation

4   If necessary, replace the front oil seal by carefully prying it out of the cover with a large screwdriver. Don't distort the cover.

5   Install the new seal with the spring side toward the inside of the cover. Drive the seal into place using a seal installation tool or a large socket and hammer. A block of wood will also work.

6   Apply a 1/4 inch wide by 1/8 inch thick bead of RTV sealant to the front cover-to-block mating surface.

7   Apply a 3/8 inch wide by 3/16 inch thick bead of RTV sealant to the oil pan-to-front cover mating surface.

8   Place the cover in position over the dowel pins on the block. Slide the crankshaft

pulley onto the end of the crankshaft to align the cover.

9   Install the bolts that secure the cover to the block, tightening them a little at a time until the cover is seated, then tighten all of them to the torque listed in this Chapter's Specifications. Follow a criss-cross pattern to avoid distorting the cover.

10   Install the crankshaft pulley.

Timing chain and sprockets (1991 and 1992 only)

Inspection

11   The timing chain should be replaced with a new one if the engine has high mileage, the chain has visible damage, or total freeplay midway between the sprockets exceeds one-inch. **Caution:** *Failure to replace a worn timing chain may result in erratic engine performance, loss of power and decreased fuel mileage. Loose chains can "jump" timing. In the worst case, chain "jumping" or breakage will result in severe engine damage.*

12   Inspect the sprockets for wear and damage. Look for teeth that are deformed, chipped, pitted and cracked.

13   Inspect the timing chain tensioner for cracks or wear and replace it if necessary.

Removal

14   Loosen the camshaft bolt.

15   Turn the engine to Top Dead Center (TDC) and check that the camshaft and crankshaft timing marks are aligned.

16   Remove the camshaft sprocket bolt. Do not turn the camshaft in the process (if you do, realign the timing marks before the bolt is removed).

17   Slip the timing chain and sprocket assembly off the engine.

18   Timing chains and sprockets should be replaced in sets. Be sure to align the key in the crankshaft with the keyway in the sprocket during installation.

19   Clean the timing chain and sprockets with solvent and dry them with compressed air (if available). **Warning:** *Wear eye protection when using compressed air.*

Installation

20   Installation is the reverse of removal. Be sure to tighten fasteners to the torques listed in this Chapter's Specifications and lubricate the chain and sprockets with clean engine oil before installing the timing chain cover.

---

13   Camshaft and bearings - removal, inspection and installation

Due to the fact the engine is mounted transversely in the vehicle, there isn't enough room to remove the camshaft with the engine in place. Therefore, the procedure is covered in Chapter 2, Part H.

14.18 Oil pan mounting bolt locations (some bolts are not visible)

---

14   Oil pan - removal and installation

Refer to illustration 14.18

Removal

1   Warm up the engine, then drain the oil and remove the oil filter (see Chapter 1).

2   Detach the cable from the negative battery terminal. **Caution:** *On models equipped with the Theftlock audio system, be sure the lockout feature is turned off before performing any procedure which requires disconnecting the battery.*

3   Remove the coolant reservoir (see Chapter 3).

4   Remove the engine torque strut.

5   Remove the air cleaner assembly and the air inlet tube (see Chapter 4).

6   Remove the drivebelt (see Chapter 1).

7   Remove the dipstick tube.

8   Raise the vehicle and support it securely on jackstands. Support the transaxle and engine assembly with a floor jack and a piece of wood placed under the transaxle.

9   On air conditioned models, remove the air conditioner from the brackets and set it aside, without disconnecting the hoses (see Chapter 3).

10   Remove the starter (see Chapter 5).

11   Remove the lower bellhousing cover.

12   Turn the front wheels all the way to the right and remove the engine wiring harness retaining screws under the oil pan on the right and left sides.

13   Remove the splash pan from the right side of the engine.

14   Remove the front engine mount bracket bolts and nuts.

15   Remove the transaxle mount nuts and raise the engine and transaxle assembly approximately 2 inches with the floor jack.

16   Remove the front engine mount and bracket.

17   Loosen the frame bolts.

18   Remove the bolts and nuts securing the oil pan to the engine block **(see illustration)**.

19   Tap on the pan with a soft-face hammer to break the gasket seal, then detach the oil pan from the engine. Don't pry between the oil

pan and the block, as the pan could become bent or the block could become gouged.

20   Using a gasket scraper, remove all traces of old sealant from the engine block and oil pan. Make sure the threaded bolt holes in the block are clean. Wash the oil pan with solvent and dry it thoroughly.

Installation

21   Check the sealing flanges for distortion, particularly around the bolt holes. If necessary, place the pan on a block of wood and use a hammer to flatten and restore the gasket surfaces. Clean the mating surfaces with lacquer thinner or acetone.

22   Place a continuous bead of RTV sealant on the oil pan-to-block sealing flanges and the oil pan-to-front cover surface. Do not apply excessive amounts of the sealer and make sure the sealer is applied to the inside of the bolt holes.

23   Apply a thin coat of RTV sealant to the ends of the rear oil pan seal down to the ears.

24   Carefully place the oil pan against the block.

25   Install the bolts and tighten them in 1/4-turn increments to the torque listed in this Chapter's Specifications. Start with the bolts closest to the center of the pan and work out in a spiral pattern. Don't overtighten them or leakage may occur.

26   Reinstall components removed for access to the oil pan.

27   Add oil and install a new filter, run the engine and check for oil leaks.

---

15   Oil pump - removal and installation

Removal

1   Remove the oil pan (see Section 14).

2   Place a large drain pan under the engine.

3   Unbolt the oil pump cover from the force balancer assembly. **Warning:** *Use caution if you remove the pressure regulator valve - it is under considerable spring pressure.*

4   Lower the pump cover from the force

17.2 Most driveplates have locating dowels (arrow) - if the one you're working on doesn't have one, make some marks to ensure correct installation

17.3 A large screwdriver wedged in one of the holes in the driveplate can be used to keep the driveplate from turning as the mounting bolts are removed and installed

balancer assembly, then remove the gears from the balancer housing.

Installation

5   Pack the cavities between the gears with petroleum jelly to prime it.
6   Attach the oil pump to the force balancer assembly. Align the top end of the oil pump drive with the lower end of the oil pump. When aligned properly, it should slip into place easily.
7   Install the pump mounting bolts and tighten them to the torque listed in this Chapter's Specifications.
8   Install the oil pan and add oil (see Section 14).

16   Crankshaft force balancer - removal and installation

Removal

1   Remove the oil pan (see Section 14).
2   Remove the bolts that retain the force balancer assembly to the engine block and carefully lower the assembly.

Installation

3   Rotate the engine until number 1 or 4 cylinder is at Top Dead Center (see Chapter 2H).
4   Install the balancer assembly with the balance weights at BDC (plus or minus one-half gear tooth). **Note:** *When installing the force balancer assembly, the end of the housing without the dowel pins must contact the engine block surface evenly. If it loses contact, the gears will not engage properly and the unit will become defective.*
5   Install the retaining bolts and tighten them to the torque listed in this Chapter's Specifications, using an "X" crossover pattern.
6   Install the oil pan (see Section 14).

17   Driveplate - removal and installation

Refer to illustrations 17.2 and 17.3
1   Raise the vehicle and support it securely on jackstands, then refer to Chapter 7 and remove the transaxle. If it's leaking, now would be a very good time to replace the front pump seal and O-ring (automatic trans-

axle only).
2   If there is no dowel pin, make some marks on the driveplate and crankshaft to ensure correct alignment during reinstallation **(see illustration)**.
3   Remove the bolts that secure the driveplate to the crankshaft **(see illustration)**. If the crankshaft turns, wedge a screwdriver through the openings in the driveplate. Since the driveplate is fairly heavy, be sure to support it while removing the last bolt.
4   Remove the driveplate from the crankshaft.
5   Clean the driveplate to remove grease and oil. Inspect it for cracks and cracked and broken ring gear teeth. Lay the driveplate on a flat surface and use a straightedge to check for warpage.
6   Clean and inspect the mating surfaces of the driveplate and the crankshaft. If the crankshaft rear seal is leaking, replace it before reinstalling the driveplate.
7   Position the driveplate against the crankshaft. Be sure to align the dowel or marks made during removal. Before installing the bolts, apply thread locking compound to the threads.
8   Keep the driveplate from turning as described above while you tighten the bolts to the torque listed in this Chapter's Specifications.
9   The remainder of installation is the reverse of the removal procedure.

18   Rear main oil seal - replacement

Refer to illustration 18.2
1   Remove the driveplate (see Section 17).
2   Using a thin screwdriver or seal removal tool, carefully remove the oil seal from the engine block **(see illustration)**. Be very careful not to damage the crankshaft surface while prying the seal out.
3   Clean the bore in the block and the seal contact surface on the crankshaft. Check the seal contact surface on the crankshaft for

18.2 Carefully pry the old oil seal out

19.9a Details of the front engine mount

1	Four-cylinder engine mounting nuts	2	V6 engine mounting nuts

19.9b Transaxle mount bolts (arrows)

scratches and nicks that could damage the new seal lip and cause oil leaks - if the crankshaft is damaged, the only alternative is a new or different crankshaft. Inspect the seal bore for nicks and scratches. Carefully smooth it with a fine file if necessary, but don't nick the crankshaft in the process.

4   A special tool is recommended to install the new oil seal. Lubricate the oil seal lips. Slide the seal onto the mandril until the dust lip bottoms squarely against the collar of the tool. **Note:** *If the special tool isn't available, carefully work the seal lip over the crankshaft and tap it into place with a hammer and punch.*

5   Align the dowel pin on the tool with the dowel pin hole in the crankshaft and attach the tool to the crankshaft by hand-tightening the bolts.

6   Turn the tool handle until the collar bottoms against the case, seating the seal.

7   Loosen the tool handle and remove the bolts. Remove the tool.

8   Check the seal and make sure it's seated squarely in the bore.

9   Install the driveplate (see Section 17).

10   Install the transaxle.

19 Engine mounts - check and replacement

Refer to illustrations 19.9a and 19.9b

Warning: *A special tool is available to support the engine during repair operations. Similar fixtures are available from rental yards. Improper lifting methods or devices are hazardous and could result in severe injury or death. DO NOT place any part of your body under the engine/transaxle when it's supported only by a jack. Failure of the lifting device could result in severe injury or death.*

1   Engine mounts seldom require attention, but broken or deteriorated mounts should be replaced immediately or the added strain placed on the driveline components may cause damage or wear.

Check

2   During the check, the engine must be raised slightly to remove the weight from the mounts.

3   Raise the vehicle and support it securely on jackstands, then position a jack under the engine oil pan. Place a large block of wood between the jack head and the oil pan, then carefully raise the engine just enough to take the weight off the mounts.

4   Check the mounts to see if the rubber is

cracked, hardened or separated from the metal plates. Sometimes the rubber will split right down the center.

5   Check for relative movement between the mount plates and the engine or frame (use a large screwdriver or pry bar to attempt to move the mounts). If movement is noted, lower the engine and tighten the mount fasteners.

6   Rubber preservative should be applied to the mounts to slow deterioration.

Replacement

7   Disconnect the negative battery cable from the battery, then raise the vehicle and support it securely on jackstands (if not already done). **Caution:** *On models equipped with the Theftlock audio system, be sure the lockout feature is turned off before performing any procedure which requires disconnecting the battery.*

8   Remove the engine torque strut **(see illustration 6.9)**.

9   Raise the engine slightly with a jack or hoist. Remove the fasteners and detach the mount from the frame **(see illustrations)**.

10   Remove the mount-to-block bracket bolts/nuts and detach the mount.

11   Installation is the reverse of removal. Use thread locking compound on the threads and be sure to tighten everything securely.

Chapter 2 Part C
2.3 liter four-cylinder (Quad-4) engine

Contents

	Section
Camshaft, lifters and housing - removal, inspection and installation	9
Crankshaft front oil seal - replacement	6
Crankshaft pulley - removal and installation	5
Cylinder compression check	See Chapter 2H
Cylinder head - removal and installation	11
Drivebelt check, adjustment and replacement	See Chapter 1
Engine mounts - check and replacement	16
Engine oil and filter change	See Chapter 1
Engine overhaul - general information	See Chapter 2H
Engine - removal and installation	See Chapter 2H
Exhaust manifold - removal and installation	4
Flywheel - removal and installation	14
General information	1

	Section
Intake manifold - removal and installation	3
Oil pan - removal and installation	12
Oil pump - removal, inspection and installation	13
Rear main oil seal - replacement	15
Repair operations possible with the engine in the vehicle	2
Spark plug replacement	See Chapter 1
Timing chain and sprockets - removal, inspection and installation	7
Timing chain housing - removal and installation	8
Top Dead Center (TDC) for number one piston - locating	See Chapter 2H
Valve springs, retainers and seals - replacement	10
Water pump - removal and installation	See Chapter 3

Specifications

General
Cylinder numbers (timing chain end-to-transaxle end)	1-2-3-4
Firing order	1-3-4-2

FRONT ↓ ❶②③④
2.3L engine
Cylinder location

Camshafts and housings
Lobe lift (intake and exhaust)
VIN D	0.3750 in (9.525 mm)
VIN A	0.4100 in (10.414 mm)
Lobe taper limit	0.0018 to 0.0033 inch per 0.5512 in (0.046 to 0.083 mm per 14.0 mm)
Endplay	0.0009 to 0.0088 in (0.025 to 0.225 mm)

Journal diameter
No. 1	1.5728 to 1.5720 in (39.95 to 39.93 mm)
All others	1.3751 to 1.3760 in (34.93 to 34.95 mm)
Bearing oil clearance	0.0019 to 0.0043 in (0.050 to 0.110 mm)

Lifters
Bore diameter	1.3775 to 1.3787 in (34.989 to 34.019 mm)
Outside diameter	1.3763 to 1.3770 in (34.959 to 34.975 mm)
Lifter-to-bore clearance	0.0006 to 0.0024 in (0.014 to 0.060 mm)
Camshaft housing warpage limit	0.001 inch per 3.937 in (0.025 mm per 100 mm)

Oil pump gear backlash
0.0091 to 0.0201 in (0.23 to 0.51 mm)

Torque specifications

Ft-lbs (unless otherwise indicated)

Note: *One foot-pound (ft-lb) of torque is equivalent to 12 inch-pounds (in-lbs) of torque. Torque values below approximately 15 foot-pounds are expressed in inch-pounds, because most foot-pound torque wrenches are not accurate at these smaller values.*

Camshaft housing-to-cylinder head bolts	
Step 1	11
Step 2	Turn bolts an additional 75-degrees
Camshaft sprocket-to-camshaft bolt	40
Crankshaft pulley-to-crankshaft bolt	
Step 1	74
Step 2	Turn bolt an additional 90-degrees
Crankshaft rear main oil seal housing bolts	106 in-lbs
Cylinder head bolts	
Short bolts	
Step 1	26
Step 2	Turn bolts an additional 100-degrees
Long bolts	
Step 1	26
Step 2	Turn bolts an additional 110-degrees
Exhaust manifold-to-cylinder head nuts	27
Flywheel-to-crankshaft bolts	
Step 1	22
Step 2	Turn bolts an additional 45-degrees
Intake manifold-to-cylinder head nuts/bolts	18
Oil pan baffle nuts/bolts	30
Oil pan bolts	
6 mm	106 in-lbs
8 mm	17
Oil pump-to-block bolts	33
Oil pump cover-to-oil pump body bolts	106 in-lbs
Oil pump screen assembly-to-pump bolts	22
Oil pump screen assembly-to-brace bolts	106 in-lbs
Timing chain cover-to-housing bolts	106 in-lbs
Timing chain housing bolts	19
Timing chain housing-to-block stud	19
Timing chain tensioner bolts	115 in-lbs

1   General information

This Part of Chapter 2 is devoted to in-vehicle repair procedures for the 2.3 liter four-cylinder (Quad-4) engine. The 2.3L Quad-4 engine became available in 1990 and 1991, in the Pontiac Grand Prix and Oldsmobile Cutlass Supreme models only. Information concerning engine removal and installation and engine overhaul can be found in Part H of this Chapter.

The following repair procedures are based on the assumption the engine is installed in the vehicle. If the engine has been removed from the vehicle and mounted on a stand, many of the steps outlined in this Part of Chapter 2 will not apply.

The Quad-4 engine utilizes a number of advanced design features to increase power output and improve durability. The aluminum cylinder head contains four valves per cylinder. A double-row timing chain drives two overhead camshafts - one for intake and one for exhaust. Lightweight bucket-type hydraulic lifters actuate the valves. Rotators are used on all valves for extended service life.

The Quad-4 engine is easily identified by the designation molded onto the ignition module cover. It can also be identified by the vehicle identification number on the left front corner of the instrument panel. This plate is visi-ble from outside the vehicle (**see illustration 1.1** in Chapter 2, Part B). The eighth character in the sequence is the engine designation:

A or D = 2.3L four-cylinder, Quad-4 engine

2   Repair operations possible with the engine in the vehicle

Many major repair operations can be accomplished without removing the engine from the vehicle.

Clean the engine compartment and the exterior of the engine with some type of degreaser before any work is done. It'll make the job easier and help keep dirt out of the internal areas of the engine.

Depending on the components involved, it may be helpful to remove the hood to improve access to the engine as repairs are performed (refer to Chapter 11 if necessary). Cover the fenders to prevent damage to the paint. Special pads are available, but an old bedspread or blanket will also work.

If vacuum, exhaust, oil or coolant leaks develop, indicating a need for gasket or seal replacement, the repairs can generally be made with the engine in the vehicle. The intake and exhaust manifold gaskets, timing chain housing gasket, oil pan gasket, crankshaft oil seals and cylinder head gasket are all accessible with the engine in place.

Exterior engine components, such as the intake and exhaust manifolds, the oil pan (and the oil pump), the water pump, the starter motor, the alternator and the fuel system components can be removed for repair with the engine in place.

Since the cylinder head can be removed without pulling the engine, camshaft and valve component servicing can also be accomplished with the engine in the vehicle. Replacement of the timing chain and sprockets is also possible with the engine in the vehicle.

In extreme cases caused by a lack of necessary equipment, repair or replacement of piston rings, pistons, connecting rods and rod bearings is possible with the engine in the vehicle. However, this practice is not recommended because of the cleaning and preparation work that must be done to the components involved.

3   Intake manifold - removal and installation

Removal

Refer to illustration 3.6

1   Relieve the fuel system pressure as described in Chapter 4.

3.6 Oil fill tube components

1   Oil fill cap and dipstick
2   Oil fill tube
3   Bolt

2   Disconnect the negative battery cable from the battery, then refer to Chapter 1 and drain the cooling system. **Caution:** *On models equipped with the Theftlock audio system, be sure the lockout feature is turned off before performing any procedure which requires disconnecting the battery.*
3   Remove the throttle body (see Chapter 4).
4   Label and disconnect the vacuum and breather hoses and electrical wires.
5   Remove the oil/air separator (see Chapter 6).
6   Remove the oil fill cap and dipstick assembly **(see illustration)**.
7   Unbolt the oil fill tube and detach it from the engine block, rotating it as necessary to gain clearance between the intake tubes.
8   Remove the intake manifold brace **(see illustration)**.
9   Loosen the manifold mounting nuts/bolts in 1/4-turn increments until they can be removed by hand.
10   The manifold will probably be stuck to the cylinder head and force may be required to break the gasket seal. If necessary, dislodge the manifold with a soft-face hammer. **Caution:** *Don't pry between the head and manifold or damage to the gasket sealing surfaces will result and vacuum leaks could develop.*

Installation

Refer to illustration 3.16
Note: *The mating surfaces of the cylinder head and manifold must be perfectly clean when the manifold is installed. Gasket removal solvents in aerosol cans are available at most auto parts stores and may be helpful when removing old gasket material stuck to the head and manifold (since the components are made of aluminum, aggressive scraping can cause damage). Be sure to follow the directions printed on the container.*

3.16 Intake manifold bolt/nut tightening sequence

11   Use a gasket scraper to remove all traces of sealant and old gasket material, then clean the mating surfaces with lacquer thinner or acetone. If there's old sealant or oil on the mating surfaces when the manifold is reinstalled, vacuum leaks may develop.
12   Use a tap of the correct size to chase the threads in the bolt holes, then use compressed air (if available) to remove the debris from the holes. **Warning:** *Wear safety glasses or a face shield to protect your eyes when using compressed air. Use a die to clean and restore the stud threads.*
13   Position the gasket on the cylinder head. Make sure all intake port openings, coolant passage holes and bolt holes are aligned correctly. **Note:** *Install the new manifold gasket with the numbers that are stamped on the gasket faced toward the manifold surface.*
14   Install the manifold, taking care to avoid damaging the gasket.
15   Thread the nuts/bolts into place by hand.
16   Tighten the nuts/bolts to the torque listed in this Chapter's Specifications following the recommended sequence **(see illustration)**. Work up to the final torque in three steps.
17   The remaining installation steps are the reverse of removal. Start the engine and check carefully for leaks at the intake manifold joints.

---

4   Exhaust manifold - removal and installation

Refer to illustrations 4.4 and 4.10

Removal

Warning: *Allow the engine to cool completely before performing this procedure.*
1   Disconnect the negative battery cable from the battery. **Caution:** *On models equipped with the Theftlock audio system, be sure the lockout feature is turned off before performing any procedure which requires disconnecting the battery.*
2   Unplug the oxygen sensor (see Chapter 6).
3   Remove the manifold heat shields.
4   Raise the vehicle and support it securely on jackstands, then remove the exhaust pipe-to-manifold nuts. The nuts are usually rusted

in place, so penetrating oil should be applied to the stud threads before attempting to remove them. Loosen them a little at a time, working from side-to-side to prevent the flange from jamming **(see illustration)**.
5   Remove the exhaust manifold brace.
6   Separate the exhaust pipe flange nuts (spring loaded) from the manifold studs, then pull the pipe down slightly to break the seal at the manifold joint.
7   Loosen the exhaust manifold mounting nuts 1/4-turn at a time each, working from the inside out, until they can be removed by hand.
8   Separate the manifold from the head and remove it.

Installation

9   The manifold and cylinder head mating surfaces must be clean when the manifold is reinstalled. Use a gasket scraper to remove all traces of old gasket material and carbon deposits.
10   Using a new gasket, install the manifold and hand tighten the fasteners. Working from the center out following the recommended sequence **(see illustration)**, tighten the bolts/nuts to the torque listed in this Chapter's Specifications.
11   The remaining installation steps are the reverse of removal.

4.4 Exhaust pipe-to-exhaust manifold flange bolts - make sure you do not lose the springs when removing the bolts

5   Crankshaft pulley - removal and installation

Refer to illustrations 5.4, 5.5 and 5.8

1   Remove the cable from the negative battery terminal. **Caution:** *On models equipped with the Theftlock audio system, be sure the lockout feature is turned off before performing any procedure which requires disconnecting the battery.*
2   Remove the drivebelt (see Chapter 1).
3   With the parking brake applied and the shifter in Park (automatic) or in gear (manual), raise the front of the vehicle and support it securely on jackstands.
4   Remove the bolt from the front of the crankshaft. A breaker bar will probably be necessary, since the bolt is very tight. Use GM special tool J-38122 (or equivalent) to keep the crankshaft from turning. If the special tool isn't available, insert a bar through a hole in the pulley to prevent the crankshaft from turning **(see illustration)**.
5   Using a puller (tool J-24420-B or equivalent), remove the crankshaft pulley from the crankshaft **(see illustration)**.

4.10 Exhaust manifold bolt tightening sequence

6   Check the oil seal and replace it if necessary. Refer to Section 8.
7   Apply a thin layer of clean multi-purpose grease to the seal contact surface of the crankshaft pulley hub.
8   Position the pulley on the crankshaft and slide it through the seal until it bottoms against the crankshaft sprocket. Note that the slot (keyway) in the hub must be aligned with the Woodruff key in the end of the crankshaft **(see illustration)**. The crankshaft bolt can also be used

to press the pulley into position.
9   Tighten the crankshaft bolt to the torque and angle of rotation listed in this Chapter's Specifications.
10   The remaining installation steps are the reverse of removal.

6   Crankshaft front oil seal - replacement

Refer to illustrations 6.2 and 6.5

1   Remove the crankshaft pulley (see Section 5).
2   Pry the old oil seal out with a seal removal tool **(see illustration)** or a screwdriver. Be very careful not to nick or otherwise damage the crankshaft in the process and don't distort the timing chain cover.
3   Apply a thin coat of RTV-type sealant to the outer edge of the new seal. Lubricate the seal lip with moly-base grease or clean engine oil.
4   Place the seal squarely in position in the bore with the spring side facing in.
5   Carefully tap the seal into place with a large socket or section of pipe and a hammer **(see illustration)**. The outer diameter of the socket or pipe should be the same size as the seal outer diameter.

5.4 The crankshaft pulley can be kept from turning with a bar while the bolt is loosened/tightened

5.5 Use a bolt-type puller hub as shown here - if a jaw-type puller that applies force to the outer edge is used, the pulley will be damaged

5.8 Align the keyway in the crankshaft pulley hub with the Woodruff key in the crankshaft (arrow)

6.2 Pry the old seal out with a seal removal tool (shown here) or a screwdriver

6.5 Install the new seal with a large socket or piece of pipe and a hammer

7.3 Remove the vent hose and engine lifting bracket bolts

1   Vent hose fitting   2   Engine lifting bracket bolts

7.5 Timing chain cover fastener locations (arrows)

6   Install the crankshaft pulley (see Section 5).

7   Start the engine and check for oil leaks at the seal.

7   Timing chain and sprockets - removal, inspection and installation

Note: *Special tools are required for this procedure, so read through it before beginning work.*

Removal

> ** CAUTION **
>
> The timing system is complex. Severe engine damage will occur if you make any mistakes. Do not attempt this procedure unless you are highly experienced with this type of repair. If you are at all unsure of your abilities, consult an expert. Double-check all your work and be sure everything is correct before you attempt to start the engine.

Refer to illustrations 7.3, 7.5, 7.8, 7.10, 7.11, 7.12, 7.14, 7.17 and 7.18

1   Disconnect the negative battery cable from the battery. **Caution:** *On models equipped with the Theftlock audio system, be sure the lockout feature is turned off before performing any procedure which requires disconnecting the battery.*

2   Remove the coolant reservoir (see Chapter 3).

3   Detach the timing chain cover vent hose and unbolt the engine lifting bracket at the drivebelt end of the engine **(see illustration)**.

4   Remove the crankshaft pulley (see Section 5).

5   Working from above, remove the upper timing chain cover fasteners **(see illustration)**.

6   Working from below, remove the lower timing chain cover fasteners.

7   Detach the cover and gaskets from the housing.

8   Slide the oil slinger off the crankshaft **(see illustration)**.

9   Temporarily reinstall the crankshaft pulley bolt to use when turning the crankshaft.

10   Turn the crankshaft clockwise until the camshaft sprocket's timing pin holes line up

7.8 Note how it's installed, then remove the oil slinger (arrow) from the crankshaft

7.10 Insert 8 mm (5/16-inch) bolts (arrows) or pins to hold the camshaft sprockets

7.11 The mark on the crankshaft sprocket must align with the mark on the block (arrows)

7.12 The timing chain guides are wedged into the housing at four points (arrows) - just pull them out

7.14 The timing chain tensioner shoe is held in place by an E-clip

1   Tensioner mounting bolts   2   E-clip

with the holes in the timing chain housing. Insert 8 mm pins or bolts into the holes to maintain alignment **(see illustration)**.

11 The mark on the crankshaft sprocket should line up with the mark on the engine block **(see illustration)**. The crankshaft sprocket keyway should point up and line up with the centerline of the cylinder bores.

12 Remove the three timing chain guides **(see illustration)**.

13 Detach the timing chain tensioner sleeve and spring.

14 Make sure all the slack in the timing chain is above the tensioner assembly, then remove the chain tensioner shoe **(see illustration)**. The timing chain must be disengaged from the wear grooves in the tensioner shoe in order to remove the shoe. Slide a screwdriver blade under the timing chain while pulling the shoe out. **Note:** *If difficulty is*

7.17 Begin removing the chain at the exhaust camshaft sprocket

encountered when removing the chain tensioner shoe, proceed as follows:

a) *Hold the intake camshaft sprocket with a special tool and remove the sprocket bolt and washer.*

b) *Remove the washer from the bolt and thread the bolt back into the camshaft by hand.*

c) *Remove the intake camshaft sprocket, using a three-jaw puller in the three relief holes in the sprocket, if necessary.* **Caution:** *Don't try to pry the sprocket off the camshaft or damage to the sprocket could occur.*

15 Remove the tensioner assembly retaining bolts and tensioner. The spring can be caged with a special anti-release tool **(see illustration 7.31). Warning:** *The tensioner plunger is spring loaded and could come out with great force, causing personal injury.*

16 Remove the chain housing-to-block stud (timing chain tensioner shoe pivot).

17 Slip the timing chain off the sprockets **(see illustration)**.

18 To remove the camshaft sprockets (if not already done), loosen the bolts while the pins

7.18 Mark the sprockets, then remove the bolts and pull the sprockets off

7.22 The camshaft sprocket locating dowels should be near the top (arrows) prior to sprocket installation

are still in place. Mark the sprockets for identi-fication (see illustration), remove the bolts and pins, then pull on the sprockets by hand until they slip off the dowels.

19   The crankshaft sprocket will slip off the crankshaft by hand.

20   The idler sprocket and bearing are pressed into place. If replacement is neces-sary, remove the timing chain housing (see Section 8) and take it to a dealer service department or automotive machine shop. Special tools are required and the bearing must be replaced each time it's pressed out.

Inspection

21   Visually inspect all parts for wear and damage. Look for loose pins, cracks, worn rollers and side plates. Check the sprockets for hook-shaped, chipped and broken teeth. Note: Some scoring of the timing chain shoe and guides is normal. Replace the timing chain, sprockets, chain shoe and guides as a set if the engine has high mileage or fails the visual parts inspection.

Installation

> ** CAUTION **
> Before starting the engine, carefully rotate the crankshaft by hand through at least two full revolutions (use a socket and breaker bar on the crankshaft pulley center bolt). If you feel any resistance, STOP! There is something wrong - most likely, valves are contacting the pistons. You must find the problem before proceeding. Check your work and see if any updated repair information is available.

Refer to illustrations 7.22, 7.23 and 7.31

22   Turn the camshafts until the dowel pins are at the top (see illustration). Install both camshaft sprockets (if removed). Apply seal-

ant to the camshaft sprocket bolt threads and make sure the washers are in place. Keep the camshaft from turning with 8 mm bolts). Tighten the bolts to the torque listed in this Chapter's Specifications.

23   Recheck the positions of the camshaft and crankshaft sprockets for correct valve timing (see illustration). Note: If the cam-shafts are out of position and must be rotated more than 1/8-turn in order to install the align-ment dowel pins:

a)   The crankshaft must be rotated 90-de-grees clockwise past Top Dead Center to give the valves adequate clearance to open.

b)   Once the camshafts are in position and the dowels installed, rotate the crank-shaft counterclockwise back to Top Dead Center. Caution: Do not rotate the crankshaft clockwise to TDC (valve or piston damage could occur).

24   Slip the timing chain over the exhaust camshaft sprocket, then around the idler and crankshaft sprocket.

25   Remove the alignment dowel pin from the intake camshaft. Using a special sprocket rotating tool, rotate the intake camshaft sprocket counterclockwise enough to mesh the timing chain with it. Release the special tool. The chain run between the two camshaft sprockets will tighten. If the valve timing is correct, the intake cam alignment dowel pin should slide in easily. If it doesn't index, the camshafts aren't timed correctly; repeat the procedure.

26   Leave the dowel pins installed for now. Working under the vehicle, check the timing marks. With slack removed from the timing chain between the intake cam sprocket and the crankshaft sprocket, the timing marks on the crankshaft sprocket and the engine block should be aligned. If the marks aren't aligned, move the chain one tooth forward or back-ward, remove the slack and recheck the marks.

27   Install the chain housing-to-block stud

7.23 Make sure the alignment holes on the camshaft align with the dowel holes (arrows) and the crankshaft gear mark aligns with the mark on the case (arrows)

(timing chain tensioner shoe pivot), and tighten it to the torque listed in this Chapter's Specifications.

28   Reload the timing chain tensioner assembly to its "zero" position as follows:

a)   Assemble the restraint cylinder, spring and nylon plug in the plunger. While rotating the restraint cylinder clockwise, push it into the plunger until it bottoms. Keep rotating the restraint cylinder clock-wise, but allow the spring to push it out of the plunger. The pin in the plunger will lock the restraint cylinder in the loaded position.

b)   Position a special tensioner anti-release tool onto the plunger.

c)   Install the plunger assembly in the ten-sioner body with the long end toward the crankshaft when installed.

29   Install the tensioner assembly in the chain housing. Tighten the bolts to the torque

7.31 Remove the anti-release device from the tensioner and depress the shoe once to release the tensioner

1   Tensioner mounting bolts   2   Tensioner anti-release tool

8.14 Position a new gasket over the dowel pins (arrows)

listed in this Chapter's Specifications. **Note:** *Recheck the plunger assembly installation - it's correctly installed when the long end is toward the crankshaft.*

30   Install the tensioner shoe, spring and sleeve.

31   Remove tensioner anti-release tool and squeeze the plunger assembly into the tensioner body to unload the plunger assembly **(see illustration)**.

32   Remove the alignment pins.

33   Slowly rotate the crankshaft clockwise two full turns (720-degrees). Do not force it; if resistance is felt, back up and recheck the installation procedure. Align the crankshaft timing mark with the mark on the engine block and temporarily reinstall the 8 mm alignment pins. The pins should slide in easily if the valve timing is correct. **Caution:** *If the valve timing is incorrect, severe engine damage could occur.*

34   Install the remaining components in the reverse order of removal. Check fluid levels, start the engine and check for proper operation and coolant/oil leaks.

8   Timing chain housing - removal and installation

Refer to illustration 8.14

1   Remove the timing chain and sprockets (see Section 7).

2   Remove the exhaust manifold (see Section 4).

3   If you're installing a replacement timing chain housing, remove the water pump (see Chapter 3).

4   Remove the timing chain housing-to-belt tensioner bracket brace.

5   Remove the four oil pan-to-timing chain housing bolts.

6   Remove the timing chain housing-to-block lower fasteners.

7   Remove the lowest cover retaining stud from the timing chain housing.

8   Remove the rear engine mount nut (see Section 16).

9   Loosen the front engine mount nut, leaving about three threads remaining in contact.

10   Remove the eight chain housing-to-cam-

shaft housing bolts.

11   Position a floor jack under the oil pan, using an 18-inch long piece of wood (2x4) on the jack pad to distribute the weight.

12   Raise the engine off the front and rear mounts until the front mount bracket contacts the nut.

13   Remove the timing chain housing and gaskets. Thoroughly clean the mating surfaces to remove any traces of old sealant or gasket material.

14   Install the timing chain housing with new gaskets **(see illustration)**. Tighten the bolts to the torque listed in this Chapter's Specifications.

15   The remaining steps are the reverse of removal.

9   Camshaft, lifters and housing - removal, inspection and installation

Note: *Special tools are required for this procedure, so read through it before beginning work.*

Removal

Refer to illustrations 9.7, 9.10, 9.11 and 9.14

1   Disconnect the cable from the negative battery terminal. **Caution:** *On models equipped with the Theftlock audio system, be sure the lockout feature is turned off before performing any procedure which requires disconnecting the battery.*

2   Remove the timing chain and sprockets (see Section 7).

3   Remove the timing chain housing-to-camshaft housing bolts (see Section 8).

4   Remove the ignition coil and module assembly (see Chapter 5).

Intake (front)

5   Disconnect the idle speed power steering pressure switch.

9.7 The power steering pump drive pulley must be removed with a puller

9.10 Oil pressure sending unit mounting hole (1) and engine lifting bracket bolts (2)

9.11 Gently lift the camshaft housing off the cylinder head and turn it over so the lifters won't fall out

9.14 Remove the oil seal (arrow) from the intake camshaft

9.17a Check the camshaft lobe surfaces and the bore surfaces (arrows) of the lifters for wear

6   Remove the power steering pump and brackets (see Chapter 10).

7   Remove the power steering pump drive pulley **(see illustration)**. **Caution:** *The power steering pump drive pulley must be removed following this procedure or damage to the pulley will result. If any other removal procedure is used, a new pulley must be installed.*

8   Remove the oil/air separator (PCV System) as an assembly, with the hoses attached (see Chapter 6).

9   Remove the fuel rail from the cylinder head and set it aside (see Chapter 4).

Exhaust (rear)

10   Unplug the oil pressure sending unit wire and unbolt the engine lifting bracket **(see illustration)**.

Intake and exhaust

11   Loosen the camshaft housing-to-cylinder head bolts in 1/4-turn increments, following the tightening sequence in reverse **(see illustration 9.28)**. Leave the two cover-to-housing bolts in place temporarily. Lift the housing off

the cylinder head **(see illustration)**.

12   Remove the two camshaft cover-to-housing bolts. Push the cover off the housing by threading four of the housing-to-head bolts into the tapped holes in the cover. Carefully lift the camshaft out of the housing.

13   Remove all traces of old gasket material from the mating surfaces and clean them with lacquer thinner or acetone to remove any traces of oil.

14   Remove the oil seal from the intake camshaft **(see illustration)** and discard it.

15   Remove the lifters and store them in order so they can be reinstalled in their original locations. To minimize lifter bleed-down, store the lifters valve-side up, submerged in clean engine oil.

Inspection

Refer to illustrations 9.17a, 9.17b, 9.18 and 9.19

16   Refer to Chapter 2, Part H, for camshaft inspection procedures, but use this Chapter's Specifications. Do not attempt to salvage camshafts. Whenever a camshaft is replaced,

replace all the lifters actuated by the camshaft as well.

17   Visually inspect the lifters for wear, galling, score marks and discoloration from overheating **(see illustrations)**.

9.17b Check the valve-side of the lifters too

9.18 Use a telescoping gauge and micrometer to measure the lifter bores . . .

9.19 . . . then measure the lifters with a micrometer - subtract each lifter diameter from the corresponding bore diameter to obtain the lifter-to-bore clearances

9.24 The dowel pins (arrows) should be at the top (12 o'clock position)

9.28 Camshaft housing-to-cylinder head bolt tightening sequence

18   Measure each lifter bore inside diameter and record the results **(see illustration)**.
19   Measure each lifter outside diameter and record the results **(see illustration)**.
20   Subtract the lifter outside diameter from the corresponding bore inside diameter to determine the clearance. Compare the results to this Chapter's Specifications and replace parts as necessary.

Installation

Refer to illustrations 9.24, 9.28 and 9.29
21   Using a new gasket, position the camshaft housing on the cylinder head and temporarily hold it in place with one bolt.
22   Coat the camshaft journals and lobes and the lifters with Camshaft and Lifter Prelube or equivalent and install them in their original locations.
23   On the intake camshaft only, lubricate the lip of the oil seal, then position the seal on the camshaft journal with the spring side facing in.
24   Install the camshaft in the housing with the sprocket dowel pin UP (12 o'clock position) **(see illustration)**. Position the cover on the housing, holding it in place with the two bolts, as described above.
25   Apply Pipe Sealant or equivalent to the

threads of the camshaft housing and cover bolts.
26   Install new housing seals. Each seal is pre-fit.
27   Install the camshaft cover and bolts while positioning the oil seal (intake side only). Be sure the seal is installed to the depth of 0.020 inch (0.50 mm) into the cover and cylinder head.
28   Tighten the bolts in the sequence shown **(see illustration)** to the torque and angle of rotation listed in this Chapter's Specifications.
29   Install the power steering pump pulley with a special tool **(see illustration)**.
30   Install the remaining parts in the reverse order of removal.
31   Change the oil and filter (see Chapter 1).
Note: *If new lifters have been installed or the lifters bled down while the engine was disassembled, excessive lifter noise may be experienced after startup - this is normal. Use the following procedure to purge the lifters of air:*

a) *Start the engine and allow it to warm up for five minutes.*
b) *Increase engine speed to 2000 rpm until the lifter noise is gone.*

32   Road test the vehicle and check for oil and coolant leaks.

9.29 The power steering pump drive pulley must be pressed on with a special tool

10.5 This is what the air hose adapter that threads into the spark plug hole looks like - they're commonly available from auto parts stores

10.18 Apply a small dab of grease to each keeper before installation to hold it in place on the valve stem until the spring is released

10 Valve springs, retainers and seals - replacement

Refer to illustrations 10.5 and 10.18

Note: *Broken valve springs and defective valve stem seals can be replaced without removing the cylinder head. Two special tools and a compressed air source are normally required to perform this operation, so read through this Section carefully and rent or buy the tools before beginning the job. If compressed air isn't available, a length of nylon rope can be used to keep the valves from falling into the cylinder during this procedure.*

1   Remove the spark plug from the cylinder which has the defective part. Due to the design of this engine, the intake and exhaust camshaft housings can be removed separately to service their respective components. If all of the valve stem seals are being replaced, all of the spark plugs and both camshaft housings should be removed.

2   Refer to Chapter 5 and remove the ignition coil assembly.

3   Remove the camshaft(s), lifters and housing(s) as described in Section 9.

4   Turn the crankshaft until the piston in the affected cylinder is at top dead center on the compression stroke (refer to Chapter 2, Part H, for instructions). If you're replacing all of the valve stem seals, begin with cylinder number one and work on the valves for one cylinder at a time. Move from cylinder-to-cylinder following the firing order sequence (see this Chapter's Specifications).

5   Thread an adapter into the spark plug hole **(see illustration)** and connect an air hose from a compressed air source to it. Most auto parts stores can supply the air hose adapter. **Note:** *Many cylinder compression gauges utilize a screw-in fitting that may work with your air hose quick-disconnect fitting.*

6   Apply compressed air to the cylinder. **Warning:** *The piston may be forced down by compressed air, causing the crankshaft to turn suddenly. If the wrench used when positioning the number one piston at TDC is still attached to the bolt in the crankshaft nose, it could cause damage or injury when the crankshaft moves.*

7   The valves should be held in place by the air pressure. If the valve faces or seats are in poor condition, leaks may prevent air pressure from retaining the valves - in this case a "valve job" is needed.

8   If you don't have access to compressed air, an alternative method can be used. Position the piston at a point just before TDC on the compression stroke, then feed a long piece of nylon rope through the spark plug hole until it fills the combustion chamber. Be sure to leave the end of the rope hanging out of the engine so it can be removed easily. Use a large ratchet and socket to rotate the crankshaft in the normal direction of rotation (clockwise) until slight resistance is felt.

9   Stuff shop rags into the cylinder head holes adjacent to the valves to prevent parts and tools from falling into the engine, then use a valve spring compressor to compress the spring. Remove the keepers with small needle-nose pliers or a magnet.

10   Remove the retainer and valve spring, then remove the valve guide seal and rotator. **Note:** *If air pressure fails to hold the valve in the closed position during this operation, the valve face or seat is probably damaged. If so, the cylinder head will have to be removed for additional repair operations.*

11   Wrap a rubber band or tape around the top of the valve stem so the valve won't fall into the combustion chamber, then release the air pressure. **Note:** *If a rope was used instead of air pressure, turn the crankshaft slightly in a counterclockwise direction (opposite normal rotation).*

12   Inspect the valve stem for damage. Rotate the valve in the guide and check the end for eccentric movement, which would indicate the valve stem is bent.

13   Move the valve up-and-down in the guide and make sure it doesn't bind. If the valve stem binds, either the valve is bent or the guide is damaged. In either case, the head will have to be removed for repair.

14   Reapply air pressure to the cylinder to retain the valve in the closed position, then remove the tape or rubber band from the valve stem. If a rope was used instead of air pressure, rotate the crankshaft in the normal direction of rotation until slight resistance is felt.

15   Reinstall the valve rotator.

16   Lubricate the valve stem with engine oil and install a new guide seal.

17   Install the spring in position over the valve.

18   Install the valve spring retainer. Compress the valve spring and carefully install the keepers in the groove. Apply a small dab of grease to the inside of each keeper to hold it in place if necessary **(see illustration)**. Remove the pressure from the spring tool and make sure the keepers are seated.

19   Disconnect the air hose and remove the adapter from the spark plug hole. If a rope was used in place of air pressure, pull it out of the cylinder.

20   Refer to Section 9 and install the camshaft(s), lifters and housing(s).

21   Install the spark plug(s) and coil assembly.

22   Start and run the engine, then check for oil leaks and unusual sounds coming from the camshaft housings.

11 Cylinder head - removal and installation

Removal

1   Disconnect the negative cable from the battery. **Caution:** *On models equipped with the Theftlock audio system, be sure the lockout feature is turned off before performing any procedure which requires disconnecting the battery.*

2   Refer to Section 3 and remove the intake manifold. The cooling system must be drained to prevent coolant from getting into internal areas of the engine when the head is removed.

3   Refer to Section 4 and detach the exhaust manifold.

4   Remove the camshafts and housings as described in Section 9.

5   Make a holder for the head bolts. Using the new head gasket, outline the cylinders and bolt pattern on a piece of cardboard. Be sure to indicate the front of the engine for reference. Punch holes at the bolt locations **(see illustration 8.11 in Part B)**.

11.10 Remove the old gasket and clean the head thoroughly

11.15 Cylinder head bolt TIGHTENING sequence

6   Loosen the head bolts in 1/4-turn increments until they can be removed by hand. Work from bolt-to-bolt in a pattern that's the reverse of the tightening sequence **(see illustration 11.15)**. Store the bolts in the cardboard holder as they're removed - this will ensure they are reinstalled in their original locations.

7   Lift the head off the engine. If resistance is felt, don't pry between the head and block as damage to the mating surfaces will result. To dislodge the head, place a block of wood against the end of it and strike the wood block with a hammer.

8   Store the head on blocks of wood to prevent damage to the gasket sealing surfaces.

12.11 The oil pan baffle is held in place by four bolts (arrows)

Installation
Refer to illustrations 11.10 and 11.15

9   The mating surfaces of the cylinder head and block must be perfectly clean when the head is installed.

10   Use a gasket scraper to remove all traces of carbon and old gasket material **(see illustration)**, then clean the mating surfaces with lacquer thinner or acetone. If there's oil on the mating surfaces when the head is installed, the gasket may not seal correctly and leaks could develop. **Note:** *Since the head is made of aluminum, aggressive scraping can cause damage. Be extra careful not to nick or gouge the mating surface with the scraper. Use a vacuum cleaner to remove debris that falls into the cylinders.*

11   Check the block and head mating surfaces for nicks, deep scratches and other damage. If damage is slight, it can be removed with a flat mill file; if it's excessive, machining may be the only alternative.

12   Use a tap of the correct size to chase the threads in the head bolt holes. Mount each bolt in a vise and run a die down the threads to remove corrosion and restore the threads. Dirt, corrosion, sealant and damaged threads will affect torque readings.

13   Position the new gasket over the dowel pins in the block.

14   Carefully position the head on the block without disturbing the gasket.

15   Install the bolts in their original locations and tighten them finger tight. Following the recommended sequence **(see illustration)**, tighten the bolts in several steps to the torque and angle of rotation listed in this Chapter's Specifications.

16   The remaining installation steps are the reverse of removal.

17   Refill the cooling system and change the oil and filter (see Chapter 1, if necessary).

18   Run the engine and check for leaks and proper operation.

12 Oil pan - removal and installation

Refer to illustrations 12.11 and 12.15
Note: *The following procedure is based on the assumption the engine is in place in the vehicle. If its been removed, simply unbolt the oil pan and detach it from the block.*

Removal

1   Disconnect the negative battery cable from the battery, then refer to Chapter 1 and drain the oil. **Caution:** *On models equipped with the Theftlock audio system, be sure the lockout feature is turned off before performing any procedure which requires disconnecting the battery.*

2   Remove the lower splash shield.

3   Detach the lower bellhousing cover.

4   Unbolt the exhaust manifold brace (manual transaxle models only - see Section 4).

5   Remove the radiator outlet pipe-to-oil pan bolt.

6   On manual transaxle equipped models, remove the transaxle-to-oil pan nut and stud with a 7 mm socket.

7   Gently pry the spacer out from between the oil pan and transaxle.

8   Remove the oil pan-to-transaxle bolt.

9   Remove the oil pan mounting bolts.

10   Carefully separate the pan from the block. Don't pry between the block and pan or damage to the sealing surfaces may result and oil leaks may develop. **Note:** *The crankshaft may have to be rotated to gain clearance for oil pan removal.*

11   If you need to get at the crankshaft or other lower end components, remove the oil pan baffle **(see illustration)**.

Installation

12   Clean the sealing surfaces with lacquer thinner or acetone. Make sure the bolt holes in the block are clean.

12.15 Oil pan bolt locations - viewed from below

13.5 Check the oil pump drive gear (arrow) and driven gear for
wear and damage

13   The gasket should be checked carefully and replaced with a new one if damage is noted. Minor imperfections can be repaired with silicone sealant. **Caution:** *Use only enough sealant to restore the gasket to its original size and shape. Excess sealant may cause part misalignment and oil leaks.*
14   Reinstall the oil pan baffle, if removed. With the gasket in position, carefully hold the pan against the block and install the bolts finger tight.
15   Tighten the bolts in three steps to the torque listed in this Chapter's Specifications **(see illustration)**. Start at the center of the pan and work out toward the ends in a spiral pattern. Note that the bolts are not all tightened to the same torque value.
16   The remaining steps are the reverse of removal. **Caution:** *Don't forget to refill the engine with oil before starting it* (see Chapter 1).
17   Start the engine and check carefully for oil leaks at the oil pan.

13   Oil pump - removal, inspection and installation

Refer to illustration 13.5

Removal
1   Remove the oil pan as described in Section 12.
2   While supporting the oil pump, remove the mounting bolts.
3   Lower the pump from the engine.

Inspection
4   Clean all parts thoroughly and remove the cover.
5   Visually inspect all parts for wear, cracks and other damage **(see illustration)**. Replace the pump if it's defective, if the engine has high mileage or if the engine is being rebuilt.

Installation
6   Position the pump on the engine and

install the mounting bolts. Tighten them to the torque listed in this Chapter's Specifications.
7   Oil pump drive gear backlash must be checked whenever the oil pump, crankshaft or engine block is replaced. Mount a dial indicator on the engine with the indicator stem touching the oil pump driven gear. Check the backlash and compare it to the Specifications in this Chapter. If the clearance is not correct, replace the oil pump.
8   Install the oil pan (and baffle, if removed).
9   Add oil and run the engine. Check for oil pressure and leaks.

14   Flywheel - removal and installation

This procedure is essentially the same for all engines. Refer to Part B and follow the driveplate removal and installation procedure outlined there. Check the surface of the flywheel for cracks, rivet grooves and other signs of damage. If necessary, have the flywheel machined by an automotive machine shop. Be sure to use the bolt torque listed in this Chapter's Specifications.

15   Rear main oil seal - replacement

Refer to illustrations 15.5, 15.6, 15.7 and 15.8
Warning: *A special tool is available to support the engine during repair operations. Similar fixtures are available from rental yards. Improper lifting methods or devices are hazardous and could result in severe injury or death. DO NOT place any part of your body under the engine/transaxle when it's supported only by a jack. Failure of the lifting device could result in serious injury or death.*
Note: *The rear main (crankshaft) oil seal is a one-piece unit that can be replaced without removing the engine. However, the transaxle must be removed and the engine must be supported as this procedure is done. A special tool is available for seal installation, but the procedure outlined here was devised to avoid having to use the tool.*
1   Remove the transaxle (see Chapter 7).
2   Remove the pressure plate and clutch disc (see Chapter 8).
3   Remove the flywheel (see Section 14).
4   Remove the oil pan (see Section 12).
5   After the oil pan has been removed, remove the bolts **(see illustration)**, detach the seal housing and peel off all the old gasket material.

15.5 Remove the seal housing bolts (arrows)

15.6 After removing the housing from the engine, support it on wood blocks and drive out the old seal with a punch and hammer

15.7 Drive the new seal into the housing with a block of wood or a section of pipe, if you have one large enough - don't cock the seal in the housing bore

15.8 Lubricate the seal journal and lip, then position a new gasket over the dowel pins (arrows)

16.7 Upper torque strut mounting bolt locations (arrows)

6   Position the seal housing on a couple of wood blocks on a workbench and drive the old seal out from the back side with a punch and hammer **(see illustration)**.
7   Drive the new seal into the housing with a wood block **(see illustration)**.
8   Lubricate the crankshaft seal journal and the lip of the new seal with moly-base grease. Position a new gasket on the engine block **(see illustration)**.
9   Slowly and carefully push the new seal onto the crankshaft. The seal lip is stiff, so work it onto the crankshaft with a smooth object such as the end of an extension as you push the housing against the block.
10   Install and tighten the housing bolts to the torque listed in this Chapter's Specifications.
11   Install the flywheel and clutch components.
12   Reinstall the transaxle.

16   Engine mounts - check and replacement

Refer to illustrations 16.7, 16.8 and 16.13
Warning: *A special tool is available to support the engine during repair operations. Similar fixtures are available from rental yards. Improper lifting methods or devices are hazardous and could result in severe injury or death. DO NOT place any part of your body under the engine/transaxle when it's supported only by a jack. Failure of the lifting device could result in serious injury or death.*
1   Engine mounts seldom require attention, but broken or deteriorated mounts should be replaced immediately or the added strain placed on the driveline components may cause damage or wear.

Check

2   During the check, the engine must be raised slightly to remove the weight from the mounts.
3   Raise the vehicle and support it securely on jackstands. Support the engine as described above. If the special support fixture is unavailable, position a jack under the engine oil pan. Place a large block of wood between the jack head and the oil pan, then carefully raise the engine just enough to take the weight off the mounts. **Warning:** *DO NOT place any part of your body under the engine when it's supported only by a jack!*
4   Check the mounts to see if the rubber is cracked, hardened or separated from the metal plates. Sometimes the rubber will split right down the center.
5   Check for movement between the mount plates and the engine or frame (use a large

16.8 Torque strut to body bracket bolts

16.13 Engine mount bolt locations (arrows)

screwdriver or pry bar to attempt to move the mounts). If movement is noted, lower the engine and tighten the mount fasteners.

6   Rubber preservative should be applied to the mounts to slow deterioration.

Replacement

Upper mount (torque strut)

7   Detach the negative battery cable from the battery. Remove the upper torque strut bracket bolt **(see illustration)**. **Caution:** *On models equipped with the Theftlock audio system, be sure the lockout feature is turned*

off before performing any procedure which requires disconnecting the battery.

8   Remove the torque strut-to-body mount bolts **(see illustration)**.

9   Remove the torque strut.

10   Place the new torque strut in position and install the bolts. Tighten the nuts securely.

11   Reconnect the negative battery cable.

Lower mount

12   Detach the negative battery cable from the battery. **Caution:** *On models equipped with the Theftlock audio system, be sure the*

lockout feature is turned off before performing any procedure which requires disconnecting the battery.

13   Working under the frame mounting bracket, remove the nuts from the engine mount **(see illustration)**.

14   Raise the engine off the mount.

15   Remove the mount-to-bracket nuts.

16   Remove the mount from the vehicle.

17   Installation is the reverse of removal.

18   Gently lower the engine.

19   Tighten the nuts securely.

20   Reconnect the negative battery cable.

2C-16 Chapter 2 Part C 2.3 liter four-cylinder (Quad-4) engine

Notes

Chapter 2 Part D
2.8L, 3.1L and 3100 V6 engines

Contents

	Section
Camshaft and bearings - removal, inspection and installation	See Chapter 2H
Crankshaft front oil seal - replacement	11
Cylinder compression check	See Chapter 2H
Cylinder heads - removal and installation	8
Drivebelt check, adjustment and replacement	See Chapter 1
Engine mounts - check and replacement	18
Engine oil and filter change	See Chapter 1
Engine overhaul - general information	See Chapter 2H
Engine - removal and installation	See Chapter 2H
Exhaust manifolds - removal and installation	7
Flywheel/driveplate - removal and installation	16
General information	1
Hydraulic lifters - removal, inspection and installation	9
Intake manifold - removal and installation	6
Oil pan - removal and installation	14

	Section
Oil pump - removal and installation	15
Rear main oil seal - replacement	17
Repair operations possible with the engine in the vehicle	2
Rocker arms and pushrods - removal, inspection and installation	4
Spark plug replacement	See Chapter 1
Timing chain and sprockets - inspection, removal and installation	13
Timing chain cover - removal and installation	12
Top Dead Center (TDC) for number one piston - locating	See Chapter 2H
Valve covers - removal and installation	3
Valve springs, retainers and seals - replacement	5
Vibration damper - removal and installation	10
Water pump - removal and installation	See Chapter 3

Specifications

General
Cylinder numbers (drivebelt end-to-transaxle end)
Front bank (radiator side) ... 2-4-6
Rear bank ... 1-3-5
Firing order ... 1-2-3-4-5-6

Torque specifications

Note: *One foot-pound (ft-lb) of torque is equivalent to 12 inch-pounds (in-lbs) of torque. Torque values below approximately 15 foot-pounds are expressed in inch-pounds, because most foot-pound torque wrenches are not accurate at these smaller values.*

Ft-lbs (unless otherwise indicated)

Camshaft sprocket bolts
  2.8L and 3.1L
    1989 and earlier ... 18
    1990 and later ... 21
  3100
    1995 and earlier ... 74
    1996 and 1997 ... 81
    1998 and later ... 103

Cylinder head bolts
  Step 1
    1997 and earlier ... 33
    1998 through 2001 ... 37
    2002 and later ... 44
  Step 2
    2001 and earlier ... Rotate an additional 90-degrees (1/4-turn)
    2002 and later ... Rotate an additional 95-degrees

Exhaust manifold-to-cylinder head bolts
  2.8L and 3.1L ... 18
  3100 ... 144 in-lbs

Flywheel/driveplate-to-crankshaft bolts
  2.8L and 3.1L ... 52
  3100
    1995 and earlier ... 59
    1996 and 1997 ... 61
    1998 and later ... 52

Lower intake manifold-to-cylinder head bolts/nuts
  2.8L and 3.1L
    Step one ... 15
    Step two ... 24

FRONT

2.8L and 3.1L V6 engines

1 4 6 3 2 5

1994 and later 3100 V6 engine

FRONT OF VEHICLE

Cylinder and coil terminal locations

Torque specifications (continued)

Ft-lbs (unless otherwise indicated)

Note: *One foot-pound (ft-lb) of torque is equivalent to 12 inch-pounds (in-lbs) of torque. Torque values below approximately 15 foot-pounds are expressed in inch-pounds, because most foot-pound torque wrenches are not accurate at these smaller values.*

Lower intake manifold-to-cylinder head bolts/nuts (continued)

3100	
Step 1	62 in-lbs
Step 2	115 in-lbs
Oil pan bolts/nuts	
2.8L and 3.1L	
Left (transaxle end) two bolts............................	18
All others	89 in-lbs
3100	
Retaining..	18
Side..	37
Oil pump mounting bolts..	30
Oil pump drive bolt (3100)	27
Rocker arm nuts/bolts	
1995 and earlier (nuts)...	18
1996 and 1997 (bolts)	89 in-lbs plus an additional 30 degrees
1998 and later (bolts)	168 in-lbs plus an additional 30 degrees
Timing chain cover bolts **(see illustration 12.16)**	
2.8L and 3.1L	
6 mm (number 3)	20
8 mm (number 4)	28
3100	
1997 and earlier	
Small	15
Large	35
1998 through 2000	
Small	15
Medium..	35
Large	41
2001	
Small	20
Medium..	41
Large	41
2002 and later	
Small	20
Large	41
Timing chain damper bolt	
2.8L and 3.1L	15
3100	
1995 and earlier...	18
1996 and later..	15
Valve cover-to-cylinder head bolts..............................	89 in-lbs
Vibration damper bolt	76
Front engine mount-to-bracket nuts	35
Front mount bracket-to-oil pan bolts............................	43
Rear engine mount nuts to transaxle bracket..............	35
Rear engine mount-to-chassis nuts.............................	35
Torque strut through-bolt nuts.....................................	35
Left strut mount to cylinder head bolts........................	52
Right strut mount to block...	37

1   General information

Refer to illustration 1.2

This Part of Chapter 2 is devoted to in-vehicle repair procedures for the 2.8L, 3.1L and 3100 V6 engines. The 2.8L engine became available in 1988 and 1989, in the Pontiac Grand Prix, Oldsmobile Cutlass Supreme and the Buick Regal models only. The 3.1L engine became available in 1989 and was produced through 1994, in all four models covered by this manual. The 3100 engine became available in 1994 and later, it is utilized in the Pontiac Grand Prix, Oldsmobile Cutlass Supreme and the Buick Regal models only. These engines utilize cast-iron blocks with six cylinders arranged in a "V" shape at a 60-degree angle between the two banks. The overhead valve aluminum cylinder heads are equipped with replaceable valve guides and seats. Hydraulic lifters actuate the valves through tubular pushrods.

The engines are easily identified by looking for the designations printed on the alumi-num intake plenum, directly on the top **(see illustration)**. To positively identify these engines, locate the vehicle identification number on the left front corner of the instrument panel. This plate is visible from outside the vehicle **(see illustration 1.1** in Chapter 2, Part B). The eighth character in the sequence is the engine designation:

W = 2.8L V6 engine
T = 3.1L V6 engine
V = 3.1L Turbocharged V6 engine
M = 3100 V6 engine

1.2 3.1L Multi Port Fuel Injected engine (2.8L and 3100 similar)

3.10 Some valve cover mounting bolts (arrows) require a Torx bit for removal and installation

Information concerning engine removal and installation and engine overhaul can be found in Part H of this Chapter. The following repair procedures are based on the assumption the engine is installed in the vehicle. If the engine has been removed from the vehicle and mounted on a stand, many of the steps outlined in this Part of Chapter 2 will not apply.

2   Repair operations possible with the engine in the vehicle

Many major repair operations can be accomplished without removing the engine from the vehicle.

Clean the engine compartment and the exterior of the engine with some type of degreaser before any work is done. It'll make the job easier and help keep dirt out of the internal areas of the engine.

Depending on the components involved, it may be helpful to remove the hood to improve access to the engine as repairs are performed (refer to Chapter 11 if necessary). Cover the fenders to prevent damage to the paint. Special pads are available, but an old bedspread or blanket will also work.

If vacuum, exhaust, oil or coolant leaks develop, indicating a need for gasket or seal replacement, the repairs can generally be done with the engine in the vehicle. The intake and exhaust manifold gaskets, timing chain cover gasket, oil pan gasket, crankshaft oil seals and cylinder head gaskets are all accessible with the engine in place.

Exterior engine components, such as the intake and exhaust manifolds, the oil pan (and the oil pump), the water pump, the starter motor, the alternator and the fuel system components can be removed for repair with the engine in place.

Since the cylinder heads can be removed without pulling the engine, valve component servicing can also be accomplished with the engine in the vehicle. Replacement of the timing chain and sprockets is also possible with the engine in the vehicle.

In extreme cases caused by a lack of necessary equipment, repair or replacement of piston rings, pistons, connecting rods and rod bearings is possible with the engine in the vehicle. However, this practice is not recommended because of the cleaning and preparation work that must be done to the components involved.

3   Valve covers - removal and installation

Removal
Front cover
Refer to illustration 3.10

1   Disconnect the negative battery cable from the battery. **Caution:** *On models equipped with the Theftlock audio system, be sure the lockout feature is turned off before performing any procedure which requires disconnecting the battery.*
2   Remove the air cleaner assembly (see Chapter 4).
3   On the 3100, remove the thermostat bypass pipe clip nut.
4   On the 3100, remove the automatic transaxle vacuum modulator pipe assembly.
5   On the 3100, disconnect the right engine mount strut at the engine.
6   If necessary, remove the spark plug wires from the spark plugs (see Chapter 1). Be sure each wire is labeled before removal to ensure correct reinstallation.
7   Detach the spark plug wire harness clamps from the coolant tube.
8   Remove the PCV tube from the valve cover.
9   Drain the coolant (see Chapter 1).
10   Remove the valve cover mounting bolts. **Note:** *Some models are equipped with special bolts. Remove them with a T-30 Torx driver* (see illustration).
11   Detach the valve cover. **Note:** *If the cover sticks to the cylinder head, use a block of wood and a hammer to dislodge it. If the cover still won't come loose, pry on it carefully, but don't distort the sealing flange.*

Rear cover
12   Disconnect the negative battery cable from the battery. **Caution:** *On models equipped with the Theftlock audio system, be sure the lockout feature is turned off before performing any procedure which requires disconnecting the battery.*
13   Remove the air cleaner assembly (see Chapter 4).
14   On the 2.8L and 3.1L, drain the coolant (see Chapter 1). Remove the coolant hoses at the base of the throttle valve.
15   Rotate the engine (see Chapter 1).
16   Detach the vacuum hoses at the plenum. Also, disconnect the brake booster vacuum supply at the plenum.
17   Remove the EGR tube at the crossover pipe. On the 3100, disconnect the EGR valve and move it aside.
18   Disconnect the ignition wire guide and harness at the plenum. On the 3100, remove the ignition coil-pack, which on later models includes the solenoids for the vacuum canister and purge control solenoids. On these models, tag and disconnect the wires and hoses to the solenoids.
19   If necessary, remove the bracket at the right side of the plenum.
20   Remove the serpentine drivebelt (see Chapter 1).
21   On the 3100, remove the black plastic cover from the shock tower.
22   Remove the alternator and loosen the alternator bracket (see Chapter 5).
23   Detach the breather hose from the PCV valve.
24   Remove the spark plug wires from the spark plugs (see Chapter 1). Be sure each wire is labeled before removal to ensure correct reinstallation.
25   Remove the accelerator cable, T.V. cable and also the cruise control cable, as necessary.
26   Detach the valve cover. **Note 1:** *If the cover sticks to the cylinder head, use a block of wood and a hammer to dislodge it. If the cover still won't come loose, pry on it carefully, but don't distort the sealing flange.* **Note 2:** *Some models are equipped with spe-*

4.2a On 1995 and earlier models remove the rocker arm nuts (arrows)

4.2b 1996 and later engines use rocker arm bolts, stamped roller rocker arms, and rocker arm pedestals - they are kept as an assembly by a small sleeve between the bolt and the pedestal - note the projections on the pedestal; they fit into grooves in the head

A   Rocker arm bolt
B   Rocker arm
C   Rocker arm pedestal
D   Pedestal projections
E   Grooves in the head

cial bolts. Remove them with a T-30 Torx driver **(see illustration 3.10)**.

Installation

27   The mating surfaces of each cylinder head and valve cover must be perfectly clean when the covers are installed. Use a gasket scraper to remove all traces of sealant or old gasket material, then clean the mating surfaces with lacquer thinner or acetone (if there's sealant or oil on the mating surfaces when the cover is installed, oil leaks may develop). The valve covers are made of aluminum, so be extra careful not to nick or gouge the mating surfaces with the scraper.

28   Clean the mounting bolt threads with a die if necessary to remove any corrosion and restore damaged threads. Use a tap to clean the threaded holes in the heads.

29   Place the valve cover and new gasket in position, then install the bolts. Tighten the bolts in several steps to the torque listed in this Chapter's Specifications.

30   Complete the installation by reversing the removal procedure. Start the engine and check carefully for oil leaks at the valve cover-to-head joints.

4.3 A perforated cardboard box can be used to store the pushrods to ensure they are reinstalled in their original locations - note the label indicating the transaxle end of the engine

4   Rocker arms and pushrods - removal, inspection and installation

Refer to illustrations 4.2a, 4.2b and 4.3

Removal

1   Remove the valve cover(s) (see Section 3).

2   On 1995 and earlier models, the rocker arms are retained by nuts with a pivot ball between the nut and the rocker. The 1996 and later engines have the rocker arm on a pedestal, with a bolt through the rocker arm and pedestal. Beginning at the drivebelt end of one cylinder head, remove the rocker arm mounting nuts/bolts one at a time and detach the rocker arms, nuts, and pivot balls/pedestals **(see illustrations)**. Store each set of rocker arm components separately in a marked plastic bag to ensure they're reinstalled in their original locations. The 1996 and later rocker arms have the pedestal mount "captured" on the rocker arm bolt by a metal sleeve inside. The components can be separated if necessary by tapping the bolt out of the pedestal, but normally all components for a particular valve will stay as an assembly. **Note:** *If you only need to remove the pushrods, loosen the rocker arm nuts/bolts and turn the rocker arms to allow room for pushrod removal.*

3   Remove the pushrods and store them separately to make sure they don't get mixed up during installation **(see illustration). Note:** *Intake and exhaust pushrods are different lengths. The intake pushrods are shorter and the exhaust pushrods are longer in length. On 1995 and earlier models the pushrods may be color coded with several paint stripes to help distinguish the intake (red or orange striped) pushrods from the exhaust (blue striped) pushrods. Never mix-up the pushrods and always install them in the original position from which they were removed or engine damage may occur.*

Inspection

4   Inspect each rocker arm for wear, cracks and other damage, especially where the push-

rods and valve stems make contact.

5   Check the pivot seat in each rocker arm and the pivot ball faces. Look for galling, stress cracks and unusual wear patterns. If the rocker arms are worn or damaged, replace them with new ones and install new pivot balls as well.

6   Make sure the hole at the pushrod end of each rocker arm is open.

7   Inspect the pushrods for cracks and excessive wear at the ends. Roll each pushrod across a piece of plate glass to see if it's bent (if it wobbles, it's bent).

Installation

8   Lubricate the lower end of each pushrod with clean engine oil or moly-base grease and install them in their original locations. Make sure each pushrod seats completely in the lifter socket.

9   Apply moly-base grease to the ends of the valve stems and the upper ends of the pushrods.

10   Apply moly-base grease to the pivot balls to prevent damage to the mating surfaces before engine oil pressure builds up. Install the rocker arms, pivot balls and nuts and tighten the nuts to the torque listed in this Chapter's Specifications. As the nuts are tightened, make sure the pushrods engage properly in the rocker arms.

11   Install the valve covers and the remaining components detached during valve cover removal (see Section 3). Start the engine and check for any unusual noises coming from the valve cover area.

6.9 Label (arrow) and disconnect all remaining hoses and lines

6.11a Intake manifold mounting bolt/nut locations - models through 1995

5   Valve springs, retainers and seals - replacement

This procedure is essentially the same as the procedure for the 2.5 liter four-cylinder engine. Refer to Part B and follow the procedure outlined there.

6   Intake manifold - removal and installation

Removal

Refer to illustrations 6.9, 6.11a, 6.11b and 6.11c

1   Relieve the fuel system pressure (see Chapter 4).
2   Disconnect the negative battery cable from the battery. **Caution:** *On models equipped with the Theftlock audio system, be sure the lockout feature is turned off before performing any procedure which requires disconnecting the battery.*

3   Remove the EGR valve (see Chapter 4) at the plenum.
4   Remove the plenum, fuel rail and injectors (see Chapter 4). When disconnecting fuel line fittings, be prepared to catch some fuel with a rag, then cap the fittings to prevent contamination.
5   Remove the serpentine drivebelt and drain the cooling system (see Chapter 1).
6   Remove the alternator and loosen the bracket (see Chapter 5).
7   Unbolt the power steering pump (if equipped) and set it aside without disconnecting the hoses.
8   Disconnect the coolant tubes and hoses as necessary.
9   Label and disconnect any remaining fuel and vacuum lines **(see illustration)** and wires from the manifold.
10   Remove the valve covers (see Section 3).
11   Remove the manifold mounting bolts and nuts, then separate the manifold from the engine **(see illustrations)**. Don't pry between the manifold and heads, as damage to the

soft aluminum gasket sealing surfaces may result. If you're installing a new manifold, transfer all fittings and sensors to the new manifold.
12   Loosen the rocker arm nuts/bolts, rotate the rocker arms out of the way and remove the pushrods that go through the manifold gasket (see Section 4).

Installation

Refer to illustration 6.16
Note: *The mating surfaces of the cylinder heads, block and manifold must be perfectly clean when the manifold is installed. Gasket removal solvents are available at most auto parts stores and may be helpful when removing old gasket material that's stuck to the heads and manifold (since the manifold is made of aluminum, aggressive scraping can cause damage). Be sure to follow the directions printed on the container.*
13   Lift the old gasket off. Use a gasket scraper to remove all traces of sealant and old gasket material, then clean the mating surfaces with lacquer thinner or acetone. If

6.11b Pry the manifold loose at a casting boss - don't pry between the gasket surfaces!

6.11c Intake manifold TIGHTENING sequence, 1996 and later models - make sure the bolts in the center (1 through 4) are completely tightened before tightening the end bolts (5 through 8)

6.16 Apply a bead of sealant to, or position an end seal on, the ridges between the heads (arrows)

7.12 On early models the exhaust crossover pipe is secured by four nuts; the upper nuts (arrows) are visible here

there's old sealant or oil on the mating surfaces when the manifold is installed, oil or vacuum leaks may develop. Use a vacuum cleaner to remove any gasket material that falls into the intake ports or the lifter valley.

14   Use a tap of the correct size to chase the threads in the bolt holes, if necessary, then use compressed air (if available) to remove the debris from the holes. **Warning:** *Wear safety glasses or a face shield to protect your eyes when using compressed air!*

15   Apply a 3/16-inch (5 mm) bead of RTV sealant or equivalent to the front and rear ridges of the engine block between the heads. **Note:** *Some gasket sets include end seals.*

16   Install the intake manifold gasket **(see illustration)**.

17   Install the pushrods and rocker arms (see Section 4).

18   Carefully lower the manifold into place and install the mounting bolts/nuts finger tight. First tighten the four vertical bolts (in the middle of the manifold) then the four angled bolts (at the ends) **(see illustration 6.11a)**. **Note:** *Coat the bolt threads with pipe thread sealant.*

19   Tighten the mounting bolts until they're all at the torque listed in this Chapter's Specifications. **Caution:** *To prevent oil leaks, tighten the vertical bolts first to ensure that the lower manifold stays centered on the gaskets, then tighten the angled bolts.*

20   Install the remaining components in the reverse order of removal.

21   Change the oil and filter and refill the cooling system (see Chapter 1). Start the engine and check for leaks.

7   Exhaust manifolds - removal and installation

Front manifold

Refer to illustrations 7.12, 7.13 and 7.14

1   Disconnect the negative battery cable from the battery. **Caution:** *On models equipped with the Theftlock audio system, be sure the lockout feature is turned off before performing any procedure which requires disconnecting the battery.*

2   Remove the air cleaner assembly, inlet hose and mass air flow sensor (see Chapter 4).

3   Allow the engine to cool completely, then drain the coolant (see Chapter 1) and disconnect the coolant bypass tube, if necessary.

4   On 3100 engines through 1998, remove the upper and lower radiator hoses and the coolant bypass pipe from the front exhaust manifold and water pump.

5   On the 3100, remove the tie straps from the heater outlet pipe and ignition wire harness, and remove the heater outlet pipe.

6   On the 3100, remove the automatic transaxle vacuum modulator pipe if equipped.

7   Remove the coolant reservoir (see Chapter 3).

8   Remove the serpentine drivebelt (see Chapter 1).

9   On models through 1996, remove the air conditioning compressor, leaving the hoses connected to it (see Chapter 3).

10   Remove the torque strut from the right side, if necessary (see Section 18).

11   Remove the torque strut bracket, and on models through 1996, the air conditioning compressor bracket.

12   Unbolt the crossover pipe where it joins

the front manifold **(see illustration)**. **Note:** *On later models it will be necessary to remove the crossover pipe heat shield to allow access to the crossover pipe mounting nuts. The crossover pipe heat shield is mounted to the left and right exhaust manifolds by two bolts on each side (four bolts total).*

13   Remove the manifold heat shield **(see illustration)**.

14   Remove the mounting bolts and detach the manifold from the cylinder head **(see illustration)**.

15   Clean the mating surfaces to remove all traces of old gasket material, then inspect the manifold for distortion and cracks. Warpage can be checked with a precision straightedge held against the mating flange. If a feeler gauge thicker than 0.030-inch can be inserted between the straight edge and flange surface, take the manifold to an automotive machine shop for resurfacing.

16   Place the manifold in position with a new gasket and install the mounting bolts finger tight.

17   Starting in the middle and working out toward the ends, tighten the mounting bolts a little at a time until all of them are at the torque listed in this Chapter's Specifications.

7.13 Exhaust manifold heat shield mounting bolts (arrows) (3.1L engine shown, 2.8L and 3100 engine similar)

7.14 Exhaust manifold bolt locations (arrows)

18 Install the remaining components in the reverse order of removal.
19 Start the engine and check for exhaust leaks between the manifold and cylinder head and between the manifold and exhaust pipe.

Rear manifold

20 Disconnect the negative battery cable from the battery. **Caution:** *On models equipped with the Theftlock audio system, be sure the lockout feature is turned off before performing any procedure which requires disconnecting the battery.*
21 Allow the engine to cool completely, then drain the coolant (see Chapter 1).
22 Remove the coolant reservoir, if necessary (see Chapter 3).
23 Rotate the engine to gain working clearance at the rear of the engine (see Chapter 1).
24 Remove the air cleaner assembly (see Chapter 4).
25 On some models it may be necessary to remove the accelerator cable and T.V. cable and brackets for clearance (see Chapters 4 and 7).
26 Unbolt the crossover pipe (or front manifold extension pipe) where it joins the rear manifold **(see illustration 7.12)**.
27 Remove the exhaust manifold heat shield **(see illustration 7.13)**. Note that the rear manifold heat shield typically has two bolts retaining it to the manifold, not three bolts like the front manifold heat shield.
28 Set the parking brake, block the rear wheels and raise the front of the vehicle, supporting it securely on jackstands.
29 Working under the vehicle with the engine completely cool, remove the exhaust pipe-to-manifold bolts.. You may have to apply penetrating oil to the fastener threads - they're usually rusted. **Note:** *On 1997 and later models the catalytic converter is bolted to the rear exhaust manifold.*
30 On the 3100, it may be necessary to lower the drivetrain/front suspension frame assembly. Place a floor jack under the frame front center crossmember. Loosen the rear frame bolts - DO NOT REMOVE THEM! Remove the front frame bolts and lower the front of the frame.
31 On the 3100, disconnect the EGR tube assembly from the exhaust manifold.
32 On the 3100, remove the automatic transaxle vacuum modulator pipe (if equipped) and the filler tube.
33 Remove the oxygen sensor from the manifold if equipped.
34 Unbolt and remove the exhaust manifold **(see illustration 7.14)**.
35 Clean the mating surfaces to remove all traces of old sealant, then check for warpage and cracks. Warpage can be checked with a precision straightedge held against the mating flange. If a feeler gauge thicker than 0.030-inch can be inserted between the straightedge and flange surface, take the manifold to an automotive machine shop for resurfacing.
36 Place the manifold in position with a new gasket and install the bolts finger tight.

8.3 Remove the oil dipstick tube mounting bolt (arrow)

37 Starting in the middle and working out toward the ends, tighten the mounting bolts a little at a time until all of them are at the torque listed in this Chapter's Specifications.
38 Install the remaining components in the reverse order of removal.
39 Start the engine and check for exhaust leaks between the manifold and cylinder head and between the manifold and exhaust pipe.

8 Cylinder heads - removal and installation

Refer to illustrations 8.3, 8.13, 8.16a, 8.16b, 8.18 and 8.19
Caution: *Allow the engine to cool completely before loosening the cylinder head bolts.*
Note: *On engines with high mileage and during an overhaul, camshaft lobe height should be checked prior to cylinder head removal (see Chapter 2, Part H for instructions).*

Removal

1 Disconnect the negative battery cable from the battery. **Caution:** *On models equipped with the Theftlock audio system, be sure the lockout feature is turned off before performing any procedure which requires disconnecting the battery.*
2 Remove the air cleaner assembly (see Chapter 4) and then remove the intake manifold as described in Section 8. On 2002 models, remove the oil splash shield by bending the spring clips that secure the shield to the cylinder heads.
3 If you're removing the front cylinder head, remove the oil dipstick tube mounting bolt **(see illustration)**.
4 Disconnect all wires and vacuum hoses from the cylinder head(s). Be sure to label them to simplify reinstallation.
5 Disconnect the spark plug wires and remove the spark plugs (see Chapter 1). Be sure the plug wires are labeled to simplify reinstallation.
6 Detach the exhaust manifold from the cylinder head being removed (see Section 7).
7 Remove the valve cover(s) (see Section 3).

8.13 Remove the old gasket and carefully scrape off all old gasket material and sealant

8 Remove the rocker arms and pushrods (see Section 4).
9 Using the new head gasket, outline the cylinders and bolt pattern on a piece of cardboard **(see illustration 8.11 in Part B)**. Be sure to indicate the front (drivebelt end) of the engine for reference. Punch holes at the bolt locations. Loosen each of the cylinder head mounting bolts 1/4-turn at a time until they can be removed by hand - work from bolt-to-bolt in a pattern that's the *reverse* of the tightening sequence **(see illustration 8.19)**. Store the bolts in the cardboard holder as they're removed - this will ensure they are reinstalled in their original locations, which is absolutely essential.
10 Lift the head(s) off the engine. If resistance is felt, don't pry between the head and block as damage to the mating surfaces will result. Recheck for head bolts that may have been overlooked, then use a hammer and block of wood to tap up on the head and break the gasket seal. Be careful because there are locating dowels in the block which position each head. As a last resort, pry each head up at the rear corner only and be careful not to damage anything.
11 After removal, place the head on blocks of wood to prevent damage to the gasket surfaces.

Installation

12 The mating surfaces of each cylinder head and block must be perfectly clean when the head is installed.
13 Use a gasket scraper to remove all traces of carbon and old gasket material **(see illustration)**, then clean the mating surfaces with lacquer thinner or acetone. If there's oil on the mating surfaces when the head is installed, the gasket may not seal correctly and leaks may develop. When working on the block, it's a good idea to cover the lifter valley with shop rags to keep debris out of the engine. Use a shop rag or vacuum cleaner to remove any debris that falls into the cylinders.
14 Check the block and head mating surfaces for nicks, deep scratches and other damage. If damage is slight, it can be removed

8.16a Position the new gasket over the dowel pins (arrows) . . .

8.16b . . . with the correct side facing up

with a file; if it's excessive, machining may be the only alternative.

15   Use a tap of the correct size to chase the threads in the head bolt holes. Dirt, corrosion, sealant and damaged threads will affect torque readings.

16   Position the new gasket over the dowel pins in the block. Some gaskets are marked TOP or THIS SIDE UP to ensure correct installation **(see illustrations)**.

17   Carefully position the head on the block without disturbing the gasket.

18   Apply RTV sealant or equivalent to the threads and the undersides of the bolt heads. Install the bolts in the correct locations - two different lengths are used **(see illustration)**. Here's where the cardboard holder comes in handy.

19   Tighten the bolts, using the recommended sequence **(see illustration)**, to the torque listed in this Chapter's Specifications. Then, using the same sequence, turn each bolt the amount of angle listed in this Chapter's Specifications.

20   The remaining installation steps are the reverse of removal.

21   Change the engine oil and filter (see Chapter 1).

9   Hydraulic lifters - removal, inspection and installation

Refer to illustrations 9.4, 9.5 and 9.6

1   A noisy valve lifter can be isolated when the engine is idling. Hold a mechanic's stethoscope or a length of hose near the location of each valve while listening at the other end. Another method is to remove the valve cover and, with the engine idling, touch each of the valve spring retainers, one at a time. If a valve lifter is defective, it'll be evident from the shock felt at the retainer each time the valve seats.

2   The most likely causes of noisy valve lifters are dirt trapped inside the lifter and lack of oil flow, viscosity or pressure. Before condemning the lifters, check the oil for fuel contamination, correct level, cleanliness and correct viscosity.

Removal

3   Remove the valve cover(s) and intake manifold as described in Sections 3 and 6.

4   Remove the rocker arms and pushrods (see Section 4). On 3100 engines, remove the bolts holding the roller lifter guide to the block, and remove the two roller lifter guides **(see illustration)**. Mark the guides as to which side

8.18 Two different length cylinder head bolts are used - apply sealant to the threads and the undersides of the bolt heads (arrows)

they came from. **Note:** On 2002 3.1L models, first remove the oil splash shield by bending the spring clips that secure the shield to the cylinder heads.

5   There are several ways to extract the lifters from the bores. A special tool designed to grip and remove lifters is manufactured by many tool companies and is widely available, but it may not be required in every case. On newer engines without a lot of varnish buildup, the lifters can often be removed with a small

8.19 Cylinder head bolt TIGHTENING SEQUENCE (reverse the sequence when loosening the bolts)

9.4 Remove the bolts (A) and pull up the roller lifter guides (B)

9.5 A magnetic pick-up tool or a scribe can be used to remove the lifters

9.6 Store the lifters in a box like this to ensure installation in their original locations

10.7 Remove the vibration damper-to-crankshaft bolt (arrow) - it's very tight, so use a six-point socket and a breaker bar

magnet or even with your fingers. A machinist's scribe with a bent end can be used to pull the lifters out by positioning the point under the retainer ring in the top of each lifter **(see illustration)**. **Caution:** *Don't use pliers to remove the lifters unless you intend to replace them with new ones (along with the camshaft). The pliers may damage the precision machined and hardened lifters, rendering them useless.*

6   Before removing the lifters, arrange to store them in a clearly labeled box to ensure they're reinstalled in their original locations. Remove the lifters and store them where they won't get dirty **(see illustration)**. **Note:** *Some engines may have both standard and 0.010-inch oversize lifters installed at the factory. They are marked on the block at the lifter boss and will have 0.25 mm OS stamped on it.*

Inspection and installation

7   Parts for valve lifters are not available separately. The work required to remove them from the engine again if cleaning is unsuccessful outweighs any potential savings from repairing them. Refer to Chapter 2, Part B, for lifter inspection procedures and Part H for camshaft inspection procedures. If the lifters are worn, they must be replaced with new ones. **Note:** *If the lifters are non-roller type, the camshaft must be replaced as well - never install used non-roller lifters with a new camshaft or new non-roller lifters with a used camshaft.*

8   When reinstalling used lifters, make sure they're replaced in their original bores. Soak new lifters in oil to remove trapped air. Coat all lifters with moly-base grease or engine assembly lube prior to installation.

9   The remaining installation steps are the reverse of removal.

10   Run the engine and check for oil leaks.

10 Vibration damper - removal and installation

Refer to illustrations 10.7, 10.8 and 10.9
Caution: *On some engines a rubber sleeve connects the inertia weight to the vibration damper. Take care when working on the vibration damper that you do not accidentally shift*

the inertia weight's position relative to the sleeve or damper, as this will upset the tuning of the vibration damper.

Removal

1   Disconnect the negative battery cable from the battery. **Caution:** *On models equipped with the Theftlock audio system, be sure the lockout feature is turned off before performing any procedure which requires disconnecting the battery.*

2   Loosen the lug nuts on the right front wheel.

3   Raise the vehicle and support it securely on jackstands.

4   Remove the right front wheel.

5   Remove the right front inner fender splash shield.

6   Remove the serpentine drivebelt (see Chapter 1).

7   On automatic transaxle equipped models, remove the driveplate cover and position a large screwdriver in the ring gear teeth to keep the crankshaft from turning while an assistant removes the vibration damper-to-crankshaft bolt **(see illustration)**. On manual transaxle equipped models, engage high gear and apply the brakes while an assistant

removes the vibration damper bolt. The bolt is normally very tight, so use a large breaker bar and a six-point socket. **Note:** *On later models it may be necessary to lower the right side of the subframe to allow access to the vibration damper bolt. Place a floor jack under the subframe's front center crossmember. Loosen the left side bolts (DO NOT REMOVE THEM!) then remove the right side bolts and lower the right side to access the damper.*

8   Pull the damper off the crankshaft with a bolt-type puller **(see illustration)**. Leave the Woodruff key in place in the end of the crankshaft.

Installation

9   Installation is the reverse of removal. Be sure to apply moly-base grease to the seal contact surface of the damper hub (if it isn't lubricated, the seal lip could be damaged and oil leakage would result). Align the damper hub keyway with the Woodruff key **(see illustration)**.

10   Tighten the vibration damper-to-crankshaft bolt to the torque listed in this Chapter's Specifications.

11   Reinstall the remaining parts in the reverse order of removal.

10.8 Use a puller that bolts to the vibration damper hub; jaw-type pullers will damage the vibration damper

10.9 The damper keyway must be aligned with the woodruff key (arrow) in the crankshaft nose

11.2 Carefully pry the old seal out of the timing chain cover - don't damage the crankshaft in the process

11.3 Drive the new seal into place with a large socket and hammer

11 Crankshaft front oil seal - replacement

Refer to illustrations 11.2 and 11.3

1   Remove the vibration damper (see Section 10).

2   Note how the seal is installed - the new one must be installed to the same depth and facing the same way. Carefully pry the oil seal out of the cover with a seal puller or a large screwdriver **(see illustration)**. Be very careful not to distort the cover or scratch the crankshaft! Wrap electrician's tape around the tip of the screwdriver to avoid damage to the crankshaft.

3   Apply clean engine oil or multi-purpose grease to the outer edge of the new seal, then install it in the cover with the lip (spring side) facing IN. Drive the seal into place **(see illustration)** with a large socket and a hammer (if a large socket isn't available, a piece of pipe will also work). Make sure the seal enters the bore squarely and stop when the front face is at the proper depth.

4   Reinstall the vibration damper.

12 Timing chain cover - removal and installation

Refer to illustrations 12.5 and 12.16

1   Disconnect the negative battery cable from the battery. **Caution:** *On models equipped with the Theftlock audio system, be sure the lockout feature is turned off before performing any procedure which requires disconnecting the battery.*

2   Loosen, but do not remove, the water pump pulley bolts, then remove the serpentine drivebelt (see Chapter 1).

3   Remove the water pump pulley (see Chapter 3).

4   Remove the vibration damper (see Section 10).

5   Unbolt the drivebelt tensioner **(see illustration)** and idler, if equipped.

6   Drain the coolant and engine oil (see Chapter 1).

7   Remove the alternator and loosen the mounting bracket (see Chapter 5).

8   Unbolt the power steering pump (if equipped) and tie it aside (see Chapter 10). Leave the hoses connected.

9   Unbolt the flywheel/driveplate cover below the transaxle.

10   Remove the starter (see Chapter 5).

11   Remove the oil pan (see Section 14).

12   Disconnect the coolant hoses from the fill pipe and water pump.

13   Unbolt the spark plug wire shield at the water pump.

14   Disconnect the canister purge hose and tie it aside.

15   If necessary, remove the crankshaft position sensor assembly from the timing chain cover (see Chapter 6).

16   Remove the timing chain cover-to-engine block bolts **(see illustration)**. Note that some of the bolts require T-40 and T-50 Torx bits for removal.

17   Separate the cover from the engine. If it's stuck, tap it with a soft-face hammer, but don't try to pry it off.

18   Use a gasket scraper to remove all traces of old gasket material and sealant from the cover and engine block. The cover is made of aluminum, so be careful not to nick or gouge it. Clean the gasket sealing surfaces with lacquer thinner or acetone.

19   Apply a thin layer of RTV sealant or equivalent to both sides of the new gasket, then position the gasket on the engine block (the dowel pins should keep it in place). Attach the cover to the engine and install the bolts.

20   Apply sealant to the bottom of the gasket. Follow a criss-cross pattern when tightening the fasteners and work up to the torque listed in this Chapter's Specifications in three steps.

21   The remainder of installation is the reverse of removal.

22   Add oil and coolant, start the engine and check for leaks.

13 Timing chain and sprockets - inspection, removal and installation

Refer to illustrations 13.3a and 13.3b

Inspection

1   The timing chain should be replaced with a new one if the engine has high mileage, the chain has visible damage, or total freeplay midway between the sprockets exceeds one-inch. Failure to replace a worn timing chain may result in erratic engine performance, loss of power and decreased fuel mileage. Loose chains can jump timing. In the worst case, chain jumping or breakage will result in severe engine damage.

Removal

2   Remove the timing chain cover (see Section 12) and loosen the camshaft sprocket bolt(s) two turns but do not remove them. **Note:** *Earlier models use three bolts to retain the camshaft sprocket while later models use a single bolt to retain the camshaft sprocket.*

3   Temporarily install the vibration damper bolt and turn the crankshaft with the bolt to align the timing marks on the crankshaft and camshaft sprockets **(see illustrations)**. On early models the timing marks should be at the top (12 o'clock position). On later models when number 1 piston is at TDC, the crankshaft sprocket timing mark should align at the 12 o'clock position with the mark on the bottom of the chain tensioner plate, and the small hole in the camshaft sprocket should be at the

12.5 The drivebelt tensioner is secured to the timing chain cover by a bolt (arrow)

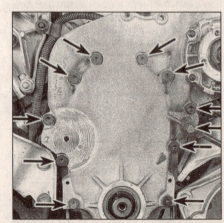

12.16 Timing chain cover bolt locations (arrows)

13.3a On early models the timing marks (arrows) on the sprockets should be at the top (12 o'clock position) - a straight line should pass through the camshaft sprocket timing mark, the center of the camshaft, the crankshaft sprocket timing mark and the center of the crankshaft

6 o'clock position, aligned with the timing mark in the top of the chain tensioner plate.

4   Remove the camshaft sprocket bolts. Do not turn the camshaft in the process (if you do, realign the timing marks before the bolts are removed).

5   Use two large screwdrivers to carefully pry the camshaft sprocket off the camshaft dowel pin. Slip the timing chain and camshaft sprocket off the engine.

6   Timing chains and sprockets should be replaced in sets. If you intend to install a new timing chain, remove the crankshaft sprocket with a puller and install a new one. Be sure to align the key in the crankshaft with the keyway in the sprocket during installation.

7   Inspect the timing chain damper (guide) for cracks and wear and replace it if necessary. The damper is mounted in between camshaft and crankshaft sprockets and is held to the engine block by two bolts **(see illustrations 13.3a or 13.3b).**

8   Clean the timing chain and sprockets

13.3b On later models the timing marks on the sprockets should align as shown - a straight line should pass through the center of the camshaft, camshaft sprocket timing hole (A), the upper mark on the tensioner (B), the lower mark on the tensioner (C), the crankshaft sprocket timing mark (D) and the center of the crankshaft

with solvent and dry them with compressed air (if available). **Warning:** *Wear eye protection when using compressed air.*

9   Inspect the components for wear and damage. Look for teeth that are deformed, chipped, pitted and cracked.

Installation

10   If the camshaft was moved during this procedure, rotate the camshaft to position the dowel pin at 9 o'clock on early models or at 3 o'clock on late models engines. Mesh the timing chain with the camshaft sprocket, then engage it with the crankshaft sprocket. The timing marks should be aligned as shown in **illustration 13.3a and 13.3b. Note:** *If the crankshaft has been disturbed, turn it until the*

"O" stamped on the crankshaft sprocket is exactly at the top.

11   Install the camshaft sprocket bolt(s) and tighten them to the torque listed in this Chapter's Specifications.

12   Lubricate the chain and sprocket with clean engine oil. Install the timing chain cover (see Section 12).

13   The remaining installation steps are the reverse of removal.

14   Oil pan - removal and installation

Refer to illustrations 14.14, 14.15a and 14.15b
Note: *On some early models with automatic transaxle, it may be necessary to remove the transaxle (see Chapter 7) to make clearance for oil pan removal.*

Removal

1   Disconnect the negative cable from the battery (see Chapter 1). **Note:** The following procedure requires that the engine be supported from above with an engine support fixture **(see illustration). Caution:** *On models equipped with the Theftlock audio system, be sure the lockout feature is turned off before performing any procedure which requires disconnecting battery.*

2   Remove the serpentine drivebelt (see Chapter 1).

3   Remove the air conditioning compressor, and the compressor bracket if equipped.

4   On the 3100, remove the electric cooling fan assemblies.

5   Raise the front of the vehicle and place it securely on jackstands. Apply the parking brake and block the rear wheels to keep it from rolling off the stands. Remove the lower splash pan and drain the engine oil (refer to Chapter 1 if necessary).

6   On the 3100, remove the front exhaust pipe and disconnect the connector from the oil level sensor at the bottom of the oil pan. Then remove the transaxle to oil pan braces, if equipped.

7   Remove the steering gear pinch bolt (see Chapter 10). **Caution:** *Be sure to separate the steering gear from the rack and pinion stub shaft to avoid damage to the steering gear and intermediate shaft.*

8   Remove the transaxle mount to frame retaining nuts (see Section 18), then remove the engine-to-frame mount retaining nuts.

9   On 2.8L and 3.1L engines remove the engine mount bracket (horse shoe type bracket) from the front of the engine block (see Section 18).

10   Remove the flywheel/driveplate lower cover.

11   Remove the starter (see Chapter 5).

12   Place a floor jack under the frame front center crossmember.

13   Loosen (but do not remove) the rear drivetrain/front suspension frame bolts, then remove the front frame bolts and lower the front of the frame.

14   On 3100 engines remove the front engine mount from the oil pan **(see illustration).**

14.1 Support the engine with an engine support fixture and chains to the front and rear engine lifting eyes - these tools can be rented

14.14 The front engine mount (A) is between the front of the oil pan and the chassis - remove the bolts (arrows) holding the bracket to the oil pan

14.15a On 2.8L and 3.1L engines simply remove the bolts around the perimeter of the oil pan

14.15b On 3100 engines remove six oil pan side bolts (A indicates three bolts on the radiator side) - also remove the oil filter shield bolts (B) and the nuts and bolts around the perimeter of the oil pan (C)

15   On models equipped with an oil level sensor in the oil pan, disconnect the electrical connector at the sensor and remove the sensor before attempting to remove the oil pan. Remove the oil pan bolts and nuts, then carefully separate the oil pan from the block (see illustrations). Note: *The oil pan rear side bolts on 3100 engines, are difficult to remove, but a box wrench with the correct offset can remove them.* Don't pry between the block and the pan or damage to the sealing surfaces could occur and oil leaks may develop. Instead, tap the pan with a soft-face hammer to break the gasket seal. Don't pry between the block and the pan or damage to the sealing surfaces could occur and oil leaks may develop. Instead, tap the pan with a soft-face hammer to break the gasket seal.

Installation

16   Clean the pan with solvent and remove all old sealant and gasket material from the block and pan mating surfaces. Clean the mating surfaces with lacquer thinner or acetone and make sure the bolt holes in the block are clear. Check the oil pan flange for distortion, particularly around the bolt holes. If necessary, place the pan on a block of wood and use a hammer to flatten and restore the gasket surface.
17   Always use a new gasket whenever the oil pan is installed. Apply a bead of RTV seal-

ant to the front of the gasket, where it contacts the front cover.
18   Place the oil pan in position on the block and install the nuts/bolts finger tight.
19   After the fasteners are installed, tighten them to the torque listed in this Chapter's Specifications. Starting at the center, follow a criss-cross pattern and work up to the final torque in three steps. Note: *On 3100 engines it will be necessary to tighten all the bolts around the perimeter (vertical mounted bolts) of the oil pan first and tighten the side bolts (horizontal mounted bolts) last.*
20   The remaining steps are the reverse of the removal procedure.
21   Refill the engine with oil, run it until normal operating temperature is reached and check for leaks.

15   Oil pump - removal and installation

Refer to illustration 15.2
Refer to illustration 15.2
1   Remove the oil pan (see Section 14).
2   Unbolt the oil pump and lower it from the engine (see illustration). Note: *The oil pump driveshaft will come out with the pump as you lower it. It's a rod with a flat-sided portion at each end.*
3   If the pump is defective, replace it with a

new one - don't reuse the original or attempt to rebuild it. Inspect the ends of the oil pump driveshaft and the plastic collar that retains the driveshaft to the oil pump. If there are signs of wear on the shaft or if the plastic collar is cracked or missing, replace the shaft with a new one. Note: *The plastic collar centers the oil pump driveshaft over the oil pump shaft. If the collar is not used or is missing, damage to the oil pump driveshaft and the oil pump will occur. A new plastic collar is usually included with a new oil pump or driveshaft.*
4   Prime the pump by pouring clean engine oil into the pick-up screen while turning the pump driveshaft.
5   To install the pump, turn the flat on the driveshaft so it mates with the slot in the oil pump shaft. Make sure the plastic collar is fitted over the oil pump-to-oil pump driveshaft joint, then install the oil pump and driveshaft assembly into the block while engaging the upper end of the oil pump driveshaft into the oil pump drive.
6   Install the pump mounting bolt and tighten it to the torque listed in this Chapter's Specifications.
7   The remainder of assembly is the reverse of the removal procedure.

16   Flywheel/driveplate - removal and installation

Refer to Part B and follow the procedure outlined there. However, use the bolt torque listed in this Chapter's Specifications.

17   Rear main oil seal - replacement

Refer to Part B and follow the procedure outlined there.

18   Engine mounts - check and replacement

Refer to illustration 18.1
Refer to Part B and follow the procedure outlined there.

15.2 Oil pump mounting bolt location (arrow)

18.1 V6 engine torque strut (front)

Chapter 2 Part E
3.4 liter V6 engine

Contents

	Section
Camshaft carrier - removal and installation	12
Camshaft carrier cover - removal and installation	11
Camshafts, lifters, sprockets and oil seals - removal, inspection and installation	13
Camshaft timing procedure	14
Crankshaft front oil seal - replacement	6
Crankshaft pulley and vibration damper – removal and installation	5
Cylinder compression check	See Chapter 2H
Cylinder head - removal and installation	16
Drivebelt check, adjustment and replacement	See Chapter 1
Engine mounts - check and replacement	24
Engine oil and filter change	See Chapter 1
Engine overhaul - general information	See Chapter 2H
Engine - removal and installation	See Chapter 2H
Exhaust manifolds - removal and installation	4
Flywheel/driveplate - removal and installation	22
General information	1
Intake manifold - removal and installation	3
Intermediate shaft timing belt sprocket and oil seal - removal and installation	17

	Section
Oil pan - removal and installation	20
Oil pump - removal, inspection and installation	21
Rear main oil seal - replacement	23
Repair operations possible with the engine in the vehicle	2
Spark plug replacement	See Chapter 1
Timing belt covers - removal and installation	7
Timing belt - inspection, removal and installation	9
Timing belt tensioner plate and actuator- removal and installation	8
Timing belt tensioner pulley and arm assembly - removal and installation	10
Timing chain, sprockets and tensioner - inspection, removal and installation	19
Timing chain cover - removal and installation	18
Top Dead Center (TDC) for number one piston - locating	See Chapter 2H
Valve springs, retainers and seals - replacement	15
Water pump - removal and installation	See Chapter 3

Specifications

General
Cylinder numbers (drivebelt end-to-transaxle end)	
Front bank (radiator side)	2-4-6
Rear bank	1-3-5
Firing order	1-2-3-4-5-6

Camshafts
Lobe lift	
Intake	0.370 in
Exhaust	0.370 in
Journal diameter	
1994 and earlier	2.165 to 2.166 in
1995 and later	2.1643 to 2.154 in
Journal clearance	
1994 and earlier	0.0015 to 0.0035 in
1995 and later	0.0019 to 0.0040 in

Oil pump
Gear backlash	0.0037 to 0.0077 in
Gear length	1.199 to 1.200 in
Gear diameter	1.498 to 1.500 in
Gear housing depth	1.202 to 1.205 in
Gear housing inner diameter	1.504 to 1.506 in
Gear side clearance	0.003 to 0.004 in
Gear end clearance	0.002 to 0.006 in
Pressure valve-to-bore clearance	0.0015 to 0.0035 in

1996 3.4L V6 engine

Cylinder and coil terminal locations

Torque specifications   Ft-lbs (unless otherwise indicated)

Note: One foot-pound (ft-lb) of torque is equivalent to 12 inch-pounds (in-lbs) of torque. Torque values below approximately 15 foot-pounds are expressed in inch-pounds, because most foot-pound torque wrenches are not accurate at these smaller values.

Cam carrier cover bolts	97 in-lb
Cam carrier-to-cylinder head bolts	20
Camshaft sprocket bolts	96
Cylinder head bolts	
First step	44
Second step	Rotate an additional 90-degrees (1/4-turn)
Exhaust manifold-to-cylinder head bolts	
Nut	
1995 and earlier	18
1996 and later	116 in-lbs
Stud	13
Flywheel/driveplate-to-crankshaft bolts	60
Intake manifold-to-cylinder head bolts/nuts	
1994 and earlier	30
1995	22
1996 and later	116 in-lbs
Oil pan bolts/nuts	
Pan bolt (two at transaxle end)	18 to 20
Others	
1994 and earlier	89 in-lbs
1995 and later	97 in-lbs
Oil pump	
Mounting bolt	40 to 43
Drive bolt	27
Cover bolt	89 in-lbs
Timing belt cover bolts	89 in-lbs
Timing chain tensioner bolt	20
Vibration damper bolt	79

1   General information

Refer to illustration 1.4

This Part of Chapter 2 is devoted to in-vehicle repair procedures for the 3.4 liter V6 engine. The 3.4L engine became available in 1990 and was produced through 1996; it is utilized in the Pontiac Grand Prix, Oldsmobile Cutlass Supreme and the Chevrolet Lumina models only. This engine utilizes a cast-iron block with six cylinders arranged in a "V" shape at a 60-degree angle between the two banks.

The overhead cam aluminum cylinder heads have two exhaust valves and two intake valves for each cylinder, and have pressed-in valve guides and valve seats.

The camshafts are located inside aluminum cam carrier housings that are located on top of each cylinder head. Each cam carrier contains two camshafts, one for the exhaust valves and one for the intake valves. The camshaft thrust plates are at rear of the carriers. The aluminum of the carriers serves as the bearing surface for the camshafts.

The engine is easily identified by looking at the designation printed on the fuel rail cover **(see illustration)**. To positively identify this engine, locate the vehicle identification number on the left front corner of the instrument panel. This plate is visible frcm outside the vehicle (**see illustration 1.1** in Chapter 2, Part B). The eighth character in the sequence is the engine designation:

X = 3.4L DOHC V6 engine

Information concerning engine removal and installation and engine overhaul can be found in Part H of this Chapter. The following repair procedures are based on the assumption the engine is installed in the vehicle. If the engine has been removed from the vehicle and mounted on a stand, many of the steps outlined in this Part of Chapter 2 will not apply.

2   Repair operations possible with the engine in the vehicle

Many major repair operations can be accomplished without removing the engine from the vehicle.

Clean the engine compartment and the exterior of the engine with some type of degreaser before any work is done. It'll make the job easier and help keep dirt out of the internal areas of the engine.

Depending on the components involved, it may be helpful to remove the hood to improve access to the engine as repairs are performed (refer to Chapter 11 if necessary). Cover the fenders to prevent damage to the paint. Special pads are available, but an old bedspread or blanket will also work.

If vacuum, exhaust, oil or coolant leaks develop, indicating a need for gasket or seal replacement, the repairs can generally be done with the engine in the vehicle. The intake and exhaust manifold gaskets, timing chain cover gasket, oil pan gasket, crankshaft oil seals and

1.4 3.4 liter double overhead cam (DOHC) V6 engine

cylinder head gaskets are all accessible with the engine in place.

Exterior engine components, such as the intake and exhaust manifolds, the oil pan (and the oil pump), the water pump, the starter motor, the alternator and the fuel system components can be removed for repair with the engine in place.

Since the cylinder heads can be removed without pulling the engine, valve component servicing can also be accomplished with the engine in the vehicle. Replacement of the timing chain and sprockets is also possible with the engine in the vehicle.

In extreme cases caused by a lack of necessary equipment, repair or replacement

3.4 Thermostat housing outlet (arrow)

4.3 Remove the exhaust crossover pipe from the manifold

1   *Exhaust manifold*
2   *Exhaust crossover pipe*
3   *Engine torque strut*

4.15 The exhaust crossover pipe (upper arrow) attaches to each exhaust manifold with nuts (lower arrows)

of piston rings, pistons, connecting rods and rod bearings is possible with the engine in the vehicle. However, this practice is not recommended because of the cleaning and preparation work that must be done to the components involved.

3   Intake manifold - removal and installation

Removal

Refer to illustration 3.4

1   Disconnect the negative battery cable from the battery. **Caution:** *On models equipped with the Theftlock audio system, be sure the lockout feature is turned off before performing any procedure which requires disconnecting the battery.*
2   Relieve the fuel system pressure, then remove the fuel rail (see Chapter 4). **Note:** *When disconnecting fuel line fittings, be prepared to catch some fuel with a rag, then cap the fittings to prevent contamination.*
3   Remove the plenum (see Chapter 4).
4   Remove the radiator hose from the thermostat housing **(see illustration)**.
5   Remove the connector from the coolant temperature sensor.
6   Remove the heater pipe nut at the throttle body.
7   Remove the manifold mounting bolts and nuts, then separate the manifold from the engine. Don't pry between the manifold and heads, as damage to the soft aluminum gasket sealing surfaces may result. If you're installing a new manifold, transfer all fittings and sensors to the new manifold.

Installation

Note: *The mating surfaces of the cylinder heads, block and manifold must be perfectly clean when the manifold is installed. Gasket removal solvents are available at most auto parts stores and may be helpful when removing old gasket material that's stuck to the heads and manifold (since the manifold is made of aluminum, aggressive scraping can cause damage). Be sure to follow the directions printed on the container.*
8   Lift the old gasket off. Use a gasket scraper to remove all traces of sealant and old gasket material, then clean the mating surfaces with lacquer thinner or acetone. If there's old sealant or oil on the mating surfaces when the manifold is installed, oil or vacuum leaks may develop. Use a vacuum cleaner to remove any gasket material that falls into the intake ports or the lifter valley.
9   Use a tap of the correct size to chase the threads in the bolt holes, if necessary, then use compressed air (if available) to remove the debris from the holes. **Warning:** *Wear safety glasses or a face shield to protect your eyes when using compressed air!*
10   Install the intake manifold gasket **(see illustration 3.8)**.
11   Carefully lower the manifold into place and install the mounting bolts/nuts finger tight. **Note:** *To ease reassembly, you can temporarily install two M8 x 1.25 x 50 mm bolts, with washers, in the vertical holes in the intake manifold. This will help align the intake bolt grommet bores with the threaded holes in the cylinder heads.*
12   Tighten the mounting bolts/nuts in two steps, working from the center out, in a circular pattern, until they're all at the torque listed in this Chapter's Specifications. If necessary, remove the two bolts from the vertical holes in the intake manifold.
13   Install the remaining components in the reverse order of removal.
14   Change the oil and filter and refill the cooling system (see Chapter 1). Start the engine and check for leaks.

4   Exhaust manifolds - removal and installation

Front Manifold

Refer to illustration 4.3

1   Disconnect the negative battery cable from the battery. **Caution:** *On models equipped with the Theftlock audio system, be sure the lockout feature is turned off before*

performing any procedure which requires disconnecting the battery.
2   Remove the air cleaner assembly (see Chapter 4).
3   Remove the exhaust crossover pipe from the manifold **(see illustration)**.
4   Remove the cooling fans (see Chapter 3).
5   On manual transmission cars, remove the front hose from the air pipe.
6   Remove the mounting nuts, then remove the front exhaust manifold from the cylinder head.
7   Clean the mating surfaces to remove all traces of old gasket material, then inspect the manifold for distortion and cracks. Warpage can be checked with a precision straightedge held against the mating flange. if a feeler gauge thicker than 0.030-inch can be inserted between the straightedge and flange surface, take the manifold to an automotive machine shop for resurfacing.
8   Place the manifold in position with a new gasket and install the mounting nuts finger tight.
9   Starting in the middle and working out toward the ends, tighten the mounting nuts a little at a time until all of them are at the torque listed in this Chapter's Specifications.
10   Install the remaining components in the reverse order of removal.
11   Start the engine and check for exhaust leaks between the manifold and cylinder head and between the manifold and exhaust pipe.

Rear manifold

Refer to illustration 4.15

12   Disconnect the negative battery cable from the battery. **Caution:** *On models equipped with the Theftlock audio system, be sure the lockout feature is turned off before performing any procedure which requires disconnecting the battery.*
13   Remove the air cleaner and duct assembly.
14   If the car is equipped with an automatic transaxle, remove the rear cam carrier (see Section 12).
15   Remove the exhaust crossover pipe from the manifold **(see illustration)**.

16   Remove the EGR tube from the exhaust manifold (see Chapter 4).
17   Set the parking brake, block the rear wheels and raise the front of the car supporting it securely on jackstands.
18   Remove the front exhaust pipe and catalytic converter assembly.
19   Remove the oxygen sensor.
20   On manual transaxle cars, remove the exhaust pipe front heat shield.
21   If necessary, remove the rear alternator bracket.
22   On automatic transaxle cars, remove the dipstick tube.
23   If necessary, remove the steering gear intermediate shaft.
24   Remove the exhaust manifold nuts.
25   If necessary, support the engine from underneath, remove the rear cradle bolts, then lower the engine and remove the steering gear heat shield.
26   Remove the exhaust manifold.
27   Clean the mating surfaces to remove all traces of old gasket material, then inspect the manifold for distortion and cracks. Warpage can be checked with a precision straightedge held against the mating flange. If a feeler gauge thicker than 0.030-inch can be inserted between the straightedge and flange surface, take the manifold to an automotive machine shop for resurfacing.
28   Place the manifold in position with a new gasket and install the mounting nuts finger tight.
29   Starting in the middle and working out toward the ends, tighten the mounting nuts a little at a time until all of them are at the torque listed in this Chapter's Specifications.
30   Install the remaining components in the reverse order of removal.
31   Start the engine and check for exhaust leaks between the manifold and cylinder head and between the manifold and exhaust pipe.

5   Crankshaft pulley and vibration damper - removal and installation

Removal

Refer to illustrations 5.7 and 5.9
1   Disconnect the negative battery cable from the battery. **Caution:** *On models equipped with the Theftlock audio system, be sure the lockout feature is turned off before performing any procedure which requires disconnecting the battery.*
2   Loosen the lug nuts on the right front wheel.
3   Raise the vehicle and support it securely on jackstands.
4   Remove the right front wheel.
5   Remove the right front inner fender splash shield.
6   Remove the serpentine drivebelt (see Chapter 1).
7   On automatic transaxle equipped models, remove the driveplate cover and position a large screwdriver in the ring gear teeth to

5.7 Have an assistant hold the ring gear with a large screwdriver as the pulley-to-crankshaft bolt is loosened/tightened

keep the crankshaft from turning while an assistant removes the crankshaft bolt **(see illustration)**. On manual transaxle equipped models, engage high gear and apply the brakes while an assistant removes the damper bolt. **Note:** *The bolt is normally very tight, so use a large breaker bar and a six-point socket.*
8   Remove the pulley-to-damper bolts, then remove the pulley from the damper.
9   Pull the damper off the crankshaft with a bolt-type puller **(see illustration)**. Leave the Woodruff key in place in the end of the crankshaft.

Installation

10   Installation is the reverse of removal. Be sure to apply moly-base grease to the seal contact surface of the damper hub (if it isn't lubricated, the seal lip could be damaged and oil leakage would result). Align the hub keyway with the Woodruff key.
11   Tighten the damper-to-crankshaft bolt to the torque listed in this Chapter's Specifications.
12   Install the pulley on the damper and torque its bolts to 37 ft-lb.

5.9 Use a puller that bolts to the vibration damper hub; jaw type pullers will damage the vibration damper

13   Reinstall the remaining parts in the reverse order of removal.

6   Crankshaft front oil seal - replacement

Refer to illustrations 6.2 and 6.3
1   Remove the crankshaft pulley and vibration damper (see Section 5).
2   Note how the seal is installed - the new one must be installed to the same depth and facing the same way. Carefully pry the oil seal out of the cover with a seal puller **(see illustration)** or a large screwdriver. Be very careful not to distort the cover or scratch the crankshaft! Wrap electrician's tape around the tip of the screwdriver to avoid damage to the crankshaft.
3   Apply clean engine oil or multi-purpose grease to the outer edge of the new seal, then install it in the cover with the lip (spring side) facing IN. Drive the seal into place **(see illustration)** with a large socket and a hammer (if a large socket isn't available, a piece of pipe will also work). Make sure the seal enters the

6.2 Carefully pry the old seal out with a seal removal tool (shown) or a large screwdriver

6.3 Drive the new seal into place with a large socket and hammer

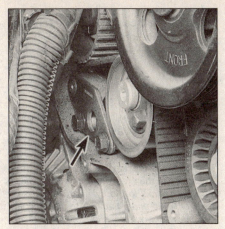

8.8 Timing belt tensioner side plate (arrow)

bore squarely; stop when the front face is at the proper depth.
4   Reinstall the vibration damper and the crankshaft pulley.

7   Timing belt covers - removal and installation

Front and rear covers
1   Remove the spark plug wire cover (front cover only). On 1996 and later models remove the ignition coils and the coil mounting bracket to access the rear cover.
2   Remove the retaining bolts.
3   Remove the covers.

Center Cover
4   Remove the ECM harness cover.
5   Remove the serpentine belt (see Chapter 1) and the serpentine belt tensioner.
6   Remove the clip holding the power steering line at the alternator.
7   Remove the cover bolts, then the cover.
8   Installation is the reverse of removal.

8   Timing belt tensioner plate and actuator - removal and installation

Removal
Refer to illustration 8.8
1   Remove the plenum (see Chapter 4).
2   Remove the serpentine belt (see Chapter 1).
3   If necessary, move the ECM aside, then remove its mounting bracket.
4   Remove the timing belt covers (see Section 7).
5   Align the timing marks (see Section 14).
6   Loosely clamp the two camshaft sprockets on each side of the engine together using clamping pliers or equivalent.
7   If the timing belt is not going to be removed, use a C-clamp and a protective cloth to hold the belt in position on the rear

exhaust cam sprocket. **Note:** *Make sure there is no deflection in the sprocket. If there is, set up your clamp again.*
8   Remove the retaining bolts from the tensioner side plate, then remove the side plate **(see illustration)**.
9   Remove the tensioner actuator from its base with a rotating motion. **Note:** *When you do this the tensioner will extend to its maximum travel.* **Caution:** *A tapered bushing is positioned between the actuator and the mounting base; be careful not to lose it when removing the actuator.*

Installation
10   Lightly clamp the body of the tensioner actuator in a vise with its rod tip facing down. **Caution:** *Do not position the actuator in a manner that will cause damage to the rod tip or the rubber boot.*
11   Leave the actuator in this position for at least five minutes to allow the oil to drain into the boot end.
12   Find a standard paper clip - one with no serrations - and straighten it out so that you have a length of about one inch. Form the remaining portion of the paper clip into a loop.
13   Remove the rubber end plug from the rear of the actuator. Do not remove the vent plug.
14   Push your paper clip through the center hole in the vent plug, and on into the pilot hole.
15   Retract the tensioner plunger by pushing the rod tip against a table top while turning the screw at the rear of the actuator clockwise.
16   When the tensioner plunger is fully retracted, align the screw slot with the vent hole and push the paper clip into the slot to retain the plunger.
17   If oil was lost from the tensioner, fill it to the bottom of the plug hole with a synthetic 5W-30 engine oil. **Note:** *Fill the tensioner only when it is fully retracted and the paper clip is installed.*
18   Install the rubber end plug; be sure it is snapped fully into place and fits flush against the body of the tensioner.
19   Check to be sure that all bushings and the holes they fit into are in good condition

and properly installed, then fit the actuator onto its base. Be sure the actuator is free and can rotate under its own weight. **Note:** *Do not oil the bushings.* **Caution:** *Make sure the tensioner's tapered fulcrum is properly seated in its bushing.*
20   Install the tensioner plate assembly and tighten the bolts to the torque listed in this Part's Specifications.
21   Make sure the actuator rod tip is seated in the tensioner pulley socket, then remove the paper clip; this will allow the actuator to extend to its normal position.
22   Gently rotate the pulley counterclockwise into the belt.
23   Remove the clamps from the sprockets and belt.
24   Seat the belt by rotating the engine three full turns clockwise (the direction of crankshaft rotation). **Caution:** *Do not rotate the engine counterclockwise.*
25   Align the timing marks on the crankshaft pulley and timing chain cover, then inspect the camshaft timing marks to be sure the cam timing is correct.
26   Reassembly is reverse of disassembly.

9   Timing belt - inspection, removal and installation

Refer to illustration 9.3

Inspection
1   Remove the timing belt covers (see Section 7).
2   Inspect the timing belt for signs of wear, such as cracks or tears, and for oil contamination. Make sure the belt's teeth are in good condition. Check also for fraying or for wear around one edge of the belt, which would indicate misalignment of cam/belt drive components. Replace the belt as necessary.
3   Check the camshaft belt length. Insert a very thin, narrow ruler under the tensioner pulley until it contacts the tensioner base **(see illustration)**. If the belt is too long, the ruler will drop into the groove in the tensioner bracket. Check this by recording the length indicated on the ruler. If the depth from the edge of the pulley to the base of the tensioner

9.3 To check the camshaft timing belt length, insert a small ruler between the tensioner pulley and the front cover flange, and measure the depth

1   *Tensioner pulley*
2   *Intermediate shaft sprocket*

10.4 After you get the pivot bolt started, rotate the arm counterclockwise until the square lug is at the 6 o'clock position

11.3 Remove the camshaft carrier cover bolts with a socket, ratchet and extension

measures 42.6 mm or less, the length of the belt is OK. If the ruler shows 45.1 mm or more, it means it dropped into the groove in the tensioner bracket, indicating that the belt is too long and must be replaced.

Removal

> ## ** CAUTION **
> The timing system is complex. Severe engine damage will occur if you make any mistakes. Do not attempt this procedure unless you are highly experienced with this type of repair. If you are at all unsure of your abilities, consult an expert. Double-check all your work and be sure everything is correct before you attempt to start the engine.

4   Remove the timing belt tensioner and pulley (see Section 8).
5   If you're going to reuse the belt, mark the direction of rotation on the belt.
6   Remove the belt by sliding it carefully off the sprockets and pulleys. **Caution:** *Do not kink, fold, twist or pry on the belt or you will cause damage.*

Installation

> ## ** CAUTION **
> Before starting the engine, carefully rotate the crankshaft by hand through at least two full revolutions (use a socket and breaker bar on the crankshaft pulley center bolt). If you feel any resistance, STOP! There is something wrong - most likely valves are contacting the pistons. You must find the problem before proceeding. Check your work and see if any updated repair information is available.

7   Start at the intermediate shaft sprocket **(see illustration 9.3)** and route the belt around the other sprockets or pulleys in a counterclockwise direction. **Note:** *Make sure*

you accumulate slack in the belt as you go.
8   Install the tensioner assembly and complete the procedure by following steps 20 through 26 of Section 8.

10 Timing belt tensioner pulley and arm assembly - removal and installation

Removal

1   Remove the timing belt tensioner plate and actuator (see Section 8).
2   Remove the tensioner pulley **(see illustration 9.3)**. **Note:** *The pivot bushing inside the pulley can fall out. Hold it in place with tape or a magnet.*

Installation

Refer to illustration 10.4
Note: *The timing belt should be in place before you install the pulley assembly.*
3   Use a magnet or tape to hold the tensioner pulley's pivot tube in place while you fit the pulley into position. Remove the magnet or tape and thread the pivot bolt into it's hole.
4   After you get the pivot bolt started, rotate the arm counterclockwise until the square lug **(see illustration)** is at the 6 O'clock position. **Note:** *The pivot bushing and tube should be clean, but should not be lubricated.*
5   Tighten the tensioner pulley pivot bolt to 37 ft-lb (50 Nm).
6   Install the timing belt tensioner plate and actuator (see Section 8).

11 Camshaft carrier cover - removal and installation

Removal

Front cover
Refer to illustration 11.3
1   Remove the breather hose from the cover.
2   Remove the spark plug wires from the spark plugs. **Note:** *Be sure each wire is labeled before removal to ensure correct reinstallation.*
3   Remove the carrier cover bolts **(see illustration)**, then remove the cover. **Note:** *If the cover sticks to the cylinder head, use a block of wood and a hammer to dislodge it. If the cover still won't come loose, pry on it carefully, but don't distort the sealing flange.*
4   Remove the gasket and O-rings from the cover.

Rear Cover
5   Remove the plenum (see Chapter 4).
6   Remove the rear timing belt cover (see Section 7).
7   Remove the spark plug wires from the spark plugs (see Chapter 1). **Note:** *Be sure each wire is labeled before removal to ensure correct reinstallation.*
8   Remove the breather hose from the cover.
9   Remove the carrier cover bolts, then remove the cover. **Note:** *If the cover sticks to the cylinder head, use a block of wood and a hammer to dislodge it. If the cover still won't come loose, pry on it carefully, but don't distort the sealing flange.*
10   Remove the gasket and O-rings from the cover.

Installation
Refer to illustration 11.11
11   Installation is the reverse of removal. When installing the cover retaining bolts, be sure the bolt isolators **(see illustration)** are fully seated in the cover, then tighten the bolts to 89 lb-in.

12 Camshaft carrier - removal and installation

Removal

Front camshaft carrier
Refer to illustration 12.10
1   Remove the front camshaft carrier cover (see Section 11).

11.11 Make sure bolt isolators (arrows) are fully seated before installing the cover

12.10 Camshaft carrier with cover removed. The thrust plate cover is the "cap" at the back of the housing (arrow)

2   Remove the timing belt (see Section 9).
3   Remove the exhaust crossover pipe.
4   Drain the coolant and remove the upper radiator hose.
5   Remove the heater pipe hose at the plenum.
6   Remove the front exhaust manifold (see Section 4).
7   Remove the engine torque strut **(see illustration 4.3)**.
8   Remove the front engine coolant pipe.
9   Install fuel line hoses under the camshafts and between the lifters to hold the lifters in place when the carrier is removed. **Note:** *You will need 6 lengths of hose. On the exhaust side the hose dimensions should be 6 x 3/16 inch. On the intake side the hose dimensions should be 3 x 5/32 inch.*
10   Remove the cam carrier mounting bolts, then remove the cam carrier **(see illustration)**.

Rear camshaft carrier

11   Remove the rear camshaft carrier cover (see Section 11).
12   Remove the timing belt (see Section 9).
13   Install fuel line hoses under the camshafts and between the lifters to hold the lifters in place when the carrier is removed (see Step 9). **Note:** *You will need 6 lengths of hose. On the exhaust side, the hose dimensions should be 6 x 3/16 inch. On the intake side, the hose dimensions should be 3 x 5/32 inch.*
14   Remove the camshaft carrier mounting bolts, then remove the cam carrier **(see illustration 12.10)**.

Installation

15   Installation is the reverse of removal. **Caution:** *Before installing the cam carrier, be sure to remove any oil that seeped into the cam carrier-to-cylinder head bolt holes.*

13   Camshaft, lifters, sprockets and oil seal - removal, inspection and installation

Note: *This procedure will require special tools available at automotive tool companies and*

some auto part stores. If the specialty tools, camshaft timing clamps, camshaft sprocket holding tool and camshaft and intermediate shaft sprocket remover, are not available, obtain similar tools and adapt them for this application.*

Removal

1   Remove the cam carrier (see Section 12).
2   Remove the lifters from the cam carrier housing. **Note:** *Keep the lifters in order so that they can be replaced in their original positions.*
3   Turn the camshafts so the "flats" are facing up, then install the special camshaft timing clamp tool (see Step 9 in Section 12).
4   Remove the camshaft sprocket bolts. Use special sprocket holding tool to hold the sprockets while you loosen the bolts.
5   Remove the sprockets with a puller, then remove the flat ring from the sprocket bore.
6   Remove the camshaft thrust plate cover, then the thrust plate **(see illustration 12.10)**.
7   Remove the timing clamp, then remove the camshafts by carefully withdrawing them through the back of the cam carrier. **Caution:** *Be sure you don't damage the camshaft journals inside the carrier when you remove the camshafts.*
8   Remove the seals from the carrier by carefully prying them it out with a screwdriver. **Caution:** *The aluminum seal seating surface in the carrier is easily damaged.*

Inspection

9   Check for damage or pitting on the camshaft lobes. Check the nose of the camshaft for brinelling. Check the camshaft journals inside the carrier for wear or damage. For camshaft inspection, refer to Part H, Section 9. For lifter inspection, refer to Part C, Section 9.

Installation

Caution: *When installing the camshaft, exercise care to avoid damaging the seal.*
Note: *Coat the camshaft lobes and journals with moly-base grease or engine assembly lube prior to installation. When installing the thrust plate, be sure the arrow points up.*
10   Install the camshaft seal using a large socket and a hammer (if a large socket isn't available, a piece of pipe will also work). Make sure the seal enters the bore squarely; stop when the front face is at the same depth as the original seal was. **Note:** *Coat the seal with clean engine oil or multi-purpose grease prior to installation.*
11   The remainder of installation is the reverse of removal. Be sure to check cam timing after reassembly and before starting the engine (see Section 14).

14   Camshaft timing procedure

Refer to illustrations 14.1a and 14.1b
Note: *This procedure will require special tools available at automotive tool companies and some auto part stores. If the specialty tools, camshaft timing clamps, camshaft sprocket holding tool and camshaft and intermediate shaft sprocket remover, are not available, obtain similar tools and adapt them for this application.*
1   Some special tools and procedures are required to adjust the camshaft timing. If you suspect that the camshaft timing is out of adjustment, check to see if the timing marks on the camshaft sprockets are properly aligned when the engine is at top dead center (TDC) on the number 1 cylinder's exhaust stroke. When at #1 TDC exhaust, the timing marks should be aligned **(see illustrations)**. If the timing marks are not aligned as shown, first try to determine if the cause is a slipped

14.1a Timing marks at #1 TDC on exhaust stroke

1   *Camshaft sprocket timing marks (front bank shown). Make sure the camshafts are aligned this way.*
2   *Intermediate shaft sprocket timing mark*
3   *Engine front cover mark*

timing belt. If the belt has slipped, find the cause and replace the belt as required (see Section 9 for belt inspection and replacement). If the belt is good and you suspect the camshafts are out of time, they will have to checked and/or adjusted as follows. **Note:** *The following procedure is based on the timing belt and tensioner already being in place on the engine.*

2   Turn the camshafts so the "flats" are facing up, then install the timing clamps (see Section 13).

3   Loosen the camshaft sprockets bolts so the sprockets can "freewheel." Use special camshaft timing clamp tools to hold the sprockets while you loosen the bolts.

4   Position the crankshaft timing mark at the TDC position **(see illustration 14.1b)**.

5   If necessary, scribe new timing marks on the camshaft sprockets using a straight-edge and a scribe, and remove the old timing marks.

6   Tighten the sprocket bolts at the rear bank camshafts and remove the timing clamp. **Note:** *The "running torque" (the torque required to turn the bolt before it is seated) should be 44-66 lb-ft. If the running torque is either more or less than this specification, replace the shim ring and lock ring and inspect the camshaft for brinelling or damaged threads. The sprocket bolt is fully seated when the edge of the lock ring is flush with the sprocket.*

7   Turn the crankshaft 360 degrees and realign the crankshaft timing mark. **Note:** *The camshafts on the rear bank should now turn with the crankshaft, while the camshafts sprockets on the front bank should still freewheel.*

8   Repeat steps 5 and 6 on the front bank. **Note:** *When the cam timing procedure is complete, the position of the timing flats on the front bank of camshafts should differ from those of the rear bank camshafts by 180 degrees.*

15 Valve springs, retainers and seals - replacement

Refer to illustrations 15.4, 15.8 and 15.16
Note: *Broken valve springs and defective valve stem seals can be replaced without removing the cylinder head. Two special tools and a compressed air source are normally required to perform this operation, so read through this Section carefully and rent or buy the tools before beginning the job. If compressed air isn't available, a length of nylon rope can be used to keep the valves from falling into the cylinder during this procedure.*

1   Remove the cam carrier (see Section 12).

2   Remove the spark plugs from the cylinders which have the defective components. If all of the valve stem seals are being replaced, all of the spark plugs should be removed.

3   Turn the crankshaft until the piston in the

14.1b When the camshaft and intermediate sprocket timing marks are aligned as shown in figure 14.1a, the crank timing mark should be aligned with the pointer on the front cover (arrow)

affected cylinder is at top dead center. If you're replacing all of the valve stem seals, begin with cylinder number one and work on the valves for one cylinder at a time. Move from cylinder-to-cylinder following the firing order sequence (see this Chapter's Specifications).

4   Thread an adapter into the spark plug hole **(see illustration)** and connect an air hose from a compressed air source to it. Most auto parts stores can supply the air hose adapter. **Note:** *Many cylinder compression gauges utilize a screw-in fitting that may work with your air hose quick-disconnect fitting.*

5   Apply compressed air to the cylinder. **Warning:** *The piston may be forced down by compressed air, causing the crankshaft to turn suddenly. If the wrench used when positioning the number one piston at TDC is still attached to the bolt in the crankshaft nose, it could cause damage or injury when the crankshaft moves.*

6   The valves should be held in place by the air pressure. If the valve faces or seats are in poor condition, leaks may prevent air

15.4 This is what the typical air hose adapter that threads into the spark plug hole looks like - they're commonly available at auto parts stores

pressure from retaining the valves - a "valve job" is necessary to correct this problem.

7   If you don't have access to compressed air, an alternative method can be used. Position the piston at a point just before TDC on the compression stroke, then feed a long piece of nylon rope through the spark plug hole until it fills the combustion chamber. Be sure to leave the end of the rope hanging out of the engine so it can be removed easily. Rotate the crankshaft in the normal direction of rotation (clockwise) until slight resistance is felt.

8   Stuff shop rags into the cylinder head holes above and below the valves to prevent parts and tools from falling into the engine, then use a valve spring compressor to compress the spring. Remove the keepers **(see illustration)** with small needle-nose pliers or a magnet.

9   Remove the spring retainer and valve spring, then remove the valve guide seal.

10   Wrap a rubber band or tape around the top of the valve stem so the valve won't fall into the combustion chamber, then release the air pressure. **Note:** *If a rope was used instead of air pressure, turn the crankshaft slightly in the direction opposite normal rotation.*

11   Inspect the valve stem for damage. Rotate the valve in the guide and check the

15.8 Typical engine valves and related components

1   *Keepers*
2   *Retainer*
3   *Oil shield*
4   *O-ring stem seal*
5   *Umbrella or positive type seal*
6   *Spring and damper*
7   *Intake valve*
8   *Retainer/rotator*
9   *Exhaust valve*

15.16 Keepers don't always stay in place, so apply a small dab of grease to each one as shown here before installation - the grease will hold the keepers in place on the valve stem

16.12 Position the new gasket over the dowel pins (arrows)

end for eccentric movement, which would indicate the valve stem is bent.

12   Move the valve up-and-down in the guide and make sure it doesn't bind. If the valve stem binds, either the valve is bent or the guide is damaged. In either case, the head will have to be removed for repair.

13   Reapply air pressure to the cylinder to retain the valve in the closed position, then remove the tape or rubber band from the valve stem. If a rope was used instead of air pressure, rotate the crankshaft in the normal direction of rotation until slight resistance is felt.

14   Lubricate the valve stem with engine oil and install a new valve guide seal.

15   Install the spring in position over the valve.

16   Install the valve spring retainer. Compress the valve spring and carefully install the keepers in the groove. Apply a small dab of grease to the inside of each keeper to hold it in place if necessary (see illustration). Remove the pressure from the spring tool and make sure the keepers are seated.

17   Disconnect the air hose and remove the adapter from the spark plug hole. If a rope was used in place of air pressure, pull it out of the cylinder.

18   Install the spark plug(s) and hook up the wire(s).

19   Install the cam carrier.

20   Start and run the engine, then check for oil leaks and unusual sounds coming from the valve cover area.

16 Cylinder head - removal and installation

Refer to illustrations 16.12 and 16.14
Caution: Allow the engine to cool completely before loosening the cylinder head bolts.
Note: On engines with high mileage and during an overhaul, camshaft lobe height should be checked prior to cylinder head removal (see Part H for instructions).

Removal

1   Remove the cam carrier (see Section 12).

2   Remove the intake manifold (see Section 3).

3   If you're removing the front cylinder head, remove the oil dipstick tube mounting bolt and the electrical connector for the temperature sender. If your removing the rear cylinder head, remove the electrical connector for the oxygen sensor.

4   If you're removing the front cylinder head, remove the exhaust manifold (see Section 4). If you're removing the rear cylinder head, remove the exhaust crossover pipe, separate the exhaust pipe at the exhaust manifold and, on manual transmission cars, remove the rear air hose from the air pipe.

5   If you're removing the rear cylinder head, remove the timing belt tensioner bracket (see Section 8).

6   Lift the head off the engine. If resistance is felt, don't pry between the head and block as damage to the mating surfaces will result. Recheck for head bolts that may have been overlooked, then use a hammer and block of wood to tap up on the head and break the gasket seal. Be careful because there are locating dowels in the block which position each head. As a last resort, pry each head up at the rear corner only and be careful not to damage anything.

7   After removal, place the head on blocks of wood to prevent damage to the gasket surfaces.

Installation

8   The mating surfaces of each cylinder head and block must be perfectly clean when the head is installed.

9   Use a gasket scraper to remove all traces of carbon and old gasket material, then clean the mating surfaces with lacquer thinner or acetone. If there's oil on the mating surfaces when the head is installed, the gasket may not seal correctly and leaks may develop. When working on the block, it's a good idea to cover any holes with shop rags to keep debris out of the engine. Use a shop rag or vacuum cleaner to remove any debris that falls into the cylinders.

TIGHTENING SEQUENCE

1671-2e-16.14 HAYNES

16.14 Cylinder head bolt tightening sequence

10   Check the block and head mating surfaces for nicks, deep scratches and other damage. If damage is slight, it can be removed with a file; if it's excessive, machining may be the only alternative.

11   Use a tap of the correct size to chase the threads in the head bolt holes. Dirt, corrosion, sealant and damaged threads will affect torque readings.

12   Position the new gasket over the dowel pins in the block (see illustration). Be sure the metal tabs between the cylinders are facing up.

13   Carefully position the head on the block without disturbing the gasket.

14   Install the bolts and tighten them in the sequence shown (see illustration) to the torque listed in this Chapter's Specifications. Then, using the same sequence, turn each bolt the amount of angle listed in this Chapter's Specifications.

15   The remaining installation steps are the reverse of removal.

16   Change the engine oil and filter (see Chapter 1).

17 Intermediate shaft timing belt sprocket and oil seal - removal and installation

Removal

1   Align the cam timing marks by turning the engine to cylinder #1 Top Dead Center on the exhaust stroke, then remove the timing belt (see Section 9).

18.5 Engine lift bracket (arrow)

18.16 Unbolt the air conditioning compressor and lay it aside, but DO NOT disconnect the refrigerant lines (arrow)

2   Raise the car and support it on jack-stands.
3   Remove the flywheel inspection cover.
4   On cars with automatic transaxle, position a large screwdriver in the ring gear teeth to keep the crankshaft from turning while an assistant removes the intermediate shaft timing belt sprocket bolt **(see illustration 9.3)**. On cars with manual transaxle, engage high gear and apply the brakes while an assistant removes the sprocket bolt. **Note:** *The intermediate shaft timing belt sprocket bolt is normally very tight, so use a large breaker bar and a six-point socket.*
5   Note the relationship of the sprocket's timing mark to the timing chain cover, then remove the sprocket with a puller. **Caution:** *Avoid pounding on the intermediate shaft or prying on the sprocket as these actions can damage the thrust bearing.*
6   Note how the oil seal is installed - the new one must be installed to the same depth and facing the same way. Carefully pry the oil seal out of the cover with a seal puller or a large screwdriver **(see illustration 6.2)**. Be very careful not to distort the cover or scratch the intermediate shaft! Wrap electrician's tape around the tip of the screwdriver to avoid damage to the intermediate shaft.

Installation

7   Apply clean engine oil or multi-purpose grease to the outer edge of the new seal, then install it in the cover with the lip (spring side) facing IN. Drive the seal into place with a large socket and a hammer **(see illustration 6.3)**. If a large socket isn't available, a piece of pipe will also work. Make sure the seal enters the bore squarely and stop when the front face is at the proper depth.
8   Lubricate the seal "running surface" of the sprocket, then carefully fit the sprocket onto the intermediate shaft, through the seal and into the timing chain cover. **Note:** *Be sure the locating tangs of the intermediate shaft timing belt sprocket align with those on the timing chain sprocket (hidden behind the timing chain cover). To be sure the tangs are*

aligned, measure the distance from the front of the intermediate shaft sprocket to the timing chain cover. If the distance is more than 42 mm, the tangs are not aligned.
9   Check that the timing mark on the sprocket is aligned with the reference mark on the timing chain cover **(see illustration 14.1a)**. If necessary, reposition the sprocket.
10   Lubricate the intermediate shaft O-ring with clean engine oil, then carefully place it into position on the end of the shaft.
11   Put a little clean engine oil on the threads of the sprocket bolt, then install the sprocket bolt and washer. Torque the bolt to 96 ft-lb while an assistant prevents the crankshaft from turning.
12   The remainder of installation is the reverse of removal.

18   Timing chain cover - removal and installation

Removal

Refer to illustrations 18.5 and 18.16

1   Disconnect the negative battery cable. **Caution:** *On models equipped with the Theft-lock audio system, be sure the lockout feature is turned off before performing any procedure which requires disconnecting the battery.*
2   Remove the serpentine drivebelt (see Chapter 1).
3   Remove the camshaft timing belt tensioner and it's bracket (see Section 8).
4   Remove the timing belt (see Section 9) and the timing belt idler pulleys. **Note:** *Mark the direction of rotation on the timing belt before removing it.*
5   Remove the front engine lift bracket **(see illustration)**.
6   Remove the cooling fans.
7   Disconnect the coolant hoses from the water pump.
8   Remove the heater pipe retaining screws from the frame.
9   Remove the starter (see Chapter 5).

10   Remove the vibration damper (see Section 5).
11   Remove the alternator (see Chapter 5).
12   On manual transmission cars, remove the front-to-rear engine mount bracket brace.
13   Remove the oil filter.
14   Remove the oil cooler assembly.
15   Remove the oil pan front nuts and bolts, and loosen the remaining oil pan fasteners.
16   Remove the air conditioning compressor and lay it aside without disconnecting the refrigerant lines **(see illustration)**.
17   Remove the lower timing chain cover bolts.
18   Remove the intermediate shaft timing belt sprocket (see Section 17).
19   Remove the water pump pulley.
20   On manual transmission cars, remove the front exhaust air pipe check valve.
21   Remove any wiring or relays that will interfere with removal of the cover.
22   Remove the timing chain cover-to-engine block bolts.
23   Separate the cover from the engine. If it's stuck, tap it with a soft-face hammer, but don't try to pry it off.
24   Use a gasket scraper to remove all traces of old gasket material and sealant from the cover and engine block. The cover is made of aluminum, so be careful not to nick or gouge it. Clean the gasket sealing surfaces with lacquer thinner or acetone.

Installation

25   Install the new gasket.
26   Apply a thin layer of RTV sealant or equivalent to the lower edges of the timing chain cover, then install the cover.
27   Apply thread sealant to the upper timing chain cover bolts then install them. Draw the timing chain cover against the block by tightening the bolts in a criss-cross pattern. Tighten the bolts to the torque listed in this Chapter's Specifications.
28   The remainder of installation is the reverse of removal.
29   Add oil and coolant, start the engine and check for leaks.

20.15a Remove the bolts and nuts from around the perimeter of the oil pan . . .

20.15b . . . then carefully separate the oil pan from the block

19 Timing chain, sprockets and tensioner - inspection, removal and installation

Note: *This procedure will require special tools available at automotive tool companies and some auto part stores. If the specialty tools, camshaft timing clamps, camshaft sprocket holding tool, camshaft and intermediate shaft sprocket remover and tensioner retractor tool, are not available, obtain similar tools and adapt them for this application.*

Inspection

1   The timing chain should be replaced with a new one if the engine has high mileage, the chain has visible damage, or has too much freeplay. Failure to replace a worn timing chain may result in erratic engine performance, loss of power and decreased fuel mileage. A worn, damaged or loose chain can break or "jump" time. In the worst case, chain breakage or "jumping" will result in severe engine damage.
2   The timing chain tensioner should be replaced if it is worn, cracked, or displays other damage.

Removal

3   Remove the timing chain cover (see Section 18).
4   Mark the positions of the sprockets to the chain.
5   Remove the timing chain tensioner bolts.
6   Remove the chain and sprockets as an assembly using special camshaft sprocket tools to pull the crankshaft sprocket off the crankshaft.
7   Remove the timing chain tensioner.

Installation

8   Install the tensioner on the block. **Note:** *Use the upper attaching bolt as the primary locator.*
9   Thread the remaining tensioner bolts into their holes finger tight.

10   Torque the bolt in the slotted hole in the tensioner to 20 ft-lb, then torque the remaining bolts to 18 ft-lb.
11   Retract the tensioner shoe using special timing chain tensioner retractor tool, and insert an appropriately-sized rivet or nail into the spring pin hole in the tensioner to hold it in position. **Caution:** *Avoid using any type of tool that will damage the tensioner or mar the surface of the tensioner shoe.* **Note:** *Be sure the rivet or nail is stout enough to maintain the shoe in it's retracted position.*
12 Apply a light coating of clean engine oil to the tensioner's chain contact surfaces
13   Carefully install the timing chain and sprockets assembly. **Note:** *Try to keep the two sprockets parallel as you install them on their respective shafts. The crank sprocket should be installed with it's large chamfer and counterbore toward the crankshaft. The intermediate shaft sprocket should be installed with it's splines facing away from the block. The crankshaft sprocket will need to be pressed on for the last 8 mm of it's travel; use a special tool. Finally, be sure the timing marks are aligned after installation.*
Caution: *Be sure the tensioner shoe and guide do not become dislodged or damaged during installation of the sprocket and chain assembly.*
14   When the sprockets and chain assembly are in place and properly timed, remove the retaining pin from the tensioner.
15   Install the timing chain cover in the reverse order of removal.

20 Oil pan - removal and installation

Note: *On vehicles equipped with an automatic transaxle, it may be necessary to remove the transaxle (see Chapter 7) to make clearance for the oil pan.*

Removal

Refer to illustrations 20.15a and 20.15b

1   Disconnect the cable from the negative battery terminal. **Caution:** *On models equipped with the Theftlock audio system, be sure the lockout feature is turned off before performing any procedure which requires disconnecting the battery.*
2   Raise the front of the vehicle and place it securely on jackstands. Apply the parking brake and block the rear wheels to keep it from rolling off the stands.
3   Remove the front wheels and remove the lower splash pan.
4   Drain the engine oil (see Chapter 1) and remove the oil filter, the oil cooler assembly, and the oil level sensor.
5   Drain the coolant (see Chapter 1) and remove the coolant recovery tank.
6   Remove the steering gear bolts and use some wire to hang the steering gear from the body.
7   Remove the right and left lower ball joint nuts, then separate the ball joints from the control arms.
8   Disconnect the power steering cooler line clamps at the frame.
9   Remove the engine mount nuts at the frame.
10   If necessary, remove the flywheel/driveplate lower cover.
11   Remove the starter (see Chapter 5).
12   Place a floor jack under the frame front center crossmember.
13   Loosen the rear frame bolts - DO NOT REMOVE THEM!
14   Remove the front frame bolts and lower the front of the frame.
15   Remove the bolts and nuts, then carefully separate the oil pan from the block **(see illustrations)**. Don't pry between the block and the pan or damage to the sealing surfaces could occur and oil leaks may develop. Instead, tap the pan with a soft-face hammer to break the gasket seal.

Installation

16   Clean the pan with solvent and remove all old sealant and gasket material from the block and pan mating surfaces. Clean the mating surfaces with lacquer thinner or acetone and make sure the bolt holes in the block

are clear. Check the oil pan flange for distortion, particularly around the bolt holes. If necessary, place the pan on a block of wood and use a hammer to flatten and restore the gasket surface.

17   Always use a new gasket whenever the oil pan is installed. Apply a bead of RTV sealant to the front of the gasket, where it contacts the timing chain cover.

18   Place the oil pan in position on the block and install the nuts/bolts.

19   After the fasteners are installed, tighten them to the torque listed in this Chapter's Specifications. Starting at the center, follow a criss-cross pattern and work up to the final torque in three steps.

20   The remaining steps are the reverse of the removal procedure.

21   Refill the engine with oil, run it until normal operating temperature is reached and check for leaks.

21   Oil pump - removal, inspection and installation

Refer to illustration 21.2

1   Remove the oil pan (see Section 20) and the oil pan baffle.

2   Unbolt the oil pump and lower it from the engine **(see illustration)** along with the drive extension.

3   Inspect the pump body and cover for cracks, scoring or other damage.

4   Remove the pump cover and the gears. Check the gears for wear, galling or chips. Check the length and diameter of the gears. Check the lash between the gears with a feeler gauge. Compare your measurements with the dimensions given in this Chapter's Specifications.

5   Check the idler gear shaft and the drive shaft extension for looseness.

6   Check the pressure regulator for scoring or sticking, and check it's spring for tension.

7   Check that the suction pipe is not bent or otherwise damaged.

8   If the pump is found defective in any of the checks above, replace it with a new one - don't reuse the original or attempt to rebuild it.

9   Prime the pump by pouring motor oil into the pick-up screen while turning the pump driveshaft.

10   To install the pump, turn the hexagonal driveshaft so it mates with the oil pump drive.

11   Install the pump mounting bolt and tighten it to the torque listed in this Chapter's Specifications.

22   Flywheel/driveplate - removal and installation

This procedure is essentially the same as for the 2.5L four-cylinder engine. Refer to

21.2 Oil pump mounting bolt (arrow)

Part B and follow the procedure outlined there. However, use the bolt torque listed in this Chapter's Specifications.

23   Rear main oil seal - replacement

This procedure is essentially the same as that for the 2.5L four-cylinder engine. Refer to Part B and follow the procedure outlined there.

24   Engine mounts - check and replacement

1   There are four mounts that connect the drivetrain to the chassis, two at the timing chain end (a front and a rear), one at the transaxle end, and one upper mount connecting the engine torque strut to the body near the top of the radiator.

2   Engine mounts seldom require attention, but broken or deteriorated mounts should be replaced immediately or the added strain placed on the driveline components may cause damage or wear.

Check

3   During the check, the engine must be raised slightly to remove the weight from the mounts.

4   Raise the vehicle and support it securely on jackstands, then position a jack under the engine oil pan. Place a large block of wood between the jack head and the oil pan, then carefully raise the engine just enough to take the weight off the mounts. **Warning:** *DO NOT place any part of your body under the engine when it's supported only by a jack!*

5   Check the mount insulators (the rubber part between the engine and the chassis brackets) to see if the rubber is cracked, hardened or separated from the metal plates. Sometimes the rubber will split right down the center.

6   Check for relative movement between the mount plates and the engine or frame (use

a large screwdriver or prybar to attempt to move the mounts). If movement is noted, lower the engine and tighten the mount fasteners.

7   Rubber preservative should be applied to the insulators to slow deterioration.

Replacement

8   Disconnect the negative battery cable from the battery, then raise the vehicle and support it securely on jackstands (if not already done). **Caution:** *On models equipped with a Delco Theftlock audio system, be sure the lockout feature is turned off before performing any procedure which requires disconnecting the battery.*

All except the right (rear) engine mount

9   Raise the engine slightly with a jack or hoist. Remove the bolts/nuts holding the mount to the engine and to the chassis brackets, then raise the engine more until you can remove the mount nuts, remove the old mount and insert the new one, then lower the engine and tighten the nuts to Specifications.

Right (rear) engine mount

10   The procedure for replacing the rear engine mount is more involved. The hood must be removed and a three-bar engine support must be used to support the engine from above. Raise and support the front of the vehicle on jackstands.

11   Refer to Chapter 3 and remove the engine cooling fan.

12   Disconnect the engine torque strut from its mount.

13   Refer to Chapter 8 and remove the right driveaxle, then refer to Chapter 10 and disconnect the right balljoint at the control arm.

14   Remove the nuts from the right engine mount (it attaches the transaxle-to-engine brace to the front subframe), raise the engine and replace the mount.

15   Installation is the reverse of removal. Use thread-locking compound on the mount bolts and be sure to tighten them securely to this Chapter's Specifications.

Chapter 2 Part F
3800 V6 Engine

Contents

	Section
Camshaft, balance shaft and bearings - removal, inspection and installation	See Chapter 2H
Crankshaft front oil seal - replacement	12
Crankshaft rear oil seal - replacement	20
Cylinder compression check	See Chapter 2H
Cylinder heads - removal and installation	10
Drivebelt check, adjustment and replacement	See Chapter 1
Driveplate - removal and installation	19
Engine mount - check and replacement	21
Engine oil and filter change	See Chapter 1
Engine overhaul - general information	See Chapter 2H
Engine - removal and installation	See Chapter 2H
Exhaust manifolds - removal and installation	9
General information	1
Intake manifold - removal and installation	7
Oil filter adapter and pressure regulator valve - removal and installation	14
Oil pan - removal and installation	17
Oil pump pickup tube and screen assembly - removal and installation	18
Oil pump - removal, inspection and installation	15
Repair operations possible with the engine in the vehicle	2
Rocker arms and pushrods - removal, inspection and installation	5
Rocker arm covers - removal and installation	4
Spark plug replacement	See Chapter 1
Timing chain and sprockets - removal and installation	16
Timing chain cover - removal and installation	13
Top Dead Center (TDC) for number one piston - locating	3
Valve lifters - removal, inspection and installation	8
Valve springs, retainers and seals - replacement	6
Vibration damper - removal and installation	11
Water pump - removal and installation	See Chapter 3

Specifications

General

Cylinder numbers (drivebelt end-to-transaxle end)

Front bank (radiator side) ... 1-3-5

Rear bank ... 2-4-6

Firing order ... 1-6-5-4-3-2

Cylinder and coil terminal locations

Valve lifters

Diameter ... 0.8420 to 0.8427 in

Lifter-to-bore clearance ... 0.0008 to 0.0025 in

Oil pump

Outer gear-to-housing clearance ... 0.008 to 0.015 in

Inner gear-to-outer gear clearance ... 0.006 in

Gear end clearance ... 0.001 to 0.0035 in

Pump cover warpage limit ... 0.002 in

Torque specifications

Ft-lbs (unless otherwise indicated)

Note: One foot-pound (ft-lb) of torque is equivalent to 12 inch-pounds (in-lbs) of torque. Torque values below approximately 15 foot-pounds are expressed in inch-pounds, because most foot-pound torque wrenches are not accurate at these smaller values.

Camshaft sprocket bolts

1990 and 1991

Step one ... 52

Step two ... Turn an additional 110-degrees

1992

Step one ... 74

Step two ... Turn an additional 105-degrees

1993 and later

Step one ... 74

Step two ... Turn an additional 90-degrees

Cylinder head bolts

1994 and earlier

Step one ... 35

Step two ... Tighten an additional 130-degrees

Step three ... Turn an additional 30 degrees

1995 and later

Step one ... 37

Step two ... Tighten an additional 120-degrees

1997 VIN (1)

Step one ... 37

Step two ... Tighten an additional 120-degrees

Step three (only the center four bolts!) ... Tighten an additional 30-degrees

Torque specifications (continued)

Ft-lbs (unless otherwise indicated)

Note: One foot-pound (ft-lb) of torque is equivalent to 12 inch-pounds (in-lbs) of torque. Torque values below approximately 15 foot-pounds are expressed in inch-pounds, because most foot-pound torque wrenches are not accurate at these smaller values.

Driveplate-to-crankshaft bolts	
1991	
Step one	89 in-lbs
Step two	Turn an additional 90-degrees
1992 and later	
Step one	11
Step two	Turn an additional 50-degrees
Exhaust manifold-to-cylinder head bolts	
1995 and earlier	38
1996 and later	22
Intake manifold-to-cylinder head bolts	
1992 and earlier	89 in-lbs
1993 and later	132 in-lbs
Lifter guide bolts	22
Oil pan bolts	120 to 125 in-lbs
Oil filter adapter to timing chain cover bolts	
Through 1997	24
1998 and later models	
Step 1	132 in-lbs
Step 2	Tighten an additional 50-degrees
Oil pump	
Cover-to-timing chain cover bolts	96 to 98 in-lbs
Pickup tube and screen assembly bolts	
1995 and earlier	96 in-lbs
1996 and later	132 in-lbs
Rocker arm cover nuts/bolts	89 in-lbs
Rocker arm pivot bolts	
1991 and 1992	28
1993 through 1995	
Step one	18
Step two	Turn an additional 70-degrees
1996 and later	
Step one	11
Step two	Turn an additional 90-degrees
Supercharger mounting bolts	17
Timing chain cover bolts	
1995 and earlier	22
1996 through 1998	
To block	
Step one	133 in-lbs
Step two	Tighten an additional 40 degrees
To pan	125 in-lbs
1999 and later models	
To block	
Step one	177 in-lbs
Step two	Tighten an additional 40 degrees
To pan	125 in-lbs
Timing chain damper bolt	16
Vibration damper-to-crankshaft bolt	
1990	219
1991	
Step one	105
Step two	Turn an additional 56-degrees
1992 and later	
Step one	111
Step two	Turn an additional 76-degrees

1   General information

Note: On models equipped with the Delco Loc II audio system, be sure the lockout feature is turned off before performing any procedure which requires disconnecting the battery.

This Part of Chapter 2 is devoted to in-vehicle repair procedures for the "3800" V6 engines. The 3800 engine was available from 1991 through 1999, it is utilized in the Pontiac Grand Prix and the Buick Regal models only. This engine utilizes a cast-iron block with six cylinders arranged in a "V" shape at a 60-degree angle between the two banks. The overhead valve cast iron cylinder heads are equipped with integral valve guides and seats. Hydraulic lifters actuate the valves through tubular pushrods.

3.6 Hold a finger over the spark plug opening until you feel air escaping . . .

3.8 . . . then insert a soft plastic pen into the hole to detect piston movement

4.2 Unclip the harness cover

The engines are easily identified by looking for the designations printed on the upper intake plenum or cover. To positively identify this engine, locate the vehicle identification number on the left front corner of the instrument panel. This plate is visible from outside the vehicle (see illustration 1.1 in Chapter 2, Part B). The eighth character in the sequence is the engine designation:

L or K = 3800 V6 engine
1 = 3800 Supercharged V6 engine

Information concerning camshaft, balance shaft and engine removal and installation, as well as engine overhaul is in Part H of this Chapter.

The following repair procedures are based on the assumption the engine is installed in the vehicle. If the engine has been removed from the vehicle and mounted on a stand, many of the steps included in this Part of Chapter 2 will not apply.

2 Repair operations possible with the engine in the vehicle

Many major repair operations can be accomplished without removing the engine from the vehicle.

Clean the engine compartment and the exterior of the engine with some type of pressure washer before any work is done. A clean engine will make the job easier and will help keep dirt out of the internal areas of the engine.

Depending on the components involved, it may be a good idea to remove the hood to improve access to the engine as repairs are performed (refer to Chapter 11 if necessary).

If vacuum, exhaust, oil or coolant leaks develop, indicating a need for gasket or seal replacement, the repairs can generally be made with the engine in the vehicle. The intake and exhaust manifold gaskets, oil pan gasket and cylinder head gaskets are all accessible with the engine in place.

Exterior engine components such as the intake and exhaust manifolds, the oil pan, the

oil pump, the water pump, the starter motor, the alternator and the fuel injection system can be removed for repair with the engine in place. The timing chain and sprockets can also be replaced with the engine in the vehicle, but the camshaft and balance shaft cannot be removed with the engine in place.

Since the cylinder heads can be removed without pulling the engine, valve component servicing can also be accomplished with the engine in the vehicle.

In extreme cases caused by a lack of necessary equipment, repair or replacement of piston rings, pistons, connecting rods and rod bearings is possible with the engine in the vehicle. However, this practice is not recommended because of the cleaning and preparation work that must be done to the components involved.

3 Top Dead Center (TDC) for number one piston - locating

Refer to illustrations 3.6 and 3.8

1   Top Dead Center (TDC) is the highest point in the cylinder each piston reaches as it travels up-and-down when the crankshaft turns. Each piston reaches TDC on the compression stroke and again on the exhaust stroke, but TDC generally refers to piston position on the compression stroke.

2   Positioning the piston(s) at TDC is an essential part of certain procedures such as timing chain/sprocket removal and camshaft removal.

3   Before beginning this procedure, be sure to place the transaxle in Park, apply the parking brake and block the rear wheels. Raise the front of the vehicle and support it securely on jackstands.

4   Remove the spark plugs (see Chapter 1).

5   When looking at the drivebelt end of the engine, normal crankshaft rotation is clockwise. In order to bring any piston to TDC, the crankshaft must be turned with a socket and ratchet attached to the bolt threaded into the

center of the vibration damper on the crankshaft.

6   Have an assistant turn the crankshaft with a socket and ratchet as described above while you hold a finger over the number one spark plug hole (see illustration). Note: *See the cylinder numbering diagram in the specifications for this Chapter.*

7   When the piston approaches TDC, air pressure will be felt at the spark plug hole. Instruct your assistant to turn the crankshaft slowly.

8   Insert a plastic pen into the spark plug hole (see illustration). As the piston rises the pen will be pushed out. Note the point where the pen stops moving out - this is TDC.

9   After the number one piston has been positioned at TDC on the compression stroke, TDC for any of the remaining pistons can be located by repeating the procedure described above and following the firing order.

4 Rocker arm covers - removal and installation

Refer to illustrations 4.2, 4.4 and 4.5

Front cover removal

1   Disconnect the negative battery cable from the battery. **Caution:** *On models equipped with the Theftlock audio system, be sure the lockout feature is turned off before performing any procedure which requires disconnecting the battery.*

2   Remove the spark plug wires from the spark plugs and remove the harness cover (see illustration). Number each wire before removal to ensure correct reinstallation.

3   On models through 1996, remove the drivebelt (see Chapter 1) and the alternator brace.

4   Remove the acoustic cover on top of the intake plenum. On 1996 and later models, it will be necessary to twist out the oil filler tube from the front valve cover, pull up the front of the acoustic cover (also called the fuel injection sight shield) and pull it forward (toward

4.4 Remove the acoustic engine cover from the top of the plenum - On 1996 and later models twist out the oil filler neck, then pull up and forward on the cover to remove it

4.5 Remove the valve cover bolts (arrows)

5.2a First loosen the rocker arm bolts

5.2b Typical rocker arm components

1. *Rocker arm*
2. *Rocker arm shaft mounting bolt*
3. *Rocker arm shaft*
4. *Rocker arm retainer*

the radiator) to release it from the bracket at the rear of the plenum **(see illustration)**. On supercharged models, also remove the bolt securing the acoustic cover to the top of the supercharger housing.

5   Remove the engine lift bracket from the front exhaust manifold. Remove the rocker arm cover mounting bolts/nuts **(see illustration)**.

6   Detach the rocker arm cover. **Note:** *If the cover sticks to the cylinder head, use a soft-face hammer to dislodge it.*

Rear cover removal

7   Disconnect the negative battery cable from the battery. **Caution:** *On models equipped with the Theftlock audio system, be sure the lockout feature is turned off before performing any procedure which requires disconnecting the battery.*

8   Remove the spark plug wires from the spark plugs and remove the wire holder. Be sure each wire is labeled before removal to ensure correct reinstallation.

9   On models through 1996, remove the serpentine drivebelt (see Chapter 1) and the power steering pump, if necessary (see Chapter 10). Remove the rear alternator bracket on 1997 through 2000 models (see Chapter 5).

10   Remove the acoustic engine cover if equipped (see Step 4 and the EGR pipe, valve and adapter (see Chapter 6). On 1999 and later models, remove the EVAP purge solenoid and bracket.

11   Remove the engine lift bracket from the rear exhaust manifold. Remove the rocker arm cover mounting bolts/nuts.

12   Detach the rocker arm cover. **Note:** *If the cover sticks to the cylinder head, use a soft-face hammer to dislodge it.*

Installation

13   The mating surfaces of the cylinder head and rocker arm cover must be perfectly clean when the covers are installed. Use a gasket scraper to remove all traces of sealant or old gasket, then clean the mating surfaces with

lacquer thinner or acetone (if there's sealant or oil on the mating surfaces when the cover is installed, oil leaks may develop). The rocker arm covers are made of aluminum, so be extra careful not to nick or gouge the mating surfaces with the scraper.

14   Apply a thread sealer to the mounting bolt threads. Place the rocker arm cover and new gasket in position, then install the bolts.

15   Tighten the bolts/nuts in several steps to the torque listed in this Chapter's specifications.

16   Complete the installation by reversing the removal procedure. Be sure to add coolant if it was drained.

17   Start the engine and check for oil leaks at the rocker arm cover-to-head joints.

---

5   Rocker arms and pushrods - removal, inspection and installation

Refer to illustrations 5.2a, 5.2b and 5.3

Removal

1   Refer to Section 4 and detach the rocker arm covers from the cylinder heads.

2   On models with pedestal-mounted rocker arms, loosen the rocker arm pivot bolts one at a time and detach the rocker arms, bolts, pivots and pivot retainers **(see illustrations)**. On models with rocker arm shafts, loosen the

three bolts on each shaft a little at a time, working from the center out. Keep track of the rocker arm positions, since they must be returned to the same locations. Store each set of rocker components separately in a marked plastic bag to ensure that they're reinstalled in their original locations. **Note:** *If all rocker arms are removed, remove the pushrod guide plate beneath the rocker arms.*

3   Remove the pushrods and store them separately to make sure they don't get mixed up during installation **(see illustration)**.

5.3 If more than one pushrod is being removed, store them in a perforated cardboard box to prevent mix-ups during installation - note the label indicating the front of the engine

6.4 This is what the air hose adapter that threads into the spark plug hole looks like - they're commonly available from auto parts stores

6.8 After compressing the valve spring, remove the keepers with a magnet (as shown here) or small needle-nose pliers

6.9 Typical engine valve and related components

1 Keepers
2 Retainer
3 Spring and damper
4 Umbrella seal
5 Valve

Inspection

4   Check each rocker arm for wear, cracks and other damage, especially where the pushrods and valve stems contact the rocker arm.
5   Check the pivot seat in each rocker arm and the pivot faces. Look for galling, stress cracks and unusual wear patterns. If the rocker arms are worn or damaged, replace them with new ones and install new pivots or shafts as well.
6   Make sure the hole at the pushrod end of each rocker arm is open.
7   Inspect the pushrods for cracks and excessive wear at the ends. Roll each pushrod across a piece of plate glass to see if it's bent (if it wobbles, it's bent).

Installation

8   Lubricate the lower end of each pushrod with clean engine oil or moly-base grease and install them in their original locations. Make sure each pushrod seats completely in the lifter socket.
9   Apply moly-base grease to the ends of the valve stems, the upper ends of the pushrods and to the pivot faces to prevent damage to the mating surfaces before engine oil pressure builds up.
10   Coat the rocker arm pivot bolts with moly-base grease. Install the pushrod guide plates, rocker arms, pivots and pivot retainers. Tighten the bolts to the torque listed in this Chapter's specifications. As the bolts are tightened, make sure the pushrods seat properly in the rocker arms.
11   Install the rocker arm covers (see Section 4).

6   Valve springs, retainers and seals - replacement

Refer to illustrations 6.4, 6.8, 6.9 and 6.17
Note: *Broken valve springs and defective valve stem seals can be replaced without removing the cylinder heads. Two special tools and a compressed air source are normally required to perform this operation, so read through this Section carefully and rent or buy the tools before beginning the job. If compressed air is not available, a length of nylon rope can be used to keep the valves from falling into the cylinder during this procedure.*
1   Refer to Section 4 and remove the rocker arm cover from the affected cylinder head. If all of the valve stem seals are being replaced, remove both rocker arm covers.
2   Remove the spark plug from the cylinder which has the defective component. If all of the valve stem seals are being replaced, all of the spark plugs should be removed.
3   Turn the crankshaft until the piston in the affected cylinder is at Top Dead Center on the compression stroke (refer to Section 3 for instructions). If you're replacing all of the valve stem seals, begin with cylinder number one and work on the valves for one cylinder at a time. Move from cylinder-to-cylinder following the firing order sequence (1-6-5-4-3-2).
4   Thread an adapter into the spark plug hole **(see illustration)** and connect an air hose from a compressed air source to it. Most auto parts stores can supply the air hose adapter. **Note:** *Many cylinder compression gauges utilize a screw-in fitting that may work with your air hose quick-disconnect fitting.*
5   Remove the bolt, pivot and rocker arm for the valve with the defective part and pull out the pushrod (see Section 5). If all of the valve stem seals are being replaced, all of the rocker arms and pushrods should be removed.
6   Apply compressed air to the cylinder. The valves should be held in place by the air pressure. If the valve faces or seats are in poor condition, leaks may prevent the air pressure from retaining the valves - refer to the alternative procedure below.
7   If you don't have access to compressed air, an alternative method can be used. Position the piston at a point just before TDC on the compression stroke, then feed a long piece of nylon rope through the spark plug hole until it fills the combustion chamber. Be sure to leave the end of the rope hanging out of the engine so it can be removed easily. Use a large breaker bar and socket to rotate the crankshaft in the normal direction of rotation until slight resistance is felt.
8   Stuff shop rags into the cylinder head holes above and below the valves to prevent parts and tools from falling into the engine, then use a valve spring compressor to compress the spring. Remove the keepers with small needle-nose pliers or a magnet **(see illustration)**. **Note:** *A couple of different types of tools are available for compressing the valve springs with the head in place. One type grips the lower spring coils and presses on the retainer as the knob is turned, while the other type, shown here, utilizes the rocker arm bolt for leverage. Both types work very well, although the lever type is usually less expensive.*
9   Remove the spring retainer and valve spring, then remove the guide seal **(see illustration)**. **Note:** *If air pressure fails to hold the valve in the closed position during this operation, the valve face or seat is probably damaged. If so, the cylinder head will have to be removed for additional repair operations.*
10   Wrap a rubber band or tape around the top of the valve stem so the valve won't fall into the combustion chamber, then release the air pressure. **Note:** *If a rope was used instead of air pressure, turn the crankshaft slightly in the direction opposite normal rotation.*
11   Inspect the valve stem for damage. Rotate the valve in the guide and check the end for eccentric movement, which would indicate that the valve is bent.
12   Move the valve up-and-down in the guide and make sure it doesn't bind. If the valve stem binds, either the valve is bent or the guide is damaged. In either case, the head will have to be removed for repair.
13   Reapply air pressure to the cylinder to retain the valve in the closed position, then remove the tape or rubber band from the valve stem. If a rope was used instead of air pressure, rotate the crankshaft in the normal direction of rotation until slight resistance is felt.

6.17 Apply a small dab of grease to each keeper as shown here before installation - it will hold them in place on the valve stem as the spring is released

7.6 Pinch the tabs (arrows) together with pliers to detach the cables from the bracket

7.12 Unplug the electrical connectors (arrows) and move the harness aside

14   Lubricate the valve stem with clean engine oil and install a new valve guide seal. Using a hammer and a deep socket or seal installation tool, gently tap the seal into place until it's completely seated on the guide.

15   Install the spring in position over the valve.

16   Install the valve spring retainer and compress the valve spring.

17   Position the keepers in the upper groove. Apply a small dab of grease to the inside of each keeper to hold it in place if necessary **(see illustration)**. Remove the pressure from the spring tool and make sure the keepers are seated.

18   Disconnect the air hose and remove the adapter from the spark plug hole. If a rope was used in place of air pressure, pull it out of the cylinder.

19   Install the rocker arm(s) and pushrod(s).

20   Install the spark plug(s) and connect the wire(s).

21   Refer to Section 4 and install the rocker arm cover(s).

22   Start and run the engine, then check for oil leaks and unusual sounds coming from the rocker arm cover area.

7   Intake manifold - removal and installation

Refer to illustrations 7.6, 7.12, 7.14, 7.15, 7.19a and 7.19b

Removal

1   Relieve the fuel system pressure (see Chapter 4).

2   Disconnect the negative battery cable from the battery. **Caution:** *On models equipped with the Theftlock audio system, be sure the lockout feature is turned off before performing any procedure which requires disconnecting the battery.*

3   Remove the air intake duct, the mass airflow sensor and the throttle body (see Chapter 4). If you're working on a supercharged model, remove the supercharger

(see Chapter 4).

4   Remove the power steering pump-to-manifold brace (Chapter 10). On 1995 and later models remove the acoustic cover **(see illustration 4.4).**

5   Referring to Chapter 4, remove the fuel rail and injectors. On 1995 and later models remove the upper plenum.

6   Remove the control cables from their brackets **(see illustration)**.

7   Remove the drivebelt (see Chapter 1).

8   Disconnect and remove the alternator and brackets (see Chapter 5).

9   Drain the cooling system (see Chapter 1).

10   Disconnect the coolant tubes and hoses at the manifold.

11   Remove the ignition module/coil assembly (See Chapter 5). On 1995 and later engines remove the EGR tube from the lower manifold if equipped.

12   Label and disconnect the vacuum and electrical connectors at the intake manifold.

13   Remove the manifold mounting bolts.

14   Separate the manifold from the engine **(see illustration)**. Do not pry between the manifold and heads, as damage to the gasket sealing surfaces may result. If you're installing a new manifold, transfer all fittings and sensors to the new manifold.

Installation

Note: *The mating surfaces of the cylinder heads, block and manifold must be perfectly clean when the manifold is installed. Gasket removal solvents in aerosol cans are available at most auto parts stores and may be helpful when removing old gasket material that's stuck to the heads and manifold (since the manifold is made of aluminum, aggressive scraping can cause damage). Be sure to follow the directions printed on the container.*

15   Use a gasket scraper to remove all traces of sealant and old gasket material **(see illustration)**, then clean the mating surfaces with lacquer thinner or acetone. If there's old sealant or oil on the mating surfaces when the manifold is installed, oil or vacuum leaks may develop. Use a vacuum cleaner to remove any gasket material that falls into the intake ports or the lifter valley.

16   Use a tap of the correct size to chase the threads in the bolt holes, then use compressed air (if available) to remove the debris from the holes. **Warning:** *Wear safety glasses or a face shield to protect your eyes when using compressed air.*

17   If steel manifold gaskets are used, apply contact cement or a spray adhesive to both sides of the gaskets before positioning them on

7.14 Carefully pry up on a casting boss - don't pry between gasket surfaces

7.15 Remove all traces of gasket material, but don't gouge the soft aluminum

7.19a Intake manifold tightening sequence (1994 and earlier)

7.19b Intake manifold tightening sequence (1995 and later)

8.6a The guide plate is held in place by two bolts (arrows)

8.6b The lifter guides slip over the lifters

8.6c On 1995 and later engines the roller lifters are retained by guides bolted to the sides of the lifter valley - remove the four bolts to take off the guides and remove the lifters

the heads. Apply RTV sealant to the ends of the new manifold-to-block seals, then install them. Make sure the pointed end of the seal fits snugly against both the head and block.

18   Carefully lower the manifold into place. Apply thread lock compound to the mounting bolt threads and install the bolts finger tight.

19   Tighten the mounting bolts in two stages, following the recommended sequence **(see illustrations)**, until they're all at the torque listed in this Chapter's specifications.

20   Install the remaining components in the reverse order of removal. Install a new plenum-to-lower intake gasket when installing the plenum or supercharger.

21   Change the oil and filter and fill the cooling system (see Chapter 1). Start the engine and check for oil and vacuum leaks.

8   Valve lifters - removal, inspection and installation

Refer to illustrations 8.6a, 8.6b, 8.6c, 8.7, 8.8, 8.11 and 8.12

1   A noisy valve lifter can be isolated when the engine is idling. Hold a mechanic's stethoscope or a length of hose near the position of each valve while listening at the other end.

2   The most likely causes of noisy valve lifters are dirt trapped between the plunger and the lifter body or lack of oil flow, viscosity or pressure. Before condemning the lifters, we recommend checking the oil for fuel contamination, proper level, cleanliness and correct viscosity.

Removal

3   Remove the rocker arm cover(s) as described in Section 4.

4   Remove the rocker arms and pushrods (see Section 5).

5   Remove the intake manifold as described in Section 7.

6   Earlier models have conventional lifters. Later production engines have roller lifters. Roller lifters are kept from turning by a guide plate and lifter guide **(see illustrations)**, which must be removed to access the lifters.

7   There are several ways to extract the lifters from the bores. A special tool designed to grip and remove lifters is manufactured by many tool companies and is widely available, but it may not be required in every case **(see illustration)**. On newer engines without a lot of varnish buildup, the lifters can often be removed with a small magnet or even with your fingers. A machinist's scribe with a bent

end can be used to pull the lifters out by positioning the point under the retainer ring in the top of each lifter. **Caution:** *Don't use pliers to remove the lifters unless you intend to replace them with new ones. The pliers will damage the precision machined and hardened lifters, rendering them useless.*

8.7 Often you can remove the lifters by hand

8.8 The lifters on an engine that has accumulated many miles may have to be removed with a special tool - be sure to store the lifters in an organized manner to make sure they're reinstalled in their original locations

8.11 Check the pushrod seat (arrow) in the top of each lifter for wear

8.12 The roller must turn freely - check for wear and excessive play as well

8   Before removing the lifters, arrange to store them in a clearly labeled box to ensure that they're reinstalled in their original locations. Remove the lifters and store them where they won't get dirty **(see illustration)**.

Inspection

9   Parts for valve lifters are not available separately. The work required to remove them from the engine again if repair is unsuccessful outweighs any potential savings from repairing them.
10   Clean the lifters with solvent and dry them thoroughly without mixing them up.

Conventional lifters

11   Check each lifter wall, pushrod seat and foot for scuffing, score marks and uneven wear **(see illustration)**. Each lifter foot (the surface that rides on the cam lobe) must be slightly convex, although this can be difficult to determine by eye. If the base of the lifter is concave, the lifters and camshaft must be replaced. If the lifter walls are damaged or worn (which isn't very likely), inspect the lifter bores in the engine block as well. If the pushrod seats **(see illustration)** are worn, check the pushrod ends.

Roller lifters

12   Check the rollers carefully for wear and damage and make sure they turn freely without excessive play **(see illustration)**. The inspection procedure for conventional lifters also applies to roller lifters.

Installation

13   Used roller lifters can be reinstalled with a new camshaft and the original camshaft can be used if new lifters are installed.
14   If the conventional lifters are worn, they must be replaced with new ones and the camshaft must be replaced as well - never install used conventional lifters with a new camshaft or new lifters with a used camshaft.

9.4 The exhaust manifolds are bolted to the crossover pipe (arrows)

15   When reinstalling used lifters, make sure they're replaced in their original bores. Soak new lifters in oil to remove trapped air. Coat all lifters with moly-base grease or engine assembly lube prior to installation.
16   The remaining installation steps are the reverse of removal.
17   Run the engine and check for oil leaks.

9   Exhaust manifolds - removal and installation

Warning: *Allow the engine to cool completely before beginning this procedure.*
Note: *Exhaust system fasteners are frequently difficult to remove - they get frozen in place because of the heating/cooling cycle to which they're constantly exposed. To ease removal, apply penetrating oil to the threads of all exhaust manifold and exhaust pipe fasteners and allow it to soak in.*

Removal - front manifold

Refer to illustrations 9.4 and 9.8
1   Disconnect the negative battery cable.
Caution: *On models equipped with the Theftlock audio system, be sure the lockout feature is turned off before performing any procedure*

9.8 Remove the front exhaust manifold bolts/studs (arrows) - 3 bolts (out of 6 total) visible in this photo

which requires disconnecting the battery.
2   Remove the cooling fan for access (see Chapter 3).
3   Remove the mass airflow sensor, air duct and crankcase ventilation pipe, if necessary (see Chapter 4). Remove the engine mount struts. On 1996 and later models remove the acoustic cover **(see illustration 4.4)**.
4   Unbolt the manifold from the crossover pipe **(see illustration)**.
5   Remove the dipstick tube hold-down nut and wiggle the dipstick tube out of the block.
6   Detach the spark plug wires from the front spark plugs (see Chapter 1).
7   Remove the exhaust manifold heat shield, if equipped, then remove the nuts and the engine lifting bracket.
8   Unbolt and remove the exhaust manifold **(see illustration)**.

Removal - rear manifold

9   Disconnect the negative battery cable.
Caution: *On models equipped with the Theftlock audio system, be sure the lockout feature is turned off before performing any procedure which requires disconnecting the battery.*
10   Drain the coolant from the radiator (see Chapter 1).

11   Remove the mass airflow sensor, air duct and crankcase ventilation pipe, if necessary (see Chapter 4).

12   Remove the two nuts attaching the crossover pipe to the rear exhaust manifold.

13   Disconnect the spark plug wires from the rear spark plugs (see Chapter 1).

14   Remove the EGR pipe and transaxle dipstick tube if it's in the way (see Chapters 6 and 7).

15   Unbolt the power steering pump (some models) without removing the hoses and hold it to one side with wire (see Chapter 10).

16   Detach the alternator support bracket. Refer to Chapter 5 as necessary.

17   Remove the heater hoses and coolant tube brackets and tubing above the exhaust manifold. On 1996 and later models remove the acoustic cover (**see illustration 4.4**) and the acoustic cover mounting bracket.

18   Remove the exhaust manifold heat shield, if equipped, then remove the nuts and the engine lifting bracket.

19   Detach the IAC wiring from the throttle body.

20   Set the parking brake, block the rear wheels and raise the front of the vehicle, supporting it securely on jackstands.

21   Working under the vehicle, remove the two exhaust pipe-to-manifold bolts.

22   Disconnect the oxygen sensor electrical connector at the rear manifold. Remove the oxygen sensor from the exhaust manifold (see Chapter 6) to prevent damaging the sensor during manifold removal.

23   Remove the six bolts and detach the manifold from the head.

Installation

24   Clean the mating surfaces of the manifold and cylinder head to remove all traces of old gasket material, then check the manifold for warpage and cracks. If the manifold gasket was blown, take the manifold to an automotive machine shop for resurfacing.

25   Place the manifold in position with a new gasket and install the bolts finger tight.

26   Starting in the middle and working out toward the ends, tighten the mounting bolts a little at a time until all of them are at the specified torque.

10.3a The alternator bracket is attached to the cylinder head with two nuts (arrows)

27   Install the remaining components in the reverse order of removal.

28   Start the engine and check for exhaust leaks between the manifold and cylinder head and between the manifold and exhaust pipe.

10   Cylinder heads - removal and installation

Refer to illustrations 10.3a, 10.3b, 10.3c, 10.9, 10.10, 10.13, 10.16 and 10.19

Removal

1   Disconnect the negative battery cable at the battery. **Caution:** *On models equipped with the Theftlock audio system, be sure the lockout feature is turned off before performing any procedure which requires disconnecting the battery.*

2   Disconnect the spark plug wires and remove the spark plugs (see Chapter 1). Be sure to label the plug wires to simplify reinstallation. Refer to Chapter 1 and drain the engine oil.

3   Remove the nuts/bolts holding the brackets to the head **(see illustrations)**.

4   Disconnect all wires and hoses from the cylinder head(s). Be sure to label them to simplify reinstallation.

10.3b On some models, the air conditioner compressor bracket is attached to the cylinder head with one Torx T-50 bolt (arrow)

5   Remove the intake manifold as described in Section 7.

6   Detach the exhaust manifold(s) from the cylinder head(s) being removed (see Section 9).

7   Remove the rocker arm cover(s) (see Section 4).

8   Remove the rocker arms and pushrods (see Section 5). If removing the rear cylinder head, remove the alternator (1999 and 2000 models, see Chapter 5), on 2001 and later models, remove the power steering pump and set it aside without disconnecting the hoses (see Chapter 10). Remove the water bypass hoses from the belt tensioner and remove the belt tensioner.

9   Loosen the head bolts in 1/4-turn increments until they can be removed by hand. Work from bolt-to-bolt as shown **(see illustration)**.

10   Lift the head off the engine. If resistance is felt, don't pry between the head and block as damage to the mating surfaces will result. Recheck for head bolts that may have been overlooked, then use a hammer and block of wood to tap the head and break the gasket seal. Be careful because there are locating dowels in the block which position each head. As a last resort, pry each head up at the rear

10.3c Drivebelt tensioner bolt locations (arrows)

10.9 Cylinder head bolt LOOSENING sequence

10.10 Pry carefully - don't force a tool between the gasket surfaces

10.13 Carefully remove all traces of old gasket material

10.16 Look for gasket marks (arrow) to ensure correct installation

corner only and be careful not to damage anything **(see illustration)**.

11   After removal, place the head on blocks of wood to prevent damage to the gasket surfaces.

Installation

12   The mating surfaces of the cylinder heads and block must be perfectly clean when the heads are installed.

13   Use a gasket scraper to remove all traces of carbon and old gasket material **(see illustration)**, then clean the mating surfaces with lacquer thinner or acetone. If there's oil on the mating surfaces when the heads are installed, the gaskets may not seal correctly and leaks may develop. When working on the block, it's a good idea to cover the lifter valley with shop rags to keep debris out of the engine. Use a shop rag or vacuum cleaner to remove any debris that falls into the cylinders.

14   Check the block and head mating surfaces for nicks, deep scratches and other damage. If damage is slight, it can be removed with a file; if it's excessive, machining may be the only alternative.

15   Use a tap of the correct size to chase the threads in the head bolt holes. Dirt, corrosion, sealant and damaged threads will affect torque readings.

16   Position the new gaskets over the dowel pins in the block. If steel gaskets are used, apply contact cement or spray adhesive. Install "non-retorquing" type gaskets dry (no sealant), unless the manufacturer states otherwise. Most gaskets are marked UP or TOP **(see illustration)** because they must be installed a certain way.

17   Carefully position the heads on the block without disturbing the gaskets.

18   Use NEW head bolts - don't reinstall the old ones - and apply thread sealer to the threads and the undersides of the bolt heads.

19   Tighten the bolts as directed in this Chapter's specifications in the sequence shown **(see illustration)**. This must be done in three steps, following the sequence each time.

10.19 Cylinder head bolt TIGHTENING sequence

11.7a Wedge a large screwdriver in the teeth to hold the flywheel/driveplate in place

20   The remaining installation steps are the reverse of removal.

21   Change the oil and filter (see Chapter 1).

---

11   Vibration damper - removal and installation

Refer to illustrations 11.7a, 11.7b and 11.9

Caution: *The vibration damper is serviced as an assembly. Do not attempt to separate the pulley from the balancer hub.*

1   Disconnect the negative cable from the battery. **Caution:** *On models equipped with the Theftlock audio system, be sure the lockout feature is turned off before performing any*

11.7b Remove the bolt in the center of the hub (arrow)

procedure which requires disconnecting the battery.

2   Loosen the lug nuts on the right front wheel.

3   Raise the vehicle and support it securely on jackstands.

4   Remove the right front wheel.

5   Remove the right front fender inner splash shield.

6   Remove the drivebelt (see Chapter 1).

7   Remove the lower bellhousing cover plate and hold the crankshaft with a special flywheel locking tool. If this tool is unavailable, position a large screwdriver in the ring gear teeth **(see illustration)** to keep the crankshaft from turning while an assistant removes the crankshaft balancer bolt **(see illustration)**. The bolt is

11.9 Be sure to align the keyway (arrow) with the key in the crankshaft

12.2 Pry out the old seal with a seal removal tool (shown here) or a screwdriver

12.5 Gently drive the new seal into place with a hammer and large socket

normally quite tight, so use a large breaker bar and a six-point socket. **Note:** *On later models it may be necessary to lower the right side of the drivetrain/front suspension frame assembly to allow access to the vibration damper bolt. Place a floor jack under the frame front center crossmember. Loosen the right side frame bolts - DO NOT REMOVE THEM! - and lower the right side of the frame to access the vibration damper.*

8   The damper should pull off the crankshaft by hand. Leave the Woodruff key in place in the end of the crankshaft. **Note:** *On 1997 and later models a special crankshaft pulley puller is needed to remove the damper. Check your local tool rental store for availability.*

9   Installation is the reverse of removal. Align the keyway with the key **(see illustration)** and avoid bending the metal tabs. Be sure to apply moly-base grease to the seal contact surface on the back side of the damper (if it isn't lubricated, the seal lip could be damaged and oil leakage would result).

10   Apply sealant to the threads and tighten the crankshaft bolt to the torque listed in this Chapter's Specifications.

11   Reinstall the remaining components in the reverse order of removal.

12   Crankshaft front oil seal - replacement

Refer to illustrations 12.2 and 12.5

1   Remove the vibration damper (see Section 11) and the crankshaft position sensor shield if equipped. If there's a groove worn into the seal contact surface on the vibration damper, sleeves are available that fit over the groove, restoring the contact surface to like-new condition. These sleeves are sometimes included with the seal kit. Check with your parts supplier for details.

2   Pry the old oil seal out with a seal removal tool or a screwdriver **(see illustration)**. Be very careful not to nick or otherwise damage the crankshaft in the process.

3   Apply a thin coat of RTV-type sealant to the outer edge of the new seal. Lubricate the

seal lip with moly-base grease or clean engine oil.

4   Place the seal squarely in position in the bore and press it into place with special tool. Make sure the seal enters the bore squarely and seats completely.

5   If the special tool is unavailable, carefully guide the seal into place with a large socket or piece of pipe and a hammer **(see illustration)**. The outer diameter of the socket or pipe should be the same size as the seal outer diameter.

6   Install the vibration damper (see Section 11).

7   Reinstall the remaining parts in the reverse order of removal.

8   Start the engine and check for oil leaks at the seal.

13   Timing chain cover - removal and installation

Refer to illustrations 13.9, 13.10, 13.11 and 13.12

1   Disconnect the negative battery cable from the battery. **Caution:** *On models equipped with the Theftlock audio system, be sure the lockout feature is turned off before*

performing any procedure which requires disconnecting the battery.

2   Set the parking brake and put the transmission in Park. Raise the front of the vehicle and support it securely on jackstands. Remove the splash shield from the right inner fender.

3   Drain the oil and coolant (see Chapter 1).

4   Remove the coolant hoses from the timing chain cover.

5   Remove the large (8 mm) water pump-to-block bolts, leaving the smaller (6 mm) diameter bolts in place.

6   Remove the vibration damper (see Section 11) and the crankshaft position sensor shield if equipped.

7   Unplug the connectors from the oil pressure, camshaft and crankshaft sensors on distributorless ignition models or remove the distributor, if equipped (see Chapter 5).

8   Remove the oil pan (see Section 17).

9   Remove the timing chain cover-to-engine block bolts **(see illustration)**. Note that two of the bolts also secure the crankshaft sensor. Lift the sensor off when removing these bolts.

10   Separate the cover from the front of the engine. On earlier models there is a spring and button that controls camshaft end play inside the cam sprocket. If they are missing,

13.9 Timing chain cover bolt locations (arrows)

13.10 Once the timing cover has been removed, remove the camshaft button from the end of the camshaft (1994 and earlier models)

13.11 Remove all traces of old gasket material

13.12 The camshaft thrust surface on this cover is worn away (arrow) which means that a new cover must be installed (1994 and earlier models)

look for them in the oil pan **(see illustration)**.

11   Use a gasket scraper to remove all traces of old gasket material and sealant from the cover and engine block **(see illustration)**. The cover is made of aluminum, so be careful not to nick or gouge it. Clean the gasket sealing surfaces with lacquer thinner or acetone.

12   On 1994 and earlier models check the camshaft thrust surface in the cover for excessive wear **(see illustration)**. If it's worn, a new cover will be required (see the note at the beginning of this Section).

13   The oil pump cover must be removed and the cavity packed with petroleum jelly as described in Section 15 before the cover is installed.

14   Apply a thin layer of RTV sealant to both sides of the new gasket, then position the gasket on the engine block (the dowel pins should keep it in place). Make sure the spring and button are in place in the end of the camshaft (hold them in place with grease), then attach the cover to the engine. The oil pump drive must engage with the crankshaft or distributor gear.

15   Apply thread sealant to the bolt threads, then install them finger tight. Install the crankshaft sensor, but leave the bolts finger tight until Step 16. Follow a criss-cross pattern when tightening the other bolts and work up to the torque listed in this Chapter's specifications in three steps to avoid warping the cover.

16   Use a special crankshaft sensor adjuster tool to position the crankshaft sensor on the timing cover. Tighten the bolts to the torque listed in this Chapter's specifications for the timing chain cover.

17   The remainder of installation is the reverse of removal.

18   Add oil and coolant, start the engine and check for leaks.

---

14   Oil filter adapter and pressure regulator valve - removal and installation

Refer to illustrations 14.3 and 14.4

1   Raise the vehicle and support it securely on jackstands. Remove the engine oil filter. Remove the right front wheel and inner fender liner (see Chapter 11).

2   Remove the engine splash shield from below. On 2001 and later models, remove the right-side driveaxle (see Chapter 8).

3   Remove the four bolts holding the oil filter adapter to the timing chain cover **(see illustration)**. The cover is spring loaded, so remove the bolts while keeping pressure on the cover, then release the spring pressure carefully.

4   Remove the pressure regulator valve and spring **(see illustration)**. Use a gasket scraper to remove all traces of the old gasket.

5   Clean all parts with solvent and dry them with compressed air (if available). **Warning:** *Wear eye protection. Check for wear, score marks and valve binding.*

6   Installation is the reverse of removal. Be sure to use a new gasket. **Caution:** *If a new timing chain cover is being installed on the engine, make sure the oil pressure relief valve supplied with the new cover is used. If the old style relief valve is installed in a new cover, oil pressure problems will result.*

7   Tighten the bolts to the torque listed in this Chapter's Specifications.

8   Run the engine and check for oil leaks.

14.3 Carefully pull the oil filter adapter away from the timing cover - the pressure regulator (arrow) is spring loaded and may spring out when the adapter is removed

14.4 Remove the pressure regulator valve and spring, then check the valve for wear and damage

15.4 The oil pump cover is attached to the inside of the timing chain cover - a T-30 Torx driver is required for removal of the screws

15.10 Measuring the outer gear-to-housing clearance with a feeler gauge

15.11 Measuring the inner gear-to-outer gear clearance with a feeler gauge

15 Oil pump - removal, inspection and installation

Refer to illustrations 15.4, 15.10 and 15.11

Removal

1   Remove the oil filter (see Chapter 1).
2   Disconnect the oil cooler lines (if equipped) and the oil pressure sensor electrical connector.
3   Remove the timing chain cover (see Section 13).
4   Remove the oil pump cover-to-timing chain cover bolts **(see illustration)**.
5   Lift out the cover and oil pump gears as an assembly.

Inspection

6   Clean the parts with solvent and dry them with compressed air (if available). **Warning:** *Wear eye protection!*
7   Inspect all components for wear and score marks. Replace any worn out or damaged parts.
8   Refer to Section 14 for bypass valve information.

9   Reinstall the gears in the timing chain cover.
10   Measure the outer gear-to-housing clearance with a feeler gauge **(see illustration)**.
11   Measure the inner gear-to-outer gear clearance at several points **(see illustration)**.
12   Use a dial indicator or straightedge and feeler gauges to measure the gear end clearance (distance from the gear to the gasket surface of the cover).
13   Check for pump cover warpage by laying a precision straightedge across the cover and trying to slip a feeler gauge between the cover and straightedge.
14   Compare the measurements to this Chapter's Specifications. Replace all worn or damaged components with new ones.

Installation

15   Remove the gears and pack the pump cavity with petroleum jelly.
16   Install the gears - make sure petroleum jelly is forced into every cavity. Failure to do so could cause the pump to lose its prime when the engine is started, causing damage from lack of oil pressure.
17   Install the pump cover, using a new gasket only - its thickness is critical for maintaining the correct clearances.

18   Install the pressure regulator spring and valve.
19   Install the timing chain cover.
20   Install the oil filter and check the oil level. Start and run the engine and check for correct oil pressure, then look carefully for oil leaks at the timing chain cover.

16 Timing chain and sprockets - removal and installation

Refer to illustrations 16.1, 16.3, 16.4, 16.5 and 16.6

Removal

1   Remove the timing chain cover (see Section 13), then slide the shim off the nose of the crankshaft **(see illustration)**.
2   The timing chain should be replaced with a new one if the total free play midway between the sprockets exceeds one inch. Failure to replace the timing chain may result in erratic engine performance, loss of power and lowered fuel mileage.
3   Temporarily install the vibration damper bolt and turn the crankshaft clockwise to align the timing marks on the crankshaft and camshaft sprockets directly opposite each other **(see illustration)**.

16.1 The shim has a notch in it to fit over the key in the crankshaft (1994 and earlier models)

16.3 The marks on the crankshaft and camshaft sprockets (arrows) must be aligned adjacent to each other as shown here (the mark on the camshaft sprocket is a dimple - the one on the crankshaft sprocket is a raised dot)

16.4 Carefully release the spring with needle-nose pliers

16.5 Earlier models use two bolts (arrows) to retain the camshaft sprocket while later model engines use a single bolt to retain the sprocket

16.6 Guide the chain and sprockets off as an assembly

4   Remove the timing chain damper. **Note:** *On some earlier models it will be necessary to detach the spring and rotate the damper out of the way* **(see illustration)**. *On all other models simply remove the damper bolt to detach it from the block.*

5   Remove the camshaft sprocket bolts **(see illustration)**. Try not to turn the camshaft in the process (if you do, realign the timing marks after the bolts are loosened).

6   Alternately pull the camshaft sprocket and then the crankshaft sprocket forward and remove the sprockets and timing chain as an assembly **(see illustration)**.

7   Remove the camshaft gear.

8   Clean the timing chain components with solvent and dry them with compressed air (if available). **Warning:** *Wear eye protection.*

9   Inspect the components for wear and damage. Look for teeth that are deformed, chipped, pitted, polished or discolored.

Installation

Note: *If the crankshaft has been disturbed, install the sprocket temporarily and turn the crankshaft until the mark on the crankshaft sprocket is exactly at the top. If the camshaft was disturbed, install the sprocket temporarily and turn the camshaft until the timing mark is at the bottom, opposite the mark on the crankshaft sprocket* **(see illustration 16.3)**.

10   Assemble the timing chain on the sprockets, then slide the sprocket and chain assembly onto the shafts with the timing marks aligned as shown in **illustration 16.3**. **Note:** *Be sure the timing marks on the balance shaft gears are aligned before installing the camshaft timing chain sprocket. Alignment of the balance shaft gears is covered in Chapter 2H.*

11   Install the camshaft sprocket bolt(s) and tighten them to the torque listed in this Chapter's specifications.

12   Attach the timing chain damper assembly to the block and install the spring.

13   On 1994 and earlier models, install the camshaft thrust button and spring. Hold it in place with grease.

14   Lubricate the chain and sprocket with

clean engine oil and install the timing chain cover (see Section 13). Remember to lubricate the oil pump cavity before installing the cover (see Section 15).

17   Oil pan - removal and installation

Refer to illustration 17.4

1   Disconnect the cable from the negative battery terminal. **Caution:** *On models equipped with the Theftlock audio system, be sure the lockout feature is turned off before performing any procedure which requires disconnecting the battery.*

2   Raise the vehicle and place it securely on jackstands. Drain the engine oil and replace the oil filter (refer to Chapter 1 if necessary). On 1995 and later models, remove the front exhaust pipe.

3   Remove the driveplate inspection cover and starter, if necessary (refer to Chapter 5). On 1992 and later models, disconnect the electrical connector from the oil level sensor and remove the sensor. The sensor will be damaged if the pan is removed with the sensor in place. On 1995 and later models, support the engine from above with an engine

support fixture (see illustration 14.1 in Part D of this Chapter). Remove the front and rear engine mounts and the torque strut arms, by removing the throughbolts and the bolts attaching the struts to the mounts on the radiator support. Use a floorjack under the transaxle to raise the engine. **Note:** *When reinstalling the torque strut mounts, you may have to use a prybar to rotate the engine toward or away from the radiator to align the throughbolts.*

4   Remove the oil pan mounting bolts **(see illustration)** and carefully separate the oil pan from the block. Don't pry between the block and the pan or damage to the sealing surfaces may result and oil leaks may develop. Instead, tap the pan with a soft-face hammer to break the gasket seal.

5   Clean the pan with solvent and remove all old sealant and gasket material from the block and pan mating surfaces. Clean the mating surfaces with lacquer thinner or acetone and make sure the bolt holes in the block are clear. Check the oil pan flange for distortion, particularly around the bolt holes. If necessary, place the pan on a block of wood and use a hammer to flatten and restore the gasket surface.

6   Always use a new gasket whenever the oil pan is installed.

17.4 The oil pan bolts (arrows) are located around the perimeter of the oil pan (viewed from below)

18.2 Remove the bolts and lower the pickup tube and screen assembly

19.2 Place a prybar or large screwdriver through one of the holes in the driveplate to keep the crankshaft from turning as the bolts are loosened/tightened

7   Place the oil pan in position on the block and install the bolts.

8   After the bolts are installed, tighten them to the torque listed in this Chapter's specifications. Starting at the center, follow a crisscross pattern and work up to the final torque in three steps.

9   The remaining steps are the reverse of the removal procedure.

10   Refill the engine with oil. Run the engine until normal operating temperature is reached and check for leaks.

18   Oil pump pickup tube and screen assembly - removal and installation

Refer to illustration 18.2

1   Remove the oil pan (see Section 17).

2   Unbolt the oil pump pickup tube and screen assembly and detach it from the engine **(see illustration)**.

3   Clean the screen and housing assembly with solvent and dry it with compressed air, if available. **Warning:** *Wear eye protection.*

4   If the oil screen is damaged or has metal chips in it, replace it. An abundance of metal chips indicates a major engine problem which must be corrected.

5   Make sure the mating surfaces of the pipe flange and the engine block are clean and free of nicks and install the screen assembly with a new gasket.

6   Install the oil pan (see Section 17).

7   Be sure to refill the engine with oil before starting it.

19   Driveplate - removal and installation

Refer to illustration 19.2

1   Refer to Chapter 7 and remove the transaxle.

2   Place a prybar or large screwdriver

through a hole in the driveplate to keep the crankshaft from turning, then remove the mounting bolts **(see illustration)**.

3   Pull straight back on the driveplate to detach it from the crankshaft. Inspect the driveplate for cracks and chipped teeth. Replace it if it's damaged.

4   Reinstall the driveplate. The holes in the driveplate are staggered to ensure correct positioning on the crankshaft. Use Locktite on the bolt threads and tighten them to the specified torque in a crisscross pattern.

5   Reinstall the transaxle (see Chapter 7).

20   Crankshaft rear oil seal - replacement

Refer to illustration 20.3

1   Remove the transaxle (see Chapter 7).

2   Remove the driveplate (see Section 19).

3   Using a thin screwdriver or seal removal tool, carefully remove the oil seal from the engine block **(see illustration)**. Be very careful not to damage the crankshaft surface while prying the seal out.

4   Clean the bore in the block and the seal contact surface on the crankshaft. Check the seal contact surface on the crankshaft for scratches and nicks that could damage the new seal lip and cause oil leaks - if the crankshaft is damaged, the only alternative is a new or different crankshaft. Inspect the seal bore for nicks and scratches. Carefully smooth if with a fine file if necessary, but don't nick the crankshaft in the process.

5   A special tool is recommended to install the new oil seal. Lubricate the lips of the seal with clean engine oil. Slide the seal onto the mandril until the dust lip bottoms squarely against the collar of the tool. **Note:** *If the special tool isn't available, carefully work the seal lip over the crankshaft and tap it into place with a hammer and punch.*

6   Align the dowel pin on the tool with the dowel pin hole in the crankshaft and attach the tool to the crankshaft by hand-tightening

the bolts.

7   Turn the tool handle until the collar bottoms against the case, seating the seal.

8   Loosen the tool handle and remove the bolts. Remove the tool.

9   Check the seal and make sure it's seated squarely in the bore.

10   Install the driveplate (see Section 19).

11   Install the transaxle (see Chapter 7).

21   Engine mount - check and replacement

Refer to illustrations 21.4, 21.10 and 21.11
Note: *See Chapter 7 for transaxle mount information.*
Warning: *A special engine support fixture should be used to support the engine during repair operations. Similar fixtures are available from rental yards. Improper lifting methods or devices are hazardous and could result in severe injury or death. DO NOT place any part of your body under the engine/transaxle when it's supported only by a jack. Failure of the lifting device could result in serious injury or death.*

20.3 Carefully pry the old oil seal out

21.4 Broken engine mount (removed from vehicle for clarity)

21.10 The front engine mount (A) is located between the front subframe and the engine front mount cradle (B) - remove the two nuts (C) at the cradle and two nuts below the subframe to remove the mount

1   Engine mounts seldom require attention, but broken or deteriorated mounts should be replaced immediately or the added strain placed on the driveline components may cause damage or wear. The 3800 engine has a transaxle mount (see Chapter 7), two engine torque struts and a mount at the front (timing belt end) of the engine that attaches to a cradle type bracket under the front of the oil pan.

Check

2   During the check, the engine must be raised slightly to remove the weight from the mounts.
3   Raise the vehicle and support it securely on jackstands, then position a jack under the engine oil pan. Place a large block of wood between the jack head and the oil pan, then carefully raise the engine just enough to take the weight off the mounts. **Warning:** *DO NOT place any part of your body under the engine when it's supported only by a jack!*
4   Check the mounts to see if the rubber is cracked, hardened or separated from the metal plates. Sometimes the rubber will split right down the center **(see illustration)**.
5   Check for relative movement between the mount plates and the engine or frame (use a large screwdriver or prybar to attempt to move the mounts). If movement is noted, lower the engine and tighten the mount fasteners.

6   Rubber preservative may be applied to the mounts to slow deterioration.

Replacement

7   Disconnect the negative battery cable from the battery, then raise the vehicle and support it securely on jackstands (if not already done). **Caution:** *On models equipped with the Theftlock audio system, be sure the lockout feature is turned off before performing any procedure which requires disconnecting the battery.*
8   On 1996 and later models remove the right front wheel and loosen the inner fender splash panel.
9   Raise the engine slightly with a jack or hoist. Install an engine support as described in the **Warning** above **(see illustration 14.1 in Part D of this Chapter)**. Remove the fasteners and detach the mount from the frame bracket.
10   Remove the mount-to-block bracket bolts/nuts and detach the mount. **Note:** *1995 and earlier models are equipped with a front and rear engine mounts while 1996 and later models are equipped with a single mount and bracket located directly below the crankshaft balancer* **(see illustration)**.
11   The engine torque struts mount between the engine and the upper radiator support on the body **(see illustration)**. They can be replaced without jacking up the engine, by

removing the throughbolts and the bolts attaching the struts to the mounts on the radiator support. **Note:** *When reinstalling the mounts, you may have to use a prybar to rotate the engine toward or away from the radiator to align the throughbolts.*
12   Installation is the reverse of removal. Use thread locking compound on the threads and be sure to tighten everything securely.

21.11 Remove the throughbolts (A) and the engine torque struts (B) for replacement

Chapter 2 Part G
V8 engine

Contents

	Section
Camshaft and lifters - removal and installation	13
CHECK ENGINE light on	See Chapter 6
Crankshaft balancer - removal and installation	10
Crankshaft front oil seal - removal and installation	11
Cylinder compression check	See Chapter 2H
Cylinder heads - removal and installation	9
Drivebelt check, adjustment and replacement	See Chapter 1
Driveplate - removal and installation	16
Engine - removal and installation	See Chapter 2H
Engine mounts - check and replacement	18
Engine overhaul	See Chapter 2H
Exhaust manifolds - removal and installation	8

	Section
General information	1
Intake manifold - removal and installation	7
Oil pan - removal and installation	14
Oil pump - removal, inspection and installation	15
Rear main oil seal - replacement	17
Repair operations possible with the engine in the vehicle	2
Rocker arms and pushrods - removal, inspection and installation	5
Timing chain - removal, inspection and installation	12
Top Dead Center (TDC) for number one piston - locating	3
Valve covers - removal and installation	4
Valve springs, retainers and seals - replacement	6
Water pump - removal and installation	See Chapter 3

Specifications

General
Displacement	(5.3L) 325 cubic inches
Bore and stroke	3.779 x 3.622 inches
Cylinder numbers (front-to-rear)	
Front cylinder bank	1-3-5-7
Rear cylinder bank	2-4-6-8
Firing order	1-8-7-2-6-5-4-3
Cylinder compression pressure	
Minimum	100 psi
Maximum variation between cylinders	25 percent from the highest reading

Camshaft
Displacement on Demand cylinders	1, 4, 6 and 7
Lobe lift	
Cylinders 2, 3, 5 and 8	0.283 inch
Cylinders 1, 4, 6 and 7	0.289 inch

Front of vehicle

24017-1-B HAYNES

Cylinder numbering

Torque specifications*

Ft-lbs (unless otherwise indicated)

Note: *One foot-pound (ft-lb) of torque is equivalent to 12 inch-pounds (in-lbs) of torque. Torque values below approximately 15 ft-lbs are expressed in inch-pounds, since most foot-pound torque wrenches are not accurate at these smaller values.*

Camshaft sprocket bolts	26
Camshaft retainer bolts	
Torx head	132 in-lbs
Hex head	18
Crankshaft balancer bolt	
Step one (use old bolt)	240
Step two (use new bolt)	37
Step three (use new bolt)	Tighten an additional 140 degrees
Cylinder head bolts (in sequence - **see illustration 9.17**)**	
Step 1	
All 11 mm bolts (1 through 10)	22
Step 2	
All 11 mm bolts (1 through 10)	Tighten an additional 90 degrees
Step 3	
All 11 mm bolts (1 through 10)	Tighten an additional 70 degrees
Step 4	
All 8 mm bolts (11 through 15)	22
Engine mount retaining bolts	37
Exhaust manifold bolts	
Step one	132 in-lbs
Step two	15
Exhaust manifold heat shield bolt	80 in-lbs
Exhaust pipe flange nuts	18
Displacement-on-demand assembly bolts	18
Driveplate bolts	
Step one	15
Step two	37
Step three	74
Intake manifold bolts	
Step one	44 in-lbs
Step two	89 in-lbs
Oil pan baffle bolts	106 in-lbs
Oil pan drain plug	18
Oil pan rear access plugs	80 in-lbs
Oil pan bolts	
Step 1 (to engine and front cover)	18
Step 2 (to rear cover)	106 in-lbs
Step 3 (bellhousing, converter cover and transmission bolts)	37
Oil pump cover bolts	106 in-lbs
Oil pump mounting bolts	18
Rocker arm bolts	22
Front timing chain cover bolts	18
Valve cover bolts	106 in-lbs
Vapor vent pipe bolts	106 in-lbs
Water pump manifold bolts	
M10 bolts	44
M8 bolts	22

*Note: *Refer to Part H for additional specifications.*

**Use NEW bolts

1 General information

This Part of Chapter 2 is devoted to in-vehicle repair procedures for the 5.3L V8 engine. This engine uses an aluminum block and heads with eight cylinders arranged in a "V" shape at a 90-degree angle between the two banks. The aluminum cylinder heads have an overhead valve arrangement with pressed-in valve guides and hardened valve seats. Hydraulic roller lifters actuate the valves through tubular pushrods and rocker arms. The oil pump is mounted at the front of the engine behind the timing chain cover and is driven by the crankshaft. The engine uses a Displacement on Demand system that allows it to operate on four cylinders when driveability conditions permit.

Information concerning engine removal and installation and engine overhaul can be found in Part H of this Chapter. The following repair procedures are based on the assumption that the engine is installed in the vehicle. If the engine has been removed from the vehicle and mounted on a stand, many of the steps outlined in this Part of Chapter 2 will not apply.

2 Repair operations possible with the engine in the vehicle

Many major repair operations can be accomplished without removing the engine from the vehicle.

Clean the engine compartment and the exterior of the engine with some type of pressure washer before any work is done. A clean engine will make the job easier and will help keep dirt out of the internal areas of the engine.

Depending on the components involved, it may be a good idea to remove the hood to improve access to the engine as repairs are performed (refer to Chapter 11 if necessary).

If oil or coolant leaks develop, indicating a need for gasket or seal replacement, the repairs can generally be made with the engine in the vehicle. The cylinder head gaskets, intake and exhaust manifold gaskets, and the crankshaft oil seals are all accessible with the engine in place.

Exterior engine components, such as the water pump, the starter motor, the alternator and the fuel injection components, as well as the intake and exhaust manifolds, can be removed for repair with the engine in place.

Since the cylinder heads can be removed without removing the engine, valve component servicing can also be accomplished with the engine in the vehicle.

Camshaft removal and timing chain removal require that the engine be removed from the vehicle. These procedures are traditionally included in this Chapter because engine removal is not necessary for working on them in most vehicles. There are other procedures such as oil pan removal and driveplate removal that require the engine subframe to be removed. This is a difficult procedure and it is sometimes easier to simply remove the entire engine and transmission assembly instead.

3 Top Dead Center (TDC) for number one piston - locating

Refer to illustration 3.6

1   Top Dead Center (TDC) is the highest point in the cylinder that each piston reaches as it travels up the cylinder bore. Each piston reaches TDC on the compression stroke and again on the exhaust stroke, but TDC generally refers to piston position on the compression stroke.

2   Positioning the piston(s) at TDC is an essential part of certain procedures, such as timing chain/sprocket removal.

3   Before beginning this procedure, be sure to place the transmission in Park and apply the parking brake or block the front wheels. Also, disable the ignition system by disconnecting the primary electrical connectors at the ignition coil packs, then remove the spark plugs (see Chapter 1).

4   In order to bring any piston to TDC, the crankshaft must be turned using one of the methods outlined below. When looking at the front of the engine, normal crankshaft rotation is clockwise. **Warning:** *If method b) or c) is used, disable the fuel system (see Chapter 4, Section 2).*

a) *The preferred method is to turn the crankshaft with a socket and ratchet attached to the bolt threaded into the front of the crankshaft. Turn the bolt in a clockwise direction.*

b) *A remote starter switch, which may save some time, can also be used. Follow the instructions included with the switch. Once the piston is close to TDC, use a socket and ratchet as described in the previous paragraph.*

c) *If an assistant is available to turn the ignition switch to the Start position in short bursts, you can get the piston close to TDC without a remote starter switch. Make sure your assistant is out of the vehicle, away from the ignition switch, then use a socket and ratchet as described in Paragraph (a) to complete the procedure.*

5   Install a compression gauge in the No. 1 spark plug hole. It should be a gauge with a screw-in type fitting and a hose at least six inches long. Rotate the crankshaft using one of the methods described above while observing for pressure on the compression gauge. The moment the gauge shows pressure indicates that the No. 1 cylinder has begun the compression stroke.

6   To bring the piston to the top of the cylinder, insert a long screwdriver into the number one spark plug hole until it touches the top of the piston. **Note:** *Make sure to wrap the tip of the screwdriver with tape to avoid scratching the top of the piston and the cylinder walls.* Use the screwdriver (as a feeler gauge) to tell where the top of the piston is located in the cylinder while slowly rotating the crankshaft with a socket and breaker bar on the crankshaft pulley bolt **(see illustration).** As the piston rises, the screwdriver will be pushed out. The point at which the screwdriver stops moving outward is TDC. **Note:** *Always hold the screwdriver upright while the engine is being rotated so that the screwdriver will not get wedged as the piston travels upward.*

7   If you go past TDC, rotate the crankshaft counterclockwise until the piston is approximately one inch below TDC, then slowly rotate the crankshaft clockwise again until TDC is reached.

8   After the number one piston has been positioned at TDC on the compression stroke, TDC for any of the remaining pistons can be located by turning the crankshaft 90-degrees (1/4 turn) at a time and following the firing order.

3.6 A long screwdriver inserted in the number one spark plug hole can be used to determine the highest point reached by that piston - make sure to wrap the tip of the screwdriver with tape to avoid scratching the top of the piston or the cylinder walls

4.4 Valve cover mounting bolts (arrows)

4.7 Position the new gasket in the valve cover lip

4   Valve covers - removal and installation

Removal

Refer to illustration 4.4

1   Disconnect the cable from the negative terminal of the battery.
2   Pull the engine top cover from its mounting studs. Disconnect the wiring harness from the ignition coil assembly. Pull the harness out of the way.
3   Disconnect the spark plug wires from the ignition coils.
4   Remove the ignition coil bracket along with all of the coils mounted to it. Remove the interfering PCV tube. Remove the valve cover bolts **(see illustration)**, then detach the cover from the cylinder head. **Note:** *If the cover is stuck to the cylinder head, bump one end with a block of wood and a hammer to jar it loose. If that doesn't work, try to slip a flexible putty knife between the cylinder head and cover to break the gasket seal. Don't pry at the cover-to-head joint or damage to the sealing surfaces may occur (leading to oil leaks in the future).*

Installation

Refer to illustration 4.7

5   The mating surfaces of each cylinder head and valve cover must be perfectly clean when the covers are installed. Use a gasket scraper to remove all traces of sealant and old gasket material, then clean the mating surfaces with lacquer thinner or acetone. If there's sealant or oil on the mating surfaces when the cover is installed, oil leaks may develop.
6   Clean the mounting bolt threads with a die to remove any corrosion and restore damaged threads. Make sure the threaded holes in the cylinder head are clean - run a tap into them to remove corrosion and restore damaged threads.
7   The gaskets should be mated to the covers before the covers are installed. Position the gasket inside the cover lip **(see illustration)**. If the gasket will not stay in place in the cover lip, apply a thin coat of RTV sealant to the cover flange, then allow the sealant to set up so the gasket adheres to the cover.
8   Inspect the valve cover bolt grommets for damage. If the grommets aren't damaged they can be reused. Carefully position the valve cover(s) on the cylinder head and install

the bolts and grommets. **Note:** *Do not remove the oil filler tube unless service is required. If the oil filler tube is removed, replace it with a new one.*
9   Tighten the bolts in three or four steps to the torque listed in this Chapter's Specifications.
10   The remaining installation steps are the reverse of removal.
11   Start the engine and check carefully for oil leaks as the engine warms up.

5   Rocker arms and pushrods - removal, inspection and installation

Removal

Refer to illustrations 5.2 and 5.3

1   Refer to Section 4 and detach the valve covers from the cylinder heads.
2   Loosen the rocker arm pivot bolts one at a time and detach the rocker arms and bolts, then detach the pivot support pedestal **(see illustration)**. Keep track of the rocker arm positions, since they must be returned to the

5.2 Remove the mounting bolts (A) and rocker arms, then remove the pivot support pedestal (B)

5.3 Store the pushrods and rocker arms in order to ensure they are reinstalled in their original locations - note the arrow indicating the front of the engine

5.4 Rocker arm wear points

A   Pushrod socket
B   Pivot bearings
C   Valve stem contact point

ber 1, 3, 4, and 5 cylinders and the exhaust rocker arms for the Number 1, 2, 7, and 8 cylinders. Tighten each of the specified rocker arm bolts to the torque listed in this Chapter's Specifications.
11   Rotate the crankshaft 360 degrees. Tighten the intake valve rocker arms for the Number 2, 6, 7, and 8 cylinders and the exhaust rocker arms for the Number 3, 4, 5, and 6 cylinders. Tighten each of the rocker arm bolts to the torque listed in this Chapter's Specifications.
12   Refer to Section 4 and install the valve covers. Start the engine, listen for unusual valve train noses and check for oil leaks at the valve cover gaskets.

same locations. Store each set of rocker components separately in a marked plastic bag to ensure that they're reinstalled in their original locations.
3   Remove the pushrods and store them separately to make sure they don't get mixed up during installation **(see illustration)**.

Inspection

Refer to illustration 5.4
4   Check each rocker arm for wear, cracks and other damage, especially where the push-rods and valve stems contact the rocker arm **(see illustration)**.
5   Check the pivot bearings for binding and roughness. If the bearings are worn or damaged, replacement of the entire rocker arm will be necessary. **Note:** *Keep in mind that there is no valve adjustment on these engines, so excessive wear or damage in the valve train can easily result in excessive valve clearance, which in turn will cause valve noise when the engine is running.* Also check the rocker arm pivot support pedestal for cracks and other obvious damage.
6   Make sure the hole at the pushrod end of each rocker arm is open.

7   Inspect the pushrods for cracks and excessive wear at the ends, also check that the oil hole running through each pushrod is not clogged. Roll each pushrod across a piece of plate glass to see if it's bent (if it wobbles, it's bent).

Installation

Refer to illustration 5.9
8   Lubricate the lower end of each pushrod with clean engine oil or engine assembly lube and install them in their original locations. Make sure each pushrod seats completely in the lifter socket.
9   Apply engine assembly lube to the ends of the valve stems and to the upper ends of the pushrods to prevent damage to the mating surfaces on initial start-up **(see illustration)**. Also apply clean engine oil to the pivot shaft and bearing of each rocker arm and install the rocker arms loosely in their original locations. DO NOT tighten the bolts at this time!
10   Rotate the crankshaft until the number one piston is at TDC (see Section 3). With the number one piston is at TDC, tighten the intake valve rocker arms for the Num-

6   Valve springs, retainers and seals - replacement

Refer to illustrations 6.5, 6.8, 6.10, 6.15a, 6.15b and 6.19

Note: *Broken valve springs and defective valve stem seals can be replaced without removing the cylinder head. Two special tools and a compressed air source are normally required to perform this operation, so read through this Section carefully and rent or buy the tools before beginning the job.*
1   Remove the spark plugs (see Chapter 1).
2   Remove the valve covers (see Section 4).
3   Rotate the crankshaft until the number one piston is at top dead center on the compression stroke (see Section 3).
4   Remove the rocker arms for the number one piston.
5   Thread an adapter into the spark plug hole and connect an air hose from a compressed air source to it **(see illustration)**. Most auto parts stores can supply the air hose adapter. **Note:** *Many cylinder compression gauges utilize a screw-in fitting that may work with your air hose quick-disconnect fitting. If a cylinder compression gauge fitting is used*

5.9 Lubricate the pushrod ends and the valve stems with engine assembly lube before installing the rocker arms

6.5 This is what the air hose adapter that fits into the spark plug hole looks like - they're commonly available from auto parts stores

6.8 Once the spring is depressed, the keepers can be removed with a small magnet or needle-nose pliers (a magnet is preferred to prevent dropping the keepers)

6.10 Use a pair of needle nose pliers to remove the valve seals

6.15a Be sure to install the seals on the correct valve stems

1   Intake valve seal
2   Exhaust valve seal

it will be necessary to remove the Schrader valve from the end of the fitting before using it in this procedure.

6   Apply compressed air to the cylinder. The valves should be held in place by the air pressure. **Warning:** *If the cylinder isn't exactly at TDC, air pressure may force the piston down, causing the engine to quickly rotate. DO NOT leave a wrench on the crankshaft balancer bolt or you may be injured by the tool.*

7   Stuff shop rags into the cylinder head holes around the valves to prevent parts and tools from falling into the engine.

8   Using a socket and a hammer gently tap on the top of each valve spring retainer several times (this will break the seal between the valve keeper and the spring retainer and allow the keeper to separate from the valve spring retainer as the valve spring is compressed), then use a valve spring compressor to compress the spring. Remove the keepers with small needle-nose pliers or a magnet **(see illustration)**. **Note:** *Several different types of tools are available for compressing the valve springs with the head in place. One type grips the lower spring coils and presses on the retainer as the knob is turned, while the lever-type shown here utilizes the rocker arm bolt for leverage. Both types work very well, although the lever type is usually less expensive.*

9   Remove the valve spring and retainer. **Note:** *If air pressure fails to retain the valve in the closed position during this operation, the valve face or seat may be damaged. If so, the cylinder head will have to be removed for repair.*

10   Remove the old valve stem seals, noting differences between the intake and exhaust seals **(see illustration)**.

11   Wrap a rubber band or tape around the top of the valve stem so the valve won't fall into the combustion chamber, then release the air pressure.

12   Inspect the valve stem for damage. Rotate the valve in the guide and check the end for eccentric movement, which would

indicate that the valve is bent.

13   Move the valve up-and-down in the guide and make sure it does not bind. If the valve stem binds, either the valve is bent or the guide is damaged. In either case, the head will have to be removed for repair.

14   Reapply air pressure to the cylinder to retain the valve in the closed position, then remove the tape or rubber band from the valve stem.

15   If you're working on an exhaust valve, install the new exhaust valve seal on the valve stem and press it down over the valve guide to the specified depth. Don't force the seal against the top of the guide **(see illustrations)**. **Note:** *Be sure to take this measurement from the steel spring seat to the top edge of the intake and exhaust valve seals, not from the aluminum seat on the head!*

16   If you're working on an intake valve, install a new intake valve stem seal over the valve stem and press it down over the valve guide to the specified depth. Don't force the

intake valve seal against the top of the guide. **Caution:** *Do not install an exhaust valve seal on an intake valve, as high oil consumption will result.*

17   Install the spring and retainer in position over the valve.

18   Compress the valve spring assembly only enough to install the keepers in the valve stem.

19   Position the keepers in the valve stem groove. Apply a small dab of grease to the inside of each keeper to hold it in place if necessary **(see illustration)**. Remove the pressure from the spring tool and make sure the keepers are seated.

20   Disconnect the air hose and remove the adapter from the spark plug hole.

21   Repeat the above procedure on the remaining cylinders, following the firing order sequence (see this Chapter's Specifications). Bring each piston to top dead center on the compression stroke before applying air pressure (see Section 3).

6.15b Install the intake and exhaust valve seals to the specified depth - measure from the spring seat to the top edge of the valve seal

0.712 to 0.752

6.19 Apply small dab of grease to each keeper as shown here before installation - it'll hold them in place on the valve stem as the spring is released

7.10a Displacement on Demand assembly mounting bolts

7.10b The Displacement on Demand assembly gasket (A) can be re-used if it's in good condition. Don't pick up the assembly by the electrical lead frame (B)

22   Reinstall the rocker arm assemblies and the valve covers (see Sections 4 and 5).

23   Start the engine, then check for oil leaks and unusual sounds coming from the valve cover area. Allow the engine to idle for at least five minutes before revving the engine.

7   Intake manifold - removal and installation

Warning: *Wait until the engine is completely cool before starting this procedure.*

Removal

Refer to illustrations 7.10a and 7.10b

1   Disconnect the cable from the negative terminal of the battery.

2   Remove the plastic engine cover by pulling it from its mounting studs.

3   Remove the vacuum line that attaches to the brake booster.

4   Remove both PCV air tubes. Disconnect the fuel supply line from the fuel rail (see Chapter 4).

5   Disconnect the EVAP tube from the purge solenoid and move it aside.

6   Label and disconnect all interfering wiring connectors. Free the large wiring harness from the plastic clips on the fuel rail.

7   Remove the MAP sensor from the top of the intake manifold. Pull the EVAP purge solenoid valve from its bracket, then remove the bracket.

8   Loosen the intake manifold mounting bolts in 1/4-turn increments in the reverse order of the tightening sequence until they can be removed by hand **(see illustration 7.15).**

9   Lift the manifold from the engine. The intake manifold can be removed with the throttle body, fuel rail and injectors all in place. **Caution:** *Do not pry between the manifold and the heads or damage to the gasket seal-*

ing surfaces may result and vacuum leaks could develop. Also, don't use too much force - the manifold is made of a plastic composite and could crack.

10   As the manifold is lifted from the engine, be sure to check for and disconnect anything still attached to the manifold. The Displacement on Demand assembly can be removed at this time **(see illustrations)**. This component de-energizes cylinders when there is no demand for their power.

Installation

Refer to illustrations 7.13 and 7.15

Note: *The mating surfaces of the cylinder heads, block and manifold must be perfectly clean when the manifold is installed.*

11   Carefully remove all traces of old gasket material. Note that the intake manifold is made of a composite material and the cylinder heads on 5.3L engines are made of aluminum, therefore aggressive scraping is not suggested and will damage the sealing surfaces. After the gasket surfaces are cleaned and free of any gasket

material wipe the mating surfaces with a cloth saturated with safety solvent. If there is old sealant or oil on the mating surfaces when the manifold is installed, oil or vacuum leaks may develop. Use a vacuum cleaner to remove any gasket material that falls into the intake ports in the heads.

12   Use a tap of the correct size to chase the threads in the bolt holes, then use compressed air (if available) to remove the debris from the holes. **Warning:** *Wear safety glasses or a face shield to protect your eyes when using compressed air.*

13   Position the new gaskets on the intake manifold **(see illustration)**. Note that the gaskets are equipped with installation tabs that must snap into place on the intake manifold. The words "Manifold Side" may appear on the gasket, If so, this will ensure proper installation. Make sure the gaskets snap into place and all intake port openings align.

14   Carefully set the manifold in place.

15   Apply medium-strength thread locking compound to the threads of the bolts. Install the bolts and tighten them following the rec-

7.13 Align the tabs on the intake gaskets with the tabs on the manifold and snap the gasket into place

7.15 Intake manifold bolt tightening sequence

8.7 Exhaust crossover pipe nuts (A) and manifold mounting bolts (B) (front manifold shown, rear manifold similar)

ommended sequence **(see illustration)** to the torque listed in this Chapter's Specifications. Do not overtighten the bolts or gasket leaks may develop.

16   The remaining installation steps are the reverse of removal. Check the coolant level, adding as necessary (see Chapter 1). Start the engine and check carefully for vacuum leaks at the intake manifold joints.

8   Exhaust manifolds - removal and installation

Removal

Refer to illustration 8.7

Warning: *Use caution when working around the exhaust manifolds - the sheetmetal heat shields can be sharp on the edges. Also, the engine should be cold when this procedure is followed.*

1   Disconnect the cable from the negative terminal of the battery.

Rear side

2   Raise the vehicle and support it securely on jackstands. Disconnect the exhaust pipe from the rear exhaust manifold. Support the weight of the exhaust system with wire.

3   Remove the ignition coils from the rear cylinder bank.

4   Remove the oxygen sensor (see Chapter 6).

Front side

5   Remove the dipstick tube.

Both manifolds

6   Remove the spark plugs.

7   Disconnect the exhaust crossover pipe from the manifold to be removed **(see illustration)**.

8   Remove the exhaust manifold heat shield if necessary for working room.

9   Remove the exhaust manifold mounting

bolts and separate the manifold from the cylinder head.

Installation

10   Check the manifold for cracks and make sure the bolt threads are clean and undamaged. The manifold and cylinder head mating surfaces must be clean before the manifolds are reinstalled - use a gasket scraper to remove all carbon deposits and gasket material. **Note:** *The cylinder heads are made of aluminum, therefore aggressive scraping is not suggested and will damage the sealing surfaces.*

11   Install the heat shields, then install the bolts and gaskets onto the manifold. Retaining tabs surrounding the gasket bolt holes should hold the assembly together as the manifold is installed.

12   Starting at the fourth thread, apply a 1/4-inch wide band of medium-strength threadlocking compound to the threads of the bolts. **Note:** *The manufacturer recommends not applying threadlocking compound on the first three threads.*

13   Place the manifold on the cylinder head and install the mounting bolts finger tight.

14   When tightening the mounting bolts, work from the center to the ends and be sure to use a torque wrench. Tighten the bolts in two steps to the torque listed in this Chapter's Specifications. If required, bend the exposed end of the exhaust manifold gasket back against the cylinder head.

15   The remaining installation steps are the reverse of removal.

16   Start the engine and check for exhaust leaks.

9   Cylinder heads - removal and installation

Note: *It will be necessary to purchase a new set of 11 mm head bolts before or during this procedure.*

Removal

Refer to illustration 9.12

1   Disconnect the cable from the negative terminal of the battery and drain the cooling system (see Chapter 1).

2   Remove the intake manifold (see Section 7) and the coolant air bleed pipe.

3   Detach both exhaust manifolds from the cylinder heads (see Section 8). It is not necessary to disconnect the manifolds from the exhaust pipes.

4   Remove the valve covers (see Section 4).

5   Remove the rocker arms and pushrods (see Section 5). **Caution:** *Again, as mentioned in Section 5, keep all the parts in order so they are reinstalled in the same location.*

Rear side

6   Remove the drivebelt (see Chapter 1) and the drivebelt idler pulley, then remove the alternator (see Chapter 5) and the alternator bracket. **Note:** *Rotate the drivebelt tensioner to access the lower alternator mounting bracket bolt.*

Front side

7   Remove the top engine mount strut.

8   Remove the drivebelt (see Chapter 1).

9   Using the correct power steering pulley removal tool, remove the pulley for access to the bolt behind its rim. (These removal tools can be rented at most auto supply stores if you don't already have one.) Alternatively, you can unbolt the power steering pump and pull it upward to get enough clearance for bolt removal.

10   Remove the three coolant manifold bolts that attach to the left end of the cylinder head.

Both sides

11   Loosen the head bolts in 1/4-turn increments in the reverse order of the tightening sequence **(see illustration 9.21)** until they can be removed by hand. **Note:** *There will*

9.12 Using a prybar inserted into an intake port to break the head loose - do not use excessive force or damage to the head may result

9.18 Position the head gasket over the dowels at each end of the cylinder head with the mark (arrow) facing the front of the vehicle

be different length and size head bolts for different locations. Make a note of the different sizes and lengths and where they go when removing the bolts to ensure correct installation of the new bolts.

12   Lift the head(s) off the engine. If resistance is felt, do not pry between the head and block as damage to the mating surfaces will result. To dislodge the head, place a pry bar or long screwdriver into the intake port and carefully pry the head off the engine **(see illustration)**.

13   Store the heads on blocks of wood to prevent damage to the gasket sealing surfaces.

Installation

Refer to illustrations 9.18 and 9.21

14   The mating surfaces of the cylinder heads and block must be perfectly clean when the heads are installed. Gasket removal solvents are available at auto parts stores and may prove helpful.

15   Use a gasket scraper to remove all traces of carbon and old gasket material, then wipe the mating surfaces with a cloth saturated with lacquer thinner or acetone. **Note:**

The cylinder heads are made of aluminum, therefore aggressive scraping is not suggested and will damage the sealing surfaces. If there is oil on the mating surfaces when the heads are installed, the gaskets may not seal correctly and leaks may develop. When working on the block, use a vacuum cleaner to remove any debris that falls into the cylinders.

16   Check the block and head mating surfaces for nicks, deep scratches and other damage. If damage is slight, it can be removed with emery cloth. If it is excessive, machining may be the only alternative.

17   Use a tap of the correct size to chase the threads in the head bolt holes in the block. If a tap is not available, spray a liberal amount of brake cleaner into each hole. Use compressed air (if available) to remove the debris from the holes. **Warning:** *Wear safety glasses or a face shield to protect your eyes when using compressed air.* All cylinder head bolts should be replaced with **New** bolts.

18   Position the new gaskets over the dowels in the block **(see illustration)**.

19   Carefully position the heads on the block without disturbing the gaskets.

20   Before installing the 8mm head bolts,

coat the threads with a medium-strength threadlocking compound. Then install the **New** 8mm head bolts (bolts 11 through 15).

21   Install **New** 11 mm head bolts (bolts 1 through 10) and tighten them finger tight. Following the recommended sequence **(see illustration)**, tighten the bolts in four steps to the torque listed in this Chapter's Specifications. **Warning:** *DO NOT reuse head bolts - always replace them with new ones.*

22   The remaining installation steps are the reverse of removal.

23   Add coolant and change the oil and filter (see Chapter 1). Start the engine and check for proper operation and coolant or oil leaks.

10   Crankshaft balancer - removal and installation

Refer to illustrations 10.16, 10.17 and 10.20

Note: *This procedure requires a special balancer installation tool that is available through specialized tool manufacturers only and a new crankshaft balancer bolt. Read through the entire procedure and obtain the tool and materials before proceeding.*

1   Disconnect the cable from the negative terminal of the battery.

2   Raise the front of the vehicle and support it securely on jackstands. Then apply the parking brake.

3   Refer to Chapter 1 and remove the drivebelt.

4   Remove the upper part of the air filter housing (see Chapter 1).

5   Remove the top engine mounting strut.

6   Remove the inner plastic inner fender from the right side of the vehicle (see Chapter 11).

7   Disconnect the transmission cooler tubes from the transmission. Pull back the plastic covers and pry out the small wire retainers from each fitting with a screwdriver. Note that each clip engages in the fitting in a particular orientation.

8   Disconnect the stabilizer bar links at their lower points.

9   Pry up the plastic cover from the steering shaft and remove the pinch bolt (see Chapter 10). Push the steering shaft off of the lower shaft.

10   Refer to Chapter 11 and remove the lower air dam and its braces.

11   Remove the braces that attach the radiator to the lower engine frame.

12   Install an engine support fixture of the type that straddles the top of the engine onto the fender edges and attaches to the top of the engine to take its weight. These can be rented at most rental yards. Bolt it securely to the engine and tighten it to lift the weight of the engine off of its mounts.

13   Carefully remove the four engine-support frame bolts.

14   Remove the right front wheel.

9.21 Cylinder head bolt tightening sequence

10.16 Use a strap wrench to hold the crankshaft balancer while removing the center bolt (a chain-type wrench may be used if you wrap a section of old drivebelt or rag around the balancer first)

10.17 The use of a three jaw puller will be necessary to remove the crankshaft balancer - always place the puller jaws around the hub, not the outer ring

15   Using the engine-support fixture, slowly and carefully lower the engine until there is enough clearance for removal of the crank-shaft balancer/pulley.
16   Remove the bolt from the balancer. The easiest way to do this is with a heavy-duty impact gun. It can be done by hand, but it will be necessary to have an assistant hold the crankshaft from turning with a strap wrench around the balancer **(see illustration)**. If this doesn't provide enough turning resistance, remove the inspection cover from the flywheel and hold a prybar meshed into the flywheel teeth to hold the crankshaft in place.
17   Pull the balancer off the crankshaft with a puller **(see illustration)**. **Note:** *An Allen-head bolt should be inserted into the crank-shaft nose for the puller's tapered tip to push against to prevent damage to the crank-shaft threads.*

18   Position the crankshaft pulley/balancer on the crankshaft and slide it on as far as it will go.
19   Using the specialized crankshaft bal-ancer installation tool, press the crankshaft pulley/balancer onto the crankshaft.
20   Install the old crankshaft balancer bolt and tighten the crankshaft bolt to 240 ft-lbs. Remove the old bolt and measure the dis-tance from the snout of the crankshaft to the balancer hub **(see illustration)**. When properly installed, the balancer hub should extend 3/32 to 11/64-inch past the crank-shaft snout. If the measurement is incorrect, reinstall the balancer installation tool and press the balancer on the crankshaft until the measurement is correct.
21   Install a **New** crankshaft balancer bolt and tighten it in two steps to the torque and angle of rotation listed in this Chapter's Speci-fications.
22   The remaining installation steps are the reverse of removal.

11   Crankshaft front oil seal - removal and installation

Refer to illustrations 11.2, 11.4 and 11.5
1   Remove the crankshaft balancer (see Section 10).
2   Note how the seal is installed - the new one must be installed to the same depth and facing the same way. Carefully pry the oil seal out of the cover with a seal puller or a large screwdriver **(see illustration)**. Be very careful not to distort the cover or scratch the crank-shaft! Wrap electrician's tape around the tip of the screwdriver to avoid damage to the crank-shaft.
3   If the seal is being replaced with the tim-ing chain cover removed, support the cover on top of two blocks of wood and drive the seal out from the backside with a hammer and punch. **Caution:** *Be careful not to scratch, gouge or distort the area that the seal fits into or a leak will develop.*

10.20 Before the new crankshaft bolt is installed and tightened, the balancer must be measured for proper installation - when properly installed, the balancer hub should extend 3/32 to 11/64-inch past the crankshaft snout (early-style balancer shown)

11.2 Carefully pry the old seal out of the timing chain cover - don't damage the crankshaft in the process

11.4 Drive the new seal into place with a large socket and hammer

11.5 If the sealing surface of the pulley hub has a wear groove from contact with the seal, repair sleeves are available at most auto parts stores

12.9 Detach the hoses, then remove the bolts and lift off the water pump manifold (engine removed for clarity)

12.13 Timing chain cover mounting bolts (arrows)

4   Apply clean engine oil or multi-purpose grease to the outer edge of the new seal, then install it in the cover with the lip (spring side) facing IN. Drive the seal into place **(see illustration)** with a large socket and a hammer (if a large socket isn't available, a piece of pipe will also work). Make sure the seal enters the bore squarely and stop when the front face is at the proper depth.

5   Check the surface on the balancer hub that the oil seal rides on. If the surface has been grooved from long-time contact with the seal, a press-on sleeve may be available to renew the sealing surface **(see illustration)**. This sleeve is pressed into place with a hammer and a block of wood and is commonly available at auto parts stores for various applications.

6   Lubricate the balancer hub with clean engine oil and reinstall the crankshaft balancer as described in Section 10.

7   The remainder of installation is the reverse of the removal.

12   Timing chain - removal, inspection and installation

Removal and inspection

Refer to illustrations 12.9, 12.13, 12.16 and 12.19

1   Disconnect the cable from the negative terminal of the battery.

2   Refer to Chapter 1 and drain the cooling system and engine oil.

3   Refer to Chapter 5 and remove the alternator.

4   Remove the power steering pump (see Chapter 10).

5   Refer to Chapter 3 and remove the water pump.

6   Remove the camshaft position sensor (see Chapter 6).

7   Disconnect the hoses from the coolant air bleed pipe.

8   Disconnect all of the hoses from the

coolant manifold and secure them out of the way using wire.

9   Using the correct power steering pulley removal tool, remove the pulley for access to the bolt behind its rim. (These removal tools can be rented at most auto supply stores if you don't already have one). Alternatively, you can unbolt the power steering pump and pull it upward to get enough clearance for bolt removal. Remove the water pump manifold **(see illustration)**.

10   Refer to Section 10 and remove the crankshaft balancer.

11   Remove one of the belt tensioner bolts and move the tensioner for access to the timing chain cover bolts.

12   Remove the bolts that attach the timing chain cover to the oil pan.

13   Remove the timing chain cover mounting bolts and separate the timing chain cover from the block **(see illustration)**. The cover may be stuck; if so, use a putty knife to break the gasket seal. Since the cover is made of aluminum it can easily be damaged, so DO NOT attempt to pry it off.

14   Remove the oil pump (see Section 15).

15   Measure the timing chain freeplay. If it is more than 5/8 inch, the chain and both sprockets should be replaced.

16   Loosen the camshaft sprocket bolts one

12.16 Timing chain alignment marks (arrows) - when properly aligned, the crankshaft gear should be in the 12 o'clock position, the camshaft gear should be in the 6 o'clock position and the number one piston should be at TDC

turn, then screw the crankshaft balancer bolt into the end of the crankshaft and rotate the crankshaft in the normal direction of rotation (clockwise) until the timing marks align **(see illustration)**. Verify that the number one piston is at TDC.

12.19 The sprocket on the crankshaft can be removed with a two or three-jaw puller

12.22 Slip the chain and camshaft sprocket in place over the crankshaft sprocket with the camshaft sprocket timing mark (arrow) at the bottom

17   Remove the three bolts from the end of the camshaft, then detach the camshaft sprocket and chain as an assembly. **Caution:** *Never rotate the crankshaft with the timing chain removed. The pistons may contact the valves and bend them.*
18   Inspect the camshaft and crankshaft sprockets for damage or wear.
19   If replacement of the timing chain is necessary, remove the sprocket on the crankshaft with a two-or three-jaw puller, but be careful not to damage the threads in the end of crankshaft **(see illustration)**.

Installation

Refer to illustrations 12.22, 12.26 and 12.27

Note: *Timing chains must be replaced as a set with the camshaft and crankshaft sprockets. Never put a new chain on old sprockets.*
20   Use a gasket scraper to remove all traces of old gasket material and sealant from the cover and engine block.
21   Align the crankshaft sprocket with the Woodruff key and press the sprocket onto the crankshaft (if removed) with the vibration damper bolt, a large socket and some washers or tap it gently into place until it is completely seated. **Caution:** *If resistance is encountered, do not hammer the sprocket onto the crankshaft. It may eventually move onto the shaft, but it may be cracked in the process and fail later, causing extensive engine damage.*
22   Loop the new chain over the camshaft sprocket, then turn the sprocket until the timing mark is at the bottom **(see illustration)**. Mesh the chain with the crankshaft sprocket and position the camshaft sprocket on the end of the camshaft. If necessary, turn the camshaft so the dowel in the camshaft fits into the hole in the sprocket with the timing mark in the 6 o'clock position **(see illustration 12.16)**. When the chain is installed, the timing marks MUST align as shown.

23   Apply a thread locking compound to the camshaft sprocket bolt threads and tighten the bolts to the torque listed in this Chapter's Specifications.
24   Lubricate the chain with clean engine oil.
25   Install the oil pump and the oil pick up tube onto the engine (see Section 15). Now would be a good time to replace the crankshaft front oil seal (see Section 11).
26   Install the timing chain cover on the engine loosely using a new gasket **(see illustration)**.
27   Align the timing chain cover as follows:
a) *Install the crankshaft balancer on the engine as described in Section 10. This Step will align the front oil seal with the balancer hub.*
b) *Place a straightedge on the engine block oil pan rail. Measure the distance on each side of the block from the oil pan rail to the timing chain cover with a feeler gauge* **(see illustration)**. *This Step mea-*

12.26 Install the timing chain cover with a new gasket onto the engine block LOOSELY - the cover must be aligned properly before final installation

12.27 With the crankshaft balancer in place and the front cover bolts installed LOOSELY, measure the distance between the oil pan rail and the front cover sealing surface on each side (arrows) - then adjust the cover so the measurements are even on both sides before tightening the cover bolts

13.3 Remove the bolts (arrows) and take off the camshaft retainer plate, noting which side faces the block

13.8a The roller lifters are held in place by retainers - remove the retainer bolts and remove the retainers and the lifters as an assembly - note that each retainer houses four individual lifters and they must be installed back in their original locations if they're going to be reused

sures the difference between the sealing surface of the oil pan and the sealing surface of the timing chain cover in relationship to each other.

c) Tilt the timing chain cover as necessary to achieve an even measurement on each side. This Step properly aligns the front timing cover to oil pan sealing surfaces. Typically 0.000 to 0.020 inch is an acceptable tolerance. Note: Ideally the timing chain cover should be flush with the oil pan rail, but because of the differences in seal thickness, this may not always be obtainable. That is why there is a tolerance of 0.000 to 0.020 inch. Always let the front seal center itself around the crankshaft balancer hub and tilt the cover from side to side to even up the measurement at both oil pan rails. Never push downward on the front timing cover in an attempt to make the oil pan sealing surface flush, as this will distort the front oil seal and eventually lead to an oil leak!

d) With the timing chain cover properly aligned, tighten the cover bolts to the torque listed in this Chapter's Specifications.

13.8b Once the lifters and retainers are removed from the block, they can be marked (for location and installation purposes) and inspected

28   Apply a thin layer of RTV sealant to the areas where the timing chain cover and cylinder block meet, then install the oil pan as described in Section 14.

29   The remaining installation steps are the reverse of removal.

30   Add coolant and oil to the engine (see Chapter 1). Run the engine and check for oil and coolant leaks.

---

13   Camshaft and lifters - removal and installation

Note: *The camshaft should always be thoroughly inspected before installation and camshaft endplay should always be checked prior to camshaft removal. Refer to Chapter 2H for the camshaft and lifter inspection procedures.*

Removal

Refer to illustrations 13.3, 13.8a and 13.8b

1   Refer to Chapter 2H and remove the engine from the vehicle.

2   Refer to Section 12 and remove the timing chain and the camshaft sprocket.

3   Remove the camshaft retaining plate **(see illustration)** from the front of the engine block and screw long bolts into the front of the camshaft to aid in extracting it.

4   Remove the valve covers (see Section 4). Remove the rocker arms and the pushrods (see Section 5). Be sure to keep all components in order so they can be installed in their original positions.

5   If you wish to replace the camshaft only and not the lifters, this can be done on this engine. **Note:** *The manufacturer recommends that the lifters be replaced any time the camshaft is replaced.* Before the camshaft can be removed, the lifters must be placed at their highest point of travel for clearance or else the cylinder heads can be removed and the lifters can be taken out completely. Refer to Section 9 if you elect to remove the cylinder heads, lifter trays and lifters.

6   If you decide to keep the heads on the engine during camshaft removal, purchase special lifter supporting rods (JPR rods are available from Thunder Racing) or obtain two pieces of 5/16" metal rod about 24 inches long. Grind or file one end of each rod to a bullet-nose shape.

7   Grease the tips of the rods and insert them through the holes in the front of the engine so that they engage the flat parts of the lifters as you slowly rotate the camshaft. They should hold the lifters in the up position. Any lifters that drop down can be raised using mechanic's retractable pen magnets, securing the magnets with a clothespin to hold them up.

8   If you've removed the heads, unscrew the bolts and remove the lifter retainers and lifters **(see illustrations)**. Put the lifters and lifter trays in a clearly labeled box to ensure that they can be installed in their original locations.

9   If the engine is worn, the lifters may not come out with the lifter retainers. If so, there are several ways to extract them from their bores. Several manufacturers make a spe-

13.11 Be sure to apply camshaft assembly lube to the cam lobes and bearing journals before installing the camshaft

14.15 Subframe mounting bolts

cial tool but it may not be necessary. In newer models without a lot of varnish build-up, the mechanic's retractable pen magnet or even your fingers can be used. A machinist's scribe with a bent end can be used to pull the lifters out also.

10   Whether or not the heads have been removed, be very careful as you slowly rotate the camshaft while drawing it out of the engine. It is easy to nick the bearings with the camshaft so take your time and if you feel resistance, back off, keep the camshaft in line with the bore, rotate the camshaft more and continue.

Installation

Refer to illustration 13.11

11   Lubricate the camshaft bearing journals and cam lobes with camshaft and lifter assembly lube **(see illustration)**.

12   Slide the camshaft into the engine. Support the cam near the block and be careful not to scrape or nick the bearings.

13   Turn the camshaft until the dowel pin is in the 3 o'clock position, and install the camshaft thrust plate, tighten the bolts to the torque listed in this Chapter's Specifications. Make sure the gasket surface on the camshaft thrust plate and the engine block are free from oil and dirt.

14   Install the timing chain and sprockets (see Section 12). Also install the camshaft position sensor using a new O-ring (see Chapter 6).

15   Lubricate the lifters with clean engine oil and install them in the lifter retainers. Be sure to align the flats on the lifters with the flats in the lifter retainers. **Note:** *The displacement-on-demand lifters have a raised area that must align with a notch in the lifter tray.* Install the retainer and lifters into the engine block as an assembly. If the original lifters are being reinstalled, be sure to return them to their original locations. If a new camshaft is being installed, install new lifters as well. Tighten the lifter retainer bolts to the torque listed in this

Chapter's Specifications.

16   The remaining installation steps are the reverse of removal.

17   Before starting and running the engine, change the oil and install a new oil filter (see Chapter 1).

14   Oil pan - removal and installation

Removal

Refer to illustration 14.15

1   Disconnect the cable from the negative terminal of the battery.

2   Loosen the front wheel lug nuts. Raise the vehicle and support it securely on jackstands, then refer to Chapter 1 and drain the engine oil and remove the oil filter.

3   Install an engine support fixture of the type that straddles the top of the engine onto the fender edges and attaches to the top of the engine to take its weight. These can be rented at most rental yards. Bolt it securely to the engine and tighten it to lift the weight of the engine off of its mounts.

4   Remove the front wheels.

5   Refer to Chapter 11 and remove the lower air dam and its braces. Remove the engine drivebelt (see Chapter 1).

6   Move the battery cable harness clear of the subframe.

7   Disconnect the steering fluid cooler tube from the subframe.

8   Disconnect the stabilizer bar links and turn the stabilizer bar to provide access to the steering gear bolts.

9   Unbolt the power steering gear and tie it aside.

10   Unbolt the engine and transmission mounts from the frame.

11   Disconnect the front wheel speed sensor harnesses and release the harnesses from the control arms.

12   Disconnect the lower control arms from the subframe (see Chapter 10).

13   Support the subframe with two floor

14.21 The manufacturer uses rivets to hold the gasket to the oil pan during assembly - carefully drill them out (it isn't necessary to rivet the new gasket to the oil pan)

jacks - one placed on each side.

14   Remove the two subframe reinforcement plates.

15   Remove the four subframe bolts **(see illustration)**.

16   Carefully lower the subframe.

17   Remove the plastic cover from the torque converter.

18   Disconnect the wiring and wiring harness from the oil pan.

19   Remove the bolt from the lower drivebelt tensioner and push the tensioner aside for access to the oil pan bolt.

20   Remove the oil pan bolts and lower the oil pan. The pan will probably stick to the engine, so strike the pan with a rubber mallet until it breaks the gasket seal. **Caution:** *Before using force on the oil pan, be sure all the bolts have been removed.* Carefully slide the oil pan down and out, to the rear.

Installation

Refer to illustrations 14.21 and 14.24

21   Drill out the rivets securing the oil pan gasket to the oil pan and remove the old gas-

14.24 Oil pan TIGHTENING sequence - all V8 engines

15.4 Remove the bolt (arrow) securing the oil pick-up tube to the oil pump and remove it from the engine

ket **(see illustration)**. Wash out the oil pan with solvent.

22   Thoroughly clean the mounting surfaces of the oil pan and engine block of old gasket material and sealer. Wipe the gasket surfaces clean with a rag soaked in lacquer thinner, acetone or brake system cleaner.

23   Apply a 3/16-inch wide, one inch long bead of RTV sealant to the corners of the block where the front cover and the rear cover meet the engine block. Then attach the new gasket to the pan, install the pan and tighten the bolts finger-tight. Be sure the oil gallery passages in the pan and the gasket are aligned properly. **Note:** *Oil pan gasket rivets do not need to be installed on assembly.*

24   The alignment of the rear face of the aluminum pan to the rear of the block is important. Measure between the rear face of the pan and the front face of the transmission bellhousing with feeler gauges. Clearance should ideally be flush, but a gap of up to 0.010-inch is allowable. If the clearance is OK, tighten the pan bolts/studs in sequence to the torque listed in this Chapter's Specifi-

cations **(see illustration)**. If the clearance is not acceptable, install the two lower oil pan-to-bellhousing bolts and tighten them finger tight. This should draw the oil pan flush with the bellhousing. **Caution:** *The rear of the oil pan should never protrude rearward of the bellhousing plane of the block.*

25   The remainder of installation is the reverse of removal. Tighten the bolts to the torque listed in this Chapter's Specifications.

26   Add the proper type and quantity of oil (see Chapter 1), start the engine and check for leaks before placing the vehicle back in service.

15 Oil pump - removal, inspection and installation

Removal

Refer to illustrations 15.4 and 15.5

1   Refer to the Section 12 and remove the timing chain cover.

2   Raise the vehicle and support it securely

on jackstands. Refer to Section 14 and disconnect or remove all of the components such as wiring harnesses that interfere with lowering of the oil pan.

3   Remove all of the oil pan bolts except the rear two; loosen them a few turns. This will allow the oil pan to drop at the front end, giving enough room to reach the oil pump pick-up bolt at the oil pump.

4   Remove the oil pump pick-up bolt, being careful to avoid dropping it into the pan **(see illustration)**. You can place a rag between the oil pan and the oil pump to avoid losing the bolt or the O-ring.

5   Remove the oil pump bolts **(see illustration)** and slide the pump off of the crankshaft along with the pick-up tube O-ring.

Inspection

Refer to illustration 15.6

6   Remove the oil pump cover and withdraw the rotors from the pump body **(see illustration)**. Clean the components with solvent, dry them thoroughly and inspect for any obvious damage. Also check the bolt holes for

15.5 Oil pump mounting bolts (arrows)

15.6 Oil pump cover-to-oil pump housing mounting bolts (arrows)

15.10 Always install a new O-ring on the oil pump pick up tube

damaged threads and the splined surfaces on the crankshaft sprocket for any apparent damage. If any of the components are scored, scratched or worn, replace the entire oil pump assembly. There are no serviceable parts currently available.

Installation

Refer to illustration 15.10

7   Prime the pump by pouring clean motor oil into the pick-up tube hole, while turning the pump by hand.
8   Position the oil pump over the end of the crankshaft and align the teeth on the crankshaft sprocket with the teeth on the oil pump drive gear. Making sure the pump is fully seated against the block.
9   Install the oil pump mounting bolts and tighten them to the torque listed in this Chapter's Specifications.
10   Install a new O-ring on the oil pump pick-up tube, then fasten it to the oil pump and the

engine block main studs **(see illustration)**. **Caution:** *Be absolutely certain that the pick-up tube-to-oil pump bolts are properly tightened so that no air can be sucked into the oiling system at this connection.*
11   Install and align the timing chain cover, then install the oil pan. Refer to Sections 12 and 14 for the installation procedures.
12   The remainder of installation is the reverse of removal.
13   Add oil and coolant as necessary. Run the engine and check for oil and coolant leaks. Also check the oil pressure as described in Chapter 2H.

16   Driveplate - removal and installation

1   Refer to Chapter 7 and remove the transaxle.
2   Remove the driveplate and inspect it for wear and damage.
3   Before installing the bolts, apply locking compound to the bolt threads.
4   Set the driveplate in place and tighten the bolts to the torque values listed in this Chapter's Specifications. Make sure you tighten the bolts in three steps in a criss-cross pattern.
5   The remainder of the installation procedure is the reverse of removal.

17   Rear main oil seal - replacement

Refer to illustrations 17.3 and 17.4

Note: *If you're installing a new rear seal during a complete engine overhaul, refer to the procedure in Chapter 2H.*
1   Remove the transaxle (see Chapter 7).
2   Remove the driveplate (see Section 16).
3   Pry the oil seal from the rear cover with a

screwdriver **(see illustration)**. Be careful not to nick or scratch the crankshaft or the seal bore. Be sure to note how far it's recessed into the housing bore before removal so the new seal can be installed to the same depth. Thoroughly clean the seal bore in the block with a shop towel. Remove all traces of oil and dirt.
4   Lubricate the outside diameter of the seal and install the seal over the end of the crankshaft. Make sure the lip of the seal points toward the engine. Preferably, a seal installation tool (available at most auto parts store) should be used to press the new seal back into place. If the proper seal installation tool is unavailable, use a large socket, section of pipe or a blunt tool and carefully drive the new seal squarely into the seal bore and flush with the rear cover **(see illustration)**.
5   Install the driveplate (see Section 16).
6   Install the transmission (see Chapter 7).

18   Engine mounts - check and replacement

1   Engine mounts seldom require attention, but broken or deteriorated mounts should be replaced immediately or the added strain placed on the driveline components may cause damage.

Check

2   During the check, the engine must be raised slightly to remove the weight from the mounts.
3   Raise the vehicle and support it securely on jackstands, then position the jack under the engine oil pan. Place a large block of wood between the jack head and the oil pan, then carefully raise the engine just enough to take the weight off the mounts. Do not use the jack to support the entire weight of the engine.

17.3 Carefully pry the old seal out with a screwdriver at the notches provided in the rear cover

17.4 The rear oil seal can be pressed into place with a seal installation tool, a section of pipe or a blunt object shown here - in any case be sure the seal is installed squarely into the seal bore and flush with the rear cover

4   Check the mounts to see if the rubber is cracked, hardened or separated from the metal plates. Sometimes the rubber will split right down the center.

5   Check for relative movement between the mount plates and the engine or frame (use a large screwdriver or prybar to attempt to move the mounts). If movement is noted, check the tightness of the mount fasteners first before condemning the mounts. Usually when engine mounts are broken, they are very obvious as the engine will easily move away from the mount when pried or under load.

Replacement

Refer to illustration 18.7

6   Disconnect the cable from the negative terminal of the battery, then raise the vehicle and support it securely on jackstands.

7   Raise the vehicle and support it securely on jackstands. Remove the nuts that attach the mount studs to the engine subframe **(see illustration)**.

8   Attach an engine hoist to the top of the engine for lifting; do not use a jack under the oil pan to support the entire weight of the engine

18.7 Engine mount-to-subframe nuts (right side shown)

or the oil pump pick-up could be damaged. **Note:** *If a hoist is not available, casting lugs on each side of the engine block can be used to support the entire weight of the engine while the engine mounts are being replaced.*

9   Raise the engine slightly until the engine mount can be unbolted from the block. Unbolt

the mount from the engine block and remove it from the vehicle.

10   Installation is the reverse of removal. Use non-hardening thread-locking compound on the mount bolts and be sure to tighten them to the torque listed in this Chapter's Specifications.

Notes

Chapter 2 Part H
General engine overhaul procedures

Contents

	Section			Section
Camshaft, intermediate shaft (3.4L) and balance shaft (3800) - removal, inspection and installation	9	Engine rebuilding alternatives		5
CHECK ENGINE light on	See Chapter 6	Engine removal - methods and precautions		6
Crankshaft - removal and installation	11	General information - engine overhaul		1
Cylinder compression check	3	Initial start-up and break-in after overhaul		13
Engine - removal and installation	7	Oil pressure check		2
Engine overhaul - disassembly sequence	8	Pistons and connecting rods - removal and installation		10
Engine overhaul - reassembly sequence	12	Vacuum gauge diagnostic checks		4

Specifications

General

Displacement
2.2L four-cylinder	134 cubic inches
2.5L four-cylinder	151 cubic inches
2.3L four-cylinder (Quad four)	138 cubic inches
2.8L V6	173 cubic inches
3.1L (or 3100) V6	192 cubic inches
3.4L V6	204 cubic inches
3800 V6	231 cubic inches
5.3L V8	325 cubic inches

Cylinder compression pressure
Minimum	100 psi
Maximum	25 percent from highest reading

Oil pressure (minimum, at operating temperature)
1000 rpm	6 psi
2000 rpm	18 psi
4000 rpm	24 psi

Torque specifications   Ft-lbs (unless otherwise indicated)

Note: *One foot-pound (ft-lb) of torque is equivalent to 12 inch-pounds (in-lbs) of torque. Torque values below approximately 15 ft-lbs are expressed in inch-pounds, since most foot-pound torque wrenches are not accurate at these smaller values.*

Subframe/engine cradle mounting bolts (V8 models)
Front	107
Rear	118
Driveplate-to-torque converter bolts	46

Torque specifications (continued)

Ft-lbs (unless otherwise indicated)

Note: *One foot-pound (ft-lb) of torque is equivalent to 12 inch-pounds (in-lbs) of torque. Torque values below approximately 15 ft-lbs are expressed in inch-pounds, since most foot-pound torque wrenches are not accurate at these smaller values.*

Connecting rod bearing cap bolts
 2.2L four-cylinder
  Step 1 20
  Step 2 .... Tighten an additional 50-degrees
 2.5L four-cylinder 29
 2.3L four-cylinder (Quad four)
  Step 1 18
  Step 2 .... Tighten an additional 80-degrees
 2.8L V6
  1989 and earlier.. 37
  1990 and later... 39
 3.1L (or 3100) and 3.4L V6
  Step 1 15
  Step 2 .... Tighten an additional 75-degrees
 3800 V6
  Step 1 20
  Step 2 .... Tighten an additional 50-degrees
 V8
  Step 1 15
  Step 2 .... Tighten an additional 85-degrees
Main bearing cap bolts
 2.2L four-cylinder 66
 2.5L four-cylinder 65
 2.3L four-cylinder (Quad four)
  Step 1 15
  Step 2 .... Tighten an additional 90-degrees
 2.8L V6
  1989 and earlier.. 70
  19090 and later... 73
 3.1L (or 3100)
  Step 1 37
  Step 2 .... Tighten an additional 77-degrees
 3.4L
  Bolts
   Step 1 37
   Step 2 .... Tighten an additional 75-degrees
  Studs
   Step 1 37
   Step 2 .... Tighten an additional 77-degrees
 3800 V6
  1995 and earlier
   Step 1 26
   Step 2 .... Tighten an additional 45-degrees
  1996 and later
   Step 1 30
   Step 2 .... Tighten an additional 110-degrees
  Side bolts
   Step 1 11
   Step 2 .... Tighten an additional 45-degrees
 V8
  Bolts 1 through 10
   Step 1 15
   Step 2 .... Tighten an additional 80-degrees
  Bolts 11 through 20
   Step 1 15
   Step 2 .... Tighten an additional 51-degrees
  Bolts 21 through 30.. 18*
Camshaft retainer bolts
 2.2L four-cylinder 9
 2.5L four-cylinder .... 89 in-lbs
3800 V6 balance shaft retainer bolt... 22
3800 V6 balance shaft driven gear bolt
 Step 1 16
 Step 2 .... Tighten an additional 70-degrees
Transmission-to-engine bolts 55

Must be replaced with new bolts

1.1 An engine block being bored. An engine rebuilder will use special machinery to recondition the cylinder bores

1.2 If the cylinders are bored, the machine shop will normally hone the engine on a machine like this

1   General information - engine overhaul

Refer to illustrations 1.1, 1.2, 1.3, 1.4, 1.5 and 1.6

Included in this portion of Chapter 2 are general information and diagnostic testing procedures for determining the overall mechanical condition of your engine.

The information ranges from advice concerning preparation for an overhaul and the purchase of replacement parts and/or components to detailed, step-by-step procedures covering removal and installation.

The following Sections have been written to help you determine whether your engine needs to be overhauled and how to remove and install it once you've determined it needs to be rebuilt. For information concerning in-vehicle engine repair, see Chapter 2A, 2B, 2C, 2D, 2E, 2F or 2G.

It's not always easy to determine when, or if, an engine should be completely over-

hauled, because a number of factors must be considered.

High mileage is not necessarily an indication that an overhaul is needed, while low mileage doesn't preclude the need for an overhaul. Frequency of servicing is probably the most important consideration. An engine that's had regular and frequent oil and filter changes, as well as other required maintenance, will most likely give many thousands of miles of reliable service. Conversely, a neglected engine may require an overhaul very early in its service life.

Excessive oil consumption is an indication that piston rings, valve seals and/or valve guides are in need of attention. Make sure that oil leaks aren't responsible before deciding that the rings and/or guides are bad. Perform a cylinder compression check to determine the extent of the work required (see Section 3). Also check the vacuum readings under various conditions (see Section 4).

Check the oil pressure with a gauge

installed in place of the oil pressure sending unit and compare it to this Chapter's Specifications (see Section 2). If it's extremely low, the bearings and/or oil pump are probably worn out.

Loss of power, rough running, knocking or metallic engine noises, excessive valve train noise and high fuel consumption rates may also point to the need for an overhaul, especially if they're all present at the same time. If a complete tune-up doesn't remedy the situation, major mechanical work is the only solution.

An engine overhaul involves restoring the internal parts to the specifications of a new engine. During an overhaul, the piston rings are replaced and the cylinder walls are reconditioned (rebored and/or honed) **(see illustrations 1.1 and 1.2)**. If a rebore is done by an automotive machine shop, new oversize pistons will also be installed. The main bearings, connecting rod bearings and camshaft bearings are generally replaced with new

1:3 A crankshaft having a main bearing journal ground

1.4 A machinist checks for a bent connecting rod, using specialized equipment

ones and, if necessary, the crankshaft may be reground to restore the journals **(see illustration 1.3)**. Generally, the valves are serviced as well, since they're usually in less-than-perfect condition at this point. While the engine is being overhauled, other components, such as the distributor, starter and alternator, can be rebuilt as well. The end result should be similar to a new engine that will give many trouble free miles. **Note:** *Critical cooling system components such as the hoses, drivebelts, thermostat and water pump should be replaced with new parts when an engine is overhauled. The radiator should be checked carefully to ensure that it isn't clogged or leaking (see Chapter 3). If you purchase a rebuilt engine or short block, some rebuilders will not warranty their engines unless the radiator has been professionally flushed. Also, we don't recommend overhauling the oil pump - always install a new one when an engine is rebuilt.*

Overhauling the internal components on today's engines is a difficult and time-consuming task which requires a significant amount of specialty tools and is best left to a professional engine rebuilder **(see illustrations 1.4, 1.5 and 1.6)**. A competent engine rebuilder will handle the inspection of your old parts and offer advice concerning the reconditioning or replacement of the original engine, never purchase parts or have machine work done on other components until the block has been thoroughly inspected by a professional machine shop. As a general rule, time is the primary cost of an overhaul, especially since the vehicle may be tied up for a minimum of two weeks or more. Be aware that some engine builders only have the capability to rebuild the engine you bring them while other rebuilders have a large inventory of rebuilt exchange engines in stock. Also be aware that many machine shops could take as much as two weeks time to completely rebuild your engine depending on shop workload. Sometimes it makes more sense to simply exchange your engine for another engine that's already rebuilt to save time.

2   Oil pressure check

Refer to illustrations 2.2a, 2.2b, 2.2c, 2.2d and 2.3

1   Low engine oil pressure can be a sign of an engine in need of rebuilding. A low oil pressure indicator (often called an "idiot light") is not a test of the oiling system. Such indicators only come on when the oil pressure is dangerously low. Even a factory oil pressure gauge in the instrument panel is only a relative indication, although much better for driver information than a warning light. A better test is with a mechanical (not electrical) oil pressure gauge.

2   Locate the engine oil pressure sending unit on the engine block:

a) *On V8 engines, the oil pressure sender is located at the end of the intake manifold near the throttle body. It screws into the displacement-on-demand valley cover* **(see illustration)**.

1.5 A bore gauge being used to check the main bearing bore

1.6 Uneven piston wear like this indicates a bent connecting rod

2.2a On V8 engines the oil pressure sending unit is located at the left end (driver's side) of the engine, between the throttle body and intake manifold

2.2b On V6 engines, the oil pressure sending unit (arrow) is located adjacent to the oil filter housing (typical V6 shown)

2.2c On 2.2 and 2.5 liter four-cylinder engines, the oil pressure sending unit is located at the lower center edge of the hydraulic lifter and valve cover (arrow) (view with intake manifold removed)

2.2d On the Quad-4 engine, the oil pressure sending unit is located in the transaxle end of the cylinder head

b) On V6 engines, the oil pressure sending unit is located near the oil filter housing on the front side of the engine (see illustration). Note: On some models a heat shield will have to be removed for access to the sending unit.

c) On 2.2 and 2.5 liter four-cylinder engines, the oil pressure sending unit is located at the lower center edge of the hydraulic lifter and valve cover, and on the Quad-4 engine it's located in the trasaxle end of the cylinder head (see illustrations 2.2c and 2.2d).

3 Unscrew and remove the oil pressure sending unit and screw in the hose for your oil pressure gauge (see illustration). If necessary, install an adapter fitting. Use Teflon tape or thread sealant on the threads of the adapter and/or the fitting on the end of your gauge's hose.

4 Connect an accurate tachometer to the engine, according to the tachometer manu-

facturer's instructions.

5 Check the oil pressure with the engine running (normal operating temperature) at the specified engine speed, and compare it to this Chapter's Specifications. If it's extremely low, the bearings and/or oil pump are probably worn out.

3 Cylinder compression check

Refer to illustration 3.6

1 A compression check will tell you what mechanical condition the upper end of your engine (pistons, rings, valves, head gaskets) is in. Specifically, it can tell you if the compression is down due to leakage caused by worn piston rings, defective valves and seats or a blown head gasket. Note: *The engine must be at normal operating temperature and the battery must be fully charged for this check.*

2 Begin by cleaning the area around the

spark plugs before you remove them (compressed air should be used, if available). The idea is to prevent dirt from getting into the cylinders as the compression check is being done.

3 Remove all of the spark plugs from the engine (see Chapter 1).

4 Remove the air intake duct (see Chapter 4) and block the throttle plate wide open.

5 On V6 models, disable the ignition system by disconnecting the primary (low voltage) wiring from the coil pack. On V8 engines, disconnect the large electrical connector for each ignition coil harness. On all models, disable the fuel system by removing the fuel pump fuse (see Chapter 4, Section 2).

6 Install a compression gauge in the number one cylinder spark plug hole (see illustration).

7 Crank the engine over at least seven compression strokes and watch the gauge. The compression should build up quickly in a healthy engine. Low compression on the first

2.3 Remove the oil pressure sending unit and install an oil pressure gauge

3.6 Use a compression gauge with a threaded fitting for the spark plug hole, not the type that requires hand pressure to maintain the seal

stroke, followed by gradually increasing pressure on successive strokes, indicates worn piston rings. A low compression reading on the first stroke, which doesn't build up during successive strokes, indicates leaking valves or a blown head gasket (a cracked head could also be the cause). Deposits on the undersides of the valve heads can also cause low compression. Record the highest gauge reading obtained.

8   Repeat the procedure for the remaining cylinders and compare the results to this Chapter's Specifications.

9   Add some engine oil (about three squirts from a plunger-type oil can) to each cylinder, through the spark plug hole, and repeat the test.

10   If the compression increases after the oil is added, the piston rings are definitely worn. If the compression doesn't increase significantly, the leakage is occurring at the valves or head gasket. Leakage past the valves may be caused by burned valve seats and/or faces or warped, cracked or bent valves.

11   If two adjacent cylinders have equally low compression, there's a strong possibility that the head gasket between them is blown. The appearance of coolant in the combustion chambers or the crankcase would verify this condition.

12   If one cylinder is slightly lower than the others, and the engine has a slightly rough idle, a worn lobe on the camshaft could be the cause.

13   If the compression is unusually high, the combustion chambers are probably coated with carbon deposits. If that's the case, the cylinder head(s) should be removed and decarbonized.

14   If compression is way down or varies greatly between cylinders, it would be a good idea to have a leak-down test performed by an automotive repair shop. This test will pinpoint exactly where the leakage is occurring and how severe it is.

4   Vacuum gauge diagnostic checks

Refer to illustration 4.6

A vacuum gauge provides inexpensive but valuable information about what is going on in the engine. You can check for worn rings or cylinder walls, leaking head or intake manifold gaskets, incorrect carburetor adjustments, restricted exhaust, stuck or burned valves, weak valve springs, improper ignition or valve timing and ignition problems.

Unfortunately, vacuum gauge readings are easy to misinterpret, so they should be used in conjunction with other tests to confirm the diagnosis.

Both the absolute readings and the rate of needle movement are important for accurate interpretation. Most gauges measure vacuum in inches of mercury (in-Hg). The following references to vacuum assume the diagnosis is being performed at sea level. As elevation increases (or atmospheric pressure

Low, steady reading — Low, fluctuating needle — Regular drops

Irregular drops — Rapid vibration

Large fluctuation — Slow fluctuation

STD-O-OBR HAYNES

4.6 Typical vacuum gauge readings

decreases), the reading will decrease. For every 1,000 foot increase in elevation above approximately 2,000 feet, the gauge readings will decrease about one inch of mercury.

Connect the vacuum gauge directly to the intake manifold vacuum, not to ported (throttle body) vacuum. Be sure no hoses are left disconnected during the test or false readings will result.

Before you begin the test, allow the engine to warm up completely. Block the wheels and set the parking brake. With the transaxle in Park, start the engine and allow it to run at normal idle speed. **Warning:** *Keep your hands and the vacuum gauge clear of the fans.*

Read the vacuum gauge; an average, healthy engine should normally produce about 17 to 22 in-Hg with a fairly steady needle **(see illustration)**. Refer to the following vacuum gauge readings and what they indicate about the engine's condition:

1   A low steady reading usually indicates a leaking gasket between the intake manifold and cylinder head(s) or throttle body, a leaky vacuum hose, late ignition timing or incorrect camshaft timing. Check ignition timing with a timing light and eliminate all other possible causes, utilizing the tests provided in this Chapter before you remove the timing chain cover to check the timing marks.

2   If the reading is three to eight inches below normal and it fluctuates at that low reading, suspect an intake manifold gasket leak at an intake port or a faulty fuel injector.

3   If the needle has regular drops of about two-to-four inches at a steady rate, the valves are probably leaking. Perform a compression check or leak-down test to confirm this.

4   An irregular drop or down-flick of the needle can be caused by a sticking valve or an ignition misfire. Perform a compression check or leak-down test and read the spark plugs.

5   A rapid vibration of about four in-Hg vibration at idle combined with exhaust smoke indicates worn valve guides. Perform a leak-down test to confirm this. If the rapid vibration occurs with an increase in engine speed, check for a leaking intake manifold gasket or head gasket, weak valve springs, burned valves or ignition misfire.

6   A slight fluctuation, say one inch up and down, may mean ignition problems. Check all the usual tune-up items and, if necessary, run the engine on an ignition analyzer.

7   If there is a large fluctuation, perform a compression or leak-down test to look for a weak or dead cylinder or a blown head gasket.

8   If the needle moves slowly through a wide range, check for a clogged PCV system, incorrect idle fuel mixture, throttle body or intake manifold gasket leaks.

6.3 Get an engine stand sturdy enough to firmly support the engine while you're working on it. Stay away from three-wheeled models; they have a tendency to tip over more easily, so get a four-wheeled unit

6.4 Since many of the fasteners on these engines are tightened using the "angle torque" method, a torque angle gauge is essential for proper assembly

9   Check for a slow return after revving the engine by quickly snapping the throttle open until the engine reaches about 2,500 rpm and let it shut. Normally the reading should drop to near zero, rise above normal idle reading (about 5 in-Hg over) and return to the previous idle reading. If the vacuum returns slowly and doesn't peak when the throttle is snapped shut, the rings may be worn. If there is a long delay, look for a restricted exhaust system (often the muffler or catalytic converter). An easy way to check this is to temporarily disconnect the exhaust ahead of the suspected part and redo the test.

5   Engine rebuilding alternatives

The do-it-yourselfer is faced with a number of options when purchasing a rebuilt engine. The major considerations are cost, warranty, parts availability and the time required for the rebuilder to complete the project. The decision to replace the engine block, piston/connecting rod assemblies and crankshaft depends on the final inspection results of your engine. Only then can you make a cost effective decision whether to have your engine overhauled or simply purchase an exchange engine for your vehicle.

Some of the rebuilding alternatives include:

Individual parts - If the inspection procedures reveal that the engine block and most engine components are in reusable condition, purchasing individual parts and having a rebuilder rebuild your engine may be the most economical alternative. The block, crankshaft and piston/connecting rod assemblies should all be inspected carefully by a machine shop first.

Short block - A short block consists of an engine block with a crankshaft and piston/connecting rod assemblies already installed. All new bearings are incorporated and all

clearances will be correct. The existing camshafts, valve train components, cylinder head and external parts can be bolted to the short block with little or no machine shop work necessary.

Long block - A long block consists of a short block plus an oil pump, oil pan, cylinder head, valve cover, camshaft and valve train components, timing sprockets and chain or gears and timing cover. All components are installed with new bearings, seals and gaskets incorporated throughout. The installation of manifolds and external parts is all that's necessary.

Low mileage used engines - Some companies now offer low mileage used engines which is a very cost effective way to get your vehicle up and running again. These engines often come from vehicles which have been in totaled in accidents or come from other countries which have a higher vehicle turn over rate. A low mileage used engine also usually has a similar warranty like the newly remanufactured engines.

Give careful thought to which alternative is best for you and discuss the situation with local automotive machine shops, auto parts dealers and experienced rebuilders before ordering or purchasing replacement parts.

6   Engine removal - methods and precautions

Refer to illustrations 6.3 and 6.4

If you've decided that an engine must be removed for overhaul or major repair work, several preliminary steps should be taken. Read all removal and installation procedures carefully prior to committing to this job.

Locating a suitable place to work is extremely important. Adequate work space, along with storage space for the vehicle, will be needed. If a shop or garage isn't available,

at the very least a flat, level, clean work surface made of concrete or asphalt is required.

Cleaning the engine compartment and engine before beginning the removal procedure will help keep tools clean and organized.

An engine hoist will also be necessary. Make sure the hoist is rated in excess of the combined weight of the engine and transaxle. Safety is of primary importance, considering the potential hazards involved in removing the engine from the vehicle.

A vehicle hoist will be necessary for engine removal on V8 engines, since the engine and transaxle are removed as an assembly out the bottom of the vehicle. On V6 models, the engine is removed out the top.

If you're a novice at engine removal, get at least one helper. One person cannot easily do all the things you need to do to remove a big heavy engine and transaxle assembly from the engine compartment. Also helpful is to seek advice and assistance from someone who's experienced in engine removal.

Plan the operation ahead of time. Arrange for or obtain all of the tools and equipment you'll need prior to beginning the job **(see illustrations 6.3 and 6.4)**. Some of the equipment necessary to perform engine removal and installation safely and with relative ease are (in addition to a vehicle hoist and an engine hoist) a heavy duty floor jack (preferably fitted with a transaxle jack head adapter), complete sets of wrenches and sockets as described in the front of this manual, wooden blocks, plenty of rags and cleaning solvent for mopping up spilled oil, coolant and gasoline.

Plan for the vehicle to be out of use for quite a while. A machine shop can do the work that is beyond the scope of the home mechanic. Machine shops often have a busy schedule, so before removing the engine, consult the shop for an estimate of how long it will take to rebuild or repair the components that may need work.

7.5a Label both ends of each wire and hose before disconnecting it

7.5b On models through 1996, the ECM is located on the right side of the engine compartment ahead of the shock tower, on later models, it is located on the driver's side, next to or inside the air cleaner housing

7   Engine - removal and installation

Warning 1: *Gasoline is extremely flammable, so take extra precautions when you work on any part of the fuel system. Don't smoke or allow open flames or bare light bulbs near the work area, and don't work in a garage where a gas-type appliance (such as a water heater or clothes dryer) is present. Since gasoline is carcinogenic, wear fuel-resistant gloves when there's a·possibility of being exposed to fuel, and, if you spill any fuel on your skin, rinse it off immediately with soap and water. Mop up any spills immediately and do not store fuel-soaked rags where they could ignite. The fuel system is under constant pressure, so, if any fuel lines are to be disconnected, the fuel pressure in the system must be relieved first (see Chapter 4 for more information). When you perform any kind of work on the fuel system, wear safety glasses and have a Class B type fire extinguisher on hand.*
Warning 2: *The engine must be completely cool before beginning this procedure.*

7.13 Unbolt the power steering pump and move it aside, then use wire or rope to hold it in place (typical V6 engine shown, others similar)

All models except 5.3L V8

Refer to illustrations 7.5a, 7.5b, 7.13, 7.23 and 7.30

Removal

1   Carefully inspect the routing of the air conditioning system refrigerant lines before beginning the engine removal to see if line disconnection, and therefore professional discharging, is necessary. Have the air conditioning system discharged by a dealer service department or service station.

All models

2   Refer to Chapter 4 and relieve the fuel system pressure, then disconnect the negative cable from the battery. **Caution:** *On models equipped with the Theftlock audio system, be sure the lockout feature is turned off before performing any procedure which requires disconnecting the battery.*
3   Cover the fenders and cowl and remove the hood (see Chapter 11). Special pads are available to protect the fenders, but an old bedspread or blanket will also work.
4   Remove the air cleaner assembly (and MAF sensor on V6 models so equipped) (see Chapter 4).
5   Remove the plastic firewall covers. Label the vacuum lines, emissions system hoses, wiring connectors, ground straps and fuel lines to ensure correct reinstallation, then detach them. The relay panel and bracket can be detached as an assembly. Pieces of masking tape with numbers or letters written on them work well **(see illustration)**. If there's any possibility of confusion, make a sketch of the engine compartment and clearly label the lines, hoses and wires. **Note 1:** *The ECM wiring can be unplugged and the harness pulled through the firewall. The engine harness plugs into the firewall connector.* **Note 2:** *On some models, the plastic wire harness must be detached from the body and the ECM and the fuse block placed on top of the engine* **(see illustration)**.
6   Raise the vehicle and support it securely on jackstands. Drain the cooling system (see Chapter 1).
7   Label and detach all coolant hoses from the engine.
8   Remove the coolant reservoir, cooling fan, shroud and radiator (see Chapter 3).
9   Remove the drivebelt and idler, if equipped (see Chapter 1). On 2.5L four-cylinder and V6 models, remove the crankshaft pulley/vibration damper (see Parts A through F of this Chapter, depending on engine type/size).
10   Disconnect the fuel lines running from the engine to the chassis (see Chapter 4). Plug or cap all open fittings/lines.
11   Remove the torque struts on the engine (see *Engine mounts - removal and installation* in Parts A through F of this Chapter, depending on engine type/size).
12   Disconnect the accelerator cable (and TV cable/cruise control cable, if equipped)

7.23 Attach the chain or hoist cable to the engine brackets (arrows)

7.30 Lift the engine off the mounts and guide it carefully around any obstacles as an assistant raises the hoist until it clears the front of the vehicle

from the engine (see Chapters 4 and 7).

13   Unbolt the power steering pump and set it aside (see Chapter 10). Leave the lines/hoses attached and make sure the pump is kept in an upright position in the engine compartment **(see illustration)**.

14   Remove the steering gear pinch bolt and separate the intermediate shaft from the rack and pinion stub shaft (steering gear). **Caution:** *Be sure to separate the steering gear from the rack and pinion stub shaft to avoid damage to the steering gear and intermediate shaft. This damage could cause loss of steering control which could result in injury.*

15   Unbolt the air conditioning compressor (see Chapter 3) and set it aside.

16   Drain the engine oil and remove the filter (see Chapter 1).

17   Remove the starter and the alternator (see Chapter 5).

18   On Quad-4 models, remove the oil/air separator (see Chapter 6).

19   Check for clearance and remove the brake master cylinder, if necessary, to allow clearance for the transaxle (see Chapter 9).

20   Disconnect the exhaust system from the engine (see Chapter 4). On Quad-4 models, remove the exhaust manifold (see Chapter 2C). **Note:** *On V6 and Quad-4 models, the engine and transaxle are removed from the vehicle as a unit. 2.5 liter four-cylinder engines should be removed from the vehicle after the transaxle has been removed.*

V6 and Quad-4 models only

21   Disconnect all the components attaching the transaxle to the vehicle (including driveaxles, intermediate shaft, cables, wiring, linkage, etc. - see Chapter 7).

22   Support the transaxle with a jack. Position a block of wood on the jack head to prevent damage to the transaxle.

All models

23   Attach an engine sling or a length of chain to the lifting brackets on the engine **(see illustration)**. **Note:** *On 1996 and later V6 models, the transaxle may be supported by a jack and left in the vehicle while the engine is removed.*

24   Roll the hoist into position and connect the sling to it. Take up the slack in the sling or chain, but don't lift the engine. **Warning:** *DO NOT place any part of your body under the engine when it's supported only by a hoist or other lifting device.*

25   If you're working on a vehicle with an automatic transaxle, refer to Chapter 7 and remove the torque converter-to-driveplate fasteners.

26   Remove the transaxle-to-body mount nuts and pry the mount out of the frame bracket.

27   On 2.5 liter four-cylinder models, remove the transaxle (see Chapter 7).

28   Remove the engine mount-to-chassis bolts/nuts.

29   Recheck to be sure nothing is still connecting the engine to the vehicle. Disconnect anything still remaining.

30   Raise the engine (or engine/transaxle assembly) slightly to disengage the mounts. Slowly raise the engine out of the vehicle **(see illustration)**. Check carefully to make sure nothing is hanging up as the hoist is raised.

31   If the engine and transaxle were removed as a unit, set the engine/transaxle on the floor with wooded block to keep either unit from falling. Remove the engine-to-transaxle mounting bolts. Carefully separate the engine from the transaxle. If you're working on a vehicle with an automatic transaxle, be sure the torque converter stays in place (clamp a pair of locking pliers to the housing to keep the converter from sliding out). If you're working on a vehicle with a manual transaxle, the input shaft must be completely disengaged from the clutch.

32   Remove the clutch and flywheel or driveplate and mount the engine on an engine stand.

Installation

33   Check the engine and transaxle mounts. If they're worn or damaged, replace them.

34   If you're working on a manual transaxle equipped vehicle, install the clutch and pressure plate (see Chapter 7). Now is a good time to install new clutch components. Apply a dab of high-temperature grease to the input shaft.

35   **Caution:** *DO NOT use the transaxle-to-engine bolts to force the transaxle and engine together. If you're working on an automatic transaxle equipped vehicle, take great care when installing the torque converter, following the procedure outlined in Chapter 7.*

36   Carefully lower the engine into the engine compartment - make sure the mounts line up. Reinstall the remaining components in the reverse order of removal. Double-check to make sure everything is hooked up correctly.

37   Add coolant, oil, power steering and transmission fluid as needed. If the brake master cylinder was removed, bleed the brakes (see Chapter 9). Recheck the fluid level and test the brakes.

38   Run the engine and check for leaks and proper operation of all accessories, then install the hood and test drive the vehicle.

39   If the air conditioning system was discharged, have it evacuated, recharged and leak tested by the shop that discharged it.

V8 models

Refer to illustrations 7.54, 7.55, 7.57, 7.60, 7.62, 7.64, 7.74, 7.75 and 7.79

Note 1: *The engine is removed from the bottom of the engine compartment on V8 models. This procedure requires the use of a vehicle hoist. Only begin this procedure if all of the necessary equipment is at hand. With only*

7.54 Remove the bolts from the fuse/relay block . . .

7.55 . . . then separate the fuse/relay block and detach the four large electrical connectors from the back

a floor jack and jackstands, the vehicle can't safely be raised high enough for the engine/ transmission to slide out from underneath.

Note 2: *Read through the entire Section before beginning this procedure. The engine and transmission are removed as a unit from below and then separated once clear of the vehicle.*

40   Have the air conditioning refrigerant evacuated at an approved service facility.

41   Park the vehicle squarely on a frame-contact type hoist and adjust the hoist arms to correctly align with the jacking points of the vehicle. Point the wheels straight ahead. **Warning:** *Tie the front of the body down to the hoist so the car doesn't tilt back and fall off the hoist when the weight of the engine and transmission is removed.*

42   Remove the engine top cover. Relieve the fuel system pressure (see Chapter 4).

43   Disconnect the cable from the negative battery terminal (see Chapter 5, Section 4).

44   Loosen the front wheel lug nuts. Raise the vehicle and remove the front wheels.

45   Drain the engine oil and coolant (see Chapter 1).

46   Disconnect the radiator hoses at the engine.

47   Disconnect the air conditioning lines near the left side of the radiator.

48   Disconnect the power brake booster vacuum hose from the intake manifold.

49   Suction the fluid from the master cylinder, then remove the two brake lines.

50   Remove the master cylinder (see Chapter 9).

51   Disconnect the fuel supply tube from the intake manifold (see Chapter 4).

52   Remove the EVAP line from the purge solenoid.

53   Remove both fender braces.

54   Remove the cover from the electrical cen-ter, then unscrew the four captive bolts in the center of the fuse block **(see illustration)**.

55   Disconnect the four large harness connectors from the back of the fuse block **(see illustration)**.

56   Disconnect the wiring from the ABS controller, the camshaft position (CMP) sensor and the brake booster vacuum sensor. Also disconnect the two large electrical connectors at the left strut tower.

57   Remove the upper part of the air cleaner assembly, exposing the electronic modules in its base. Disconnect the harnesses from the modules and move them from the housing **(see illustration)**.

58   Disconnect the remaining wiring and harness clips running between the engine and the chassis (the wiring harnesses will be removed with the engine/transaxle assembly).

59   Use a screwdriver to pry the shifter cable

7.57 Flip the locking levers back, then disconnect the electrical connectors from the PCM and TCM

7.60 Remove the heat shield from over the vehicle speed sensor, then disconnect the electrical connector

7.62 Remove the steering shaft pinch bolt

7.64 Squeeze the clamps and slide them back on the hoses, then disconnect the heater hoses from the pipes

from the transmission shift lever and then disconnect the cable from the bracket.

60   Working through the right-side wheel well, remove the heat shield from the vehicle speed sensor and then disconnect the sensor **(see illustration)**.

61   Make sure all the wiring is disconnected and put the harnesses where they will not be damaged during engine removal.

62   Pull up the plastic cover from the steering shaft, then remove the shaft pinch bolt **(see illustration)**. Push the steering shaft off of the steering rack. **Note:** *The shaft might not come off all the way at this time; you may have to detach it as the vehicle is being raised from the engine/transaxle assembly.*

63   Disconnect the front wheel speed sensors at the hubs and release the wiring from the control arms.

64   Disconnect the heater hoses **(see illustration)**.

65   Disconnect the stabilizer bar links, the outer tie-rod ends and the lower ball joints (see Chapter 10).

66   Disconnect the power steering hoses as required.

67   Remove both driveaxles (see Chapter 8).

68   Disconnect the cooler lines from the transmission.

69   Disconnect the starter wiring and the grounds in the vicinity of the starter (see Chapter 5). Also disconnect the harnesses from the subframe.

70   Remove the catalytic converter (see Chapter 4).

71   Remove the torque converter bolt access cover, then remove the torque converter bolts.

72   Remove the lower air dam from beneath the front bumper (see Chapter 11).

73   Place four jackstands under the subframe and lower the vehicle slightly to put some weight on the jackstands.

74   Remove the four subframe bolts **(see illustration)**. Verify that there are no harnesses, hoses, etc. that will interfere with raising the vehicle off of the engine/transmission module.

75   Slowly raise the vehicle while checking for obstructions **(see illustration)**. Make sure that the engine and transmission are secure.

76   Attach an engine hoist to the engine and raise it just enough to take weight off of the engine mounts.

77   Disconnect both engine mounts from the subframe.

78   Remove the transaxle bolts.

7.74 Locations of the subframe mounting bolts

7.75 Once it has been confirmed that nothing is still attached between the engine/transaxle/subframe and the rest of the chassis, the vehicle can be raised on the hoist

7.79 Attach an engine hoist to the engine, remove the transaxle-to-engine bolts, then carefully lift the engine up and away from the transaxle

7.81 Use a plumb-bob to get the engine/transaxle/subframe lined-up with the bolt holes in the body

79   Slowly and carefully lift the engine away from the transaxle and off of the subframe **(see illustration)**.

80   Remove the driveplate and mount the engine on an engine stand.

Installation

Refer to illustration 7.81

81   Installation is the reverse of the removal process, noting the following points:

a) *Check the engine and transmission mounts. If they're worn, replace them.*

b) *When positioning the subframe beneath the vehicle, make a plumb-bob from a piece of string and a nut. Hold the string at each subframe bolt hole on the body and verify that its corresponding sub-frame bolt hole is directly below it. This will eliminate trying to adjust the sub-frame as the vehicle is lowered over it* **(see illustration)**.

c) *Tighten the subframe mounting bolts to the torque listed in this Chapter's Speci-fications.*

d) *Tighten the torque converter bolts to the torque listed in this Chapter's Specifica-tions.*

e) *Refill the cooling system with the proper mixture of coolant and refill the engine with the recommended oil (see Chapter 1).*

f) *Check the transmission fluid level and add fluid as necessary.*

g) *Have the air conditioning system recharged by the shop that discharged it.*

8   Engine overhaul - disassembly sequence

1   It's much easier to remove the external components if the engine is mounted on a portable engine stand. A stand can often be rented quite cheaply from an equipment rental yard. Before the engine is mounted on a stand, the driveplate should be removed from the engine.

2   If a stand isn't available, it's possible to remove the external engine components with it blocked up on the floor. Be extra careful not to tip or drop the engine when working without a stand.

3   If you're going to obtain a rebuilt engine, all external components must come off first, to be transferred to the replacement engine. These components include:

> *Driveplate*
> *Ignition system components*
> *Emissions-related components*
> *Engine mounts and mount brackets*
> *Engine rear cover (spacer plate between driveplate and engine block), if equipped*
> *Intake/exhaust manifolds*
> *Fuel injection components*
> *Oil filter*
> *Spark plugs and ignition coil pack (and spark plug wires) or coil-over plug assemblies*
> *Thermostat and housing assembly*
> *Water pump*

Note: *When removing the external compo-nents from the engine, pay close attention to details that may be helpful or important during*

9.3 When checking the camshaft lobe lift, the dial indicator plunger must be positioned directly above and in line with the pushrod

installation. Note the installed position of gas-kets, seals, spacers, pins, brackets, washers, bolts and other small items.

4   If you're going to obtain a short block (assembled engine block, crankshaft, pistons and connecting rods), then remove the tim-ing chain or belt, cylinder head(s), oil pan, oil pump pick-up tube, oil pump and water pump from your engine so that you can turn in your old short block to the rebuilder as a core. See *Engine rebuilding alternatives* for additional information regarding the different possibili-ties to be considered.

9   Camshaft, intermediate shaft (3.4L) and balance shaft (3800) - removal, inspection and installation

Camshaft lobe lift check

With cylinder head installed

Refer to illustration 9.3

1   In order to determine the extent of cam lobe wear, the lobe lift should be checked prior to camshaft removal. Refer to Part A, B, D or F and remove the valve cover(s).

2   Position the number one piston at TDC on the compression stroke (see Section 4).

3   Beginning with the number one cylinder valves, mount a dial indicator on the engine and position the plunger against the top surface of the first rocker arm. The plunger should be directly above and in line with the pushrod **(see illustration)**.

4   Zero the dial indicator, then very slowly turn the crankshaft in the normal direction of rotation (clockwise) until the indicator needle stops and begins to move in the opposite direction. The point at which it stops indicates maximum cam lobe lift.

5   Record this figure for future reference, then reposition the piston at TDC on the com-pression stroke.

6   Move the dial indicator to the remaining

9.9 To verify camshaft lobe lift, measure the major (A) and minor (B) diameters of each lobe with a micrometer or vernier caliper - subtract each minor diameter from the major diameter to arrive at the lobe lift

9.12a The V6 engine oil pump drive (arrow) is located at the transaxle-end of the block

number one cylinder rocker arm and repeat the check. Be sure to record the results for each valve.

7   Repeat the check for the remaining valves. Since each piston must be at TDC on the compression stroke for this procedure, work from cylinder-to-cylinder following the firing order sequence.

8   After the check is complete, compare the results to determine if one or more readings is dramatically less than the others. Normally when a camshaft wears out, one lobe is virtually destroyed and there is much more damage than simply increased wear.

With cylinder head removed

Refer to illustration 9.9

9   If the cylinder head(s) have already been removed, an alternate method of lobe

measurement can be used. Remove the camshaft as described below. Using a micrometer, measure the lobe at its highest point. Then measure the base circle perpendicular (90-degrees) to the lobe **(see illustration)**. Do this for each lobe and record the results.

10   Subtract the base circle measurement from the lobe height. The difference is the lobe lift. See Step 8 above.

Removal
Camshaft (all engines except Quad-4 and 3.4L) and intermediate shaft (3.4L)

Refer to illustrations 9.12a, 9.12b, 9.12c, 9.13, 9.14 and 19.15

Note 1: *The intermediate shaft on 3.4L engines is removed and installed much like a*

conventional camshaft, although it does not operate the lifters or valves.
Note 2: *For camshaft removal procedures on Quad-4 and 3.4L engines, refer to Chapter 2C or 2E.*

11   Remove the lifters and pushrods. On models so equipped, remove the timing chain and sprockets. Refer to the appropriate Section in Parts A, B, D or F, depending on the engine.

12   On the 2.2L four-cylinder and on V6 engines (except 3800), remove the oil pump drive **(see illustration)**. If it's stuck, remove the oil pump and push the drive out with a long socket extension (see illustration). Be sure to replace the O-ring before reassembly **(see illustration)**.

13   On the 2.2L four-cylinder and on V6 engines, thread long bolts into the camshaft

9.12b If the oil pump drive is stuck, remove the pump and push the drive out with a long socket extension

9.12c Be sure to replace the O-ring (arrow)

9.13 Thread long bolts into the sprocket bolt holes to use as a handle when removing and installing the camshaft (V6 engine)

9.14 On 2.5L engines the camshaft thrust plate bolts can be removed through the access holes in the camshaft timing gear

9.15 Support the camshaft near the block to avoid damaging the bearings

sprocket bolt holes to use as a handle when removing the camshaft from the block **(see illustration)**. On 3800 engines check the balance shaft drive gear back lash, then remove the drive gear before removing the camshaft (see Steps 16 through 18).

14   Remove the camshaft thrust plate. On 2.5L engines through 1990, rotate the camshaft so that you can get access to the thrust plate bolts through the holes in the timing gear **(see illustration)**.

15   Slide the camshaft or intermediate shaft straight out of the engine. Support the shaft near the block and be careful not to scrape or nick the bearings **(see illustration)**.

Balance shaft (3800 only)

Refer to illustrations 9.19 and 9.20

16   Refer to Chapter 2 Part F and remove the timing chain and sprockets (lifters should already be removed and stored in marked plastic bags).

17   Check the gear backlash between the balance shaft drive gear (behind the camshaft sprocket) and the balance shaft driven gear. Set up a dial indicator against the top teeth of the balance shaft driven gear (the one on the front of the balance shaft) and rock the gear by hand. Compare the backlash to this Chapter's Specifications. The gears will have to be replaced if the backlash is greater than specified.

18   Remove the balance shaft drive gear (behind the camshaft sprocket). Set up a dial indicator on the nose of the balance shaft and zero it. Reaching inside the lifter valley, grab the balance shaft and move it forward and back in the block while watching the dial indicator. Compare this endplay measurement with this Chapter's Specifications. If it is incor-

rect, a new balance shaft thrust plate will have to be installed.

19   Remove the two balance shaft thrust plate bolts and take off the thrust plate **(see illustration)**.

20   The balance shaft's front bearing fits tightly into the front of the block, and a slide hammer must be used to remove the shaft and its bearing **(see illustration)**. Once the bearing is free of the block, withdraw the balance shaft straight out by hand, being careful to not cock it against its rear bearing.

Inspection

Refer to illustration 9.24

21   After the camshaft, intermediate shaft or balance shaft has been removed, clean it with solvent and dry it, then inspect the bearing journals for uneven wear, pitting and evidence

9.19 Remove the retaining bolts and the balance shaft thrust plate

9.20 A slide hammer must be threaded into the front of the balance shaft to pull the balance shaft front bearing out of the block

9.24 The camshaft bearing journal diameters are checked to pinpoint excessive wear and out-of-round conditions

of seizure. If the journals are damaged, the bearing inserts in the block are probably damaged as well. Both the shaft and bearings will have to be replaced.

22   On 2.5L engines through 1990, if the timing gear must be removed from the camshaft, it must be pressed off. If you don't have access to a press, take it to an automotive machine shop. The thrust plate must be positioned so the Woodruff key in the shaft does not damage it when the shaft is pressed off.

23   If the gear has been removed, it must be pressed back on prior to installation of the camshaft.

a) Support the camshaft in a press by placing press plate adapters behind the front journal.
b) Place the gear spacer ring and the thrust plate over the end of the shaft.
c) Install the Woodruff key in the shaft keyway.
d) Position the camshaft gear and press it onto the shaft until it bottoms against the gear spacer ring.

e) Use a feeler gauge to check the end clearance. It should be 0.0015 to 0.0050 inch. If the clearance is less than 0.0015 inch, the spacer ring should be replaced. If the clearance is more than 0.0050 inch, the thrust plate should be replaced.

24   Measure the bearing journals with a micrometer (see illustration) to determine if they're excessively worn or out-of-round. Visually inspect them for grooves and other damage.

25   Check the camshaft lobes and oil pump drive and driven gears for heat discoloration, score marks, chipped areas, pitting and uneven wear. If the lobes and gears are in good condition and if the lobe lift measurements are as specified, the components can be reused.

26   Check the bearings in the block for wear and damage. Look for galling, pitting and discolored areas.

27   The inside diameter of each bearing can be determined with a small hole gauge and outside micrometer or an inside micrometer. Subtract the camshaft bearing journal

diameter(s) from the corresponding bearing inside diameter(s) to obtain the bearing oil clearance. If it's excessive, new bearings will be required regardless of the condition of the originals. Typical clearances should be no more than 0.005-inch.

28   Camshaft and balance shaft bearing replacement requires special tools and expertise that place it outside the scope of the home mechanic. Take the block to an automotive machine shop to ensure the job is done correctly.

Installation

Camshaft and intermediate shaft (3.4L)

Refer to illustrations 9.29 and 9.30

Note: *For camshaft installation procedures on Quad-4 and 3.4L engines, refer to Chapter 2C or 2E.*

29   Lubricate the camshaft bearing journals and cam lobes with moly-base grease or engine assembly lube (see illustration).

30   Slide the camshaft into the engine, using a long bolt (the same thread as the camshaft sprocket bolt) screwed into the front of the camshaft as a handle. Support the cam near the block and be careful not to scrape or nick the bearings. Install the camshaft retainer plate or intermediate shaft plate (3.4L) and tighten the bolts to the torque listed in this Chapter's Specifications. On 2.5L engines through 1990, align the timing marks on the camshaft gear and the crankshaft gear (see illustration). Install the thrust plate bolts and tighten them to the torque listed in this Chapter's Specifications.

31   On 2.2L four cylinder and V6 engines (except 3800), dip the gear portion of the oil pump drive in engine oil and insert it into the block. It should be flush with its mounting boss before inserting the retaining bolt. **Note:** *Position a new O-ring on the oil pump driveshaft*

9.29 Be sure to prelube the bearing journals and lobes prior to camshaft installation

9.30 On 2.5L engines, the camshaft and crankshaft gears must be positioned so the timing marks (arrows) line up

9.33 Drive the front balance shaft bearing in (it's attached to the balance shaft) just until the retainer plate can be installed

9.36 The balance shaft gear mark (arrow) should point straight down

before installation.

32   Refer to Part A, B, D or F (depending on engine type and size) to complete the installation of the lifters, timing chain and sprockets. On 3800 engines, perform the following procedure for balance shaft installation before installing the timing chain and sprockets.

Balance shaft (3800 only)

Refer to illustrations 9.33, 9.36 and 9.37

33   Lubricate the front bearing and rear journal of the balance shaft with engine oil and insert the balance shaft carefully into the block. When the front bearing approaches the insert in the front of the block, use a hammer and an appropriate-size socket to drive the front bearing into its insert. Drive it in just enough to allow installation of the balance shaft bearing retainer **(see illustration)**. Tighten the balance shaft retainer bolts to the

torque listed in this Chapter's Specifications.
34   Install the balance shaft driven gear and its bolt.
35   Turn the camshaft so that with the camshaft sprocket temporarily installed, the timing mark is straight down.
36   With the camshaft sprocket and the camshaft gear removed, turn the balance shaft so the timing mark on the gear points straight down **(see illustration)**.
37   Install the camshaft gear (that drives the balance shaft) onto the cam, aligning it with the keyway and align the marks on the balance shaft gear and the camshaft gear **(see illustration)** by turning the balance shaft.
38   After the camshaft sprocket, crankshaft sprocket and timing chain have been installed (see Chapter 2, Part F), tighten the balance shaft driven gear bolt to the torque listed in this Chapter's Specifications.

10   Pistons and connecting rods - removal and installation

Removal

Refer to illustrations 10.1, 10.3 and 10.4

Note: *Prior to removing the piston/connecting rod assemblies, remove the cylinder head and oil pan (see Chapter 2A).*

1   Use your fingernail to feel if a ridge has formed at the upper limit of ring travel (about 1/4-inch down from the top of each cylinder). If carbon deposits or cylinder wear have produced ridges, they must be completely removed with a special tool **(see illustration)**. Follow the manufacturer's instructions provided with the tool. Failure to remove the ridges before attempting to remove the piston/connecting rod assemblies may result in pis-

9.37 Align the marks (arrows) on both balance shaft gears as shown

10.1 A ridge reamer is required to remove the ridge from the top of each cylinder - do this before removing the pistons!

10.3 Check the connecting rod endplay with a feeler gauge as shown

10.4 If the connecting rods and caps are not marked, use paint to mark the caps to the rods by cylinder number (for example, this would be the No. 4 connecting rod)

ton breakage.

2   After the cylinder ridges have been removed, turn the engine so the crankshaft is facing up.

3   Before the main bearing cap assembly and connecting rods are removed, check the connecting rod endplay with feeler gauges. Slide them between the first connecting rod and the crankshaft throw until the play is removed **(see illustration)**. Repeat this procedure for each connecting rod. The endplay is equal to the thickness of the feeler gauge(s). Check with an automotive machine shop for the endplay service limit (a typical endplay limit should measure between 0.005 to 0.015 inch [0.127 to 0.396 mm]). If the play exceeds the service limit, new connecting rods will be required. If new rods (or a new crankshaft) are installed, the endplay may fall under the minimum allowable. If it does, the rods will have to be machined to restore it. If necessary, consult an automotive machine shop for advice.

4   Check the connecting rods and caps for identification marks. If they aren't plainly marked, use paint or marker to clearly identify each rod and cap (1, 2, 3, etc., depending on the cylinder they're associated with) **(see illustration)**.

5   Remove the connecting rod cap bolts.

6   Remove the number one connecting rod cap and bearing insert. Don't drop the bearing insert out of the cap.

7   Remove the bearing insert and push the connecting rod/piston assembly out through the top of the engine. Use a wooden or plastic hammer handle to push on the upper bearing surface in the connecting rod. If resistance is felt, double-check to make sure that all of the ridge was removed from the cylinder.

8   Repeat the procedure for the remaining cylinders.

9   After removal, reassemble the connecting rod caps and bearing inserts in their respective connecting rods and install the cap bolts finger tight. Leaving the old bearing inserts in place until reassembly will help prevent the connecting rod bearing surfaces from being accidentally nicked or gouged.

10   The pistons and connecting rods are now ready for inspection and overhaul at an automotive machine shop.

Piston ring installation

Refer to illustrations 10.13, 10.14, 10.15, 10.19a, 10.19b and 10.22

11   Before installing the new piston rings,

the ring end gaps must be checked. It's assumed that the piston ring side clearance has been checked and verified correct. **Note:** *V6 engines are equipped with two different brand pistons. The correct piston rings must match the piston. To identify the piston brand, turn the piston over and look between the pin bores for a FM mark (Federal Mogul) or a no mark (Mahle) brand type. Use only the correct type of piston rings that match the piston manufacturer.*

12   Lay out the piston/connecting rod assemblies and the new ring sets so the ring sets will be matched with the same piston and cylinder during the end gap measurement and engine assembly.

13   Insert the top (number one) ring into the first cylinder and square it up with the cylinder walls by pushing it in with the top of the piston **(see illustration)**. The ring should be near the bottom of the cylinder, at the lower limit of ring travel.

14   To measure the end gap, slip feeler gauges between the ends of the ring until a gauge equal to the gap width is found **(see illustration)**. The feeler gauge should slide between the ring ends with a slight amount of drag. A typical ring gap should fall between 0.010 and 0.020 inch [0.25 to 0.50 mm] for

10.13 Install the piston ring into the cylinder then push it down into position using a piston so the ring will be square in the cylinder

10.14 With the ring square in the cylinder, measure the ring end gap with a feeler gauge

10.15 If the ring end gap is too small, clamp a file in a vise as shown and file the piston ring ends - be sure to remove all raised material

10.19a Installing the spacer/expander in the oil ring groove

compression rings and up to 0.030 inch [0.76 mm] for the oil ring steel rails. If the gap is larger or smaller than specified, double-check to make sure you have the correct rings before proceeding.

15   If the gap is too small, it must be enlarged or the ring ends may come in contact with each other during engine operation, which can cause serious damage to the engine. If necessary, increase the end gaps by filing the ring ends very carefully with a fine file. Mount the file in a vise equipped with soft jaws, slip the ring over the file with the ends contacting the file face and slowly move the ring to remove material from the ends. When performing this operation, file only by pushing the ring from the outside end of the file towards the vise **(see illustration)**.

16   Excess end gap isn't critical unless it's greater than 0.040 inch (1.01 mm). Again, double-check to make sure you have the correct ring type.

17   Repeat the procedure for each ring that will be installed in the first cylinder and for each ring in the remaining cylinders. Remember to keep rings, pistons and cylinders matched up.

18   Once the ring end gaps have been checked/corrected, the rings can be installed on the pistons.

19   The oil control ring (lowest one on the piston) is usually installed first. It's composed of three separate components. Slip the spacer/expander into the groove **(see illustration)**. If an anti-rotation tang is used, make sure it's inserted into the drilled hole in the ring groove. Next, install the upper side rail in the same manner **(see illustration)**. Don't use a piston ring installation tool on the oil ring side rails, as they may be damaged. Instead, place one end of the side rail into the groove between the spacer/expander and the ring land, hold it firmly in place and slide a finger around the piston while pushing the rail into the groove.

Finally, install the lower side rail.

20   After the three oil ring components have been installed, check to make sure that both the upper and lower side rails can be rotated smoothly inside the ring grooves.

21   The number two (middle) ring is installed next. It's usually stamped with a mark which must face up, toward the top of the piston. Do not mix up the top and middle rings, as they have different cross-sections. **Note 1:** *Always follow the instructions printed on the ring package or box - different manufacturers may require different approaches.*

22   Use a piston ring installation tool and make sure the identification mark is facing the top of the piston, then slip the ring into the middle groove on the piston **(see illustration)**. Don't expand the ring any more than necessary to slide it over the piston.

23   Install the number one (top) ring in the same manner. Make sure the mark is facing up. Be careful not to confuse the number one

10.19b DO NOT use a piston ring installation tool when installing the oil control side rails

10.22 Use a piston ring installation tool to install the number 2 and the number 1 (top) rings - be sure the directional mark on the piston ring(s) is facing toward the top of the piston

10.30 Piston ring end gap positions

10.35 Use a plastic or wooden hammer handle to push the piston into the cylinder

and number two rings.

24 Repeat the procedure for the remaining pistons and rings.

Installation

25 Before installing the piston/connecting rod assemblies, the cylinder walls must be perfectly clean, the top edge of each cylinder bore must be chamfered, and the crankshaft must be in place.

26 Remove the cap from the end of the number one connecting rod (refer to the marks made during removal). Remove the original bearing inserts and wipe the bearing surfaces of the connecting rod and cap with a clean, lint-free cloth. They must be kept spotlessly clean.

Connecting rod bearing oil clearance check

Refer to illustrations 10.30, 10.35, 10.37 and 10.41

27 Clean the back side of the new upper bearing insert, then lay it in place in the connecting rod.

10.37 Place Plastigage on each connecting rod bearing journal parallel to the crankshaft centerline

28 Make sure the tab on the bearing fits into the recess in the rod. Don't hammer the bearing insert into place and be very careful not to nick or gouge the bearing face. Don't lubricate the bearing at this time.

29 Clean the back side of the other bearing insert and install it in the rod cap. Again, make sure the tab on the bearing fits into the recess in the cap, and don't apply any lubricant. It's critically important that the mating surfaces of the bearing and connecting rod are perfectly clean and oil free when they're assembled.

30 Position the piston ring gaps at the specified intervals around the piston as shown **(see illustration)**.

31 Lubricate the piston and rings with clean engine oil and attach a piston ring compressor to the piston. Leave the skirt protruding about 1/4-inch to guide the piston into the cylinder. The rings must be compressed until they're flush with the piston.

32 Rotate the crankshaft until the number one connecting rod journal is at BDC (bottom dead center) and apply a liberal coat of engine oil to the cylinder walls.

33 With the arrow on top of the piston facing the front (timing chain) of the engine, gently insert the piston/connecting rod assembly into the number one cylinder bore and rest the bottom edge of the ring compressor on the engine block.

34 Tap the top edge of the ring compressor to make sure it's contacting the block around its entire circumference.

35 Gently tap on the top of the piston with the end of a wooden or plastic hammer handle **(see illustration)** while guiding the end of the connecting rod into place on the crankshaft journal. The piston rings may try to pop out of the ring compressor just before entering the cylinder bore, so keep some downward pressure on the ring compressor. Work slowly, and if any resistance is felt as the piston enters the cylinder, stop immediately. Find out what's hanging up and fix it before proceeding. Do not, for any reason, force the piston into the cylinder - you might break a ring and/or the piston.

36 Once the piston/connecting rod assembly is installed, the connecting rod bearing oil clearance must be checked before the rod cap is permanently installed.

37 Cut a piece of the appropriate size Plastigage slightly shorter than the width of the connecting rod bearing and lay it in place on the number one connecting rod journal, parallel with the journal axis **(see illustration)**.

38 Clean the connecting rod cap bearing face and install the rod cap. Make sure the mating mark on the cap is on the same side as the mark on the connecting rod **(see illustration 10,4)**.

39 Install the rod bolts, and tighten them to the torque listed in this Chapter's Specifications. **Note:** *Use a thin-wall socket to avoid erroneous torque readings that can result if the socket is wedged between the rod cap and the bolt. If the socket tends to wedge itself between the fastener and the cap, lift up on it slightly until it no longer contacts the cap. DO NOT rotate the crankshaft at any time during this operation.*

ENGINE BEARING ANALYSIS

Debris

Aluminum bearing embedded with glass beads

Babbitt bearing embedded with debris from machinings

Microscopic detail of debris

Microscopic detail of gouges

Overplated copper alloy bearing gouged by cast iron debris

Damaged lining caused by dirt left on the bearing back

Microscopic detail of glass beads

Misassembly

Result of a lower half assembled as an upper - blocking the oil flow

Excessive oil clearance is indicated by a short contact arc

Polished and oil-stained backs are a result of a poor fit in the housing bore

Result of a wrong, reversed, or shifted cap

Overloading

Damage from excessive idling which resulted in an oil film unable to support the load imposed

Damaged upper connecting rod bearings caused by engine lugging; the lower main bearings (not shown) were similarly affected

The damage shown in these upper and lower connecting rod bearings was caused by engine operation at a higher-than-rated speed under load

Misalignment

A warped crankshaft caused this pattern of severe wear in the center, diminishing toward the ends

A poorly finished crankshaft caused the equally spaced scoring shown

A tapered housing bore caused the damage along one edge of this pair

A bent connecting rod led to the damage in the "V" pattern

Lubrication

Result of dry start: The bearings on the left, farthest from the oil pump, show more damage

Result of a low oil supply or oil starvation

Severe wear as a result of inadequate oil clearance

Corrosion

Microscopic detail of corrosion

Corrosion is an acid attack on the bearing lining generally caused by inadequate maintenance, extremely hot or cold operation, or inferior oils or fuels

Microscopic detail of cavitation

Example of cavitation - a surface erosion caused by pressure changes in the oil film

Damage from excessive thrust or insufficient axial clearance

Bearing affected by oil dilution caused by excessive blow-by or a rich mixture

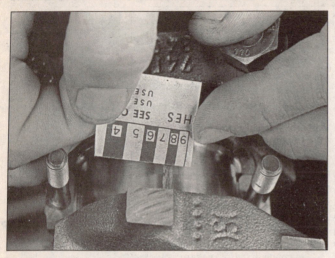

10.41 Use the scale on the Plastigage package to determine the bearing oil clearance - be sure to measure the widest part of the Plastigage and use the correct scale; it comes with both standard and metric scales

11.1 Checking crankshaft endplay with a dial indicator

40   Remove the fasteners and detach the rod cap, being very careful not to disturb the Plastigage.
41   Compare the width of the crushed Plastigage to the scale printed on the Plastigage envelope to obtain the oil clearance **(see illustration)**. The connecting rod oil clearance is usually about 0.001 to 0.002 inch. Consult an automotive machine shop for the clearance specified for the rod bearings on your engine.
42   If the clearance is not as specified, the bearing inserts may be the wrong size (which means different ones will be required). Before deciding that different inserts are needed, make sure that no dirt or oil was between the bearing inserts and the connecting rod or cap when the clearance was measured. Also, recheck the journal diameter. If the Plastigage was wider at one end than the other, the journal may be tapered. If the clearance still exceeds the limit specified, the bearing will have to be replaced with an undersize bearing. **Caution:** *When installing a new crankshaft always use a standard size bearing.*

Final installation

43   Carefully scrape all traces of the Plastigage material off the rod journal and/or bearing face. Be very careful not to scratch the bearing - use your fingernail or the edge of a plastic card.
44   Make sure the bearing faces are perfectly clean, then apply a uniform layer of clean moly-base grease or engine assembly lube to both of them. You'll have to push the piston into the cylinder to expose the face of the bearing insert in the connecting rod.
45   Slide the connecting rod back into place on the journal, install the rod cap, install the bolts and tighten them to the torque listed in this Chapter's Specifications.
46   Repeat the entire procedure for the remaining pistons/connecting rods.
47   The important points to remember are:

a) Keep the back sides of the bearing inserts and the insides of the connecting rods and caps perfectly clean when assembling them.
b) Make sure you have the correct piston/ rod assembly for each cylinder.
c) The arrow on the piston must face the front (timing chain) of the engine.
d) Lubricate the cylinder walls liberally with clean oil.
e) Lubricate the bearing faces when installing the rod caps after the oil clearance has been checked.

48   After all the piston/connecting rod assemblies have been correctly installed, rotate the crankshaft a number of times by hand to check for any obvious binding.
49   As a final step, check the connecting rod endplay as described in Step 3. If it was correct before disassembly and the original crankshaft and rods were reinstalled, it should still be correct. If new rods or a new crankshaft were installed, the endplay may be inadequate. If so, the rods will have to be removed and taken to an automotive machine shop for resizing.

---

11   Crankshaft - removal and installation

Removal

Refer to illustrations 11.1 and 11.3
Note: *The crankshaft can be removed only after the engine has been removed from the vehicle. It's assumed that the driveplate, crankshaft pulley, timing chain, oil pan, oil pump body, oil filter and piston/connecting rod assemblies have already been removed. The rear main oil seal retainer must be unbolted and separated from the block before proceeding with crankshaft removal.*
1   Before the crankshaft is removed, mea-

sure the endplay. Mount a dial indicator with the indicator in line with the crankshaft and just touching the end of the crankshaft as shown **(see illustration)**.
2   Pry the crankshaft all the way to the rear and zero the dial indicator. Next, pry the crankshaft to the front as far as possible and check the reading on the dial indicator. The distance traveled is the endplay. A typical crankshaft endplay will fall between 0.003 to 0.010 inch (0.076 to 0.254 mm). If it is greater than that, check the crankshaft thrust surfaces for wear after it's removed. If no wear is evident, new main bearings should correct the endplay.
3   If a dial indicator isn't available, feeler gauges can be used. Gently pry the crankshaft all the way to the front of the engine. Slip feeler gauges between the crankshaft and the front face of the thrust bearing or washer to determine the clearance **(see illustration)**.
4   Loosen the main bearing cap bolts 1/4-turn at a time each, until they can be removed by hand.
5   Remove the main bearing caps. Pull the main bearing cap straight up and off the

11.3 Checking the crankshaft endplay with feeler gauges at the thrust bearing journal

11.17 Place the Plastigage onto the crankshaft bearing journal as shown

11.21 Use the scale on the Plastigage package to determine the bearing oil clearance - be sure to measure the widest part of the Plastigage and use the correct scale; it comes with both standard and metric scales

cylinder block. Removing the caps from a V8 engine may require a special slide-hammer removal tool that threads into the caps. Gently tap the main bearing cap with a soft-face hammer, if necessary.

6   Carefully lift the crankshaft out of the engine. It may be a good idea to have an assistant available, since the crankshaft is quite heavy and awkward to handle. With the bearing inserts in place inside the engine block and main bearing caps, reinstall the main bearing caps onto the engine block and tighten the bolts finger tight. Make sure the caps are in the exact order they were removed with the arrow pointing toward the front (timing chain and front cover) of the engine.

Installation

7   Crankshaft installation is the first step in engine reassembly. It's assumed at this point that the engine block and crankshaft have been cleaned, inspected and repaired or reconditioned.

8   Position the engine block with the bottom facing up.

9   Remove the bolts and lift off the main bearing caps.

10   If they're still in place, remove the original bearing inserts from the block and from the main bearing caps. Wipe the bearing surfaces of the block and main bearing cap assembly with a clean, lint-free cloth. They must be kept spotlessly clean. This is critical for determining the correct bearing oil clearance.

Main bearing oil clearance check

Refer to illustrations 11.17 and 11.21

11   Without mixing them up, clean the back sides of the new upper main bearing inserts (with grooves and oil holes) and lay one in each main bearing saddle in the engine block. Each upper bearing (engine block) has an oil groove and oil hole in it. **Caution:**

The oil holes in the block must line up with the oil holes in the engine block inserts. The thrust washer or thrust bearing insert must be installed in the correct location. **Note:** *The thrust bearing is located on the 3rd journal in the main bearing cap journals (counting from the front).* Clean the back sides of the lower main bearing inserts and lay them in the corresponding location in the main bearing caps. Make sure the tab on the bearing insert fits into the recess in the block or main bearing caps. **Caution:** *Do not hammer the bearing insert into place and don't nick or gouge the bearing faces. DO NOT apply any lubrication at this time.*

12   Clean the faces of the bearing inserts in the block and the crankshaft main bearing journals with a clean, lint-free cloth.

13   Check or clean the oil holes in the crankshaft, as any dirt here can go only one way - straight through the new bearings.

14   Once you're certain the crankshaft is clean, carefully lay it in position in the cylinder block.

15   Before the crankshaft can be permanently installed, the main bearing oil clearance must be checked.

16   Cut several strips of the appropriate size of Plastigage. They must be slightly shorter than the width of the main bearing journal.

17   Place one piece on each crankshaft main bearing journal, parallel with the journal axis as shown **(see illustration)**.

18   Clean the faces of the bearing inserts in the main bearing caps or lower crankcase. Install the caps without disturbing the Plastigage.

19   Apply clean engine oil to all bolt threads prior to installation, install all bolts finger-tight, then tighten them to the torque listed in this Chapter's Specifications. DO NOT rotate the crankshaft at any time during this operation. **Note:** *On V8 engines, follow the correct torque sequence* **(see illustration 10.30)**, *but note that it isn't necessary to install the side*

bolts at this time (just bolts 1 through 20).

20   Remove the bolts and carefully lift the main bearing caps straight up and off the block. Do not disturb the Plastigage or rotate the crankshaft.

21   Compare the width of the crushed Plastigage on each journal to the scale printed on the Plastigage envelope to determine the main bearing oil clearance **(see illustration)**. Check with an automotive machine shop for the crankshaft bearing oil clearance for your engine.

22   If the clearance is not as specified, the bearing inserts may be the wrong size (which means different ones will be required). Before deciding if different inserts are needed, make sure that no dirt or oil was between the bearing inserts and the caps or block when the clearance was measured. If the Plastigage was wider at one end than the other, the crankshaft journal may be tapered. If the clearance still exceeds the limit specified, the bearing insert(s) will have to be replaced with an undersize bearing insert(s). **Caution:** *When installing a new crankshaft always install a standard bearing insert set.*

23   Carefully scrape all traces of the Plastigage material off the main bearing journals and/or the bearing insert faces. Be sure to remove all residue from the oil holes. Use your fingernail or the edge of a plastic card - don't nick or scratch the bearing faces.

Final installation

Refer to illustration 11.30

24   Carefully lift the crankshaft out of the cylinder block.

25   Clean the bearing insert faces in the cylinder block, then apply a thin, uniform layer of moly-base grease or engine assembly lube to each of the bearing surfaces. Be sure to coat the thrust faces as well as the journal face of the thrust bearing.

26   Make sure the crankshaft journals are clean, then lay the crankshaft back in place in

the cylinder block.

27   Clean the bearing insert faces and apply the same lubricant to them. Clean the engine block and the bearing cap mating surfaces thoroughly. The surfaces must be free of oil residue.

28   Prior to installation, apply clean engine oil to all bolt threads wiping off any excess, then install all bolts finger-tight.

29   On all engines except the 5.3L V8, tighten the main bearing cap bolts to the torque listed in this Chapter's Specifications.

30   On V8 engines, tighten bolts one through ten to the torque listed in Step 1 of this Chapter's Specifications. Be sure to follow the correct sequence **(see illustration)**. Tap the crankshaft to the rear and then to the front to align the thrust bearing on V8 engines. The last tap must be in the forward direction.

31   Proceed with the rest of the fastener tightening steps listed in this Chapter's Specifications for the V8 engine, ending with the tightening of the NEW side bolts.

32   Recheck the crankshaft endplay with a feeler gauge or a dial indicator. The endplay should be correct if the crankshaft thrust faces aren't worn or damaged and if new bearings have been installed.

33   Rotate the crankshaft a number of times by hand to check for any obvious binding. It should rotate with a running torque of 50 in-lbs or less. If the running torque is too high, correct the problem at this time.

34   Install the new rear main oil seal (see Chapter 2A, 2B, 2C, 2D, 2E, 2F or 2G).

11.30 Main bearing cap tightening sequence - V8 engine

12 Engine overhaul - reassembly sequence

1   Before beginning engine reassembly, make sure you have all the necessary new parts, gaskets and seals as well as the following items on hand:

   Common hand tools
   A 1/2-inch drive torque wrench
   New engine oil
   Gasket sealant
   Thread locking compound

2   If you obtained a short block it will be necessary to install the cylinder head, the oil pump and pick-up tube, the oil pan, the water pump, the timing belt and timing cover, and the valve cover (see Chapter 2A, 2B, 2C, 2D, 2E, 2F or 2G). In order to save time and avoid problems, the external components must be installed in the following general order:

   Thermostat and housing cover
   Water pump
   Intake and exhaust manifolds
   Fuel injection components
   Emission control components
   Spark plugs
   Ignition coils or coil pack and spark plug wires
   Oil filter
   Engine mounts and mount brackets
   Driveplate

13 Initial start-up and break-in after overhaul

Warning: *Have a fire extinguisher handy when starting the engine for the first time.*

1   Once the engine has been installed in the vehicle, double-check the engine oil and coolant levels.

2   With the spark plugs out of the engine and the ignition system and fuel pump disabled, crank the engine until oil pressure registers on the gauge or the light goes out.

3   Install the spark plugs, hook up the plug wires and restore the ignition system and fuel pump functions.

4   Start the engine. It may take a few moments for the fuel system to build up pressure, but the engine should start without a great deal of effort.

5   After the engine starts, it should be allowed to warm up to normal operating temperature. While the engine is warming up, make a thorough check for fuel, oil and coolant leaks.

6   Shut the engine off and recheck the engine oil and coolant levels.

7   Drive the vehicle to an area with minimum traffic, accelerate from 30 to 50 mph, then allow the vehicle to slow to 30 mph with the throttle closed. Repeat the procedure 10 or 12 times. This will load the piston rings and cause them to seat properly against the cylinder walls. Check again for oil and coolant leaks.

8   Drive the vehicle gently for the first 500 miles (no sustained high speeds) and keep a constant check on the oil level. It is not unusual for an engine to use oil during the break-in period.

9   At approximately 500 to 600 miles, change the oil and filter.

10   For the next few hundred miles, drive the vehicle normally. Do not pamper it or abuse it.

11   After 2,000 miles, change the oil and filter again and consider the engine broken in.

COMMON ENGINE OVERHAUL TERMS

B

Backlash - The amount of play between two parts. Usually refers to how much one gear can be moved back and forth without moving the gear with which it's meshed.

Bearing Caps - The caps held in place by nuts or bolts which, in turn, hold the bearing surface. This space is for lubricating oil to enter.

Bearing clearance - The amount of space left between shaft and bearing surface. This space is for lubricating oil to enter.

Bearing crush - The additional height which is purposely manufactured into each bearing half to ensure complete contact of the bearing back with the housing bore when the engine is assembled.

Bearing knock - The noise created by movement of a part in a loose or worn bearing.

Blueprinting - Dismantling an engine and reassembling it to EXACT specifications.

Bore - An engine cylinder, or any cylindrical hole; also used to describe the process of enlarging or accurately refinishing a hole with a cutting tool, as to bore an engine cylinder. The bore size is the diameter of the hole.

Boring - Renewing the cylinders by cutting them out to a specified size. A boring bar is used to make the cut.

Bottom end - A term which refers collectively to the engine block, crankshaft, main bearings and the big ends of the connecting rods.

Break-in - The period of operation between installation of new or rebuilt parts and time in which parts are worn to the correct fit. Driving at reduced and varying speed for a specified mileage to permit parts to wear to the correct fit.

Bushing - A one-piece sleeve placed in a bore to serve as a bearing surface for shaft, piston pin, etc. Usually replaceable.

C

Camshaft - The shaft in the engine, on which a series of lobes are located for operating the valve mechanisms. The camshaft is driven by gears or sprockets and a timing chain. Usually referred to simply as the cam.

Carbon - Hard, or soft, black deposits found in combustion chamber, on plugs, under rings, on and under valve heads.

Cast iron - An alloy of iron and more than two percent carbon, used for engine blocks and heads because it's relatively inexpensive and easy to mold into complex shapes.

Chamfer - To bevel across (or a bevel on) the sharp edge of an object.

Chase - To repair damaged threads with a tap or die.

Combustion chamber - The space between the piston and the cylinder head, with the piston at top dead center, in which air-fuel mixture is burned.

Compression ratio - The relationship between cylinder volume (clearance volume) when the piston is at top dead center and cylinder volume when the piston is at bottom dead center.

Connecting rod - The rod that connects the crank on the crankshaft with the piston. Sometimes called a con rod.

Connecting rod cap - The part of the connecting rod assembly that attaches the rod to the crankpin.

Core plug - Soft metal plug used to plug the casting holes for the coolant passages in the block.

Crankcase - The lower part of the engine in which the crankshaft rotates; includes the lower section of the cylinder block and the oil pan.

Crank kit - A reground or reconditioned crankshaft and new main and connecting rod bearings.

Crankpin - The part of a crankshaft to which a connecting rod is attached.

Crankshaft - The main rotating member, or shaft, running the length of the crankcase, with offset throws to which the connecting rods are attached; changes the reciprocating motion of the pistons into rotating motion.

Cylinder sleeve - A replaceable sleeve, or liner, pressed into the cylinder block to form the cylinder bore.

D

Deburring - Removing the burrs (rough edges or areas) from a bearing.

Deglazer - A tool, rotated by an electric motor, used to remove glaze from cylinder walls so a new set of rings will seat.

E

Endplay - The amount of lengthwise movement between two parts. As applied to a crankshaft, the distance that the crankshaft can move forward and back in the cylinder block.

F

Face - A machinist's term that refers to removing metal from the end of a shaft or the face of a larger part, such as a flywheel.

Fatigue - A breakdown of material through a large number of loading and unloading cycles. The first signs are cracks followed shortly by breaks.

Feeler gauge - A thin strip of hardened steel, ground to an exact thickness, used to check clearances between parts.

Free height - The unloaded length or height of a spring.

Freeplay - The looseness in a linkage, or an assembly of parts, between the initial application of force and actual movement. Usually perceived as slop or slight delay.

Freeze plug - See Core plug.

G

Gallery - A large passage in the block that forms a reservoir for engine oil pressure.

Glaze - The very smooth, glassy finish that develops on cylinder walls while an engine is in service.

H

Heli-Coil - A rethreading device used when threads are worn or damaged. The device is installed in a retapped hole to reduce the thread size to the original size.

I

Installed height - The spring's measured length or height, as installed on the cylinder head. Installed height is measured from the spring seat to the underside of the spring retainer.

J

Journal - The surface of a rotating shaft which turns in a bearing.

K

Keeper - The split lock that holds the valve spring retainer in position on the valve stem.

Key - A small piece of metal inserted into matching grooves machined into two parts fitted together - such as a gear pressed onto a shaft - which prevents slippage between the two parts.

Knock - The heavy metallic engine sound, produced in the combustion chamber as a result of abnormal combustion - usually detonation. Knock is usually caused by a loose or worn bearing. Also referred to as detonation, pinging and spark knock. Connecting rod or main bearing knocks are created by too much oil clearance or insufficient lubrication.

L

Lands - The portions of metal between the piston ring grooves.

Lapping the valves - Grinding a valve face and its seat together with lapping compound.

Lash - The amount of free motion in a gear train, between gears, or in a mechanical assembly, that occurs before movement can begin. Usually refers to the lash in a valve train.

Lifter - The part that rides against the cam to transfer motion to the rest of the valve train.

M

Machining - The process of using a machine to remove metal from a metal part.

Main bearings - The plain, or babbit, bearings that support the crankshaft.

Main bearing caps - The cast iron caps, bolted to the bottom of the block, that support the main bearings.

Chapter 3
Cooling, heating and air conditioning systems

Contents

	Section
Air conditioning accumulator - removal and installation	14
Air conditioning compressor - removal and installation	15
Air conditioning condenser - removal and installation	16
Air conditioning expansion (orifice) tube - removal and installation	17
Air conditioning system - check and maintenance	13
Antifreeze - general information	2
Coolant level check	See Chapter 1
Coolant reservoir - removal and installation	6
Coolant temperature sending unit or low coolant sensor - check and replacement	9
Cooling system check	See Chapter 1

	Section
Cooling system servicing	See Chapter 1
Engine cooling fan - check and replacement	4
General information	1
Heater and air conditioner blower motor - removal and installation	10
Heater and air conditioner control assembly - removal and installation	12
Heater core - removal and installation	11
Radiator - removal and installation	5
Thermostat - check and replacement	3
Water pump - check	7
Water pump - removal and installation	8

Specifications

General

Radiator cap pressure rating	See Chapter 1
Thermostat rating	195-degrees F
Coolant temperature fan switch rating	230-degrees F (110-degrees C)
Drivebelt tension	See Chapter 1

Torque specifications

Ft-lbs (unless otherwise specified)

Note: *One foot-pound (ft-lb) of torque is equivalent to 12 inch-pounds (in-lbs) of torque. Torque values below approximately 15 foot-pounds are expressed in inch-pounds, because most foot-pound torque wrenches are not accurate at these smaller values.*

Compressor mounting bolts
3.1L	
Models through 2000, both bolts	37
2001 and later models	
Upper bolts	37
Lower bolts	22
3.4L	
Front bolts	36
Rear bolts	19
3.8L	
Models through 1996	
Front bolts	35
Rear bolts	19
1997 through 2000	
Front nuts	74
Upper bolt	36
Lower bolt	59
Rear bracket bolts	23
2001 and later models, front and rear bolts	37
5.3L V8	36
Oil cooler connector	37

Thermostat cover bolts
2.2 liter four-cylinder engines	89 in-lbs
2.5 liter four-cylinder engines	17
2.3 liter four-cylinder (Quad-4) engine	19
3800 V6	20
Other V6 engines	18
5.3L V8	11

Water pump mounting bolts/nuts
2.2 liter four-cylinder engines	18
2.5 liter four-cylinder engines	24
2.3 liter four-cylinder (Quad-4) engine	19
3.1L and 3.4L	89 in-lbs

Torque specifications (continued)

Ft-lbs (unless otherwise specified)

Note: *One foot-pound (ft-lb) of torque is equivalent to 12 inch-pounds (in-lbs) of torque. Torque values below approximately 15 foot-pounds are expressed in inch-pounds, because most foot-pound torque wrenches are not accurate at these smaller values.*

Water pump mounting bolts/nuts (continued)

3.8L

Models through 1996

Short bolts, Step 1	132 in-lbs
Short bolts, Step 2	tighten an additional 80 degrees
Long bolts	22

1997 through 2001

Short bolts

Step 1	132 in-lbs
Step 2	Tighten an additional 80-degrees

Long bolts

Step 1	15
Step 2	Tighten an additional 40-degrees

2002 and later

Long bolts	25
Short bolts	16
5.3L V8	106 in-lbs

Water pump pulley bolts

3.1L and 3.4L	18
3.8L	115 in-lbs

---

1   General information

Engine cooling system

All vehicles covered by this manual employ a pressurized engine cooling system with thermostatically controlled coolant circulation. An impeller type water pump mounted on the engine block pumps coolant through the engine and radiator. The coolant flows around each cylinder and back to the radiator. Cast-in coolant passages direct coolant around the intake and exhaust ports, near the spark plug areas and the exhaust valve guides.

A wax pellet type thermostat is located in a housing connected to the upper radiator hose. During warm up the closed thermostat prevents coolant from circulating through the radiator. As the engine nears normal operating temperature, the thermostat opens and allows hot coolant to travel through the radiator, where it's cooled before returning to the engine.

The cooling system is sealed by a pressure-type radiator cap, which raises the boiling point of the coolant and increases the cooling efficiency of the radiator. If the system pressure exceeds the cap pressure relief value, the excess pressure in the system forces the spring-loaded valve inside the cap off its seat and allows the coolant to escape through a hose into a coolant reservoir. When the system cools, the excess coolant is automatically drawn from the reservoir back into the radiator.

The coolant reservoir does double duty as both the point at which fresh coolant is added to the cooling system to maintain the proper level and as a holding tank for expelled coolant.

This type of cooling system is known as a closed design because coolant that escapes past the pressure cap is saved and reused.

Heating system

The heating system consists of a blower fan and heater core located in the heater box, the hoses connecting the heater core to the engine cooling system and the heater/air conditioning control head on the dashboard. Hot engine coolant is circulated through the heater core. When the heater mode is activated, a trap door opens to expose the heater box to the passenger compartment. A fan switch on the control head activates the blower motor, which forces air through the core, heating the air.

Air conditioning system

The air conditioning system consists of a condenser mounted in front of the radiator, an evaporator mounted adjacent to the heater core, a compressor mounted on the engine, a filter-drier (accumulator), which contains a high pressure relief valve, and the hoses and lines connecting all of the above components.

A blower fan forces the warmer air of the passenger compartment through the evaporator core (sort of a radiator-in-reverse), transferring the heat from the air to the refrigerant. The liquid refrigerant boils off into low pressure vapor, taking the heat with it when it leaves the evaporator. **Warning:** *Most models covered by this manual are equipped with airbags. Always disable the airbag system before working in the vicinity of the impact sensors, steering column or instrument panel to avoid the possibility of accidental deployment of the airbag(s), which could cause personal injury (see Chapter 12). The yellow wires and connectors routed through the instrument panel are for this system. Do not use electrical test equipment on these yellow wires or tamper with them in any way while working under the instrument panel.*

---

2   Antifreeze - general information

Warning: *Don't allow antifreeze to come in contact with your skin or painted surfaces of the vehicle. Rinse off spills immediately with plenty of water. Antifreeze is highly toxic if ingested. Never leave antifreeze lying around in an open container or in puddles on the floor; children and pets are attracted by its sweet smell and may drink it. Check with local authorities about disposing of used antifreeze. Many communities have collection centers, which will see that antifreeze is disposed of safely. Antifreeze is also combustible, so don't store or use it near open flames.* **Caution:** *Never mix green-colored ethylene glycol antifreeze and orange-colored "DEX-COOL" silicate-free coolant because doing so will destroy the efficiency of the "DEX-COOL" coolant which is designed to last for 100,000 miles or five years.*

The cooling system should be filled with a water/ethylene glycol based antifreeze solution, which will prevent freezing down to at least -20-degrees F, or lower if local climate requires it. It also provides protection against corrosion and increases the coolant boiling point.

3.8 Thermostat details -
3.4 liter V6 engine

1   Upper radiator hose
2   Thermostat outlet pipe

3.13a Quad-4 (2.3L) thermostat housing mounting bolt locations (arrows) - the coolant temperature sensor is mounted on the right side of the assembly

3.13b V6 (2.8L and 3.1L) thermostat housing mounting bolt locations (arrows)

3.14a 2.5L four-cylinder thermostat housing components - first, twist the cap off . . .

3.14b . . . and then remove the thermostat by the bail

The cooling system should be drained, flushed and refilled at least every other year (see Chapter 1). The use of antifreeze solutions for periods of longer than two years is likely to cause damage and encourage the formation of rust and scale in the system. However, 1996 and later models are filled with a new, long-life coolant called "DEX-COOL", with a manufacturer recommended maintenance interval of five years.

Before adding antifreeze, check all hose connections, because antifreeze tends to leak through very minute openings. Engines don't normally consume coolant, so if the level goes down, find the cause and correct it.

The exact mixture of antifreeze-to-water you should use depends on the relative weather conditions. The mixture should contain at least 50 percent antifreeze, but should never contain more than 70 percent antifreeze. Consult the mixture ratio chart on the antifreeze container before adding coolant. Hydrometers are available at most auto parts stores to test the coolant. Use antifreeze that meets the vehicle manufacturer's specifications.

3 Thermostat - check and replacement

Warning: *DO NOT remove the radiator cap, drain the coolant or replace the thermostat until the engine has cooled completely.*

Check

1   Before assuming the thermostat is to blame for a cooling system problem, check the coolant level, drivebelt tension (see Chapter 1) and temperature gauge (or light) operation.
2   If the engine seems to be taking a long time to warm up (based on heater output or temperature gauge operation), the thermostat is probably stuck open. Replace the thermostat with a new one.
3   If the engine runs hot, use your hand to check the temperature of the upper radiator hose. If the hose isn't hot, but the engine is, the thermostat is probably stuck closed, preventing the coolant inside the engine from escaping to

the radiator. Replace the thermostat. **Caution:** *Don't drive the vehicle without a thermostat. The computer may stay in open loop and emissions and fuel economy will suffer.*
4   If the upper radiator hose is hot, it means the coolant is flowing and the thermostat is open. Consult the Troubleshooting Section at the front of this manual for cooling system diagnosis.

Replacement

Refer to illustrations 3.8, 3.13a, 3.13b, 3.14a, 3.14b, 3.15, 3.16 and 3.17
5   Disconnect the negative battery cable from the battery and drain the cooling system (see Chapter 1). If the coolant is relatively new or in good condition, save it and reuse it. **Caution:** *On models equipped with the Theft-lock audio system, be sure the lockout feature is turned off before performing any procedure which requires disconnecting the battery.*
6   Remove the air cleaner assembly, if necessary for access (see Chapter 4).
7   On the 3.4L V6, remove the torque strut at the engine. On 5.3L V8 models, remove the radiator lower air deflector.
8   Follow the upper radiator hose to the engine to locate the thermostat cover **(see illustration)**.
9   On all models except those equipped with a 2.5L four-cylinder engine, loosen the hose clamp, then detach the hose from the fitting. If the hose sticks, grasp it near the end with a pair of adjustable pliers and twist it to break the seal, then pull it off. If the hose is old or deteriorated, cut it off and install a new one. **Note:** *2.3L Quad-4 engines have two hoses and a wire harness connected to the thermostat cover - remove all of these.*
10   If the outer surface of the large fitting that mates with the hose is deteriorated (corroded, pitted, etc.) it may be damaged further by hose removal. If it is, the thermostat cover will have to be replaced.
11   On the 3.4L V6, relieve the fuel system pressure (see Chapter 4), then disconnect the fuel lines at the fuel rail.
12   On the 3.4L V6, remove the heater hose bracket at the thermostat housing stud, and the heater hose at the throttle body.
13   On all models except those equipped

with a 2.5L four-cylinder engine, remove the bolts/nuts and detach the thermostat cover **(see illustrations)**. If the cover is stuck, tap it with a soft-face hammer to jar it loose. Be prepared for some coolant to spill as the gasket seal is broken.
14   Note how it's installed (which end is facing up), then remove the thermostat. **Note:** *On 2.5L engines, the thermostat is removed by simply twisting the cap off the thermostat housing and pulling up on the bail that attaches to the thermostat* **(see illustrations)**.
15   Remove all traces of old gasket material and sealant from the housing and cover with a gasket scraper **(see illustration)**. Clean the

3.15 Remove all traces of gasket material (Quad-4 shown)

3.16 Some models use a rubber gasket around the circumference of the thermostat

3.17 Position the thermostat in the housing as shown here (V6 shown, others similar)

4.1 The motor may be tested by running fused jumper wires directly from the battery to the motor terminals (arrow)

gasket mating surfaces with lacquer thinner or acetone.

16   Some models are equipped with a rubber gasket around the circumference of the thermostat (**see illustration**). If the vehicle you are working on is equipped with this type of thermostat, replace the rubber gasket.

17   Install the new thermostat in the housing. Make sure the correct end faces up - the spring end is normally directed into the engine (**see illustration**).

18   On 2.3L Quad-4 models, apply a thin, uniform layer of RTV sealant to both sides of the new gasket and position it on the housing.

19   Install the cover and bolts/nuts. On the 3.4L and 3800 V6 engines, put RTV sealer around the bolt threads. Tighten the bolts to the torque figure listed in this Chapter's Specifications.

20   The remaining steps are the reverse of removal.

21   Refill the cooling system (see Chapter 1). **Note:** *Be sure to bleed the system of air.*

22   Start the engine and allow it to reach normal operating temperature, then check for leaks and proper thermostat operation (as described in Steps 2 through 4).

4.6 Cooling fan bolt locations (arrows) - (early models shown, bolt locations on later models will vary slightly)

4   Engine cooling fan - check and replacement

Check

Refer to illustration 4.1

1   To test the fan motor, unplug the electrical connector at the motor and use jumper wires to connect the fan directly to the battery (**see illustration**). If the fan still doesn't work, replace the motor.

2   If the motor tested OK, the fault lies in the coolant temperature switch, the relay or the wiring which connects the components. Carefully check all wiring and connections. If no obvious problems are found, further diagnosis should be done by a dealer service department or a repair shop.

Replacement

Refer to illustrations 4.6 and 4.7

3   Disconnect the negative battery cable from the battery. **Caution:** *On models equipped with the Theftlock audio system, be sure the lockout feature is turned off before performing any procedure which requires disconnecting the battery.*

4   Remove the air cleaner assembly (see Chapter 4). Remove the engine torque struts (see Chapter 2). On 2002 models, partially drain the cooling system and disconnect the

upper radiator hose from the radiator.

5   Insert a small screwdriver into the connector to lift the lock tab and unplug the fan wire harness. Disconnect the coolant reservoir tubing from the shroud on later models. Disconnect the transaxle fluid cooler tube from the radiator if it interferes.

6   Unbolt the fan assembly (**see illustration**), then carefully lift it out of the engine compartment.

7   To detach the fan from the motor, remove the motor shaft nut (**see illustration**). **Note:** *This nut may have left-hand threads. Check the hub of the fan for marks that may indicate which way to loosen the nut.*

8   To remove the fan motor from the bracket, remove the mounting bolts/nuts.

9   Installation is the reverse of removal.

5   Radiator - removal and installation

Refer to illustrations 5.2, 5.4a, 5.4b, 5.4c, 5.7 and 5.9

Warning: *Wait until the engine is completely cool before beginning this procedure.*

Removal

1   Disconnect the negative battery cable. On 2002 models, remove both battery cables and the battery (see Chapter 5). **Caution:** *On*

4.7 Remove the motor shaft nut (arrow) - note the left-hand threads

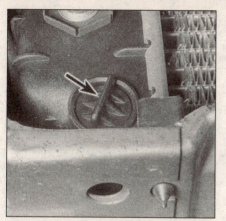

5.2 Do not strip or ruin the coolant drain plug (arrow) - it's made of plastic

5.4a The transaxle cooler lines (arrow) are located in the upper . . .

5.4b . . . and lower left corners of the radiator (viewed from below)

5.4c On later models, unsnap the plastic collar, then pry off the retaining clip from the quick-connect fitting to disconnect transmission and engine oil cooler lines

5.6 Use a pair of adjustable pliers to squeeze the ends of the hose clamp (arrow) and slide the clamp down the hose

5.7 The coolant reservoir hose (arrow) connects to the right side of the radiator

models equipped with a Theftlock audio system, be sure the lockout feature is turned off before performing any procedure which requires disconnecting the battery.

2   Drain the cooling system (see Chapter 1). If the coolant is relatively new or in good condition, save it and reuse it. **Note:** *Be careful not to ruin the plastic drain plug when removing it* (see illustration).

3   Remove the air cleaner assembly (see Chapter 4).

4   If the vehicle is equipped with an automatic transaxle, disconnect the cooler lines from the radiator (see illustrations), then cap the ends to prevent excessive fluid loss and contamination. Use a drip pan to catch spilled fluid. **Note:** *Later models have quick-connect fittings on the cooler lines. Do not remove the clips by pulling straight out. Hold one side in with your fingers while using a pick (with a bent tip) to pull the other side out, then rotate the clip off. Install clips the same way, not straight on.*

5   Remove the engine cooling fan assembly (see Section 4). On 2004 and later models, remove the wiring clips and brackets from the shroud. Also remove the bracket from the radiator and condenser.

6   Loosen the hose clamps, then detach the radiator hoses from the fittings (see illustration). If they're stuck, grasp each hose near the end with a pair of adjustable pliers and twist it to break the seal, then pull it off - be careful not to distort the radiator fittings! If the hoses are old or deteriorated, cut them off and install new ones.

7   Disconnect the reservoir hose from the radiator neck (see illustration).

8   Plug the lines and fittings to prevent the spillage of coolant or ATF as the radiator is removed.

9   Remove the bolts from the radiator mounting panel (see illustration).

10   Remove the panel, if equipped, and tilt the radiator to the rear. On 2004 and later models, lift the condenser from the radiator mounting tabs and position it aside. Don't spill coolant on the vehicle or scratch the paint.

11   With the radiator removed, it can be inspected for leaks and damage. If it needs

5.9 Radiator mounting bolt locations (arrows) (early models shown, bolt locations on later models will vary slightly)

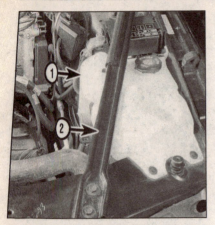

6.3 3.4 liter V6 engine coolant reservoir details

1   *Coolant reservoir*
2   *Front fender upper rail*

6.4 Coolant reservoir (typical) - remove the mounting bolts (arrows) and lift the reservoir out

7.4 If the pump is leaking through the vent hole, stains will form below the shaft (arrow) - pump removed for clarity

repair, have a radiator shop or dealer service department perform the work, as special techniques are required.

12   Bugs and dirt can be removed from the radiator with compressed air and a soft brush. Don't bend the cooling fins as this is done.

13   Check the radiator mounts for deterioration and make sure there's nothing in them when the radiator is installed.

Installation

14   Installation is the reverse of the removal procedure. Install the cooler line retaining clips onto the quick-connect fitting before installing the lines, then snap the cooler lines into place on the quick-connect fittings. Be sure to reinstall the plastic collars on the quick-connect fittings, as they lock the retaining clips in place.

15   After installation, fill the cooling system with the proper mixture of antifreeze and water. Be sure to bleed the system of air (see Chapter 1).

16   Start the engine and check for leaks. Allow the engine to reach normal operating temperature, indicated by the upper radiator hose becoming hot. Recheck the coolant level and add more if required.

17   If you're working on an automatic transaxle equipped vehicle, check and add fluid as needed.

6   Coolant reservoir - removal and installation

Refer to illustrations 6.3 and 6.4

1   Detach the hose from the windshield washer fluid reservoir cap if it interferes.

2   Disconnect the radiator overflow hose from the top of the radiator.

3   Remove the front fender upper rail, if necessary **(see illustration)**.

4   Remove the mounting bolts and lift the coolant reservoir from the vehicle **(see illustration)**.

5   Installation is the reverse of removal.

7   Water pump - check

Refer to illustrations 7.4 and 7.5

1   A failure in the water pump can cause serious engine damage due to overheating.

2   There are three ways to check the operation of the water pump while it's installed on the engine. If the pump is defective, it should be replaced with a new or rebuilt unit.

3   With the engine running at normal operating temperature, squeeze the upper radiator hose. If the water pump is working properly, a pressure surge should be felt as the hose is released. **Warning:** *Keep your hands away from the fan blades!*

4   Water pumps are equipped with weep or vent holes. If a failure occurs in the pump seal, coolant will leak from the hole **(see illustration)**. In most cases you'll need a flashlight and mirror to find the hole on the under side of the water pump to check for leaks.

5   If the water pump shaft bearings fail there may be a howling sound coming from the drivebelt area while the engine is running. Shaft wear can be felt if the water pump pulley is rocked up-and-down **(see illustration)**. Don't mistake drivebelt slippage, which causes a squealing sound, for water pump bearing failure.

8   Water pump - removal and installation

Refer to illustrations 8.10a, 8.10b, 8.10c and 8.15
Warning: *Wait until the engine is completely cool before beginning this procedure.*

Removal

1   Disconnect the negative battery cable from the battery. **Caution:** *On models equipped with the Theftlock audio system, be sure the lockout feature is turned off before performing any procedure which requires disconnecting the battery.*

2   Drain the cooling system (see Chap-

ter 1). If the coolant is relatively new or in good condition, save it and reuse it. **Note:** *On Quad-4 models, disconnect the heater hose from the thermostat housing for more complete coolant drain.*

3   Remove the air cleaner if necessary.

4   Remove the windshield washer reservoir and the coolant recovery reservoir (see Section 6), as necessary. Remove the battery and the battery tray on later models where it interferes.

5   Remove the serpentine belt and tensioner (see Chapter 1).

6   Remove the alternator and its brackets and the air conditioner compressor, as necessary.

Quad-4 equipped models only

7   Remove the exhaust manifold heat shields (see Chapter 2C) and the exhaust manifold.

8   Remove the radiator outlet pipe-to-radiator pump cover bolts, leaving the lower radiator hose attached. Pull down on the radiator outlet pipe to disengage it from the water pump and detach the pipe from the oil pan and transaxle.

9   Remove the water pump cover-to-cylinder block bolts.

All models

10   On 3.1L engines, remove the small belt

7.5 Rock the pulley back and forth to check for bearing play

8.10a Typical V6 water pump mounting details (except 3800) - the mounting bolts are located around the perimeter of the pump

8.10b Pull the pump off - if it's stuck, tap it with a soft-face hammer

8.10c Water pump mounting details - 3800 V6

8.15 On Quad-4 models, lubricate the splines (arrow) with grease

9.1a Coolant temperature sending unit location (arrow) - 2.5 liter four cylinder engine - the sending unit on the 2.2 liter engine is located on the engine's coolant outlet

9.1b On 2.8, 3.1 and 3.4 liter V6 engines, the coolant temperature sensor (arrow) is adjacent to the EGR pipe (On the 3100 V6, the coolant temperature sensor is located next to the ignition control module)

guard just above the water pump. Remove the bolts/nuts and detach the water pump from the engine **(see illustrations)**.

11   Clean the fastener threads and any threaded holes in the engine to remove corrosion and sealant.

12   Compare the new pump to the old one to make sure they're identical.

13   Remove all traces of old gasket material from the engine with a gasket scraper.

14   Clean the engine and water pump mating surfaces with lacquer thinner or acetone.

Installation

15   Carefully attach the pump and gasket to the engine and start the bolts/nuts finger tight. **Note:** *On Quad-4 models, lubricate the splines of the water pump drive* **(see illustration)** *with chassis grease prior to installation. Lubricate the O-ring on the radiator outlet pipe with antifreeze solution before installing.*

16   Tighten the fasteners in 1/4-turn increments to the torque figure listed in this Chapter's Specifications. Don't overtighten them or the pump may be distorted. **Note:** *On Quad-4 models, tighten the fasteners in this order:*

a) *Pump-to-chain housing*
b) *Pump cover-to-pump assembly*
c) *Cover-to-block, bottom bolt first*
d) *Radiator outlet pipe-to-water pump cover*

17   Reinstall all parts removed for access to the pump.

18   Refill the cooling system (see Chapter 1). Run the engine and check for leaks.

9   Coolant temperature sending unit or Low Coolant sensor - check and replacement

Refer to illustrations 9.1a, 9.1b and 9.1c
Warning: *Wait until the engine is completely*

cool before beginning this procedure.

1   The coolant temperature indicator system is composed of a light or temperature gauge mounted in the instrument panel and a coolant temperature sending unit mounted on the engine **(see illustrations)**. (Some vehicles have more than one sending unit, but the one used for the indicator system has only one wire). **Note:** *Refer to* **illustration 3.13a** *for the location of the coolant temperature sending unit on the Quad-4 engine. On some models a low coolant warning system is also*

9.1c Location of the sending unit (arrow) on the 3800 engine

10.3 Detach the electrical connector and remove the mounting screws from the blower assembly

| 1 | *Electrical connector* | 2 | *Blower mounting screw* |

10.4 The convenience center is located at the passenger side knee bolster (1996 and earlier models only)

used. This system is composed of a warning light in the instrument panel and a low coolant sensor mounted on the side of the radiator.

2   If the light or gauge indicates the engine is overheating or that the coolant is low, check the coolant level in the system and then make sure the wiring between the light or gauge and the sending unit is secure and all fuses are intact.

3   When the ignition switch is turned on and the starter motor is turning, the indicator lights (if equipped) should be on (overheated engine or low coolant indication).

4   If either of the lights isn't on, the bulb may be burned out, the ignition switch may be faulty or the circuit may be open. Test the circuit by grounding the wire to the sending unit while the ignition is on (engine not running for safety). If the gauge deflects full scale or the light comes on, replace the sending unit.

5   As soon as the engine starts, the light should go out and remain out unless the engine overheats or, in the case of the low coolant sensor, the coolant level becomes low. Failure of the light to go out may be due to a grounded wire between the light and the sending unit, a defective sending unit or a

faulty ignition switch. If the problem is with the temperature sender, check the coolant to make sure it's the proper type. Plain water may have too low a boiling point to activate the sending unit.

6   If the temperature sending unit must be replaced, simply unscrew it from the engine and install the replacement. Use a light coat of sealant on the threads. Make sure the engine is cool before removing the defective sending unit. If the low coolant sensor must be replaced, drain some coolant from the radiator (see Chapter 1), disconnect the connector then unsnap the sensor from it's mount on the radiator.

7   Check the coolant level after the replacement has been installed and refill as necessary.

10   Heater and air conditioner blower motor - removal and installation

Refer to illustrations 10.3, 10.4, 10.5 and 10.6

1   Disconnect the cable from the negative battery terminal. **Caution:** *On models equipped with the Theftlock audio system, be sure the lockout feature is turned off before*

performing any procedure which requires disconnecting the battery. **Warning:** *Most models covered by this manual are equipped with airbags. Always disable the airbag system before working in the vicinity of the impact sensors, steering column or instrument panel to avoid the possibility of accidental deployment of the airbag(s), which could cause personal injury (see Chapter 12). The yellow wires and connectors routed through the instrument panel are for this system. Do not use electrical test equipment on these yellow wires or tamper with them in any way while working under the instrument panel.*

2   Working in the passenger compartment, remove the panel below the glove compartment.

3   Pull down the carpet as necessary so that you can see the blower motor, then disconnect the wires from the blower motor **(see illustration)**.

4   On early models, remove the convenience center rear screws, loosen the front screw and slide the convenience center out **(see illustration)**.

5   Remove the blower motor mounting bolts and separate the motor/fan assembly from the housing **(see illustration)**.

6   Remove the retaining nut, if so equipped

10.5 2004 and later blower motor location with the glove box removed

10.6 Remove the nut (arrow) and slip the fan off the motor shaft

11.6 Heater/air conditioning duct mounting screws (arrows)

11.7 Heater core cover mounting screws (arrows)

(see illustration) and slide the blower fan off the motor shaft. **Note:** *If the blower fan is pressed onto the shaft, it can be removed by cutting through the plastic shaft sleeve with a "hot-knife" until it splits, or by pressing it off.*

7   Installation is the reverse of the removal procedure.

11   Heater core - removal and installation

Refer to illustrations 11.6, 11.7, 11.9a and 11.9b

1   Disconnect the cable from the negative terminal of the battery. **Caution:** *On models equipped with the Theftlock audio system, be sure the lockout feature is turned off before performing any procedure which requires disconnecting the battery.* **Warning:** *Most models covered by this manual are equipped with airbags. Always disable the airbag system before working in the vicinity of the impact sensors, steering column or instrument panel to avoid the possibility of accidental deployment of the airbag(s), which could cause personal injury (see Chapter 12). The yellow wires and connectors routed through the instrument panel are for this system. Do not use electrical test equipment on these yellow wires' or tamper with them in any way while working under the instrument panel.*

2003 and earlier models

2   Raise the front of the vehicle and support it securely on jackstands. Apply the parking brake and block the rear wheels to keep the vehicle from rolling off the jackstands.

3   Drain the cooling system (see Chapter 1).

4   Remove the drain hose from the bottom of the heater case.

5   Working in the passenger compartment, remove the panels from under the dash and the steering column trim covers. Also remove the floor console, if equipped (see Chapter 11).

6   Remove the heater outlet duct and glove box **(see illustration)**.

7   Remove the heater core cover **(see illustration)**.

8   Disconnect the heater hoses from the heater core. **Note:** *The heater hoses and clamps are accessible from inside the engine compartment on the firewall. On the 3100, you may have to rotate the engine forward to gain access (see Chapter 1). On the 3.4 liter, you may have to remove the plenum, the fuel lines, the exhaust crossover pipe and the transmission dipstick tube (see Chapter 4). On 2002 models, remove the cross-beam (between the shock towers) in the engine compartment for access to the heater hose connections from the engine side.*

9   On models where the heater pipes are not integral with the core, remove the metal clips where the heater core pipes enter the core, then twist and pull the two pipes out of the core. Remove the heater core **(see illustrations)**. **Caution:** *Have plenty of old towels on the floor to protect the carpet from spilled coolant.*

10   Installation is the reverse of removal. Refill the cooling system (see Chapter 1).

2004 and later models

Refer to illustrations 11.12, 11.17a, 11.17b, 11.18a, 11.18b, 11.19, 11.20a and 11.20b

11   Drain the cooling system (see Chapter 1). If the coolant is fairly fresh, it can be saved and reused. **Warning:** *Be sure to clean up any spilled coolant immediately.*

12   Disconnect the heater hoses from the nipples on the firewall **(see illustration)**.

13   Remove the panels from the bottom of each side of the instrument panel.

14   Remove the front seats, the kick trim panels and the console (see Chapter 11).

15   Detach the carpet fasteners and pull back the carpet for access to the center duct that's below the console.

16   Separate the center air duct that leads to the rear from the heater core cover.

11.9a Heater core mounting clip and screw locations (arrows)

11.9b Handle the heater core by the upper and lower edges (arrows)

11.12 The heater hoses are connected to the heater core pipes next to the brake booster

11.17a Screw (A) and heat stake (B) locations viewed from the right

11.17b Screw (A) and heat stake (B) locations viewed from the left

11.18a Screw (A) and heat stake (B) locations viewed from the left with the outer cover removed

11.18b Remove the two bottom screws for the inner cover

11.19 Carefully remove the heater core from the housing while withdrawing the pipes from the firewall and seal

11.20a The inner cover mounting hole drill locations

11.20b The outer cover mounting hole drill locations

12.4 Automatic air conditioning control assembly mounting screw locations (arrows)

17   Remove the screws and heat stakes that hold the outer cover in place **(see illustrations)**. Use a small chisel or a screwdriver with a thin, sharp blade to remove the plastic heat stakes. **Caution:** *The bottom mounting tabs use a heat stake and a screw on each tab. Avoid breaking a tab by confirming that the screws and heat stake on each tab are removed before trying to detach the cover.*

18   Use the same method to remove the inner heater core cover **(see illustrations)**.

19   Remove the heater core from the housing **(see illustration)**. Place rags under the heater core pipes.

20   Installation is the reverse of removal. **Note:** *The heater core covers are designed to be reinstalled onto the housing with screws. These can be obtained at a dealership parts department. Mounting holes will need to be drilled on the covers; they are clearly marked* **(see illustrations)**.

21   Refill the cooling system and reconnect the battery when you're done (see Chapter 1).

12   Heater and air conditioner control assembly - removal and installation

Refer to illustration 12.4

1   Disconnect the cable from the negative terminal of the battery. **Caution:** *On models equipped with the Theftlock audio system, be sure the lockout feature is turned off before performing any procedure which requires disconnecting the battery.* **Warning:** *Most models covered by this manual are equipped with airbags. Always disable the airbag system before working in the vicinity of the impact sensors, steering column or instrument panel to avoid the possibility of accidental deployment of the airbag(s), which could cause personal injury (see Chapter 12). The yellow wires and connectors routed through the instrument panel are for this system. Do not use electrical test equipment on these yellow wires or tamper with them in any way while working under the instrument panel.*

2   Remove the trim plates from the dash

(see Chapter 11).

3   If equipped, pull the control knobs off the face of the control assembly.

4   Remove the screws on each side of the control assembly **(see illustration)**.

5   Disconnect the electrical connectors at the rear of the control assembly.

6   Installation is the reverse of removal.

13   Air conditioning system - check and maintenance

Warning: *The air conditioning system is under high pressure. DO NOT loosen any fittings or remove any components until after the system has been discharged. Air conditioning refrigerant should be properly discharged into an EPA-approved recovery container at a dealership service department or an automotive air conditioning repair facility. Always wear eye protection when disconnecting air conditioning system fittings.*

1   The following maintenance steps should be performed on a regular basis to ensure that the air conditioner continues to operate at peak efficiency:

a)   *Check the drivebelt (see Chapter 1).*

b)   *Check the condition of the hoses. Look for cracks, hardening and deterioration. Look at potential leak areas (hoses and fittings) for signs of refrigerant oil leaking out.* **Warning:** *Do not replace air conditioning hoses until the system has been discharged by a dealership or air conditioning repair facility.*

c)   *Check the fins of the condenser for leaves, bugs and other foreign material. A soft brush and compressed air can be used to remove them.*

d)   *Check the wire harness for correct routing, broken wires, damaged insulation, etc. Make sure the electrical connectors are clean and tight.*

e)   *Maintain the correct refrigerant charge.*

2   The system should be run for about 10 minutes at least once a month. This is particularly important during the winter months because long-term non-use can cause hard-

ening of the internal seals.

3   Because of the complexity of the air conditioning system and the special equipment required to effectively work on it, accurate troubleshooting of the system should be left to a certified air conditioning technician.

4   If the air conditioning system doesn't operate at all, check the fuse panel. Check the HVAC fuse and the air conditioning compressor relay.

5   Watch the air conditioning compressor while the system is on. The clutch at the front of the compressor should be engaged and turning. If it is not, connect a jumper wire with battery voltage to the clutch electrical connector. If it still doesn't operate, connect another jumper wire from the ground side of the clutch's electrical connector to an engine ground. If it still fails to engage, the clutch needs repair or replacement, both of which should be handled by a dealer service department or air conditioning repair shop.

6   If the compressor clutch did operate when the voltage was applied, check the low-pressure cycling switch (not on all models), located in the low-pressure line near or on the accumulator. Pull the electrical connector off and insert a short jumper wire (a paper clip formed into a U-shape will work) to connect both terminals. If the compressor clutch now engages, the refrigerant is probably low, see recharging procedure below.

7   The most common cause of poor cooling is simply a low system refrigerant charge. If a noticeable drop in cool air output occurs, the following quick check will help you determine if the refrigerant level is low. For more complete information on the air conditioning system, refer to the *Haynes Automotive Heating and Air Conditioning Manual*.

Checking the refrigerant charge

Refer to illustration 13.11

8   Warm the engine up to normal operating temperature.

9   Place the air conditioning temperature selector at the coldest setting and the blower at the highest setting. Open the doors (to

13.11 Use a thermometer in the center dash vent while the air conditioning is ON to check for cooling efficiency

13.12 A basic charging kit for R-134a systems is available at most auto parts stores

make sure the air conditioning system doesn't cycle off as soon as it cools the passenger compartment).

10   With the compressor engaged - the clutch will make an audible click and the center of the clutch will rotate - feel the surface of the accumulator and the evaporator inlet pipe. **Note:** *The 3800 V6 uses a type of compressor that does not cycle; it changes its stroke to match system demand. If the smaller diameter line feels warm and the receiver/drier feels cool, the system is properly charged. On 3800 V6 models, feel the pipe on either side of the expansion tube - there should be a noticeable difference in temperature.*

11   Place a thermometer in the dashboard vent nearest the evaporator and add refrigerant to the system until the indicated temperature is around 40 to 45-degrees F **(see illustration)**. If the ambient (outside) air temperature is very high, say 110-degrees F, the duct air temperature will probably be higher, but generally the air conditioning is 30 to 40-degrees F cooler than the ambient air. **Note:** *Humidity of the ambient air also affects the*

cooling capacity of the system. Higher ambient humidity lowers the effectiveness of the air conditioning system.

Adding refrigerant

Refer to illustrations 13.12 and 13.15

Note: *There are two types of refrigerant; R-12, used on earlier models, and the more environmentally friendly R-134a used on 1994 and later models. These two refrigerants (and their appropriate refrigerant oils) are not compatible and must never be mixed or components will be damaged. Vehicles using R-12 refrigerant will have to be brought to a dealer or air-conditioning shop for recharging, as R-12 is no longer available to the public. Since the dwindling supplies of R-12 are very expensive, it may be cheaper to have the shop convert your vehicle to R-134a.*

12   For later models, buy an R-134a automotive charging kit at an auto parts store. A charging kit includes a 14-ounce can of refrigerant, a tap valve and a short section of hose that can be attached between the tap valve and the system low side service valve **(see illustration)**. Because one can of refrigerant

may not be sufficient to bring the system charge up to the proper level, it's a good idea to buy an extra can. Make sure that one of the cans contains red refrigerant dye. If the system is leaking, the red dye will leak out with the refrigerant and help you pinpoint the location of the leak.

13   Hook up the charging kit by following the manufacturer's instructions. **Warning:** *DO NOT hook the charging kit hose to the system high side! The fittings on the charging kit are designed to fit **only** on the low side of the system.*

14   Back off the valve handle on the charging kit and screw the kit onto the refrigerant can, making sure first that the O-ring or rubber seal inside the threaded portion of the kit is in place. **Warning:** *Wear protective eyewear when dealing with pressurized refrigerant cans.*

15   Remove the dust cap from the low-side charging connection and attach the quick-connect fitting on the kit hose **(see illustration)**.

16   Warm up the engine and turn on the air conditioner. Keep the charging kit hose away from the fan and other moving parts. **Note:**

13.15 Add refrigerant to the low-side port only (arrow) - the procedure is easier if you wrap the can with a warm, wet towel to prevent icing

13.25 Check that the evaporator drain tube (arrow) on the firewall is not plugged

The charging process requires the compressor to be running. Your compressor may cycle off if the pressure is low due to a low charge. If the clutch cycles off, you can pull the low-pressure cycling switch plug from the evaporator inlet line and attach a jumper wire across the terminals. This will keep the compressor ON.

17   Turn the valve handle on the kit until the stem pierces the can, then back the handle out to release the refrigerant. You should be able to hear the rush of gas. Add refrigerant to the low side of the system until both the accumulator surface and the evaporator inlet pipe feel about the same temperature. Allow stabilization time between each addition.

18   If you have an accurate thermometer, you can place it in the center air conditioning duct inside the vehicle and keep track of the "conditioned" air temperature. A charged system that is working properly should put out air that is 40-degrees F. If the ambient (outside) air temperature is very high, say 110-degrees F, the duct air temperature will probably be higher, but generally the air conditioning is 30 to 40-degrees-F cooler than the ambient air.

19   When the can is empty, turn the valve handle to the closed position and release the connection from the low-side port. Replace the dust cap. **Warning:** *Never add more than one can of refrigerant to the system (if more than one can is required, the system should be evacuated and leak tested).*

20   Remove the charging kit from the can and store the kit for future use with the piercing valve in the UP position, to prevent inadvertently piercing the can on the next use.

Heating systems

21   If the carpet under the heater core is damp, or if antifreeze vapor or steam is coming through the vents, the heater core is leaking. Remove it (see Section 12) and install a new unit (most radiator shops will not repair a leaking heater core).

22   If the air coming out of the heater vents isn't hot, the problem could stem from any of the following causes:

a) *The thermostat is stuck open, preventing the engine coolant from warming up enough to carry heat to the heater core. Replace the thermostat (see Section 3).*

b) *A heater hose is blocked, preventing the flow of coolant through the heater core. Feel both heater hoses at the firewall. They should be hot. If one of them is cold, there is an obstruction in one of the hoses or in the heater core, or the heater control valve is shut. Detach the hoses and back flush the heater core with a water hose. If the heater core is clear but circulation is impeded, remove the two hoses and flush them out with a water hose.*

c) *If flushing fails to remove the blockage from the heater core, the core must be replaced (see Section 12).*

23   If the blower motor speed does not correspond to the setting selected on the blower

switch, the problem could be a bad fuse, circuit, control panel or blower resistor (see Section 10).

24   If there isn't any air coming out of the vents:

a) *Turn the ignition ON and activate the fan control. Place your ear at the heating/air conditioning register (vent) and listen. Most motors are audible. Can you hear the motor running?*

b) *If you can't (and have already verified that the blower switch and the blower motor resistor are good), the blower motor itself is probably bad (see Section 11).*

25   Inspect the drain hose from the heater/evaporator assembly at the right-center of the firewall, make sure it is not clogged **(see illustration)**. If there is a humid mist coming from the system ducts, this hose may be plugged with leaves or road debris.

Eliminating air conditioning odors

26   Unpleasant odors that often develop in air conditioning systems are caused by the growth of a fungus, usually on the surface of the evaporator core. The warm, humid environment there is a perfect breeding ground for mildew to develop.

27   The evaporator core on most vehicles is difficult to access, and factory dealerships have a lengthy, expensive process for eliminating the fungus by opening up the evaporator case and using a powerful disinfectant and rinse on the core until the fungus is gone. You can service your own system at home, but it takes something much stronger than basic household germ-killers or deodorizers.

28   Aerosol disinfectants for automotive air conditioning systems are available in most auto parts stores, but remember when shopping for them that the most effective treatments are also the most expensive. The basic procedure for using these sprays is to start by running the system in the RECIRC mode for ten minutes with the blower on its highest speed. Use the highest heat mode to dry out the system and keep the compressor from engaging by disconnecting the wiring connector at the compressor (see Section 16).

29   The disinfectant can usually comes with a long spray hose. Remove the blower motor resistor (see Section 11), point the nozzle inside the hole and spray, according to the manufacturer's recommendations. Try to cover the whole surface of the evaporator core, by aiming the spray up, down and sideways. Follow the manufacturer's recommendations for the length of spray and waiting time between applications.

30   Once the evaporator has been cleaned, the best way to prevent the mildew from coming back again is to make sure your evaporator housing drain tube is clear **(see illustration 13.25)**.

14   Air conditioning accumulator - removal and installation

Refer to illustrations 14.4 and 14.6

Warning: *The air conditioning system is under high pressure. DO NOT loosen any hose or line fittings or remove any components until after the system has been discharged. Air conditioning refrigerant should be properly discharged into an approved container at a dealer service department or an automotive air conditioning repair facility. Always wear eye protection when disconnecting air conditioning system fittings.*

Note: *Later models do not have an accumulator.*

1   Have the system discharged (see **Warning** above).

2   Disconnect the negative battery cable from the battery. **Caution:** *On models equipped with the Theftlock audio system, be sure the lockout feature is turned off before performing any procedure which requires disconnecting the battery.*

3   Remove the air cleaner and intake tube assembly (see Chapter 4).

4   Disconnect the refrigerant lines from the accumulator **(see illustration)**. On the 3800, remove the pressure switch from the accumulator if necessary. **Caution:** *Use a back-up wrench when removing the refrigerant lines to prevent twisting the tubing.*

5   Plug the open fittings to prevent entry of dirt and moisture.

14.4 The accumulator is usually located in the left front corner of the engine compartment below the air cleaner

14.6 Remove the air cleaner housing to access the A/C
accumulator mounting bolt (arrow)

15.7 Disconnect the compressor clutch wiring harness (arrow) -
oil filter removed for clarity (V6 shown)

6   Loosen or remove the mounting bracket and bolts **(see illustration)** and remove the accumulator.

7   If a new accumulator is being installed, remove the Schrader valve and pour the oil out into a measuring cup, noting the amount. Add fresh refrigerant oil to the new accumulator equal to the amount removed from the old unit, plus one ounce. **Caution:** *Air conditioner systems equipped with R-134a refrigerant use a special oil designed specifically for use in such systems.*

8   Installation is the reverse of removal.

9   Have the system evacuated, recharged and leak tested by the shop that discharged it.

15   Air conditioning compressor - removal and installation

Refer to illustrations 15.7, 15.14a and 15.14b
Warning: *The air conditioning system is under high pressure. DO NOT loosen any*
hose or line fittings or remove any components until after the system has been discharged. Air conditioning refrigerant should be properly discharged into an approved container at a dealer service department or an automotive air conditioning repair facility. Always wear eye protection when disconnecting air conditioning system fittings.
Note: *The accumulator (see Section 14) should be replaced whenever the compressor is replaced.*

1   Have the system discharged (see Warning above).

2   Disconnect the negative battery cable from the battery. **Caution:** *On models equipped with the Theftlock audio system, be sure the lockout feature is turned off before performing any procedure which requires disconnecting the battery.*

3   Remove the coolant recovery reservoir (see Section 6). On 2002 models, , remove the cross-beam (between the shock towers) in the engine compartment.

4   Set the parking brake and block the rear wheels. Raise the front of the vehicle and support it securely on jackstands.

5   Remove the right lower splash shield.

6   Refer to Chapter 1 and remove the drivebelt (and oil filter, if necessary for clearance). On the 3.4 liter, remove the engine torque strut and bracket. On the 3.4 liter and the 3800, remove the cooling fan assembly.

7   Disconnect the compressor clutch wiring harness **(see illustration)**.

5.3L V8 models

8   Remove the lower radiator air deflector and the engine splash shield.

9   Disconnect the hoses from the compressor and remove the hose mounting stud. Plug all openings to prevent contamination.

10   Remove the rear mounting bolt from the compressor and remove the front mounting bolt, nut and stud.

11   Place a floor jack under the right front portion of the engine subframe.

FRONT MOUNTING BOLTS

REAR MOUNTING BOLT

15.14a A/C compressor front and rear mounting bolts

15.14b On 3100 engines disconnect the electrical connector (A) from the air conditioning compressor and remove the mounting bolts (B)

16.8 Remove the bolt (arrow) to disconnect the refrigerant lines

12   Loosen the right front subframe bolt and use the jack to carefully lower the subframe as much as possible.

All models

13   Disconnect the refrigerant lines from the rear of the compressor. Plug the open fittings to prevent entry of dirt and moisture.
14   Unbolt the compressor from the mounting brackets and lift it out of the vehicle (see illustrations).
15   If a new compressor is being installed, follow the directions with the compressor regarding the draining of excess oil prior to installation.
16   The clutch may have to be transferred from the original to the new compressor.
17   Installation is the reverse of removal. Replace all O-rings with new ones specifically made for air conditioning system in your car and lubricate them with the appropriate refrigerant oil.
18   Have the system evacuated, recharged and leak tested by the shop that discharged it.

16   Air conditioning condenser - removal and installation

Refer to illustrations 16.8 and 16.10
Warning: The air conditioning system is under high pressure. DO NOT loosen any hose or line fittings or remove any components until after the system has been discharged. Air conditioning refrigerant should be properly discharged into an approved container at a dealer service department or an automotive air conditioning repair facility. Always wear eye protection when disconnecting air conditioning system fittings.
Note: The accumulator (see Section 14) should be replaced whenever the condenser is replaced.

Removal

1   Have the air conditioning system discharged (see Warning above).
2   Disconnect the negative cable from the battery. Caution: On models equipped with the Theftlock audio system, be sure the lock-out feature is turned off before performing any procedure which requires disconnecting the battery.
3   Remove the air cleaner assembly and the air cleaner duct(s) (see Chapter 4). Note: On the 2.5L engine, remove the air intake resonator mounting bolt.
4   Remove the torque struts (upper engine mounts) from the engine (see Chapter 2).
5   Remove the coolant reservoir (see Section 6).
6   Remove the cooling fan (see Section 4).
7   Remove the radiator (see Section 5).
8   Disconnect the refrigerant lines from the condenser (see illustration). Plug the lines to keep dirt and moisture out. On 2004 and later models, disconnect the condenser tube from the evaporator tube by removing the line coupling and pulling the tubes apart. Use a small flat-blade screwdriver to release the locking tabs of the coupling.
9   Remove any radiator mounting panels from above the condenser (see illustration 5.9).
10   Remove any bolts and clamps and lift out the condenser (see illustration).
11   If the original condenser will be reinstalled, plug the line fittings to prevent oil from draining out.

Installation

12   If a new condenser is being installed, pour one ounce of refrigerant oil into it prior to installation.
13   Reinstall the components in the reverse order of removal. Be sure the rubber pads are in place under the condenser.
14   Have the system evacuated, recharged

and leak tested by the shop that discharged it.

17   Air conditioning expansion (orifice) tube - removal and installation

Refer to illustrations 17.3 and 17.4
Warning: The air conditioning system is under high pressure. DO NOT loosen any fittings or remove any components until after the system has been discharged. Air conditioning refrigerant should be properly discharged into an EPA-approved container at a dealership service department or an automotive air conditioning repair facility. Always wear eye protection when disconnecting air conditioning system fittings.
Note: Whenever the expansion tube is replaced, the accumulator-drier should also be replaced (see Section 15).
1   Have the air conditioning system dis-

16.10 The condenser has rubber mounts at the corners (arrow) - be sure they're in place properly during reassembly

17.3 Disconnect the high-pressure line at this fitting (arrow) to replace the expansion (orifice) tube

17.4 Expansion (orifice) tube details

charged and the refrigerant recovered (see **Warning** above). Disconnect the cable from the negative terminal of the battery. **Caution:** *On models equipped with a Theftlock audio system, be sure the lockout feature is turned off before performing any procedure which requires disconnecting the battery.*

2003 and earlier models

2   Remove the air cleaner and duct (see Chapter 4).

3   Disconnect the refrigerant high-pressure line at the fitting right over the transaxle, about ten inches behind the accumulator/drier **(see illustration)**.

4   The expansion *(orifice)* tube is a tube with a fixed-diameter orifice and a mesh filter at each end **(see illustration)**. When you separate the pipe at the fitting you will see one end of the orifice tube inside the pipe leading to the evaporator. Use needle-nose pliers to remove the orifice tube.

5   The orifice tube acts to meter the refrigerant, changing it from high-pressure liquid to low-pressure liquid. It is possible to reuse the orifice tube if:

   a) *The screens aren't plugged with grit or foreign material*
   b) *Neither screen is torn*
   c) *The plastic housing over the screens is intact*
   d) *The brass orifice inside the plastic housing is unrestricted*

6   Installation is the reverse of removal. Be sure to insert the expansion tube with the shorter end in first, toward the evaporator. **Caution:** *Always use a new O-ring when installing the expansion tube.*

7   Retighten the fitting and refrigerant line, then have the system evacuated, recharged and leak-tested by the shop that discharged it.

2004 and later models

8   Remove the nut holding the air conditioner lines to the fitting at the firewall. Pull the lines from the fitting and discard the O-rings. Plug the line openings to prevent contamination.

9   Remove the two small screws that secure the expansion valve. Lift the expansion valve off and discard the O-rings. Replace the expansion valve with a new one.

10   Installation is the reverse of removal. Be sure to replace the O-rings that were removed with new ones.

Chapter 4
Fuel and exhaust systems

Contents

	Section
Accelerator cable - removal and installation	14
Air and PCV filter replacement	See Chapter 1
Air cleaner housing - removal and installation	8
Exhaust system check	See Chapter 1
Exhaust system servicing - general information	15
Fuel filter replacement	See Chapter 1
Fuel injection system - check	10
Fuel injection system - general information	9
Fuel lines and fittings - repair and replacement	4
Fuel pressure relief procedure	2
Fuel pump/fuel pressure - testing	3
Fuel pump - removal and installation	7
Fuel tank - removal and installation	5

	Section
Fuel tank cleaning and repair - general information	6
General information	1
Port Fuel Injection (PFI) and Sequential Fuel Injection (SFI) – component removal and installation	13
Supercharger - general information	19
Supercharger - removal and installation	20
Throttle Body Injection (TBI) assembly - removal and installation	11
Throttle Body Injection (TBI) - component replacement	12
Turbocharger - general information	16
Turbocharger - inspection	17
Turbocharger - removal and installation	18

Specifications

Fuel pressure (key On, engine not running)

Throttle Body Injection (TBI)	26 to 32 psi
1997 through 1999	
3.1L	41 to 47 psi
3.8L	48 to 55 psi
2000 through 2003	
3.1L	52 to 59 psi
3.8L	48 to 55 psi
2004 and later	50 to 62 psi
All other engines	40 to 47 psi
Fuel pressure at idle (with vacuum to fuel pressure regulator)	3 to 10 psi less than KOEO test

Torque specifications

Ft-lbs (unless otherwise indicated)

Note: *One foot-pound (ft-lb) of torque is equivalent to 12 inch-pounds (in-lbs) of torque. Torque values below approximately 15 foot-pounds are expressed in inch-pounds, because most foot-pound torque wrenches are not accurate at these smaller values.*

TBI throttle body mounting bolts	18
PFI/SFI throttle body bolts/nuts	
3.1L	21
3.8L V6 and 5.3L V8	89 in-lbs
Plenum-to-intake manifold bolts	
3800	
1992 and earlier	89 in-lbs
1993 and later	132 in-lbs
All other V6 engines	16 to 18
Injector retainer screws (2.2L 4-cylinder)	31 in-lbs
Supercharger mounting bolts	17

1   General information

The fuel system consists of a fuel tank, an electric fuel pump, a fuel pump relay, an air cleaner assembly and either a Throttle Body Injection (TBI) system, a Port Fuel Injection (PFI) system or a Sequential Fuel Injection (SFI) system. The basic differences between the three types of fuel injection system are in the number of injectors, the location of injectors and the sequence in which they inject fuel.

Throttle Body Injection (TBI) system

The throttle body system utilizes one injector, centrally mounted in a carburetor-like housing. The injector is an electrical solenoid, with fuel delivered to the injector at a constant pressure level. To maintain the fuel pressure at a constant level, excess fuel is returned to the fuel tank.

A signal from the ECM opens the solenoid, allowing fuel to spray through the injector into the throttle body. The amount of time the injector is held open by the ECM determines the fuel/air mixture ratio. This system is used on some Lumina models through 1992.

Port Fuel Injection (PFI) system

The port system utilizes four or six injectors similar in operation to the throttle body injector and the fuel/air ratio is controlled in the same manner. Instead of a single injector mounted in a centrally located throttle body, one injector is installed above each intake port. The throttle body serves only to control the amount of air passing into the system. Because each cylinder is equipped with an injector mounted immediately adjacent to the intake valve, much better control of the fuel/air mixture ratio is possible.

This system is used on various Lumina, Regal, Cutlass and Monte Carlo models through 1994.

Sequential Fuel Injection (SFI) system

The sequential system is like the port fuel injection system in that it has one injector per cylinder. However, in the sequential system the opening of each injector is synchronized with the opening of each intake valve.

Variations of this system are used on all Regal models with the 3800 engine, on 1993 California-specification Regals with the 3.1 liter engine, all 1994 models with the 3100 or 3.4 liter engines, and all 1995 and later models.

2   Fuel pressure relief procedure

Refer to illustration 2.4
Warning: *Gasoline is extremely flammable, so take extra precautions when you work on any part of the fuel system. Don't smoke or allow open flames or bare light bulbs near the work area, and don't work in a garage where a natural gas-type appliance (such as a water heater or a clothes dryer) with a pilot light is present. Since gasoline is carcinogenic, wear latex gloves when there's a possibility of being exposed to fuel, and, if you spill any fuel on your skin, rinse it off immediately with soap and water. Mop up any spills immediately and do not store fuel-soaked rags where they could ignite. When you perform any kind of work on the fuel system, wear safety glasses and have a Class B type fire extinguisher on hand.*
Caution: *On models equipped with the Theft-lock audio system, be sure the lockout feature is turned off before performing any procedure which requires disconnecting the battery.*
Note: *After the fuel pressure has been relieved, it's a good idea to use a shop towel around any fuel connection to absorb the residual fuel that may leak out when servicing the fuel system.*

1   Before servicing any fuel system component, you must relieve the fuel pressure to minimize the risk of fire or personal injury.
2   Remove the fuel filler cap - this will relieve any pressure built up in the tank.
3   On models with Throttle Body Injection, remove the fuel pump fuse and run the engine until it stalls, then crank the engine for three seconds. Disconnect the cable from the negative terminal of the battery.
4   On models with Port or Sequential Fuel Injection, use one of the two following methods:

   a) *Disconnect the fuel pump electrical connector at the fuel tank (lower the tank if necessary). Run the engine until it stops, then engage the starter again for another three seconds. With the ignition turned*

Off, reconnect the fuel tank electrical connector, then disconnect the cable from the negative terminal of the battery.
   b) *Loosen the fuel filler cap. Attach a fuel pressure gauge to the Schrader valve on the fuel rail (see illustration). Place the gauge bleeder hose in an approved fuel container. Open the valve on the gauge to relieve pressure, then disconnect the cable from the negative terminal of the battery.*

5   Unless this procedure is followed before servicing fuel lines or connections, fuel spray (and possible injury) may occur.

3   Fuel pump/fuel pressure - testing

Warning: *Gasoline is extremely flammable, so extra precautions must be taken when working on any part of the fuel system. See the* **Warning** *in Section 2.*
Note: *In order to perform the fuel pressure test, you will need to obtain a fuel pressure gauge and adapter set for the fuel injection system being tested.*

Preliminary inspection (all vehicles)

1   Should the fuel system fail to deliver the proper amount of fuel, or any fuel at all, to the fuel injection system, inspect it as follows.
2   Always make certain there is fuel in the tank.
3   With the engine running, inspect for leaks at the threaded fittings at both ends of the fuel line (see Chapter 1). Tighten any loose connections. Inspect all hoses for flattening or kinks which would restrict the flow of fuel.

Pressure check

4   Relieve the fuel system pressure (see Section 2).

Models with Port Fuel Injection (PFI) or Sequential Fuel Injection (SFI)

5   Install a fuel pressure gauge at the connection on the fuel rail **(see illustration 2.4)**.

2003 and earlier models

6   Turn the ignition switch ON with the air conditioning off. The fuel pump should run for about two seconds - note the reading on the gauge. After the pump stops running the pressure should hold steady. It should be within the range listed in this Chapter's Specifications.
7   Start the engine and let it idle at normal operating temperature. The pressure should be lower by 3 to 10 psi. If all the pressure readings are within the limits listed in this Chapter's Specifications, the system is operating properly.
8   If the pressure did not drop by 3 to 10 psi after starting the engine, apply 10 inches of vacuum to the pressure regulator. If the pressure drops, repair the vacuum source to the regulator. If the pressure does not drop, replace the regulator.
9   If the fuel pressure is not within specifi-

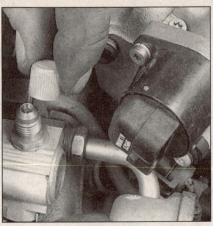

2.4 Remove the cap to the Schrader valve for connecting a fuel pressure gauge

cations, check the following:

   a) *If the pressure is higher than specified, check for a faulty regulator or a pinched or clogged fuel return hose or pipe.*
   b) *If the pressure is lower than specified:*
   c) *Inspect the fuel filter - make sure it's not clogged.*
   d) *Look for a pinched or clogged fuel hose between the fuel tank and the fuel rail.*
   e) *Check the pressure regulator for a malfunction.*
   f) *Look for leaks in the fuel line.*
   g) *Look for a pinched, broken or disconnected regulator vacuum hose.*
   h) *Check for leaking injectors.*
   i) *Check the in-tank fuel pump check valve.*

10   After the testing is done, relieve the fuel pressure (see Section 2) and remove the fuel pressure gauge.
11   If there are no problems with any of the above-listed components, check the fuel pump (see below).

2004 and later models

12   Start the engine and allow it to idle. Note the gauge reading as soon as the pressure stabilizes, and compare it with the pressure listed in this Chapter's Specifications.

   a) *If the pressure is lower than specified, check for a restriction in the fuel system. Two likely suspects are the fuel inlet strainer at the base of the fuel pump module in the left fuel tank, or a faulty fuel pressure regulator.* **Note:** *Neither of these components can be inspected or replaced separately. It's also possible that there is a restriction in the fuel line (a blockage or a kink).*
   b) *If the fuel pressure is higher than specified, replace the fuel pressure regulator, which is part of the left fuel pump module (see Section 7).*

13   Turn off the engine. Verify that the fuel pressure loses no more than 8 psi for five minutes after the engine is turned off.
14   Relieve the fuel pressure (see Section 2), then disconnect the fuel pressure gauge and

3.18 The fuel pump test terminal is located near the left front strut tower

3.25a On earlier models the fuel pump fuse and fuel pump relay are in the holder near the left front strut tower

1   *Fuel pump relay*
2   *Fuel pump fuse*

3.25b On later models the ECM or PCM BAT (fuel pump) fuse (A) and the fuel pump relay (B) locations are clearly marked on the cover of the fuse/relay control box in the engine compartment (typical)

screw on the test port cap. Clean up any spilled gasoline.

15   Start the engine and verify that there are no fuel leaks.

Models with Throttle Body Injection (TBI)

Refer to illustration 3.18

16   Relieve fuel system pressure (see Section 2).

17   Install a fuel pressure gauge between the fuel feed hose and the inlet fitting of the throttle body. The fuel hoses will be under high pressure during this check, so make your connections secure, with no possibility of leaks.

18   With the ignition OFF, use a fused jumper wire from a 12 volt source, jump the fuel pump test terminal and note the pressure reading **(see illustration)**.

19   If the pressure is within the limits listed in this Chapter's Specifications, no further testing is necessary.

20   If the pressure was higher than specified, check for a restricted fuel return line. If the line is OK, then replace the pressure regulator.

21   If the pressure was less than specified, slowly pinch the hose between the gauge and the TBI unit and note the pressure. If the pressure goes above 9 psi, then replace the pressure regulator. If there is not any pressure, then check for a plugged fuel filter, plugged fuel pump inlet filter or a restricted fuel line.

22   After testing is completed, relieve the fuel pressure and remove the fuel pressure gauge.

23   If no problems are found with any of the above listed components, check the fuel pump (see below).

Fuel pump check

Refer to illustration 3.25a and 3.25b

24   The fuel pump is located inside the fuel tank, which muffles its sound when the engine is running. But you can actually hear the fuel pump. Sit inside the vehicle with the windows closed, turn the ignition key to ON (not START) and listen carefully for a whirring sound made by the fuel pump as it's briefly turned on by the

PCM to pressurize the fuel system prior to starting the engine. You will only hear the sound for a second or two, but that sound tells you that the pump is working. If you can't hear the pump, remove the fuel filler cap, then have an assistant turn the ignition switch to ON while you listen for the sound of the pump operating for a couple of seconds. **Note:** *If the fuel system is already pressurized, the pump won't come on.*

25   If the pump does not come on when the ignition key is turned to ON, check the fuel pump fuse and relay **(see illustrations)**. If the fuse and relay are okay, check the wiring back to the fuel pump. If the fuse, relay and wiring are okay, the fuel pump is probably defective.

---

4   Fuel lines and fittings - repair and replacement

Refer to illustrations 4.4a, 4.4b, 4.5, 4.6, 4.16, 4.18 and 4.19

Warning: *Gasoline is extremely flammable, so extra precautions must be taken when*

4.4a Quick-connect fitting (arrow) - plastic collar-type shown

working on any part of the fuel system. See the **Warning** *in Section 2.*

1   Always relieve the fuel pressure before servicing fuel lines or fittings (see Section 2).

2   The fuel feed, return and vapor lines extend from the fuel tank to the engine compartment. The lines are secured to the underbody with clip and screw assemblies. These lines must be occasionally inspected for leaks, kinks and dents.

3   If evidence of dirt is found in the system or fuel filter during disassembly, the line should be disconnected and blown out. Check the fuel strainer on the fuel gauge sending unit (see Section 7) for damage and deterioration.

Quick-connect fittings

4   Beginning in model year 1989, "quick-connect fittings" were adopted for certain fuel line connections. Quick-connect fittings come in two varieties. Some have a plastic collar while others have a metal collar **(see illustrations)**. The kind your car is equipped with will depend on the model.

4.4b On quick-connect fuel lines, use a special tool and push them into the connector (arrows) to separate the fuel lines

4.5 Some models are equipped with fuel lines that can be disconnected by pinching the tabs and separating each connector

A   *Fuel return line*   B   *Fuel feed line*

4.6 3/8 and 5/16-inch fuel line disconnect tools

5   To disconnect a plastic quick-connect fitting, simply squeeze the retaining tabs and pull the fitting apart **(see illustration)**.

6   To disconnect a metal quick-connect fitting, a special tool (fuel line separator) is required **(see illustration)**. Slide back the quick-connect fitting's dust cover, then twist the fitting to dislodge any dirt. Use compressed air to blow any dirt away. Install the special tool on the male pipe end and push it in to release the fitting.

7   To reconnect the quick-connect fitting, apply a few drops of clean engine oil to the male pipe end, then push both sides of the fitting together until the retaining tabs snap into place. Make sure the fitting is securely snapped into place by tugging on each end.

Steel tubing

8   If replacement of a fuel line or emission line is called for, use original equipment replacement parts from the dealer parts department.

9   Don't use copper or aluminum tubing to replace steel tubing. These materials cannot withstand normal vehicle vibration.

10   Because fuel lines used on fuel-injected vehicles are under high pressure, they require special consideration.

11   Most fuel lines have threaded fittings with

O-rings. Any time the fittings are loosened to service or replace components:

a) *Use a backup wrench while loosening and tightening the fittings.*
b) *Check all O-rings for cuts, cracks and deterioration. Replace any that appear worn or damaged.*
c) *If the lines are replaced, always use original equipment parts, or parts that meet the GM standards specified in this Section.*

Nylon fuel lines

12   Steel or rubber fuel lines can sometimes be replaced with nylon fuel lines. These are designed so that they can be used in fuel injection systems and typically come with a 3/8" inner diameter (for fuel feed) or a 5/16" inner diameter (for fuel return).

13   New nylon fuel lines are flexible enough to be formed around slight bends. If bent too sharply, however, they will kink. Old nylon lines that are to be re-used are less pliable that new ones and are liable to kink more easily, so beware.

Rubber hose

14   When rubber hose is used to replace a metal line, use reinforced, fuel resistant hose marked specifically for use in fuel-injected

applications. Ask a dealer parts department for replacement parts. Hose(s) not clearly marked like this could fail prematurely and could fail to meet Federal emission standards. Hose inside diameter must match line outside diameter.

15   Don't use rubber hose within four inches of any part of the exhaust system or within ten inches of the catalytic converter. Metal lines and rubber hoses must never be allowed to chafe against the frame. A minimum of 1/4-inch clearance must be maintained around a line or hose to prevent contact with the frame.

Removal and installation

Note: *The following procedure and accompanying illustrations are typical for vehicles covered by this manual.*

16   Relieve the fuel pressure (see Section 2) and disconnect the fuel feed, return or vapor line at the fuel tank **(see illustration)**.

17   Remove all fasteners attaching the lines to the vehicle body.

18   Detach the fitting(s) that attach the metal lines to the engine compartment fuel hoses **(see illustration)**.

19   Installation is the reverse of removal. Be sure to use new O-rings at the threaded fittings **(see illustration)**.

4.16 The fuel return (A), vapor (B), and feed lines (C) at the fuel tank

4.18 Typical feed and return line threaded fittings in the engine compartment

4.19 Always replace the fuel line O-rings

5.9 Location of the fuel tank strap mounting bolts (arrows)

7.3 Remove the nuts (arrows) and the fuel pump access cover in the trunk

5 Fuel tank - removal and installation

Refer to illustration 5.9

Warning: *Gasoline is extremely flammable, so extra precautions must be taken when working on any part of the fuel system. See the* **Warning** *in Section 2.* **Note:** *Don't begin this procedure until the fuel gauge indicates the tank is empty or nearly empty. If the tank must be removed when it's full (for example, if the fuel pump malfunctions), siphon any remaining fuel from the tank prior to removal.*

1   Unless the vehicle has been driven far enough to completely empty the tank, it's a good idea to siphon the residual fuel out before removing the tank from the vehicle. **Warning:** *DO NOT start the siphoning action by mouth! Use a siphoning kit, available at most auto parts stores.*

2   Relieve the fuel pressure (see Section 2).

3   Detach the cable from the negative terminal of the battery. **Caution:** *On models equipped with the Theftlock audio system, be sure the lockout feature is turned off before performing any procedure which requires disconnecting the battery.*

4   Raise the vehicle and place it securely on jackstands.

5   Locate the electrical connector for the electric fuel pump and fuel gauge sending unit in front of the tank, and unplug it. If the vehicle doesn't have a connector, see Step 9 below. **Note:** *On some models, it is necessary to remove the rubber exhaust system hangers and drop the exhaust to get adequate clearance.*

6   Disconnect the fuel feed and return lines (see Section 4), the vapor return line and the filler neck and vent tubes. Refer to Section 4 for information on the fittings used.

7   If necessary, remove the rubber exhaust pipe hangers to allow the exhaust to drop slightly, then remove the exhaust pipe and heat shield.

8   On 2001 and later models, remove the plastic pushpins securing the fuel tank shield, then remove the shield. Support the fuel tank with a floor jack.

9   Disconnect both fuel tank retaining straps **(see illustration)**.

10   Lower the tank enough to disconnect the wires and ground strap from the fuel pump/fuel gauge sending unit, if you haven't already done so.

11   Remove the tank from the vehicle.

12   Installation is the reverse of removal.

6 Fuel tank cleaning and repair - general information

1   All repairs to the fuel tank or filler neck should be carried out by a professional who has experience in this critical and potentially dangerous work. Even after cleaning and flushing of the fuel system, explosive fumes can remain and ignite during repair of the tank.

2   If the fuel tank is removed from the vehicle, it should not be placed in an area where sparks or open flames could ignite the fumes coming out of the tank. Be especially careful inside garages where a natural gas-type appliance is located, because the pilot light could cause an explosion.

7 Fuel pump - removal and installation

Refer to illustrations 7.3, 7.5a, 7.5b and 7.8

Warning: *Gasoline is extremely flammable,*

7.5a On some models the fuel pump is retained by a lock ring; carefully tap the lock ring counterclockwise until the locking tabs align with the slots in the fuel tank

so extra precautions must be taken when working on any part of the fuel system. See the **Warning** *in Section 2.*

Removal

1   Relieve the fuel pressure (see Section 2).

2   Remove the cable from the negative battery terminal. **Caution:** *On models equipped with the Theftlock audio system, be sure the lockout feature is turned off before performing any procedure which requires disconnecting the battery.*

3   On many 1997 through 2003 models, there is a fuel pump access cover in the trunk floor **(see illustration).** On all other models, you must remove the fuel tank to proceed.

4   The fuel pump/sending unit assembly is located inside the fuel tank. It's held in place by a cam lock ring mechanism consisting of an inner ring with three locking cams and an outer ring with three retaining tangs.

5   To unlock the fuel pump/sending unit assembly, turn the inner ring clockwise until the locking cams are free of the retaining tangs **(see illustrations).** **Note:** *If the rings are locked together too tightly to release by hand, tap them gently with a rubber or brass hammer. On later models, the ring is usually extremely tight; there is a special tool for removing it, but if you must use a brass hammer and a punch, take all possible pre-*

7.5b On other models, use a pair of snap-ring pliers to remove the retaining collar from the fuel pump assembly

7.8 Inspect the fuel strainer for dirt; if necessary, carefully pry the strainer from the inlet pipe using a screwdriver

8.4 Air intake details - 3.4 liter V6 shown (others similar)

1   Mass air flow sensor
2   Intake air temperature sensor
3   Air intake hose clamp

8.8a Removing the upper air cleaner housing on a 2.3L (Quad 4) engine

8.8b Upper air cleaner housing mounting details (typical V6 engine)

1   IAT sending unit
2   Housing mounting screws
3   Upper air filter housing

cautions to avoid damaging the tank and ring. After removing the ring, check it for straightness on a flat surface. There should be less than 0.018-inch bend in it. If there is more, replace it with a new one. **Warning**: *Do not use a steel hammer - a spark could cause an explosion!*

6   Pull the fuel pump/sending unit assembly out of the tank. **Caution:** *The fuel level float and sending unit are delicate. Don't bump them into the lock ring during removal or the accuracy of the sending unit may be affected, and don't lift or support the fuel gauge sending unit assembly by the fuel pipes as this could damage the solder joints.*

7   Check the condition of the rubber O-ring around the mouth of the lock ring mechanism. If it's dried out, cracked or deteriorated, replace it.

8   Inspect the filter on the lower end of the fuel pump **(see illustration)**. If it's dirty, remove it, clean it with solvent and blow it out with compressed air. If it's too dirty to be cleaned, replace it.

9   If you have to separate the fuel pump and sending unit, pull the fuel pump assembly into the rubber connector and slide the pump away from the bottom support. Care should be taken to prevent damage to the rubber insulator and fuel strainer during removal. After the pump is clear of the bottom support, pull it out of the rubber connector. **Note:** *2004 and later models don't have fuel pumps that can be serviced separately - you must buy a complete fuel pump module.*

Installation

10   Position the rubber gasket around the opening in the fuel tank and guide the fuel pump/sending unit assembly into the tank.

11   Turn the inner lock ring counterclockwise until the locking cams are fully engaged by the retaining tangs. **Note:** *If you've installed a new O-ring, it may be necessary to push down on the inner lock ring until the locking cams slide under the retaining tangs.*

8   Air cleaner housing - removal and installation

Refer to illustrations 8.4, 8.8a and 8.8b

1   Detach the cable from the negative terminal of the battery. **Caution:** *On models equipped with the Theftlock audio system, be sure the lockout feature is turned off before performing any procedure which requires disconnecting the battery.*

2   On models through 1995, remove the battery and the engine compartment diagonal support brace, if necessary (see Chapter 5).

3   Remove the air cleaner element (see Chapter 1).

4   Unplug the connector from the intake air temperature sender if necessary **(see illustration)**.

5   Unplug the electrical connector and unclamp the air duct from the Mass Air Flow (MAF) sensor, if equipped.

6   Unclamp the air duct from the housing and detach any other fasteners retaining the duct. On 1997 and later models, remove the PCM and its wiring harness from the air filter housing.

7   Remove the crankcase vent tube (if equipped).

8   Remove the housing mounting bolts and lift the housing from the vehicle **(see illustrations)**.

9   Installation is the reverse of removal.

9   Fuel injection system - general information

Electronic fuel injection provides optimum fuel/air mixture ratios at all stages of combustion and offers immediate throttle response characteristics. It also enables the engine to run at the leanest possible fuel/air mixture ratio, reducing exhaust gas emissions.

On models equipped with a 2.5L four-cylinder engine, the Throttle Body Injection (TBI) unit replaces a conventional carburetor atop the intake manifold. All other models are fitted with either a Port Fuel Injection (PFI) system or a Sequential Fuel Injection (SFI) system. All three systems are controlled by an Electronic Control Module (ECM), which monitors engine performance and adjusts the air/fuel mixture accordingly (see Chapter 6 for a complete

> Chapter 4 Fuel and exhaust systems

4-7

An electric fuel pump located in the fuel tank with the fuel gauge sending unit pumps fuel to the fuel injection system through the fuel feed line and an in-line fuel filter. A pressure regulator keeps fuel available at a constant pressure. Fuel in excess of injector needs is returned to the fuel tank by a separate line.

The basic TBI unit is made up of two major casting assemblies - a throttle body with an Idle Air Control (IAC) valve controls air flow and a Throttle Position Sensor (TPS) monitors throttle angle. The fuel body consists of a fuel meter with a built-in pressure regulator and a fuel injector to supply fuel to the engine.

The fuel injector is a solenoid operated device controlled by the ECM. The ECM turns on the solenoid, which lifts a normally closed ball valve off its seat. The fuel, which is under pressure, is injected in a conical spray pattern at the walls of the throttle body bore above the throttle valve. The fuel which is not used by the injector passes through the pressure regulator before being returned to the fuel tank.

On all port fuel injection systems, the throttle body has a throttle valve to control the amount of air delivered to the engine. The valve is operated by a cable attached to the accelerator pedal (early models) or electrically by the PCM. On these later models, the driver's accelerator pedal only operates an accelerator pedal position sensor - there is no direct mechanical connection between the pedal and the throttle valve.

The throttle position sensor is located on the throttle body. 2003 and earlier models with mechanically-operated throttles also have an Idle Air Control (IAC) valve mounted on the throttle body.

The fuel rail is mounted on top of the engine. It distributes fuel to the individual injectors.

Fuel is delivered to the inlet end of the rail by the fuel supply line. 2003 and earlier models also use a pressure regulator mounted on the fuel rail and a fuel return line

that directs excess fuel back to the fuel tank. This regulator keeps the pressure at the injectors at a constant level. 2004 and later models use a returnless fuel system with a pressure regulator located at the fuel tank module.

10 Fuel injection system - check

Warning: *Gasoline is extremely flammable, so extra precautions must be taken when working on any part of the fuel system. See the* **Warning** *in Section 2.*
Note: *The following procedure is based on the assumption that the fuel pump is working and the fuel pressure is adequate (see Section 3).*

Preliminary checks

1   Check all electrical connectors that are related to the system. Loose connectors and poor grounds can cause many problems that resemble more serious malfunctions.
2   Check to see that the battery is fully charged, as the control unit and sensors depend on an accurate supply of voltage in order to properly meter the fuel.
3   Check the air filter element - a dirty or partially blocked filter will severely impede performance and economy (see Chapter 1).
4   If a blown fuse is found, replace it with a fuse of the same amp rating and see if it blows again. If it does, search for a grounded wire in the harness to the fuel pump.

Port Fuel and Sequential Injection only

5   Check the air intake duct from the mass airflow sensor (if equipped) to the intake manifold for leaks, which will result in an excessively lean mixture. Also check the condition of the vacuum hoses connected to the intake manifold.
6   Remove the air intake duct from the throttle body and check for dirt, carbon or other residue build-up. If it's dirty, clean it with carburetor cleaner and a toothbrush.

7   With the engine running, place a screwdriver against each injector, one at a time, and listen through the handle for a clicking sound, indicating operation.
8   The remainder of the system checks should be left to a GM service department or other qualified repair shop, as there is a chance that the control unit may be damaged if the checks are not performed properly.

11 Throttle Body Injection (TBI) assembly - removal and installation

Refer to illustrations 11.4a and 11.4b
Warning: *Gasoline is extremely flammable, so extra precautions must be taken when working on any part of the fuel system. See the* **Warning** *in Section 2.*
Note: *The fuel injector, pressure regulator, throttle position sensor and the idle air control valve can be replaced without removing the throttle body assembly.*
1   Relieve the fuel system pressure (see Section 2).
2   Disconnect the cable from the negative battery terminal. **Caution:** *On models equipped with the Theftlock audio system, be sure the lockout feature is turned off before performing any procedure which requires disconnecting the battery.*
3   Remove the air cleaner housing (see Section 8).
4   Unplug the electrical connectors from the idle air control valve, throttle position sensor and fuel injector **(see illustrations)**.
5   Remove the wiring harness and insulating grommet from the throttle body.
6   Remove the throttle linkage and return spring, transmission control and cruise control cables (if applicable).
7   Using pieces of numbered tape, mark all of the vacuum hoses to the throttle body and disconnect them.
8   Disconnect the fuel inlet and return lines. Use a backup wrench on the inlet and return

11.4a Typical location of the IAC valve and the fuel injector electrical connectors (arrows) on a Model 300 TBI unit

1   *Fuel injector electrical connector*
2   *Idle air control valve electrical connector*

11.4b Typical location of the TPS (arrow) on a Model 700 TBI unit

12.4 The best way to remove the fuel injector is to pry on it with a screwdriver, using a second screwdriver as a fulcrum

12.25 The idle air control (IAC) valve pintle must not extend more than 1-1/8 inch - also, replace the O-ring if it is brittle

A   Distance of pintle   B   O-ring
*   extension*

fitting nuts to prevent damage to the throttle body and fuel lines. Remove the fuel fitting O-rings and discard them.

9   Remove the TBI assembly mounting bolts and lift the unit from the intake manifold. It is a good idea to stuff a rag into the intake manifold opening to prevent foreign matter from falling in.

10   Installation is the reverse of the removal procedure. Be sure to install a new throttle body-to-intake manifold gasket, new fuel line O-rings and tighten the mounting bolts to the torque listed in this Chapter's Specifications.

11   Turn the ignition switch to the "ON" position without starting the engine and check for fuel leaks.

12   Check to see if the accelerator pedal is free by depressing the pedal to the floor and releasing it with the ignition switch in the "OFF" position.

12   Throttle Body Injection (TBI) - component replacement

Warning: *Gasoline is extremely flammable, so extra precautions must be taken when working on any part of the fuel system. See the* **Warning** *in Section 2.*

Fuel injector

Refer to illustration 12.4

1   Disconnect the negative battery cable. **Caution:** *On models equipped with the Theft-lock audio system, be sure the lockout feature is turned off before performing any procedure which requires disconnecting the battery.*

2   Unplug the electrical connector at the injector.

3   Remove the injector retainer screw and the retainer **(refer to illustration 11.4a)**.

4   Using one screwdriver as a fulcrum on the fuel meter body, place another screwdriver tip under the ridge on the fuel injector

opposite the electrical connector end and gently pry the injector out **(see illustration)**.

5   If the injector is to be reused, replace the upper and lower O-rings on the injector and in the fuel injector cavity. Install the upper O-ring in the groove on the injector and the lower O-ring flush against the filter element.

6   Install the injector assembly in the fuel meter body by pushing it straight down. Make sure the connector end is facing in the direction of the opening in the fuel meter body for the wire harness grommet.

7   Install the injector retainer and screw. Use a thread locking compound or Loctite 262 on the retainer screw.

8   Reconnect the negative battery cable. Pressurize the fuel system by turning the ignition key to the On position and inspect the area around the injector for leaks.

9   Plug the electrical connector into the injector and start the engine to check for correct operation.

Fuel Pressure Regulator Diaphragm

10   Disconnect the battery negative cable. **Caution:** *On models equipped with the Theft-lock audio system, be sure the lockout feature is turned off before performing any procedure which requires disconnecting the battery.*

11   Relieve the fuel system pressure.

12   Remove the air intake duct.

13   Remove the pressure regulator cover screws. **Caution:** *Apply pressure to the cover while you're removing the screws or the spring inside will force the cover off before you're ready for it.*

14   Carefully remove the regulator cover, then the spring, spring seat and diaphragm assembly.

15   Inspect the regulator valve seat for damage. The throttle body will have to be replaced if damage exists.

16   On reassembly, install a new diaphragm. **Note:** *The diaphragm must be replaced when-*

ever the regulator cover is removed.

17   Check that the regulator cover screws still retain some thread-locking material on the threads. If necessary apply Loctite 262 to the threads before installing the screws.

18   Reassembly is the reverse of disassembly. Be sure to replace all gaskets and O-ring seals, otherwise a dangerous fuel leak may develop.

19   Turn the ignition switch to the "ON" position without starting the engine and check for fuel leaks.

Idle Air Control (IAC) valve

Refer to illustrations 12.25 and 12.26

20   Unplug the electrical connector from the Idle Air Control (IAC) valve assembly.

21   Remove the two IAC valve attaching screws and withdraw the valve. **Note:** *You may need a Torx bit to remove the screws.*

22   Remove the IAC valve assembly. Check the rubber O-ring for damage and replace it if necessary. **Caution:** *If the IAC valve is to be reused, do not push or pull the IAC valve pintle, as this may damage the threads of the worm drive.*

23   Clean the sealing surface and the bore of the idle air/vacuum signal housing assembly to ensure a good seal. **Caution:** *The IAC valve assembly itself is an electrical component and must not be soaked in any liquid cleaner or solvent or damage may result.*

24   Before installing a new IAC valve assembly, the position of the pintle must be checked. If the pintle is extended too far, damage to the assembly may occur.

25   Measure the distance from the gasket mounting surface of the IAC valve assembly to the tip of the pintle **(see illustration)**.

26   If the distance is greater than 1-1/8 inch, reduce it by applying a firm hand pressure on the pintle to retract it **(see illustration)**.

27   Position the O-ring seal on the IAC valve assembly. Lubricate the O-ring with clean engine oil.

12.26 To reduce the IAC valve pintle extension, grasp the valve and depress the pintle using a slight side-to-side motion

12.33 The throttle position sensor (TPS) mounts to the side of the throttle body with two screws (arrows) and is not adjustable

28   Install the IAC valve in the idle air/vacuum signal housing assembly and tighten it securely.

29   Plug in the electrical connector at the IAC valve assembly. **Note:** *The IAC resetting is controlled by the ECM. To initiate this process, turn the ignition on for five seconds, turn it off for ten seconds, then start the engine and check for proper idle.*

Throttle Position Sensor (TPS)

Refer to illustration 12.33

30   Disconnect the cable from the negative battery terminal. **Caution:** *On models equipped with the Theftlock audio system, be sure the lockout feature is turned off before performing any procedure which requires disconnecting the battery.*

31   Remove the air cleaner housing.

32   Unplug the electrical connector from the throttle position sensor.

33   Remove the two sensor mounting screws and pull the sensor from the throttle body **(see illustration)**.

34   To install the TPS, align the slot in the rear of the sensor with the throttle shaft and insert the sensor into the throttle body. Install the mounting screws. This style TPS is not adjustable.

35   The remainder of installation is the reverse of the removal procedure.

13   Port Fuel Injection (PFI) and Sequential Fuel Injection (SFI) - component removal and installation

Warning: *Gasoline is extremely flammable, so extra precautions must be taken when working on any part of the fuel system. See the **Warning** in Section 2.*

Note: *Relieve the fuel system pressure before servicing any fuel system component (see Section 2).*

Throttle Body

Refer to illustrations 13.3, 13.4 and 13.8

Note: *The throttle body on the 1995 and ear-*

lier model 3.4 liter engine is integral with the plenum. See Plenum in this Section.

1   Disconnect the cable from the negative terminal of the battery. On later engines, remove the acoustic cover from the top of the engine (see Chapter 2F). **Caution:** *On models equipped with the Theftlock audio system, be sure the lockout feature is turned off before performing any procedure which requires disconnecting the battery.*

2   Remove the engine top cover on models so equipped.

3   Disconnect all electrical connectors from the throttle body assembly **(see illustration)**.

4   Disconnect all vacuum and vapor hoses (see illustration).

5   Disconnect the throttle cable and cruise control cable on early models so equipped (see Section 14). On 3100 engines, remove the throttle cable bracket.

6   Remove the air inlet duct.

7   On models with heated throttle bodies, drain some coolant and disconnect the two coolant hoses from the throttle body.

8   Remove the throttle body mounting bolts

13.3 Using a small screwdriver, release the locking tab and remove the electrical connector

13.4 Using a small screwdriver, remove the vacuum line assembly from the throttle body

13.8 To detach the throttle body from the plenum, remove these two bolts (arrows) (V6 engine is shown)

13.18 Location of the plenum mounting bolts (arrows) for a V6 engine (2.8L engine shown, others are similar)

and detach it **(see illustration)**.

9   Installation is the reverse of removal. Be sure to replace the gasket if there is any indication of damage.

10   Tighten the fasteners to the torque listed in this Chapter's Specifications.

Idle Air Control (IAC) valve

See Section 12.

Throttle Position Sensor (TPS)

11   Most of the models covered by this manual are equipped with non-adjustable TP sensors, however other models may require adjustment after sensor replacement. The adjustable type of TP sensor is easily identifiable by the elongated slots surrounding the sensor mounting holes. Non-adjustable type TP sensors have round mounting holes that are just slightly larger than the mounting screws that are used to fasten the sensor. To replace non-adjustable type TP sensors refer to Section 12. On adjustable type TP sensors replacement of this component should be performed by a dealer service department or repair shop equipped with a "scan" tool to properly adjust the TPS.

Plenum (2.2L four-cylinder and 2.8L, 3.1L and 3100 V6)

Refer to illustration 13.18

Note: Some models may require that the engine be rotated (refer to Chapter 1)

12   Remove the cable from the negative terminal of the battery. **Caution:** On models equipped with the Theftlock audio system, be sure the lockout feature is turned off before performing any procedure which requires disconnecting the battery.

13   Mark and remove all of the vacuum lines that may interfere, then remove the throttle cable bracket nuts.

14   On V6 models, remove the EGR valve (see Chapter 6). On 2.2L four cylinder models, unscrew the EGR tube fitting.

15   On V6 models, remove the throttle body.

16   If necessary, remove the bolts which

13.27 Remove the air cleaner assembly and air intake hose

secure the plastic spark plug wire shield.

17   On the 3100, remove the ignition coil and bracket, the braces to the alternator, and the MAP sensor and bracket.

18   Remove the plenum bolts **(see illustration)**.

19   Remove the plenum and gaskets. If the plenum sticks, use a block of wood and a rubber mallet to dislodge it. Do not pry between the sealing flanges, as this will damage the machined surfaces and vacuum leaks may develop.

20   Remove all traces of old gasket material from the plenum and intake manifold mating surfaces. It is a good idea to stuff rags into the intake manifold openings to prevent debris and old gasket material from falling in.

21   Install the new gaskets and set the plenum into position.

22   Install the plenum bolts and tighten them to the torque listed in this Chapter's Specifications.

23   The rest of the procedure is the reverse of removal.

Plenum (3.4 liter V6)

Refer to illustrations 13.27, 13.30 and 13.36

Note: An eight digit identification number is

13.30 3.4L V6 EGR details

1   *EGR valve assembly*
2   *EGR Tube*

affixed to the plenum adjacent to the EGR valve flange. Refer to this number if servicing or parts replacement is required.

24   Remove the cable from the negative terminal of the battery. **Caution:** On models equipped with the Theftlock audio system, be sure the lockout feature is turned off before performing any procedure which requires disconnecting the battery.

25   Drain the coolant (see Chapter 1).

26   Remove the throttle cable (see Section 14) and cruise control cable from the throttle lever cam.

27   Remove the air cleaner assembly and air intake hose **(see illustration)**.

28   Remove the vacuum hoses for the brakes and crankcase ventilation valve at the plenum.

29   Disconnect the connectors for the Idle Air Control (IAC) valve and Throttle Position (TP) sensor.

30   Remove the EGR valve and the EGR tube **(see illustration)**. **Caution:** Avoid bending the EGR tube during removal as this will damage the tube or prevent you from being able to align it during reassembly.

31   If necessary, remove the bolt that secures the coolant tube to the throttle cable bracket.

32   Remove the fuel pipe clip.

13.36 3.4L V6 plenum details

1 Engine identification cover
2 Plenum bolts
3 Fuel injectors
4 Fuel rail

13.54 Remove the upper plenum (arrow) (1995 and later 3800 V6)

33   Loosen the clamp that secures the coolant hose to the plenum, then slide the clamp down the hose.
34   Disconnect the crankcase vent hose at the front camshaft cover.
35   Remove the vacuum hoses from the vacuum module. **Note:** *Mark the hoses for reassembly.*
36   Remove the engine identification cover **(see illustration)**.
37   Remove the wires from the rear spark plugs.
38   Remove the bolts and nuts that secure the plenum.
39   Lift the plenum off the intake manifold. If the plenum sticks, use a block of wood and a rubber mallet to dislodge it. **Caution:** *Do not pry between the sealing flanges, as this will damage the machined surfaces and vacuum leaks may develop. Remove the coolant hose as you lift the plenum.*
40   Remove all traces of old gasket material from the plenum and intake manifold mating surfaces, and remove the remove and discard the coolant O-ring. It is a good idea to stuff rags into the intake manifold openings to prevent debris and old gasket material from falling in.
41   Install the new gaskets and O-ring and set the plenum into position.
42   Install the plenum bolts and tighten them to the torque listed in this Chapter's Specifications.
43   The rest of the procedure is the reverse of removal.

Plenum (1995 and later 3800 V6)

Refer to illustration 13.54

44   Disconnect the negative battery cable from the battery. **Caution:** *On models equipped with the Theftlock audio system, be sure the lockout feature is turned off before performing any procedure which requires disconnecting the battery.*
45   Detach the air intake duct (see Section 9).
46   Remove the acoustic cover over the plenum **(see Chapter 2 Part F illustration 4.4)**.
47   Detach the spark plug wires from the spark plugs and set them aside.

48   Unplug the Idle Air Control (IAC) valve, the Throttle Position Sensor (TPS) and the Mass Air Flow sensor (MAF) electrical connectors (see Chapter 6).
49   Mark and disconnect any vacuum hoses connected to the throttle body and the upper plenum. Also detach the breather hose, if equipped.
50   Disconnect the accelerator cable and the cruise control cable (see Section 14) from the throttle lever.
51   Detach the lower throttle body support bracket.
52   Refer to Section 2 to relieve the fuel system pressure then remove the the fuel rail and injectors
53   Refer to Chapter 6 and remove the EGR valve from the manifold.
54   Remove the upper intake plenum mounting bolts and separate the plenum from the engine **(see illustration)**. Do not pry between the manifold and the plenum, as damage to the gasket sealing surfaces may result. If you're installing a new manifold, transfer all fittings and the throttle body to the new manifold. **Note:** *On 3.8L Regal models with supercharger, remove the supercharger drivebelt, disconnect the wires and hoses from the throttle body, and remove the supercharger*

mounting bolts and the supercharger. On these models, the supercharger takes the place of a plenum.

Fuel rail and related components (All except 2.2L four-cylinder)

Refer to illustrations 13.57a, 13.57b, 13.60a, 13.60b, 13.60c, 13.61 and 13.62
Warning: *Before any work is performed on the fuel lines, fuel rail or injectors, the fuel system pressure must be relieved (refer to the fuel pressure relief procedure in Section 2).*
55   Detach the negative battery cable from the battery. **Caution:** *On models equipped with the Theftlock audio system, be sure the lockout feature is turned off before performing any procedure which requires disconnecting the battery.*
56   Remove the plenum, if equipped (see Plenum).
57   Using a backup wrench, remove the fuel lines at the fuel rail **(see illustration)**. **Note:** *Some models use "quick-connect" fittings on some fuel line connections. These require a special tool to remove **(see illustration)**. Tool set J 37088-a includes the tools for different sizes of quick-connect fittings.*

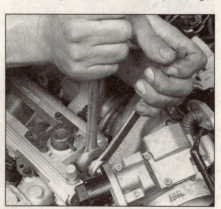

13.57a Use a backup wrench when disconnecting the fuel lines (typical V6 engine shown)

13.57b Use a special fuel line disconnect tool to release the quick-connect fuel line couplers (arrows) from the fuel rail (3.1L engine shown)

13.60a Before removing the injector electrical connector, label the connector according to the cylinder number

13.60b To remove the connector, push in the retaining clip and pull up

13.60c Sometimes after removing the connector the insulator will pop out - if it does, be sure to reinstall it

58   On models with Quad-4 engines, remove the air/oil separator (see Chapter 6).
59   Remove the vacuum line at the fuel pressure regulator, if so equipped.
60   Label and unplug the injector electrical connectors **(see illustrations)**.
61   Remove the fuel rail retaining bolts **(see accompanying illustration and illustration 13.36)**.
62   Carefully remove the fuel rail with the injectors **(see illustration)**. **Caution:** *Use care when handling the fuel rail assembly to avoid damaging the injectors.*
63   On reassembly, be sure to replace the fuel pipe O-rings with new ones.

Fuel rail (2.2L four-cylinder)
64   The fuel rail on the 2.2L four-cylinder is integral with the intake manifold (refer to Chapter 2).

Fuel injectors (All except 2.2L four-cylinder)
Refer to illustrations 13.65 and 13.66
Caution: *To prevent dirt from entering the*

engine, the area around the injectors should be cleaned before servicing.
65   To remove the fuel injectors, spread open the end of the injector clip slightly and remove it from the fuel rail, then extract the injector **(see illustration)**.
66   Inspect the injector O-ring seal(s). These should be replaced whenever the fuel rail is removed **(see illustration)**.
67   Install the new O-ring seals on the injectors and lubricate them with engine oil. **Note 1:** *It is recommended that all of the O-rings be replaced whenever the fuel rail is removed.* **Note 2:** *The upper and lower O-rings are made of different materials and usually are different colors. Always use the same color O-ring in the same positions (i.e. black on top, brown on the bottom).*
68   Install the injectors on the fuel rail.
69   Secure the injectors with the retainer clips.

Fuel Injectors (2.2L four-cylinder)
Warning: *Before any work is performed on*

the fuel lines or injectors, the fuel system pressure must be relieved (refer to the fuel pressure relief procedure in Section 2).
70   Disconnect the negative battery cable.

13.61 To remove the fuel rail assembly, remove the retaining bolts (arrows) (typical V6 engine shown)

13.62 Use a gentle side-to-side rocking motion while pulling straight up to release the injectors from their bores in the intake manifold (typical V6 shown)

13.65 To remove an injector from the fuel rail assembly, spread the spring clip with a small screwdriver (typical V6 shown)

13.66 If you plan to reuse the same injector, always replace the O-ring with a new one

13.84 Details of the Quad-4 engine fuel pressure regulator

1   *Fuel pressure regulator vacuum hose*
2   *Retainer bracket screws*
3   *Fuel pressure regulator*

13.85a A Torx bit or screwdriver is needed to remove the pressure regulator mounting bolts (arrows)

13.85b Separate the fuel rail(s) from the regulator

13.86 Always replace all O-rings when replacing the regulator

Caution: *On models equipped with the Theft-lock audio system, be sure the lockout feature is turned off before performing any procedure which requires disconnecting the battery.*

71   Remove the plenum (see Plenum).
72   Remove the fuel return line retaining bracket and move it away from the fuel pressure regulator.
73   Remove the fuel pressure regulator.
74   Remove the injector retainer bracket.
75   Label then remove the injector connectors.
76   Remove the injectors. **Note:** *Be sure that the small injector O-rings do not remain inside the manifold after the injectors have been removed.*
77   On reassembly, if you're going to reinstall the original injectors, be sure to use new O-rings, lubricated with engine oil. **Note 1:** *It is recommended that all of the O-rings be replaced whenever the fuel rail is removed.* **Note 2:** *The upper and lower O-rings are made of different materials and usually are different colors. Always use the same color O-ring in the same positions (i.e. black on top, brown on the bottom).*
78   Apply a light film of clean engine oil to the O-rings.
79   Install the injectors in their holes using a twisting motion.
80   Plug in the electrical connectors, then

install the injector retainer, making sure that each injector fits properly into its retaining slot.
81   Apply a non-hardening thread locking compound to the retainer screws and tighten the screws to the torque listed in this chapter's Specifications.
82   The remainder of the installation is the reverse of removal. Be sure to check for leaks before returning the car to normal service.

Fuel pressure regulator (Quad-4, 2.8L and 3.1L V6)

Refer to illustrations 13.84, 13.85a, 13.85b and 13.86

83   On V6 models, to remove the fuel pressure regulator from the fuel rail, remove the two fuel line fittings and gaskets.
84   On models with a Quad-4 engine, remove the pressure regulator mounting bracket screws and detach it from the fuel rail **(see illustration)**.
85   On V6 models, detach the pressure regulator mounting bolts and separate the two fuel rails from the pressure regulator assembly **(see illustrations)**.
86   On all models, reassembly is the reverse of disassembly. Be sure to replace all gaskets and O-ring seals **(see illustration)**, otherwise a dangerous fuel leak may develop.
87   Before installing the fuel rail, lubricate all

injector O-ring seals with engine oil.
88   Turn the ignition switch to the "ON" position without starting the engine and check for fuel leaks.

Fuel pressure regulator (2.2L four-cylinder and 3.4L, 3100, and 3800 V6)

Refer to illustrations 13.92 and 13.94
Note: *2004 and later 3800 V6 models and 5.3L V8 models with returnless fuel systems don't have a serviceable fuel pressure regulator (it's part of the fuel pump assembly).*
89   Disconnect the battery negative cable.
Caution: *On models equipped with the Theft-lock audio system, be sure the lockout feature is turned off before performing any procedure which requires disconnecting the battery.*
90   Relieve the fuel system pressure.
91   On the 3100, remove the throttle body (see Throttle Body, in this Section). On the 3.4L, remove the plenum (see Plenum, in this Section).
92   Detach the vacuum hose from the regulator **(see illustration)**.

13.92 Fuel pressure regulator details (typical V6 shown - four-cylinder similar)

A   *Vacuum hose*
B   *Fuel return line fitting*
C   *Mounting bolts*

13.94 On 1996 and later 3.4L engines and all 3800 engines, remove the snap-ring (arrow) from the top of the pressure regulator

13.99 On 1995 and later 3800 engines, remove the retaining screws (arrows) securing the MAF sensor to the throttle body

93   On the 3800, clean the area around the snap ring that holds the regulator in place. On others, detach the fuel return line from the regulator. **Caution:** *Be sure to use a back-up wrench.*

94   On the 3800, remove the snap ring that holds the regulator in place **(see illustration)**. On others, remove the screw holding the regulator onto the fuel rail.

95   Remove the regulator using a twisting motion. **Note:** *Fuel is likely to spill when you remove the regulator, so place a towel under the regulator before removing it.*

96   On the 3800, cover the regulator housing to prevent contamination of the fuel system.

97   Reassembly is the reverse of disassembly. Be sure to replace all gaskets and O-ring seals otherwise a dangerous fuel leak may develop.

98   Turn the ignition switch to the "ON" position without starting the engine and check for fuel leaks.

Mass Air Flow (MAF) sensor

Refer to illustration 13.99

99   On 1995 through 2003 3800 V6 models, the MAF is attached to the throttle body. To remove it, unplug the connector then remove the two MAF sensor screws **(see illustration)**.

100 On others so equipped, the MAF sensor is located between the air intake duct and the air cleaner housing **(see illustration 8.4)**. To remove the sensor, loosen the clamp securing it to the air duct, then loosen the clamp attaching the MAF sensor to the air cleaner housing. Unplug the connector and remove the MAF sensor. **Caution:** *The MAF sensor is delicate - if you plan to reinstall the existing unit, handle it carefully.*

101 Installation is the reverse of the removal procedure.

14   Accelerator cable - removal and installation

Refer to illustrations 14.2, 14.7

Note: *2004 and later models don't have an accelerator cable. The throttle is controlled electrically.*

Removal

1   Detach the screws and the clip retaining the lower instrument panel trim and lower the trim (if necessary).

2   Detach the accelerator cable from the accelerator pedal **(see illustration)**.

3   Squeeze the accelerator cable cover tangs and push the cable through the firewall into the engine compartment.

4   Remove the cable clamp attaching screws and the cable clamp (if equipped).

5   Detach the routing clip and the accelerator cable (if equipped).

6   On 3.4L V6 models, remove the air cleaner duct.

7   Detach the accelerator cable-to-throttle lever retainer and detach the accelerator cable from the throttle body lever **(see illustration)**.

8   On 3.4L V6 models, turn the throttle body accelerator cam counterclockwise and hold it there while you disconnect the cable **(see illustration)**.

9   Squeeze the accelerator cable retaining tangs and push the cable through the accelerator cable bracket.

14.2 To detach the accelerator cable at the pedal, pull the spring cup (arrow) toward the end of the cable and slide the cable out of the slot

14.7 If your vehicle has this type of retainer, pop off the retaining clip from the throttle lever arm

14.8 Throttle body accelerator cam (arrow) - 3.4 liter V6 - turn counterclockwise and hold it there while you disconnect the cable

15.1 To detach this rubber block type hanger, remove the bolt

Installation

10   Installation is the reverse of removal.
Caution: *To prevent possible interference, flexible components (hoses, wires, etc.) must not be routed within two inches of moving parts, unless routing is controlled.*
11   Operate the accelerator pedal and check for any binding condition by completely opening and closing the throttle.
12   At the engine compartment side of the firewall, apply sealant around the accelerator cable.

15 Exhaust system servicing - general information

Refer to illustration 15.1
Warning: *Inspection and repair of exhaust system components should be done only after enough time has elapsed after driving the vehicle to allow the system components to cool completely. Also, when working under the vehicle, make sure it is securely supported on jackstands.*
1   The exhaust system consists of the exhaust manifold(s), the catalytic converter, the muffler, the tailpipe and all connecting pipes, brackets, hangers and clamps. The exhaust system is attached to the body with mounting brackets and rubber hangers **(see illustration)**. If any of the parts are improperly installed, excessive noise and vibration will be transmitted to the body.
2   Conduct regular inspections of the exhaust system to keep it safe and quiet. Look for any damaged or bent parts, open seams, holes, loose connections, excessive corrosion or other defects which could allow exhaust fumes to enter the vehicle. Deteriorated exhaust system components should not be repaired; they should be replaced with new parts.
3   If the exhaust system components are extremely corroded or rusted together, welding equipment will probably be required to remove them. The convenient way to accom-

plish this is to have a muffler repair shop remove the corroded sections with a cutting torch. If, however, you want to save money by doing it yourself (and you don't have a welding outfit with a cutting torch), simply cut off the old components with a hacksaw. If you have compressed air, special pneumatic cutting chisels can also be used. If you do decide to tackle the job at home, be sure to wear safety goggles to protect your eyes from metal chips and work gloves to protect your hands.
4   Here are some simple guidelines to follow when repairing the exhaust system:

  a) *Work from the back to the front when removing exhaust system components.*
  b) *Apply penetrating oil to the exhaust system component fasteners to make them easier to remove.*
  c) *Use new gaskets, hangers and clamps when installing exhaust systems components.*
  d) *Apply anti-seize compound to the threads of all exhaust system fasteners during reassembly.*
  e) *Be sure to allow sufficient clearance between newly installed parts and all points on the underbody to avoid overheating the floor pan and possibly damaging the interior carpet and insulation. Pay particularly close attention to the catalytic converter and heat shield.*

16 Turbocharger - general information

A turbocharger is used on some models to increase power. As increased power is required and the throttle is opened, more air/fuel mixture is forced into the combustion chambers by the turbocharger.
A turbine wheel in the turbocharger is driven by the exhaust stream and is connected by a shaft to drive a compressor wheel (fan) to pressurized the intake air stream. The amount of pressurized air allowed into the engine is controlled by an exhaust by-

pass valve, or wastegate. In this system, the wastegate is controlled by a solenoid which is controlled by the ECM.
This system also incorporates an air-to-air intercooler (similar to a radiator). The function of the intercooler is to cool the pressurized air from the turbocharger. This cooling of the pressurized air allows for a higher compression ratio (without pre-ignition occurring). This, in turn, will increase power by approximately 15-percent.

17 Turbocharger - inspection

Caution: *Operation of the turbocharger without all the ducts and filters installed can result in personal injury, and/or allow foreign objects to damage the turbine blades.*
Note: *The turbocharger is not serviceable and must be replaced as a unit.*
1   Every turbocharger has its own noise level when operating. If the noise level changes, suspect a problem. If the sound of the turbocharger goes up and down in pitch, check for heavy dirt buildup in the compressor housing and on the compressor wheel, or for an air inlet restriction. If the noise level is a high pitch or whistling sound, look for an inlet air or exhaust gas leak.
2   With the engine off and the turbocharger stopped, make a visual inspection of the turbocharger and components.
3   Check for loose duct connections from the air cleaner to the turbocharger.
4   Be sure the cross-over duct from the turbocharger-to-intake system is not loose.
5   Visually check the wheels of the turbocharger for damage from foreign objects.
6   Look for evidence of wheel-to-housing contact.
7   Be sure the shaft rotates freely. Rotating stiffness could indicate the presence of sludged oil or coking (hardened oil deposits) from overheating.
8   Push in on one of the shaft wheels while turning it. Be sure the wheels turn freely with-

out contacting the housings, the backplate or the shroud.

9   Be sure the exhaust manifold has no loose connections or cracks.

10   Check the oil drain line for any restrictions.

11   Visually inspect the actuator and wastegate linkage for damage.

12   Check the hose from the throttle body-to-wastegate solenoid and from the wastegate solenoid-to-actuator assembly.

13   Using a pump, apply 3.5 to 4.5 psi to the actuator assembly. The actuator rod end should move 1/64 inch to actuate the wastegate linkage. If not, replace the actuator assembly and recheck.

14   Remove test equipment and reconnect the hose.

18 Turbocharger - removal and installation

Removal

1   Detach the negative cable from the battery. **Caution:** *On models equipped with the Theftlock audio system, be sure the lockout feature is turned off before performing any procedure which requires disconnecting the battery.*

2   Drain the coolant from the radiator.

3   Remove the bolt attaching the intercooler to the intake manifold duct.

4   Detach the intercooler-to-intake manifold duct.

5   At the turbocharger, detach the air cleaner-to-turbocharger duct.

6   Detach the air cleaner inlet duct.

7   Remove the air cleaner and duct assembly.

8   At the turbocharger, detach the turbocharger-to-intercooler duct.

9   Remove the turbocharger heat covers.

10   Disconnect the electrical connector for the oxygen sensor.

11   Remove the oxygen sensor.

12   At the turbocharger, detach the coolant return line, the turbocharger oil supply line and the vacuum line.

13   At the actuator, detach the vacuum line. Remove the actuator arm-to-wastegate retaining clip. Detach the actuator arm from the wastegate. Remove the wastegate actuator from the turbocharger.

14   Remove the cruise control servo and place out of the work area.

15   At the turbocharger, detach the downpipe, the coolant supply hose, the oil drain hose (at the drain pipe).

16   Remove the bolt attaching the turbocharger to the exhaust crossover.

17   Remove the turbocharger. **Caution:** *Do not attempt to repair the turbocharger. It is serviced as a unit only.*

Installation

18   Installation is the reverse of removal. Be sure to transfer the oil and water lines to the new turbocharger.

19   Be sure to prime the turbocharger with oil before running the engine. Crank the engine with the fuel pump fuse removed until normal operating oil pressure is reached.

20   Start the engine and check for fluid leaks.

19 Supercharger - general information

A supercharger is used on some models to increase performance. It differs from the turbocharger (see Section 16) in that the supercharger is driven by a belt from the engine, rather than exhaust gasses, which drive the turbocharger. Inside the supercharger housing are two three-lobe rotors that are driven by gears.

The rotors draw air/fuel through the throttle body and force the mixture into the engine, pumping more air/fuel than the engine could "suck in" by itself. Unlike the turbocharger that takes a little time to "spool up" and add the extra power, the supercharger is always making some boost, which goes up with engine rpm. Maximum boost is 7-9 psi.

The internal gears and rotor bearings are lubricated by synthetic oil in a reservoir within the supercharger.

There are some driving conditions in which boost is not needed, and the supercharger boost is diverted. At idle or low-throttle cruise conditions, the excess air is routed through a bypass passage. The amount and timing of the bypass is controlled by a vacuum-operated valve, similar in operation to the wastegate on a turbocharged engine. This valve, in turn, is electronically controlled by the PCM.

The supercharger is considered a unit for service purposes and when defective, must be replaced, not rebuilt. Whenever the fuel injection sight shield is removed from the engine inspect the supercharger for signs of oil leakage. At the front of the drive-end of the supercharger, remove the threaded plug at the top of the housing and check the lubricant level. It should be at the bottom of the threads in the hole. If necessary, top off the lubricant with synthetic oil (GM p/n 12345982). Supercharged models require premium unleaded fuel and are not designed for gasoline mixes that contain methanol.

20 Supercharger - removal and installation

Removal

1   Relieve the fuel system pressure (see Section 2).

2   Disconnect the cable from the negative battery terminal. Remove the plastic engine cover.

3   Remove the fasteners securing the fuel injector sight shield and the EGR valve heat shield, then remove the shields.

4   Using a 15 mm box-end wrench, rotate the supercharger drivebelt tensioner and remove the belt. Use the wrench on the pulley nut.

5   Disconnect the right side (rear) spark plug wires from the ignition control module.

6   Disconnect the vacuum hoses and electrical connector from the EVAP purge valve, remove the fasteners securing the valve, then remove the valve.

7   Remove the engine drivebelt (see Chapter 1).

8   Detach the electrical connectors from the alternator. Remove the bolts securing the alternator and bracket, then remove the alternator and bracket from the vehicle (see Chapter 5).

9   Remove the MAP sensor. Detach the vacuum hose, unplug the electrical connector and remove the mounting screws.

10   Remove the fuel rail and injectors (see Section 13).

11   Disconnect the vacuum hoses and electrical connector from the boost control solenoid. Remove the fastener securing the solenoid, then remove the solenoid.

12   Unclamp the air duct from the throttle body.

13   Loosen the supercharger mounting bolts in 1/4-turn increments until they can be removed by hand. Remove the supercharger. As the supercharger is lifted from the intake manifold, be sure to check for and disconnect anything still attached to the manifold.

14   Remove the gasket and supercharger O-rings from the intake manifold.

Installation.

Note: *The mating surfaces of the cylinder heads, block and manifold must be perfectly clean when the manifold is installed.*

15   Position the new O-rings and gasket on the intake manifold.

16   Carefully set the supercharger in place and tighten the mounting bolts to the torque listed in this Chapter's Specifications. Make sure you tighten the bolts in three steps in a criss-cross pattern.

17   The remainder of installation is the reverse of removal.

Chapter 5
Engine electrical systems

Contents

	Section
Alternator - removal and installation	9
Battery cables - check and replacement	4
Battery check and maintenance	See Chapter 1
Battery - emergency jump starting	3
Battery - removal and installation	2
Charging system - check	8
Charging system - general information and precautions	7
Drivebelt check, adjustment and replacement	See Chapter 1

	Section
Ignition coil and module - removal and installation	6
Ignition system - check	5
Ignition system - general information	1
Spark plug replacement	See Chapter 1
Starter motor - removal and installation	11
Starter solenoid - removal and installation	12
Starting system - general information and precautions	10

Specifications

General

Cylinder numbers	See Chapter 2
Firing order	See Chapter 2
Ignition coil	
DIS system (except 5.3L engine)	
Primary resistance	0.50 to 0.90 ohms @ 70 to 80-degrees F
Secondary resistance	5,000 to 10,000 ohms
IDI system	
Primary resistance	0.40 to 0.80 ohms @ 70 to 80-degrees F
Secondary resistance	4,000 to 8,000 ohms

Charging system

Alternator charging output	13 to 14.5 volts

1 Ignition system - general information

The engines covered in this manual are equipped with either a Distributorless Ignition System (DIS), on all engines except the Quad-4, or an Integrated Direct Ignition System (IDI) on the Quad-4.

All except 5.3L models

The DIS and IDI systems use a "waste spark" method of spark distribution. Each cylinder is paired with its opposing cylinder in the firing order (1-4, 2-3 on a four cylinder, 1-4, 2-5, 3-6 on a V6) so one cylinder under compression fires simultaneously with its opposing cylinder, where the piston is on the exhaust stroke. Since the cylinder on the exhaust stroke requires very little of the available voltage to fire its plug, most of the voltage is used to fire the plug of the cylinder on the compression stroke.

The DIS system includes a coil pack, an ignition module, a crankshaft reluctor ring, a magnetic sensor, spark plug wires, and the ECM. The IDI system is the same except that it does not have spark plug wires. The ignition module is located under the coil pack and is connected to the ECM.

The magnetic crankshaft sensor is mounted on the bottom of the engine block, just above the oil pan rail, or on the timing chain cover, near the vibration damper. The reluctor ring is a special disc, either cast onto the crankshaft or attached to the vibration damper, which acts as a signal generator for the ignition timing. (Some models also have a camshaft position sensor that is used to determine fuel injection timing.)

The ignition system uses Electronic Spark Timing (EST) and control wires from the ECM, just like conventional distributor systems.

5.3L models

All 5.3L engines are equipped with an ignition coil mounted near each cylinder. Short spark plug wires attach the coils to their respective spark plugs. Each coil is energized by the ECM in a manner very similar to the earlier DIS system.

2 Battery - removal and installation

Refer to illustration 2.2

Caution 1: *Always disconnect the negative cable first and hook it up last or the battery may be shorted by the tool being used to loosen the cable clamps.* **Caution 2:** *On models equipped with the Theftlock audio system, be sure the lockout feature is turned off before performing any procedure which requires disconnecting the battery.*

1   Disconnect both cables from the battery terminals.

2   Detach any brackets or braces that would interfere with the removal of the battery, then remove the battery hold-down clamp or strap **(see illustration)**. On models through 1998, remove the windshield washer tank.

2.2 Remove the battery hold-down clamp bolt (arrow) from the battery carrier

3   Lift out the battery. Be careful - it's heavy. **Note:** *On some models it may be necessary to remove the air cleaner housing and to position the engine compartment fuse/junction block aside.*

4   While the battery is out, inspect the carrier (tray) for corrosion (see Chapter 1).

5   If you are replacing the battery, make sure that you get one that's identical, with the same dimensions, amperage rating, cold cranking rating, etc.

6   Installation is the reverse of removal.

3   Battery - emergency jump starting

Refer to the *Booster battery (jump) start-ing* procedure at the front of this manual.

4   Battery cables - check and replacement

Refer to illustration 4.2

1   Periodically inspect the entire length of each battery cable for damage, cracked or

Terminal end corrosion or damage.

Insulation cracks.

Chafed insulation or exposed wires.

Burned or melted insulation.

4.2 Inspect the battery cables for these common problems

burned insulation and corrosion. Poor battery cable connections can cause starting problems and decreased engine performance.

2   Check the cable-to-terminal connections at the ends of the cables for cracks, loose wire strands and corrosion **(see illustration)**. The presence of white, fluffy deposits under the insulation at the cable terminal connection is a sign that the cable is corroded and should be replaced. Check the terminals for distortion, missing mounting bolts and corrosion.

3   When removing the cables, always disconnect the negative cable first and hook it up last or the battery may be shorted by the tool used to loosen the cable clamps. Even if only the positive cable is being replaced, be sure to disconnect the negative cable from the battery first (see Chapter 1 for further information regarding battery cable removal). **Caution:** *On models equipped with the Theftlock audio system, be sure the lockout feature is turned off before performing any procedure which requires disconnecting the battery.* **Note:** *5.3L models have battery current sensors that must be carefully removed from the battery cables. Replacing the cables on these vehicles also requires partially disassembling and repositioning the underhood electrical center. These later-model cables are routed and retained in a complicated manner and it's usually necessary to raise the vehicle and support it securely on jackstands to access the lower portions.*

4   Disconnect the old cables from the battery, then trace each of them to their opposite ends and detach them from the starter solenoid and ground terminals. Note the routing of each cable to ensure correct installation.

5   If you are replacing either or both of the old cables, take them with you when buying new cables. It is vitally important that you replace the cables with identical parts. Cables have characteristics that make them easy to identify: positive cables are usually red, larger in cross-section and have a larger diameter battery post clamp; ground cables are usually black, and are smaller in cross-section.

6   Clean the threads of the solenoid or ground connection with a wire brush to

5.2 To use a calibrated ignition tester, simply disconnect a spark plug wire, clip the tester to a convenient ground (like a rocker arm cover bolt) and operate the starter - if there's enough power to fire the plug, sparks will be visible between the electrode tip and the tester body

remove rust and corrosion. Apply a light coat of battery terminal corrosion inhibitor, or petroleum jelly, to the threads to prevent future corrosion.

7   Attach the cable to the solenoid or ground connection and tighten the mounting nut/bolt securely.

8   Before connecting a new cable to the battery, make sure that it reaches the battery post without having to be stretched.

9   Connect the positive cable first, followed by the negative cable.

5   Ignition system - check

Warning: *Because of the very high voltage generated by the ignition system, extreme care should be taken whenever an operation is performed involving ignition components. This not only includes the coils, control module and spark plug wires (all engines, except Quad-4), but related items connected to the system as well, such as the plug connections, tachometer and any test equipment.*

1   If the engine turns over, but won't start, check for spark at the spark plug by installing a calibrated ignition system tester to one of the spark plug wire/boot terminals. Calibrated ignition testers are available at most auto parts stores in several different types. One type of spark tester has a short center electrode extending from the insulator and is intended for use on breaker-point and older electronic ignitions. The other type does not have a visible center electrode and is for use on high-voltage ignition systems. Be sure to use the high-voltage ignition tester on these models.

All engines (except Quad-4 and 5.3L V8 models)

Refer to illustrations 5.2, 5.5, 5.6, 5.7a and 5.7b

2   Insert the ignition tester into the number one spark plug boot terminal. Connect the clip on the tester to a ground such as a metal bracket or valve cover bolt, crank the engine

5.5 Check for battery voltage to the ignition module from the ignition key (all engines, except Quad-4 and 5.3L)

5.6 On all engines except Quad-4 and 5.3L V8 models, remove the coil pack from the module assembly and check for a trigger signal between the module terminals with a test light while an assistant cranks the engine over

5.7a Check the secondary coil resistance across the towers on each coil pack (all engines, except Quad-4 and 5.3L models)

5.7b Checking the coil primary resistance (all engines, except Quad-4 and 5.3L models)

and watch the end of the tester for bright blue, well defined sparks **(see illustration)**.

3   If sparks occur, sufficient voltage is reaching the plugs to fire the engine. However the plugs themselves may be fouled, so remove and check them as described in Chapter 1 or replace them with new ones.

4   If no sparks or intermittent sparks occur, check for a bad spark plug wire by swapping wires or by using an ohmmeter to measure the resistance between the spark plug wire terminal ends. There should be approximately 5000 ohms of resistance per foot.

5   Check the primary wire connections at the ignition control module to make sure they are clean and tight. Refer to the wiring diagrams (see Chapter 12) and check for battery voltage to the ignition control module from the IGN-MOD fuse **(see illustration)**. Battery voltage should be available to the ignition control module with the ignition switch ON. **Note:** *If no voltage is available check the ignition system fuses (see Chapter 12). If the reading is 7 volts or less, repair the primary circuit from the ignition switch to the ignition control module.*

6   If voltage is available at the ignition control module and there's still no spark, check for a trigger signal from the ignition module. Remove the coil pack from the ignition module to expose the module terminals (see Section 7). Connect a test light between each of the module terminals and have an assistant crank the engine over **(see illustration)**. The test light should blink quickly and constantly as each coil pack is triggered to fire by the switching signal from the ignition module. This test checks for the trigger signal (ground) from the computer and Ignition Control Module. **Caution:** *Use only an LED test light to avoid damaging the PCM.*

7   If a trigger signal is present at the coil, the computer and the Ignition Control Module are functioning properly and the problem lies in the ignition coils. Check the primary and

secondary resistance of the ignition coils and compare it to the Specifications at the beginning of this Chapter **(see illustrations)**.

8   If the test light does not flash, the ignition module is most likely the problem but not always. **Note:** *Refer to Chapter 6 for additional information on the crankshaft and the camshaft sensors. It will be necessary to verify that the crankshaft sensors and camshaft sensor is operating correctly before changing the ignition module. A defective ignition module can only be diagnosed by process of elimination.*

9   Have the crankshaft sensor(s), the camshaft sensor and the PCM, checked by a dealer service department or other qualified automotive repair shop.

Quad-4 engines

Refer to illustrations 5.12, 5.15, 5.16a, 5.16b, 5.17a and 5.17b

Note: *This procedure is difficult to perform on Quad-4 engines but it is possible with the correct set-up.*

10   Remove the ignition coil/module housing from the cylinder head (see Section 6). Turn the ignition coil/module assembly upside down and bolt it (module cover) to the engine block using the bolt hole in the cover that the ground strap is attached too, then recon-

nect the ignition module connector. This will ground the assembly to the engine for testing purposes.

11   Insert the ignition tester into the number one spark plug terminal on the coil assembly, then connect a ground wire from the ignition tester to the engine block.

12   Construct three makeshift spark plug wires from a spare wire set that can be connected to the remaining spark plugs and to each of their corresponding spark plug terminals on the coil assembly **(see illustration)**.

13   Disable the fuel pump (see Chapter 4) and crank the engine over to check for spark at the ignition tester. Test each cylinder one-by-one making sure to ground the remaining spark plugs not being tested before cranking the engine over. Failure to ground the three spark plugs not being tested may result in ignition control module damage!

14   If sparks occur, sufficient voltage is reaching the plugs to fire the engine. However the plugs themselves may be fouled, so remove and check them as described in Chapter 1 or replace them with new ones.

15   If no sparks or intermittent sparks occur, check the primary wire connections at the ignition control module to make sure they are clean and tight. Refer to the wiring diagrams (see Chapter 12) and check for battery voltage to the ignition control module from the

5.12 To use a calibrated ignition tester on Quad-4 engines, it will be necessary to flip the coil assembly over and bolt it to engine while grounding the ignition cover - then fabricate three spark plug wires which connect from the remaining spark plug boot terminals on the coil assembly and to spark plugs not being tested

5.15 Check for battery voltage to the ignition module connector (arrow) from the ignition key (Quad-4 engines)

5.16a On Quad-4 engines, first disconnect the ignition coil to ignition module connector and check for battery voltage to the coil with the ignition key On . . .

5.16b . . . then connect an LED test light to the positive terminal of the battery and to each of the coil negative (-) terminals on the ignition module and watch for a blinking light when the engine is cranked

5.17a To check the primary resistance of the ignition coil on Quad-4 engines, connect the positive probe to the positive (+) terminal and the negative probe to each of negative (-) terminals of the coil connector - the resistance should be the same for each check

5.17b Checking the secondary coil resistance (Quad-4 engines) - be sure the probes touch the contact in the center of each socket

IGN-MOD fuse **(see illustration)**. Battery voltage should be available to the ignition control module with the ignition switch ON. **Note:** *If no voltage is available check the ignition system fuses (see Chapter 12). If the reading is 7 volts or less, repair the primary circuit from the ignition switch to the ignition control module.*

16   If voltage is available at the ignition control module and there's still no spark, check for a trigger signal from the ignition module. Remove the coil housing cover and the ignition coil to ignition module electrical connector to expose the module output terminals (see Section 7). First check for battery voltage to the coils with the ignition key On, then connect a test light to the positive terminal of the battery and to each of the coil/module negative terminals and have an assistant crank the engine over **(see illustrations)**. The test light should blink quickly and constantly as each coil pack is triggered to fire by the switching signal from the ignition module. This test checks for the trigger signal (ground) from the computer and Ignition Control Module. **Caution:** *Use only an LED test light to avoid dam-*

aging the PCM

17   If a trigger signal is present at the coil, the computer and the Ignition Control Module are functioning properly and the problem lies in the ignition coils or the wiring to the ignition coils. Check the primary and secondary resistance of the ignition coils and compare it to the Specifications at the beginning of this Chapter **(see illustrations)**. **Note:** *On Quad-4 engines, primary resistance can be checked at the coil/ ignition module connector or at the bottom of each coil. Always verify that the wires leading to the coils are not defective (have continuity) before replacing an ignition coil.*

18   If the test light does not flash, the ignition module is most likely the problem but not always. **Note:** *Refer to Chapter 6 for additional information on the crankshaft and the camshaft sensors. It will be necessary to verify that the crankshaft sensors and camshaft sensor is operating correctly before changing the ignition module. A defective ignition module can only be diagnosed by process of elimination.*

19   Have the crankshaft sensor(s), the camshaft sensor and the PCM, checked by a dealer service department or other qualified automotive repair shop.

5.3L engines

20   Check the spark at each spark plug (see Steps 2 through 4).

21   If there are no sparks at any cylinders, check all fuses that are connected with the ignition system.

22   If only one (or a few) of the cylinders have no spark, check the primary wiring to the coils involved. All wiring must be clean and all connections tight. Check for chafed or broken wires.

23   If the primary wiring is good, then try swapping ignition coils between good and bad cylinders. If the miss follows a coil as it is moved, replace that coil.

24   Try the same system with the spark plug wires (see Step 4). If exchanging the spark plug wires makes a difference, consider purchasing a complete new set.

6.4 Coils and plug wires are numbered according to their associated cylinders

6.5 Mounting bolt locations (arrows) for the module/coil assemblies on a V6 engine

6.6 A 5.5 mm socket is required to remove the coil mounting bolts (arrows)

6.8 When installing a coil, make sure that it plugs into the module completely

6   Ignition coil and module - removal and installation

Refer to illustrations 6.4, 6.5, 6.6, 6.8, 6.11 and 6.13

Direct Ignition System (DIS) (all except Quad-4 and 5.3L engines)

1   Refer to the previous Section for checking procedures.

2   Detach the cable from the negative terminal of the battery. **Caution:** *On models equipped with the Theftlock audio system, be sure the lockout feature is turned off before performing any procedure which requires disconnecting the battery.*

3   Unplug the electrical connectors from the module.

4   If the plug wires are not numbered, label them and detach the plug wires at the coil assembly **(see illustration)**.

5   Remove the module/coil assembly mounting bolts and lift the assembly from the vehicle **(see illustrations)**.

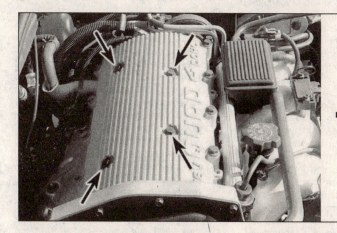

6.11 The Quad-4 ignition coil and module retaining bolt locations (arrows)

6   Remove the bolts attaching the coils to the module and separate them **(see illustration)**.

7   Installation is the reverse of removal.

8   When installing the coils, make sure they are connected properly **(see illustration)**.

Integrated Direct Ignition (IDI) (Quad 4 engines)

9   Detach the cable from the negative terminal of the battery. **Caution:** *On models equipped with the Theftlock audio system, be sure the lockout feature is turned off before performing any procedure which requires disconnecting the battery.*

10   Disconnect the IDI electrical connector.

11   Remove the ignition system assembly-to-camshaft housing bolts **(see illustration)**.

12   Lift the ignition system assembly from the engine.

13   Detach the coil housing-to-cover screws

and remove the housing from the cover **(see illustration)**.

14   Detach the coil electrical connectors.

15   Remove the coils.

16   Remove the module-to-cover screws and detach the module from the cover.

17   Installation is the reverse of removal.

5.3L engines

18   Remove the engine cover. Pull the small safety retainer out of the wiring connector of the ignition coil to be replaced. Disconnect the wiring connector from the coil.

19   Disconnect the spark plug wire from the coil. Be sure to pull only on the boot, not the wire.

20   Remove the retaining screws and lift off the coil.

21   Installation is the reverse of removal.

7   Charging system - general information and precautions

Caution: *On models equipped with the Theft-lock audio system, be sure the lockout feature is turned off before performing any procedure which requires disconnecting the battery.*

The charging system includes the alternator, an internal voltage regulator, a charge indicator, the battery, a fusible link and the wiring between all the components. The charging system supplies electrical power for the ignition system, the lights, the radio, etc. The alternator is driven by a drivebelt at the front of the engine.

The purpose of the voltage regulator is to limit the alternator's voltage to a preset value. This prevents power surges, circuit overloads, etc., during peak voltage output.

The fusible link is a short length of insulated wire integral with the engine compartment wiring harness. The link is four wire gauges smaller in diameter than the circuit it protects. Production fusible links and their identification flags are identified by the flag color. See Chapter 12 for additional information regarding fusible links.

The charging system doesn't ordinarily require periodic maintenance. However, the drivebelt, battery and wires and connections should be inspected at the intervals outlined in Chapter 1.

The dashboard warning light should come on when the ignition key is turned to Start, then go off immediately. If it remains on, there is a malfunction in the charging system (see Section 8). Some vehicles are also equipped with a voltmeter. If the voltmeter indicates abnormally high or low voltage, check the charging system (see Section 8).

Be very careful when making electrical circuit connections to a vehicle equipped with an alternator and note the following:

a) *When reconnecting wires to the alternator from the battery, be sure to note the polarity.*

b) *Before using arc welding equipment to repair any part of the vehicle, disconnect*

6.13 Exploded view of the ignition module/coil assemblies on the 2.3L Quad 4 engine

A   Cover
B   Ignition module
C   Coil housing

the wires from the alternator and the battery terminals.

c) *Never start the engine with a battery charger connected.*

d) *Always disconnect both battery leads before using a battery charger.*

e) *The alternator is turned by an engine drivebelt which could cause serious injury if your hands, hair or clothes become entangled in it with the engine running.*

f) *Because the alternator is connected directly to the battery, it could arc or cause a fire if overloaded or shorted out.*

g) *Wrap a plastic bag over the alternator and secure it with rubberbands before steam cleaning the engine.*

8   Charging system - check

1   If a malfunction occurs in the charging circuit, don't automatically assume that the alternator is causing the problem. First check the following items:

a) *Check the drivebelt tension and condition (see Chapter 1). Replace it if it's worn or deteriorated.*

b) *Make sure the alternator mounting and adjustment bolts are tight.*

c) *Inspect the alternator wiring harness and the electrical connectors at the alternator and voltage regulator. They must be in good condition and tight.*

d) *Check the fusible link (if equipped) located between the starter solenoid and the alternator. If it's burned, determine the cause, repair the circuit and replace the link (the vehicle won't start and/or the accessories won't work if the fusible link blows). Sometimes a fusible link may look good, but still be bad. If in doubt, remove it and check for continuity.*

e) *Start the engine and check the alternator for abnormal noises (a shrieking or squealing sound indicates a bad bearing).*

f) *Check the specific gravity of the battery electrolyte. If it's low, charge the battery (doesn't apply to maintenance free batteries).*

g) *Make sure the battery is fully charged (one bad cell in a battery can cause overcharging by the alternator).*

h) *Disconnect the battery cables (negative first, then positive). Inspect the battery posts and the cable clamps for corrosion. Clean them thoroughly if necessary (see Chapter 1). Reconnect the cable to the positive terminal.* **Caution:** *On models equipped with the Theftlock audio system, be sure the lockout feature is turned off before performing any procedure which requires disconnecting the battery.*

i) *With the key off, connect a test light between the negative battery post and the disconnected negative cable clamp.*

   1) *If the test light does not come on, reattach the clamp and proceed to the next Step.*

   2) *If the test light comes on, there is a short (drain) in the electrical system of the vehicle. The short must be repaired before the charging system can be checked.*

   3) *Disconnect the alternator wiring harness.*

      (a) *If the light goes out, the alternator is bad.*

      (b) *If the light stays on, pull each fuse until the light goes out (this will tell you which component is shorted).*

2   Using a voltmeter, check the battery voltage with the engine off. It should be approximately 12 volts.

3   Start the engine and check the battery voltage again. It should now be approximately 14 to 15 volts.

4   Turn on the headlights. The voltage should drop, and then come back up, if the charging system is working properly.

5   If the voltage reading is more or less than the specified charging voltage, alternator replacement is necessary (refer to Section 9).

9   Alternator - removal and installation

All except 3.4 liter V6

Refer to illustrations 9.4a and 9.4b

1   Detach the cable from the negative terminal of the battery. **Caution:** *On models equipped with the Theftlock audio system, be*

9.4a Alternator mounting bolts (arrows) (typical four-cylinder engine)

9.4b Alternator mounting bolts (arrows) (typical V6 engine)

sure the lockout feature is turned off before performing any procedure which requires disconnecting the battery.

2   Detach the electrical connectors from the alternator.

3   On some models it will be necessary to loosen the adjustment and pivots to remove the drivebelt. On other models it will be necessary to rotate the drivebelt tensioner to remove the drivebelt (see Chapter 1).

4   Remove the alternator support brackets if equipped, then remove the alternator mounting bolts **(see illustrations)**.

3.4 liter V6

5   Remove the air cleaner and duct assembly (see Chapter 4).

6   Detach the cable from the negative terminal of the battery. **Caution:** *On models equipped with the Theftlock audio system, be sure the lockout feature is turned off before performing any procedure which requires disconnecting the battery.*

7   Remove the coolant recovery tank (see Chapter 3).

8   Remove the drivebelt (see Chapter 1).

9   Loosen the wheel lug nuts and the right-side driveaxle/hub nut. Raise the front of the vehicle and support it securely on jackstands, then remove the wheels.

10   Remove the under-vehicle splash shield. Also remove the right inner fender splash shield (see Chapter 11, Section 12).

11   Remove the front exhaust pipe and catalytic converter (see Chapter 4).

12   Remove the right driveaxle (see Chapter 8).

13   Also remove the driveaxle shield.

14   Remove the steering gear heat shield.

15   Unplug the electrical connector from the knock sensor (see Chapter 6, Section 7).

16   Remove the alternator cooling duct, if so equipped.

17   Remove the alternator rear brace bolt and nut.

18   Unscrew the nut and detach the power steering line from the alternator upper mounting stud.

19   Detach the electrical connector and battery terminal from the rear of the alternator.

20   Unscrew the alternator lower mounting bolt. Be careful not to lose any spacers or washers that may be present.

21   Unscrew the upper mounting bolt/stud and remove the alternator.

All engines

22   Because of the expense and the limited availability of internal repair parts, it is usually not practical for the home mechanic to rebuild the alternator. New and rebuilt units are readily available at auto parts stores. If you're replacing the alternator, take the old one with you when purchasing the new one. Make sure the new/rebuilt unit is identical to the old alternator. Look at the terminals - they should be the same in number, size and location as the terminals on the old alternator. Finally, look at the identification numbers - they'll be stamped into the housing or printed on a tag attached to the housing. Make sure the numbers are the same on both alternators.

23   Some new alternators DO NOT have a pulley installed, so you may have to switch the pulley from the old unit to the new/rebuilt one. When buying an alternator, find out the shop's policy regarding pulleys - some shops will perform this service free of charge.

24   Installation is the reverse of removal.

25   After installation, adjust the drive belt tension (see Chapter 1).

26   Check the charging voltage to verify proper operation of the alternator (see Section 8).

10   Starting system - general information and precautions

The starting system consists of the battery, the starter motor, the starter solenoid and the wires connecting them. The solenoid is mounted directly on the starter motor. The solenoid/starter motor assembly is installed on the lower part of the engine, next to the transmission bellhousing.

When the ignition key is turned to the "Start" position, the starter solenoid is actuated through the starter control circuit. The starter solenoid then connects the battery to the starter. The battery supplies the electrical energy to the starter motor, which does the actual work of cranking the engine.

The starter motor on a vehicle equipped with a manual transaxle can only be operated when the clutch pedal is depressed; the starter on a vehicle equipped with an automatic transaxle can only be operated when the selector lever is in Park or Neutral.

Always observe the following precautions when working on the starting system:

a)   *Excessive cranking of the starter motor can overheat it and cause serious damage. Never operate the starter motor for more than 15 seconds at a time without pausing to allow it to cool for at least two minutes.*

b)   *The starter is connected directly to the battery and could arc or cause a fire if mishandled, overloaded or shorted out.*

c)   *Always detach the cable from the negative terminal of the battery before working on the starting system.* **Caution:** *On models equipped with the Theftlock audio system, be sure the lockout feature is turned off before performing any procedure which requires disconnecting the battery.*

11   Starter motor - removal and installation

Refer to illustrations 11.8 and 11.9

Note: *On some vehicles it may be necessary to remove the exhaust pipe(s) or frame crossmember to gain access to the starter motor. In extreme cases it may even be necessary to unbolt the mounts and raise the engine slightly to get the starter out.*

1   Detach the negative cable from the battery. **Caution:** *On models equipped with the Theftlock audio system, be sure the lockout feature*

11.8 Disconnect the battery terminal (A) and the switch terminal (B) from the starter solenoid

11.9 Typical starter motor mounting bolt locations (arrows)

12.3 Disconnect the solenoid-to-starter motor strap by removing the retaining bolt (arrow)

12.5 To remove the solenoid housing from the starter (models up to 1997), remove the screws and turn it clockwise

tration). Note the location of any shims used.
10   Installation is the reverse of removal.

12   Starter solenoid - removal and installation

Refer to illustrations 12.3 and 12.5

1   Disconnect the cable from the negative terminal of the battery. **Caution:** *On models equipped with the Theftlock audio system, be sure the lockout feature is turned off before performing any procedure which requires disconnecting the battery.* **Note:** *On 1996 3.4L models and all 1998 and later models, the starter solenoid is not serviceable. If it's bad, the whole starter must be replaced.*
2   Remove the starter motor (see Section 12).
3   Disconnect the strap from the solenoid to the starter motor terminal **(see illustration)**.
4   Remove the screws which secure the solenoid to the starter motor.
5   Twist the solenoid in a clockwise direction to disengage the flange from the starter body **(see illustration)**.
6   Installation is the reverse of removal.

is turned off before performing any procedure which requires disconnecting the battery.
2   Remove the air cleaner and duct assembly, as necessary.
3   On the 3800, remove the upper mounting bracket, the cooling fan, and the oil cooler lines from the radiator.
4   Except on 5.3L models, raise the vehicle and support it securely on jackstands.
5   On 3.4 liter, 3800 and 3100 V6 engines with 4T60-E/4T65-E transaxles, remove the flywheel inspection cover. On 5.3L models,

remove the air filter housing (see Chapter 4).
6   Remove the oil filter splash shield, if necessary. On later 3800 V6 models, remove the front lower air deflector for additional clearance.
7   On the 3800, remove the engine harness retainers and position the harness away from the starter.
8   Clearly label, then detach, the electrical connectors from the starter **(see illustration)**.
9   Remove the mounting bolts and nuts (if equipped), then remove the starter **(see illus-**

Chapter 6
Emissions and engine control systems

Contents

	Section		Section
Air Injection Reactor (AIR) system	12	General information	1
Catalytic converter	11	Information sensors - general information and testing	4
CHECK ENGINE light	See Section 2	Information sensors - replacement	5
Electronic Spark Control (ESC)	7	On Board Diagnostic (OBD) system and trouble codes	2
Electronic Spark Timing (EST)	6	Positive Crankcase Ventilation (PCV) system	10
Evaporative Emissions Control (EECS or EVAP) System	9	Powertrain Control Module (PCM/ECM) - replacement	3
Exhaust Gas Recirculation (EGR) system	8		

Specifications

Torque specifications

Note: *One foot-pound (ft-lb) of torque is equivalent to 12 inch-pounds (in-lbs) of torque. Torque values below approximately 15 ft-lbs are expressed in inch-pounds, since most foot-pound torque wrenches are not accurate at these smaller values.*

Crankshaft position sensor bolts
  1995 and earlier
    3X or 7X sensors
      2.5L .... 20 in-lbs
      All others .... 70 to 85 in-lbs
    24X sensor .... 96 in-lbs
  1996 and later
    3100 and 3.4L engines
      7X sensors .... 70 in-lbs
      24X sensor .... 96 in-lbs
    3800 engine .... 14 to 28 ft-lbs
    5.3L engine .... 18 ft-lbs
Camshaft position sensor bolts
  3100 and 3.4L engines .... 96 in-lbs
  3800 engine .... 35 to 53 in-lbs
  5.3L engine .... 106 in-lbs

1 General information

Refer to illustration 1.5

To prevent pollution of the atmosphere from burned and evaporating gases, a number of emissions control systems are incorporated on the vehicles covered by this manual. The combination of systems used depends on the year in which the vehicle was manufactured, the locality to which it was originally delivered and the engine type. The major systems incorporated on the vehicles with which this manual is concerned include the:

Fuel Control System
Exhaust Gas Recirculation (EGR) system
Evaporative Emissions Control (EVAP) system
Transmission Converter Clutch (TCC) system
Positive Crankcase Ventilation (PCV) system
Catalytic converter
Secondary air injection system (some 2000 and later models)

All of these systems are linked, directly or indirectly, to the On Board Diagnostic (OBD) system. The Sections in this Chapter include general descriptions, checking procedures (where possible) and component replacement procedures (where applicable) for each of the systems listed above.

Before assuming that an emissions control system is malfunctioning, check the fuel and ignition systems carefully. In some cases special tools and equipment, as well as specialized training, are required to accurately diagnose the causes of a rough running or difficult to start engine. If checking and servicing become too difficult, or if a procedure is beyond the scope of the home mechanic, consult your dealer service department or other qualified repair shop. This does not necessarily mean, however, that the emissions control systems are particularly difficult to maintain and repair. You can quickly and easily perform many checks and do most (if not all) of the regular maintenance at home with common tune-up and hand tools. **Note:** *The most frequent cause of emissions system problems is simply a loose or broken vacuum hose or wiring connection. Therefore, always check the hose and wiring connections first.*

Pay close attention to any special precautions outlined in this Chapter. It should be noted that the illustrations of the various systems may not exactly match the system installed on your particular vehicle due to changes made by the manufacturer during production or from year to year.

A Vehicle Emissions Control Information (VECI) label is located in the engine compartment of all vehicles with which this manual is concerned **(see illustration)**. This label contains important emissions specifications and setting procedures, as well as a vacuum hose schematic with emissions components identified. When servicing the engine or emissions systems, the VECI label in your particular vehicle should always be checked for up-to-date information. **Note:** *Because of a federally mandated extended warranty which covers the emission control system components (and any components which have a primary purpose other than emission control but have*

1.5 Typical Vehicle Emission Control Information (VECI) label that shows emission hose routing

2.1 Digital multimeters can be used for testing all types of circuits; because of their high impedance, they are much more accurate than analog meters for measuring millivolts in low-voltage computer circuits

significant effects on emissions), check with your dealer about warranty coverage before working on any emission related systems.

The number of emissions control system components on later model fuel-injected vehicles has actually decreased due to the high efficiency of the new fuel injection and ignition systems. These models are equipped with a three way catalytic converter containing beads which are coated with a catalyst material containing platinum, palladium and rhodium to reduce the level of nitrogen oxides.

2 On Board Diagnostic (OBD) system and trouble codes

Note: *All 1995 and earlier models (except 1994 and later 3.4L and 1995 3800 models) are equipped with OBD I self diagnosis system, while 1994 and later 3.4L and 1995 3800 models and all 1996 and later models are equipped with OBD II self diagnosis system. Both systems require the use of a Scan tool to access trouble codes. However, many of the information sensor checks and replacement procedures do apply to both systems. Because OBD I and OBD II systems require a special SCAN tool to access the trouble codes, have the vehicle diagnosed by a dealer service department or other qualified automotive repair facility if the proper SCAN tool is not available. The codes indicated in the text are designed and mandated by the EPA for all*

OBD I and OBD II vehicles produced by automobile manufacturers. These generic trouble codes do not include the manufacturer's specific trouble codes. Consult a dealer service department or other qualified repair shop for additional information. Refer to the troubleshooting tips in the beginning of this manual to gain some insight to the most likely causes of a problem.

Diagnostic tool information

Refer to illustrations 2.1, 2.2 and 2.4

1   A digital multimeter is a necessary tool for checking fuel injection and emission related components **(see illustration)**. A digital voltohmmeter is preferred over the older style analog multimeter for several reasons. The analog multimeter cannot display the voltsohms or amps measurement in hundredths and thousandths increments. When working with electronic circuits which are often very low voltage, this accurate reading is most important. Another good reason for the digital multimeter is the high impedance circuit. The digital multimeter is equipped with a high resistance internal circuitry (10 million ohms). Because a voltmeter is hooked up in parallel with the circuit when testing, it is vital that none of the voltage being measured should be allowed to travel the parallel path set up by the meter itself. This dilemma does not show itself when measuring larger amounts of voltage (9 to 12 volt circuits) but if you are measuring a low voltage circuit such as the oxy-

gen sensor signal voltage, a fraction of a volt may be a significant amount when diagnosing a problem.

2   Hand-held scanners are the most powerful and versatile tools for analyzing engine management systems used on later model vehicles **(see illustration)**. Early model scanners handle codes and some diagnostics for many OBD I systems. Each brand scan tool must be examined carefully to match the year, make and model of the vehicle you are working on. Often interchangeable cartridges are available to access the particular manufacturer; Ford, GM, Chrysler, etc.). Some manufacturers will specify by continent; Asia, Europe, USA, etc. Seek the advice of your local parts retailer.

3   With arrival of the federally mandated emission control system (OBD-II), specially designed scanners have been developed. These scanners are considerably more expensive.

2.2 Scanners like these from Actron and AutoXray are powerful diagnostic aids - they can tell you just about anything you want to know about your engine management system

2.4 Trouble code tools simplify the task of extracting the trouble codes on OBD I systems

2.5a Typical engine control components – Quad-4 engine

1 Vehicle speed sensor (on transaxle)	5 IAC valve and TPS sensor (on throttle body)
2 Oxygen sensor (on exhaust manifold)	6 MAT sensor
3 Coolant temperature sensor	7 MAP sensor
4 Power steering pressure switch (on steering gear)	

4   Another type of code reader and less expensive is available at parts stores **(see illustration)**. These tools simplify the procedure for extracting codes from the engine management computer on earlier models by simply "plugging in" to the diagnostic connector on the vehicle wiring harness.

OBD system general description

Refer to illustrations 2.5a, 2.5b, 2.5c, 2.5d and 2.5e

5   The electronically controlled fuel and emissions system is linked with many other related engine management systems. It consists mainly of sensors, output actuators and a Powertrain Control Module (PCM) **(see illustrations)**. Completing the system are various other components which respond to commands from the PCM.

6   In many ways, this system can be compared to the central nervous system in the human body. The sensors (nerve endings) constantly gather information and send this data to the PCM (brain), which processes the data and, if necessary, sends out a command for some type of vehicle change (limbs).

7   Here's a specific example of how one portion of this system operates: An oxygen sensor, mounted in the exhaust manifold and

protruding into the exhaust gas stream, constantly monitors the oxygen content of the exhaust gas as it travels through the exhaust pipe. If the percentage of oxygen in the exhaust gas is incorrect, an electrical signal is sent to the PCM. The PCM takes this information, processes it and then sends a command to the fuel injectors, telling it to change the fuel/air mixture. To be effective, all this happens in a fraction of a second, and it goes on continuously while the engine is running. The end result is a fuel/air mixture which is constantly kept at a predetermined ratio, regardless of driving conditions.

Obtaining trouble codes

Refer to illustrations 2.11a and 2.11b

8   One might think that a system which uses exotic electrical sensors and is controlled by an on-board computer would be difficult to diagnose. This is not necessarily the case.

9   The On Board Diagnostic (OBD) system has a built-in self-diagnostic system, which indicates a problem by turning on a "SERVICE ENGINE SOON" light on the instrument panel when a fault has been detected. **Note:** *Since some of the trouble codes do not set the 'SERVICE ENGINE SOON' light,*

2.5b Typical engine control components – 3.1L engine (1990 and later)

1   MAP sensor
2   IAC valve
3   Throttle body
4   Fuel pump relay
5   MAT sensor
6   PCV valve
7   Relay control center

2.5c Typical engine control components - 3100 engine (1994 through 1997)

1   Manifold Absolute Pressure sensor
2   Digital EGR valve
3   Idle Air Control valve
4   Throttle Position Sensor (not visible)

5   Intake Air Temperature sensor
6   Mass Air Flow sensor
7   Engine Coolant Temperature sensor
    (not visible)

8   PCV valve
9   Powertrain Control Module
10 Camshaft position sensor (not visible)

2.5d Typical engine control components - 3800 engine (1995 through 1997)

1   Digital EGR valve
2   Idle Air Control valve
3   Mass Air Flow sensor

4   Intake Air Temperature sensor
5   Throttle Position Sensor
6   Engine Coolant Temperature sensor
    (not visible)

7   Powertrain Control Module
8   PCV valve (underneath MAP sensor)
9   Manifold Absolute Pressure sensor

2.5e Typical engine control components – 1998 and later V6 models

1   Manifold Absolute Pressure sensor
2   Digital EGR valve
3   Intake Air Temperature sensor

4   Mass Air Flow sensor
5   Powertrain Control Module (inside air filter box)

6   PCV valve
7   Camshaft position sensor (not visible)

it is a good idea to access the OBD system and look for any trouble codes that may have been recorded and need tending.

10   Perhaps more importantly, the PCM will recognize this fault, in a particular system monitored by one of the various information sensors, and store it in its memory in the form of a trouble code. Although the trouble code cannot reveal the exact cause of the malfunction, it greatly facilitates diagnosis as you or a dealer mechanic can "tap into" the PCM's memory and be directed to the problem area.

11   To retrieve this information from the PCM on most OBD I and all OBD II systems, a SCAN tool must be connected to the Data Link Connector (DLC) **(see illustrations)**. The SCAN tool is a hand-held digital computer scanner that interfaces with the on-board computer. The SCAN tool is a very powerful tool; it not only reads the trouble codes but also displays the actual operating conditions of the sensors and actuators. SCAN tools are expensive, but they are necessary to accurately diagnose a modern computerized fuel-injected engine. SCAN tools are available from automotive parts stores and specialty tool companies. **Note 1:** On some OBD I models with a 12-pin Data Link Connector, trouble codes can be access by connecting terminal B to terminal A with a jumper wire with the ignition key in the ON position, and the codes can be read by watching the flashes of the SERVICE ENGINE SOON light on the instrument panel (for example, one flash, pause, followed by four flashes would indicate a code 14). It should be noted,

however, that some models with a 12-pin diagnostic connector do not have a terminal B present in the connector. On these models a scan tool is required to access trouble codes. **Note 2:** Even the expensive scan tools can't access some proprietary manufacturers' OBD II codes, but the federally-mandated codes can be obtained from all vehicles. If you don't have access to a scan tool for an OBD II model, consider having the system scanned at a dealership or other repair facility.
Caution: Don't crank or start the engine when terminals A and B are connected by the jumper wire.

12   The self-diagnosis feature built into this

system does not detect all possible faults. If you suspect a problem with the On Board Diagnostic (OBD) system, but the SERVICE ENGINE SOON light has not come on and no trouble codes have been stored, take the vehicle to a dealer service department or other qualified repair shop for diagnosis.

13   Furthermore, when diagnosing an engine performance, fuel economy or exhaust emissions problem (which is not accompanied by a SERVICE ENGINE SOON light) do not automatically assume the fault lies in this system. Perform all standard troubleshooting procedures, as indicated elsewhere in this manual, before turning to the On Board Diag-

2.11a The 12-pin Data Link Connector (DLC) found on models equipped with OBD I engine control system is located under the dash

A   Ground
B   Diagnostic test terminal (not present on all models)

2.11b The 16-pin Data Link Connector (DLC) found on models equipped with OBD II - the DLC (arrow) is located under the instrument panel

nostic (OBD) system.

14   Finally, since this is an electronic system, you should have a basic knowledge of automotive electronics before attempting any diagnosis. Damage to the PCM, Programmable Read Only Memory (PROM) calibration unit or related components can easily occur if care is not exercised.

Clearing trouble codes

15   To clear the codes from the PCM memory, install the SCAN tool, scroll the menu for the function that describes "CLEARING CODES" and follow the prescribed method for that particular SCAN tool or momentarily remove the PCM/IGN fuse from the fuse box for 30 seconds. Clearing codes may also be accomplished by removing the fusible link (main power fuse) located near the battery positive terminal (see Chapter 12) or by disconnecting the cable from the positive terminal (+) of the battery. **Caution:** *On models equipped with a Theftlock audio system, be sure the lockout feature is turned off before disconnecting the battery cable.* Disconnecting the power to the PCM to clear the memory can be an important diagnostic tool, especially on intermittent problems. **Caution:** *To prevent damage to the PCM, the ignition switch must be OFF when disconnecting or connecting power to the PCM.* **Note:** *Disconnecting the negative battery terminal will erase any radio preset codes that have been stored.*

Trouble Code Identification

16   Following is a list of the typical Trouble Codes which may be encountered while diagnosing the On Board Diagnostic (OBD I and OBD II) system. Also included are simplified troubleshooting procedures. If the problem persists after these checks have been made, the vehicle must be diagnosed by a professional mechanic who can use specialized diagnostic tools and advanced troubleshooting methods to check the system. Procedures marked with an asterisk (*) indicate component replacements which may not cure the problem in all cases. For this reason, you may want to seek professional advice before purchasing replacement parts.

OBD I Trouble Codes

Trouble codes	Circuit or system	Probable cause
Code 12 (1 flash, pause, 2 flashes)	Diagnostic	This code will flash whenever the diagnostic terminal is grounded with the ignition turned On and the engine not running. If additional trouble codes are stored in the ECM they will appear after this code has flashed three times.
Code 13 (1 flash, pause, 3 flashes)	Oxygen sensor circuit (open circuit)	Check the wiring and connectors from the oxygen sensor. Replace the oxygen sensor.*
Code 14 (1 flash, pause, 4 flashes)	Coolant sensor circuit (high temperature)	If the engine is experiencing overheating problems, the problem must be rectified before continuing. Check all wiring and connectors associated with the coolant temperature sensor. Replace the coolant temperature sensor.*
Code 15 (Except 2.2L) (1 flash, pause, 5 flashes)	Coolant sensor circuit (low temperature)	See above, then check the wiring connections at the ECM.
Code 16 (3100, '93 3.1 Calif.) (1 flash, pause 6 flashes)	System voltage low	This code will set when the voltage on the ignition feed is 8 volts or less. Check the wiring and ground connections at the ECM, and check for open or chafed wiring.
Code 17 (3100 V6, '93 3.1 Calif.) (1 flash, pause, 7 flashes)	Cam position sensor circuit	Check the wiring and connections between the camshaft position sensor and the ECM.
Code 18 ('93 3800 V6) (1 flash, pause, 8 flashes)	Cam/Crank sensor circuit	Check the connections at the ECM, the crank position flash, sensor and the ignition control module. Also check for opens or shorts in the sensor wiring. Check for bent vanes in the interrupter ring on the vibration damper, and check that the crank sensor is not damaged or misaligned.
Code 21 (2 flashes, pause, 1 flash)	Throttle position sensor	Check for a sticking or misadjusted TPS plunger. Check all wiring and connections between the TPS and the ECM. Adjust or replace the TPS (see Chapter 4).*
Code 22 (Except 2.2L) (2 flashes, pause, 2 flashes)	Throttle position sensor	Check the TPS adjustment (Chapter 4). Check the ECM connector. Replace the TPS (Chapter 4).*
Code 23 (2 flashes, pause, 3 flashes)	Manifold (Intake) air temperature	Check the MAT/IAT sensor, wiring and connectors for an open sensor circuit. Replace the MAT/IAT sensor.*
Code 24 (Except '93 3.1 Calif.) (2 flashes, pause, 4 flashes)	Vehicle speed sensor (3100: No voltage)	A fault in this circuit should be indicated only when the vehicle is in motion. Disregard Code 24 if it is set when the drive wheels are not turning. Check the connections at the ECM. Check the TPS setting.
Code 25 (Except 2.2L) (2 flashes, pause, 5 flashes)	Manifold (Intake) air temperature	Check the voltage signal from the MAT/IAT sensor to the ECM. It should be above 4 volts.

Trouble codes	Circuit or system	Probable cause
Code 26 (Except 2.2, 2.5, 3100, '93 3.1 Calif.) (2 flashes, pause, 6 flashes)	Quad driver circuit	Have the vehicle checked by a dealer service department.
Code 27 ('91/'92 3800 V6) (2 flashes, pause, 7 flashes)	Gear switch diagnosis	Check for poor connections at the ECM, or for mis-routed or damaged wiring.
Code 28 ('91/'92 3800 V6) (2 flashes, pause, 8 flashes)	Gear switch diagnosis	Check for poor connections at the ECM, or for mis-routed or damaged wiring.
Code 29 ('91/'92 3800 V6) (2 flashes, pause, 9 flashes)	Gear switch diagnosis	Check for poor connections at the ECM, or for mis-routed or damaged wiring.
Code 31 (Turbo models) (3 flashes, pause, 1 flash)	Turbo overboost	Wastegate system malfunction. Have the vehicle checked by a dealer service department.
Code 32 (Except '93 3.1L for Calif.) (3 flashes, pause, 2 flashes)	EGR system	Check vacuum hoses and connections for leaks and restrictions. Replace the EGR valve.*
Code 33 (1988 models) (3 flashes, pause, 3 flashes)	MAF sensor	Replace MAF sensor.*
Code 33 (1989 On) (3 flashes, pause, 3 flashes)	MAP sensor	Check the vacuum hoses from the MAP sensor. Check the electrical connections at the ECM. Replace the MAP sensor.*
Code 34 (1988 models and 3800 through 1993) (3 flashes, pause, 4 flashes)	MAF sensor	Check for loose or damaged air duct, misadjusted minimum idle speed and vacuum leaks. Inspect the MAF sensor and the electrical connections.
Code 34 (1989 on, except 2.2L) (3 flashes, pause, 4 flashes)	MAP sensor	Code 34 will set when the signal voltage from the MAP sensor is too low. Instead the ECM will substitute a fixed MAP value and use the TPS to control fuel delivery. Replace the MAP sensor.*
Code 35 (Except 2.2L) (3 flashes, pause, 5 flashes)	Idle speed error	Code 35 will set when the closed throttle speed is 300 rpm above or below the correct idle speed for 5 seconds. Replace the IAC.*
Code 36 (3100, '93 3.1 Calif.) (3 flashes, pause, 6 flashes)	Ignition control 24X reference	Check the connections between the ECM and the crankshaft position sensor.
Code 36 ('93 3800 V6 only) (3 flashes, pause, 6 flashes)	Transaxle shift control	Check wiring for opens or shorts. Check connectors at transaxle as well as the solenoids. If these are all good, the problem may be an internal hydraulic or mechanical failure.
Code 37 (3100 V6) (3 flashes, pause, 7 flashes)	TCC/Brake switch	Check the connections at the stop lamp/torque converter clutch/cruise control switch, and check the adjustment of the switch.
Code 39 ('92/'93 3.4L V6 only) (3 flashes, pause, 9 flashes)	Transaxle clutch switch	Check for a short to ground between the ECM and the clutch switch, bad connections at the ECM, and make sure that the clutch switch is securely fastened.
Code 41 (V6 through '93 except 3800 and '93 3.1 Calif.) (4 flashes, pause, 1 flash)	Cylinder select error	Check for faulty connections at MEM-CAL or incorrect MEM-CAL installed in ECM. Replace the MEM-CAL.*
Code 41 (Quad-4 engine) (4 flashes, pause, 1 flash)	1X reference	Check the ignition module and ECM connections.
Code 41 (3100 V6) (4 flashes, pause, 1 flash)	Ignition control	Look for an open circuit between the ignition control module and the powertrain control module.
Code 41 (3800 through '93) (4 flashes, pause, 1 flash)	Camshaft position sensor	Check the connections and wiring at the camshaft position sensor and ignition control module. Check for a missing camshaft magnet, or a damaged or faulty sensor.

OBD I Trouble Codes (continued)

Trouble codes	Circuit or system	Probable cause
Code 42 (4 flashes, pause, 2 flashes)	Electronic Spark Timing (Ignition control circuit)	Faulty connections or ignition module.
Code 43 (Except 2.2L, 2.5L) (4 flashes, pause, 3 flashes)	Electronic spark control (Knock sensor circuit)	Faulty knock sensor or MEM-CAL.*
Code 44 (4 flashes, pause, 4 flashes)	Lean exhaust	Check the ECM wiring connections. Check for vacuum leaks at the hoses and intake manifold gasket.*
Code 45 (4 flashes, pause, 5 flashes)	Rich exhaust	Check the evaporative charcoal canister and its components for the presence of fuel.
Code 46 (3100 V6) (4 flashes, pause, 6 flashes)	Security system error	Check for an open or short circuit between the theft deterrent module and the powertrain control module.
Code 51 (5 flashes, pause, 1 flash)	MEM-CAL or PROM	Make sure the MEM-CAL or PROM is properly installed in the ECM. Replace the MEM-CAL or PROM.*
Code 53 (Except 2.2L and '93 3800 V6) (5 flashes, pause, 3 flashes)	System over-voltage	Code 53 will set if the voltage at ECM terminal B2 is greater than 17.1 volts for 2 seconds. Check the charging system.
Code 53 ('93 3800 V6) (5 flashes, pause, 3 flashes)	EGR system	If the EGR valve shows signs of excessive heat, the exhaust system may have a blockage, such as a plugged converter. Also, check the wiring between the EGR valve and the ECM. Check for a blockage in the EGR passage too.
Code 54 (V6 except '93 3800) (5 flashes, pause, 4 flashes)	Fuel pump	Check for a faulty fuel pump relay.
Code 54 ('93 3800 V6) (5 flashes, pause, 4 flashes)	EGR system	If the EGR valve shows signs of excessive heat, the exhaust system may have a blockage, such as a plugged converter. Also, check the wiring between the EGR valve and the ECM. Check for a blockage in the EGR passage too.
Code 55 (Except 2.2, 2.5, '93 3800, and '93 3.1 Calif.) (5 flashes, pause, 5 flashes)	ECM	Check the ECM grounds and the MEM-CAL or PROM seating. Replace the ECM *
Code 55 ('93 3800 V6) (5 flashes, pause, 5 flashes)	EGR system	If the EGR valve shows signs of excessive heat, the exhaust system may have a blockage, such as a plugged converter. Also, check the wiring between the EGR valve and the ECM. Check for a blockage in the EGR passage too.
Code 56 ('93 3800 V6 only) (5 flashes, pause, 6 flashes)	Quad driver	Have the vehicle checked by a dealer service department.
Code 58 (3100 V6) (5 flashes, pause, 8 flashes)	Transaxle fluid temperature	A low voltage signal indicates high transaxle fluid temperature, or a circuit (low voltage) failure in the sensor circuit. Check for a short circuit between the transaxle fluid temperature sensor and the control unit, or a bad control unit.
Code 59 (3100 V6) (5 flashes, pause, 9 flashes)	Transaxle fluid temperature circuit (high voltage)	A high voltage signal indicates low transaxle fluid temperature, or a failure in the circuit. Check for an open circuit between the transaxle fluid temperature sensor and the control unit, a bad sensor ground, or a bad control unit.
Code 61 (V6 except '93 3800 and 3.1 Calif.) (6 flashes, pause, 1 flash)	Degraded oxygen sensor	Check for contaminated fuel. Replace the sensor.*

Trouble codes	Circuit or system	Probable cause
Code 61 ('93 3800 V6 only) (6 flashes, pause, 1 flash)	Cruise control vent circuit	This particular trouble code will not illuminate the Service Engine Soon light. If code 61 is displayed during the course of troubleshooting, check the wiring and connections between the cruise servo and the ECM. If necessary, replace the cruise servo.*
Code 62 (Quad-4 and 3.4L V6) (6 flashes, 2 flashes)	Trans. gear switch circuit	Check electrical switching circuits of transaxle.
Code 62 ('93 3800 V6) (6 flashes, pause, 2 flashes)	Cruise control VAC solenoid	This particular trouble code will not illuminate the Service Engine Soon light. If code 62 is displayed during the course of troubleshooting, check the wiring and connections between the cruise servo and the ECM. If necessary, replace the cruise servo.*
Code 63 ('93 3800 V6) (6 flashes, pause, 3 flashes)	Cruise control system problem	This particular trouble code will not illuminate the Service Engine Soon light. If code 63 is displayed during the course of troubleshooting, check the wiring and connections between the cruise servo and the ECM. Also check for a binding cruise control throttle cable or leaking vacuum lines. If necessary, replace the cruise servo.*
Code 65 (Quad-4 engine) (6 flashes, pause, 5 flashes)	Fuel injector	Check the ECM and injector wiring and connectors.
Code 65 ('93 3800 V6) (6 flashes, pause, 5 flashes)	Cruise servo position sensor (SPS low)	This particular trouble code will not illuminate the Service Engine Soon light. If code 65 is displayed during the course of troubleshooting, check the wiring and connections between the cruise servo and the ECM. If necessary, replace the cruise servo.*
Code 66 (Quad-4, 3.1, 3.4 and 3100 V6) (6 flashes, pause, 6 flashes)	A/C pressure sensor	Check the sensor connections.
Code 66 (3800 V6) (6 flashes, pause, 6 flashes)	Excessive A/C cycling (Low refrigerant charge)	If the refrigerant pressure is low the ECM can cause the compressor to cycle too often. If excessive cycling is detected, the ECM protects the compressor by disabling the relay, and storing a code 66, until the ignition is turned off and on again. If this happens three times, the ECM will disable the A/C clutch until code 66 is cleared. If the refrigerant charge is low, check all refrigerant lines and connections for leaks. If refrigerant charge is OK, check the A/C wiring and connections. Replace the pressure switch if necessary.*
Code 67 ('93 3800 V6) (6 flashes, pause, 7 flashes)	Cruise control switches	Check the wiring and connections between the cruise engage switch and the ECM.
Code 68 ('93 3800 V6) (6 flashes, pause, 8 flashes)	Cruise servo position sensor (SPS low)	This particular trouble code will not illuminate the Service Engine Soon light. If code 68 is displayed during the course of troubleshooting, check the wiring and connections between the cruise servo and the ECM. Also check for a binding cruise control throttle cable or a blockage in the vacuum dump hose. Check that the vacuum dump valve is properly adjusted. If necessary, replace the cruise servo.*
Code 69 (3800 V6) (6 flashes, pause, 9 flashes)	A/C head pressure high	This particular trouble code will not illuminate the Service Engine Soon light. If code 69 is displayed during the course of troubleshooting, check the wiring and connections between the A/C system and the ECM.
Code 70 (3100, '93 3.1Calif.) (7 flashes)	A/C pressure sensor (high pressure)	Code 70 sets when the voltage signal from the sensor is beyond the normal range, but is not a problem in the refrigerant system. Check for an open sensor ground or a bad wiring connection. If these are good, the sensor may have to be replaced.*

OBD I Trouble Codes (continued)

Trouble codes	Circuit or system	Probable cause
Code 72 (3100 V6) (7 flashes, pause, 2 flashes)	Vehicle speed sensor (Signal error)	This code sets when the voltage signal is lost while the car is traveling at road speeds. Check for a short in the speed sensor wires. If these are good, the speed sensor or the ECM may have to be replaced.*
Code 75 (3100, '93 3.1 Calif.) (7 flashes, pause, 5 flashes)	Digital EGR # 1 solenoid	Check the wires and connections between the EGR valve and the ECM. Also check for plugged passages in the intake plenum. If these are good the EGR valve or the ECM may have to be replaced.*
Code 76 (3100, '93 3.1 Calif.) (7 flashes, pause, 6 flashes)	Digital EGR # 2 solenoid	Check the wires and connections between the EGR valve and the ECM. Also check for plugged passages in the intake plenum. If these are good the EGR valve or the ECM may have to be replaced.*
Code 77 (3100, '93 3.1 Calif.) (7 flashes, pause, 7 flashes)	Digital EGR # 3 solenoid	Check the wires and connections between the EGR valve and the ECM. Also check for plugged passages in the intake plenum. If these are good the EGR valve or the ECM may have to be replaced.*
Code 79 (3100 V6) (7 flashes, pause, 9 flashes)	Transaxle fluid (temperature high)	Certain driving conditions can cause the transaxle fluid to get too hot. For example, trailer towing and driving on steep grades.
Code 79 ('93 3.1 Calif.) (7 flashes, pause, 9 flashes)	Vehicle speed sensor (High signal voltage)	A misadjusted park/neutral switch can cause a false code 79. Also check for short circuits in the wiring between the speed sensor and the ECM.
Code 80 (3100 V6) (8 flashes)	Transaxle component error	Check torque converter clutch (TCC) fuse; if blown, check for a short circuit in the wiring between the fuse and the transaxle. If the fuse and wiring are good check for faulty terminal connections at the ECM and transaxle.
Code 80 ('93 3.1 Calif.) (8 flashes)	Vehicle speed sensor (Low signal voltage)	A misadjusted park/neutral switch can cause a false code 79. Also check for short circuits in the wiring between the speed sensor and the ECM. If necessary the vehicle speed sensor or ECM may have to be replaced.
Code 81 ('93 3.1 Calif.) (8 flashes, pause, 1 flash)	Brake switch error	Check the adjustment of the brake switch, as well as the wiring between the brake switch and the ECM.
Code 82 (3100, '93 3.1 Calif.) (8 flashes, pause, 2 flashes)	Ignition control 3X error	An open or short in the 3X signal will cause the symptom cranks but won't run. However, an intermittent problem, such as poor connections, can also set the code. If the wiring is good the problem may be in the ignition control module or the crankshaft position sensor.
Code 85 (3100, '93 3.1 Calif.) (8 flashes, pause, 5 flashes)	PROM error	Check all wiring and connections at the ECM. If these are good, the ECM may need to be reprogrammed or replaced. A replacement ECM must be reprogrammed also.
Code 86 (3100, '93 3.1 Calif.) (8 flashes, pause, 6 flashes)	Analog/Digital (A/D) error	The A/D multiplexer is a chip inside the ECM. If code 86 sets, check for and repair any other codes first. Also check the ECM terminals and wiring.
Code 87 (3100, '93 3.1 Calif.) (8 flashes, pause, 7 flashes)	EEPROM error	Check all wiring and connections at the ECM. If these are good, the ECM may need to be reprogrammed or replaced. A replacement ECM must be reprogrammed also. Reprogramming is a job for your dealer to carry out.
Code 90 (3100 V6) (9 flashes)	Torque Converter Clutch (TCC) error	Check torque converter clutch (TCC) fuse; if blown, check for a short circuit in the wiring between the fuse and the transaxle. If the fuse and wiring are good check for faulty terminal connections at the ECM and transaxle.
Code 96 (3100 V6) (9 flashes, pause, 6 flashes)	Transaxle low voltage	Check the charging system, as well as the wiring and connections at the ECM.

Trouble codes	Circuit or system	Probable cause
Code 98 (3100 V6) (9 flashes, pause, 8 flashes)	Invalid ECM program	The ECM may have to be reprogrammed.
Code 99 (3100, '93 3800 V6) (9 flashes, pause, 9 flashes)	Invalid ECM program	The ECM may have to be reprogrammed.

Component replacement may not cure the problem in all cases. For this reason, you may want to seek professional advice before purchasing replacement parts.

OBD II Trouble Codes

Note: *Not all trouble codes apply to all models.*

Code	Code Identification
P0016	Crankshaft position/camshaft position, bank 1, sensor A - correlation
P0030	HO2S heater control circuit (bank 1, sensor 1)
P0033	Turbocharger bypass valve control circuit
P0036	HO2S heater control circuit (bank 1 sensor 2)
P0053	HO2S heater resistance (bank 1, sensor 1)
P0054	HO2S heater resistance (bank 1, sensor 2)
P0068	Throttle position (TP) sensor inconsistent with mass air flow (MAF) sensor
P0069	Manifold pressure (MAP) sensor - barometric pressure correlation
P0101	Mass air flow sensor circuit, range or performance problem
P0102	Mass air flow sensor circuit, low input
P0103	Mass air flow sensor circuit, high input
P0105	Manifold absolute pressure sensor or throttle position sensor circuit malfunction
P0106	Manifold absolute pressure sensor circuit, range or performance problem
P0107	Manifold absolute pressure sensor circuit, low input
P0108	Manifold absolute pressure sensor circuit, high input
P0112	Intake air temperature circuit, low input
P0113	Intake air temperature circuit, high input
P0116	Engine coolant temperature circuit range/performance problem
P0117	Engine coolant temperature circuit, low input
P0118	Engine coolant temperature circuit, high input
P0120	Throttle position or pedal position sensor/switch circuit malfunction

Code	Code Identification
P0121	Throttle position or pedal position sensor/switch circuit, range or performance problem
P0122	Throttle position sensor circuit, low input
P0123	Throttle position sensor circuit, high input
P0125	Insufficient coolant temperature for closed loop fuel control
P0128	Coolant thermostat (coolant temperature below thermostat regulating temperature)
P0130	O2 sensor circuit malfunction (bank 1, sensor 1)
P0131	Oxygen sensor circuit, low voltage (upstream sensor)
P0132	Oxygen sensor circuit, high voltage (upstream sensor)
P0133	Oxygen sensor circuit, slow response (upstream sensor)
P0134	Oxygen sensor circuit - no activity detected (upstream sensor)
P0135	O2 sensor heater circuit malfunction (bank 1, sensor 1)
P0137	Oxygen sensor circuit, low voltage (downstream sensor)
P0138	Oxygen sensor circuit, high voltage (downstream sensor)
P0140	Oxygen sensor circuit - no activity detected (downstream sensor)
P0141	O2 sensor heater circuit malfunction (bank 1, sensor 2)
P0171	System too lean
P0172	System too rich
P0200	Injector circuit malfunction
P0201	Injector circuit malfunction - cylinder no. 1
P0202	Injector circuit malfunction - cylinder no. 2
P0203	Injector circuit malfunction - cylinder no. 3
P0204	Injector circuit malfunction - cylinder no. 4

OBD II Trouble Codes (continued)

Code	Code Identification
P0205	Injector circuit malfunction - cylinder no. 5
P0206	Injector circuit malfunction - cylinder no. 6
P0207	Injector circuit malfunction - cylinder no. 7
P0208	Injector circuit malfunction - cylinder no. 8
P0218	Transaxle fluid over temperature
P0220	Throttle position or pedal position sensor/switch B circuit malfunction
P0223	Throttle position or pedal position sensor/switch B circuit, high input
P0230	Fuel pump primary circuit malfunction
P0300	Random/multiple cylinder misfire detected
P0301	Cylinder no. 1 misfire detected
P0302	Cylinder no. 2 misfire detected
P0303	Cylinder no. 3 misfire detected
P0304	Cylinder no. 4 misfire detected
P0305	Cylinder no. 5 misfire detected
P0306	Cylinder no. 6 misfire detected
P0307	Cylinder no. 7 misfire detected
P0308	Cylinder no. 8 misfire detected
P0315	Crankshaft position system - variation not learned
P0324	Knock control system error
P0325	Knock sensor circuit malfunction
P0326	Knock sensor no. 1 circuit, range or performance problem (bank 1 or single sensor)
P0327	Knock sensor circuit, low input
P0328	Knock sensor no. 1 circuit, high input (bank 1 or single sensor)
P0330	Knock sensor no. 2 circuit malfunction (bank 2)
P0332	Knock sensor no. 2 circuit, low input (bank 2)
P0333	Knock sensor no. 2 circuit, high input (bank 2)
P0335	Crankshaft position sensor circuit malfunction
P0336	Crankshaft position sensor circuit, range or performance problem
P0340	Camshaft position sensor "A", circuit malfunction (bank 1)
P0341	Camshaft position sensor circuit, range or performance problem
P0342	Camshaft position sensor circuit, low input
P0350	Ignition coil primary or secondary circuit malfunction

Code	Code Identification
P0351	Ignition coil A primary or secondary circuit malfunction
P0352	Ignition coil B primary or secondary circuit malfunction
P0353	Ignition coil C primary or secondary circuit malfunction
P0354	Ignition coil D primary or secondary circuit malfunction
P0355	Ignition coil E primary or secondary circuit malfunction
P0356	Ignition coil F primary or secondary circuit malfunction
P0357	Ignition coil G primary or secondary circuit malfunction
P0358	Ignition coil H primary or secondary circuit malfunction
P0385	Crankshaft position sensor B circuit malfunction
P0386	Crankshaft position sensor B circuit, range or performance problem
P0401	Exhaust gas recirculation, insufficient flow detected
P0403	Exhaust gas recirculation circuit malfunction
P0404	Exhaust gas recirculation circuit, range or performance problem
P0405	Exhaust gas recirculation sensor circuit low
P0406	Exhaust gas recirculation valve position sensor A circuit high
P0410	Secondary air injection system
P0411	Secondary air injection system, incorrect flow detected
P0412	Secondary air injection solenoid control circuit
P0418	Secondary air injection pump relay control circuit
P0420	Catalyst system efficiency below threshold
P0440	Evaporative emission control system malfunction
P0442	Evaporative emission control system, small leak detected
P0443	Evaporative emission control system, purge control circuit malfunction
P0446	Evaporative emission control system, vent system performance
P0449	Evaporative emission control system, vent control circuit malfunction
P0451	Evaporative emission control system, pressure sensor range or performance problem
P0452	Evaporative emission control system, pressure sensor low input
P0453	Evaporative emission control system, pressure sensor high input
P0454	Evaporative emission control system, pressure sensor intermittent
P0455	Evaporative emission (EVAP) control system leak detected (no purge flow or large leak)

Code	Code Identification
P0460	Fuel level sensor circuit malfunction
P0461	Fuel level sensor circuit, range or performance problem
P0462	Fuel level sensor circuit, low input
P0463	Fuel level sensor circuit, high input
P0480	Cooling fan control circuit malfunction
P0481	Cooling fan control circuit malfunction
P0496	Evaporative emission system - high purge flow
P0502	Vehicle speed sensor circuit low output
P0503	Vehicle speed sensor signal intermittent
P0506	Idle control system, rpm lower than expected
P0507	Idle control system, rpm higher than expected
P0530	Air conditioning refrigerant pressure sensor, circuit malfunction
P0560	System voltage malfunction
P0562	System voltage low
P0563	System voltage high
P0601	Internal control module, memory error
P0602	Control module, programming error
P0603	Internal control module, keep alive memory (KAM) error
P0604	Internal control module, random access memory (RAM) error
P0605	Internal control module, read only memory (ROM) error
P0606	PCM processor fault
P0607	Control module performance
P0620	Charging system performance
P0641	Sensor reference voltage A - circuit open
P0650	Malfunction Indicator Light (MIL) control circuit
P0651	Sensor reference voltage B - circuit open
P0654	Tachometer control circuit
P0685	EGM power relay, control - circuit open
P0689	ECM power relay sense - circuit low
P0690	ECM power relay sense - circuit high
P0700	Transmission control system malfunction
P0705	Transmission range sensor, circuit malfunction (PRNDL input)
P0706	Transaxle range switch performance
P0711	Fluid temperature sensor circuit out-of-range
P0712	Fluid temperature sensor circuit low input

Code	Code Identification
P0713	Fluid temperature sensor circuit high input
P0716	Input speed sensor circuit out-of-range
P0717	Input speed sensor circuit no signal
P0719	Torque converter clutch brake switch circuit low
P0724	Torque converter clutch brake switch circuit high
P0730	Incorrect gear ratio
P0741	Torque converter clutch system stuck off
P0742	Torque converter clutch system stuck on
P0748	Pressure control solenoid valve circuit
P0751	1-2 shift solenoid performance
P0753	1-2 shift solenoid circuit
P0756	2-3 shift solenoid performance
P0758	2-3 shift solenoid circuit
P1106	Manifold absolute pressure sensor circuit intermittent high voltage
P1107	Manifold absolute pressure sensor circuit intermittent low voltage
P1111	Intake air temperature sensor circuit intermittent high voltage
P1112	Intake air temperature sensor circuit intermittent low voltage
P1114	Engine coolant temperature sensor circuit intermittent low voltage
P1115	Engine coolant temperature sensor circuit intermittent high voltage
P1121	Throttle position sensor circuit intermittent high voltage
P1122	Throttle position sensor circuit intermittent low voltage
P1133	Oxygen sensor insufficient switching (upstream sensor)
P1134	Oxygen sensor transition time ratio (upstream sensor)
P1171	Fuel system lean during acceleration
P1200	Fuel injector control circuit
P1336	Crankshaft position sensor system variation not learned
P1350	By-pass line monitor
P1351	Ignition control circuit open
P1352	Ignition by-pass circuit open
P1361	Ignition control circuit not switching
P1362	Ignition by-pass circuit shorted
P1374	Crankshaft position sensor 3X reference circuit
P1380	Electronic brake control module rough road sensing error

OBD II Trouble Codes (continued)

Code	Code Identification
P1381	No serial data from electronic brake control module
P1404	EGR valve closed pintle position
P1406	EGR valve pintle position circuit
P1441	EVAP system flow during non-purge
P1554	Cruise control status circuit
P1573	Serial data communication failure with electronic brake and traction control module
P1601	Serial communication malfunction
P1602	Serial data communication failure with electronic brake control module
P1610	Serial data communication failure with body function controller
P1621	PCM memory performance
P1626	Serial data communication failure with vehicle theft deterrent controller (no password)
P1630	Theft deterrent PCM in learn mode
P1631	Theft deterrent password incorrect
P1632	Theft deterrent fuel disabled
P1635	5-volt reference circuit
P1639	5-volt reference circuit
P1641	Malfunction indicator light control circuit
P1651	Electric cooling fan relay control circuit
P1652	Electric cooling fan relay control circuit
P1654	Air conditioning relay control circuit
P1655	Evaporative emission control system, purge valve solenoid control circuit
P1662	Cruise control inhibit control circuit
P1665	Evaporative emission control system, vent valve solenoid control circuit
P1671	Malfunction indicator light control circuit
P1675	Evaporative emission control system, vent solenoid control circuit
P1676	Evaporative emission control system, purge valve solenoid control circuit
P1810	Pressure switch assembly malfunction
P1811	Long shift time
P1860	Torque converter clutch pulse width modulator solenoid circuit
P1887	Torque converter clutch release switch malfunction
P2101	Throttle actuator control (TAC) motor - range/performance

Code	Code Identification
P2107	Throttle actuator control (TAC) module - processor fault
P2108	Throttle actuator control (TAC) module - performance problem
P2119	Throttle actuator control throttle body range/performance
P2120	Throttle/pedal position sensor/switch "D" circuit
P2122	Throttle/pedal position sensor/switch "D" circuit low input
P2123	Throttle/pedal position sensor/switch "D" circuit high input
P2125	Throttle/pedal position sensor/switch "E" circuit
P2127	Throttle/pedal position sensor/switch "E" circuit low input
P2128	Throttle/pedal position sensor/switch "E" circuit high input
P2135	Throttle/pedal position sensor/switch "A"/ "B" voltage correlation
P2138	Throttle/pedal position sensor/switch "D" / "E" voltage correlation
P2176	Throttle actuator control (TAC) system - idle position not learned
P2227	Barometric pressure (BARO) sensor - range/performance sensor - circuit low
P2229	Barometric pressure (BARO) sensor - circuit high
P2430	Secondary air injection (AIR) system, air flow / pressure sensor, bank 1 - circuit malfunction
P2431	Secondary air injection (AIR) system, air flow / pressure sensor, bank 1 - range/performance
P2432	Secondary air injection (AIR) system, air flow / pressure sensor, bank 1 - circuit low
P2433	Secondary air injection (AIR) system, air flow / pressure sensor, bank 1 - circuit high
P2440	Secondary air injection (AIR) switching valve, bank 1 - valve stuck open
P2444	Secondary air injection (AIR) pump, bank 1 - pump stuck on
P2544	Torque management request, input signal A - malfunction
P2610	Engine control module (ECM) - internal engine timer performance
P3400	Cylinder deactivation system bank 1
P3401	Cylinder 1 deactivation/intake valve control circuit/open
P3425	Cylinder 4 deactivation/intake valve control circuit/open
P3441	Cylinder 6 deactivation/intake valve control circuit/open
P3449	Cylinder 7 deactivation/intake valve control circuit/open

Component replacement may not cure the problem in all cases. For this reason, you may want to seek professional advice before purchasing replacement parts.

3.3a On some models it will be necessary to detach the clasps (arrows) from the PCM cover

3.3b Location of the ECM mounting screws (arrows)

3.3c On later models, remove the top of the air filter housing to access the PCM (arrow)

3 Powertrain Control Module (PCM/ECM) - replacement

Note 1: *All vehicles equipped with OBD I diagnostic system have a replaceable PROM or MEM-CAL in the PCM that must be installed into the new PCM when exchanged. All vehicles equipped with OBD II diagnostic system are equipped with (non-replaceable) EEPROM that must be recalibrated with a special factory SCAN tool after replacement of the PCM.*

Note 2: *1995 3100 engines and all 1996 and 1997 models are equipped with a replaceable Knock sensor (KS) module in the PCM that must be installed into the new PCM when exchanged.*

Note 3: *The Powertrain Control Module (PCM) is often referred to as the Electronic Control Module (ECM) in several instances throughout this manual. For clarification purposes the PCM is the same component as the ECM. When electronic engine control systems where first introduced, the manufacturers named this control unit the ECM, as the engine control systems became more advanced with the additional sensors and related components the manufacturers renamed this control unit the PCM.*

PCM/ECM replacement

Refer to illustrations 3.3a, 3.3b and 3.3c

Caution: *The ignition switch must be turned off when disconnecting or plugging in the electrical connectors to prevent damage to the PCM.*

1   The Powertrain Control Module (PCM) on 1997 and earlier models is located in the engine compartment in front of the right front strut tower. The Powertrain Control Module (PCM) on 1998 and later models is located at the left front corner of the engine compartment in the air cleaner housing.

2   Disconnect the negative battery cable from the battery. **Caution:** *On models equipped with the Theftlock audio system, be sure the lockout feature is turned off before*

3.6 Two typical Electronic Control Modules (ECM)

performing any procedure which requires disconnecting the battery.

3   On 1997 and earlier models remove the retaining nuts **(see illustrations)**. On 1998 and later models remove the air intake duct, the upper air cleaner housing and the air filter **(see illustration)**.

4   Detach the PCM from the inner fender well (1997 and earlier) or air cleaner housing (1998 and later) and unplug the electrical connectors from the PCM.

5   Installation is the reverse of removal.

MEM-CAL or PROM replacement (OBD I diagnostic system)

Refer to illustration 3.6

6   To allow one model of PCM to be used for many different vehicles, a device called a MEM-CAL (MEMory and CALibration) or PROM (Programmable Read Only Memory) is used **(see illustration)**. This device is located inside the PCM and contains information on the vehicle's weight, engine, transaxle, axle ratio, etc. One PCM part number can be used by many GM vehicles but the MEM-CAL or PROM is very specific and must be used only in the vehicle for which it was designed. For this reason, it's essential to check the latest parts book and Service Bulletin information for the correct part number when replacing a MEM-CAL or PROM. A PCM purchased at a dealer doesn't come with a MEM-CAL or

PROM. The MEM-CAL or PROM from the old PCM must be carefully removed and installed in the new PCM.

MEM-CAL

Refer to illustrations 3.8 and 3.11

7   Remove the MEM-CAL access cover.

8   Using two fingers, push both retaining clips back away from the MEM-CAL **(see illustration)**. At the same time, grasp the MEM-CAL at both ends and lift it up out of the socket. Don't remove the MEM-CAL cover

3.8 Using two fingers, push the retaining clips (arrows) away from the MEM-CAL and simultaneously grasp it at both ends and lift it up, out of the socket

3.11 To install the MEM-CAL, press only on the ends until the retaining clips snap into the ends of the MEM-CAL - make sure the notches in the MEM-CAL are aligned with the small notches in the socket

3.14 Note how the notch in the PROM is matched up with the smaller notch in the carrier

3.15 Press only on the ends of the PROM carrier - pressure on the area in between could result in bent or broken pins or damage to the PROM

itself. **Caution:** *Use of unapproved removal or installation methods may damage the MEM-CAL or socket.*

9   Verify that the numbers on the old PCM and new PCM match up (or that the numbers of the old and new MEM-CALs match up, depending on the component(s) being replaced).

10   To install the MEM-CAL, press only on the ends.

11   The small notches in the MEM-CAL must be aligned with the small notches in the MEM-CAL socket. Press on the ends of the MEM-CAL until the retaining clips snap into the ends of the MEM-CAL. Don't press on the middle of the MEM-CAL - press only on the ends **(see illustration)**.

12   The remainder of the installation is the reverse of removal.

PROM

Refer to illustrations 3.14 and 3.15

13   To remove the PROM a special tool should be used. These are usually supplied when a replacement PCM is purchased. **Caution:** *Removal without this tool or with any other tool may cause damage.* Grasp the PROM carrier at the narrow ends. Gently rock the carrier from end-to-end while carefully pulling up.

14   Note the reference end of the PROM carrier **(see illustration)** before setting it aside.

15   Position the PROM and carrier assembly squarely over the socket with the small notched end of the carrier aligned with the small notch in the socket **(see illustration)**. **Caution:** *Don't press on the PROM; press only on the carrier. Also, if the unit is installed backwards it will be destroyed when the ignition is turned on.*

Final Installation

16   Once the new MEM-CAL or PROM is installed in the old PCM (or the old MEM-CAL or PROM is installed in the new PCM), check the installation to verify its been installed prop-

erly by doing the following test:

a) *Turn the ignition switch on.*
b) *Enter the diagnostics mode at the ALDL (data link connector) (see Section 2).*
c) *Allow Code 12 to flash four times to verify that no other codes are present. This indicates the MEM-CAL or PROM is installed properly and the PCM is functioning properly.*

17   If trouble codes 41, 42, 43, 51 or 55 (41, 43, or 51 on Quad-4 engine) occur, or if the Service Engine Soon or Check Engine light is on constantly but isn't flashing any codes, the MEM-CAL or PROM is either not completely seated or it's defective. If it's not seated, press firmly on the ends of the MEM-CAL or PROM. If it's necessary to remove the MEM-CAL or PROM, follow the above Steps again.

EEPROM reprogramming (OBD II diagnostic system)

18   The 1995 models equipped with 3100 engines and all 1996 and later models are equipped with Electrical Erasable Programmable Read Only Memory (EEPROM) chip that is permanently soldered to the PCM

circuit board. The EEPROM can be reprogrammed using the GM TECH 1 scan tool. Do not attempt to remove this component from the PCM. Have the EEPROM reprogrammed at a dealer service department or other qualified repair shop.

Knock Sensor (KS) module replacement

Refer to illustrations 3.21 and 3.22

19   1995 3100 engine, and all 1996 and 1997 models are equipped with a knock sensor (KS) module. New PCMs are not supplied with a KS module, therefore it is necessary to remove the original and install it into the new PCM. Use care not to damage the KS module when working with these delicate electrical components.

20   Remove the PCM from the engine compartment (see Step 4).

21   Remove the screws and detach the access cover from the PCM **(see illustration)**.

22   Using two fingers, carefully squeeze the retaining clips together and lift the KS module straight out of the PCM **(see illustration)**.

23   Installation is the reverse of removal. Be

3.21 Remove the screws and lift the cover to expose the knock sensor module

3.22 Pinch the tabs and lift the knock sensor module from the PCM

4.1a Be sure the ohmmeter probes make clean contact with the terminals of the sensor when checking the resistance (thermistor type sensor shown)

Temperature (degrees-F)	Resistance (ohms)
212	176
194	240
176	332
158	458
140	668
122	972
112	1182
104	1458
95	1800
86	2238
76	2795
68	3520
58	4450
50	5670
40	7280
32	9420

4.1b Coolant temperature and intake air temperature sensors approximate temperature vs. resistance relationships

4.3 Carefully backprobe the GROUND (-) and the SIGNAL (+) terminals using straight pins to make contact without disconnecting the harness connector (potentiometer type sensor shown)

sure to use the alignment notches in the seat area of the PCM when sliding the KS module back in place. Press only on the end of the KS module assembly until it snaps back into place.

4   Information sensors - general information and testing

Caution 1: *When performing the following tests, use only a high-impedance (10 mega ohms) digital multi-meter to prevent damage to the PCM.*
Caution 2: *On models equipped with a Theft-lock audio system, be sure the lockout feature is turned off before disconnecting the battery cable.*
Note 1: *Because this system requires a special TECH 1 SCAN tool to access the self-diagnosis system, have the vehicle codes extracted by a dealer service department or other qualified repair facility if the SCAN tool is not available for diagnostic purposes. There are several checks the home mechanic can perform to test for a NO START condition but in the event the driveability symptoms are intermittent or varied, it will be necessary to monitor the operation of the sensor(s) with a SCAN tool or oscilloscope.*
Note 2: *Refer to Chapter 5 for additional information concerning the ignition system and the crankshaft sensor diagnostics.*

Thermistor (two-wire) sensors (coolant temperature, intake air temperature, etc.)

Refer to illustrations 4.1a and 4.1b
1   Thermistors are variable resistors that sense temperature level changes and convert them to a voltage signal. The engine coolant temperature sensor (ECT) and the intake air temperature sensor (IAT) are thermistor type sensors. As the sensor temperature

DECREASES, the resistance will INCREASE. As the sensor temperature INCREASES, the resistance will DECREASE. to check thermistor type sensors select the ohms range on the multi-meter, disconnect the harness connector at the sensor and connect the test probes to the sensor terminals **(see illustration)**. The resistance reading (ohms) should be high when the sensor is cold, and low when the sensor is hot **(see illustration)**. Be sure the tips of the probe make clean contact with the terminals inside the sensor to insure an accurate reading.
2   After the resistance of the sensor has been checked, test the system for the proper reference voltage from the computer. Simply disconnect the harness connector at the sensor, select the voltage range on the multi-meter and probe the terminals on the harness for the voltage signal. Reference voltage should be approximately 5.0 volts. The ignition switch must be in the ON position (engine not running). If there is no reference voltage available to the sensor, then the circuit and the computer must be checked.

Potentiometers (three-wire) sensors (TPS, EGR valve position sensor)

Refer to illustration 4.3
3   The potentiometer is a variable resistor that converts the voltage signal by varying the resistance according to the driving situation. The signal the potentiometer generates is used by the computer to determine position and direction of the device within the component. Although it is possible to measure resistance changes of the sensor, it is best to measure voltage changes as the end result of the potentiometer's performance. Select the DC volts function on the multi-meter, carefully backprobe the harness connector using straight pins inserted into the correct terminals and connect the meter probes to the pins. Connect the negative probe (-) to the ground

terminal and the positive probe to the SIGNAL terminal. It will be necessary to refer to the wiring diagrams at the end of this manual for the correct terminals. Observe the meter as the signal arm is moved through its complete range (sweep). The voltage should vary as the arm is moved through its range. These sensors are often used as the throttle position sensor or the EGR valve position sensor. Most of these type sensors will vary from as little as 0.2 volts, up to 5.0 volts (closed to open).
4   After the SIGNAL voltage has been checked, test the system for the proper reference voltage from the computer. Simply disconnect the harness connector at the sensor, select the voltage range on the rotary switch on the volt/ohmmeter and probe the correct terminals on the harness for the voltage signal. Reference voltage should be approximately 5.0 volts. The ignition switch must be in the ON position (engine not running). If there is no reference voltage available to the sensor, then the circuit and the computer must be checked.

Pressure/vacuum (three-wire) sensors (MAP, BARO, vacuum sensors, etc.)

Refer to illustrations 4.5a and 4.5b
5   The pressure/vacuum sensors monitor the intake manifold pressure changes resulting from changes in engine load and speed and converts the information into a voltage output. The PCM uses the sensor to control fuel delivery and ignition timing. The sensor SIGNAL voltage to the PCM varies from below 2.0 volts at idle (high vacuum) to above 4.0 volts with the ignition key ON (engine not running) or wide open throttle (WOT) (low vacuum). These values correspond with the alti-

VOLTAGE RANGE	ALTITUDE
3.8 - 5.5V	Below 1,000
3.6 - 5.3V	1,000 - 2,000
3.5 - 5.1V	2.000 - 3,000
3.3 - 5.0V	3,000 - 4,000
3.2 - 4.8V	4,000 - 5,000
3.0 - 4.6V	5,000 - 6,000
2.9 - 4.5V	6,000 - 7,000
2.8 - 4.3V	7,000 - 8,000
2.6 - 4.2V	8,000 - 9,000
2.5 - 4.0V	9,000 - 10,000 FEET

LOW ALTITUDE = HIGH PRESSURE = HIGH VOLTAGE

24071-6-4.09 HAYNES

4.5a Typical Manifold Absolute Pressure (MAP) sensor altitude (pressure) vs. voltage values

24048-6-4.5b HAYNES

4.5b It will be necessary to run the engine to check for voltage fluctuations in order to create pressure and vacuum changes within the system (pressure/vacuum type sensor shown)

24048-6-4.7 HAYNES

4.7 Connect the probes of the volt meter directly to the VSS and observe AC voltage fluctuations as the drive gear is slowly rotated

tude and pressure changes the vehicle experiences while driving **(see illustration)**. Select the DC volts function on the meter, carefully backprobe the harness connector terminals using straight pins and connect the voltmeter probes to the pins **(see illustration)**. Connect the negative probe (-) to the ground terminal and the positive probe to the SIGNAL terminal. It will be necessary to refer to the manufacturer's schematic or wiring diagram for the correct terminals. Observe the meter as the engine idles and then slowly raise the engine rpm to wide open throttle. The voltage should increase from approximately 0.5 to 1.5 volts (high vacuum) to 5.0 volts (low vacuum). If the engine stalls or runs roughly, it is possible to simulate conditions by attaching a hand-held vacuum pump to the pressure/vacuum sensor to simulate running conditions. Also, be sure the manufacturer specifies the type of pressure/vacuum sensor installed on the vehicle. Some manufacturers equip the fuel injection system with a voltage varying sensor while others use a frequency varying sensor. The latter type must be checked using the frequency (Hz) scale on the meter.

6   If SIGNAL voltage does not exist, test the system for the proper reference voltage from the computer. Simply disconnect the harness connector at the sensor, select the voltage range on the meter and probe the correct terminals on the harness for the voltage signal. Reference voltage should be approximately 5.0 volts. The ignition switch must be in the ON position (engine not running). If there is no reference voltage available to the sensor, then the circuit and the computer must be checked.

Magnetic reluctance (two-wire) sensors (crankshaft, vehicle speed, etc.)

Refer to illustration 4.7

7   Magnetic reluctance type sensors consist of a permanent magnet with a coil wire wound around the assembly. Crankshaft sensors and vehicle speed sensors are common applications of this type sensor. A steel disk

mounted on a gear (crankshaft, input shaft, etc.) has tabs that pass between the pole pieces of the magnet causing a break in the magnetic field when passed near the sensor. This break in the field causes a magnetic flux producing reluctance (resistance) thereby changing the voltage signal. This voltage signal is used to determine crankshaft position, vehicle speed, etc. Because magnetic energy is a free-standing source of energy and does not require battery power to produce voltage, this type of sensor must be checked by observing voltage fluctuations with an AC volt meter. Simply switch the voltmeter to the AC scale and connect the probes to the sensor. On vehicle speed sensors it will be necessary to place the transmission in neutral, then with the help of an assistant, hold one tire still while spinning the other tire (approximately 2 MPH or faster) and, observe the voltage fluctuations. This test can also be performed with the sensor removed from the vehicle, by turning the sensor's drive gear **(see illustration)**. **Note:** *Some vehicle speed sensors don't have a drive gear - this type of sensor will have to be checked in place.* On crankshaft position sensors it will be necessary to have an assistant crank the engine over in short bursts at the ignition key while you observe the voltage fluctuations. The meter should register slight voltage fluctuations that are constant and relatively the same range. These small voltage fluctuations indicate that the magnetic portion of the sensor is producing a magnetic field and "sensing" engine parameters for the computer.

Hall effect (three-wire) sensors (crankshaft, camshaft, etc.)

Refer to illustration 4.9

8   These sensors consist of a single hall effect switch, and a magnet which are separated by an air gap. The hall effect switch completes the ground circuit when a magnetic field is present. As the engine rotates, these

sensors will produce ON OFF signals to the PCM to determine crankshaft and camshaft position and speed. Hall effect crankshaft sensors generally use an interrupter ring located on the back of the crankshaft balancer to disrupt the ground signal from the sensor. Always be sure to check the interrupter ring for damage while diagnosing a faulty crankshaft position sensor. Hall effect camshaft sensors typically use a rotating magnet on the camshaft sprocket or in the sensor housing to complete the hall effect switch ground signal. The PCM uses the sensors to control fuel delivery and ignition timing. The camshaft sensor typically produces only one ON OFF signal per camshaft revolution while the crankshaft sensor produces as many as thirty ON OFF signals per crankshaft revolution depending on the make and manufacturer of the vehicle.

9   To check Hall effect type sensors, select the DC volts function on the multi-meter, carefully backprobe the harness connector terminals using pins and connect the voltmeter probes to the pins **(see illustration)**. Connect the negative probe (-) to the ground connection and the positive probe to the SIGNAL terminal. It will be necessary to refer to the wiring diagrams at the back of this manual for the correct terminals. With the ignition key in the ON position and the engine OFF, rotate the engine crankshaft by hand (one full turn) and observe the voltmeter. If the sensor is operating properly it should trigger ON OFF voltage readings on the voltmeter while the engine is being rotated. Depending on the make and model of the vehicle, there should be 5.0 to 12 volts of signal voltage. **Note:** *When testing camshaft sensors it may be necessary to have an assistant crank the engine over in short bursts at the ignition key (detach the primary (low-voltage) wires from the coil to prevent the engine from starting) while observing the voltmeter. It could take as many as two complete crankshaft revolutions before a camshaft sensor signal is detected.*

10   If SIGNAL voltage does not exist, test the

4.9 Carefully backprobe the GROUND (-) and the SIGNAL (+) terminals using sewing pins to make contact without disconnecting the harness connector (Hall effect type sensor shown)

system for the proper reference voltage from the computer. Simply disconnect the harness connector at the sensor, select the voltage range on the rotary switch on the volt/ohm-meter and probe the correct terminals on the harness for the reference signal. Depending on the make and model of the vehicle there should be 5.0 to 12 volts of reference voltage (5 volts is the most common). The ignition switch must be in the ON position (engine not running). If there is no reference voltage available to the sensor, the circuit and the computer must be checked.

Dual Hall effect (four-wire) sensors (crankshaft)

11   Dual Hall effect sensors consist of two hall-effect switches and a shared magnet mounted between them. The magnet and each Hall-effect switch are separated by an air gap. Each hall effect switch completes the ground circuit when a magnetic field is present. Dual hall effect sensors are often used as a crank-shaft sensor in place of two single hall effect switches described above. Typically the crank-shaft balancer is equipped with two "interrupter rings" (each having a different number of inter-rupter blades) which create two separate ON OFF signal patterns that can be used for the timing and the ignition sequence.

12   To check dual hall effect type sensors, select the DC volts function with the rotary switch, carefully backprobe the harness con-nector terminals using pins and position the voltmeter probes onto the pins **(see illustra-tion 4.9)**. Connect the negative probe (-) to the ground connection and the positive probe to one SIGNAL terminal. It will be neces-sary to refer to the manufacturer's schematic or wiring diagram for the correct terminals. With the ignition key in the ON position and the engine OFF, rotate the engine crankshaft

by hand (one full turn) and observe the volt meter. Next, connect the positive probe to the second SIGNAL terminal. If the sensor is operating properly it should trigger ON OFF voltage readings on the voltmeter from both SIGNAL terminals while the engine is being rotated. Depending on the make and model of the vehicle, there should be 5 to 12 volts of signal voltage at each terminal.

13   If SIGNAL voltage does not exist, test the system for the proper reference voltage from the computer. Simply disconnect the harness connector at the sensor, select the voltage range on the rotary switch on the volt/ohm-meter and probe the correct terminals on the harness for the reference signal. Depending on the make and model of the vehicle there should be 5.0 to 12 volts of reference voltage (5 volts is the most common). The ignition switch must be in the ON position (engine not running). If there is no reference voltage available to the sensor, the circuit and the com-puter must be checked.

Oxygen (O2) sensors

14   The oxygen sensor(s) monitors the oxy-gen content of the exhaust gas stream. The oxygen content in the exhaust reacts with the oxygen sensor to produce a voltage output which varies from 0.1-volt (high oxygen, lean mixture) to 0.9-volts (low oxygen, rich mix-ture). The PCM constantly monitors this vari-able voltage output to determine the ratio of oxygen to fuel in the mixture. The PCM alters the air/fuel mixture ratio by controlling the pulse width (open time) of the fuel injectors. The PCM and the oxygen sensor(s) attempt to maintain a mixture ratio of 14.7 parts air to 1 part ratio of fuel at all times. The oxygen sensor produces no voltage when it is below its normal operating temperature of about 600-degrees F. During this initial period before warm-up, the PCM operates in OPEN LOOP mode. When checking the oxygen sensor system, it will be necessary to test all oxygen sensors. **Note:** *Because the oxygen sensor(s) are difficult to access, probing the harness electrical connectors for testing purposes will require patience. The exhaust manifolds and pipes are extremely hot and will melt stray electrical probes and leads that touch the sur-face during testing. If possible, use a SCAN tool that plugs into the DLC (diagnostic link). This tool will access the PCM data stream and indicates the millivolt changes for each individual oxygen sensor.*

15   Check the oxygen sensor millivolt signal. Locate the oxygen sensor electrical connector and carefully backprobe it using a long pin(s) into the appropriate wire terminals. In most models, connect the positive probe (+) of a voltmeter onto the SIGNAL wire and the nega-tive probe (-) to the ground wire. Consult the wiring diagrams at the end of Chapter 12 for additional information on the oxygen sensor electrical connector wire color designations. **Note:** *Downstream oxygen sensors will pro-duce much slower fluctuating voltage values to reflect the results of the catalyzed exhaust mixture from rich or lean to less presence of*

CO, HC and Nox molecules. Here the CO_2 and H_2O gaseous forms do not register or react with the oxygen sensors to such a large degree. Monitor the SIGNAL voltage (milli-volts) as the engine goes from cold to warm.

16   The oxygen sensor will produce a steady voltage signal of approximately 0.1 to 0.2 volts (100 to 200 millivolts) with the engine cold (open loop). After a period of approximately two minutes, the engine will reach operating temperature and the oxygen sensor will start to fluctuate between 0.1 to 0.9 volts (100 to 900 millivolts) (closed loop). If the oxygen sensor fails to reach the closed loop mode or there is a very long period of time until it does switch into closed loop mode, replace the oxygen sensor with a new part. **Note:** *Downstream oxygen sensors will not change voltage values as quickly as upstream oxy-gen sensors. Because the downstream oxy-gen sensors detect oxygen content after the exhaust has been catalyzed, voltage values should fluctuate much slower and deliberate.*

17   Also inspect the oxygen sensor heater. Disconnect the oxygen sensor electrical con-nector and working on the oxygen sensor side, connect an ohmmeter between the black wire (-) and brown wire (+). It should measure approximately 5 to 7 ohms. **Note:** *The wire colors often change from the harness con-nector to the oxygen sensor connector wires according to manufacturer's specifications. Follow the wire colors to the oxygen sensor electrical connector and determine the match-ing wires and their colors before testing the heater resistance.*

18   Check for proper supply voltage to the heater. Disconnect the oxygen sensor electri-cal connector and working on the engine side of the harness, measure the voltage between the black wire (-) and brown wire (+) on the oxygen sensor electrical connector. There should be battery voltage with the ignition key ON (engine not running). If there is no volt-age, check the circuit between the main relay, the fuse and the sensor. **Note:** *It is important to remember that supply voltage will only reach the O_2 sensor with the ignition key ON (engine not running).*

19   If the oxygen sensor fails any of these tests, replace it with a new part.

Mass Air Flow (MAF) sensors

20   The MAF sensor measures the amount of air passing through the sensor body and ulti-mately entering the engine through the throttle body. The PCM uses this information to control fuel delivery - the more air entering the engine (acceleration), the more fuel needed.

21   A SCAN tool is necessary to check the output of the MAF sensor. The SCAN tool dis-plays the sensor output in grams per second. With the engine idling at normal operating temperature, the display should read 4 to 7 grams per second. When the engine is accel-erated the values should raise and remain steady at any given RPM. A failure in the MAF sensor or circuit will also set a diagnostic trou-ble code.

5.2 To prevent coolant leakage, be sure to wrap the temperature sensor threads with Teflon tape before installation

5.3 A typical engine coolant temperature sensor (1) - electrical connector (2) has a locking tab (3) that must be released to unplug the connector

Knock sensors

22   Knock sensors detect abnormal vibration in the engine. The knock control system is designed to reduce spark knock during periods of heavy detonation. This allows the engine to use maximum spark advance to improve driveability. Knock sensors produce AC output voltage which increases with the severity of the knock. The signal is fed into the PCM and the timing is retarded to compensate for the severe detonation.

23   To check a knock sensor, disconnect the electrical connector and drain the engine coolant as described in Chapter 1. Remove the sensor from the engine block, then reconnect the wiring harness to it. **Note:** *Most knock sensors have a 1/4-inch pipe thread, use a pipe plug of the same size to thread into the engine block as the sensor is removed. This will relieve the task of draining the coolant with minimal coolant loss.* These type of sensors must be checked by observing voltage fluctuations with a voltmeter. Simply switch the voltmeter to the lowest voltage scale and connect the negative probe (-) to the sensor body (ground) and the positive probe to the sensor terminal. With the voltmeter connected to the sensor, gently tap on the bottom of the knock sensor with a hammer or similar device (this simulates the knock from the engine) and observe voltage fluctuations on the meter. If no voltage fluctuations can be detected, the sensor is bad and should be replaced with a new part.

Neutral Start switch

24   The Neutral Start switch or Transaxle range sensor, located on the rear upper part of the automatic transaxle, indicates to the PCM when the transaxle is in Park or Neutral. This information is used for Transaxle Converter Clutch (TCC), Exhaust Gas Recirculation (EGR) and Idle Air Control (IAC) valve operation. **Caution:** *The vehicle should not be driven with the Neutral Start switch disconnected because idle quality will be adversely affected.*

25   For more information regarding the Neu-

tral Start switch, which is part of the Neutral start and back-up light switch assembly, see Chapter 7.

Air conditioning control

26   During air conditioning operation, the PCM controls the application of the air conditioning compressor clutch. The PCM controls the air conditioning clutch control relay to delay clutch engagement after the air conditioning is turned ON to allow the IAC valve to adjust the idle speed of the engine to compensate for the additional load. The PCM also controls the relay to disengage the clutch on WOT (wide open throttle) to prevent excessively high rpm on the compressor. Be sure to check the air conditioning system as detailed in Chapter 3 before attempting to diagnose the air conditioning clutch or electrical system.

Power steering pressure sensor

27   Turning the steering wheel increases power steering fluid pressure and engine load. The pressure switch will close before the load can cause an idle problem. A pressure switch that will not open or an open circuit from the PCM will cause timing to retard at idle and this will affect idle quality. A pressure switch that will not close or an open circuit may cause the engine to die when the power steering system is used heavily. Any problems with the power steering pressure switch or circuit should be repaired by a dealer service department or other qualified repair shop.

Fuel Tank Pressure (FTP) sensor

28   The fuel tank pressure (FTP) sensor is used to monitor the fuel tank pressure or vacuum during the OBD II test portion for emissions integrity. This test scans various sensors and output actuators to detect abnormal amounts of fuel vapors that may not be purging into the canister and/or the intake system for recycling. The FTP sensor helps the PCM monitor this pressure differential (pressure vs. vacuum) inside the fuel tank. Any problems

with the fuel tank pressure (FTP) sensor or circuit should be repaired by a dealer service department or other qualified repair shop.

Transaxle Converter Clutch (TCC) system

29   The purpose of the Torque Converter Clutch (TCC) system, equipped in automatic transaxles, is to eliminate the power loss of the torque converter stage when the vehicle is in the cruising mode (usually above 35 mph). This economizes the automatic transaxle to the fuel economy of the manual transaxle. The lock-up mode is controlled by the PCM through the activation of the TCC apply solenoid which is built into the automatic transaxle. When the vehicle reaches a specified speed, the PCM energizes the solenoid and allows the torque converter to lock-up and mechanically couple the engine to the transaxle, under which conditions emissions are at their minimum. However, because of other operating condition demands (deceleration, passing, idle, etc.), the transaxle must also function in its normal, fluid-coupled mode. When such latter conditions exist, the solenoid de-energizes, returning the torque converter to normal operation. The converter also returns to normal operation whenever the brake pedal is depressed.

30   Due to the requirement of special diagnostic equipment for the testing of this system, and the possible requirement for dismantling of the automatic transaxle to replace components of this system, checking and replacing of the components should be handled by a dealer service department or other qualified repair facility.

5   Information sensors - replacement

Engine Coolant Temperature (ECT) sensor

Refer to illustrations 5.2 and 5.3

Warning: *Wait until the engine is completely cool before beginning this procedure.*

1   The coolant temperature sensor is typically located in the thermostat housing or near the thermostat. On the 3.4L engine it is located on the lower intake manifold at the rear of the right cylinder head (facing the firewall). The coolant temperature sensor is a thermistor (a resistor which varies the value of its resistance in accordance with temperature changes). Refer to Section 4 for the checking procedures.

2   Before installing the new sensor, wrap the threads with Teflon sealing tape to prevent leakage and thread corrosion **(see illustration)**.

3   To remove the sensor, release the locking tab, unplug the electrical connector **(see illustration)**, then carefully unscrew the sensor. **Caution:** *Handle the coolant sensor with care. Damage to this sensor will affect the operation of the entire fuel injection system.*

5.7 Typical Mass Air Flow (MAF) sensor installation (arrow)

5.8 On the 1995 and later 3800 engines, remove the screws (arrows) securing the MAF sensor to the throttle body

5.10 Typical MAP sensor mounting details

1   MAP sensor assembly
2   Mounting screws
3   Vacuum line
4   Electrical connector

4   Installation is the reverse of removal. Check the coolant level and add some, if necessary (see Chapter 1).

Mass Airflow (MAF) sensor

Refer to illustrations 5.7 and 5.8

5   The Mass Airflow Sensor (MAF) is typically located in the air intake duct between the throttle body and the air cleaner housing. On 1995 and later 3800 engines the MAF sensor is located on the throttle body. The MAF sensor is a hot-wire type sensor and is used to measure the amount of air entering the engine. Refer to Section 4 for the checking procedures. **Note** : *Not all engines are equipped with a MAF sensor, engines not equipped with a MAF sensor will be equipped with a MAP sensor.*

6   Disconnect the electrical connector from the MAF sensor.

7   Loosen the clamps securing the MAF sensor to the air intake duct and remove the sensor from the vehicle **(see illustration)**.

8   On 1995 and later 3800 engines, remove the screws and lift the MAF sensor from the throttle body **(see illustration)**.

9   Installation is the reverse of removal.

Manifold Absolute Pressure (MAP) sensor

Refer to illustrations 5.10 and 5.13

10   The Manifold Absolute Pressure (MAP) sensor is typically mounted to the upper intake manifold or to the firewall **(see illustration)**. On the 1995 and later 3800 engines it is located at the front of the engine underneath the fuel injector (acoustic) trim cover. On 5.3L engines it is mounted at the downstream end of the throttle body. This sensor is a pressure/vacuum type sensor which monitors the intake manifold pressure changes resulting from changes in engine load and speed. Refer to Section 4 for the checking procedures.

11   To replace the sensor, detach the vacuum hose, unplug the electrical connector and remove the mounting screws.

12   To replace the sensor on 3.4L models, unplug the electrical connector and remove the sensor retaining bracket and bolt. Then pull straight up to remove it.

13   To replace the sensor on 1995 and later 3800 engines, unplug the electrical connector and detach the retaining clips to remove it **(see illustration)**.

14   Installation is the reverse of removal.

Intake Air Temperature (IAT) sensor

Refer to illustrations 5.15a and 5.15b

15   The Intake Air Temperature (IAT) sensor is located inside the air duct directly downstream of the air filter housing or in the air cleaner housing **(see illustrations)**. On earlier models this sensor is also referred to as a Manifold Air Temperature (MAT) sensor. The IAT or MAT sensor is a thermistor (a resistor which varies the value of its resistance in accordance with temperature changes). Refer to Section 4 for the checking procedures.

16   To remove an IAT or MAT sensor, unplug the electrical connector and remove the sensor from the air intake duct or the air cleaner housing. On sensors located in the air intake duct carefully twist the sensor to release it from the rubber boot. Sensors mounted to the air cleaner housing will require a wrench to unscrew them.

17   Installation is the reverse of removal.

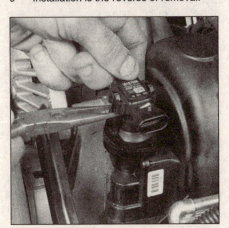

5.13 On 1995 and later 3800 engines, squeeze the clips and disengage the MAP sensor from the PCV valve housing

5.15a On some models the Intake Air Temperature (IAT) sensor (arrow) is mounted in the air intake duct

5.15b On other models the Intake Air Temperature (IAT) sensor (arrow) is mounted in the air cleaner housing

5.18a The oxygen sensor (arrow) is located in the exhaust manifold

5.18b Location of the downstream oxygen sensor – OBD II engine control systems

5.23 Use a special slotted socket to remove the oxygen sensor from the exhaust manifold or exhaust pipe

Oxygen sensor(s)

Refer to illustrations 5.18a, 5.18b and 5.23

Note: *Because it is installed in the exhaust manifold or pipe, which contracts when cool, the oxygen sensor may be very difficult to loosen when the engine is cold. Rather than risk damage to the sensor (assuming you are planning to reuse it in another manifold or pipe) or the threads, which it screws into, start and run the engine for a minute or two, then shut it off. Be careful not to burn yourself during the following procedure.*

18   Vehicles equipped with OBD-I engine control systems have a single heated oxygen sensor located in the exhaust manifold. Vehicles equipped with OBD-II engine control systems have an upstream O2 sensor (before the catalytic converter in the rear exhaust manifold) and a downstream O2 sensor (after the catalytic converter) **(see illustration)**. The oxygen sensor(s) monitors the oxygen content of the exhaust gas stream. Oxygen content in the exhaust reacts with the oxygen sensor to produce a voltage output which allows the PCM to change the air fuel ratio in the engine. Refer to Section 4 for the checking procedures.

19   The following is a list of special precautions which must be taken whenever the sensor is serviced.

a) *The oxygen sensor has a permanently attached pigtail and electrical connector which should not be removed from the sensor. Damage or removal of the pigtail or electrical connector can adversely affect operation of the sensor.*

b) *Grease, dirt and other contaminants should be kept away from the electrical connector and the louvered end of the sensor.*

c) *Do not use cleaning solvents of any kind on the oxygen sensor.*

d) *Do not drop or roughly handle the sensor.*

e) *The silicone boot must be installed in the correct position to prevent the boot from being melted and to allow the sensor to operate properly.*

f) *The sensor is designed to allow air circulation to the internal portion of the sensor. Whenever the sensor is removed and installed or replaced, make sure the air passages are not restricted.*

20   Disconnect the cable from the negative terminal of the battery. **Caution:** *On models equipped with a Theftlock audio system, be sure the lockout feature is turned off before disconnecting the battery cable.*

21   Raise the vehicle and place it securely on jackstands.

22   Remove any exhaust heat shields which would interfere with the removal of the oxygen sensor(s), then disconnect the electrical connector from the sensor.

23   Carefully unscrew the sensor from the exhaust manifold or the exhaust pipe **(see illustration)**.

24   Anti-seize compound must be used on the threads of the sensor to facilitate future removal. The threads of new sensors will already be coated with this compound, but if an old sensor is removed and reinstalled, re-coat the threads.

25   Install the sensor and tighten it securely.

26   Reconnect the electrical connector of the pigtail lead to the main engine wiring harness.

27   Lower the vehicle, take it on a test drive and check to see that no trouble codes set.

Throttle Position Sensor (TPS)

28   The Throttle Position Sensor (TPS) is located on the end of the throttle shaft on the throttle body regardless of whether the engine is equipped with a Throttle Body Injection (TBI), Port Fuel Injection (PFI) or a Sequential Fuel Injection (SFI) system. The TPS is a potentiometer type sensor and is used to measure the throttle valve position and angle. Refer to Section 4 of this Chapter for the checking procedures of the TPS or to Chapter 4 for the removal and installation procedures of the TPS.

Crankshaft position sensor(s)

Refer to illustrations 5.29 and 5.30

29   2.2L, 2.3L (Quad-4) and 2.5L four cylinder engines and 2.8L, 3.1L and 1993 and

5.29 3X or 7X crankshaft position sensors (arrow) receive pulses from a magnet on the crankshaft and are mounted to the side of the engine block - do not confuse the CKP sensor with a knock sensor which is threaded into a coolant passage

earlier 3.4L V6 engines are equipped with a single 3X or 7X crankshaft position sensor (CKP) which is mounted on the side of the engine block **(see illustration)**. 3X and 7X sensors are hall effect type sensors that produce 7 ON/OFF signals per crankshaft revolution. This sensor monitors crankshaft position and speed for the Ignition control module which then in turn sends a signal to the PCM to control the ignition and fuel systems. Refer to Section 4 for the checking procedures.

30   3100 and 1994 and later 3.4L V6 engines are equipped with two crankshaft position sensor(s), the first crankshaft sensor (24X sensor) is mounted at the front of the engine behind the crankshaft balancer **(see illustration)**. The 24X sensor is a hall effect type sensor that produces 24 ON/OFF signals per crankshaft revolution. This sensor monitors crankshaft position and speed to improve idle spark control below 1250 RPM. The second crankshaft sensor on 3100 and 1994 and later 3.4L engines (3X sensor on 1995 models or a 7X sensor on 1996 and later models) is mounted on the side of the engine block **(see illustration 5.29)**. 3X and 7X sensors are hall effect type sensors that

5.30 24X and dual hall effect crankshaft sensors (arrow) are mounted at the front of the engine behind the crankshaft balancer (3800 engine shown)

5.42a On 3100 engines, follow the cam sensor wiring harness (arrows) to locate the cam sensor

5.42b On the 3800 engine, the camshaft sensor (arrow) is located on the front cover (view from below)

5.47a Typical Vehicle Speed Sensor (VSS) found on 3T40 transaxles - the speed sensor is located at the rear of the transaxle housing near the right driveaxle

5.47b Typical Vehicle Speed Sensor (VSS) found on 4T60-E and 4T65-E transaxle

produce 7 ON/OFF signals per crankshaft revolution and are the same sensors used on four cylinder engines and earlier V6 engines. This sensor monitors crankshaft position and speed for the Ignition control module which then in turn sends a signal to the PCM to control the ignition and fuel systems. Refer to Section 4 for the checking procedures

31   3800 models are equipped with a dual (18X and 3X) crankshaft position sensor which is mounted at the front of the engine behind the crankshaft balancer **(see illustration 5.30)**. This sensor is a dual hall effect type sensor that can produce two signal patterns (outputs) at the same time. The 18X portion of the switch will produce 18 ON/OFF signals per crankshaft revolution while the 3X portion of the switch will produce 3 ON/OFF signals per crankshaft revolution. Refer to Section 4 for the checking procedures.

24X and dual hall effect sensor replacement

32   Disconnect the negative terminal from the battery. **Caution:** *On models equipped with a Theftlock audio system, be sure the lockout feature is turned off before disconnecting the battery cable.*
33   Disconnect the electrical connector from the crankshaft sensor.
34   Remove the crankshaft balancer (see Chapter 2).
35   On 3800 models, carefully pry off the sensor cover. On 3100 and 3.4L models, remove the connector retaining bracket.
36   Remove the bolts securing the sensor to the front cover **(see illustration 5.30)**.
37   Installation is the reverse of removal. Tighten the bolts to the torque listed in this Chapter's Specifications.

3X and 7X sensor replacement

38   Disconnect the negative terminal from the battery. **Caution:** *On models equipped with a Theftlock audio system, be sure the lockout feature is turned off before disconnecting the battery cable.*
39   Disconnect the electrical connector from

the crankshaft sensor.
40   Remove the bolt from the crankshaft sensor and remove the sensor from the side of the engine block **(see illustration 5.29)**. **Note:** *On 2.5L four cylinder engines, remove the ignition coil and module assembly from the side of the engine block then detach the crankshaft sensor from the bottom of the ignition module assembly.*
41   Installation is the reverse of removal. Tighten the bolts to the torque listed in this Chapter's Specifications.

Camshaft position sensor

Refer to illustration 5.42a and 5.42b
42   The camshaft sensor on 3100 models is mounted at the front of the engine block in between the cylinder heads **(see illustration)**. The camshaft sensor on 3.4L models is mounted to the top of the left cylinder head at the rear of the engine. The camshaft sensor on 3800 models is mounted in the front cover of the engine above the crankshaft sensor **(see illustration)**. On 5.3L engines it is mounted on the end of the engine facing the right fender. The camshaft sensor is a hall effect type sensor

which produces 1 ON/OFF signal for every two crankshaft revolutions. This signal tells the PCM that the No. 1 piston is on the intake stroke. Refer to Section 4 for the checking procedures.
43   Disconnect the negative terminal from the battery. **Caution:** *On models equipped with a Theftlock audio system, be sure the lockout feature is turned off before disconnecting the battery cable.*
44   Disconnect the electrical connector from the camshaft sensor. **Note:** *On 3100 models it may be necessary remove the power steering pump to allow access to the camshaft sensor.*
45   Remove the bolt from the camshaft sensor and remove the sensor.
46   Installation is the reverse of removal. Tighten the bolts to the torque listed in this Chapter's Specifications.

Vehicle Speed Sensor (VSS)

Refer to illustrations 5.47a and 5.47b
47   The Vehicle Speed Sensor (VSS) is located at the rear the transaxle housing near the right drive axle **(see illustrations)**. This sensor is a magnetic reluctance type sensor which sends a pulsing voltage signal to the PCM, which the PCM converts to miles per hour. The VSS is a major component in the

5.50 The Park/Neutral switch is located on the upper rear part of the automatic transaxle - arrows are pointing to mounting bolts

7.3 The Electronic Spark Control (ESC) knock sensor (arrow) is located on the engine block

Transaxle Converter Clutch (TCC) system. Refer to Section 4 for the checking procedures.

48   To replace the VSS, detach the sensor retaining bolt(s) and or bracket, unplug the sensor and remove it from the transaxle.

49   Installation is the reverse of removal.

Park/Neutral switch

Refer to illustration 5.50

50   The Park/Neutral (P/N) switch, located on the upper rear part of the automatic transaxle **(see illustration)**, indicates to the PCM when the transaxle is in Park or Neutral. This information is used for Torque Converter Clutch (TCC), Exhaust Gas Recirculation (EGR) and Idle Air Control (IAC) valve operation. **Caution:** *The vehicle should not be driven with the Park/Neutral switch disconnected because idle quality will be adversely affected and a trouble code may be set.*

51   For more information regarding the P/N switch, which is part of the Neutral/start and back-up light switch assembly, see Chapter 7 Part B.

Power Steering Pressure Switch

52   This sensor located in the steering gear tells the PCM when the pressure in the steering hydraulic system exceeds a certain pressure. If the engine is at idle the air conditioner will be shut off and the idle speed will increase. To replace this sensor, disconnect the electrical connector and unscrew the sensor from the steering gear.

6   Electronic Spark Timing (EST)

1   To provide improved engine performance, fuel economy and control of exhaust emissions, the Electronic Control Module (ECM) controls spark advance (ignition timing) with the Electronic Spark Timing (EST) system.

2   The PCM receives a reference pulse from

the crankshaft sensor **(see illustrations 5.29 and 5.30),** and/or cam sensor (if equipped) which indicate engine rpm, crankshaft position and/or camshaft position. The PCM then determines the proper spark advance for the engine operating conditions and sends an EST pulse to the ignition module. A fault in the EST system will usually set a trouble code.

7   Electronic Spark Control (ESC) system

Refer to illustration 7.3

General description

1   Irregular octane levels in modern gasoline can cause detonation in an engine. Detonation is sometimes referred to as "spark knock."

2   The Electronic Spark Control (ESC) system is designed to retard spark timing up to 15-degrees to reduce spark knock in the engine. This allows the engine to use maximum spark advance to improve driveability and fuel economy.

3   The ESC knock sensor, which is located on the engine block **(see illustration)**, creates and sends an alternating current voltage signal to the PCM. The PCM then retards the timing until spark knock is eliminated.

4   Loss of the ESC signal to the PCM will cause the PCM to constantly retard EST. This will result in sluggish performance and cause the PCM to set a trouble code.

Knock sensor replacement

5   Detach the cable from the negative terminal of the battery. **Caution:** *On models equipped with the Theftlock audio system, be sure the lockout feature is turned off before performing any procedure which requires disconnecting the battery.*

6   Disconnect the electrical connector from the knock sensor. On later-model 3800 engines, remove the heat shield over the sensor first.

7   Unscrew the sensor from the block.

8   Installation is the reverse of the removal procedure.

8   Exhaust Gas Recirculation (EGR) system

General description

1   The Exhaust Gas Recirculation (EGR) system is used to lower NOx (oxides of nitrogen) emission levels caused by high combustion temperatures. It does this by decreasing combustion temperature. The main element of the system is the EGR valve, which feeds small amounts of exhaust gas back into the combustion chamber.

2   The EGR valve is usually open during warm engine operation and anytime the engine is running above idle speed. The amount of gas recirculated is controlled by variations in vacuum and exhaust backpressure.

3   There are three types of EGR valves. Their names refer to the means by which they are controlled:

     Digital/Linear EGR valve *(Quad-4 and 1990 and later non-turbo V6 engines)*
     Negative backpressure EGR valve *(2.2L and 2.5L engines)*
     Integrated electronic EGR valve *(turbo V6 engine)*

Digital/Linear EGR valve

4   The digital EGR valve feeds small amounts of exhaust gas back into the intake manifold and then into the combustion chamber.

5   The digital EGR valve is designed to accurately supply recirculated exhaust gas to an engine, independent of intake manifold vacuum. The valve controls EGR flow from the exhaust to the intake manifold through multiple orifices to produce various combinations of EGR flow. (The exact number of orifices and combinations of EGR flow depends on the year and model of the car.) When a solenoid is energized, the armature, with attached shaft and swivel pintle, is lifted, opening the orifice. The flow accuracy is dependent on metering orifice size only, which results in improved control.

6   The digital EGR valve is opened by the PCM, grounding each solenoid circuit. This activates the solenoid, raises the pintle, and allows exhaust gas flow into the intake manifold. The exhaust gas then moves with the air/fuel mixture into the combustion chamber.

Negative backpressure EGR valve

7   On the negative backpressure EGR valve, the diaphragm on this valve has an internal vacuum bleed hole which is held closed by a small spring when there is no exhaust backpressure. Engine vacuum opens the EGR valve against the pressure of a large spring. When manifold vacuum combines with negative exhaust backpressure, the vacuum bleed hole opens and the EGR valve closes.

8.12 To check for proper circulation of recirculated exhaust gas, warm up the engine and, using a rag to protect your fingers, push up on the diaphragm - the engine should stumble or stall

8.23a The EGR valve (arrow) on the Quad-4 engine is near the firewall

8.23b EGR valve mounting bolt locations (arrows) (negative backpressure type)

Integrated electronic EGR valve

8   The integrated electronic EGR valve functions like a port valve with a remote vacuum regulator, except the regulator and a pintle position sensor are sealed in the black plastic cover. The regulator and the position sensor are not serviceable.

9   This valve has a vacuum regulator, to which the PCM provides variable current. This variable current produces the desired EGR flow using inputs from the MAT sensor (MAF sensor on 1988 models), coolant temperature sensor and engine rpm.

Checking

Refer to illustration 8.12

Negative backpressure EGR valves

10   Hold the top of the EGR valve and try to rotate it back-and-forth. If play is felt, replace the valve.

11   If no play is felt, place the transaxle in Neutral (manual) or Park (automatic), run the engine at idle until it warms up to at least 195-degrees F.

12   Using a rag to protect your hand from

the engine heat, push up on the underside of the EGR valve diaphragm (see illustration). If the rpm drops, go to step 14.

13   If there's no change in rpm, clean the EGR passages and repeat step 12. If there's still no change in rpm, replace the valve.

14   If the rpm drops is step 12, check for movement of the EGR valve diaphragm as the rpm is changed from approximately 2000 rpm to idle. If the diaphragm moves, there is no problem.

15   If the diaphragm doesn't move, check the vacuum signal at the EGR valve as the engine rpm is changed from approximately 2000 rpm to idle.

16   If the vacuum is over six inches, replace the EGR valve. If it's under six inches, check the vacuum hoses for restrictions, leaks and poor connections.

Integrated electronic EGR valves

17   With the ignition off, connect a vacuum pump to the valve - apply vacuum and the valve should not move. Repeat the test with the ignition switch On. The valve should not move.

18   Ground the diagnostic terminal (see Section 2) and repeat the test. The valve should move and should be able to hold vacuum.

19   Start the engine and lift the EGR dia-

phragm using a rag to protect your fingers. The idle should roughen (see illustration 8.12).

20   Due to the complexity and the interrelationship with ECM/PCM, any further checks should be left to a dealer service department.

Digital/Linear EGR valves

21   A special "scan" tool is needed to check this valve and should be left to a dealer service department.

Component replacement

Refer to illustrations 8.23a, 8.23b, 8.23c, 8.23d and 8.24

EGR valve

22   Disconnect the vacuum hose (if equipped) from the EGR valve and disconnect the electrical connector (if equipped).

23   Remove the nuts or bolts which secure the valve to the intake manifold or adapter (see illustrations).

24   On V6 engines so equipped, disconnect the EGR pipe from the exhaust manifold (see illustration).

25   On all engines, separate the EGR valve from the engine.

8.23c EGR valve-to-intake manifold mounting nut locations (arrows) (1995 and earlier V6 engines with digital EGR)

8.23d Disconnect the electrical connector (A) and remove the valve mounting bolts (B) (linear type EGR)

8.24 On V6 engines, disconnect the EGR pipe at the exhaust manifold

9.2 Typical evaporative canister on a 1989 3.1L engine

9.4 Canister purge control valve (arrow)

9.12 Remove the access cover in the left rear wheelwell to get at the canister

EGR valve cleaning

26   Inspect the valve pintle for deposits.

27   Depress the valve diaphragm and check for deposits around the valve seat area.

28   Use a wire brush to carefully clean deposits from the pintle.

29   Remove any deposits from the valve outlet with a screwdriver.

30   If EGR passages in the intake manifold have an excessive build-up of deposits, the passages should be cleaned. Care should be taken to ensure that all loose particles are completely removed to prevent them from clogging the EGR valve or from being ingested into the engine. **Note:** *It's a good idea to place a rag in the passage opening to keep debris from entering while cleaning the manifold.*

31   Using a wire wheel, buff the exhaust deposits off the mounting surface.

32   Clean the mounting surfaces of the EGR valve. Remove all traces of old gasket material.

33   Install the new EGR valve, with a new gasket, on the intake manifold or adapter.

34   Installation is the reverse of removal.

9   Evaporative Emission Control System (EECS or EVAP)

Refer to illustrations 9.2, 9.4 and 9.12

General description

1   This system is designed to trap and store fuel vapors that evaporate from the fuel tank, throttle body and intake manifold.

2   The Evaporative Emission Control System (EECS or EVAP) consists of a charcoal-filled canister and the lines connecting the canister to the fuel tank and ported vacuum **(see illustration)**. On 1995 through 1999 models, the EVAP canister is mounted in the left-rear fenderwell. Access is by removing the fenderwell liner. On 2000 and later models, the canister is mounted on top of the fuel tank. Access on these models is achieved only by

lowering the fuel tank (see Chapter 4).

3   Fuel vapors are transferred from the fuel tank, throttle body and intake manifold to a canister where they're stored when the engine isn't running. When the engine is running, the fuel vapors are purged from the canister by intake air flow and consumed in the normal combustion process.

4   On all engines except the 2.2L and 2.5L, the ECM/PCM operates a solenoid valve which controls vacuum to the charcoal canister. Under cold engine or idle conditions, the solenoid is turned on by the PCM, which closes the valve and blocks vacuum to the canister. The PCM turns off the solenoid valve and allows purge when the engine is warm **(see illustration)**. On 3.1L engines, the purge valve solenoid is near the junction of the intake plenum and throttle body. On 3.8L engines, it is near the coil-pack at the front side of the engine.

5   On 2.2L and 2.5L engines, the purging of the canister is controlled by a purge valve located in the engine compartment in-line between the canister and the intake manifold (2.2L), or, in the case of the 2.5L, on the canister. The purge valve is opened by vacuum when the engine speed is above idle.

Checking

6   Poor idle, stalling and poor driveability can be caused by an inoperative purge valve, a damaged canister, split or cracked hoses or hoses connected to the wrong tubes.

7   Evidence of fuel loss or fuel odor can be caused by liquid fuel leaking from fuel lines or the TBI, a cracked or damaged canister, an inoperative purge valve, disconnected, misrouted, kinked, deteriorated or damaged vapor or control hoses or an improperly seated air cleaner or air cleaner gasket.

8   Inspect each hose attached to the canister for kinks, leaks and cracks along its entire length. Repair or replace as necessary.

9   Inspect the canister. If it's cracked or damaged, replace it.

10   Look for fuel leaking from the bottom of the canister. If fuel is leaking, replace the can-

ister and check the hoses and hose routing.

11   Any further testing should be left to a dealer service department.

Component replacement

Canister

12   Remove the access cover at the left rear wheel **(see illustration)**.

13   Clearly label, then detach the vacuum hoses from the canister.

14   Remove the canister.

15   Installation is the reverse of removal.

Purge valve

16   Label and disconnect the vacuum hoses from the valve.

17   If necessary, disconnect the electrical connector.

18   Unscrew the mounting bolts and remove the valve.

19   Installation is the reverse of removal.

10   Positive Crankcase Ventilation (PCV) system

General description

All models except Quad-4 engine

1   The Positive Crankcase Ventilation (PCV) system reduces hydrocarbon emissions by scavenging crankcase vapors. It does this by circulating fresh air from the air cleaner through the crankcase, where it mixes with blow-by gases and is then rerouted through a PCV valve to the intake manifold.

2   The main components of the PCV system are the PCV valve, a fresh air filtered inlet and the vacuum hoses connecting these two components with the engine.

3   To maintain idle quality, the PCV valve restricts the flow when the intake manifold vacuum is high. If abnormal operating conditions arise, the system is designed to allow excessive amounts of blow-by gases to flow back through the crankcase vent tube into the air cleaner to be consumed by normal combustion.

10.5 Typical engine oil/air separator (arrow)

12.14 Remove the AIR pump pulley bolts and separate the pulley from the pump

4   Checking and replacement of the PCV valve and filter is covered in Chapter 1.

Quad-4 engine only

Refer to illustration 10.5

5   The Quad-4 engine uses a Crankcase Ventilation (CV) system to provide scavenging of crankcase vapors. Blow-by gases are passed through a crankcase ventilation oil/air separator into the intake manifold **(see illustration)**.

6   The oil/air separator causes oil, which may be suspended in the blow-by gases, to be separated and allows it to drain back to the crankcase through a hose.

7   If the CV system becomes plugged, it must be replaced as a unit.

Oil/air separator replacement (Quad-4 engine only)

8   Label and remove all hoses from the oil/air separator.

9   Remove the mounting bolts and lift it from the vehicle.

10   Installation is the reverse of removal.

---

11   Catalytic converter

General description

1   The catalytic converter is an emission control device added to the exhaust system to reduce pollutants from the exhaust gas stream. The converter contains a honeycomb mesh.

Checking

2   The test equipment for a catalytic converter is expensive and highly sophisticated. If you suspect the converter is malfunctioning, take it to a dealer service department or authorized emissions inspection facility for diagnosis and repair.

3   Whenever the vehicle is raised for servicing of underbody components, check the converter for leaks, corrosion and other damage. If damage is discovered, the converter should be replaced.

Removal and installation

4   On some models the converter is welded to the exhaust system, so converter replacement requires removal of the exhaust pipe assembly (see Chapter 4). Take the vehicle, or the exhaust system, to a dealer service department or a muffler shop.

5   On other models, raise the car and support it securely on jack stands.

6   Unbolt the converter from the manifold and from the intermediate exhaust pipe, then remove the converter.

7   Installation is the reverse of removal.

---

12   Air Injection Reactor (AIR) system

General description

1   The AIR system is used on V6 engine models equipped with manual transaxles. The AIR system helps reduce hydrocarbons and carbon monoxide levels in the exhaust by injecting air into the exhaust ports of each cylinder.

2   The AIR system uses an air pump to force the air into the exhaust stream. An Electric Air Control (EAC) valve, controlled by the vehicle's Electronic Control Module (ECM) directs the air to the correct location, depending on engine temperature and driving conditions. During certain situations, such as deceleration, the air is diverted to the atmosphere to prevent backfiring from too much oxygen in the exhaust stream. **Note:** *The AIR system was used on early models covered by this book, then discontinued until the 2000 and later model years, on which it was used to improve the initial heating of the catalytic converter on engine startup.*

3   One-way check valves are also used in the AIR system's air lines to prevent exhaust gases from being forced back through the system.

4   The following components are utilized in the AIR system: an engine driven air pump, an Electric Air Control (EAC) valve, air hoses and a check valve. On 2000 and later models, the AIR pump is driven electrically, rather than with a belt.

Checking

5   Because of the complexity of this system it is difficult for the home mechanic to make a proper diagnosis. If the system is suspected of not operating properly, individual components can be checked.

6   Begin any inspection by carefully checking all hoses and wires. Be sure they are in good condition and that all connections are tight and clean. Also make sure that the pump drivebelt is in good condition and properly adjusted.

7   To check the pump allow the engine to reach normal operating temperature and run it at about 1500 rpm. Locate the hose running from the air pump and squeeze it to feel the pulsations. Have an assistant increase the engine speed and check for an increase in air flow. If this is observed as described, the pump is functioning properly. If it is not operating in this manner, check for proper drive belt tension. If belt tension is okay, a faulty pump is indicated.

8   The check valve can be inspected by first removing it from the air line. Attempt to blow through it from both directions. Air should only pass through it in the direction of normal air flow. If it is either stuck open or stuck closed the valve should be replaced.

9   Disconnect the vacuum signal line at the air control valve. With the engine at idle speed, 10 inches of vacuum should be present in the line.

10   When the EAC is energized (12-volts) and has good manifold vacuum to it, air from the pump should be directed to the exhaust ports. When the EAC is de-energized and good manifold vacuum to it, the air should be diverted to the atmosphere.

Component replacement

Drivebelt

11   Loosen the pump mounting bolt and the pump adjustment bracket bolt. On 2000 and later models, disconnect the electrical connector, then unbolt the pump from the engine compartment.

12   Move the pump until the belt can be removed.

13   Install the new belt and adjust it (refer to Chapter 1).

AIR pump pulley and filter (belt-driven models)

Refer to illustrations 12.14 and 12.17

14   Compress the drivebelt to keep the pulley from turning and loosen the pulley bolts **(see illustration)**.

15   Remove the drivebelt as described above.

16   Remove the mounting bolts and lift off the pulley.

**12.17 Removing the AIR pump filter
(remove as shown - do not insert any tool
behind the filter, as damage to the
pump may occur)**

17   If the fan-like filter must be removed, grasp it firmly with needle-nose pliers, and pull it from the pump **(see illustration)**. **Note:** *Do not insert a screwdriver between the filter and pump housing as the edge of the housing could be damaged. The filter will usually be distorted when it is pulled off. Be sure no fragments fall into the air intake hose.*

18   The new filter is installed by placing it in position on the pump, placing the pulley over it and tightening the pulley bolts evenly to draw the filter into the pump. Do not attempt to install a filter by pressing or hammering it into place. **Note:** *It is normal for the new filter to have an interference fit with the pump housing and, upon initial operation, it may squeal until it has worn in.*
19   Install the drivebelt and, while compressing the belt, tighten the pulley bolts.
20   Adjust the drivebelt tension.

Hoses and tubes

21   To replace any tube or hose always note how it is routed first, either with a sketch or with numbered pieces of tape.
22   Remove the defective hose or tube and replace it with a new one of the same material and size and tighten all connections.

Check valve

23   Disconnect the pump outlet hose at the check valve.
24   Remove the check valve from the pipe assembly, making sure not to bend or twist the assembly.
25   Install a new valve after making sure that it is a duplicate of the part removed, then tighten all connections.

Electric Air Control (EAC) valve

26   Disconnect the negative cable at the battery. **Caution:** *On models equipped with the Theftlock audio system, be sure the lockout feature is turned off before performing any procedure which requires disconnecting the battery.*
27   Disconnect the vacuum signal line from the valve. Also disconnect the air hoses and electrical connectors.
28   If the mounting bolts are retained by tabbed lock washers, bend the tabs back, then remove the mounting bolts and the valve.
29   Installation is the reverse of the removal procedure.

AIR pump

30   If the pulley must be removed from the pump it should be done prior to removing the drivebelt.
31   If the pulley is not being removed, remove the drivebelt.
32   Remove the pump mounting bolts and separate the pump from the engine.
33   Installation is the reverse of the removal procedure. **Note:** *Do not tighten the pump mounting bolts until all components are installed.*
34   Following installation adjust the drivebelt tension as described in Chapter 1.

Chapter 7 Part A
Manual transaxle

Contents

	Section
General information	1
Manual transaxle lubricant change................................. See Chapter 1	
Manual transaxle lubricant level check........................... See Chapter 1	
Manual transaxle mounts - check and replacement..... See Chapter 7B	
Manual transaxle overhaul - general information	6
Manual transaxle - removal and installation	5

	Section
Manual transaxle shift cables - removal and installation	2
Manual transaxle shift control - removal and installation.............	4
Manual transaxle shifter shaft seal - replacement.......................	3
Starter safety switch check....................................See Chapter 1	
Transaxle differential oil seals - replacement .... See Chapter 7B	
Transaxle mount - check and replacement .... See Chapter 7B	

Specifications

Torque specifications

	Ft-lbs
Clutch housing cover bolts	10
Transaxle-to-engine bolts/nuts	55
Transaxle mount-to-frame nut	42
Transaxle mount-transaxle bolts	35
Shift control bolts/nuts	18
Shift linkage bracket bolts...	17
Shift cable stud nuts	18

2.2a Details of the shift cables at the retainer bracket on the transaxle

1   Retainer bracket   3   Shift cables
2   Retainer mounting nut

2.2b Details of the shift cables at the transaxle shift levers

1   Shift cable-to-shift lever mounting nut
2   Shift lever-to-transaxle mounting nut
3   Shift lever

1   General information

The vehicles covered by this manual are equipped with either a five-speed manual or a three or four-speed automatic transaxle. Information on the manual transaxle is included in this Part of Chapter 7. Information on the automatic transaxle can be found in Part B of this Chapter.

The five-speed manual transaxle is essentially a transmission coupled together with a differential in one assembly.

Due to the complexity, availability of replacement parts and special tools necessary, internal repair procedures should not be attempted by the home mechanic. The information contained in this manual will be limited to general diagnosis, external adjustments and removal and installation.

Depending on the expense involved in having a faulty transaxle overhauled, it may be a good idea to consider replacing the unit with either a new or rebuilt one. Your local dealer or transmission shop should be able to supply information concerning cost, availability and exchange policy. Regardless of how you decide to remedy a faulty transaxle problem, however, you can still save money by removing and installing it yourself.

2   Manual transaxle shift cables - removal and installation

Refer to illustrations 2.2a and 2.2b

Removal

1   Disconnect the negative cable from the battery. **Caution:** *On models equipped with the Theftlock audio system, be sure the lockout feature is turned off before performing any procedure which requires disconnecting the battery.*
2   Remove the nuts retaining the selector and shift cables to the transaxle levers, and the nut securing the cable retainer bracket **(see illustrations)**.
3   Remove the console (see Chapter 11).
4   Use a small screwdriver to pry the cable free of the shift control ball sockets.
5   Remove the screws from the carpeting sill plate in the left front corner of the passenger compartment, remove the plate and then pull the carpet back for access to the cables.
6   Remove the cable retainer and grommet nuts at the floor pan and pry the two retaining tabs up.
7   Pull the cables through into the passenger compartment and remove them from the vehicle.

Installation

8   Push the cable assembly through the opening from the passenger compartment into the engine compartment.
9   Install the grommet and cable retainer nuts and bend the two retaining tabs down.
10   Install the carpet and sill plate.
11   Connect the cable ends to the shifter.
12   Install the console.
13   Connect the cable assembly to the transaxle bracket and shift levers.

3   Manual transaxle shifter shaft seal - replacement

1   Disconnect the negative cable from the battery. **Caution:** *On models equipped with the Theftlock audio system, be sure the lockout feature is turned off before performing any procedure which requires disconnecting the battery.*
2   Disconnect the shift cable(s) from the shift lever(s).
3   Remove the shift lever nut, making sure the shift lever itself doesn't move while the nut is loosened.
4   Remove the shift lever assembly, keep-

ing all of the components in order.
5   Pry out the old seal with a screwdriver.
6   Install the new seal in the bore and tap it into place with a deep socket or piece of pipe and a hammer.
7   Installation of the remaining components is the reverse of removal.

4   Manual transaxle shift control - removal and installation

Removal

1   Disconnect the negative cable from the battery. **Caution:** *On models equipped with the Theftlock audio system, be sure the lockout feature is turned off before performing any procedure which requires disconnecting the battery.*
2   Remove the console, shift boot and knob (see Chapter 11).
3   Disconnect the shift cables from the shifter (see Section 2).
4   Remove the shift cable retaining clips.
5   Remove the retaining nuts/bolts and lift the shift control assembly out of the vehicle.

Installation

6   Place the shift control assembly in position and install the retaining nuts.
7   Connect the shift cables to the shift control assembly.
8   Install the console.
9   Connect the negative battery cable.

5   Manual transaxle - removal and installation

Refer to illustration 5.7

Removal

1   Disconnect the negative cable from the battery. **Caution:** *On models equipped with*

5.7 GM recommends using a special support fixture for the engine - you can also use an engine hoist - the engine can also be supported from below, with a jack and block of wood under the oil pan, but transaxle removal will be more difficult

the Theftlock audio system, be sure the lockout feature is turned off before performing any procedure which requires disconnecting the battery.

2   Raise the vehicle and support it securely on jackstands.

3   Drain the transaxle fluid (see Chapter 1).

4   Disconnect the shift linkage from the transaxle (see Section 2), then remove the clutch master cylinder pushrod clip (near the top of the clutch pedal arm) and slide the pushrod off the pedal pin.

5   Detach the speedometer sensor and wire harness connectors from the transaxle. Remove the clutch release cylinder from the transaxle (see Chapter 8). On 1991 and later models, disconnect the release lever from the release bearing (see Chapter 8).

6   Remove the exhaust system components as necessary for clearance.

7   Support the engine. This can be done from above with an engine hoist or support fixture, or by placing a jack (with a block of wood as an insulator) under the engine oil pan **(see illustration)**. The engine must remain supported at all times while the transaxle is out of the vehicle! Be sure the engine is supported securely.

8   Remove any chassis or suspension components that will interfere with transaxle removal (see Chapter 10).

9   Disconnect the driveaxles from the transaxle (see Chapter 8).

10   Support the transaxle with a jack, preferably one designed for removing transaxles, then remove the bolts securing the transaxle to the engine.

11   Remove the transaxle mount nuts and bolts.

12   Make a final check that all wires and hoses have been disconnected from the transaxle, then carefully pull the transaxle and jack away from the engine.

13   Once the input shaft is clear, lower the transaxle and remove it from under the vehicle. **Caution:** *Do not depress the clutch pedal while the transaxle is out of the vehicle.*

14   With the transaxle removed, the clutch components are now accessible and can be inspected. In most cases, new clutch components should be routinely installed when the transaxle is removed.

Installation

15   If removed, install the clutch components (see Chapter 8.)

16   With the transaxle secured to the jack with a chain, raise it into position behind the engine, then carefully slide it forward, engaging the input shaft with the clutch plate hub splines. Do not use excessive force to install the transaxle - if the input shaft does not slide into place, readjust the angle of the transaxle so it is level and/or turn the input shaft so the splines engage properly with the clutch plate hub.

17   Install the transaxle-to-engine bolts. Tighten the bolts securely.

18   Install the transaxle mount nuts or bolts.

19   Install the chassis and suspension components which were removed. Tighten all nuts and bolts securely.

20   Remove the jacks supporting the transaxle and engine.

21   Install or reconnect the various items removed or disconnected previously, referring to Chapter 8 for installation of the driveaxles and Chapter 4 for information regarding the exhaust system components.

22   Make a final check that all wires, hoses, linkages and the speedometer sensor have been connected and that the transaxle has been filled with lubricant to the proper level (see Chapter 1).

23   Connect the negative battery cable. Road test the vehicle for proper operation and check for leaks.

6   Manual transaxle overhaul - general information

Overhauling a manual transaxle is a difficult job for the do-it-yourselfer. It involves the disassembly and reassembly of many small parts. Numerous clearances must be precisely measured and, if necessary, changed with select fit spacers and snap-rings. As a result, if transaxle problems arise, it can be removed and installed by a competent do-it-yourselfer, but overhaul should be left to a transmission repair shop. Rebuilt transaxles may be available - check with your dealer parts department and auto parts stores. At any rate, the time and money involved in an overhaul is almost sure to exceed the cost of a rebuilt unit.

Nevertheless, it's not impossible for an inexperienced mechanic to rebuild a transaxle if the special tools are available and the job is done in a deliberate step-by-step manner so nothing is overlooked.

The tools necessary for an overhaul include internal and external snap-ring pliers, a bearing puller, a slide hammer, a set of pin punches, a dial indicator and possibly a hydraulic press. In addition, a large, sturdy workbench and a vise or transaxle stand will be required.

During disassembly of the transaxle, make careful notes of how each piece comes off, where it fits in relation to other pieces and what holds it in place.

Before taking the transaxle apart for repair, it will help if you have some idea what area of the transaxle is malfunctioning. Certain problems can be closely tied to specific areas in the transaxle, which can make component examination and replacement easier. Refer to the Troubleshooting section at the front of this manual for information regarding possible sources of trouble.

Chapter 7 Part B
Automatic transaxle

Contents

	Section
Automatic transaxle floor shift control assembly - removal and installation	7
Automatic transaxle fluid and filter change	See Chapter 1
Automatic transaxle fluid level check	See Chapter 1
Automatic transaxle park/lock system - removal and installation	6
Automatic transaxle - removal and installation	10
Automatic transaxle shift cable - replacement and adjustment	5
Diagnosis - general	2
General information	1
Neutral start (starter safety) switch – replacement and adjustment	4
Neutral start (starter safety) switch check	See Chapter 1
Throttle valve (TV) cable (3T40) - replacement and adjustment	3
Transaxle differential seals - replacement	8
Transaxle mount - check and replacement	9
Vacuum Modulator (4T60-E, models through 1999) – check and replacement	9
Vehicle Speed Sensor (VSS) – removal and installation	12

Specifications

General
Fluid type and capacity .... See Chapter 1

Torque specifications
Note: *One foot-pound of torque (ft-lb) is equivalent to 12 inch-pounds (in-lbs) of torque. Torque values below approximately 15 foot-pounds are expressed in inch-pounds, because most foot-pound torque wrenches are not accurate at these smaller values.*

Ft-lbs (unless otherwise indicated)

PNP switch-to-case bolts	18
Subframe (V8 models)	
Subframe-to-body bolts	
Front	107
Rear	118
Shift control assembly nuts	18
Starter safety switch-to-case bolts	18
Transaxle-to-engine bolts	55
Torque converter-to-driveplate bolts	
3T40	44
4T60-E and 4T65-E	46
Torque converter cover bolts	
3T40	60 in-lbs
4T60-E and 4T65-E	89 in-lbs
Transaxle mount bracket-to-transaxle bolts	
3T40	
Top (12 mm)	61
Front (10 mm)	35
4T60-E and 4T65-E	70
Transaxle mount	
Mount-to-transaxle bracket nuts	
3T40	22
4T60-E and 4T65-E	35
Mount-to-crossmember bracket nuts	35
Crossmember bracket-to-frame bolts	
3T40	35
4T60-E and 4T65-E	43
Transaxle to engine support brace bolts	35
TV cable-to-transaxle case bolt	
3T40	89 in-lbs
VSS sensor bolt	97 to 106 in-lbs

1.1 An underside view of an automatic transaxle and its related components

1 Transaxle fluid pan	*2 Driveaxles*	*3 Transaxle cooler lines*

1   General information

Refer to illustration 1.1

The vehicles covered by this manual are equipped with either a five-speed manual or three or four-speed Hydra-Matic automatic transaxles **(see illustration)**. Three models of Hydra-Matic automatic transaxles are used on these vehicles: the three-speed 125C/3T40 on earlier models, and the four-speed 4T60-E and 4T65-E on later models.

Due to the complexity of the clutches and the hydraulic control system, and because of the special tools and expertise required to perform an automatic transaxle overhaul, it should not be undertaken by the home mechanic. Therefore, the procedures in this Chapter are limited to general diagnosis, routine maintenance, adjustment and transaxle removal and installation.

If the transaxle requires major repair work, it should be left to a dealer service department or an automotive or transmission repair shop. You can, however, remove and install the transaxle yourself and save the expense, even if the repair work is done by a transmission shop.

Replacement and adjustment procedures the home mechanic can perform include those involving the throttle valve (TV) cable and the shift linkage. **Caution:** *Never tow a disabled vehicle with an automatic transaxle at speeds greater than 35 mph or for distances over 50 miles if the front wheels are on the ground.*

2   Diagnosis - general

Note: *Automatic transaxle malfunctions may be caused by five general conditions: poor*

engine performance, improper adjustments, hydraulic malfunctions, mechanical malfunctions or malfunctions in the computer or its signal network. Diagnosis of these problems should always begin with a check of the easily repaired items: fluid level and condition (see Chapter 1), shift linkage adjustment and throttle linkage adjustment. Next, perform a road test to determine if the problem has been corrected or if more diagnosis is necessary. If the problem persists after the preliminary tests and corrections are completed, additional diagnosis should be done by a dealer service department or transmission repair shop. Refer to the Troubleshooting section at the front of this manual for transaxle problem diagnosis.

Preliminary checks

1   Drive the vehicle to warm the transaxle to normal operating temperature.
2   Check the fluid level as described in Chapter 1:

a) *If the fluid level is unusually low, add enough fluid to bring the level within the designated area of the dipstick, then check for external leaks.*

b) *If the fluid level is abnormally high, drain off the excess, then check the drained fluid for contamination by coolant. The presence of engine coolant in the automatic transmission fluid indicates that a failure has occurred in the internal radiator walls that separate the coolant from the transmission fluid (see Chapter 3).*

c) *If the fluid is foaming, drain it and refill the transaxle, then check for coolant in the fluid or a high fluid level.*

3   Check the engine idle speed. **Note:** *If the engine is malfunctioning, do not proceed with the preliminary checks until it has been*

repaired and runs normally.
4   Check the throttle valve cable for freedom of movement. Adjust it if necessary (see Section 3). **Note:** *The throttle valve cable may function properly when the engine is shut off and cold, but it may malfunction once the engine is hot. Check it cold and at normal engine operating temperature.*
5   Inspect the shift cable (see Section 5). Make sure that it's properly adjusted and that the linkage operates smoothly.

Fluid leak diagnosis

6   Most fluid leaks are easy to locate visually. Repair usually consists of replacing a seal or gasket. If a leak is difficult to find, the following procedure may help.
7   Identify the fluid. Make sure it's transmission fluid and not engine oil or brake fluid (automatic transmission fluid is a deep red color).
8   Try to pinpoint the source of the leak. Drive the vehicle several miles, then park it over a large sheet of cardboard. After a minute or two, you should be able to locate the leak by determining the source of the fluid dripping onto the cardboard.
9   Make a careful visual inspection of the suspected component and the area immediately around it. Pay particular attention to gasket mating surfaces. A mirror is often helpful for finding leaks in areas that are hard to see.
10   If the leak still cannot be found, clean the suspected area thoroughly with a degreaser or solvent, then dry it.
11   Drive the vehicle for several miles at normal operating temperature and varying speeds. After driving the vehicle, visually inspect the suspected component again.
12   Once the leak has been located, the cause must be determined before it can be

3.2 Use needle-nose pliers to compress the TV cable tangs, then push the housing back through the bracket

3.4 Remove the TV cable bolt and pull up on the cable until it's out of the transaxle

3.5 Hold the transaxle TV link with the needle-nose pliers and slide the cable link off the pin

properly repaired. If a gasket is replaced but the sealing flange is bent, the new gasket will not stop the leak. The bent flange must be straightened.

13   Before attempting to repair a leak, check to make sure that the following conditions are corrected or they may cause another leak. **Note:** *Some of the following conditions cannot be fixed without highly specialized tools and expertise. Such problems must be referred to a transmission shop or a dealer service department.*

Gasket leaks

14   Check the pan periodically. Make sure the bolts are tight, no bolts are missing, the gasket is in good condition and the pan is flat (dents in the pan may indicate damage to the valve body inside).

15   If the pan gasket is leaking, the fluid level or the fluid pressure may be too high, the vent may be plugged, the pan bolts may be too tight, the pan sealing flange may be warped, the sealing surface of the transaxle housing may be damaged, the gasket may be damaged or the transaxle casting may be cracked or porous. If sealant instead of gasket material has been used to form a seal between the pan and the transaxle housing, it may be the wrong sealant.

Seal leaks

16   If a transaxle seal is leaking, the fluid level or pressure may be too high, the vent may be plugged, the seal bore may be damaged, the seal itself may be damaged or improperly installed, the surface of the shaft protruding through the seal may be damaged or a loose bearing may be causing excessive shaft movement.

17   Make sure the dipstick tube seal is in good condition and the tube is properly seated. Periodically check the area around the speedometer gear or sensor for leakage. If transmission fluid is evident, check the O-ring for damage. Also inspect the side gear shaft oil seals for leakage.

Case leaks

18   If the case itself appears to be leak-

ing, the casting is porous and will have to be repaired or replaced.

19   Make sure the oil cooler hose fittings are tight and in good condition.

Fluid comes out vent pipe or fill tube

20   If this condition occurs, the transaxle is overfilled, there is coolant in the fluid, the case is porous, the dipstick is incorrect, the vent is plugged or the drain back holes are plugged.

3   Throttle valve (TV) cable (3T40) - replacement and adjustment

Refer to illustrations 3.2, 3.4, 3.5 and 3.8

Replacement

1   Disconnect the TV cable from the throttle lever by grasping the connector, pulling it forward to disconnect it and then lifting up and off the lever pin.

2   Disconnect the TV cable housing from the bracket by compressing the tangs and pushing the housing back through the bracket **(see illustration)**.

3   Disconnect any clips or straps retaining the cable to the transaxle.

4   Remove the bolt retaining the cable to the transaxle **(see illustration)**.

5   Pull up on the cover until the end of the cable can be seen, then disconnect it from the transaxle TV link **(see illustration)**. Remove the cable from the vehicle.

6   To install the cable, connect it to the transaxle TV link and push the cover securely over the cable. Route the cable to the top of the engine, push the housing through the bracket until it clicks into place, place the connector over the throttle lever pin and pull back to lock it. Secure the cable with any retaining clips or straps.

Adjustment

7   The engine MUST NOT be running during this adjustment.

8   Depress the re-adjust button and push the

3.8 TV cable adjuster details

A	TV cable	D	Cable casing
B	Locking lugs	E	Slider
C	Release tabs		

slider through the fitting (away from the throttle lever) as far as it will go **(see illustration)**.

9   Release the re-adjust button.

10   Manually turn the throttle lever to the "wide open throttle" position until the re-adjust tab makes an audible click, then release the throttle lever. The cable is now adjusted. **Note:** *Don't use excessive force at the throttle lever to adjust the TV cable. If great effort is required to adjust the cable, disconnect the cable at the transaxle end and check for free operation. If it's still difficult, replace the cable. If it's now free, suspect a bent TV link in the transaxle or a problem with the throttle lever.*

4   Neutral Start (Starter Safety) switch – replacement and adjustment

Replacement

Refer to illustration 4.4

1   Disconnect the negative cable from the battery. **Caution:** *On models equipped with the Theftlock audio system, be sure the lockout feature is turned off before performing any procedure which requires disconnecting the*

4.4 Neutral start switch installation details

1　*Neutral start switch*
2　*Neutral start switch electrical connector*

4.11 Align the outer notch of the Park/ Neutral switch with the inner notch on the shaft using a drill bit (arrow)

5.2 Disconnect the shift cable (arrow) at the shift lever and detach the cable housing from the bracket on the transaxle

battery. **Note:** *This switch is also referred to as the PNP (Park-Neutral Position) switch. This switch is not used on later models. On these models, the starter safety switch is incorporated into the vehicle computer system and is activated by the transaxle range sensor.*

2　Shift the transaxle into Neutral.

3　Raise the vehicle and support it securely on jackstands.

4　Trace the wire harness from the Neutral start switch to the connector **(see illustration)** and unplug it. Detach the wire harness from the two retention clips.

5　Lower the vehicle.

6　Disconnect the electrical and vacuum connectors from the cruise control servo (if equipped). Remove the servo and set it out of the way on the cowl.

7　Remove the nut and detach the shift lever from the transaxle.

8　Remove the bolts and detach the switch. **Note:** *If the original switch is to be reinstalled, scribe a sharp line on the switch mounting bracket around the heads of the mounting bolts, before the switch is removed. This will aid in positioning the switch on installation.*

9　To install the switch, line up the flats on the shift shaft with the flats in the switch and lower the switch onto the shaft.

10　Install the bolts. If the switch is new and the shaft hasn't been moved, tighten the bolts. If the switch requires adjustment, leave the bolts loose and follow the adjustment procedure below. The remainder of installation is the reverse of removal.

Adjustment

Refer to illustration 4.11

11　Line up the outer notch on the switch with the inner notch on the shift shaft and tighten the switch bolts **(see illustration)**.

12　Connect the negative battery cable and verify that the engine will start only in Neutral or Park.

5　Automatic transaxle shift cable - replacement and adjustment

1　Disconnect the negative cable from the battery. **Caution:** *On models equipped with the Theftlock audio system, be sure the lockout feature is turned off before performing any procedure which requires disconnecting the battery.*

Replacement

Floor shift

Refer to illustrations 5.2, 5.3 and 5.4

2　Working in the engine compartment, disconnect the shift cable from the transaxle lever and bracket **(see illustration)**.

3　Remove the shift handle and the floor console, if equipped **(see illustration)**. Refer to Chapter 11 for console removal.

4　Disconnect the shift cable from the floor shift lever and bracket **(see illustration)**.

5　Remove the right and left side sound insulators from the under dash portion of the console, then pull back the carpet for access to the cable.

6　Trace the cable up to the firewall grommet.

7　Remove the screws from the grommet retainer, detach the grommet and retainer

from the firewall and pull the cable assembly through the firewall.

8　Installation is the reverse of removal. After installation, adjust the cable as described in Step 14.

Column shift

Refer to illustration 5.11

9　Working in the engine compartment, remove the air cleaner, then disconnect the cable from the transaxle lever and bracket **(see illustration 5.2)**.

10　Working in the passenger compartment, remove the left sound insulator located under the dash.

11　Disconnect the cable bracket on the steering column and detach the cable from the column shift lever **(see illustration)**.

12　Dislodge the grommet in the firewall and withdraw the cable from the vehicle.

13　Installation is the reverse of removal. After installation, adjust the cable as described below.

Adjustment

Refer to illustration 5.14

14　The shift control cable is in two sections, joined by a coupler retained by a metal spring clip **(see illustration)**. Do not remove this

5.3 Remove the retainer (arrow) from the shift handle

5.4 Location of the shift cable (1) and the park/lock cable (2)

5.11 Location of the column shift cable (arrow)

5.14 The shift cable comes in two halves, retained by an adjuster clip (A) and a horseshoe clip (B) – do not remove either clip!

clip! If either section of the cable is damaged, replace the whole assembly as a unit. **Note:** *A new cable may come as two pieces, with instructions for the proper engagement of the two sections.*

15   Install the two sections of new cable to their respective end mountings at the transaxle and shift control. Push the adjuster clip into its first "notch" on the end of the shift control side of the coupling.

16   With both the transaxle and shift control set in the Neutral position, connect the two halves until you feel them lock together, then push the clip onto its last position. There is a smaller clip in the transaxle end of the coupler, and when fully assembled, this clip should be flush with the coupler (not sticking out at all). Pull the two halves of the cable away from each other to test that the connection is secure. Once engaged, do not remove the adjuster clip or another new cable set will have to be purchased.

6   Automatic transaxle park/lock system – removal and installation

Park/lock cable

Note: *This procedure applies only to 2000 and earlier models. Later models use an electrically-operated shift lock system (see Step 18).*

Removal

1   Disconnect the negative cable from the battery. On V6 models, remove the air cleaner. **Caution:** *On models equipped with the Theftlock audio system, be sure the lockout feature is turned off before performing any procedure which requires disconnecting the battery.*

2   Remove the console (see Chapter 11).

3   Place the shift lever in Park and the ignition switch in the Run position.

4   Insert a screwdriver blade into the slot in the ignition switch inhibitor, depress the cable latch and detach the cable.

5   Push the cable connector lock button (located at the shift control base) to the Up position and detach the cable from the park

lock lever pin. Depress the two cable connector latches and remove the cable from the shift control base.

6   Remove the cable clips.

Installation

7   Make sure the cable lock button is in the Up position and the shift lever is in Park. Snap the cable connector into the shift control base.

8   With the ignition key in the Run position (this is very important), snap the cable into the inhibitor housing.

9   Turn the ignition key to the Lock position.

10   Snap the end of the cable onto the shifter park/lock pin.

11   Push the nose of the cable connector forward to remove the slack.

12   With no load on the connector nose, snap the cable connector lock button on.

13   Check the operation of the park/lock cable as follows.

a)   *With the shift lever in Park and the key in Lock, make sure the shift lever cannot be moved to another position and the key can be removed.*

b)   *With the key in Run and the shift lever in Neutral, make sure the key cannot be turned to Lock.*

14   If it operates as described above, the park/lock cable system is properly adjusted. Proceed to Step 16.

15   If the park/lock system doesn't operate as described, return the cable connector lock to the up position and repeat the adjustment procedure. Push the cable connector down and recheck the operation.

16   If the key cannot be removed in the Park position, snap the lock button to the up position and move the nose of the cable connector to the rear until the key can be removed from the ignition switch.

17   Install the cable in the retaining clips.

Brake/Transaxle Shift Interlock (BTSI) solenoid

Note: *This system is used on most 2001 and later models.*

Check

18   Turn the ignition key to the Run position and, without depressing the brake pedal, try to move the shift lever out of Park. If you can move the lever, either the solenoid isn't receiving power, isn't grounded or is defective. The solenoid is located in the shifter assembly.

a)   *Check the fuses*

b)   *Check the adjustment of the transaxle shift cable and the operation of the transaxle range switch.*

c)   *Remove the console (see Chapter 11) and check for power to the BTSI solenoid. If voltage is not available, repair the circuit between the solenoid and the fuse block. If voltage is available, check the ground circuit for continuity. If continuity is present, replace the solenoid.*

19   Now depress the brake pedal – you should be able to move the shift lever. If you can't, then the solenoid isn't deactivating.

a)   *Unplug the wiring connector from the solenoid and check for continuity to ground on the harness terminal that does not have power to it. There should be continuity when the brake pedal is at rest and no continuity (or high resistance) when the pedal is depressed.*

b)   *If the ground path from the solenoid is cut when the brake pedal is depressed but the solenoid still doesn't release, the solenoid is stuck and must be replaced.*

Replacement

20   The solenoid is located in the shifter assembly.

21   Disconnect the cable from the negative battery terminal (see Chapter 5, Section 1).

22   Remove the console (see Chapter 11).

23   Disconnect the wiring from the solenoid.

24   Pull both ends of the solenoid from the pivots.

25   Installation is the reverse of removal.

7   Automatic transaxle floor shift control assembly - removal and installation

Refer to illustration 7.5

1   Disconnect the negative cable from the battery. **Caution:** *On models equipped with the Theftlock audio system, be sure the lockout feature is turned off before performing any procedure which requires disconnecting the battery.*

2   Remove the floor console, if equipped (see Chapter 11). Disconnect the electrical connectors from the shift control.

3   Disconnect the shift cable from the gear shift lever (see Section 5).

4   Disconnect the park/lock cable (early models) or the BTSI wiring harness (later models).

5   Remove the retaining nuts and lift the

7.5 Location of the shift assembly mounting bolts (arrows)

8.3 The rubber-type differential seal (arrow) used on earlier models can be pried out of the housing with a screwdriver - be careful not to damage the splines on the shaft (transaxle removed for clarity)

8.4 Dislodge the metal-type differential seal used on some later models by working around the outer edge with a chisel and hammer

floor shift control assembly out of the vehicle **(see illustration)**.
6   Place the floor shift control assembly in position on the mounting studs and install the nuts. Tighten the nuts to the specified torque.
7   Connect the shift cables.
8   Install the console.
9   Reconnect the negative battery cable.
10   Test the correct operation of the shift control and Park/lock system.

8   Transaxle differential seals - replacement

Refer to illustrations 8.3 and 8.4

1   Raise the vehicle and support it securely on jackstands.
2   Remove the driveaxle(s) (see Chapter 8).
3   If a rubber-type seal is involved, use a seal remover or a long screwdriver to pry it out of the transaxle. Be careful not to damage the splines on the output shaft **(see illustration)**.
4   If a metal-type seal is involved, use a hammer and chisel to pry up the outer lip of the seal to dislodge it so it can be pried out of the housing **(see illustration)**. The manufacturer recommends using a slide hammer to remove the metal-type seal.

5   Compare the new seal to the old one to make sure they're the same.
6   Coat the lips of the new seal with transmission fluid.
7   Place the new seal in position and tap it into the bore with a hammer and a large socket or a piece of pipe that's the same diameter as the outside edge of the seal.
8   Reinstall the various components in the reverse order of removal.

9   Transaxle mount - check and replacement

Refer to illustration 9.3

1   Insert a large screwdriver or prybar into the space between the transaxle bracket and the mount and try to pry the transaxle up slightly.
2   The transaxle bracket should not move away from the insulator much at all.
3   To replace the mount, remove the nuts attaching the insulator to the crossmember and the nuts attaching the insulator to the transaxle **(see illustration)**.
4   Raise the transaxle slightly with a jack

and remove the insulator, noting which holes are used in the support for proper alignment during installation.
5   Installation is the reverse of the removal procedure. Be sure to tighten the nuts/bolts securely.

10   Automatic transaxle - removal and installation

Refer to illustrations 10.4 and 10.5
Warning: *This is a difficult procedure for the home mechanic, requiring the use of several specialized tools, including a transmission jack and a three-bar engine support fixture. Such tools can be rented, but the job is still difficult to do without a hydraulic lift. Safely raising the vehicle enough for the transaxle and subframe to be pulled out from underneath is a problem without a hoist.*

Removal

1   Disconnect the negative cable from the battery. **Caution:** *On models equipped with a Theftlock audio system, be sure the lockout feature is turned off before performing any procedure which requires disconnecting the battery.*
2   Raise the vehicle and support it securely on jackstands.
3   Drain the transaxle fluid (see Chapter 1).
4   Remove the torque converter cover **(see illustration)**.
5   Mark the torque converter-to-driveplate relationship so they can be installed in the same position **(see illustration)**.
6   Remove the torque converter-to-driveplate bolts. Turn the crankshaft pulley bolt for access to each bolt.
7   Remove the starter motor (see Chapter 5).
8   Remove the driveaxles (see Chapter 8).
9   Disconnect the speed sensor (see Section 12).
10   Disconnect the electrical connectors from the transaxle.

9.3 Transaxle mount nuts (arrows)

10.4 Torque converter inspection cover mounting bolt locations (arrows)

10.5 Make alignment marks (arrows) on the flywheel and torque converter so they can be reinstalled in the same relative positions

11   On models so equipped, disconnect the vacuum hose(s).

12   Remove any exhaust components that will interfere with transaxle removal (see Chapter 4).

13   If equipped, disconnect the TV cable from the transaxle (see Section 3).

14   Disconnect the shift linkage from the transaxle (see Section 5).

15   Support the engine using a three-bar support fixture to retain the engine in the body (**see illustration 14.1** in Part D of Chapter 2). Remove the engine mount strut brackets from the radiator support (see Chapter 2, Part A or B).

16   Support the transaxle with a jack - preferably a special jack made for this purpose. Safety chains will help steady the transaxle on the jack.

17   Remove the brace between the engine and transaxle (attached to the oil pan on the right side) and the bolts securing the transaxle to the flywheel end of the engine.

18   Disconnect and plug the transaxle cooler lines. Make sure all of the fluid has drained out into a suitable container. Remove the dipstick tube. Refer to Chapter 8 and remove the driveaxles.

19   Refer to Chapter 10 and disconnect the tie rod ends, then unbolt the steering rack and hold it to the body with heavy wire, away from the chassis. On V8 models, detach the control arms from the subframe (see Chapter 10).

20   Remove the fasteners that attach the engine and transaxle mounts to the subframe. Carefully mark the position of the subframe in relation to the vehicle chassis. Thoroughly check for wiring harnesses or anything else that may be attached to the subframe. Detach them before continuing on to the next step.

21   Position one jack on each side of the subframe to support it. Place them midway between the front and rear mounting points. Remove the subframe mounting bolts. **Warning:** *Never put any part of your body under the subframe while it is unbolted from the vehicle.* Slowly lower the floor jacks until the subframe is clear of the vehicle and the floor jacks are down fully.

22   Remove the transaxle-to-engine mount-ing bolts, then remove the transaxle by sliding it away from the engine and then lowering it.

Installation

23   Prior to installation, make sure the torque converter is fully engaged in the transmission. To do this, rotate the converter while pushing it toward the transaxle. If it wasn't already fully in place, you'll feel it clunk into position as it engages with the input shaft and front pump. It may even "clunk" more than once. Lubricate the torque converter hub with multi-purpose grease.

24   With the transaxle and subframe secured to the jack, raise it evenly into position. Be sure to keep it level so the torque converter does not slide out. **Warning:** *Do not place any part of your body under the subframe until the four subframe bolts are back in place.*

25   Turn the torque converter to line up the bolt holes with the holes in the driveplate. The mark on the torque converter and the driveplate made in Step 5 must line up.

26   Move the transaxle forward carefully until the dowel pins and the torque converter are engaged.

27   Install the transaxle housing-to-engine bolts. Tighten them securely.

28   Install the torque converter-to-drive-plate bolts. Tighten the bolts to the specified torque.

29   Install the suspension and chassis components that were removed. Tighten the bolts and nuts to the specified torque.

30   Remove the jacks supporting the transaxle and the engine.

31   Install the dipstick tube.

32   Install the starter motor (see Chapter 5).

33   Connect the vacuum hose(s) (if equipped).

34   Connect the shift and TV linkage.

35   Plug in the transaxle electrical connectors.

36   Install the torque converter cover.

37   Install the driveaxles (see Chapter 8).

38   Connect the speedometer/speed sensor cable.

39   Adjust the shift linkage (see Section 5).

40   Install any exhaust system components that were removed or disconnected.

41   Lower the vehicle.

42   Fill the transaxle (see Chapter 1), run the vehicle and check for fluid leaks.

11   Vacuum modulator (4T60-E, models through 1999) - check and replacement

Check

Refer to illustration 11.2

1   The vacuum modulator is connected to engine manifold vacuum to rapidly respond to changes in engine loading, and has an important effect on shift quality. If your vehicle exhibits shifting problems such as slipping or shifts that are either too soft or too harsh, check the vacuum supply to the modulator. With the engine running, connect a vacuum gauge to the modulator's vacuum line (at the modulator). Anything less than normal engine vacuum here of 13 to 17 inches (idling hot in Drive with the brakes applied) could cause shifting problems. If vacuum is too low, find the engine problem, hose kink or hose leak that is causing the low vacuum signal.

2   Connect a hand-held vacuum pump to the vacuum connection on the modulator (removed from vehicle) and apply 15 to 20 inches of vacuum while watching the plunger **(see illustration)**. If the plunger isn't drawn in

11.2 Vacuum modulator assembly

1   *Vacuum connection*
2   *Plunger*

11.6 Disconnect the vacuum line (A) and remove the mounting bolt (B)

11.7 Remove the O-ring (arrow) from the transaxle case

11.8 A magnet can be used to reach in and extract the modulator valve (arrow)

12.2 Disconnect the electrical connector (A) from the speed sensor (B), then remove the hold-down bolt and sensor (the socket here is on the bolt)

12.4 Before reinstalling the speed sensor, replace the O-ring with a new one

as vacuum is applied, the modulator should be replaced. The modulator should be able to hold this vacuum for at least half a minute.

3   When the modulator is withdrawn from the transaxle, turn it so the vacuum pipe is down. If any oil, water or other fluid drips out, the modulator should be replaced. **Note:** *A vehicle with a modulator whose diaphragm has a leak may exhibit excessive smoking at the tailpipe, due to transaxle fluid being drawn into the engine and burned.*

4   The body of the modulator can be checked for leaks by coating the outside with soapy water and blowing (by mouth, no more than 6 psi) into the vacuum connector, using a short length of vacuum hose. Bubbles on the outside of the modulator or along the seam indicate a leak.

Replacement

Refer to illustrations 11.6, 11.7 and 11.8

5   The modulator is located on the front (radiator) side of the transaxle, below the exhaust crossover pipe.

6   Disconnect the vacuum line, and remove the mounting bolt or stud, then withdraw the modulator **(see illustration)**.

7   Remove the O-ring from the modulator cavity, using a small screwdriver or hook **(see illustration)**.

8   Use a small magnet to remove the modulator valve from the transaxle **(see illustration)**. Inspect the valve for signs of abnormal wear or scoring.

9   Installation is the reverse of the removal procedure. Always use a new O-ring and make sure the modulator valve is installed the same way it came out.

12   Vehicle Speed Sensor (VSS) - removal and installation

Refer to illustrations 12.2 and 12.4
Note: *Any time the speed sensor is removed, you MUST install a new O-ring.*

1   The speed sensor is located on the right (passenger) side of the extension housing. To determine if the O-ring is leaking, look for transmission fluid around the sensor. For testing of the VSS, refer to Chapter 6.

2   Unplug the sensor electrical connector **(see illustration)**.

3   Remove the sensor hold-down bolt and remove the sensor.

4   Remove the old O-ring **(see illustration)** and install a new O-ring on the sensor.

5   Installation is the reverse of removal. Tighten the sensor hold-down bolt securely.

Chapter 8
Clutch and driveaxles

Contents

	Section
Clutch components - removal, inspection and installation.............	6
Clutch - description and check	2
Clutch fluid level check................................... See Chapter 1	
Clutch release bearing and lever - removal and installation.........	5
Driveaxle boot check .... See Chapter 1	
Driveaxle boot replacement	10
Driveaxles - general information.......................................	8

	Section
Driveaxles - removal and installation...	9
General information..	1
Hydraulic clutch components - removal and installation................	3
Hydraulic clutch system - bleeding (1988 and 1991 through 1992 models only)..	4
Intermediate axleshaft - removal and installation (early models) ...	11
Starter/clutch interlock switch - check and replacement...............	7

Specifications

Clutch fluid type	See Chapter 1
CV joint boot dimension (collapsed)	
1997 and earlier	5 1/16 in
1998 and later	4 29/32 in

Torque specifications
Ft-lbs

Clutch pressure plate-to-flywheel bolts	
Pull-type clutches...	21
Push-type clutches..	16
Clutch release cylinder mounting nuts.....................................	18
Clutch release cylinder canister (pull-type clutches)	28
Driveaxle hub nut	
1995 and earlier	184
1996 and 1997	151
1998 through 2000	118
2001 through 2003	159
2004 and later	118
Intermediate shaft mounting bolts	37
Intermediate shaft-to-bracket bolts...	37
Intermediate shaft bracket-to-engine bolts	18
Wheel lug nuts..	See Chapter 1

1 General information

The information in this Chapter deals with the components from the rear of the engine to the drive wheels, except for the transaxle, which is covered in the previous Chapter. For the purposes of this Chapter, these components are grouped into two categories: Clutch and driveaxles. Separate Sections within this Chapter cover components in both groups.

Warning: *Since many of the procedures covered in this Chapter involve working under the vehicle, make sure it's securely supported on sturdy jackstands or on a hoist where the vehicle can easily be raised and lowered.*

2   Clutch - description and check

Refer to illustration 2.1

1   All vehicles with a manual transaxle use a single dry plate, diaphragm spring-type clutch **(see illustration)**. The clutch disc has a splined hub which allows it to slide along the splines of the transaxle input shaft. The clutch and pressure plate are held in contact by spring pressure exerted by the diaphragm in the pressure plate.

2   The clutch release system is operated by hydraulic pressure. The hydraulic release system consists of the clutch pedal, a master cylinder, the hydraulic line, a slave cylinder which actuates the clutch release lever and the clutch release (or throwout) bearing.

3   When pressure is applied to the clutch pedal to release the clutch, hydraulic pressure is exerted against the outer end of the clutch release lever. On 1990 and earlier models, the clutch uses a conventional "push-type" release mechanism. As the release lever pivots, the release bearing pushes against the fingers of the diaphragm spring in the pressure plate assembly, which in turn releases the clutch. On 1991 and later models, the clutch uses a "pull-type" mechanism. As the release lever pivots, the release bearing pulls the diaphragm spring, which in turn releases the clutch.

4   Terminology can be a problem when discussing the clutch components because common names are in some cases different from those used by the manufacturer. For example, the driven plate is also called the clutch plate or disc, the clutch release bearing is sometimes called a throwout bearing and the slave cylinder is often called an operating or release cylinder.

5   Other than to replace components with obvious damage, some preliminary checks should be performed to diagnose clutch problems.

   a) *The first check should be of the fluid level in the clutch master cylinder. If the fluid level is low, add fluid as necessary and inspect the hydraulic system for leaks. If the master cylinder reservoir has run dry, bleed the system as described in Section 4 and recheck the clutch operation.*

   b) *To check "clutch spin down time," run the engine at normal idle speed with the transaxle in Neutral (clutch pedal up - engaged). Disengage the clutch (pedal down), wait nine seconds and shift the transaxle into Reverse. No grinding noise should be heard. A grinding noise would most likely indicate a problem in the pressure plate or the clutch disc.*

   c) *To check for complete clutch release, run the engine (with the parking brake on to prevent vehicle movement) and hold the clutch pedal approximately 1/2-inch from the floor. Shift the transaxle between First gear and Reverse several times. If the shift isn't smooth, component failure is indicated. Measure the slave*

2.1 An exploded view of a typical clutch assembly

1	Clutch master cylinder	4	Pilot bearing	7	Clutch release bearing
2	Clutch pedal	5	Clutch disc	8	Clutch release cylinder
3	Flywheel	6	Clutch cover	9	Clutch release lever

cylinder pushrod travel. With the clutch pedal depressed completely the pushrod should extend about two inches. If it doesn't, check the fluid level in the clutch master cylinder.

   d) *Visually inspect the clutch pedal bushing at the top of the clutch pedal to make sure it's not sticking or worn excessively.*

3   Hydraulic clutch components - removal and installation

1988 and 1991 through 1992

Note: *The hydraulic clutch release system on these models consists of two assemblies: the master cylinder and line and the release cylinder and line. The two assemblies are joined by a quick connect fitting. Neither the master cylinder nor release cylinder are rebuildable. Replacement assemblies are filled with fluid and have been bled (to remove air) at the factory. Individual components (i.e., the master cylinder, release cylinder or lines) are not available separately. Other than replacing the cylinder/line assemblies, bleeding the system is the only service procedure that may be necessary. There are no provisions for adjustment of clutch pedal height or freeplay.*

Master cylinder

Removal

1   Disconnect the cable from the negative battery terminal. **Caution:** *On models equipped with the Theftlock audio system, be sure the lockout feature is turned off before performing any procedure which requires disconnecting the battery.*

2   Remove the left side under-dash hush panel.

3   Remove the master cylinder pushrod clip (near the top of the clutch pedal arm) and slide the pushrod off the pedal pin.

4   Using a special hydraulic line disconnect tool (available at most auto parts stores), depress the white plastic sleeve on the clutch hydraulic line to separate the quick-connect fittings.

5   Remove the mounting screws for the remote reservoir of the clutch master cylinder. Keep the reservoir upright to avoid spilling fluid.

6   Remove the anti-rotation screw located next to the master cylinder flange at the pedal support plate.

7   To release the master cylinder, use the wrench flats on the front portion of the master cylinder and rotate it 45-degrees counterclockwise.

8   Remove the master cylinder from the vehicle.

Installation

9   Place the master cylinder into the firewall opening. Using the wrench flats on the front portion of the master cylinder, rotate it 45-degrees clockwise to engage it.

10   Install the anti-rotation screw for the master cylinder.

11   Install the reservoir and tighten the mounting screws. Connect the quick-connect fittings by pressing them together until you hear a snap. Check to be sure they're secure.

12   Lubricate and install a new bushing into the master cylinder pushrod.

13   Connect the pushrod to the clutch pedal (be sure the bushing tangs snap into the pedal pin groove). Reconnect the negative battery cable.

14   If the vehicle is equipped with cruise control, make sure the cruise control system disengages when the clutch pedal is depressed. If it doesn't, check the clutch switch.

Release cylinder

Removal

15   Disconnect the cable from the negative battery terminal. **Caution:** *On models equipped with the Theftlock audio system, be sure the lockout feature is turned off before performing any procedure which requires disconnecting the battery.*
16   Remove the left side under-dash hush panel.
17   Remove the clutch master cylinder pushrod retaining clip and slide the pushrod off the pedal pin.
18   Using a special hydraulic line disconnect tool, depress the white plastic sleeve on the clutch hydraulic line to separate the quick-connect fittings.
19   On 1991 and later models, remove the nuts holding the canister on the transaxle.
20   Remove the release cylinder mounting nuts at the transaxle.
21   Remove the release cylinder.

Installation

22   Connect the hydraulic lines by inserting the release cylinder fitting into the master cylinder fitting until they snap together.
23   While guiding the pushrod bushing into the release lever pocket, attach the release cylinder to the transaxle. Tighten the nuts securely. **Caution:** *Don't remove the plastic pushrod retainer from the release cylinder pushrod. It must remain in place during installation. The straps will break during the first clutch pedal application.*
24   Lubricate and install a new bushing into the master cylinder pushrod.
25   Connect the master cylinder pushrod to the clutch pedal (be sure the bushing tangs snap into the pedal pin groove). Attach the cable to the negative battery terminal.
26   The remainder of installation is the reverse of removal.
27   Press the clutch pedal down several times. This will break the plastic retaining strap on the release cylinder pushrod. Be sure the effort is normal.
28   If the vehicle is equipped with cruise control, make sure the cruise control system disengages when the clutch pedal is de-pressed. If it doesn't, check the clutch switch.

1989 and 1990 (assembly replacement)

Note: *The hydraulic clutch release system on these models is serviced as a complete unit. New assemblies have been bled (to remove air) at the factory. Adjustment of clutch pedal height or freeplay and bleeding of the hydraulic system are therefore usually not necessary.*

Removal

29   Disconnect the cable from the negative battery terminal. **Caution:** *On models equipped with the Theftlock audio system, be sure the lockout feature is turned off before performing any procedure which requires disconnecting the battery.*
30   On V6 models, remove the air cleaner and air intake duct as an assembly (see Chapter 4).
31   On all models, remove the left side under-dash hush panel.
32   Remove the clutch master cylinder pushrod retaining clip and slide the pushrod off the pedal pin.
33   Remove the mounting screws for the remote reservoir of the clutch master cylinder. Keep the reservoir upright to avoid spilling fluid.
34   Remove the anti-rotation screw located next to the master cylinder flange at the pedal support plate.
35   To release the master cylinder, use the wrench flats on the front portion of the master cylinder and rotate it 45-degrees counterclockwise.
36   Remove the release cylinder mounting nuts at the transaxle.
37   Remove the hydraulic system as a unit from the vehicle.

Installation

38   While guiding the pushrod bushing into the pocket in the clutch release lever, attach the release cylinder to the transaxle. Tighten the nuts securely. **Caution:** *Don't remove the plastic pushrod retainer from the release cylinder pushrod. The straps will break during the first clutch pedal application.*
39   Place the master cylinder into the firewall opening. Using the wrench flats on the front portion of the master cylinder, rotate it 45-degrees clockwise to engage it.
40   Install the anti-rotation screw for the master cylinder.
41   Install the reservoir and tighten the mounting screws.
42   Lubricate and install a new bushing into the master cylinder pushrod.
43   Connect the pushrod to the clutch pedal, with the bushing tangs snapped into the pedal pin groove.
44   Press the clutch pedal down several times. This will break the plastic retaining straps on the release cylinder pushrod. Be sure the effort is normal.
45   The remainder of installation is the reverse of removal.
46   If the vehicle is equipped with cruise control, make sure the cruise control system disengages when the clutch pedal is de-pressed. If it doesn't, check the clutch switch.

---

4   Hydraulic clutch system - bleeding (1988 and 1991 through 1992 models only)

1   Using a special hydraulic line disconnect tool, depress the white plastic sleeve and disconnect the quick connect fittings.
2   Remove the cap and diaphragm and fill the reservoir with DOT 3 brake fluid.
3   Remove the upper secondary cowl on the left side of the engine compartment.
4   Remove the air from the supply hose by squeezing it until no air bubbles are seen in the reservoir.
5   Pump the clutch pedal slowly by hand until slight resistance is felt.
6   While holding pedal pressure, bleed air from the system by depressing the internal valve at the quick connect fitting. Don't use a sharp object. **Note:** *Be sure to maintain the fluid level in the master cylinder.*
7   Repeat steps 5 and 6.
8   Use a maximum of 50 pounds of force to check pedal firmness.
9   Reconnect the hydraulic line.
10   Replace the reservoir cap and diaphragm.

---

5   Clutch release bearing and lever - removal and installation

Removal

1988 through 1990 models

Refer to illustration 5.5

1   Disconnect the negative cable from the battery. **Caution:** *On models equipped with the Theftlock audio system, be sure the lockout feature is turned off before performing any procedure which requires disconnecting the battery.*
2   Remove the under-dash panel.
3   Disconnect the clutch master cylinder pushrod from the clutch pedal pin.
4   Remove the transaxle (see Chapter 7, Part A).
5   Remove the clutch release bearing from the lever shaft **(see illustration)**.
6   Hold the center of the bearing and turn the outer race. If the bearing doesn't turn smoothly or if it's noisy, replace it with a new one. Wipe the bearing with a clean rag and inspect it for damage, wear and cracks.

5.5 Before removing the release bearing from the transaxle, index the bearing pad to the clutch release fork (arrow)

5.12 Lubricate the release bearing where the release lever contacts the release bearing - also, on 1988 through 1990 models, fill the inner groove of the bearing with grease

6.3 A clutch alignment tool in position to hold the disc during removal or center the disc during installation

6.4 If you're going to re-use the same pressure plate, mark its relationship to the flywheel (arrow)

Don't immerse the bearing in solvent - it's sealed and would be ruined by the solvent. It's common practice to replace the release bearing whenever the clutch components are replaced.

1991 and later models

7   Remove the release cylinder and canister from the transaxle.
8   Remove the access plug from the transaxle clutch housing.
9   Disconnect the release lever from the release bearing by pulling the lever. **Note:** *Pull the lever perpendicular to the transaxle center line until it reaches its stop.*
10   Remove the transaxle (see Chapter 7).
11   Remove the release bearing from the pressure plate as follows: Push the bearing toward the engine, fit a large flat-blade screwdriver between the clutch wedge collar and the release bearing, then twist the screwdriver. The bearing should pop out of the wedge collar.

Installation - all models

Refer to illustration 5.12

12   Lightly lubricate the release lever ends, where they contact the bearing, with white lithium-base grease. On 1988 to 1990 models, pack the inner groove of the bearing with grease as well **(see illustration)**.
13   Install the release bearing on the lever (be sure the levers fit between the large ears and small tangs on the bearing).
14   Be sure the lever moves freely with the bearing in place.
15   Install the transaxle (see Chapter 7).
16   On models with a pull-type clutch, seat the release bearing in the wedge collar by pushing the release cylinder end of the release lever toward the engine. The release bearing should pop into the wedge collar and become locked to the diaphragm spring.
17   On models with a pull-type clutch, install the access cover in the clutch housing.

18   Install the release cylinder and, if necessary, the canister, on the transaxle.
19   Reconnect the clutch master cylinder pushrod.
20   Install the under-dash cover.
21   Attach the cable to the negative battery terminal.
22   Check the clutch operation.

---

6   Clutch components - removal, inspection and installation

Refer to illustrations 6.3, 6.4, 6.9 and 6.11
Warning: *Dust produced by clutch wear and deposited on clutch components contains asbestos, which is hazardous to your health. DO NOT blow it out with compressed air and DO NOT inhale it. DO NOT use gasoline or petroleum-based solvents to remove the dust. Brake system cleaner should be used to flush the dust into a drain pan. After the clutch components are wiped clean with a rag, dispose of the contaminated rags and cleaner in a covered, marked container.*

Removal

1   Access to the clutch components is normally accomplished by removing the transaxle, leaving the engine in the vehicle. If the engine is being removed for major overhaul, then check the clutch for wear and replace worn components as necessary.
2   Referring to Chapter 7, Part A, remove the transaxle from the vehicle. Remove the release bearing (see Section 5).
3   To support the clutch disc during removal, install a clutch alignment tool through the splined hole **(see illustration)**.
4   Check the pressure plate and flywheel for indexing marks. They're usually an X, an O or some other white letter. If no marks are visible, make some to ensure installation of the components in the same relationship to each other **(see illustration)**.
5   Loosen the pressure plate-to-flywheel

bolts in 1/4-turn increments until they can be removed by hand. Follow a criss-cross pattern to avoid warping the pressure plate assembly. Support the pressure plate and completely remove the bolts, then detach the pressure plate and clutch disc.
6   On models with pull-type clutch only, remove the wedge collar and retainer ring from the pressure plate diaphragm spring by holding the collar against the diaphragm and working the retainer ring off the wedge collar legs with a small screwdriver. When the retainer has been removed, pry the wedge collar out of the diaphragm.

Inspection

7   Ordinarily, when a problem develops with the clutch, it can be attributed to wear of the clutch driven plate assembly (clutch disc). However, all components should be inspected at this time. **Note:** *If the clutch components are contaminated with oil, there will be shiny, black glazed spots on the clutch disc lining, which will cause the clutch to slip. Replacing clutch components won't completely cure the problem - be sure to check the rear crankshaft oil seal and the transaxle input shaft seal for leaks. If it looks like a seal is leaking, be sure to install a new one to avoid the same problem with a new clutch.*
8   Inspect the flywheel for cracks, heat checking, grooves and other obvious defects. If the imperfections are slight, a machine shop can machine the surface flat and smooth, which is highly recommended regardless of the surface appearance. Refer to Chapter 2 for the flywheel removal and installation procedure.
9   Inspect the lining on the clutch disc. There should be at least 1/16-inch of lining above the rivet heads. Check for loose rivets, distortion, cracks, broken springs and other obvious damage **(see illustration)**. As mentioned above, ordinarily the clutch disc is routinely replaced, so if in doubt about its condition, replace it with a new one.
10   Ordinarily, the release bearing is also

6.9 The clutch disc

1 **Lining** - *this will wear down in use*
2 **Rivets** - *these secure the lining and will damage the flywheel or pressure plate if allowed to contact the surfaces*
3 **Index marks** - *"Flywheel side" or something similar*

6.11 Inspect the pressure plate friction surface for score marks, cracks and signs of overheating

replaced along with the clutch disc (see Section 5).

11 Check the diaphragm spring fingers and the machined surfaces of the pressure plate **(see illustration)**. Light glazing can be removed with medium grit emery cloth. If a new pressure plate is required, new and factory-rebuilt units are available.

12 Check the condition of the wedge collar and retainer ring. If any of the wedge collar legs are bent or broken, or if the retainer ring is bent or deformed in any way, they should be replaced.

Installation

13 Before installation, clean the flywheel and pressure plate machined surfaces with lacquer thinner or acetone. It's important that no oil or grease is on these surfaces or the lining of the clutch disc. Handle the parts only with clean hands.

14 On models with pull-type clutch, install the wedge collar into the diaphragm spring from the transaxle side of the pressure plate. From the disc side of the pressure plate, install the retainer ring onto the "V" bend of the wedge collar legs. **Caution:** *Be sure you don't deform or otherwise damage the retainer ring or wedge collar legs or the release bearing will pull out of the wedge collar during operation.*

15 Position the clutch disc and pressure plate against the flywheel with the clutch plate held in place with an alignment tool. Make sure it's installed properly (most replacement clutch plates will be marked "flywheel side" or something similar - if it's not marked, install it with the damper springs toward the transaxle).

16 Tighten the pressure plate-to-flywheel bolts only finger tight, working around the pressure plate.

17 Center the clutch disc by inserting the alignment tool through the splined hub and into the bore in the crankshaft. Wiggle the alignment tool up, down or from side-to-side as needed to center the clutch. Tighten the pressure plate-to-flywheel bolts a little at a

time, working in a criss-cross pattern to prevent distorting the cover. After all the bolts are snug, tighten them to the torque listed in this Chapter's Specifications. Remove the alignment tool.

18 Put some high-temperature grease on the release lever fingers. On push-type clutches, lubricate the inner groove of the release bearing also (refer to Section 5).

19 Install the clutch release bearing as described in Section 5.

20 Install the transaxle, slave cylinder and all components that were removed previously. **Caution:** *On models with pull-type clutch, be especially careful when installing the transaxle to avoid damaging the wedge collar or retainer ring with the transaxle input shaft.*

21 Adjust the shift linkage as outlined in Chapter 7.

7 Starter/clutch interlock switch - check and replacement

1 The starter/clutch interlock switch is mounted on the clutch pedal support and allows the engine to be started only with the clutch pedal fully depressed.

Check

2 Disconnect the electrical connector from the switch. The switch is located near the top of the clutch pedal arm.

3 Connect an ohmmeter or self-powered test light (continuity tester) to the two switch terminals (if there are three terminals on the switch, one is for the cruise control. You'll probably have to check a wiring diagram to determine which two terminals to connect to).

4 With the clutch pedal in it's normal position there should be no continuity (the test light should not come on or the ohmmeter should read infinity).

5 Depress the clutch pedal. There should now be continuity (the test light should come on or the ohmmeter should indicate close to zero ohms).

6 If the switch fails to operate as described, check to make sure the plunger on the switch is contacting the clutch pedal. If it is, and the pedal depresses the plunger when the pedal is released, the switch is probably faulty.

Replacement

7 Disconnect the negative cable from the battery. **Caution:** *On models equipped with the Theftlock audio system, be sure the lockout feature is turned off before performing any procedure which requires disconnecting the battery.*

8 Disconnect the electrical connector and remove the switch.

9 Reference mark the amount of the switch protruding through the mounting bracket.

10 Remove the switch from the mount.

11 Install the new switch by reversing the removal procedure. Be sure the same amount of the switch protrudes through the mounting bracket as the old switch did.

12 Connect the negative battery cable.

13 Check to be sure the engine can be started only when the clutch pedal is fully depressed. Be sure to perform this test with the transaxle in Neutral.

8 Driveaxles - general information

Power is transmitted from the transaxle to the front wheels by two driveaxles, which consist of splined solid axles with constant velocity (CV) joints at each end.

There are two types of CV joints used. On the outer joint a double-offset design using ball bearings with an inner and outer race is used to allow angular movement. On the inner CV joint is a tri-pot design, with a spider bearing assembly and tri-pot housing to allow angular movement and permit the driveaxle to slide in and out.

The CV joints are protected by rubber boots, which are retained by clamps so the joints are protected from water and dirt. The

9.2 A screwdriver inserted through the caliper and into a disc cooling vane will hold the hub stationary while loosening the hub nut

9.5 A two-jaw puller works well for pushing the axle out of the hub (models with separate strut/steering knuckle)

9.6 Remove the axles from the transaxle using a slide hammer and adapter

9.9 Hub and bearing assembly bolts (one bolt not visible in this photo)

boots should be inspected periodically (see Chapter 1). The inner boots have very small breather holes which may leak a small amount of lubricant under some circumstances, such as when the joint is compressed during removal. Damaged CV joint boots must be replaced immediately or the joints can be damaged. Boot replacement involves removing the driveaxles. It's a good idea to disassemble, clean, inspect and repack the CV joint whenever replacing a CV joint boot to make sure the joint isn't contaminated with moisture or dirt, which would cause premature failure of the CV joint.

The most common symptom of worn or damaged CV joints, besides lubricant leaks, are a clicking noise in turns, a clunk when accelerating from a coasting condition or vibration at highway speeds.

9 Driveaxles - removal and installation

Removal

1   Remove the wheel cover and loosen the hub nut. Loosen the wheel lug nuts, raise the

front of the vehicle and support it securely on jackstands. Apply the parking brake and block the rear wheels to keep the vehicle from rolling off the jackstands. Remove the front wheel. Place a drain pan under the transaxle.
2   Remove the driveaxle hub nut. To prevent the hub from turning, insert a screwdriver through the caliper and into a rotor cooling vane, then remove the nut (see illustration). Note: *If you're working on a model with an integral strut/steering knuckle assembly and you're removing the driveaxle for access to some other component (strut removal, for example), it is unnecessary to remove the driveaxle hub nut.*
3   Remove the brake caliper and disc and support the caliper out of the way with a piece of wire (see Chapter 9).

Models with separate strut/steering knuckle

Refer to illustrations 9.2, 9.5 and 9.6

4   Remove the control arm-to-steering knuckle balljoint stud nut and separate the lower arm from the steering knuckle (see Chapter 10 if necessary). On models equipped with anti-lock brakes (ABS), remove the ABS

wheel speed sensor and place it to one side.
5   Push the driveaxle out of the hub with a puller (see illustration), then support the outer end of the driveaxle with a piece of wire to prevent damage to the inner CV joint.
6   On automatic transaxle equipped models, use a slide hammer and adapter to separate the driveaxle from the transaxle (see illustration).
7   On manual transaxle equipped models, the right driveaxle connects to an intermediate shaft. Use a slide hammer and adapter to separate the right axle from the intermediate shaft and the left axle from the transaxle.
8   On all models, support the CV joints and carefully remove the driveaxle from the vehicle.

Models with integral strut/steering knuckle

Refer to illustrations 9.9, 9.10 and 9.11

9   Remove the four bolts securing the hub bearing assembly to the steering knuckle (see illustration).
10   Using a large screwdriver or prybar, carefully pry the driveaxle out of the transaxle (see illustration).

9.10 A large prybar can be used to pry the inner CV joint out of the transaxle

9.11 Carefully remove the driveaxle and hub/bearing assembly through the opening in the steering knuckle

11   Support the CV joints and carefully remove the driveaxle through the opening in the steering knuckle **(see illustration)**. **Caution:** *Be careful not to tear the boots or nick the ABS exciter ring as you withdraw the axle.*

12   If necessary, the hub can be removed from the outer CV joint using a puller, similar to the setup shown in **illustration 9.5.**

Installation

Refer to illustration 9.13

13   Lubricate the differential seal with multi-purpose grease, raise the driveaxle into position while supporting the CV joints and insert the splined end of the inner CV joint into the differential side gear. Seat the shaft in the side gear by positioning the end of a screwdriver in the groove in the CV joint and tapping it into position with a hammer **(see illustration)**. On models with an intermediate shaft, slide the driveaxle inner CV joint onto the end of the intermediate shaft.

14   On all models, grasp the inner CV joint housing (not the driveaxle) and pull out to make sure the axle has seated securely.

Models with separate strut/steering knuckle

15   Apply a light coat of multi-purpose grease to the outer CV joint splines, pull out on the strut/steering knuckle assembly and install the stub axle in the hub.

16   Insert the control arm balljoint stud into the steering knuckle and tighten the nut. Be sure to use a new cotter pin (refer to Chapter 10). If equipped with ABS, install the ABS wheel speed sensor.

Models with integral strut/steering knuckle

17   Install the hub/bearing assembly onto the steering knuckle. Tighten the mounting bolts to the torque listed in this Chapter's Specifications.

All models

18   Install the brake disc and caliper (see

9.13 A large punch or screwdriver, positioned in the groove on the CV joint housing, can be used to seat the CV joint in the transaxle

Chapter 9 if necessary).

19   Install a **new** driveaxle hub nut. Lock the disc so it can't turn, using a screwdriver or punch inserted through the caliper into a disc cooling vane, and tighten the hub nut to the torque listed in this Chapter's Specifications.

20   Check the transaxle lubricant level and add some, if necessary, to bring it to the appropriate level (see Chapter 1).

21   Install the wheel and lower the vehicle. Install the wheel cover.

---

10   Driveaxle boot replacement

Note: *If the CV joints exhibit wear indicating the need for an overhaul (usually due to torn boots), explore all options before beginning the job. Complete rebuilt driveaxles are available on an exchange basis, which eliminates a lot of time and work. Whatever is decided, check on the cost and availability of parts before disassembling the vehicle.*

1   Remove the driveaxle (see Section 9).

2   Place the driveaxle in a vise lined with rags to avoid damage to the shaft.

10.4 Snap-ring pliers should be used to remove both the inner and outer retaining rings

Inner CV joint

Refer to illustrations 10.4, 10.8, 10.9, 10.10 and 10.12

3   Cut off the boot seal retaining clamps and slide the boot towards the center of the driveaxle. Mark the tri-pot housing and driveaxle so they can be reinstalled in the same relative positions, then slide the housing off the spider assembly.

4   Remove the spider assembly from the axle by first removing the inner retaining ring and sliding the spider assembly back to expose the front retaining ring. Remove the front retaining ring and slide the joint off the driveaxle **(see illustration)**.

5   Use tape or a cloth wrapped around the spider bearing assembly to retain the bearings during removal and installation.

6   Slide the boot off the axle.

7   Clean all of the old grease out of the housing and spider assembly. Carefully disassemble each section of the spider assembly, one at a time, and clean the needle bearings with solvent. Inspect the rollers, spider cross, bearings and housing for scoring, pitting and other signs of abnormal wear. Apply a coat of CV joint grease to the inner bearing surfaces

10.8 Before installing the CV joint boot, wrap the axle splines with tape to prevent damage to the boot

10.9 When installing the spider assembly on the driveaxle, make sure the recess in the counterbore (arrow) is facing the end of the driveaxle

10.10 Pack the housing with half of the grease furnished with the new boot and place the remainder in the boot

10.12 the length of inner CV joints (A) must be adjusted before the large boot clamp is tightened - on models through 1998 A is 8.1 inches, and 4.9 inches on 1999 and later models

to hold the needle bearings in place when reassembling the spider assembly.

8   Wrap the driveaxle splines with tape to avoid damaging the boot, then slide the boot onto the axle **(see illustration)**.

9   Install the spider bearing with the recess in the counterbore facing the end of the drive-axle **(see illustration)**.

10   Pack the housing with half of the grease furnished with the new boot and place the remainder in the boot **(see illustration)**.

11   Install the tri-pot housing.

12   Seat the boot in the housing and axle seal grooves, then adjust the length of the joint **(see illustration)**.

13   Install the retaining clamps, then install the driveaxle as described in Section 9.

10.14 Carefully tap around the circumference of the seal retainer to remove it from the housing

10.16 Use snap-ring pliers to remove the inner retaining ring

10.19 Gently tap the inner race with a brass punch to tilt it enough to allow ball bearing removal

10.20 Using a dull screwdriver, carefully pry the balls out of the cage

10.21 Tilt the inner race and cage 90-degrees, then align the windows in the cage (A) with the lands (B) and rotate the inner race up and out of the outer race

10.22 Align the inner race lands (A) with the cage windows (B) and rotate the inner race out of the cage

Outer CV joint

Refer to illustrations 10.14, 10.16, 10.19, 10.20, 10.21, 10.22, 10.23a, 10.23b, 10.26, 10.27 and 10.31

14   Tap lightly around the outer circumference of the seal retainer with a hammer and punch to dislodge and remove it. Be very careful not to deform the retainer, or it won't seal properly **(see illustration)**.

15   Cut off the band retaining the boot to the shaft.

16   Remove the snap-ring and slide the joint assembly off **(see illustration)**.

17   Slide the old boot off the driveaxle.

18   Place marks on the inner race and cage so they both can be installed facing out when reassembling the joint.

19   Press down on the inner race far enough to allow a ball bearing to be removed. If it's difficult to tilt, tap the inner race with a brass punch and hammer **(see illustration)**.

20   Pry the balls out of the cage, one at a time, with a blunt screwdriver or wooden tool **(see illustration)**.

21   With all of the balls removed from the cage and the cage/inner race assembly tilted 90-degrees, align the cage windows with the

10.23a Check the inner race lands and grooves for pitting and score marks

10.23b Check the cage for cracks, pitting and score marks - shiny spots are normal and don't affect operation

outer race lands and remove the assembly from the outer race **(see illustration)**.

22   Remove the inner race from the cage by turning the inner race 90-degrees in the cage, aligning the inner lands with the cage windows and rotating the inner race out of the cage **(see illustration)**.

23   Clean the components with solvent to remove all traces of grease. Inspect the cage and races for pitting, score marks, cracks and other signs of wear and damage. Shiny, polished spots are normal and won't adversely affect CV joint operation **(see illustrations)**.

10.26 Align the cage windows and the inner and outer race grooves, then tilt the cage and inner race to insert the balls

10.27 Apply grease through the splined hole, then insert a wooden dowel (approximately 1-5/16-inch diameter) through the splined hole and push down - the dowel will force the grease into the joint

10.31 Carefully tap around the circumference of the seal retainer to install it on the housing (early model shown)

24   Install the inner race in the cage by reversing the technique described in Step 21.

25   Install the inner race and cage assembly in the outer race by reversing the procedure in Step 20. The marks that were previously applied to the inner race and cage must both be visible after the assembly is installed in the outer race.

26   Press the balls into the cage windows **(see illustration)**.

27   Pack the CV joint assembly with lubricant through the inner splined hole. Force the grease into the bearing by inserting a wooden dowel through the splined hole and pushing it to the bottom of the joint. Repeat this procedure until the bearing is completely packed **(see illustration)**.

28   Install the boot on the driveaxle as described in Step 10. Apply a liberal amount of grease to the inside of the axle boot.

29   Position the CV joint assembly on the driveaxle, aligning the splines. Using a soft-face hammer, drive the CV joint onto the driveaxle until the retaining ring is seated in the groove.

30   Seat the inner end of the boot in the seal groove and install the retaining clamp.

31   Install the seal retainer securely by tapping evenly around the outer circumference with a hammer and punch **(see illustration)**. **Note:** *Earlier models use a seal retainer while later models use boot retaining clamps on the outboard housing. Always follow the boot manufacturers instructions when installing boot clamps since several different types are available.*

32   Install the driveaxle as described in Section 9.

11   Intermediate axleshaft – removal and installation (early models)

Removal

1   Loosen the right front wheel lug nuts, raise the front of the vehicle and support it securely on jackstands. Apply the parking brake and block the rear wheels to keep the vehicle from rolling off the jackstands. Remove the right wheel.

2   Drain the transaxle.

3   Remove the right driveaxle (see Section 9).

4   Remove the bracket bolts retaining the intermediate shaft assembly.

5   Remove the bolts connecting the shaft assembly-to-transaxle.

6   Pull the shaft out of the transaxle.

Installation

7   Lubricate the lips of the differential seal with multi-purpose grease and slide the intermediate shaft into the transaxle.

8   The remainder of installation is the reverse of removal. Refill the transaxle with the special lubricant (see Chapter 1).

Chapter 9 Brakes

Contents

	Section
Anti-lock Brake System (ABS) - general information	15
Brake check	See Chapter 1
Brake disc - inspection, removal and installation	4
Brake fluid level check	See Chapter 1
Brake hoses and lines - inspection and replacement	8
Brake light switch - removal, installation and adjustment	14
Brake system bleeding	9
Disc brake caliper - removal, overhaul and installation	3
Disc brake pads (front and rear) - replacement	2

	Section
General information	1
Master cylinder - removal, overhaul and installation	7
Parking brake - adjustment	10
Parking brake cables - replacement	11
Parking brake shoes (1997 and later) - replacement	12
Power brake booster - check, removal and installation	13
Rear brake shoes - replacement	5
Rear wheel cylinder - removal, overhaul and installation	6

Specifications

General
Brake fluid type ... See Chapter 1

Disc brakes
Brake pad lining minimum thickness ... See Chapter 1
Front and rear
  Minimum thickness ... Refer to dimension stamped on disc
  Runout (maximum) ... 0.003 in
  Thickness variation limit ... 0.0005 in

Drum brakes
Brake shoe lining minimum thickness ... See Chapter 1
Maximum allowable diameter ... Cast into drum

Torque specifications
Ft-lbs (unless otherwise indicated)

Note: *One foot-pound (ft-lb) of torque is equivalent to 12 inch-pounds (in-lbs) of torque. Torque values below approximately 15 foot-pounds are expressed in inch-pounds, because most foot-pound torque wrenches are not accurate at these smaller values.*

Bleeder valve
  Front ... 115 in-lbs
  Rear
    Caliper ... 97 in-lbs
    Wheel cylinder ... 62 in-lbs
Caliper mounting (slide) bolts (1996 and earlier models, and 1997 Olds) ... 80
Caliper mounting (slide) bolts (1997 through 2000, except Olds)
  Front ... 63
  Rear ... 32
Caliper mounting bolts (2001 and later models)
  Front
    All except 5.3L models ... 70
    5.3L models ... 44
  Rear ... 32
Caliper mounting bracket bolts (1996 and earlier models, and 1997 Olds)
  Front ... 148
  Rear ... 81
Caliper mounting bracket bolts (1997 and later, except Olds)
  Front ... 133
  Rear ... 85
Brake hose-to-caliper bolt
  Front and rear (models through 1998) ... 32
  Front (1999 and later) ... 40
  Rear
    1999 through 2001 ... 32
    2002 and later ... 40
Master cylinder-to-booster nuts ... 18
Proportioner valve caps ... 20
Wheel cylinder mounting bolts ... 15
Wheel lug nuts ... See Chapter 1

2.5a Before disassembling the brake, wash it thoroughly with brake system cleaner and allow it to dry - position a drain pan under the brake to catch the residue - DO NOT use compressed air to blow off brake dust!

2.5b To make room for the new pads, use a C-clamp to depress the piston into the caliper before removing the caliper and pads - do this a little at a time, keeping an eye on the fluid level in the master cylinder to make sure it doesn't overflow

1   General information

Conventional (non-ABS) brake system

The vehicles covered by this manual are equipped with hydraulically operated front and rear brake systems. All front brake systems are disc type, while the rear brakes are either disc or drum. All brakes are self adjusting. Front and rear disc brakes automatically compensate for pad wear. Rear drum brakes incorporate an adjusting mechanism which is activated any time the service brakes are applied.

Hydraulic system

The hydraulic system consists of two separate circuits. The master cylinder has separate reservoirs for the two circuits and in the event of a leak or failure in one hydraulic circuit, the other circuit will remain operative. A visual warning of circuit failure or air in the system is given by a warning light activated on the dash.

Proportioner valves

The proportioner valves are designed to provide better front to rear braking balance with heavy brake application. These valves allow more pressure to be applied to the front brakes (under certain braking operations) due to the fact the rear of the vehicle is lighter and does not require as much braking force.

Power brake booster

The power brake booster, utilizing engine manifold vacuum and atmospheric pressure to provide assistance to the hydraulically operated brakes, is mounted on the firewall in the engine compartment.

Parking brake

The parking brake operates the rear brakes only, through cable actuation. It's activated by a pedal mounted on the left side kick panel.

2.6a On 1996 and earlier models (and 1997 Olds) remove the caliper mounting bolts (arrows) . . .

Service

After completing any operation involving disassembly of any part of the brake system, always test drive the vehicle to check for proper braking performance before resuming normal driving. When testing the brakes, perform the tests on a clean, dry flat surface. Conditions other than these can lead to inaccurate test results.

Test the brakes at various speeds with both light and heavy pedal pressure. The vehicle should stop evenly without pulling to one side or the other. Avoid locking the brakes because this slides the tires and diminishes braking efficiency and control of the vehicle.

Tires, vehicle load and front-end alignment are factors which also affect braking performance.

2   Disc brake pads (front and rear) - replacement

Warning: *Disc brake pads must be replaced on both front or rear wheels at the same time - never replace the pads on only one wheel. Also, the dust created by the brake system is*

2.6b . . . then slide the caliper out of the mounting bracket . . .

harmful to your health. Never blow it out with compressed air and don't inhale any of it. An approved filtering mask should be worn when working on the brakes. Do not, under any circumstances, use petroleum-based solvents to clean brake parts. Use brake system cleaner only!

Front

Removal

Refer to illustrations 2.5a, 2.5b, 2.6a, 2.6b, 2.6c, 2.6d, 2.6e, 2.7a, 2.7b, 2.8a, 2.8b and 2.8c

1   Remove and discard two-thirds of the brake fluid from the master cylinder.
2   Loosen the wheel lug nuts.
3   Raise the vehicle and support it securely on jackstands.
4   Remove the wheel and reinstall two lug nuts to hold the disc in position.
5   Clean the caliper, disc and other components with brake system cleaner before beginning any brake work **(see illustration)**. This should remove traces of potentially hazardous brake dust. Collect the drippings in a plastic container. Use a large C-clamp over the caliper to push the pistons back into the body of the caliper **(see illustration)**.

2.6c . . . and suspend the caliper with a piece of wire - DO NOT let the caliper hang by the hose

2.6d On 1997 and later models (except Olds), hold the caliper slide pin with an open-end wrench (A) and loosen the lower mounting bolt with another wrench (B) . . .

2.6e . . . then pivot the caliper up and support it in this position for access to the brake pads

2.7a Use a screwdriver to pry the spring of the outside pad away from the caliper while removing the pad

2.7b Unsnap the pad retainers from the pistons

6   On 1996 and earlier (and 1997 Olds) models remove the caliper mounting bolts and pull the caliper straight up and off, but do not allow it to hang by the brake hose **(see illustrations)**. On 1997 and later models (except Olds) remove the lower caliper bolt and swing the caliper upward **(see illustrations)**.
7   On 1996 and earlier models (and 1997 Olds) remove the outer pad from the caliper **(see illustration)**. If necessary, use a screwdriver to pry up on the retaining spring of the outer pad while sliding it out of the caliper.

Unclip the inner pad from the pistons **(see illustrations)**.
8   On 1997 and later models (except Olds) remove the inner and outer pads from the caliper mount then remove the pad retaining clips from the caliper mount **(see illustrations)**.

2.8a On 1997 and later models (except Olds), remove the inner brake pad . . .

2.8b . . . the outer brake pad . . .

2.8c . . . and the upper and lower pad retainers from the caliper mounting bracket

2.9a Using a "C" clamp and flat piece of wood or metal, push the pistons into the caliper

2.9b Apply anti-squeal compound to the back of both pads (let the compound "set up" a few minutes before installing them)

2.11 On some 1997 and later models, it will be necessary to check the condition of the anti-rattle spring in the center of the caliper, replacing it if necessary

2.12 Clean the caliper slide pin and inspect it for scoring and corrosion; coat the pin with high-temperature grease

Installation

Refer to illustrations 2.9a, 2.9b, 2.11 and 2.12

9   Compress the piston(s) back into the caliper bore using a "C" clamp and a block of wood (see illustration) then coat the back of the new brake pads with an anti-squeal compound (see illustration).

10   If the boots for the caliper mounting bolts are torn or damaged, pry them out with a small screwdriver and replace them with new ones.

11   To install the new inner and outer pads reverse the removal procedure. **Note:** *On 1997 and later models (except Olds) make sure the anti rattle clip (if equipped) is securely fastened in place* (see illustration).

12   Install the caliper over the disc and align the bolt holes. The rubber boots should be between the caliper and the mounting bracket. Lubricate the entire length of the mounting bolts with a thin film of silicone grease (see illustration). Be sure to tighten the caliper mounting bolts to the torque listed in this Chapter's Specifications.

13   Lower the vehicle. Fill the reservoir with the recommended fluid (see Chapter 1) and pump the brake pedal several times to bring the pads into contact with discs.

14   Road test the vehicle carefully before returning it to normal service.

Rear

Removal

Refer to illustrations 2.24, 2.31 and 2.32

15   Remove and discard two-thirds of the brake fluid from the reservoir.

16   Loosen the wheel lug nuts, raise the vehicle and support it securely on jackstands. Remove the wheel.

17   Install two lug nuts to retain the disc when the caliper is removed.

1994 and later models (except Lumina)

18   On 1996 and earlier models remove the bolt and washer attaching the cable support bracket to the caliper body.

19   On 1996 and earlier models remove the sleeve bolt from the bottom of the caliper, then pivot the caliper up. On 1997 and later models remove the upper caliper bolt and pivot the caliper downward.

20   Remove the pads and retainers from the caliper.

Others

21   Remove the bolts retaining the shield assembly, then remove the shield.

22   Loosen the tension on the parking brake cables at the equalizer (see Section 9).

23   Disconnect the cable and return spring from the parking brake lever.

24   Hold the caliper lever and remove the

locknut (see illustration). Remove the lever and the lever seal.

25   Compress the piston into the caliper bore. Using two pairs of adjustable pliers, squeeze the inner pad and the outer flanges on the caliper housing together as much as possible.

26   Reinstall the lever seal with the rubber sealing bead against the caliper housing.

27   Reinstall the lever and it's retaining nut.

28   Remove the caliper mounting bolts.

29   Detach the brake hose from the suspension bracket.

30   Remove the caliper and support it with a piece of wire.

31   Using a screwdriver, disengage the buttons on the outer pad from the holes in the caliper housing (see illustration). Remove the outer pad.

32   From the open side of the caliper, press in on the edge of the inner pad and tilt it out to release the pad from the retainer (see illustration). Remove the inner pad. Also remove the check valve from the center of the caliper piston.

Installation

Refer to illustrations 2.35, 2.38a, 2.38b, 2.43 and 2.44

33   Check the bolt boots for damage and replace them if necessary.

2.24 Parking brake lever mounting nut

2.31 Use a screwdriver to pry the outer pad from the caliper

2.32 Unclip the inner pad from the retainer

2.35 Using a pair of needle nose pliers, engage the tips of the pliers into the cutouts of the piston face, then turn the piston into the cylinder bore - after the piston bottoms out, align the cutouts in the piston 90 degrees from the centerline of the caliper mounting bolts (1994 through 1996 models and 1997 Olds)

34   Check the mounting bolts and sleeves for corrosion, replacing them if necessary. Note that the sleeves on 1994 through 1996 models are installed in the caliper and that the sleeves on 1997 and later models are installed in the caliper mount.

1994 and later models (except Lumina)

35   On 1994 through 1996 models (and 1997 Olds) bottom the piston in the caliper by threading it in using a suitable spanner-like tool **(see illustration)**. Turn the piston as necessary so that a line drawn through the piston slots would be exactly perpendicular (90 degrees) to a line drawn through the caliper mounting bolt holes.

36   On 1997 and later models (except Olds) compress the piston back into the caliper bore using a "C" clamp and a block of wood **(see illustration 2.9a)**.

37   Coat the back of the new brake pads with an anti-squeal compound **(see illustration 2.9b)**.

38   On all 1994 and later models install the pad retainers on the caliper mount **(see illustrations)**. Install the inner and outer pads in the caliper mount. **Note:** *Where equipped, the wear sensor is on the outer pad.*

39   Pivot the caliper assembly over the disc and align the bolt holes. The rubber boots should be between the caliper and the mounting bracket. Lubricate the entire length of the mounting bolts with a thin film of silicone grease **(see illustration 2.12)**.

40   The remainder of reassembly is the opposite of disassembly. Tighten fasteners to the torques listed at the beginning of this chapter. Road test the vehicle carefully before returning it to normal service. **Warning:** *Before driving the car, pump the brakes several times to seat the pads against the disc.*

Others

41   Push the sleeves into the caliper, away from the inner pad.

42   Apply a thin film of silicone grease to a new piston check valve and install it in the face of the piston.

43   With the inner pad retainer properly positioned **(see illustration)**, place the new inner pad on the piston with the tab fitting into the "D" notch in the piston face. If the tab does not line up with the notch, turn the piston with a pair of needle-nose pliers until it is in proper alignment.

2.38a Install the upper anti-rattle clip . . .

44   Install the outer pad so the spring retainer fits into the slots in the caliper housing **(see illustration)**.

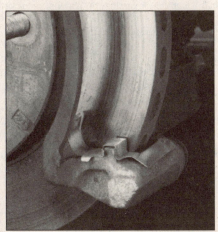

2.38b . . . and the lower anti-rattle clip in the caliper mounting bracket - make sure they're both fully seated

2.43 Position the tangs of the pad retainer as shown, then clip the pad into the retainer - make sure the tab on the retainer fits into the "D" notch in the piston face

2.44 Slide the outer pad into the caliper, making sure the ends of the retainer spring fit into the slots

45   Slide caliper over the disc. Install the mounting bolts and tighten them to the torque listed in this Chapter's Specifications.
46   Pump the brake pedal several times to seat the pads against the disc.
47   Install the bracket and retaining bolt.
48   Clean the area around the lever seal.
49   Lubricate the lever seal and install it with the sealing bead against the caliper housing.
50   Install the lever on the actuator screw hex with the lever pointing down.
51   To prevent parking brake actuation, rotate the lever back against the stop and tighten the nut.
52   Install the return spring.
53   Connect and adjust the parking brake cable (see Section 8).
54   Remove the two lug nuts used to retain the disc. Install the wheel and tighten the lug nuts to the torque listed in the Chapter 1 Specifications.

3   Disc brake caliper - removal, overhaul and installation

Warning: *Dust created by the brake system is harmful to your health. Never blow it out with compressed air and don't inhale any of it. An approved filtering mask should be worn when working on the brakes. Do not, under any circumstances, use petroleum-based solvents to clean brake parts. Use brake system cleaner only!*
Note: *If an overhaul is indicated (usually because of fluid leakage) explore all options before beginning the job. New and factory rebuilt calipers are available on an exchange basis, which makes this job quite easy. If it's decided to rebuild the calipers, make sure a rebuild kit is available before proceeding. Always rebuild the calipers in pairs - never rebuild just one of them.*

Removal

1   The removal procedure is the same as in Section 2 with the exception of disconnecting the hydraulic line from the caliper and, on 1994 through 1996 models (except Lumina),

3.4 Place a block of wood or rags in front of the pistons, then apply compressed air to the hydraulic line inlet to force the pistons out

the parking brake cable (rear disc only) and upper caliper bolts. On 1997 and later models it will be necessary to remove the hydraulic brake line and lower caliper bolt. **Warning:** *Before servicing any ABS component, it is mandatory that hydraulic pressure in the system be relieved. With ignition off, pump the brake pedal a MINÍMUM of 40 times, using full pedal strokes.*

Overhaul
Front (1996 and earlier models, and 1997 Olds)
Refer to illustrations 3.4, 3.6, 3.7a, 3.7b, 3.13 and 3.15
Note: *Due to the unavailability of overhaul kits for these models the calipers on 1997 and later models (except Olds) should be replaced with new or rebuilt units.*
2   Refer to Section 2 and remove the brake pads from the caliper.
3   Clean the exterior of the caliper with brake system cleaner. Never use gasoline, kerosene or petroleum-based cleaning solvents. Place the caliper on a clean workbench.

3.6 Use a screwdriver to pry the boots from the caliper

4   Position a wood block or several shop rags in the caliper as a cushion, then use compressed air to remove the pistons from the caliper **(see illustration)**. Use only enough air pressure to ease the pistons out of the bore. If a piston is blown out, even with the cushion in place, it may be damaged. **Warning:** *Never place your fingers in front of the pistons in an attempt to catch or protect it when applying compressed air, as serious injury could occur.*
5   If only one piston comes out it will have to be slightly reinserted. Wedge a spacer between the reinserted piston and the caliper housing. Again apply air pressure to release the frozen piston.
6   Carefully pry the dust boots out of the caliper bores **(see illustration)**.
7   Using a wood or plastic tool, remove the piston seal from the groove in the caliper bores **(see illustrations)**. Metal tools may cause bore damage.
8   Remove the caliper bleeder screw. Discard all rubber parts.
9   Clean the remaining parts with brake system cleaner and let them dry.
10   Carefully examine the pistons for nicks

3.7a Exploded view of a typical front brake caliper

A   Caliper body
B   Piston seals
C   Pistons
D   Dust boots
E   Caliper bleeder screw
F   Bleeder screw dust cap

3.7b The piston seal should be removed with a plastic or wooden tool to avoid damage to the bore and seal groove - a pencil will do the job

3.13 Lubricate the piston and insert it (with boot attached) carefully into the bore - do not twist the seal

3.15 Use the proper size driver to install the boot to the caliper

3.18 Exploded view of the rear brake caliper

1	Bolt boot	9	Balance spring and
2	Sleeve		retainer
3	Caliper body	10	Actuator screw
4	Return spring	11	Piston seal
5	Parking brake lever	12	Piston locator
6	Nut	13	Snap-ring
7	Thrust washer	14	Piston
8	Shaft seal	15	Caliper boot
		16	Check valve

and burrs and loss of plating. If surface defects are present, the parts must be replaced.

11   Check the caliper bores in a similar way. Light polishing with crocus cloth is permissible to remove light corrosion and stains. Discard the mounting bolts if they're corroded or damaged.

12   When assembling, lubricate the piston bores and seals with clean brake fluid. Position the seals in the caliper bore grooves.

13   Lubricate the pistons with clean brake fluid, then install new boots in the piston grooves with the fold toward the open end of the piston **(see illustration)**.

14   Insert the pistons squarely into the caliper bores, then apply force to bottom them.

15   Position the dust boots in the caliper counterbores, then use a driver to install them into position **(see illustration)**. If a seal driver isn't available, carefully tap around the outer circumference of the seal using a blunt punch. Make sure the boot is recessed evenly below the caliper face.

16   Install the bleeder valve.

17   Remove the bushings, support bushings

and boots from the caliper mounting bracket and install new ones **(see illustration 3.7a)**.

Rear (1993 and earlier and 1994 Lumina)

Refer to illustrations 3.18, 3.22, 3.26, 3.46 and 3.49

Note: *Later model calipers require special tools for overhaul and should be replaced with new or rebuilt units.*

18   Remove the sleeves and bolt boots **(see illustration)**.

19   Remove the pad retainer from the end of the piston by rotating the retainer until the inside tabs line up with notches in the piston.

20   Remove the lever nut, lever and lever seal.

21   Pad the interior of the caliper with rags.

22   Using a wrench to rotate the actuator screw **(see illustration)**, work the piston out of the caliper bore (in the direction the parking brake is applied).

23   Remove the balance spring.

24   Remove the actuator screw by pressing on the threaded end.

25   Remove the shaft seal and thrust washer from the actuator screw.

26   While being careful not to scratch the

3.22 Rotate the actuator screw to remove the piston

3.26 Carefully pry the dust boot out of the housing, taking care not to scratch the surface of the bore

3.46 Use a seal driver to seat the boot in the caliper housing

A

B

C

3.49 Sleeve boot installation procedure

A   *Install the sleeve boot into the groove in the sleeve bore, then push the sleeve into the boot*
B   *Install the other boot into the groove in the other side of the bore*
C   *Push the sleeve back and seat both boots into the grooves in the ends of the sleeve*

---

housing bore, remove the boot **(see illustration)**.
27   Using snap-ring pliers, remove the snap-ring.
28   Remove the piston locator.
29   Using a plastic or wooden tool (so as not to damage the bore), remove the seal from the caliper bore **(see illustration 3.7b)**.
30   Remove the bleeder valve.
31   Clean all parts not included in the repair kit with brake cleaner or denatured alcohol.
32   Dry all parts with filtered unlubricated compressed air.
33   Blow out all passages in the housing and bleeder valve.
34   Inspect all parts for wear, damage and corrosion. Replace any parts as needed. **Note:** *It is okay to remove minor corrosion from the caliper bore using crocus cloth.*
35   Lubricate all of the internal parts with clean brake fluid **(see illustration 3.18)**.
36   Install a new piston seal into the caliper bore groove. Be sure not to twist the seal.
37   Install a new piston locator on the piston.
38   Install the thrust washer on the actuator screw with the grayish side towards the caliper housing and the copper side towards the piston assembly.
39   Install the shaft seal on the actuator screw.
40   Install the actuator screw onto the piston assembly.
41   Install the balance spring and retainer into the piston recess.
42   Install the piston assembly with the actuator screws and balance spring into the lubricated bore of the caliper.
43   Push the piston into the caliper bore so the locator is past the retainer groove in the caliper bore. **Note:** *A pair of adjustable pliers might be necessary to press the piston into the caliper bore.*
44   Using snap-ring pliers, install the snap-ring.
45   With the inside lip of the boot in the piston groove and boot fold toward the end of the piston that contacts the brake pad, install the

caliper boot onto the piston **(see illustration 3.13)**.
46   Use a seal driver to seat the caliper boot into the cylinder counterbore **(see illustration)**. If a seal driver isn't available, use a blunt punch and carefully tap around the outer circumference of the seal to seat it.
47   Install the pad retainer on the piston.
48   Lubricate outside diameter of the mounting bolt sleeves and the caliper sleeve cavities with silicone grease.
49   Install one sleeve boot into a groove of the sleeve cavity **(see illustration)**.
50   Install a sleeve through the opposite side of the cavity and continue pushing sleeve until the boot lip seats in the sleeve groove.
51   Install boot in the opposite side of the sleeve cavity groove and push the sleeve through the cavity far enough for that boot lip to slip into the remaining groove of the sleeve.
52   Repeat the sleeve boot installation procedure to the remaining sleeve.

Installation

53   The installation procedure is the same as in Section 2.
54   When attaching the hydraulic line to the caliper, use new copper washers at the line-to-caliper connection.
55   Bleed the hydraulic system as described in Section 7.

---

4   Brake disc - inspection, removal and installation

Refer to illustrations 4.3, 4.4a, 4.4b, 4.5a and 4.5b

Inspection

1   Loosen the wheel lug nuts, raise the vehicle and support it securely on jackstands. Apply the parking brake and block the wheels to keep the vehicle from rolling off the jackstands. Remove the wheel and install three lug nuts to hold the disc in place.
2   Remove the brake caliper as outlined in

Section 2 (it's part of the pad replacement procedure). You don't have to disconnect the brake hose. After removing the caliper bolts, suspend the caliper out of the way with a piece of wire - DO NOT let it hang by the hose.
3   Visually inspect the disc surface for score marks and other damage. Light scratches and shallow grooves are normal and may not be detrimental to brake operation, but deep score marks - over 0.015-inch (0.38 mm) deep - require disc removal and refinishing by an automotive machine shop. Be sure to check both sides of the disc **(see illustration)**. If pulsating has been felt during application of the brakes, suspect excessive disc runout.
4   To check disc runout, mount a dial indicator with the stem resting at a point about 1/2-inch from the outer edge of the disc **(see illustration)**. Set the indicator to zero and

Chapter 9   Brakes

9-9

4.3 The brake pads on this vehicle were obviously neglected, as they wore down to the rivets and cut deep grooves into the disc - wear this severe will require replacement of the disc

4.4a Check for runout with a dial indicator - mount it with the indicator needle about 1/2-inch from the outer edge of the disc

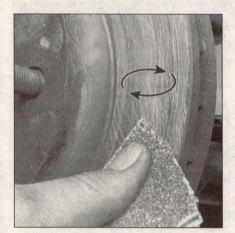

4.4b If you don't have the discs machined, at the very least be sure to remove the glaze from the disc surface with sandpaper or emery cloth (use a swirling motion as shown here)

4.5a The minimum wear (or discard) thickness (arrow) is cast into the disc

4.5b Measure the thickness of the disc at several points with a micrometer

turn the disc. The indicator reading should not exceed the specified allowable runout limit. If it does, the disc should be refinished by an automotive machine shop. **Note:** *The discs should be resurfaced, regardless of the dial indicator reading, to impart a smooth finish and ensure perfectly flat brake pad surfaces which will eliminate pedal pulsations. At the very least, if you don't have the discs resurfaced, remove the glaze with sandpaper or emery cloth using a swirling motion* **(see illustration).**

5   Never machine the disc to a thickness less than the specified minimum allowable refinish thickness. The minimum wear (or discard) thickness is cast into the disc **(see illustration).** The disc thickness can be checked with a micrometer **(see illustration).**

Removal

Refer to illustration 4.6

6   Remove the caliper mounting bracket if equipped **(see illustration). Warning:** *The manufacturer recommends replacing the caliper bracket mounting bolts if they are removed.*

Installation

7   Place the disc in position over the threaded studs.

8   Install the caliper and brake pad assembly (refer to Section 2 for the caliper installation procedure, if necessary). Tighten the caliper bolts to the torque listed in this Chapter's Specifications.

9   Install the wheel, then lower the vehicle to the ground. Tighten the lug nuts to the torque listed in the Chapter 1 Specifications. Depress the brake pedal a few times to bring the brake pads into contact with the disc. Bleeding of the system won't be necessary unless the brake hose was disconnected from the caliper. Check the operation of the brakes carefully before driving the vehicle in traffic.

---

5   Rear brake shoes - replacement

Warning: *Drum brake shoes must be replaced on both rear wheels at the same time - never replace the shoes on only one wheel. Also, the dust created by the brake system is harmful to your health. Never blow it out with compressed air and don't inhale any of it. An approved filtering mask should be worn when working on the brakes. Do not, under any circumstances, use petroleum-based solvents to clean brake parts. Use brake cleaner or denatured alcohol only!*

4.6 Remove the bolts (arrows) and detach the caliper mounting bracket

5.5a Drum brake components

1   Actuator spring
2   Trailing shoe
3   Retractor spring
4   Leading shoe
5   Adjusting screw
6   Actuator lever
7   Wheel cylinder
8   Backing plate

5.5b Use a pair of needle-nose pliers to remove the actuator spring

5.5c Wedge a flat-bladed screwdriver under the spring and pry it out of the leading brake shoe, then remove the shoe, adjusting screw and actuator lever

5.5d Lift the retractor spring from the trailing brake shoe and swing the shoe out from the hub area to gain access to the parking brake cable

Caution: *Whenever the brake shoes are replaced, the return and hold-down springs should also be replaced. Due to the continuous heating/cooling cycle the springs are subjected to, they lose tension over a period of* time and may allow the shoes to drag on the drum and wear at a much faster rate than normal. When replacing the rear brake shoes, use only high-quality, nationally-recognized brand name parts.*

Removal

Refer to illustrations 5.5a, 5.5b, 5.5c, 5.5d, 5.5e and 5.5f

1   Loosen the wheel lug nuts, raise the rear of the vehicle and support it securely on jackstands. Block the front wheels to keep the vehicle from rolling off the jackstands.

2   Release the parking brake and remove the wheel. **Note:** *All four rear shoes must be replaced at the same time, but to avoid mixing up parts, work on only one brake assembly at a time.*

3   Remove the brake drum. If it's difficult to remove, back off the parking brake cable, remove the access hole plug from the backing plate, insert a screwdriver through the hole and press in to push the parking brake lever off its stop. This will allow the brake shoes to retract slightly. Insert a punch through the hole at the bottom of the splash shield and tap gently on the punch to loosen the drum. Use a rubber mallet to tap gently on the outer rim of the drum and/or around the inner drum diameter by the spindle. Avoid using excessive force.

4   Clean the brake assembly with brake

5.5e Rotate the brake shoe to release the parking brake lever from the shoe

5.5f Use a screwdriver to pry the retractor spring over the alignment peg (arrow)

5.6a Lubricate the contact surfaces of the backing plate with high-temperature grease

5.6b Lubricate the adjuster screw with high-temperature grease prior to installation

system cleaner - DO NOT use compressed air to blow the dust out of the brake assembly.

5 Refer to the accompanying illustrations and perform the brake show removal procedure. Be sure to stay in order and to read the caption under each illustration.

Installation

Refer to illustrations 5.6a, 5.6b and 5.8
6 Installation of the shoes is the reverse of removal. Lubricate components as shown **(see illustrations)**.

7 Set the preliminary shoe adjustment by turning the star wheel on the adjuster so that the diameter of the linings is 0.05 inch less than the inner diameter of the drum.

8 Before reinstalling the drum, check it for cracks, score marks, deep scratches and hard spots, which will appear as blue discolored areas. If the hard spots can't be removed with fine emery cloth or if any of the other conditions listed above exist, the drum must be taken to an automotive machine shop to have it turned. **Note:** *The drums should be resurfaced, regardless of the surface appearance, to impart a smooth finish and ensure a perfectly round drum (which will eliminate brake pedal pulsations related to out-of-round drums). At the very least, if you don't have the drums resurfaced, remove the glaze from the surface with medium-grit emery cloth using a swirling motion. If the drum won't "clean up" before the maximum service limit is reached in the machining operation, install a new one. The maximum wear diameter is cast into each brake drum* **(see illustration)**.

9 Install the brake drum on the axle flange.
10 Mount the wheel, install the lug nuts, then lower the vehicle.
11 Apply and release the brake pedal 30 to 35 times using normal pedal force. Pause about one second between pedal applications. After adjustment, make sure that both wheels turn freely.

6 Rear wheel cylinder - removal, overhaul and installation

Refer to illustrations 6.4, 6.5 and 6.7
Note: *If an overhaul is indicated (usually because of fluid leakage or sticking brakes) explore all options before beginning the job. New wheel cylinders are available, which makes this job quite easy. If you do rebuild the wheel cylinder, make sure rebuild kits are available before proceeding.*

Removal

1 Raise the rear of the vehicle and support it securely on jackstands. Block the front wheels to keep the vehicle from rolling off the jackstands.
2 Remove the brake shoe assembly (see Section 5).
3 Carefully clean the area around the wheel cylinder on both sides of the backing plate.
4 Unscrew the brake line fitting **(see illustration)**, but don't pull the line away from the wheel cylinder.

5.8 The drum has a maximum permissible diameter cast into it which must not be exceeded when removing scoring or other imperfections in the friction surface

5 Remove the wheel cylinder retaining bolts **(see illustration)**.
6 Remove the wheel cylinder from the brake backing plate and place it on a clean

6.4 A flare-nut wrench should be used to disconnect the brake line

6.5 To remove the wheel cylinder, remove these two bolts (arrows)

6.7 Wheel cylinder components - exploded view

- A *Wheel cylinder body*
- B *Bleeder screw*
- C *Boot*
- D *Piston*
- E *Seal*
- F *Spring*

7.2 Unplug the fluid level sensor connector (arrow) and unscrew the brake line fittings (arrows)

workbench. Immediately plug the brake line to prevent fluid loss and contamination.

Overhaul

7   Remove the bleeder valve, seals, pistons, boots and spring assembly from the wheel cylinder body **(see illustration)**.
8   Clean the wheel cylinder with brake system cleaner. **Warning:** *Do not, under any circumstances, use petroleum-based solvents to clean brake parts.*
9   Check the bore for corrosion and score marks. Crocus cloth may be used to remove light corrosion and stains, but the cylinder must be replaced with a new one if the defects can't be removed easily, or if the bore is scored.
10   Lubricate the new seals with brake fluid.
11   Assemble the brake cylinder components, making sure the boots are properly seated.

Installation

12   Place the wheel cylinder in position.
13   Connect the brake line loosely.
14   Install the wheel cylinder bolts and tighten them securely.

15   Tighten the brake line fittings.
16   Install the brake shoes (see Section 5).
17   Bleed the brakes (see Section 9).

7   Master cylinder - removal, overhaul and installation

Warning: *On models through 1998 with ABS brakes, the master cylinder is combined with the ABS hydraulic unit/modulator and employ a set of spring-loaded, precision gears. The alignment and tensioning of these is a critical safety concern. While the master cylinder and ABS hydraulic unit may be unbolted from the vehicle (such as for replacement of the power brake booster), they must not be separated from each other. Only a technician with a factory scan tool can relieve the tension on these gears and safely separate the master cylinder from the ABS hydraulic unit/modulator assembly. The gear tensioning relief procedure must be performed with the master cylinder assembly installed in the vehicle, not removed from the vehicle. For this reason, it is not recommend that the home mechanic rebuild a master cylinder on these models.*

Removal

Refer to illustrations 7.2 and 7.6

1   Detach the cable from the negative battery terminal. **Caution:** *On models equipped with the Theftlock audio system, be sure the lockout feature is turned off before performing any procedure which requires disconnecting the battery.*
2   Unplug the electrical connector from the fluid level sensor switch **(see illustration)**.
3   Place rags under the line fittings and prepare caps or plastic bags to cover the ends of the lines once they're disconnected. **Caution:** *Brake fluid will damage paint. Cover all painted parts and be careful not to spill fluid during this procedure.*
4   Loosen the fittings at the ends of the brake lines where they enter the master cylinder. To prevent rounding off the flats on the fittings, use a flare-nut wrench, which wraps around the hex.
5   Pull the brake lines away from the master cylinder and plug the ends to prevent contamination.
6   Remove the two mounting nuts **(see illustration)** and detach the master cylinder from the vehicle.
7   Remove the reservoir cover and reservoir diaphragm, then discard any remaining fluid.

Overhaul

Refer to illustrations 7.9, 7.10, 7.11, 7.12, 7.16, 7.18, 7.19a, 7.19b, 7.19c, 7.19d, 7.19e, 7.19f, 7.20 and 7.32

8   Mount the master cylinder in a vise. Be sure to line the vise jaws with rags or blocks of wood to prevent damage to the cylinder body.
9   Drive out the roll pins **(see illustration)** with a 1/8-inch punch. Pull straight up on the reservoir assembly and separate it from the master cylinder body. Remove and discard the two O-rings.
10   Remove the proportioner valve caps

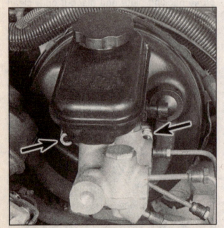

7.6 Remove the master cylinder mounting nuts (arrows)

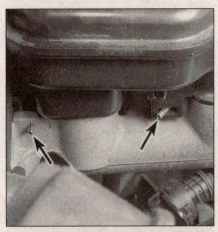

7.9 Location of the retaining roll pins (arrows) in the brake master cylinder

7.10 Remove the proportioner valve caps

7.11 Press down on the piston and remove the primary piston lock ring

7.12 Remove the primary piston assembly

7.16 The secondary piston seals must be installed with the lips facing out as shown

7.18 Install the secondary piston assembly

(see illustration). Using needle-nose pliers, carefully remove the O-rings, the springs, the proportioner valve pistons and seals. Make sure you don't scratch or otherwise damage the piston stems or the bores. Set each proportioner valve assembly aside.

11   Remove the primary piston lock ring by depressing the piston and prying the ring out with a screwdriver (see illustration).

12   Remove the primary piston assembly from the bore (see illustration).

13   Remove the secondary piston assembly from the bore. It may be necessary to remove the master cylinder from the vise and invert it, carefully tapping it against a block of wood to expel the piston.

14   Clean the master cylinder body, the primary and secondary piston assemblies, the proportioner valve assemblies and the reservoir with brake system cleaner. Warning: DO NOT, under any circumstances, use petroleum-based solvents to clean brake parts.

15   Inspect the master cylinder piston bore for corrosion and score marks. If any corrosion or damage in the bore is evident, replace the master cylinder body - don't use abrasives to try to clean it up.

16   Remove the old seals from the second-

7.19a The primary piston seal must be installed with the lip facing away from the piston

ary piston assembly and install the new seals with the cup lips facing out (see illustration).

17   Attach the spring retainer to the secondary piston assembly.

18   Lubricate the cylinder bore with clean brake fluid and install the spring and second-

7.19b Install the seal guard over the seal

ary piston assembly (see illustration).

19   Disassemble the primary piston assembly, noting the locations of the parts, then lubricate the new seals with clean brake fluid and install them on the piston (see illustrations).

7.19c Place the primary piston spring in position

7.19d Insert the spring retainer into the spring

7.19e Insert the spring retaining bolt through the retainer and spring and thread it into the piston

7.19f Lubricate the O-ring with clean brake fluid, then install it on the piston

7.20 Insert the primary piston assembly into the bore

20   Install the primary piston assembly in the cylinder bore **(see illustration)**, depress it and install the lock ring.

21   Inspect the proportioner valves for corrosion and score marks. Replace them if necessary.

22   Lubricate the new O-rings and proportioner valve seals with the silicone grease supplied with the rebuild kit. Also lubricate the stem of the proportioner valve pistons.

23   Install the new seals on the proportioner valve pistons with the seal lips facing toward the cap assembly.

24   Install the proportioner valve pistons and seals in the master cylinder body.

25   Install the springs in the master cylinder body.

26   Install the new O-rings in their respective grooves in the proportioner valve cap assemblies.

27   Install the proportioner valve caps in the master cylinder and tighten them to the torque listed in this Chapter's Specifications.

28   Inspect the reservoir for cracks and distortion. If any damage is evident, replace it.

29   Lubricate the new reservoir O-rings with clean brake fluid and press them into their respective grooves in the master cylinder body. Make sure they're properly seated.

30   Lubricate the reservoir fittings with clean brake fluid and install the reservoir on the master cylinder body by pressing it straight down.

31   Drive in new reservoir retaining (roll) pins. Make sure you don't damage the reservoir or master cylinder body.

32   Inspect the reservoir diaphragm and cover for cracks and deformation. Replace any damaged parts with new ones and attach the diaphragm to the cover **(see illustration)**. **Note:** *Whenever the master cylinder is removed, the complete hydraulic system must be bled. The time required to bleed the system can be reduced if the master cylinder is filled with fluid and bench bled (refer to Steps 33 through 36) before it's installed on the vehicle.*

33   Insert threaded plugs of the correct size into the brake line outlet holes and fill the reservoirs with brake fluid. The master cylinder should be supported so brake fluid won't spill during the bench bleeding procedure.

34   Loosen one plug at a time and push the piston assembly into the bore to force air from the master cylinder. To prevent air from being drawn back in, the appropriate plug must be replaced before allowing the piston to return to its original position.

35   Stroke the piston three or four times for each outlet to ensure that all air has been expelled.

7.32 Install the reservoir diaphragm in the cover

8.2 Using a back-up wrench on the flexible hose side of the fitting (A), loosen the tube nut (B) with a flare-nut wrench and remove the U-clip (C) from the hose fitting

36   Since high pressure isn't involved in the bench bleeding procedure, there is an alternative to the removal and replacement of the plugs with each stroke of the piston assembly. Before pushing in on the piston assembly, remove one of the plugs completely. Before releasing the piston, however, instead of replacing the plug, simply put your finger tightly over the hole to keep air from being drawn back into the master cylinder. Wait several seconds for the brake fluid to be drawn from the reservoir into the piston bore, then repeat the procedure. When you push down on the piston it'll force your finger off the hole, allowing the air inside to be expelled. When only brake fluid is being ejected from the hole, replace the plug and go on to the other port. As a third alternative, master cylinder bleeding kits are available at auto parts stores. The kit contains fittings and clear plastic tubing for bench-bleeding with little or no mess.

37   Refill the master cylinder reservoirs and install the diaphragm and cover assembly. **Note:** *The reservoirs should only be filled to the top of the reservoir divider to prevent overflowing when the cover is installed.*

Installation

38   Carefully install the master cylinder by reversing the removal steps, fill the reservoir with the recommended fluid (see Chapter 1), then bleed the brakes at each wheel (see Section 9).

8   Brake hoses and lines - inspection and replacement

Refer to illustration 8.2

Warning: *Before servicing any ABS component it is mandatory that hydraulic pressure in the system be relieved. With the ignition off, pump the brake pedal a MINIMUM of 40 times using full pedal strokes.*

1   About every six months, raise the vehicle and support it securely on jackstands, then check the flexible hoses that connect the steel brake lines to the front and rear brake assemblies. Look for cracks, chafing of the outer cover, leaks, blisters and other damage. The hoses are important and vulnerable parts of the brake system and the inspection should be thorough. A light and mirror will be helpful to see into restricted areas. If a hose exhibits any of the above conditions, replace it with a new one.

Front brake hose

2   Using a back-up wrench, disconnect the brake line from the hose fitting, being careful not to bend the frame bracket or brake line **(see illustration)**.

3   Use pliers to remove the U-clip from the female fitting at the bracket, then remove the hose from the bracket.

4   At the caliper end of the hose, remove the bolt from the fitting block, then remove the hose and the copper washers on either side of the fitting block.

5   When installing the hose, always use new copper washers on either side of the fitting block and lubricate all bolt threads with clean brake fluid.

6   With the fitting flange engaged with the caliper locating ledge, attach the hose to the caliper.

7   Without twisting the hose, install the female fitting in the hose bracket. It'll fit the bracket in only one position.

8   Install the U-clip retaining the female fitting to the frame bracket.

9   Using a back-up wrench, attach the brake line to the hose fitting.

10   When the brake hose installation is complete, there shouldn't be any kinks in the hose. Make sure the hose doesn't contact any part of the suspension. Check it by turning the wheels to the extreme left and right positions. If the hose makes contact, remove the hose and correct the installation as necessary.

Rear brake hose

11   Using a back-up wrench, disconnect the hose at both ends, being careful not to bend the bracket or steel lines.

12   Remove the U-clip with pliers and separate the female fittings from the brackets.

13   Unbolt the hose retaining clip and remove the hose.

14   Without twisting the hose, install the female ends in the frame bracket. It'll fit the bracket in only one position.

15   Install the U-clip retaining the female end to the bracket.

16   Using a back-up wrench, attach the steel line fittings to the female fittings. Again, be careful not to bend the bracket or steel line.

17   Make sure the hose installation didn't loosen the frame bracket. Tighten the bracket if necessary.

18   Fill the master cylinder reservoir and bleed the system (refer to Section 9).

Metal brake lines

19   When replacing brake lines, be sure to buy the correct replacement parts. Don't use copper or any other tubing for brake lines.

20   Prefabricated brake lines, with the ends already flared and fittings installed, are available at auto parts stores and dealer service departments. The lines are also bent to the proper shapes if necessary.

21   If prefabricated lines aren't available, obtain the recommended steel tubing and fittings to match the line to be replaced. Determine the correct length by measuring the old brake line (a piece of string can usually be used for this) and cut the new tubing to length, allowing about 1/2-inch extra for flaring the ends.

22   Install the fittings on the cut tubing and flare the ends of the line with an ISO flaring tool.

23   If necessary, carefully bend the line to the proper shape. A tube bender is recommended for this. **Caution:** *Don't crimp or damage the line.*

24   When installing the new line, make sure it's securely supported in the brackets with plenty of clearance between moving or hot components.

25   After installation, check the master cylinder fluid level and add fluid as necessary. Bleed the brake system as outlined in the next Section and test the brakes carefully before driving the vehicle in traffic.

9   Brake system bleeding

Refer to illustrations 9.8 and 9.38

Warning: *Wear eye protection when bleeding the brake system. If you get fluid in your eyes, rinse them immediately with water and seek medical attention.*

Note: *Bleeding the brakes is necessary to remove air that manages to find its way into the system when its been opened during removal and installation of a hose, line, caliper or master cylinder.*

Conventional brake system (non-ABS equipped vehicles)

1   It'll probably be necessary to bleed the system at all four brakes if air has entered the system due to low fluid level, or if the brake lines have been disconnected at the master cylinder.

9.8 When bleeding the brakes, a hose is connected to the bleeder valve at the caliper and then submerged in brake fluid - air will be seen as bubbles in the container and in the tube (all air must be expelled before continuing to the next wheel)

9.38 Later model ABS components
1   ABS control assembly
2   ABS modulator rear bleeder valve
3   ABS modulator front bleeder valve

2   If a brake line was disconnected at only one wheel, then only that caliper or wheel cylinder must be bled.

3   If a brake line is disconnected at a fitting located between the master cylinder and any of the brakes, that part of the system served by the disconnected line must be bled.

4   Remove any residual vacuum from the power brake booster by applying the brake several times with the engine off.

5   Remove the master cylinder reservoir cover and fill the reservoir with brake fluid. Reinstall the cover. **Note:** *Check the fluid level often during the bleeding procedure and add fluid as necessary to prevent the level from falling low enough to allow air bubbles into the master cylinder.*

6   Have an assistant on hand, as well as a supply of new brake fluid, an empty, clear plastic container, a length of 3/16-inch plastic, rubber or vinyl tubing to fit over the bleeder valve and a wrench to open and close the bleeder valve.

7   Beginning at the right front wheel, loosen the bleeder valve slightly, then tighten it to a point where it's snug but can still be loosened quickly and easily.

8   Place one end of the tubing over the bleeder valve and submerge the other end in brake fluid in the container **(see illustration)**.

9   Have your assistant pump the brakes slowly a few times to get pressure in the system, then hold the pedal down firmly.

10   While the pedal is held down, open the bleeder valve just enough to allow fluid to flow out of the valve. Watch for air bubbles to exit the submerged end of the tube. When the fluid slows after a couple of seconds, close the valve and have your assistant release the pedal.

11   Repeat Steps 9 and 10 until no more air is seen leaving the tube, then tighten the bleeder valve and proceed to the right rear wheel, the left front wheel and the left rear

wheel, in that order, and perform the same procedure. Be sure to check the fluid in the master cylinder reservoir frequently.

12   Never use old brake fluid. It contains moisture which can boil, rendering the brakes useless.

13   Fill the master cylinder with fluid at the end of the operation.

14   Check the operation of the brakes. The pedal should feel firm when depressed. If necessary, repeat the entire procedure. **Warning:** *Don't operate the vehicle if you're in doubt about the effectiveness of the brake system.*

Anti-lock Brake System (ABS) equipped vehicles

Warning: *Before servicing any ABS component it is mandatory that hydraulic pressure in the system be relieved. With the ignition off, pump the brake pedal a MINIMUM of 40 times using full pedal strokes.*

1991 and earlier models

15   Relieve the system pressure.

16   With the ignition off, be sure the fluid reservoir is full.

17   Connect a clear hose to the bleeder valve on the right front brake caliper and submerge the other end of the hose in a container of brake fluid **(see illustration 9.8)**.

18   Open the bleeder valve.

19   Have an assistant slowly depress the brake pedal. As the fluid flows from the caliper, tap on the caliper housing to free trapped air.

20   Close the bleeder valve and have the assistant release the brake pedal.

21   Repeat this step until air is no longer seen in the hose.

22   Repeat this procedure for the left front caliper.

23   Before bleeding the rear brakes, turn the ignition On and allow the pump motor to

charge the system. The pump motor should stop running within one minute.

24   With the reservoir full, connect the hose to the bleeder valve on the right rear caliper and submerge the other end of the hose in a container of clean brake fluid.

25   Open the bleeder valve.

26   Have an assistant slowly depress the brake pedal, part way only. Allow the fluid to flow for 15 seconds, while lightly tapping on the caliper housing to free trapped air.

27   Close the bleeder valve and have the assistant release the brake pedal.

28   Repeat this step until air is no longer seen in the hose.

29   Check the brake fluid level, then repeat this procedure for the left rear caliper.

30   Once all the calipers have been bled, the isolation valves on the ABS unit should be bled. Connect the bleeder hose to the inner side of the ABS unit and submerge the other end in the container of clean brake fluid. With the ignition still On, have an assistant apply light pressure to the brake pedal. Slowly open the bleeder valve and allow the fluid to flow until no more air bubbles are seen.

31   Repeat this procedure to the bleeder valve on the outer side of the unit.

32   Depressurize the system and check the brake fluid, adding as necessary.

33   Before turning the key On, sharply apply the brake pedal three times, using full force.

34   Turn the ignition key On and allow the pump motor to run. When the motor stops, turn the key Off.

35   Depress the brake pedal, using moderate pressure, then turn the ignition key On for three seconds. Repeat this procedure ten times.

36   Depressurize the system and recheck the fluid level.

1992 through 1997 models

37   Clean the reservoir and cap then check

that the reservoir is full of fluid.

38   Prime the ABS modulator/master cylinder assembly. **Note:** *Priming is only necessary if the assembly has been replaced or is suspected of having air trapped inside it.* First attach a bleeder hose to the rear bleeder valve **(see illustration)**. Submerge the other end of the hose in clean brake fluid. Open the bleeder valve 1/2 to 3/4 turns and have an assistant depress the brake pedal until fluid begins to flow, then close the valve. Repeat this on the front bleeder valve.

39   Check the fluid level and fill the reservoir as necessary.

40   Raise the car and support it securely on jackstands.

41   Bleed the brakes as described in steps 5 through 12 of this section. **Note:** *The recommended bleeding sequence for ABS-equipped models is right front, left front, right rear, left rear, in that order.* While bleeding each brake, be sure to allow at least five seconds to elapse between closing and re-opening the bleeder valve, and be sure to check the fluid level in the reservoir often.

42   Lower the car.

43   Attach a bleeder hose to the rear bleeder valve of the ABS modulator/master cylinder assembly **(see illustration 9.38)**. Submerge the other end of the hose in clean brake fluid.

44   Open the bleeder valve 1/2 to 3/4 turns, have an assistant depress the brake pedal until fluid begins to flow, then close the valve and allow at least five seconds to elapse.

45   Repeat step 44 until all air is purged from the system.

46   Repeat steps 43 through 45 on the front bleeder valve of the ABS modulator/master cylinder assembly.

47   Fill the reservoir as required.

48   Turn the ignition on, then apply and hold the brake pedal with moderate force.

49   If the pedal feels firm and does not have too much travel, proceed to step 50. If the pedal feels soft or has too much travel, remove your foot from the pedal, start the engine and let it run for at least 10 seconds to "initialize" the ABS. **Warning:** *Do not drive the car.* After 10 seconds, turn the ignition off. Repeat this procedure 5 times to ensure that trapped air has been dislodged, then repeat the bleeding procedure.

50   Start the engine and recheck the feel and travel of the pedal. If it continues to feel firm, road test the car and make several normal from moderate speeds stops (i.e., stops that do not require the ABS to operate) to be sure the brake system is functioning normally.

1998 and later models

51   If air entered the system due to a low fluid level, or if the hydraulic lines were disconnected from the master cylinder, bleed the master cylinder first, starting with the hydraulic line closest to the front of the vehicle, then the rear hydraulic line. To do this, have an assistant depress the brake pedal and hold it while you loosen the hydraulic line fitting with

10.7 Parking brake lever location (arrow)

a flare nut wrench until fluid begins to flow from the fitting. Tighten the fitting when the flow of fluid and air bubbles stops, then have your assistant slowly let up on the brake pedal. **Caution:** *Place rags or newspapers under and around the master cylinder to catch the fluid. Wash off any fluid that gets onto the paint with plenty of cold water.*

52   Perform Steps 5 through 13 to bleed the remainder of the hydraulic system.

53   Check the operation of the brakes thoroughly. The pedal should feel solid when depressed, with no sponginess. If necessary, repeat the entire process. **Warning:** *Do not operate the vehicle if you are in doubt about the effectiveness of the brake system. It is possible for air to become trapped in the anti-lock brake system hydraulic control unit, so, if the pedal continues to feel spongy after repeated bleedings or the BRAKE or ANTI-LOCK light stays on, have the vehicle towed to a dealer service department or other qualified shop to be bled with the aid of a scan tool.*

---

10   Parking brake - adjustment

Rear disc brakes (1996 and earlier models, and 1997 Olds)

Refer to illustration 10.7

1   Using heavy pedal pressure, depress the brake pedal three times.

2   Apply and release the parking brake three times.

3   Raise the rear of the vehicle and support it securely on jackstands.

4   Make sure the parking brake is fully released.

5   Turn the ignition key to the On position.

6   If the brake warning light is on, operate the manual brake release and pull down on the front parking brake cable to remove the slack from the pedal assembly.

7   At the rear caliper housings, the two parking brake levers should be against the lever stops **(see illustration)**. If they are not, check for binding in the rear cables and/or loosen the cables at the adjuster until both the

left and the right levers are against the stops.

8   Tighten the parking brake cable at the equalizer **(see illustration 11.2)** until either the left or right lever just begins to move off the stop.

9   Operate the parking brake to check for proper adjustment. Lower the vehicle.

Rear drum brakes and 1997 and later rear disc brakes (except Olds)

10   Adjust the rear brake shoes on drum brake equipped models (see Section 5). On 1997 and later (rear disc equipped) models adjust the rear parking brake shoes (see Section 12).

11   Apply the parking brake 10 clicks, then release it. Repeat this 5 times.

12   Make sure the parking brake is fully released. Turn the ignition on. If the brake warning light is on, operate the manual brake release and pull down on the front parking brake cable to remove slack.

13   Raise the car and support it securely on jackstands.

14   Adjust the parking brake by turning the nut on the equalizer **(see illustration 11.2)** while spinning both rear wheels. When either wheel begins to drag, stop adjusting and back off the equalizer nut one full turn.

15   Apply the parking brake 4 clicks and check the rear wheel rotation. You should not be able to turn the wheel by hand in the direction of forward movement; the wheel should drag or not turn at all when spun in the direction or rearward rotation.

16   Release the parking brake and be sure the rear wheels spin freely, then lower the car.

---

11   Parking brake cables - replacement

Refer to illustrations 11.2 and 11.13

Front cable

1   Raise and support the vehicle.

11.2 Loosen the parking brake cable adjusting nut (arrow) located at the equalizer assembly

11.13 Detach the cable from the bracket on the caliper (arrow)

2   Loosen the adjuster nut at the equalizer **(see illustration)**.
3   Detach the front cable from the retainer.
4   Remove the nut at the underbody bracket.
5   Detach the clip from the underbody.
6   Detach the cable from the parking brake lever assembly.
7   Installation is the reverse of removal.

Left rear cable

8   Raise the vehicle and support it.
9   Disconnect the spring from the equalizer, if necessary.
10   Detach the equalizer from the cable.
11   On models with rear drum brakes, detach the cable from the backing plate and parking brake lever.
12   Detach any remaining cable-to-frame brackets.
13   On 1996 and earlier rear disc models, detach the cable from the parking brake lever at the caliper. Detach the cable from the caliper bracket **(see illustration)**.
14   On 1997 and later rear disc models, detach the cable from the brake cable support bracket and from the cable actuator lever.
15   Installation is the reverse of removal.

Right rear cable

16   Raise and support the vehicle.
17   Detach the spring from the equalizer, if necessary.
18   Detach the equalizer from the cable.
19   Detach the cable from the underbody bracket.
20   Remove the bolts from the clips above the fuel tank.
21   On models with rear drum brakes, detach the cable from the backing plate and parking brake lever. On 1996 and earlier rear disc models, detach the cable from the parking brake lever at the caliper. Detach the cable from the caliper bracket. On 1997 and later rear disc models detach the cable from the brake cable support bracket and from the cable actuator lever.
22   Installation is the reverse of removal.

12   Parking brake shoes (1997 and later models, except Olds) - replacement

Note: *This procedure applies only to 1997 and later models with rear disc brakes (except Olds).*
1   Loosen the rear wheel lug nuts, raise the rear of the vehicle and support it securely on jackstands. Remove the wheels.
2   Remove the brake caliper (see Section 3) and the brake disc (see Section 4).
3   Disconnect the parking brake cable from the bracket and the actuator lever.
4   Unbolt the parking brake cable bracket.
5   Remove the rear hub and bearing assembly (see Chapter 10).
6   Remove the parking brake actuator and the parking brake shoe.
7   When installing the new shoe and lining assembly, turn the adjuster screw until the shoe lining just drags on the braking surface inside the disc. Then remove the disc and back-off the adjuster screw until the shoe lining doesn't drag when the disc is installed and turned.
8   Installation is otherwise the reverse of the removal procedure. Be sure to tighten the hub and bearing assembly bolts to the torque listed in the Chapter 10 Specifications, the caliper mounting bolts to the torque listed in the Chapter 9 Specifications, and the wheel lug nuts to the torque listed in the Chapter 1 Specifications.

13   Power brake booster - check, removal and installation

1   The power brake booster unit requires no special maintenance apart from periodic inspection of the vacuum hose and case.

Operating check

2   Depress the brake pedal several times with the engine off and make sure there is no change in the pedal reserve distance (the minimum distance to the floor).
3   Depress the pedal and start the engine. If the pedal goes down slightly, operation is normal.

Airtightness check

4   Start the engine and turn it off after one or two minutes. Depress the pedal several times slowly. If the pedal goes down farther the first time but gradually rises after the second or third depression, the booster is airtight.
5   Depress the brake pedal while the engine is running, then stop the engine with the brake pedal depressed. If there is no change in the pedal reserve travel after holding the pedal for 30 seconds, the booster is airtight.

Removal

1988 through 1990 models
Refer to illustration 13.10
6   Dismantling of the power unit requires special tools and is not ordinarily done by the home mechanic. If a problem develops, install a new or factory rebuilt unit.
7   Remove the nuts attaching the master cylinder to the booster and carefully pull the master cylinder forward until it clears the mounting studs. Be careful to avoid bending or kinking the brake lines.
8   Disconnect the vacuum hose where it attaches to the power brake booster.
9   From the passenger compartment, disconnect the power brake pushrod from the top of the brake pedal.
10   Also from this location, remove the nuts attaching the booster to the firewall **(see illustration)**.
11   Carefully lift the booster away from the firewall and out of the engine compartment.

1991 and later models
Refer to illustration 13.16
12   Dismantling of the power unit requires special tools and is not ordinarily done by the home mechanic. If a problem develops, install

13.10 Remove the retaining clip and slide the power brake pushrod off the brake pedal pin, then remove the booster-to-firewall nuts (arrows)

a new or factory rebuilt unit. On 2002 models, remove the cross-vehicle brace (between the shock towers).

13   Remove the nuts attaching the master cylinder to the booster and carefully pull the master cylinder forward until it clears the mounting studs. Be careful to avoid bending or kinking the brake lines. **Warning:** *On ABS-equipped models through 1998, do not disconnect the master cylinder from the hydraulic modulator assembly.*

14   Disconnect the vacuum hose where it attaches to the power brake booster. On 3.4L engines it may be necessary to remove the upper intake plenum (see Chapter 4). On 1996 and later 3800 engines remove the acoustic engine cover (see Chapter 2, Part F). On some models it may be necessary to remove the transaxle filler tube to allow removal of the brake booster.

15   From the passenger compartment, disconnect the brake pushrod from the top of the brake pedal. **Caution:** *Keep the pedal from moving while doing this, to avoid damage to the brake switch.*

16   The booster is mounted to the firewall with a cam-lock bracket. On the right side of the bracket, use a screwdriver to pry the booster's locking tab out of the notch on the bracket **(see illustration)**. Insert the screwdriver between the tab and the notch.

17   If you do not have access to the factory tool that holds the front of the booster for removal/installation, there are two other ways to do the job. If you have a large strap wrench, wrap it around the body of the booster. You can also install two short lengths of rubber fuel hose over the master-cylinder mounting studs at the front of the booster, and use a prybar between the two studs to turn the booster as described in the next Step.

18   While holding the tab out of the notch (toward the firewall), rotate the booster counterclockwise until it comes free of the bracket. **Caution:** *Be careful not to tear the boot (interior side of the firewall) around the booster pushrod as you remove the booster.*

Installation

19   Installation is the reverse of removal. On 1991 and later models, make sure the locking

tab is completely seated in the firewall bracket slot.

20   Carefully test the operation of the brakes before driving the car.

---

14   Brake light switch - removal, installation and adjustment

Removal

1   The brake light switch is located on a bracket at the top of the brake pedal. The switch activates the brake lights at the rear of the vehicle when the pedal is depressed.

2   Remove the under dash cover.

3   If necessary, slide the steering shaft protective sleeve towards the cowl.

4   If necessary, disconnect the vacuum hose at the cruise control cut-off switch.

5   If necessary, remove the retainer clip holding the brake light switch to the steering column bracket.

6   Detach the retainer from the four wire connector.

7   Detach the two wire connector (if equipped with cruise control).

8   If necessary, detach the switch arm from the pedal by pushing the arm to the left and towards the cowl. Release the switch by pulling down and releasing the top snap clip.

9   On later models, remove the mounting screw.

10   Detach the four wire connector and remove the switch.

Installation and adjustment

11   Installation is the reverse of removal.

12   With the brake pedal fully depressed, use a wire with a hooked end and pull on the switch set lever while listening for a click. **Note:** *If there is no click the switch may be faulty. Release the brake pedal and repeat this step.*

13   After adjustment, be sure the brake lights are functioning properly.

---

15   Anti-lock Brake System (ABS) - general information

Refer to illustrations 15.2a, 15.2b, 15.2c and 15.2d

The Anti-lock Brake System is designed to maintain vehicle steerability, directional stability and optimum deceleration under severe braking conditions on most road surfaces. It does so by monitoring the rotational speed of

13.16 "Cam-lock" booster details (1991 and later models)

A   Firewall bracket with slot
B   Tab shown locked in bracket slot
C   Booster assembly

15.2a On early models the ABS modulator/motor pack is mounted on the side of the master cylinder

15.2b Location of the ABS hydraulic unit on later models

each wheel and controlling the brake line pressure to each wheel during braking. This prevents the wheels from locking up.

The ABS system has three main components - the wheel speed sensors, the electronic control unit and the hydraulic unit **(see illustrations)**. Four wheel speed sensors - one at each wheel - send a variable voltage signal to the control unit, which monitors these signals, compares them to its program and determines whether a wheel is about to lock up. When a wheel is about to lock up, the control unit signals the hydraulic unit to reduce hydraulic pressure (or not increase it further) at that wheel's brake caliper. **Note:** *On early models the sensors are replaceable, but on later models the wheel speed sensors are integral with the hub and bearing assemblies.* Pressure modulation is handled by electrically-operated solenoid valves.

Warning lights

The ABS system has self-diagnostic capabilities. Each time the vehicle is started,

the EBCM runs a self-test. There are three warning lights on the instrument panel, a red BRAKE light, an amber ABS light and a blue LOW TRAC light, each with their own functions. During starting, the red BRAKE warning light should come on briefly then go out. If the red BRAKE light stays on, it indicates a problem with the main braking system, such as low fluid level detected or the parking brake is still on. If the lights stays on after the parking brake is released, check the brake fluid level in the master cylinder reservoir (see Chapter 1).

The amber ABS light indicates a problem with the ABS system, not the main or basic brake system. If the light stays on steadily, it indicates that there is a problem with the ABS system, but the main system is still working. If you have a steady ABS light, drive to a dealer service department or other qualified repair shop for diagnosis and repair. However, if the ABS light *flashes*, however, there is a more serious fault in the ABS system that may have affected the regular braking system. Pull over

immediately and have the vehicle towed to a dealer or other qualified repair shop for service.

Checks

Although a special electronic tester is necessary to properly diagnose the system, the home mechanic can perform a few preliminary checks before taking the vehicle to a dealer service department that is equipped with this tester:

a) *Make sure the brake calipers are in good condition.*
b) *Check the electrical connector at the controller.*
c) *Check the fuses.*
d) *Follow the wiring harness to the speed sensors and brake light switch and make sure all connections are secure and the wiring isn't damaged.*

If the above preliminary checks don't rectify the problem, the vehicle should be diagnosed by a dealer service department.

15.2c The front wheel ABS sensor (A) on early models is mounted to the hub/bearing assembly - the electrical connector (B) snaps on and the sensor is retained by a bracket and bolt (C)

15.2d An ABS sensor (arrow) is also mounted at each rear wheel, behind the brake assembly

Chapter 10
Suspension and steering systems

Contents

	Section
Balljoint - check and replacement	3
Chassis lubrication	See Chapter 1
Control arm - removal and installation	4
Front hub and wheel bearing assembly - removal and installation	7
Front stabilizer bar and bushings - removal and installation	2
Front strut - replacement	6
Front strut and spring assembly - removal, inspection and installation	5
General information	1
Power steering fluid level check	See Chapter 1
Power steering pump - removal and installation	17
Power steering system - bleeding	18
Rear suspension components - removal and installation	12
Rear hub and wheel bearing assembly - removal and installation	11

	Section
Rear strut - removal and installation	9
Rear transverse spring - removal and installation	10
Rear stabilizer bar - removal and installation	8
Steering gear boots - replacement	16
Steering gear - removal and installation	15
Steering system - general information	13
Steering wheel - removal and installation	19
Suspension and steering check	See Chapter 1
Tie-rod ends - removal and installation	14
Tire and tire pressure checks	See Chapter 1
Tire rotation	See Chapter 1
Wheel alignment - general information	22
Wheel studs - replacement	20
Wheels and tires - general information	21

Specifications

Torque specifications   Ft-lbs

Note: *One foot-pound (ft-lb) of torque is equivalent to 12 inch-pounds (in-lbs) of torque. Torque values below approximately 15 foot-pounds are expressed in inch-pounds, because most foot-pound torque wrenches are not accurate at these smaller values.*

Front suspension

Control arm pivot bolts	
1988 through 1989	52
1990 through 1993	56
1994 through 1996 (and 1997 Olds)	52
1997 (except Olds)	83
1998 through 2000	77
2001	83
2002 and later	92
Subframe-to-body bolts	
1996 and earlier	103
1997 through 2002	133
2003 and later	122
Lower balljoint nut	
1988 and 1989	
Initial	84 in-lbs
Final	Tighten an additional 120-degrees
1990 and 1991	
Initial	15
Final	Tighten an additional 90-degrees
1992 through 1996 (and 1997 Olds)	63
1997 to 1999 (except Olds)	40
2000 and later	
Step 1	15
Step 2	Tighten an additional 120 degrees
Stabilizer bar clamp nuts	35
Stabilizer bar link nuts (1997 and later, except Olds)	17
Front hub and wheel bearing assembly bolts	
1996 and earlier (and 1997 Olds)	52
1997 and later (except Olds)	96
Strut mount cover nuts	
1994 and earlier	17
1995 and later	24

Torque specifications

Ft-lbs (unless otherwise indicated)

Note: *One foot-pound of torque is equivalent to 12 inch-pounds of torque. Torque values below approximately 15 foot-pounds are expressed in inch-pounds, because most foot-pound torque wrenches are not accurate at these smaller values.*

Front suspension (continued)

Strut damper shaft nut	
1994 and earlier	72
1995	82
1996 (and 1997 Olds)	59
1997 and later (except Olds)	63
Strut cartridge nut	82
Strut-to-knuckle bolts (1997 and later, except Olds)	90
Driveaxle hub nut	See Chapter 8

Rear suspension

Rear hub and wheel bearing assembly bolts	
1996 and earlier (and 1997 Olds)	52
1997 and later (except Olds)	55
Strut-to-body bolt	34
Strut-to-knuckle nut	
1994 and earlier	133
1995 and 1996	122
1997 through 1999 (except Olds)	82
1997 Olds	90
2000 and later	90
Trailing arm-to-body nut/bolt	
1994 and earlier	48
1995 through 1996 (and 1997 Olds)	44 plus an additional 90 degrees
1997 (except Olds)	37 plus an additional 60 degrees
1998 and 1999	77
2000 and later	40
Trailing arm-to-knuckle nut/bolt	
1994 and earlier	192
1995	66 plus an additional 90 degrees
1996 and 1997	66 plus an additional 75 degrees
1998 and 1999	192
2000 through 2005	52 plus an additional 65-degrees
2006 and later	177
Suspension crossmember-to-body bolt	
1996 and earlier (and 1997 Olds)	85
1997 through 1999 (except Olds)	77
2000 and later	81
Stabilizer bar link bolt (through 1996, and 1997 Olds)	40
Stabilizer bar link nut	
1997 through 2004, except Olds	26
2005	38
Stabilizer bar clamp bolt	
Through 1996	18
1997 and later	35
Jack pad bolt	18
Spring retention plate bolt	
1994 and earlier	15
1995 and 1996 (and 1997 Olds)	22
Lateral link rod	
1988 and 1989	
To-knuckle	66 plus an additional 120-degrees (two flats)
To-crossmember (rear link rod)	66 plus an additional 120-degrees (two flats)
To-toe adjuster (front link rod)	81 plus an additional 120-degrees (two flats)
1990 through 1995	
To-knuckle	66 plus an additional 90-degrees rotation
To-crossmember	81 plus an additional 90-degrees rotation
1996 (and 1997 Olds)	
To-knuckle	177
To-crossmember	111
1997 and later (except Olds)	
To-knuckle	110
To-crossmember	103

Airbag system

Airbag module mounting screws	25 in-lbs

Steering system

Power steering pump mounting bolts	25
Steering gear mounting bolts	
2003 and earlier	59
2004 and later	
Step 1	42
Step 2	Tighten an additional 180-degrees
Tie-rod end nut	
1996 and earlier	63
1997 (except Olds)...	18 plus an additional 180-degrees rotation
1997 Olds	84 in-lbs plus an additional 210-degrees rotation
1998 and later	22 plus an additional 120-degrees rotation
Tie-rod jam nut	50
Intermediate shaft pinch-bolt	35
Steering wheel hub nut	30
Wheel lug nuts..	See Chapter 1

1.1 Front suspension components

1	*Strut/knuckle assembly*	*3*	*Control arm*	*5*	*Control arm pivot bolt*
2	*Balljoint*	*4*	*Subframe bolt*	*6*	*Stabilizer bar*

1 General information

Refer to illustrations 1.1, 1.2a and 1.2b

Warning: *Whenever any of the suspension or steering fasteners are loosened or removed, they must be inspected and, if necessary, replaced with new ones of the same part number or of original equipment quality and design. Torque specifications must be followed for proper reassembly and component retention. Never attempt to heat or straighten any suspension or steering components.*

Instead, replace any bent or damaged part with a new one.

The front suspension is a strut design that is made up of a strut supported by a coil spring. On models through 1996, the lower end of the strut body is welded to the steering knuckle, and the strut cartridge can be replaced. The strut/knuckle bearing is located under the lower spring seat, with the upper spring seat attaching to the chassis. Because of the location of the bearing, the strut cartridge on 1996 and earlier models can be removed from the engine compartment without

disassembling the spring and strut/knuckle, while on 1997 and later models, the strut cartridge is integral with the strut body. On those models, the strut is bolted to the knuckle, not welded, and the strut and coil spring can be removed. Once removed from the vehicle the spring can be removed and installed on a new strut and reinstalled on the vehicle. The strut/knuckle assemblies are connected by balljoints to the lower control arms, which are mounted to the frame. The control arms are connected by a stabilizer bar, which reduces body lean during cornering **(see illustration)**.

1.2a Rear suspension components - transversely mounted leaf spring type

1	Lateral link	3	Trailing arm	5	Knuckle
2	Auxiliary damper	4	Fiberglass spring	6	Strut

1.2b Rear suspension components - coil/strut models

1	Lateral link rods	3	Trailing arm	5	Knuckle
2	Strut	4	Coil spring	6	Stabilizer bar

2.3a Loosen the stabilizer bar bolts (arrows) on the control arm (early models)

2.3b On later models use a wrench to hold the bolt head while loosening the stabilizer link nut (arrow)

The rear suspension is independent, with earlier models having a transversely mounted fiberglass leaf spring connected to the knuckle assemblies and two shock struts (not coil over spring struts) with an auxiliary damper **(see illustration)**, while 1997 and later models use a traditional coil over spring strut connected to knuckle assemblies. Both types of suspensions are located by trailing arms and parallel lateral link rods, and a stabilizer bar.

The rack-and-pinion steering gear is located behind the engine/transaxle assembly on the firewall and actuates the steering arms that connect to the strut housings. All vehicles are equipped with power steering. The steering column is connected to the steering gear through an insulated coupler. The steering column is designed to collapse in the event of an accident.

Note: *These vehicles have a combination of standard and metric fasteners on the various suspension and steering components, so it would be a good idea to have both types of tools available when beginning work.*

2   Front stabilizer bar and bushings - removal and installation

Refer to illustrations 2.3a, 2.3b, 2.4a and 2.4b

Removal

1   Loosen the lug nuts on both front wheels, raise the vehicle and support it securely on jackstands. Remove the front wheels.
2   Remove the steering shaft pinch bolt.
3   Loosen the stabilizer bar-to-control arm nuts/bolts, or the link bolts/nuts on later models **(see illustration)**.
4   Loosen the stabilizer bar insulator-to-frame nuts/bolts **(see illustrations)**.
5   Place a jack under the rear of the subframe crossmember, then loosen the two front subframe-to-body bolts four turns. Remove the two rear subframe-to-body bolts. Slowly lower the jack and allow the rear of the sub-

frame to drop down. **Warning:** *Do not place any part of your body under the subframe assembly when it is lowered from the vehicle, even though a jack supports it.*
6   Remove the stabilizer clamps and insulators.
7   Pull the stabilizer bar to the rear, swing it down then remove it through the left side wheel well.
8   Inspect the bushings for wear and damage and replace them if necessary. To remove them, pry the bushing clamp off with a screwdriver and pull the bushings off the bar. To ease installation, spray the inside and outside of the bushings with a silicone-based lubricant. Do not use petroleum-based lubricants on any rubber suspension part!

Installation

9   Assemble the shaft bushings and clamps on the bar, guide the bar through the wheel well, over the frame and into position.
10   Install the clamps loosely to the frame and control arm and install the nuts finger tight. Tighten the bolts to the torque listed in this Chapter's Specifications.
11   Raise the frame into place while guiding

the steering shaft into position in the steering gear and install the rear bolts. Tighten the frame bolts to the torque figures listed in this Chapter's Specifications.
12   Install the pinch bolt.
13   Install the wheels and lower the vehicle. Tighten the lug nuts to the torque listed in the Chapter 1 Specifications.

3   Balljoint - check and replacement

Refer to illustrations 3.3a and 3.3b

Check

1   Raise the front of the vehicle and support it securely on jackstands. Apply the parking brake and block the rear wheels to keep the vehicle from rolling off the jackstands.
2   Visually inspect the rubber seal for damage, deterioration and leaking grease. If any of these conditions are noticed, the balljoint should be replaced.
3   Place a large pry bar under the balljoint and attempt to push the balljoint up. Next, position the pry bar between the steering knuckle and control arm and pry down **(see**

2.4a Loosen the stabilizer bar insulator-to-frame bolts (arrows) . . .

2.4b . . . and nuts (arrows), which are accessible from underneath

illustrations). If any movement is seen or felt during either of these checks, a worn out balljoint is indicated. **Note:** *On models through 1996, the balljoint is on the knuckle (with the stud pointing down into the control arm), while on 1997 and later models the balljoint is on the control arm with the stud pointing up into the knuckle.*

4   Have an assistant grasp the tire at the top and bottom and move the top of the tire in-and-out.

5   Separate the control arm from the steering knuckle (see Section 4). Using your fingers (don't use pliers), try to twist the stud in the socket. If the stud turns, replace the balljoint.

Replacement

6   Loosen the wheel lug nuts, raise the front of the vehicle and support it securely on jackstands. Apply the parking brake and block the rear wheels to keep the vehicle from rolling off the jackstands. Remove the wheel.

7   Separate the control arm from the steering knuckle (see Section 4). Temporarily insert the balljoint stud back into the control arm (loosely). This will ease balljoint removal after Step 9 has been performed, as well as hold the assembly stationary while drilling out the rivets.

8   Using a 1/8-inch drill bit, drill a pilot hole into the center of each balljoint-to-steering knuckle rivet (balljoint-to-control arm rivets on 1997 and later models).

9   Using a 1/2-inch drill bit, drill the head off each rivet. Work slowly and carefully to avoid deforming the holes in the control arm.

10   Loosen (but don't remove) the stabilizer bar-to-control arm nut. Pull the control arm down to remove the balljoint stud from the hole in the arm, then dislodge the balljoint from the steering knuckle (control arm on 1997 and later models).

11   Position the new balljoint and install the bolts (supplied in the balljoint kit) from the top of the steering knuckle (models through 1996) or the control arm (1997 and later models). Tighten the bolts to the torque specified in the new balljoint instruction sheet.

3.3a Check for movement between the balljoint and steering knuckle (arrow) when prying up

3.3b With the pry bar positioned between the steering knuckle boss and the balljoint, pry down and check for play in the balljoint - if there is any play, replace the balljoint

12   Insert the balljoint stud into its hole, install the castellated nut, tighten it to the torque listed in this Chapter's Specifications and install a new cotter pin. It may be necessary to tighten the nut some to align the cotter pin hole with an opening in the nut, which is acceptable. Never loosen the castellated nut to allow cotter pin insertion.

13   Tighten the stabilizer bar-to-control arm nut to the torque listed in this Chapter's Specifications.

14   Install the wheel, lower the vehicle and tighten the lug nuts to the torque listed in the Chapter 1 Specifications. It's a good idea to take the vehicle to a dealer service department or alignment shop to have the front end alignment checked and, if necessary, adjusted.

---

4   Control arm - removal and installation

Refer to illustration 4.5a and 4.5b

Removal

1   Loosen the wheel lug nuts, raise the front of the vehicle and support it securely on jackstands. Apply the parking brake and block the rear wheels to keep the vehicle from rolling off the jackstands. Remove the wheel.

2   If only one control arm is being removed, disconnect only that end of the stabilizer bar. If both control arms are being removed, disconnect both ends (see Section 2 if necessary).

3   Remove the balljoint stud's castellated nut and cotter pin. Disconnect any ABS wiring attached to the control arm.

4   Separate the balljoint from the control arm (from the knuckle on 1997 and later models) with a separation tool. If a tool is not available a large pry bar positioned between the control arm and steering knuckle can be used to "pop" the balljoint stud out. **Caution:** *Be careful not to overextend the inner CV joint or it may be damaged.*

5   Remove the two control arm pivot bolts and detach the control arm **(see illustrations)**.

6   The control arm bushings are replaceable, but special tools and expertise are nec-

4.5a Location of the control arm pivot bolts (arrows)

4.5b On later models the rear part of the control arm is fastened by a vertically mounted bushing bolt (arrow)

essary to do the job. Carefully inspect the bushings for hardening, excessive wear and cracks. If they appear to be worn or deteriorated, take the control arm to a dealer service department or repair shop.

Installation

7   Position the control arm in the suspension support and install the pivot bolts. Don't tighten the bolts completely yet.

8   Insert the balljoint stud into the hole in the control arm (knuckle on 1997 and later models), install the castellated nut and tighten it to the torque listed in this Chapter's Specifications. If necessary, tighten the nut a little more (but not more than one flat of the nut) if the cotter pin hole doesn't line up with an opening on the nut. Install a new cotter pin.

9   Place a floor jack under the balljoint and raise it to simulate normal ride height. Tighten the control arm pivot bolts to the torque listed in this Chapter's Specifications.

10   Install the stabilizer bar-to-control arm bolt, spacer, bushings and washers and tighten the nut to the torque listed in this Chapter's Specifications.

11   Install the wheel and lower the vehicle. Tighten the lug nuts to the torque specified in Chapter 1.

12   Drive the vehicle to a dealer service department or an alignment shop to have the front wheel alignment checked and, if necessary, adjusted.

---

5   Front strut and spring assembly - removal, inspection and installation

Refer to illustration 5.2

Note 1: *On 1996 and earlier models (and 1997 Olds) the strut cartridge can be replaced with the strut and spring assembly installed in the vehicle (see Section 6). Because it isn't necessary to remove and disassemble the strut and spring assembly for strut cartridge replacement, removal of the assembly should only be required to repair damage to the spring, seats and strut/knuckle components.*

Note 2: *On 1997 and later models (except Olds), there is no serviceable strut cartridge. If wear or damage has occurred on these models, the entire strut assembly will have to be removed and replaced (see Section 6).*

Removal

1   Loosen the wheel lug nuts, raise the front of the vehicle and support it securely on jackstands. Apply the parking brake and block the rear wheels to keep the vehicle from rolling off the jackstands. Remove the wheel.

2   Mark the position of the strut mount cover to the strut tower **(see illustration)**.

3   On 1997 and later models remove the strut to knuckle bolts **(see illustration 9.11)** and remove the strut. Be extremely careful not to over extend the CV joint or stretch the

5.2 Mark the position of the strut mount cover before removing the nuts

brake hose. If necessary support the control arm with a jack. On 1996 and earlier models separate the tie-rod end from the steering arm as described in Section 14.

4   Remove the brake caliper, bracket and disc. Hang the caliper out of the way. On models so equipped, remove the bolt and secure the ABS sensor out of the way.

5   Remove the hub and wheel bearing bolts (see Section 7).

6   Separate the balljoint from the lower control arm (see Section 4). Be careful not to overextend the inner CV joint or stretch the brake hose.

7   Remove the driveaxle (see Chapter 8).

8   Support the strut and spring assembly with one hand and remove the three strut mounting nuts. Remove the assembly out through the fenderwell.

Inspection

9   Check the strut body for leaking fluid, dents, cracks and other obvious damage that would warrant repair or replacement.

10   Check the coil spring for chips and cracks in the spring coating (this will cause premature spring failure due to corrosion). Inspect the spring seats for hardening, cracks and general deterioration.

11   Inspect the knuckle/strut for corrosion, bending or twisting.

12   If wear or damage is evident which would require removing the coil spring, take the strut and spring assembly to a dealer or properly equipped shop for repair.

Installation

13   Slide the strut assembly up into the fenderwell, align the marks and install the strut cover, then insert the three upper mounting studs through the holes in the shock tower. Once the three studs protrude from the shock tower, install the strut cover to the marked position, then the nuts so the strut won't fall back through. This may require an assistant, since the strut is quite heavy and awkward. On 1997 and later models, install the strut-to-knuckle bolts, then tighten all of the strut

6.2 Remove the strut shaft nut using this tool (arrow) with a wrench on it, and an extension with a Torx bit through the top to hold the strut shaft from turning

mounting bolts to the torque listed in this Chapter's Specifications.

14   On 1996 and earlier models, install the driveaxle.

15   Connect the lower balljoint to the control arm and install the nut. Tighten the nut to the torque listed in this Chapter's Specifications and install a new cotter pin. If the cotter pin won't pass through, tighten the nut a little more, but just enough to align the hole in the stud with a castellation on the nut (don't loosen the nut).

16   Install the hub and brake components.

17   Install the tie-rod end in the steering arm and tighten the castellated nut to the torque listed in this Chapter's Specifications. Install a new cotter pin. If the cotter pin won't pass through, tighten the nut a little more, but just enough to align the hole in the stud with a castellation on the nut (don't loosen the nut).

18   Install the wheel, lower the vehicle and tighten the lug nuts to the torque listed in the Chapter 1 Specifications.

19   Tighten the three upper mounting nuts to the torque listed in this Chapter's Specification.

---

6   Front strut - replacement

1996 and earlier models (and 1997 Olds)

Refer to illustrations 6.2, 6.3a, 6.3b, 6.4a, 6.4b and 6.5

1   Mark the position of the strut mount cover **(see illustration 5.2)** and remove the nuts and the cover. **Note:** *The vehicle should be on the ground with the full weight on the suspension.*

2   Remove the strut shaft nut, using a special tool that grips the nut while a Torx bit is installed into the shaft to prevent the shaft from turning **(see illustration)**.

3   Pry out the strut mount bushing and the

upper strut bumper (**see illustrations**). You may have to compress the strut shaft down into the cartridge using a length of pipe that just fits over the strut shaft.

4   Remove the strut cartridge nut using a special tool which engages with the slots in the nut (available at most auto parts stores) (**see illustrations**).

5   Grasp the strut cartridge and lift it out (**see illustration**).

6   If the old cartridge had been leaking oil, use a suction pump to remove the damper fluid from the strut body and pour it into an approved oil container.

7   Insert the replacement strut cartridge, which is a self-contained unit, into position and install the nut. Tighten the cartridge nut to the torque listed in this Chapter's Specifications.

8   Install the bumper.

9   Temporarily install the strut shaft nut enough to grip it with locking pliers to raise the shaft if it does not come up by itself, then remove the nut and install the bushing.

10   Install the strut shaft nut. Tighten the nut to the torque listed in this Chapter's Specifications.

11   Install the strut mount cover and nuts. Tighten the nuts to the torque listed in this Chapter's Specifications.

1997 and later models (except Olds)

12   Open the hood and loosen the three upper strut-to-body nuts (**see illustration 5.2**).

6.3a Remove the strut mount bushing (arrow) . . .

6.3b . . . and the upper strut bumper (arrow)

13   Loosen the wheel lug nuts, raise the front of the vehicle and support it securely on jackstands. Apply the parking brake and block the rear wheels to keep the vehicle from rolling off the jackstands. Remove the wheel.

14   Mark the strut-to-steering knuckle relationship by making a line around the strut-to-steering knuckle bolt heads (**see illustration 9.7**). On later models, disconnect the stabilizer bar link from the strut.

15   Remove the nuts from the strut-to-knuckle bolts and knock the bolts out with a brass punch and a hammer.

16   Separate the strut from the steering knuckle. Be careful not to overextend the inner

CV joint or stretch the brake hose. If necessary, support the control arm with a jack.

17   Support the strut and spring assembly with one hand and remove the upper strut mounting nuts and bolt. Remove the strut and spring assembly.

18   Check the strut body for leaking fluid, dents, cracks and other obvious damage, which would warrant repair or replacement.

19   Check the coil spring for chips and cracks in the spring coating (this will cause premature spring failure due to corrosion). Inspect the spring seat for hardening, cracks and general deterioration.

20   If wear or damage is evident, replace the strut and/or coil spring as necessary.

21   Mount the spring/strut in a vise, then fit the coil spring compressor tools (ensuring that they are fully engaged), and compress the spring until all tension is relieved from the upper mounting (**see illustration**).

22   Hold the strut piston rod with a Torx socket and unscrew the thrust bearing retaining nut with a box wrench.

23   Withdraw the top mounting, thrust bearing, upper spring seat and spring, followed by the boot and the bump stop.

24   If a new spring is to be installed, the original spring must now be carefully released

6.4a Strut cartridge nut removal tool - the lugs at the large end fit into the slots in the nut

6.4b In use, the tool fits down over the strut shaft and a breaker bar can be used to turn it

6.5 Lift the cartridge out

6.21 Install the spring compressor and alternately tighten each clamp to evenly compress the spring

from the compressor. If it is to be re-used, the spring can be left in compression.

25   To replace the strut, slide the spring (with the compressor tools still in place) from the old strut and slide the spring onto the new strut. Install the upper components removed in Step 12, followed by the bearing retainer nut. Tighten to the torque listed in this Chapter's Specifications.

26   With the lower spring fitted in its seat, slowly release the tension on the spring compressor, alternating side to side to release the tensioned evenly on each of the two spring tools. Remove the tools.

27   Guide the strut assembly up into the fenderwell and insert the upper mounting studs through the holes in the shock tower. Once the studs protrude from the shock tower, install the nuts so the strut won't fall back through. This may require an assistant, since the strut is quite heavy and awkward.

28   Slide the steering knuckle into the strut flange and insert the two bolts. Install the nuts, align the marks you made prior to disassembly and tighten the nuts to the torque listed in this Chapter's Specifications.

29   Install the wheel, lower the vehicle and tighten the wheel lug nuts to the torque listed in the Chapter 1 Specifications.

30   Tighten the upper mounting nuts to the torque listed in this Chapter's Specifications.

31   Drive the vehicle to a dealer service department or an alignment shop to have the front wheel alignment checked and, if necessary, adjusted (this is only necessary if the strut has been modified for camber adjustment).

7   Front hub and wheel bearing assembly - removal and installation

Refer to illustration 7.6

Note: *The front hub and wheel bearing assembly is sealed-for-life and must be replaced as a unit.*

Removal

1   Loosen the driveaxle nut one turn. Loosen the wheel lug nuts, raise the front of the vehicle and support it securely on jackstands. Apply the parking brake and block

7.6 Hub mounting bolt locations (arrows)

the rear wheels to keep the vehicle from rolling off the jackstands. Remove the wheel.

2   Disconnect the wheel speed sensor wiring on later models. On early models, disconnect the stabilizer bar from the control arm.

3   Remove the caliper and bracket from the steering knuckle and hang it out of the way with a piece of wire (see Chapter 9). On ABS-equipped models, remove the bolt and secure the sensor out of the way.

4   Pull the disc off the hub.

5   Remove the driveaxle nut.

6   Remove the hub bolts **(see illustration)**. These bolts must be discarded and replaced with new ones on all 2001 and later models. The correct bolts are available from dealer parts departments.

7   Use a puller, pull the hub/bearing assembly off the driveaxle splines and detach it from the knuckle. **Note:** *It may be necessary to tap hub and bearing assembly out of the knuckle.*

8   Wrap a rag around the end of the driveaxle to avoid damaging the splines.

Installation

9   Apply a coat of multi-purpose grease to the driveaxle splines. Carefully guide the hub/bearing assembly over the end of the driveaxle, making sure the splines engage properly. Push the hub/bearing assembly into position and install the bolts. Tighten the bolts to the torque listed in this Chapter's Specifica-

tions. Install the driveaxle hub nut and tighten it securely.

10   Install the brake disc, caliper and (if equipped) the ABS sensor (see Chapter 9).

11   Install the wheel, lower the vehicle and tighten the lug nuts to the torque listed in the Chapter 1 Specifications.

12   Tighten the driveaxle hub nut to the torque specified in Chapter 8.

8   Rear stabilizer bar - removal and installation

Refer to illustrations 8.2, 8.3a and 8.3b

1   Raise the rear of the vehicle and support it securely on jackstands. Block the front wheels to keep the vehicle from rolling off the jackstands. Remove the rear wheels if necessary for clearance.

2   On 1997 and later models remove the stabilizer shaft link from each end of the stabilizer bar, then detach the insulator brackets at the rear frame support and remove the shaft from the vehicle **(see illustration)**. On 1996 and earlier models mark the strut-to-knuckle position.

3   Remove the nuts and detach the stabilizer shaft mounting bracket **(see illustrations)**.

8.2 On 1997 and later models, remove the rear stabilizer bar link end nut (arrow)

8.3a Rear stabilizer bar details	
1	Body
2	Nut
3	Nut
4	Bracket
5	Bolt
6	Stabilizer shaft link bolt
7	Bolt
8	Link
9	Insulator
10	Stabilizer bar

8.3b On 1997 and later models, remove the one bolt/nut (arrow) at each side of the stabilizer bar

9.7 Scribe or paint around the knuckle nuts (arrow)

9.10 Location of the strut-to-body bolts (arrows)

9.11 Strut-to-knuckle mounting bolts

9.16 Location of the rear strut-to-body bolts (arrows) (coil over strut type rear suspensions)

4   Remove the two stabilizer link mounting brackets.
5   Support the left knuckle with a jack and remove the lower left knuckle mounting bolts.
6   Remove the stabilizer bar through the left side, under the knuckle.
7   Inspect the bushings for cracks, hardening and wear. Replace them if necessary.
8   Installation is the reverse of the removal procedure. Make sure the marks made in Step 2 line up before tightening the knuckle bolts.
9   Remove the strut-to-knuckle nuts and knock the bolts out with a brass, lead or plastic hammer.

9   Rear strut - removal and installation

Transversely mounted leaf spring

Refer to illustrations 9.7, 9.10 and 9.11

Note: *This procedure requires special tools to compress the auxiliary damper and the rear leaf spring. These tools are available at specialty tool suppliers. There are two different versions of the auxiliary damper compression tool, an early and late version.*

1   Loosen the wheel lug nuts, raise the rear of the vehicle and support it securely on jackstands. Block the front wheels to keep the vehicle from rolling off the jackstands. Remove the wheel.
2   Compress and remove the auxiliary damper (if equipped) using an auxiliary damper compression tool.
3   On 1991 through 1995 models (except 1995 Chevrolet) equipped with dual exhaust, remove the exhaust system as necessary.
4   On 1991 through 1995 models (except 1995 Chevrolet) remove the jack pad and retention plates from the rear transverse spring. Install a special rear leaf spring compression tool and compress, but do not remove, the leaf spring.
5   Detach the brake hose bracket.
6   Remove the brake caliper and hang it out of the way on a piece of wire.

7   Mark the strut-to-knuckle relationship and outline the knuckle nuts **(see illustration)**.
8   Detach the stabilizer bar from the knuckle.
9   Support the knuckle with a jack.
10   Remove the strut-to-body bolts **(see illustration)**.
11   Remove the strut-to-knuckle nuts and knock the bolts out with a brass, lead or plastic hammer **(see illustration)**.
12   Separate the strut from the knuckle and remove the strut from the vehicle.
13   Installation is the reverse of the removal procedure. Make sure the strut-to-knuckle alignment marks made during Step 7 line up before tightening the bolts to the torque listed in this Chapter's Specifications.

Coil over strut type suspension

Refer to illustration 9.16

Note: *This procedure applies to 1997 and later models and early Chevrolet models with coil over strut type suspensions.*

14   Loosen the wheel lug nuts, raise the rear of the vehicle and support it securely on jackstands. Block the front wheels to keep the vehicle from rolling off the jackstands. Remove the wheel.
15   Support the bottom of the knuckle with a floor jack.
16   Open the trunk and loosen the three strut-to-body nuts **(see illustration)**.
17   Detach the brake hose bracket from the strut housing if equipped.
18   Mark the relationship of the strut to the knuckle and outline the knuckle bolts/nuts.
19   Detach the stabilizer bar link from the strut (see Section 9).
20   Remove the strut-to-body nuts **(see illustration 9.14)**, and lower the strut assembly until there is no more spring pressure on the knuckle.
21   Remove the strut-to-knuckle nuts and knock the bolts out with a brass or plastic hammer **(see illustration 9.11)**.
22   Separate the strut from the knuckle and remove the strut (with coil spring assembly in place) from the vehicle.
23   If the strut is being replaced, install the

coil spring and upper strut components from the old assembly to the new strut. **Note 1:** *Replacement of the coil springs on the rear struts requires a number of special tools and a procedure that is typically beyond the scope of the home mechanic. If the coil springs are in need of replacement, take the car or the strut assembly to a dealer service department or other qualified shop.* **Note 2:** *There is no serviceable cartridge on the rear struts. The strut itself must be replaced.*

24   Installation is the reverse of the removal procedure. Make sure the strut-to-knuckle alignment marks made during Step 18 line up before tightening the bolts to the torque listed in this Chapter's Specifications.

10   Rear transverse spring - removal and installation

Refer to illustrations 10.2, 10.3 and 10.4

Warning: *Wear safety goggles and don't place any part of your body under the ends of the spring while performing this procedure.*

Note: *This procedure either requires a special tool to compress the rear leaf spring (all models except 1997 and later and early Chevrolet*

10.2 Remove the jack pad mounting bolts (arrows)

10.3 Remove the bolts and detach the spring retention plate (arrows)

10.4 Detach the right side trailing link mounting bolts (arrows)

with coil over strut type suspensions) or two floor jacks. The tool is available at most specialty tool suppliers.

Removal

Using special tool

1   Loosen the wheel lug nuts, raise the rear of the vehicle and support it securely on jackstands. Block the front wheels to keep the vehicle from rolling off the jackstands. Remove both rear wheels.
2   Remove the jack pad **(see illustration)**.
3   Remove the spring retention plates **(see illustration)**.
4   Detach the right trailing link at the knuckle **(see illustration)**.
5   Unplug the ABS electrical connectors, if equipped.
6   Attach the spring compressor tool to the center of the spring, make sure the rollers are centered, then compress the rear leaf spring.
7   Detach the spring from the right knuckle and slide it toward the left side of the vehicle. If it is necessary to pry the spring to the left using a prybar against the right knuckle, pry only on the rubber cover on the end of the spring and be very careful not to gouge or scratch the spring surface.
8   Relax the spring with the tool sufficiently to allow the spring and tool assembly to be removed from the right side of the vehicle.

Without special tool

Note: *This procedure requires the use of two floor jacks.*
9   Perform Steps 1 through 3 above.
10   Unplug the ABS electrical connectors, if equipped.
11   Loosen, but do not remove, the front and rear trailing link bolts on both sides. Remove the right side lateral link-to-knuckle bolt.
12   Disconnect the brake hoses at the rear calipers (see Chapter 9 if necessary). Plug the ends of the hoses to prevent excessive fluid loss and contamination.
13   Place a floor jack under each knuckle and raise the jacks just enough to support the knuckles.
14   Unbolt the struts from the body (see Section 9).

15   Slowly lower the jacks until the spring is no longer under tension. Remove the spring. If the ends of the spring are stuck to the knuckles, carefully pry on the rubber covers on the ends of the spring only. Be very careful not to nick or gouge the spring surface.

Installation

Using special tool

16   Compress the spring, raise it into position, then insert it into the left knuckle.
17   Compress the spring further and insert the right end into the right knuckle.
18   Center the spring and install the retention plate and bolts. Make sure the retention plate tabs line up with support so they don't contact the fuel tank. Tighten the retention plate bolts to the torque listed in this Chapter's Specifications.
19   Connect the trailing link to the right knuckle and install the bolt, but don't tighten the bolt yet. Install the jack pad.
20   If equipped, reconnect the ABS electrical harness.
21   Install the wheels and lower the vehicle. Tighten the trailing link bolt to the torque listed in this Chapter's Specifications.

Without special tool

22   Position the ends of the spring into the knuckles.
23   Slowly raise the knuckles high enough for the right side lateral links to be connected to the knuckle. Install the bolt, but don't tighten it yet. It would be helpful to have an assistant support the strut while doing this.
24   Continue to slowly raise the jacks, guide the upper mounts of the struts into position and install the bolts, tightening them to the torque listed in this Chapter's Specifications.
25   Install the spring retention plates. Make sure the retention plate tabs line up with the supports so they don't contact the fuel tank, then tighten the bolts to the torque listed in this Chapter's Specifications.
26   Connect the brake hoses to the calipers, using new copper washers, and tighten the inlet fitting bolt to the torque listed in the Chapter 9 Specifications. Bleed the brakes following the procedure in Chapter 9.

27   Reconnect the ABS electrical connectors, if equipped.
28   Install the wheels. Lower the vehicle and tighten the trailing link bolts and the lateral link-to-knuckle bolt to the torque listed in this Chapter's Specifications. Tighten the wheel lug nuts to the torque listed in the Chapter 1 Specifications.

---

11   Rear hub and wheel bearing assembly - removal and installation

Refer to illustration 11.3
Note: *The rear hub and wheel bearing assembly is sealed-for-life and must be replaced as a unit.*

Removal

1   Loosen the wheel lug nuts, raise the rear of the vehicle and support it securely on jackstands. Block the front wheels to keep the vehicle from rolling off the jackstands. Remove the wheel.
2   Remove the brake drum or the brake caliper and disc (see Chapter 9). Support the caliper with a piece of wire. If equipped, unplug the ABS electrical connector. Disconnect the parking brake cable (see Chapter 9).
3   Remove the four hub-to-knuckle bolts **(see illustration)**.

11.3 The rear hub and bearing assembly is secured to the knuckle with four bolts

12.4 Remove the trailing arm-to-knuckle bolt and nut

12.5 Use two wrenches to remove the trailing arm-to-chassis nut and bolt

4   Remove the hub and bearing assembly, maneuvering it out through the brake caliper bracket as necessary.

Installation

5   On models with rear disc brakes, transfer the parking brake actuator from the old hub to the new one. Position the hub and bearing assembly on the knuckle and align the holes. Install the bolts. After all four bolts have been installed, tighten them to the torque listed in this Chapter's Specifications.

6   Install the brake drum or the brake caliper and disc, tightening the caliper bolts to the torque listed in the Chapter 9 Specifications. Install the wheel. Lower the vehicle and tighten the wheel lug nuts to the torque listed in Chapter 1 Specifications.

12   Rear suspension components - removal and installation

1   Loosen the wheel lug nuts, raise the rear of the vehicle and support it securely on jackstands. Block the front wheels to keep the vehicle from rolling off the jackstands. Remove the wheels.

2   Remove the stabilizer bar as outlined in Section 8.

3   Remove the brake drums or calipers and discs from the hubs. See Chapter 9 if difficulty is encountered. If equipped, unplug the ABS electrical connectors.

Trailing arms (all)

Refer to illustrations 12.4 and 12.5

4   Remove the trailing arm-to-knuckle nut and bolt **(see illustration)**.

5   Remove the trailing arm-to-chassis nut and bolt **(see illustration)**.

6   Detach the trailing arm and lower it from the vehicle.

7   Installation is the reverse of removal. Do not tighten the nuts and bolts to the torque listed in this Chapters Specifications until the vehicle weight has been lowered onto the suspension.

Lateral link rods

1996 and earlier models

Refer to illustrations 12.9, 12.10 and 12.11

8   Compress and detach the auxiliary spring if equipped (see Section 9).

12.9 Lateral link rod-to-knuckle mounting bolts (arrows)

9   Remove the nuts and bolts connecting the rods to the knuckle **(see illustration)**.

10   Remove the rod inner bolts at the crossmember **(see illustration)**.

11   On 1988 and 1989 models mark the position of the toe adjusting cam to the crossmember. Remove the toe adjusting cam and push the bolt through far enough to allow the rod to be removed **(see illustration)**. (Later

12.10 Locations of the inner lateral link rod nuts (arrows)

12.11 Mark the positions of the toe adjusting cams to the crossmember

12.20 Knuckle installation details

1	Rear strut	5	Front lateral link rod	9	Washer	13	Nut
2	Knuckle	6	Auxiliary damper	10	Washer	14	Stabilizer bar
3	Trailing arm	7	Bolts	11	Bolt	15	Insulator
4	Rear lateral link rod	8	Bolt	12	Nut	16	Stabilizer bar bracket

models don't have a toe adjusting cam.) On some models it may be necessary to lower the fuel tank for access to the front rod bolt.

12   Installation is the reverse of removal. Apply thread locking compound to all bolts and don't tighten the bolts to the torque listed in this Chapter's Specifications until the vehicle weight has been lowered onto the suspension. After installation have the rear toe checked by a dealer service department or alignment shop.

1997 and later models

13   The rear suspension crossmember (steel framework that the suspension arms are bolted to at the inner ends) must be lowered for access to the inner arm bolts/nuts. Use a transmission jack under the suspension support.

14   Remove the bolts securing the suspension crossmember to the body, then lower the jack until the lateral rod inner bolts/nuts can be removed.

15   Remove the nuts and bolts connecting the rods to the knuckle **(see illustration 12.9)**.

16   Installation is the reverse of removal. Don't tighten the outer lateral rod bolts to the torque listed in this Chapter's Specifications until the vehicle weight has been lowered onto the suspension (you can simulate normal ride height by raising the suspension with a floor jack). After installation have the rear toe checked by a dealer service department or alignment shop.

Knuckle (all)

Refer to illustration 12.20

17   Mark the strut-to-knuckle relationship and make a line around the knuckle nuts **(see illustration 9.7)**.

18   Remove the rear brake drum or caliper and disc (see Chapter 9). On ABS equipped models, unplug the ABS electrical harness.

19   On cars with rear drum brakes, remove the brake shoe assembly (see Chapter 9) and the hub and bearing assembly (see Section 11). Remove the rear transverse spring, if equipped (see Section 10).

20   Remove the bolts and detach the trailing arm, lateral link rods and, if equipped, auxiliary damper and stabilizer bar from the knuckle **(see illustration)**.

21   Remove the strut-to-knuckle nuts and knock the bolts out with a brass, lead or plastic hammer.

22   Separate the knuckle from the strut and lower it from the vehicle.

23   To install the knuckle, slide it into the strut flange. If equipped, install the stabilizer bar bracket and auxiliary damper and insert the two bolts. Apply thread locking compound to the threads and install the nuts finger tight. Connect the lateral link rods and trailing arm to the knuckle. Align the marks made in Step 13 and tighten the strut-to-knuckle bolts to the torque listed in this Chapter's Specifications. The remainder of installation is the reverse of removal.

---

13 Steering system - general information

Warning: *Whenever any of the steering fasteners are removed, they must be inspected and, if necessary, replaced with new ones of the same part number or of original equipment quality and design. Torque specifications must be followed for proper reassembly and component retention. Never attempt to heat or straighten any suspension or steer-*

ing components. Instead, replace any bent or damaged part with a new one.

All vehicles covered by this manual have power rack-and-pinion steering systems. The components making up the system are the steering wheel, steering column, rack-and-pinion steering gear, tie-rods and tie-rod ends. The power steering system has a belt-driven pump to provide hydraulic pressure.

In the power steering system, the motion of turning the steering wheel is transferred through the column to the pinion shaft in the rack-and-pinion assembly. Teeth on the pinion shaft are meshed with teeth on the rack, so when the shaft is turned, the rack is moved left or right in the housing. A rotary control valve in the rack-and-pinion unit directs hydraulic fluid under pressure from the power steering pump to either side of the integral rack piston, which is connected to the rack, thereby reducing steering force. Depending on which side of the piston this hydraulic pressure is applied to, the rack will be forced either left or right, which moves the tie-rods, etc. If the power steering system loses hydraulic pressure it will still function manually, though with increased effort.

Some models are also equipped with Variable Effort Steering (VES). With VES, power assist is maximum when the vehicle is moving at low speeds, such as when parking, and minimum when the vehicle is moving at high speeds, such as highway cruising. This allows the driver to turn the steering wheel easily when it's most necessary, while still maintaining "road feel." The VES uses signals from the engine control module, the ABS control module and a steering wheel rotation sensor to control the opening of a power steering solenoid actuator. The actuator, which is located on the power steering pump on

14.3 Using white paint, mark the relationship of the tie-rod end and the threaded adjuster

15.6 Remove the pinch bolt (arrow) - this view is looking down on the steering gear below the master cylinder and booster

15.13 Disconnect the two fluid lines (arrows) from the rack - this view is looking forward from the rear of the subframe

VES-equipped cars, responds to these signals by varying the amount of power steering fluid flow. Thus, as vehicle speed decreases power steering fluid flow (and steering assist) increases, and as vehicle speed increases, fluid flow (and steering assist) decreases.

The steering column is a collapsible, energy-absorbing type, designed to compress in the event of a front end collision to minimize injury to the driver. The column also houses the ignition switch lock, key warning buzzer, turn signal controls, headlight dimmer control and windshield wiper controls. The ignition and steering wheel can both be locked while the vehicle is parked.

Due to the column's collapsible design, it's important that only the specified screws, bolts and nuts be used as designated and that they're tightened to the specified torque. Other precautions particular to this design are noted in appropriate Sections.

In addition to the standard steering column, optional tilt and key release versions are also offered. The tilt model can be set in five different positions, while with the key release model the ignition key is locked in the column until a lever is depressed to extract it.

Because disassembly of the steering column is more often performed to repair a switch or other electrical part than to correct a problem in the steering, the upper steering column disassembly and reassembly procedure is included in Chapter 12.

14   Tie-rod ends - removal and installation

Refer to illustration 14.3

Removal

1   Loosen the wheel lug nuts, raise the front of the vehicle and support it securely on jackstands. Apply the parking brake and block the rear wheels to keep the vehicle from rolling off the jackstands. Remove the wheel.
2   Loosen the tie-rod end jam nut.

3   Mark the relationship of the tie-rod end to the threaded portion of the tie-rod **(see illustration)**. This will ensure the toe-in setting is restored when reassembled.
4   Remove the cotter pin and disconnect the tie-rod from the steering knuckle arm with a puller.
5   Unscrew the tie-rod end from the tie-rod.

Installation

6   Thread the tie-rod end onto the tie-rod to the marked position and connect the tie-rod end to the steering arm. Install the castellated nut and tighten it to the torque listed in this Chapter's Specifications. Install a new cotter pin.
7   Tighten the jam nut securely and install the wheel. Lower the vehicle and tighten the lug nuts to the torque listed in the Chapter 1 Specifications.
8   Have the front end alignment checked by a dealer service department or an alignment shop.

15   Steering gear - removal and installation

Removal

Refer to illustrations 15.6, 15.13, and 15.14
Warning: *Make sure the steering shaft is not turned while the steering gear is removed or you could damage the airbag system. To prevent the shaft from turning, place the ignition key in the LOCK position or thread the seat belt through the steering wheel and clip it into place.*
1   Disconnect the cable from the negative battery terminal. **Caution:** *On models equipped with the Theftlock audio system, be sure the lockout feature is turned off before performing any procedure which requires disconnecting the battery.*
2   On models equipped with the 3.4L V6 engine, remove the air cleaner and duct assembly.
3   Loosen the front wheel lug nuts, raise

the front of the vehicle and support it securely on jackstands. Apply the parking brake and block the rear wheels to keep the vehicle from rolling off the jackstands. Remove both front wheels.
4   On models equipped with the 3.4L V6 engine, remove the right side engine splash shield.
5   On cars equipped with airbags, set the steering wheel straight ahead, check that the wide spline or "block tooth" on the upper steering shaft assembly is at the 12 o'clock position and that the ignition switch is set to "lock." **Caution:** *Failure to do this can result in damage to the airbag system's coil unit in the following steps.*
6   Roll back the boot at the bottom of the steering column to expose the flange and steering coupler assembly **(see illustration)**. Mark the coupler and steering column shaft, remove the pinch bolt and separate the steering column from the power steering input shaft.
7   Disconnect all wiring from the steering gear. Disconnect the stabilizer bar from the subframe for access, if necessary.
8   On models equipped with the 3.4L V6 engine, remove the exhaust pipe and catalytic converter assembly.
9   Separate the tie-rod ends from the steering arms (see Section 14).
10   Support the rear of the subframe assembly with a jack and remove the rear bolts. Loosen the front bolts of the subframe and lower the rear approximately five inches (three inches on models equipped with the 3.4L V6 engine). **Warning:** *Do not place any part of your body under the subframe when it is supported only by a jack.*
11   Remove the heat shield from the steering gear.
12   Remove the fluid pipe clip from the rack.
13   Place a drain pan or tray under the vehicle, positioned beneath the steering gear. Using a flare-nut wrench, disconnect the pressure and return lines from the steering gear **(see illustration)**. Plug the lines to prevent

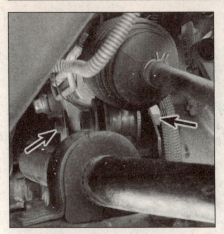

15.14 Steering rack mounting bolt/nut (arrows) - left side shown, right-side similar

17.8 Typical power steering pump details (shown with pulley removed for clarity)

1   *Pump mounting bolts*
2   *Pressure line*
3   *Return line*
4   *Pump*
5   *Reservoir*

excessive fluid loss.

14   Remove the steering gear through-bolts and nuts **(see illustration)**.

15   Lift the steering gear out of the mounts them move it forward and remove the pinch bolt from the coupler.

16   Support the steering gear and carefully maneuver the entire assembly out through the left side wheel opening.

Installation

17   Pass the steering gear assembly through the left wheel opening and place it in position in the mounts. Install the through-bolts and nuts, tightening them to the torque listed in this Chapter's Specifications.

18   Attach the pressure and return lines to the steering gear. Connect the line retainer.

19   Install the heat shield.

20   Raise the subframe into position and install the bolts. Tighten the frame bolts to the torque listed in this Chapter's Specifications.

21   Connect the tie-rod ends to the steering arms and tighten the nuts to the torque listed in this Chapter's Specifications. Install new cotter pins.

22   Install the exhaust system, if removed.

23   Center the steering gear and have an assistant guide the coupler onto the steering column shaft, with the previously applied marks aligned. Install and tighten the pinch bolt securely. **Warning:** *Be sure the shaft is seated before you install the pinch bolt or the shafts may disengage.*

24   Install the front wheels, lower the vehicle and tighten the lug nuts to the torque listed in the Chapter 1 Specifications.

25   Reconnect the negative battery cable.

26   Fill the power steering pump with the recommended fluid, bleed the system (see Section 18) and recheck the fluid level. Check for leaks.

27   Have the front end alignment checked by a dealer service department or an alignment shop.

16   Steering gear boots - replacement

1   Remove the steering gear from the vehicle (see Section 15). **Note:** *On later models, it's possible to access the steering gear boots by removing the rear subframe mounting bolts and leaving the steering gear connected to the vehicle. This avoids having to disconnect the power steering fluid lines, but it requires being under the car while servicing the boots.*

2   Remove the tie-rods ends from the steering gear (see Section 14).

3   Remove the jam nuts and outer boot clamps.

4   Cut off both inner boot clamps and discard them.

5   Mark the location of the breather tube, then remove the boots and the tube.

6   Install a new clamp on the inner end of the boot.

7   Apply multi-purpose grease to the tie-rod and the mounting groove on the steering gear.

8   Line up the breather tube with the marks made during removal and slide the boot onto the steering gear housing.

9   Make sure the boot isn't twisted, then tighten the clamp.

10   Install the outer clamps and tie-rod end jam nuts.

11   Install the tie-rod ends and tighten the nuts securely (see Section 14).

12   Install the steering gear assembly.

17   Power steering pump - removal and installation

Refer to illustration 17.8

Removal

1   Disconnect the cable from the negative battery terminal. **Caution:** *On models equipped with the Theftlock audio system, be sure the lockout feature is turned off before performing any procedure which requires disconnecting the battery.*

2   Remove the coolant recovery reservoir, if necessary.

3   On models equipped with the 3.4L V6 engine, (if necessary) remove the air cleaner and duct assembly.

4   On models equipped with the 3800 engine, remove the ECM cover.

5   Remove the pump drivebelt (see Chapter 1).

6   Position a drain pan under the vehicle. Remove as much fluid as possible with a suction pump, then remove the return line from the pump. On 5.3L engines, use a special puller to remove the pump pulley.

7   Using a flare-nut wrench and a back-up wrench, disconnect the pressure hose from the pump. **Note:** *On Quad-4 engines it may be necessary to remove the left side torque strut from the engine, disconnect the accelerator cable bracket and move it out of the way, then remove the torque strut bracket for access.*

8   Remove the pump mounting bolts and detach the pump from the engine, being careful not to spill the remaining fluid **(see illustration)**. **Note:** *The pulley may remain on the pump; there are holes through the pulley through which you can use a socket and extension to remove the pump mounting bolts. If you are installing a new pump, use a puller to remove the pulley from the old pump, and an installation tool to install it on the new pump. Many auto parts stores will make the pulley transfer for you when you buy the new pump. When shopping for the pump, ask ahead of time if the shop offers this service.*

Installation

9   Position the pump on the mounting bracket and install the bolts.

10   Connect the pressure and return lines to the pump.

11   Fill the reservoir with the recommended fluid and bleed the system, following the procedure described in the next Section.

18   Power steering system - bleeding

1   Following any operation in which the power steering fluid lines have been disconnected, the power steering system must be

19.3a Remove the airbag module retaining screws from the backside of the steering wheel (1996 and earlier models)

19.3b 1997 and later models have their airbags secured with clips; after using a mirror to see how they operate, release them using screwdrivers

bled to remove air and obtain proper steering performance.

2   With the front wheels turned all the way to the left, check the power steering fluid level and, if low, add fluid until it reaches the Cold mark on the dipstick.

3   Start the engine and allow it to run at fast idle. Recheck the fluid level and add more if necessary to reach the Cold mark on the dipstick.

4   Bleed the system by turning the wheels from side-to-side, without hitting the stops. This will work the air out of the system. Don't allow the reservoir to run out of fluid.

5   When the air is worked out of the system, return the wheels to the straight ahead position and leave the engine running for several minutes before shutting it off. Recheck the fluid level.

6   Road test the vehicle to be sure the steering system is functioning normally with no noise.

7   Recheck the fluid level to be sure it's up to the Hot mark on the dipstick while the engine is at normal operating temperature. Add fluid if necessary.

19 Steering wheel - removal and installation

Refer to illustrations 19.3a, 19.3b, 19.4, 19.5, 19.6 and 19.7

Warning: *Most models covered by this manual are equipped with Supplemental Inflatable Restraint (SIR) systems, more commonly known as airbags. The yellow wiring harnesses and connectors routed through the console and instrument panel are for this system. Do not use electrical test equipment on any of the airbag system wiring or tamper with it in any way. Always turn the steering wheel to the straight ahead position, place the ignition switch in the Lock position and disable the airbag system (see Chapter 12) before working in the vicinity of the impact sensors, steering column or instrument panel to avoid the possibility of accidental deployment of the airbag, which could cause personal injury.*

Note: *If your vehicle is not equipped with an airbag, disregard the steps that do not apply.*

1   Disconnect the cable from the negative battery terminal. **Caution:** *On models*

equipped with the Theftlock audio system, be sure the lockout feature is turned off before performing any procedure which requires disconnecting the battery.

2   Disable the airbag system (see Chapter 12).

3   On 1996 and earlier models, remove the airbag module retaining screws **(see illustration)**. On later models, there are four spring clips securing the airbag module to the steering wheel. There are openings on the back of the wheel for access. Turn the wheel until two of the slots are at the top, and use a flat-bladed tool to release the clips, then rotate the wheel for access to the other clips **(see illustration)**. First use a small mirror to view the clips so you'll be able to release them properly with a screwdriver.

4   Remove the airbag module and unplug the electrical connectors **(see illustration)**. This is a two-part disconnection, as there is a plastic clip that must be removed before the connector can be disconnected. Remove the module. **Warning:** *When carrying the airbag module, keep the driver's side of it away from your body, and when you place it on the*

19.4 Remove the airbag module and unplug the two electrical connectors (arrows)

19.5 Remove the safety clip with a pair of snap-ring pliers

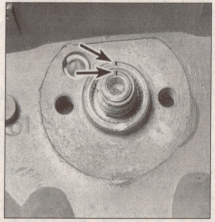

19.6 Make alignment marks (arrows) on the steering wheel and shaft, if none exist

19.7 Use a steering wheel puller to separate the steering wheel from the shaft - DO NOT attempt to remove the wheel with a hammer!

20.2 Use a special tool to push the stud out of the flange

bench, have the driver's side facing up.

5   If equipped, remove the safety clip from the steering shaft **(see illustration)**.

6   Remove the steering wheel retaining nut. Mark the relationship of the steering wheel to the steering shaft **(see illustration)**. Disconnect the horn and ground wires.

7   Remove the steering wheel with a puller **(see illustration)**. **Warning:** *Don't allow the steering shaft to turn with the steering wheel removed. If for some reason the steering shaft does turn, refer to Chapter 12, Section 8, for the airbag coil centering procedure.*

8   Installation is the reverse of removal. Be sure to tighten the steering wheel nut to the torque listed in this Chapter's Specifications.

9   To enable the airbag system, refer to Chapter 12.

20   Wheel studs - replacement

Refer to illustrations 20.2 and 20.3

Note: *This procedure applies to both the front and rear wheel studs.*

1   Install a lug nut part way onto the stud being replaced.

2   Push the stud out of the hub flange using a special tool **(see illustration)**.

3   Insert the new stud into the hub flange from the back side and install four flat washers and a lug nut on the stud **(see illustration)**.

4   Tighten the lug nut until the stud is seated in the flange.

5   Reinstall the hub and wheel bearing assembly.

21   Wheels and tires - general information

Refer to illustration 21.1

All vehicles covered by this manual are equipped with metric-size fiberglass or steel belted radial tires **(see illustration)**. The use of other size or type tires may affect the ride and handling of the vehicle. Don't mix different types of tires, such as radials and bias belted, on the same vehicle, since handling may be seriously affected. Tires should be replaced in pairs on the same axle, but if only one tire is being replaced, be sure it's the same size, structure and tread design as the other.

Because tire pressure affects handling and wear, the tire pressures should be checked at least once a month or before any extended trips (see Chapter 1).

Wheels must be replaced if they're bent, dented, leak air, have elongated bolt holes, are heavily rusted, out of vertical symmetry or if the lug nuts won't stay tight. Wheel repairs by welding or peening aren't recommended.

Tire and wheel balance is important

20.3 Install the four washers and a lug nut on the stud, then tighten the nut to draw the stud into place

METRIC TIRE SIZES

P 185 / 80 R 13

TIRE TYPE
P-PASSENGER
T-TEMPORARY
C-COMMERCIAL

ASPECT RATIO
(SECTION HEIGHT)
(SECTION WIDTH)
70
75
80

RIM DIAMETER
(INCHES)
13
14
15

SECTION WIDTH
(MILLIMETERS)
185
195
205
ETC

CONSTRUCTION TYPE
R-RADIAL
B-BIAS - BELTED
D-DIAGONAL (BIAS)

SECTION WIDTH

SECTION HEIGHT

21.1 Metric tire size code

CAMBER ANGLE (FRONT VIEW)   **CASTER ANGLE (SIDE VIEW)**

22.1 Front end alignment details

A minus B = C (degrees camber)
D = caster (expressed in degrees)
E minus F = toe-in (measured in inches)
G = toe-in (expressed in degrees)

TOE-IN (TOP VIEW)

to the overall handling, braking and performance of the vehicle. Unbalanced wheels can adversely affect handling and ride characteristics as well as tire life. Whenever a tire is installed on a wheel, the tire and wheel should be balanced by a shop with the proper equipment.

22 Wheel alignment - general information

Refer to illustration 22.1

A wheel alignment refers to the adjustments made to the wheels so they're in proper angular relationship to the suspension and the ground. Wheels that are out of proper alignment not only affect steering control, but also increase tire wear. The adjustment most commonly required is the toe-in adjustment **(see illustration)**, but camber adjustment is also possible.

Getting the proper wheel alignment is a very exacting process, one in which complicated and expensive machines are necessary to perform the job properly. Because of this, you should have a technician with the proper equipment perform these tasks. We will, however, attempt to give you a basic idea of what's involved with wheel alignment so you can better understand the process and deal intelligently with the shop that does the work.

Toe-in is the turning in of the wheels. The purpose of a toe specification is to ensure parallel rolling of the wheels. In a vehicle with zero toe-in, the distance between the front edges of the wheels will be the same as the distance between the rear edges of the wheels. The actual amount of toe-in is normally only a fraction of an inch. Incorrect toe-in will cause the tires to wear improperly by making them scrub against the road surface. On the front end, toe adjustment is controlled by the tie-rod end position on the tie-rod. On the rear on some models, toe is adjusted by turning a cam bolt

on the inner end of the front link rod. On other models, a special tool is required to reposition the front link rod at its inner mount.

Camber is the tilting of the wheels from the vertical when viewed from the front or rear of the vehicle. When the wheels tilt out at the top, the camber is said to be positive (+). When the wheels tilt in at the top the camber is negative (-). The amount of tilt is measured in degrees from the vertical and this measurement is called the camber angle. This angle affects the amount of tire tread which contacts the road and compensates for changes in the suspension geometry when the vehicle is cornering or travelling over an undulating surface. On the front end, camber can be adjusted after the strut mounting holes have been elongated with a file. On the rear, camber can be adjusted by changing the position of the rear knuckle on the strut.

Caster is not adjustable. If the caster angle is not to specification, the suspension components must be checked for damage.

Chapter 11   Body

Contents

	Section
Body repair - major damage	6
Body repair - minor damage	5
Console - removal and installation	25
Door handles - removal and installation	17
Door lock assembly - removal and installation	14
Door lock cylinder - removal and installation	18
Door lock striker - removal and installation	19
Door - removal and installation	20
Door trim panel - removal and installation	13
Door window glass - removal, installation and adjustment	15
Front fender liner - removal and installation	11
Front fender - removal and installation	12
General information	1
Hood latch and release cable - replacement	10
Hood - removal, installation and adjustment	9
Maintenance - body	2
Maintenance - hinges and locks	7
Maintenance - upholstery and carpets	3
Outside mirror - removal and installation	27
Rear lens assembly - removal and installation	24
Seat belt check	28
Seats - removal and installation	26
Trunk latch and striker - removal and installation	23
Trunk lid - removal and installation	21
Trunk lock cylinder - removal and installation	22
Vinyl trim - maintenance	4
Window regulator - removal and installation	16
Windshield and fixed glass - replacement	8

1   General information

These models are available in two-door coupe and four-door sedan body styles. The vehicle is a "unibody" type, which means the body is designed to provide vehicle rigidity so a separate frame isn't necessary. Body maintenance is an important part of the retention of the vehicle's market value. It's far less costly to handle small problems before they grow into larger ones. Major body components that are particularly vulnerable in accidents are removable. These include the hood, front fenders, grille, doors, trunk lid and tail light assembly. It's often cheaper and less time consuming to replace an entire panel than it is to attempt a restoration of the old one. However, this must be decided on a case-by-case basis.

2   Maintenance - body

1   The condition of the body is very important, because the value of the vehicle is dependent on it. It's much more difficult to repair a neglected or damaged body than it is to repair mechanical components. The hidden areas of the body, such as the fender wells and the engine compartment, are equally important, although they obviously don't require as frequent attention as the rest of the body.
2   Once a year, or every 12,000 miles, it's a good idea to have the underside of the body steam cleaned. All traces of dirt and oil will be removed and the underside can then be inspected carefully for rust, damaged brake lines, frayed electrical wiring, damaged cables and other problems.
3   At the same time, clean the engine and the engine compartment with a water soluble degreaser.
4   The fender wells should be given particular attention, as undercoating can peel away and stones and dirt thrown up by the tires can cause the paint to chip and flake, allowing rust to set in. If rust is found, clean down to the bare metal and apply an anti-rust paint.
5   The body should be washed as needed. Wet the vehicle thoroughly to soften the dirt, then wash it down with a soft sponge and plenty of clean soapy water. If the surplus dirt isn't washed off very carefully, it will in time wear down the paint.
6   Spots of tar or asphalt coating thrown up from the road should be removed with a cloth soaked in solvent.
7   Once every six months, wax the body thoroughly. If a chrome cleaner is used to remove rust from any of the vehicle's plated parts, remember that the cleaner also removes part of the chrome, so use it sparingly.

3   Maintenance - upholstery and carpets

Don't clean vinyl trim with detergents, caustic soap or petroleum-based cleaners. Plain soap and water works just fine, with a soft brush to clean dirt that may be ingrained. Wash the vinyl as frequently as the rest of the vehicle. After cleaning, application of a high-quality rubber and vinyl protectant will help prevent oxidation and cracks. The protectant can also be applied to weatherstripping, vacuum lines and rubber hoses, which often fail as a result of chemical degradation, and to the tires.

4   Vinyl trim - maintenance

1   Every three months, remove the floor-mats and clean the interior of the vehicle (more frequently if necessary). Use a stiff whisk broom to brush the carpeting and loosen dirt and dust, then vacuum the upholstery and carpets thoroughly, especially along seams and crevices.

2   Dirt and stains can be removed from carpeting with basic household or automotive carpet shampoos available in spray cans. Follow the directions and vacuum again, then use a stiff brush to bring back the "nap" of the carpet.

3   Most interiors have cloth or vinyl upholstery, either of which can be cleaned and maintained with a number of material-specific cleaners or shampoos available in auto supply stores. Follow the directions on the product for usage, and always spot-test any upholstery cleaner on an inconspicuous area (bottom edge of a back seat cushion) to ensure that it doesn't cause a color shift in the material.

4   After cleaning, vinyl upholstery should be treated with a protectant. **Note:** *Make sure the protectant container indicates the product can be used on seats - some products may make a seat too slippery.* **Caution:** *Do not use protectant on vinyl-covered steering wheels.*

5   Leather upholstery requires special care. It should be cleaned regularly with saddle-soap or leather cleaner. Never use alcohol, gasoline, nail polish remover or thinner to clean leather upholstery.

6   After cleaning, regularly treat leather upholstery with a leather conditioner, rubbed in with a soft cotton cloth. Never use car wax on leather upholstery.

7   In areas where the interior of the vehicle is subject to bright sunlight, cover leather seating areas of the seats with a sheet if the vehicle is to be left out for any length of time.

5   Body repair - minor damage

Plastic body panels

The following repair procedures are for minor scratches and gouges. Repair of more serious damage should be left to a dealer service department or qualified auto body shop. Below is a list of the equipment and materials necessary to perform the following repair procedures on plastic body panels. Although a specific brand of material may be mentioned, it should be noted that equivalent products from other manufacturers may be used instead.

  *Wax, grease and silicone
    removing solvent
  Cloth-backed body tape
  Sanding discs
  Drill motor with three-inch disc holder
  Hand sanding block
  Rubber squeegees
  Sandpaper*

  *Non-porous mixing palette
  Wood paddle or putty knife
  Curved tooth body file
Plastic body panel repair compound and material*

Flexible panels (front and rear bumper fascia)

1   Remove the damaged panel, if necessary or desirable. In most cases, repairs can be carried out with the panel installed.

2   Clean the area(s) to be repaired with a wax, grease and silicone removing solvent applied with a water-dampened cloth.

3   If the damage is structural, that is, if it extends through the panel, clean the backside of the panel area to be repaired as well. Wipe dry.

4   Sand the rear surface about 1-1/2 in beyond the break.

5   Cut two pieces of fiberglass cloth large enough to overlap the break by about 1-1/2 in. Cut only to the required length.

6   Mix the adhesive from the repair kit according to the instructions included with the kit, and apply a layer of the mixture approximately 1/8-inch thick on the backside of the panel. Overlap the break by at least 1-1/2 inches.

7   Apply one piece of fiberglass cloth to the adhesive and cover the cloth with additional adhesive. Apply a second piece of fiberglass cloth to the adhesive and immediately cover the cloth with additional adhesive insufficient quantity to fill the weave.

8   Allow the repair to cure for 20 to 30 minutes at 60-degrees to 80-degrees F.

9   If necessary, trim the excess repair material at the edge.

10   Remove all of the paint film over and around the area(s) to be repaired. The repair material should not overlap the painted surface.

11   With a drill motor and a sanding disc (or a rotary file), cut a "V" along the break line approximately 1/2-inch wide. Remove all dust and loose particles from the repair area.

12   Mix and apply the repair material. Apply a light coat first over the damaged area; then continue applying material until it reaches a level slightly higher than the surrounding finish.

13   Cure the mixture for 20 to 30 minutes at 60-degrees to 80-degrees F.

14   Roughly establish the contour of the area being repaired with a body file. If low areas or pits remain, mix and apply additional adhesive.

15   Block sand the damaged area with sandpaper to establish the actual contour of the surrounding surface.

16   If desired, the repaired area can be temporarily protected with several light coats of primer. Because of the special paints and techniques required for flexible body panels, it is recommended that the vehicle be taken to a paint shop for completion of the body repair.

Steel body panels

See photo sequence

Repair of minor scratches

17   If the scratch is superficial and does not penetrate to the metal of the body, repair is very simple. Lightly rub the scratched area with a fine rubbing compound to remove loose paint and built-up wax. Rinse the area with clean water.

18   Apply touch-up paint to the scratch, using a small brush. Continue to apply thin layers of paint until the surface of the paint in the scratch is level with the surrounding paint. Allow the new paint at least two weeks to harden, then blend it into the surrounding paint by rubbing with a very fine rubbing compound. Finally, apply a coat of wax to the scratch area.

19   If the scratch has penetrated the paint and exposed the metal of the body, causing the metal to rust, a different repair technique is required. Remove all loose rust from the bottom of the scratch with a pocket knife, then apply rust inhibiting paint to prevent the formation of rust in the future. Using a rubber or nylon applicator, coat the scratched area with glaze-type filler. If required, the filler can be mixed with thinner to provide a very thin paste, which is ideal for filling narrow scratches. Before the glaze filler in the scratch hardens, wrap a piece of smooth cotton cloth around the tip of a finger. Dip the cloth in thinner and then quickly wipe it along the surface of the scratch. This will ensure that the surface of the filler is slightly hollow. The scratch can now be painted over as described earlier in this Section.

Repair of dents

20   When repairing dents, the first job is to pull the dent out until the affected area is as close as possible to its original shape. There is no point in trying to restore the original shape completely as the metal in the damaged area will have stretched on impact and cannot be restored to its original contours. It is better to bring the level of the dent up to a point that is about 1/8-inch below the level of the surrounding metal. In cases where the dent is very shallow, it is not worth trying to pull it out at all.

21   If the back side of the dent is accessible, it can be hammered out gently from behind using a soft-face hammer. While doing this, hold a block of wood firmly against the opposite side of the metal to absorb the hammer blows and prevent the metal from being stretched.

22   If the dent is in a section of the body which has double layers, or some other factor makes it inaccessible from behind, a different technique is required. Drill several small holes through the metal inside the damaged area, particularly in the deeper sections. Screw long, self-tapping screws into the holes just enough for them to get a good grip in the metal. Now the dent can be pulled out by pull-

ing on the protruding heads of the screws with locking pliers.

23   The next stage of repair is the removal of paint from the damaged area and from an inch or so of the surrounding metal. This is done with a wire brush or sanding disk in a drill motor, although it can be done just as effectively by hand with sandpaper. To complete the preparation for filling, score the surface of the bare metal with a screwdriver or the tang of a file, or drill small holes in the affected area. This will provide a good grip for the filler material. To complete the repair, see the subsection on filling and painting later in this Section.

Repair of rust holes or gashes

24   Remove all paint from the affected area and from an inch or so of the surrounding metal using a sanding disk or wire brush mounted in a drill motor. If these are not available, a few sheets of sandpaper will do the job just as effectively.

25   With the paint removed, you will be able to determine the severity of the corrosion and decide whether to replace the whole panel, if possible, or repair the affected area. New body panels are not as expensive as most people think and it is often quicker to install a new panel than to repair large areas of rust.

26   Remove all trim pieces from the affected area except those which will act as a guide to the original shape of the damaged body, such as headlight shells, etc. Using metal snips or a hacksaw blade, remove all loose metal and any other metal that is badly affected by rust. Hammer the edges of the hole in to create a slight depression for the filler material.

27   Wire brush the affected area to remove the powdery rust from the surface of the metal. If the back of the rusted area is accessible, treat it with rust inhibiting paint.

28   Before filling is done, block the hole in some way. This can be done with sheet metal riveted or screwed into place, or by stuffing the hole with wire mesh.

29   Once the hole is blocked off, the affected area can be filled and painted. See the following subsection on filling and painting.

Filling and painting

30   Many types of body fillers are available, but generally speaking, body repair kits which contain filler paste and a tube of resin hardener are best for this type of repair work. A wide, flexible plastic or nylon applicator will be necessary for imparting a smooth and contoured finish to the surface of the filler material. Mix up a small amount of filler on a clean piece of wood or cardboard (use the hardener sparingly). Follow the manufacturer's instructions on the package, otherwise the filler will set incorrectly.

31   Using the applicator, apply the filler paste to the prepared area. Draw the applicator across the surface of the filler to achieve the desired contour and to level the filler surface. As soon as a contour that approximates the original one is achieved, stop working the paste. If you continue, the paste will begin to

stick to the applicator. Continue to add thin layers of paste at 20-minute intervals until the level of the filler is just above the surrounding metal.

32   Once the filler has hardened, the excess can be removed with a body file. From then on, progressively finer grades of sandpaper should be used, starting with a 180-grit paper and finishing with 600-grit wet-or-dry paper. Always wrap the sandpaper around a flat rubber or wooden block, otherwise the surface of the filler will not be completely flat. During the sanding of the filler surface, the wet-or-dry paper should be periodically rinsed in water. This will ensure that a very smooth finish is produced in the final stage.

33   At this point, the repair area should be surrounded by a ring of bare metal, which in turn should be encircled by the finely feathered edge of good paint. Rinse the repair area with clean water until all of the dust produced by the sanding operation is gone.

34   Spray the entire area with a light coat of primer. This will reveal any imperfections in the surface of the filler. Repair the imperfections with fresh filler paste or glaze filler and once more smooth the surface with sandpaper. Repeat this spray-and-repair procedure until you are satisfied that the surface of the filler and the feathered edge of the paint are perfect. Rinse the area with clean water and allow it to dry completely.

35   The repair area is now ready for painting. Spray painting must be carried out in a warm, dry, windless and dust free atmosphere. These conditions can be created if you have access to a large indoor work area, but if you are forced to work in the open, you will have to pick the day very carefully. If you are working indoors, dousing the floor in the work area with water will help settle the dust that would otherwise be in the air. If the repair area is confined to one body panel, mask off the surrounding panels. This will help minimize the effects of a slight mismatch in paint color. Trim pieces such as chrome strips, door handles, etc., will also need to be masked off or removed. Use masking tape and several thickness of newspaper for the masking operations.

36   Before spraying, shake the paint can thoroughly, then spray a test area until the spray painting technique is mastered. Cover the repair area with a thick coat of primer. The thickness should be built up using several thin layers of primer rather than one thick one. Using 600-grit wet-or-dry sandpaper, rub down the surface of the primer until it is very smooth. While doing this, the work area should be thoroughly rinsed with water and the wet-or-dry sandpaper periodically rinsed as well. Allow the primer to dry before spraying additional coats.

37   Spray on the top coat, again building up the thickness by using several thin layers of paint. Begin spraying in the center of the repair area and then, using a circular motion, work out until the whole repair area and about two inches of the surrounding original paint is covered. Remove all masking material 10 to

15 minutes after spraying on the final coat of paint. Allow the new paint at least two weeks to harden, then use a very fine rubbing compound to blend the edges of the new paint into the existing paint. Finally, apply a coat of wax.

6   Body repair - major damage

1   Major damage must be repaired by an auto body/frame repair shop with the necessary welding and hydraulic straightening equipment.

2   If the damage has been serious, it is vital that the structure be checked for proper alignment or the vehicle's handling characteristics may be adversely affected. Other problems, such as excessive tire wear and wear in the driveline and steering may occur.

3   Due to the fact that all of the major body components (hood, fenders, etc.) are separate and replaceable units, any seriously damaged components should be replaced rather than repaired. Sometimes these components can be found in a wrecking yard that specializes in used vehicle components, often at considerable savings over the cost of new parts.

7   Maintenance - hinges and locks

Every 3000 miles or three months, the door, hood and trunk lid hinges should be lubricated with a few drops of oil. The door striker plates should also be given a thin coat of white lithium-base grease to reduce wear and ensure free movement.

8   Windshield and fixed glass - replacement

1   Replacement of the windshield and fixed glass requires the use of special fast setting adhesive/caulk materials. These operations should be left to a dealer or a shop specializing in glass work.

2   Windshield-mounted rear view mirror support removal is also best left to experts, as the bond to the glass also requires special tools and adhesives.

9   Hood - removal, installation and adjustment

Refer to illustrations 9.2, 9.4a, 9,4b and 9.10

Note: *The hood is heavy and somewhat awkward to remove and install - at least two people should perform this procedure.*

Removal and installation

1   Use blankets or pads to cover the cowl area of the body and the fenders. This will protect the body and paint as the hood is lifted off.

These photos illustrate a method of repairing simple dents. They are intended to supplement *Body repair - minor damage* in this Chapter and should not be used as the sole instructions for body repair on these vehicles.

1 If you can't access the backside of the body panel to hammer out the dent, pull it out with a slide-hammer-type dent puller. In the deepest portion of the dent or along the crease line, drill or punch hole(s) at least one inch apart . . .

2 . . . then screw the slide-hammer into the hole and operate it. Tap with a hammer near the edge of the dent to help 'pop' the metal back to its original shape. When you're finished, the dent area should be close to its original contour and about 1/8-inch below the surface of the surrounding metal

3 Using coarse-grit sandpaper, remove the paint down to the bare metal. Hand sanding works fine, but the disc sander shown here makes the job faster. Use finer (about 320-grit) sandpaper to feather-edge the paint at least one inch around the dent area

4 When the paint is removed, touch will probably be more helpful than sight for telling if the metal is straight. Hammer down the high spots or raise the low spots as necessary. Clean the repair area with wax/silicone remover

5 Following label instructions, mix up a batch of plastic filler and hardener. The ratio of filler to hardener is critical, and, if you mix it incorrectly, it will either not cure properly or cure too quickly (you won't have time to file and sand it into shape)

6 Working quickly so the filler doesn't harden, use a plastic applicator to press the body filler firmly into the metal, assuring it bonds completely. Work the filler until it matches the original contour and is slightly above the surrounding metal

7 Let the filler harden until you can just dent it with your fingernail. Use a body file or Surform tool (shown here) to rough-shape the filler

8 Use coarse-grit sandpaper and a sanding board or block to work the filler down until it's smooth and even. Work down to finer grits of sandpaper - always using a board or block - ending up with 360 or 400 grit

9 You shouldn't be able to feel any ridge at the transition from the filler to the bare metal or from the bare metal to the old paint. As soon as the repair is flat and uniform, remove the dust and mask off the adjacent panels or trim pieces

10 Apply several layers of primer to the area. Don't spray the primer on too heavy, so it sags or runs, and make sure each coat is dry before you spray on the next one. A professional-type spray gun is being used here, but aerosol spray primer is available inexpensively from auto parts stores

11 The primer will help reveal imperfections or scratches. Fill these with glazing compound. Follow the label instructions and sand it with 360 or 400-grit sandpaper until it's smooth. Repeat the glazing, sanding and respraying until the primer reveals a perfectly smooth surface

12 Finish sand the primer with very fine sandpaper (400 or 600-grit) to remove the primer overspray. Clean the area with water and allow it to dry. Use a tack rag to remove any dust, then apply the finish coat. Don't attempt to rub out or wax the repair area until the paint has dried completely (at least two weeks)

9.2 Mark the hinge-to-hood bolt positions by drawing around the heads with a marking pen

9.4a Use a small screwdriver to pry the clip out . . .

2   Scribe or paint alignment marks around the bolt heads to insure proper alignment during installation **(see illustration)**.
3   Disconnect any cables or wire harnesses that will interfere with removal.
4   Have an assistant support the weight of the hood. Detach the upper ends of the hood support struts **(see illustrations)**.
5   Remove the hinge-to-hood bolts and lift off the hood.
6   Installation is the reverse of removal.

Adjustment

7   Fore-and-aft and side-to-side adjustment of the hood is done by moving the hood in relation to the hinge plate after loosening the bolts or nuts.
8   Scribe a line around the entire hinge plate so you can judge the amount of movement **(see illustration 9.2)**.
9   Loosen the bolts or nuts and move the hood into correct alignment. Move it only a little at a time. Tighten the hinge bolts and carefully lower the hood to check the alignment.
10   Finally, adjust the hood bumpers on the radiator support so the hood, when closed, is flush with the fenders **(see illustration)**.

11   The hood latch assembly, as well as the hinges, should be periodically lubricated with white lithium-base grease to prevent sticking and wear.

---

10   Hood latch and release cable - replacement

Cable

Refer to illustrations 10.2a, 10.2b, 10.2c, 10.3 and 10.4

1   In the passenger compartment, remove the trim panel and, if necessary, pull back the carpet.
2   Remove the latch handle retaining screws and detach the handle **(see illustrations)**. Some models have a floor-mounted handle, while most later models have the handle above the driver's kick panel.
3   In the engine compartment, detach the cable guides and grommet **(see illustration)**. Depending on the year and model of your car, you may have to remove the air cleaner and duct assembly, the diagonal brace, the head-

9.4b . . . then detach the strut from the hood

lamp access panel and/or the battery.
4   Detach the end of the cable from the latch **(see illustration)**. On some late models, the cable can be released from the latch more easily by removing the left headlight housing (see Chapter 12).

9.10 Screw the hood bumpers in or out to adjust the hood flush with the fenders

10.2a Mounting screws for the hood release handle trim cover (arrows) (floor mounted type)

10.2b Hood latch release handle mounting bolt (arrow) (floor mounted type)

10.2c Typical hood latch release handle mounting details (door pillar mounted)

10.3 Hood latch cable guide (arrow)

5   Connect a piece of string or thin wire of suitable length to the end of the cable and pull the cable through into the passenger compartment.

6   Connect the string or wire to the new cable and pull it back into the engine compartment.

7   Connect the cable and install the latch screws and trim panel.

Latch

1   Scribe a line around the latch to aid alignment when installing, then remove the retaining bolts securing the hood latch to the radiator support. Remove the latch. **Note**: *On some models, the front bumper fascia must be removed for access to the hood latch (see Section 11).*

2   Disconnect the hood release cable by disengaging the cable from the latch assembly **(see illustration 10.4)**.

3   Installation is the reverse of removal. **Note**: *Adjust the latch so the hood engages securely when closed and the hood bumpers are slightly compressed.*

11   Front fender liner - removal and installation

Refer to illustration 11.2

1   Raise the vehicle, support it securely on jackstands and remove the front wheel.

2   Remove the liner retaining screws and the nut **(see illustration)**.

3   Once all of the retainers are removed, detach the liner and remove it from the vehicle.

4   To install, place the liner in position and install the screws and nut.

12   Front fender - removal and installation

Refer to illustrations 12.7a and 12.7b

1   Loosen the wheel lug nuts, raise the front of the vehicle and support it securely on jackstands. Remove the wheel.

2   Remove the hood (see Section 9).

2003 and earlier models

3   If removing the left fender, remove the following components as required:
Left strut tower brace
Windshield washer reservoir (some models)
Battery cover
Vacuum tank

4   If removing the right fender, remove the following components as required:
Coolant recovery reservoir (some models)
Convenience center (some models)
Windshield washer reservoir

5   For either fender, remove the following components as required:
Hood
Headlamp housing
Turn signal lamp
Rocker panel and/or rocker panel finish molding
Fender liner (see Section 11)
Fender-to-fascia bolts
Fender-to-headlamp panel bolts

6   Disconnect any wiring harness connectors and other components that would interfere with fender removal.

10.4 Hood latch cable mounting clip and cable end (arrow)

11.2 Inner front fender mounting screws (arrows)

12.7a Mounting bolt locations (arrows) for the front fender (early models) (lower bolts visible from below)

12.7b On later models remove this fender-to-cowl bolt (arrow) at the rear of the fenderwell (shown with liner removed) and two bolts where the fender meets the rocker panel

7   Remove the fender mounting bolts (**see illustrations**).

2004 and later models

8   Remove the hood hinge from the vehicle.
9   Remove the fender liner (see Section 11).
10   Remove the plastic fasteners from the top of the bumper cover.
11   Remove the two bolts and two rivets from each end of the front bumper cover.
12   Lift off the front bumper cover.
13   Remove the upper support member for the front bumper cover.
14   If you're replacing the right fender, remove the windshield washer fluid bottle
15   Remove the bolt from the rear of the fender that is accessible from inside the wheel well.
16   Open the door and remove the bolt from the upper rear of the fender.
17   Remove the rocker molding at the front area, then remove the two bolts at the bottom rear part of the fender.
18   Remove the bolt from the front lower part of the fender.
19   Remove the five bolts at the top edge of the fender.

All models

20   Detach the fender. It is a good idea to have an assistant support the fender while it's being moved away from the vehicle to prevent damage to the surrounding body panels.
21   Installation is the reverse of removal.
22   Tighten all nuts, bolts and screws securely.

13   Door trim panel - removal and installation

Removal

Refer to illustrations 13.4 and 13.5

1   Disconnect the negative cable from the battery. **Caution:** *On models equipped with the Theftlock audio system, be sure the lockout feature is turned off before performing any procedure which requires disconnecting the battery.*

2003 and earlier models

2   Remove all door trim panel retaining screws and door pull/armrest assemblies. On some models it will be necessary to pry out the trim panel plugs to access the trim panel retaining screws. There is usually a screw in the inner door handle pocket, and one in the armrest/door pull pocket, under a plastic cover.

2004 and later models

3   Remove the door lock push button.
4   Use a putty knife to pry on the front edge of the door handle bezel (**see illustration**). Remove the bezel.
5   Pry the cover from the door pull handle and remove the two screws beneath it (**see illustration**).

All models

6   On manual window regulator equipped models, remove the window crank. On power regulator models, pry out the control switch assembly and unplug it.
7   On models with power mirrors, remove the mirror remote control (driver's side only).
8   Insert a putty knife between the trim panel and the door and disengage the retain-ing clips. Work around the outer edge until the panel is free.
9   Once all of the clips are disengaged, detach the trim panel, unplug any wire harness connectors and remove the trim panel from the vehicle. Lift up on the panel to disengage it from the upper part of the door.
10   Remove the door courtesy light or reflector, as necessary.
11   For access to the inner door, carefully peel back the plastic watershield and remove the energy absorber pad (if equipped).

Installation

12   Prior to installation of the door panel, be sure to reinstall any clips in the panel which may have come out during the removal procedure and remain in the door itself.
13   Plug in the wire harness connectors and place the panel in position in the door. Press the door panel into place until the clips are seated and install the armrest/door pulls. Install the manual regulator window crank or power window switch assembly.

13.4 Use a soft tool to pry the front of the handle bezel on 2004 and later models - it will then slide forward and out

13.5 There are two screws concealed under the door handle trim on 2004 and later models; the cover can be pried off

14 Door lock assembly - removal and installation

Refer to illustrations 14.3 and 14.7

Removal

1   With the window glass in the full up position, remove the door trim panel and water shield (see Section 13).
2   Remove the energy absorber pad, if equipped.
3   Disconnect spring clips from the remote control connecting rods at the lock assembly **(see illustration)**. **Note:** *Some models are equipped with non-reusable locking rod clips. On these models it will be necessary to use side cutters to cut off the clips that attach to the latch and purchase new clips.*
4   Remove any electrical connectors.
5   If necessary, remove the door lock module and separate it from the lock by bending the retaining clips or removing the rivets, as applicable.
6   As necessary, remove the inner and outer door handles.
7   Remove the lock assembly-to-door screws and lift the assembly from the door **(see illustration)**.

Installation

8   Installation is the reverse of removal.

15 Door window glass - removal, installation and adjustment

1   With the window glass in the full up position, remove the door trim panel and water shield (Section 13).

Front door glass

Refer to illustrations 15.4, 15.5a and 15.5b

2   Remove the energy absorber pad, if equipped.

14.3 After removing the cover, the door lock rod linkage is easily accessible on coupe models

3   Pry the inner (and, if necessary, outer) belt line sealing strip out of the glass opening, then remove the run channel screws.
4   If necessary, remove front run channel **(see illustration)**.
5   Raise the glass half way up, then disengage the rear run channel, if necessary,

14.7 Use a Torx-head tool to remove the door lock screws

by pushing on the rear guide retainer. Tilt the glass inboard of the door frame to remove it **(see illustration)**. **Note:** *On some later models it will only be necessary to raise the window half way up to access and remove the glass retaining bolts, then tilt the glass forward and remove the glass from the door **(see illustration)**.*

15.4 Forward run channel mounting screws

15.5a Front door glass removal

15.5b On later models raise the window just enough to access the glass retaining bolts (arrows) through the hole in the door frame

17.2a Door handle cover mounting screw locations (arrows)

17.2b Door handle linkage details

| 1 | Lock rod | 2 | Linkage |

17.3 On later models, disconnect the rods to the lock cylinder (A) and the outside handle (B), then remove the mounting bolts (C)

6   Install the glass by inserting it into the door, then engaging the regulator arm roller to the sash channel.

7   Lower the glass to the half way up position and pull the glass rearward to engage the rear guide retainer to the run channel.

8   Raise the glass to about three inches above the door belt line and install the front run channel, if removed.

9   Engage the front clip on the glass in the front run channel and tighten the bolts securely.

10   The remainder of installation is the reverse of removal.

11   If adjustment is necessary, loosen the front run channel bolts, then lower the glass fully. Tighten the top bolt finger tight and the bottom bolt securely. Raise the glass to the Up position and tighten the top bolt securely.

Rear door glass

12   Remove the inner and outer door belt sealing strips.

13   Remove the energy absorber pad, if equipped.

14   If necessary, remove the run channel from the door frame at the front and rear of the glass division channel.

15   If necessary, remove the front weatherstrip from the door.

16   Remove the sash nuts or drill out the rivets, as necessary, and lift the glass from the door. **Note:** *On some later models it will only be necessary to raise the window half way up to access and remove the glass retaining bolts, then tilt the glass forward and remove the glass from the door* **(see illustration 5.15b).**

17   Insert the glass and sash into the door and install the nuts. Tighten the nuts securely. Connect the weatherstrip and division channel, making sure to engage the glass guide securely to the channel.

18   Install the sealing strips.

19   The remainder of installation is the reverse of removal.

20   The rear door glass is not adjustable.

16   Window regulator - removal and installation

Removal

1   On power window equipped models, disconnect the negative cable at the battery. **Caution:** *On models equipped with the Theftlock audio system, be sure the lockout feature is turned off before performing any procedure which requires disconnecting the battery.*

2   On manual window glass regulator equipped models, remove the handle by pressing the bearing plate and door trim panel in and, with a piece of hooked wire, pulling off the spring clip. A special tool is available for this purpose but its use is not essential. With the clip removed, take off the handle and the bearing plate.

3   With the window glass in the full up position, remove the door trim panel and water shield (see Section 13).

4   Secure the window glass in the Up position with strong adhesive tape fastened to the glass and wrapped over the door frame (place a rag over the top of the door so the tape doesn't contact the weatherstrip).

5   Punch out the center pins of the rivets that secure the window regulator and drill the rivets out with a 1/4-inch drill bit (if equipped).

6   On power window equipped models, unplug the electrical connector.

7   Remove the retaining bolts and move the regulator until it is disengaged from the sash channel. Lift the regulator from the door.

Installation

8   Place the regulator in position in the door and engage it in the sash channel.

9   Secure the regulator to the door using 3/16-inch rivets and a rivet tool (if equipped). Instead of using rivets, you can also drill out the mounting holes and install nuts and bolts.

10   Install the bolts and tighten them securely.

11   Plug in the electrical connector (if equipped).

12   Install the water shield, door trim panel and window regulator handle. Connect the negative battery cable.

17   Door handles - removal and installation

Refer to illustrations 17.2a, 17.2b, 17.3 and 17.9

1   With the window glass in the full up position, remove the door trim panel, the energy absorber pad, if equipped, and the water shield (see Section 13).

Outside handle

Coupe models

2   On early models remove the cover assembly, if equipped **(see illustrations)**. Remove the retaining nut or drill out the rivets, as required, then detach the lock rods and remove the handle from the door.

3   On later models remove the lock rods from the latch and remove the handle retaining nuts through the opening in the door frame **(see illustration)**. Rotate the lock cylinder pawl for clearance and remove the door handle.

4   Installation is the reverse or removal.

Sedan models

5   If you're working on a rear door handles, remove the window glass (see Section 15).

6   Pry the remote rod out of the handle with a small screwdriver, remove the nuts or drill out the rivets, as required, and lift the handle off.

7   Installation is the reverse of removal.

Inside handle

8   Disconnect the rod from the handle.

9   Remove the bolt or punch out the center

17.9 The inside handle assembly is retained to the door by rivets (arrows)

20.3a Typical door check link details

| 1 | Check link assembly | 3 | Door |
| 2 | Bolt | 4 | Sealing grommet |

pins of the rivets that secure the window regulator and drill the rivets out with a 3/16-inch drill bit **(see illustration)**.
10 Lift the handle from the door.
11 To install, place the handle in position and secure it to the door, using 3/16-inch rivets and a rivet tool.
12 The remainder of installation is the reverse of removal.

18 Door lock cylinder - removal and installation

1 With the window glass in the full up position, remove the door trim panel, the energy absorber pad, if equipped, and the water shield (see Section 13).
2 If necessary, disconnect the rod from the lock cylinder and remove the anti-theft shield, if equipped.
3 Disconnect the electrical connector, if necessary.

4 Use a screwdriver to pry the retainer off and withdraw the lock cylinder from the door **Note:** *On some models it will be necessary to remove the outside door handle first (see Section 17), then pry the lock cylinder retaining clip off to remove it from the door handle.*
5 Installation is the reverse of removal.

19 Door lock striker - removal and installation

1 Mark the position of the striker bolt on the door pillar with a pencil or marking pen.
2 On most models, a Torx bit is required for removing the striker bolt. Unscrew the bolt and remove it.
3 To install, screw the lock striker bolt into the tapped cage plate in the door pillar and tighten it finger tight at the marked position. Tighten the bolt securely.

20 Door - removal and installation

Refer to illustrations 20.3a, 20.3b and 20.4

1 Unplug any electrical connectors that connect the electrical accessories and lights in the door to the dash wiring harness. Some of these may be accessible by removing the door panel - others may be tucked away behind the kick panels under the dash or behind the center pillar trim panels.
2 Open the door all the way and support it on jacks or blocks covered with cloth or pads to prevent damage to the paint.
3 On earlier models remove the door check link bolt and the hinge pin bolts, then with the help of an assistant, lift the door away **(see illustrations)**. On four-door models, open the front door to access the rear door hinge bolts at the door pillar.
4 On later models remove the hinge-to-door bolts and remove the door **(see illustration)**.
5 Install the door by reversing the removal

20.3b Location of the door hinge pin bolt (arrow)

20.4 Remove the bolts (arrows) at the door side of the hinge, not at the cowl

21.2 Typical trunk lid mounting bolt locations (arrows)

22.3a Pry the retainer clip from the trunk lock cylinder

procedure. On early models apply thread locking compound to the threads, install the hinge pin bolts and tighten the hinge pin bolts securely.

21 Trunk lid - removal and installation

Refer to illustration 21.2

1   Open the trunk lid and unplug any electrical connectors, then disconnect the solenoid (if equipped).
2   With an assistant supporting the trunk lid, detach the upper ends of the trunk support struts if equipped **(see illustrations 9.4a and 9.4b)**. then remove retaining bolts and lift the trunk lid from the vehicle **(see illustration)**.
3   Installation is the reverse of removal.

22 Trunk lock cylinder - removal and installation

Refer to illustrations 22.3a and 22.3b

1   Open the trunk lid.
2   If necessary, remove the trunk lid rear garnish by removing the bolts from inside the trunk lid. Remove the back-up lamp sockets too, if applicable.
3   Pry the retaining clip off and withdraw the lock cylinder from the vehicle **(see illustration)**. Disconnect the actuator cable (if equipped). Some retaining clips will be secured with a rivet, which must be drilled out with a 5/32-inch drill bit **(see illustration)**.
4   To install, place the lock cylinder in place and secure it with the retaining clip. On models with mounting rivets, insert new rivets or self-tapping screws to secure the clip.

23 Trunk latch and striker - removal and installation

2003 and earlier models

Refer to illustration 23.4

1   Disconnect the negative cable from the battery. **Caution:** *On models equipped with the Theftlock audio system, be sure the lockout feature is turned off before performing any procedure which requires disconnecting the battery.*
2   On models so equipped, disconnect the trunk lock cylinder cable by inserting a small screwdriver into the connector to hold the release tab down and then pull the cable out of the solenoid.
3   Remove the electronic solenoid (if equipped) and unbolt and remove the latch and (if equipped) the ajar switch. **(see illustration 22.3b)**.
4   Remove the retaining nuts and lift off the striker **(see illustration)**.
5   Installation is the reverse of removal.

2004 and later models

Latch

6   Mark the position of the latch assembly.
7   Remove the latch mounting bolts.
8   Disconnect the wiring from the latch.
9   Disconnect the lock rod and lift the latch out. Installation is the reverse of removal.

Striker

10   Remove the plastic sill from the trunk.
11   Refer to Chapter 12 and remove the tail lights.
12   Remove the trunk inner side panels, then remove the side bolts and nuts from the rear bumper cover.
13   Remove the pushpin fasteners from the

22.3b .**Typical trunk latch and lock cylinder mounting details**

1   *Screw or rivet*
2   *Lock cylinder retaining clip*
3   *Solenoid mounting bolts*
4   *Solenoid*
5   *Latch mounting bolts*
6   *Latch*

23.4 Typical trunk latch striker mounting nuts (arrows)

24.4 Remove the fasteners from the trim panel using a special tool to prevent breakage

24.6 Location of the tail light lens mounting nuts (arrows)

top edge of the bumper cover.
14   Working under the bumper, remove the bolts and the pushpin fasteners from the bumper cover.
15   Carefully lift off the bumper cover with the help of an assistant.
16   Mark the exact position of the striker.
17   Remove the mounting bolts and remove the striker. Installation is the reverse of removal.

24   Rear lens assembly - removal and installation

Refer to illustrations 24.4 and 24.6

1   Disconnect the negative cable at the battery. **Caution:** *On models equipped with the Theftlock audio system, be sure the lockout feature is turned off before performing any procedure which requires disconnecting the battery.*
2   Open the trunk lid.
3   Remove the convenience net, if equipped.
4   Remove the rear compartment trim panel **(see illustration)**.

5   Remove the bulb and socket assemblies, if necessary.
6   Unscrew the plastic wing nuts, pull the lens assembly out and lean it back **(see illustration)**. If not already removed, disconnect the bulb holders (see Chapter 12) and lift the assembly from the vehicle.
7   Installation is the reverse of removal.

25   Console - removal and installation

Refer to illustrations 25.2 and 25.4
Warning: *Most models covered by this manual are equipped with airbags. Always disable the airbag system before working in the vicinity of the impact sensors, steering column or instrument panel to avoid the possibility of accidental deployment of the airbag(s), which could cause personal injury (see Chapter 12). The yellow wires and connectors routed through the console are for this system. Do not use electrical test equipment on these yellow wires or tamper with them in any way while working around the console.*

1   Disconnect the negative cable at the battery. **Caution:** *On models equipped with the Theftlock audio system, be sure the lockout feature is turned off before performing any procedure which requires disconnecting the battery.*

Models through 1996

2   Remove the shift handle trim, the coin holder, storage compartment, armrest and shift knob and any other components which would block access to the console bolts **(see illustration)**.
3   Remove the retaining screw or pry the clip out of the automatic transaxle shift handle and manual transaxle shift handles. Pull the handle or knob off the shift lever.
4   Remove the bolts, then pull the console up **(see illustration)**.
5   Lift the console up for access and unplug the electrical connectors.
6   Installation is the reverse of removal.

1997 through 2003 models

7   Apply the parking brake lever and place the gear selector into the Low position.

25.2 Console trim mounting screws (arrows)

25.4 Typical console mounting screws (arrows)

27.3 Location of the outside mirror mounting nuts (arrows)

8   Pull the console trim bezel upward, starting at the front and working back. Then disconnect the electrical connectors and remove the bezel from the console assembly.

9   Remove the retaining screws securing the front half of the console.

10   Working in the console glove box, detach the retaining screws securing the rear half of the console.

11   Lift the console up and over the shift lever. Disconnect any electrical connections and remove the console from the vehicle.

12   Installation is the reverse of removal.

2004 and later models

13   Engage the parking brake and shift the transaxle to 2.

14   Adjust the front seats and remove the screws from the sides of the console.

15   Loosen the shifter handle screw and remove the handle.

16   Slide the console to the rear and disconnect the wiring at the front of the console.

17   Lift out the console.

18   Installation is the reverse of removal.

26   Seats - removal and installation

Warning: *2000 and later models may be equipped with side-impact airbags in the front seats. Refer to Chapter 12 and disable the airbag system before working on or in the vicinity of the front seats.*

Front seat

1   Move the seat all the way forward.

2   Remove the seat track covers and pull the carpet away from the adjuster and retaining nuts.

3   Remove the seat adjuster-to-floor panel retaining nuts.

4   Move the seat all the way to the rear.

5   Remove the front retaining nuts. Unplug the electrical connectors. Lift the seat from the vehicle.

6   Installation is the reverse of removal.

Rear seat

7   On earlier models, remove the seat cushion retaining bolts, detach the seat cush-

ion and remove it from the vehicle. On later models, just push in at the edge of the seat cushion to release the clips. Then lift up on the front edge and remove the cushion from the vehicle

8   Remove the nuts securing the bottom of the seatback, then swing the seatback up to disengage it from its upper retainers.

9   Installation is the reverse of removal.

27   Outside mirror - removal and installation

Refer to illustration 27.3

1   Remove the door trim panel (see Section 13) and the mirror reinforcement panel.

2   On power mirrors, unplug the electrical connector.

3   Remove the three nuts and lift off the mirror assembly **(see illustration)**.

4   Installation is the reverse of removal.

28   Seat belt check

1   Check the seat belts, buckles and guide loops for obvious damage and signs of wear.

2   Passive restraint type seat belts on some models are designed to lock up during a sudden stop or impact, yet allow free movement during normal driving. Verify that the retractors return the belt against your chest while driving and rewind the belt fully when the buckle is unlatched.

3   If any of the above checks reveal problems with the seat belt system, replace parts as necessary.

Chapter 12
Chassis electrical system

Contents

	Section
Airbags - general information and precautions	22
Bulb replacement	12
Circuit breakers - general information	5
Cruise control system - description and check	19
Door glass regulator - removal and installation	See Chapter 11
Door lock assembly - removal and installation	See Chapter 11
Electrical troubleshooting - general information	2
Fuses - general information	3
Fusible links - general information	4
General information	1
Headlight bulb - replacement	10
Headlights - adjustment	11
Head-up display (HUD) - general information	23
Horn - replacement	18

	Section
Ignition switch key lock cylinder - replacement	9
Instrument panel cluster - removal and installation	15
Power door lock system - description and check	21
Power window system - description and check	20
Radio and speakers - removal and installation	13
Radio antenna - removal and installation	14
Rear window defogger - check and repair	16
Relays - general information and testing	6
Starter safety switch check	See Chapter 1
Turn signal and hazard flashers - check and replacement	7
Turn signal switch assembly - removal and installation	8
Windshield wiper module and motor - removal and installation	17
Wiring diagrams - general information	24

1 General information

The electrical system is a 12-volt, negative ground type. Power for the lights and all electrical accessories is supplied by a lead/acid-type battery that is charged by the alternator.

This Chapter covers repair and service procedures for the various electrical components not associated with the engine. Information on the battery, alternator, ignition system and starter motor can be found in Chapter 5.

It should be noted that when portions of the electrical system are serviced, the negative battery cable should be disconnected from the battery to prevent electrical shorts and/or fires.

2 Electrical troubleshooting - general information

Refer to illustrations 2.5a, 2.5b, 2.6, 2.10 and 2.16

A typical electrical circuit consists of an electrical component, any switches, relays, motors, fuses, fusible links or circuit breakers related to that component and the wiring and connectors that link the component to both the battery and the chassis. To help you pinpoint an electrical circuit problem, wiring diagrams are included at the end of this book.

Before tackling any troublesome electrical circuit, first study the appropriate wiring diagrams to get a complete understanding of what makes up that individual circuit. Trouble spots, for instance, can often be narrowed down by noting if other components related to the circuit are operating properly. If several components or circuits fail at one time, chances are the problem is in a fuse or ground connection, because several circuits are often routed through the same fuse and ground connections.

Electrical problems usually stem from simple causes, such as loose or corroded connections, a blown fuse, a melted fusible link or a bad relay. Visually inspect the condition of all fuses, wires and connections in a problem circuit before troubleshooting it.

If testing instruments are going to be utilized, use the diagrams to plan ahead of time

2.5a The most useful tool for electrical troubleshooting is a digital multimeter that can measure volts, amps and resistance

2.5b A test light is a very handy tool for checking voltage

2.6 In use, the test light lead is clipped to a known good ground, then the pointed probe can test connectors, wires or electrical sockets - if the bulb lights, the circuit being tested has battery voltage

where you will make the necessary connections in order to accurately pinpoint the trouble spot.

The basic tools needed for electrical troubleshooting include a circuit tester or voltmeter (a 12-volt bulb with a set of test leads can also be used), a continuity tester, which includes a bulb, battery and set of test leads, and a jumper wire, preferably with a circuit breaker incorporated, which can be used to bypass electrical components **(see illustrations)**. Before attempting to locate a problem with test instruments, use the wiring diagram(s) to decide where to make the connections.

Voltage checks

Voltage checks should be performed if a circuit is not functioning properly. Connect one lead of a circuit tester to either the negative battery terminal or a known good ground. Connect the other lead to a connector in the circuit being tested, preferably nearest to the battery or fuse **(see illustration)**. If the bulb of the tester lights, voltage is present, which means that the part of the circuit between the connector and the battery is problem free. Continue checking the rest of the circuit in the same fashion. When you reach a point at which no voltage is present, the problem lies between that point and the last test point with voltage. Most of the time the problem can be traced to a loose connection. **Note:** *Keep in mind that some circuits receive voltage only when the ignition key is in the Accessory or Run position.*

Finding a short

One method of finding shorts in a circuit is to remove the fuse and connect a test light or voltmeter in its place to the fuse terminals. There should be no voltage present in the circuit. Move the wiring harness from side-to-side while watching the test light.

If the bulb goes on, there is a short to ground somewhere in that area, probably where the insulation has rubbed through. The

same test can be performed on each component in the circuit, even a switch.

Ground check

Perform a ground test to check whether a component is properly grounded. Disconnect the battery and connect one lead of a self-powered test light, known as a continuity tester, to a known good ground. Connect the other lead to the wire or ground connection being tested. If the bulb goes on, the ground is good. If the bulb does not go on, the ground is not good.

Continuity check

A continuity check is done to determine if there are any breaks in a circuit - if it is passing electricity properly. With the circuit off (no power in the circuit), a self-powered continuity tester can be used to check the circuit. Connect the test leads to both ends of the circuit (or to the "power" end and a good ground), and if the test light comes on the circuit is passing current properly **(see illustration)**. If the light doesn't come on, there is a break somewhere in the circuit. The same procedure can be used to test a switch, by connecting the continuity tester to the switch terminals. With the switch turned On, the test light should come on.

Finding an open circuit

When diagnosing for possible open circuits, it is often difficult to locate them by sight because oxidation or terminal misalignment are hidden by the connectors. Merely wiggling a connector on a sensor or in the wiring harness may correct the open circuit condition. Remember this when an open circuit is indicated when troubleshooting a circuit. Intermittent problems may also be caused by oxidized or loose connections.

Electrical troubleshooting is simple if you keep in mind that all electrical circuits are basically electricity running from the battery, through the wires, switches, relays, fuses and fusible links to each electrical component

(light bulb, motor, etc.) and to ground, from which it is passed back to the battery. Any electrical problem is an interruption in the flow of electricity to and from the battery.

Connectors

Most electrical connections on these vehicles are made with multiwire plastic connectors. The mating halves of many connectors are secured with locking clips molded into the plastic connector shells. The mating halves of large connectors, such as some of those under the instrument panel, are held together by a bolt through the center of the connector.

To separate a connector with locking clips, use a small screwdriver to pry the clips apart carefully, then separate the connector halves. Pull only on the shell, never pull on the wiring harness as you may damage the individual wires and terminals inside the connectors. Look at the connector closely before trying to separate the halves. Often the locking clips are engaged in a way that is not immediately clear. Additionally, many connectors have more than one set of clips.

Each pair of connector terminals has a male half and a female half. When you look at the end view of a connector in a diagram, be sure to understand whether the view shows the harness side or the component side of the connector. Connector halves are mirror images of each other, and a terminal shown on the right side end-view of one half will be on the left side end view of the other half.

Backprobing a connector

It is often necessary to take circuit voltage measurements with a connector connected. Whenever possible, carefully insert a small straight pin (not your meter probe) into the rear of the connector shell to contact the terminal inside, then clip your meter lead to the pin. This kind of connection is called "backprobing" **(see illustration)**. When inserting a test probe

2.10 With a multimeter set to the ohms scale, resistance can be checked across two terminals - when checking for continuity, a low reading indicates continuity, a high reading indicates lack of continuity

2.16 To backprobe a connector, insert a small, sharp probe (such as a straight-pin) into the back of the connector alongside the desired wire until it contacts the metal terminal inside; connect your meter leads to the probes - this allows you to test a functioning circuit

into a male terminal, be careful not to distort the terminal opening. Doing so can lead to a poor connection and corrosion at that terminal later. Using the small straight pin instead of a meter probe results in less chance of deforming the terminal connector.

3 Fuses - general information

Refer to illustrations 3.1a, 3.1b, 3.1c, 3.1d and 3.3

The electrical circuits of the vehicle are protected by a combination of fuses, circuit breakers and fusible links. The passenger compartment fuse block is located under the instrument panel on the right side of the dashboard on earlier models. It is accessible after lifting out the glove box **(see illustration)**. On later models, the interior fuse/relay panels behind a plastic cover at the right end of the dash. Open the passenger door to access the panel. On some later Grand Prix models, the interior fuse panel is located inside the glove compartment. A second fuse block is located at the right front corner of the engine compartment, under a cover **(see illustrations)**. Some models may also have other fuse blocks in the engine compartment.

Each of the fuses is designed to protect a specific circuit, and the various circuits are identified on the fuse panel itself.

Miniaturized fuses are employed in the fuse block. These compact fuses, with blade terminal design, allow removal and replacement by hand. If an electrical component fails, always check the fuse first. The easiest way to check fuses is with a test light. Check for power at the exposed terminal tips of each fuse. If power is available on one side of the fuse but not the other, the fuse is blown. A blown fuse can also be confirmed by visually

3.1a The passenger compartment fuse block is accessible after lifting out the glove box insert

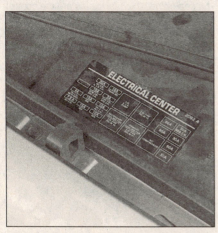

3.1b This fuse block is located under a cover in the right front corner of the engine compartment

3.1c Lift the cover off for access to the fuse block

3.1d On later models, the interior fuse/relay panel is located on the right side of the dash - remove the cover for access

3.3 When a fuse blows, the element between the terminals melts - the fuse on the left is blown, the fuse on the right is good

6.2 The convenience center is located under the right side of the dashboard and houses relays and other components

inspecting it **(see illustration)**.

Be sure to replace blown fuses with the correct type. Fuses of different ratings are physically interchangeable, but only fuses of the proper rating should be used. Replacing a fuse with one of a higher or lower value than specified is not recommended. Each electrical circuit needs a specific amount of protection. The amperage value of each fuse is molded into the fuse body.

If the replacement fuse immediately fails, don't replace it again until the cause of the problem is isolated and corrected. In most cases, the cause will be a short circuit in the wiring caused by a broken or deteriorated wire.

4   Fusible links - general information

Some circuits are protected by fusible links or fusible elements. The fusible elements used on some models are similar to a fuse and are located in the engine compartment fuse box. They are replaced in the same manner as a fuse. The fusible links are used in circuits that are not ordinarily fused, such as the ignition circuit.

Although the fusible links appear to be a heavier gauge than the wire they are protecting, the appearance is due to the thick insulation. All fusible links are several wire gauges smaller than the wire they are designed to protect.

Fusible links cannot be repaired, but a new link of the same size wire can be put in its place. The procedure is as follows:

a) *Disconnect the negative cable from the battery.* **Caution:** *On models equipped with the Theftlock audio system, be sure the lockout feature is turned off before performing any procedure which requires disconnecting the battery.*

b) *Disconnect the fusible link from the wiring harness.*

c) *Cut the damaged fusible link out of the wiring just behind the connector.*

d) *Strip the insulation back approximately 1/2-inch.*

e) *Position the connector on the new fusible link and crimp it into place.*

f) *Use rosin core solder at each end of the new link to obtain a good solder joint.*

g) *Use plenty of electrical tape around the soldered joint. No wires should be exposed.*

h) *Connect the battery ground cable. Test the circuit for proper operation.*

5   Circuit breakers - general information

Circuit breakers protect components such as power windows, power door locks and headlights. Some circuit breakers are located in the fuse block (see Section 3) and the convenience center (see Section 6).

On some models the circuit breaker resets itself automatically, so an electrical overload in a circuit breaker protected system will cause the circuit to fail momentarily, then come back on. If the circuit doesn't come back on, check it immediately. Once the condition is corrected, the circuit breaker will resume its normal function. Some circuit breakers must be reset manually.

To test a circuit breaker, hook an ohmmeter to the two terminals on the circuit breaker. No reading (infinite resistance) indicates a bad circuit breaker.

6   Relays - general information and testing

General information

Refer to illustration 6.2

1   Several electrical accessories in the vehicle use relays to transmit the electrical signal to the component. If the relay is defective, that component will not operate properly.

2   The various relays are grouped together

in several locations. Some relays are grouped together in the convenience center, which is located under the right side of the dashboard behind the sound insulator panel **(see illustration)**. On later models, the convenience center is located under the left side of the instrument panel.

Testing

Refer to illustration 6.5

3   It's best to refer to the wiring diagram for the circuit to determine the proper hook-ups for the relay you're testing. However, if you're not able to determine the correct hook-up from the wiring diagrams, you may be able to determine the test hook-ups from the information that follows.

4   On most relays, two of the terminals are the relay's control circuit (they connect to the relay coil which, when energized, closes the large contacts to complete the circuit). The other terminals are the power circuit (they are connected together within the relay when the control-circuit coil is energized).

5   Most relays are marked as an aid to help you determine which terminals are the control circuit and which are the power circuit **(see illustration)**.

6.5 Most relays are marked on the outside to easily identify the control circuit and power circuits

7.1 The turn signal flasher on some models is clipped to the steering column bracket

8.3a Remove the snap-ring and lift the airbag coil off

8.3b Use a special tool (available at most auto parts stores) to compress the lock plate for access to the retaining ring

6   Connect a fused jumper wire between one of the two control circuit terminals and the positive battery terminal. Connect another jumper wire between the other control circuit terminal and ground. When the connections are made, the relay should click. On some relays, polarity may be critical, so, if the relay doesn't click, try swapping the jumper wires on the control circuit terminals.

7   With the jumper wires connected, check for continuity between the power circuit terminals as indicated by the markings on the relay.

8   If the relay fails any of the above tests, replace it.

7   Turn signal and hazard flashers - check and replacement

Refer to illustration 7.1

Turn signal flasher

1   The turn signal flasher is a small canister-shaped or rectangular unit located under the dash, either in a clip adjacent to the steering column **(see illustration)**, or in the convenience center **(see illustration 6.2)**. **Note:** *Later models are equipped with a single combination turn signal/hazard flasher that is located behind the left kick panel.*

2   When the flasher unit is functioning properly, an audible click can be heard during its operation. If the turn signals fail on one side or the other and the flasher unit does not make its characteristic clicking sound, a faulty turn signal bulb is indicated.

3   If both turn signals fail to blink, the problem may be due to a blown fuse, a faulty flasher unit, a broken switch or a loose or open connection. If a quick check of the fuse box indicates that the turn signal fuse has blown, check the wiring for a short before installing a new fuse.

4   To replace the flasher, simply unplug it and pull it out of the clip.

5   Make sure that the replacement unit is identical to the original. Compare the old one

to the new one before installing it.

6   Installation is the reverse of removal.

Hazard flasher

7   The hazard flasher, a small canister-shaped or rectangular unit located under the dash, either in a clip adjacent to the steering **(see illustration 7.1)** or in the convenience center **(see illustration 6.2)**, flashes all four turn signals simultaneously when activated.

8   The hazard flasher is checked in a fashion similar to the turn signal flasher (see Steps 2 and 3).

9   To replace the hazard flasher, pull it from its retainer or the convenience center. **Note:** *Later models are equipped with a single combination turn signal/hazard flasher that is located behind the left kick panel.*

10   Make sure the replacement unit is identical to the one it replaces. Compare the old one to the new one before installing it.

11   Installation is the reverse of removal.

8   Turn signal switch assembly - removal and installation

Warning: *Some models covered by this manual are equipped with Supplemental Inflatable Restraint (SIR) systems, more commonly known as airbags. Always disable the airbag system before working in the vicinity of any airbag system components to avoid the possibility of accidental deployment of the airbag(s) which could cause personal injury (see Section 22). The yellow wiring harnesses and connectors routed through the console and instrument panel are for this system. Do not use electrical test equipment on any of the airbag system wiring or tamper with it in any way.*

Removal

2003 and earlier models

Refer to illustrations 8.3a, 8.3b, 8.3c, 8.4, 8.5, 8.8, 8.12 and 8.13

1   Detach the cable from the negative battery terminal and disable the airbag system, if

8.3c On later models remove the steering column cover screws (arrows) and detach the covers (lower cover shown)

equipped (see Section 22). **Caution:** *On models equipped with the Theftlock audio system, be sure the lockout feature is turned off before performing any procedure which requires disconnecting the battery.*

2   Remove the steering wheel (see Chapter 10).

3   Remove the airbag coil retaining snap-ring and remove the coil assembly. Let the coil hang by the wiring harness. Remove the wave washer. Using a lock plate removal tool, depress the lock plate for access to the retaining ring **(see illustrations)**. Use a small screwdriver to pry the retaining ring out of the groove in the steering column and remove the lock plate. **Note:** *On 1997 and later models it is not necessary to remove the airbag coil assembly, To remove the switch on these models simply remove the retaining screws from the steering column upper and lower covers and remove the covers **(see illustration)**. Then remove the switch mounting screws. The turn signal switch electrical connectors should be separated from the junction block at the bottom of the steering column and removed with the switch.*

8.4 Remove the cancel cam assembly (arrow)

8.5 Remove the hazard warning knob screw (arrow) and the knob

8.8 Remove the column housing cover plastic spacer (arrow) - don't forget this piece when reassembling the column housing

4   On earlier models remove the cancel cam assembly **(see illustration)**.
5   Remove the hazard warning knob **(see illustration)**.
6   Remove the column housing cover screw (which is longer and blue in color). Unplug the electrical connector behind the turn signal lever, grasp the lever and pull it straight out of the housing.
7   Detach the wiring protector from under the steering column, separate the wiper pulse switch wires, then unplug the connector. Remove the pulse switch pivot pin, then pull the switch wires up through the column and remove switch and wires.
8   Remove the plastic spacer in the lower left corner of the housing **(see illustration)**. Don't forget this spacer during reassembly.
9   Remove the under-dash panel below the steering column.
10   Remove the steering column bracket bolts and lower the steering column from the dash.
11   Locate the turn signal switch electrical connector. Detach the wires to the buzzer switch assembly (tan and black wire and light green wire) from the back of the connector.
12   Remove the turn signal switch mounting screws **(see illustration)**.

13   Pull the wiring harness and electrical connector up through the steering column and remove the switch assembly **(see illustration)**.

2004 and later models
14   Pull out on the tilt lever to remove it if necessary.
15   Refer to Chapter 10 and remove the steering wheel. **Note:** *It's possible to remove the steering column covers on later models without removing the steering wheel. This requires the covers to be pulled apart, then removed by bending them slightly as they are manipulated out from around the steering wheel.*
16   Remove the bolts from under the steering column and allow it to drop down enough to access the steering column covers.
17   Pull down at the rear edge of the lower column cover to detach it from the upper cover.
18   Push the lower cover forward to disconnect the lock tabs from the upper cover and remove it
19   Place the tilt mechanism into the center position.
20   Disconnect the wiring from the multi-function switch.
21   Remove the mounting screws and lift off the switch.

Installation
2003 and earlier models
Refer to illustrations 8.24, 8.26 and 8.27
22   Make sure the airbag coil is centered as described in Step 26 before installing the steering wheel. Feed the turn signal switch connector and wiring harness down through the column. Use a section of mechanics wire to pull it through, if necessary.
23   Plug in the connector and replace the wiring protector.
24   Seat the turn signal switch on the column and install the turn signal switch mounting screws and lever arm. Install the hazard knob and multi-function lever. Press the multi-function lever straight in until it snaps in place. On later models, the multi-function switch and lever are one unit, which mounts with two screws **(see illustration)**.
25   On 1996 and earlier models, install the cancel cam and the lock plate. Depress the lock plate and install the retaining ring.
26   If necessary, center the airbag coil as follows (it will only become uncentered if the spring lock is depressed and the hub rotated

8.12 Remove the two screws (arrows) . . .

8.13 . . . and detach the turn signal switch assembly

8.24 Later-model multi-function switch mounting screws (arrows)

8.26 To center the airbag coil, depress the spring lock (arrow), rotate the hub in the direction of the arrow until it stops, then back the hub off 2-1/2 turns and release the spring lock

8.27 When properly installed, the airbag coil will be centered with the marks aligned (circle) and the tab (arrow) fitted between the projections on the top of the steering column

with the coil off the column) **(see illustration)**:

a) *Turn the coil over and depress the spring lock.*

b) *Rotate the hub in the direction of the arrow until it stops.*

c) *Rotate the hub in the opposite direction 2-1/2 turns and release the spring lock.*

27   Install the wave washer and the airbag coil **(see illustration)**. Pull the slack out of airbag coil lower wiring harness to keep it tight through the steering column, or it may be cut when the steering wheel is turned. Install the airbag coil retaining snap-ring.

28   The remainder of installation is the reverse of removal.

2004 and later models

29   Installation is the reverse of removal. Be sure to center the airbag coil properly, referring to Step 26 if necessary.

---

9   Ignition switch key lock cylinder - replacement

Warning: *Some models covered by this manual are equipped with Supplemental Inflatable Restraint (SIR) systems, more commonly known as airbags. Always disable the airbag system before working in the vicinity of any airbag system components to avoid the possibility of accidental deployment of the airbag(s) which could cause personal injury (see Section 22). The yellow wiring harnesses and connectors routed through the console and instrument panel are for this system. Do not use electrical test equipment on any of the airbag system wiring or tamper with it in any way.*

1996 and earlier models (and 1997 Olds)

Fixed steering column

1   Detach the cable from the negative battery terminal. **Caution:** *On models equipped with the Theftlock audio system, be sure the lockout feature is turned off before performing*

any procedure which requires disconnecting the battery.

2   Remove the steering wheel (see Chapter 10).

3   Remove the turn signal switch assembly (see Section 8).

4   Place the lock cylinder in the Run position.

5   Remove the turn signal switch housing screws.

6   Remove the turn signal switch housing and steering shaft assembly as a complete unit.

7   Using a screwdriver, lift the switch tab, then pull gently on the buzzer switch wires and remove the buzzer switch.

8   Place the lock cylinder in the Accessory position.

9   Remove the lock cylinder retaining screw.

10   Remove the lock cylinder.

11   Installation is the reverse of removal.

Tilt steering column

12   Take the vehicle to a dealer service department or other repair shop. A special tool is needed to remove the pivot pins in the steering column housing on tilt steering columns, making key lock cylinder replacement impossible for the home mechanic.

1997 through 2003 models (except Olds)

13   Detach the cable from the negative battery terminal. **Caution:** *On models equipped with the Theftlock audio system, be sure the lockout feature is turned off before performing any procedure which requires disconnecting the battery.*

14   Remove the steering wheel (see Chapter 10).

15   Remove the steering column covers **(see illustration 8.3c)**

16   Unplug the turn signal switch connectors from the bulkhead connector. Disconnect the key alarm connector if equipped.

17   Remove the ignition switch housing screws and detach the ignition switch/alarm module from the steering column.

18   To remove the lock cylinder turn the key to the RUN position. Insert a 1/16 Allen wrench into the hole at the top of the housing and depress the lock retaining pin. Then remove the key lock cylinder from the steering column.

19   Installation is the reverse of removal.

2004 and later models

20   Disconnect the cable from the negative battery terminal (see Chapter 5, Section 4). Use a screwdriver wrapped with electrical tape to pry off the bezel from around the ignition switch.

21   Pull the center trim panel rearward to detach it from the instrument panel.

22   Disconnect the wiring from the information display, then remove the display unit.

23   Remove the center air outlet and remove the entire trim panel.

24   Remove the three pushpin fasteners from the left insulator panel, turn the light to remove it from the panel and remove the panel.

25   Remove the cover from the left end of the instrument panel by pulling it straight off.

26   Remove the data link connector from the trim panel.

27   Remove the three screws from the lower steering column filler panel and pull the top of the panel out to release it.

28   Remove the screws and bolts from the steel driver's knee bolster. Disconnect the wiring retainer and lift the knee bolster off.

29   Remove the ignition switch bolts and lower the switch.

30   Turn the switch to the On position.

31   Use a small screwdriver to hold in the detent in the hole at the bottom of the switch.

32   Pull the key and the lock cylinder out. The key can now be removed from the lock cylinder.

33   There are two retainers that secure the theft deterrent module ring. These can be unclipped and the ring removed at this time.

34   Installation is the reverse of removal.

10.3a Location of the headlight mounting bolts (arrows)

10.3b On 1997 and later Buick models, pull up the two retaining clips (arrows) to release the headlight housing (Grand Prix models mount with two screws)

10.3c On 2004 and later models, you must remove a screw, then pull the retainer upwards . . .

10.3d . . . to release the headlight assembly and access the bulbs

10.4 Unplug the electrical connector

10.5a Remove the headlight bulb holder by turning it clockwise . . .

10   Headlight bulb - replacement

Refer to illustrations 10.3a, 10.3b, 10.3c, 10.3d, 10.4, 10.5a and 10.5b

Warning: *Halogen gas filled bulbs are under pressure and may shatter if the surface is scratched or the bulb is dropped. Wear eye protection and handle the bulbs carefully, grasping only the base whenever possible. Do not touch the surface of the bulb with your fingers because the oil from your skin could cause it to overheat and fail prematurely. If you do touch the bulb surface, clean it with rubbing alcohol.*

1   Detach the cable from the negative terminal of the battery. **Caution:** *On models equipped with the Theftlock audio system, be sure the lockout feature is turned off before performing any procedure which requires disconnecting the battery.*

2   If equipped, raise the flap or remove the plastic cover over the headlight for access to the bulbs.

3   On some models it may be necessary to remove the screws or nuts and pull the headlight

assembly forward **(see illustration)**. On 1997 and later Buick models, pull up the two clips to release the headlight housing. On 1997 through 2003 Grand Prix models, remove the two mounting screws, pull the headlight housing forward and release two clips at the back **(see illustration)**. **Note:** *On Grand Prix models equipped with a center light bar, the center light bar and the side marker light will have to be removed to allow headlight housing removal. On 2004 and later models there is a single retainer that must be pulled upward to allow the headlight assembly to be pulled forward. This retainer is secured by a screw* **(see illustrations)**.

4   Unplug the electrical connector **(see illustration)**.

5   Twist the bulb lock ring counterclockwise **(see illustration)** and pull the bulb holder assembly out of the headlight **(see illustration)**.

6   Installation is the reverse of removal.

11   Headlights - adjustment

Refer to illustrations 11.1a, 11.1b and 11.3

Note: *The headlights must be aimed cor-*

rectly. If adjusted incorrectly they could blind the driver of an oncoming vehicle and cause a serious accident or seriously reduce your ability to see the road. The headlights should be checked for proper aim every 12 months

10.5b . . . and pull it out of the headlight assembly (don't try to pull the bulb out of the holder - they're sold as a single unit)

11.1a Headlight adjustment screw locations (arrows) - early models

11.1b Later model headlight adjustment screw locations (A) - B is a bubble-level for alignment

and any time a new headlight is installed or front end bodywork is performed. It should be emphasized that the following procedure is only an interim step that will provide temporary adjustment until the headlights can be adjusted by a properly equipped shop.

1   Headlights on 1996 and earlier models have two spring loaded adjusting screws, one on the top controlling up-and-down movement and one on the side controlling left-and-right movement **(see illustration)**. Later models include a bubble-level on top of the headlight housing for ease of aiming **(see illustration)**. 2004 and later models are not adjustable horizontally. There is a single screw for vertical adjustment only located at the top of the headlight assembly.

2   There are several methods of adjusting the headlights. The simplest method requires a blank wall 25-feet in front of the vehicle and a level floor.

3   Position masking tape vertically on the wall in reference to the vehicle centerline and the centerlines of both headlights **(see illustration)**.

4   Position a horizontal tape line in reference to the centerline of all the headlights. **Note:** *It may be easier to position the tape on the wall with the vehicle parked only a few inches away.*

5   Adjustment should be made with the vehicle sitting level, the gas tank half-full and no unusually heavy load in the vehicle.

6   Starting with the low beam adjustment, position the high intensity zone so it's two inches below the horizontal line and two inches to the side of the headlight vertical line, away from oncoming traffic. Adjustment is made by turning the top adjusting screw clockwise to raise the beam and counterclockwise to lower the beam. The adjusting screw on the side should be used in the same manner to move the beam left or right.

7   With the high beams on, the high intensity zone should be vertically centered with the exact center just below the horizontal line. **Note:** *It may not be possible to position the*

headlight aim exactly for both high and low beams. If a compromise must be made, keep in mind that the low beams are the most used and have the greatest effect on driver safety.

8   Have the headlights adjusted by a dealer service department or service station at the earliest opportunity.

---

12   Bulb replacement

Refer to illustrations 12.1a, 12.1b, 12.2a, 12.2b, 12.5a, 12.5b and 12.5c

1   The lenses of many lights are held in place by screws, which makes it a simple pro-

11.3 Headlight aiming details

12.1a Location of the rear side marker light mounting screws (arrows) on early models

12.1b On 2004 and later models, these bulbs are accessible after removing these screws

12.2a Press the two tabs (arrows) on the front sidemarker light assembly, then slide it forward for access to the bulb

12.2b On 1997 and later Buick models, the headlight, turn signal and marker light bulbs (arrows) are all in one headlight housing

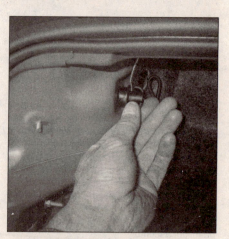

12.5a For the taillights on 2004 and later models, first pull back the trunk carpeting, then unscrew the plastic cover retainers . . .

cedure to gain access to the bulbs **(see illustrations)**.

2   On some lights, the lenses are held in place by tabs. Simply pop them off with your fingers or pry them off with a small screwdriver

(see illustration). On later model Buicks, the front side-marker bulbs are combined in one housing with the headlight bulbs **(see illustration)**, while later Grand Prix models have a separate housing (next to the headlight hous-

ing) for the marker and turn signal bulbs. On all later models, the rear side-marker bulbs are part of the taillight assembly.

3   Several types of bulbs are used. Some are removed by pushing in and turning them counterclockwise; others can simply be pulled straight out of the socket.

4   To gain access to the instrument panel lights, the instrument cluster will have to be removed first (see Section 15).

5   The taillight bulbs on 2004 and later models are accessible through the luggage compartment **(see illustrations)**.

13   Radio and speakers - removal and installation

1   Detach the cable from the negative terminal of the battery prior to performing any of the following procedures. **Caution:** *On models equipped with the Theftlock audio system, be sure the lockout feature is turned off before performing any procedure which requires disconnecting the battery.*

12.5b . . . allowing the taillight assembly to be pulled rearward

12.5c The bulb holders can then be removed for access to the bulbs

13.6 Steering column trim panel mounting screws

13.9a On 2004 and later models, the ignition switch cover can be pried off using a soft tool

Radio

Early models

Refer to illustrations 13.6

2   On these models, the radio receiver is mounted under the right side of the dashboard and is operated remotely by the radio control panel.

3   Remove the right side sound insulator or, on some models, the glove compartment.

4   Remove the radio receiver mounting nuts/screws. Lower the radio receiver from the dash

5   Reach up behind the receiver and unplug the antenna, speaker, power and ground connectors from the radio.

6   To remove the radio control panel it will be necessary to remove the steering column trim panel **(see illustration)**, the radio control knobs, instrument panel trim plate and radio control panel and on some models the heater and air conditioner control assembly as a single unit.

7   Once the assembly is removed detach the radio from the heater and air conditioner control assembly.

8   Installation is the reverse of removal.

Late models

Refer to illustrations 13.9a, 13.9b, and 13.10

9   On these models remove the accessory trim panel surrounding the radio and on some models the instrument cluster bezel. On 2004 and later models, refer to Section 9, Steps 20 through 23 for the panel removal procedure **(see illustrations)**.

10   Remove the mounting screws and the electrical connectors at the rear of the radio and the antenna lead **(see illustration)**. detach the radio from the instrument panel.

11   Installation is the reverse of removal.

Speakers

Dash mounted speakers

12   Remove the instrument panel pad (see Section 15).

13   Remove the speaker mounting screws.

14   Lift the speaker out of its enclosure, unplug the electrical connector and remove the speaker.

15   Installation is the reverse of removal.

Door mounted speakers

16   Remove the door trim panel (see Chapter 11).

17   Remove the screws securing the speakers to the door.

18   Disconnect the electrical connector and remove the speaker.

19   Installation is the reverse of removal.

Rear speakers

20   Remove the rear seat back and the seat back-to-window trim panel.

21   Remove the screws securing the speaker housing (coupe models) or the speaker itself (sedan models). Remove the speaker and detach the electrical connector. On coupe models, remove the screws and separate the speaker from the housing.

22   Installation is the reverse of removal.

13.9b After removing the ignition switch cover, pull rearward on the panel cover to release it - there is wiring at the top that must then be disconnected

13.10 Radio receiver mounting screws

14.2 To remove the standard antenna, simply unscrew it

15.2 Instrument bezel mounting screws (arrows)

14   Radio antenna - removal and installation

Refer to illustration 14.2

1   Disconnect the negative battery cable. **Caution:** *On models equipped with the Theftlock audio system, be sure the lockout feature is turned off before performing any procedure which requires disconnecting the battery.*

Standard antenna

2   Simply use a small wrench to unscrew the antenna from the base and screw on a new antenna **(see illustration)**. To remove the base, use snap-ring pliers to remove the base retaining nut.

Power antenna

3   Open the trunk and remove the trim panel.
4   Unscrew the escutcheon from the fender.
5   Unplug the electrical connector, disconnect the ground and relay cables, drain tube and antenna lead, then remove the antenna and motor assembly.
6   Installation is the reverse or removal.

Digital antenna

7   This type of antenna is used on most 2004 and later models. For access, first release and lower the rear of the headliner. This involves the removal of several interior trim panels that vary between years and models. If there are no screws apparent in an interior trim panel, it can usually be removed by pulling it directly outward. **Caution:** *Don't use excessive force, as there may be hidden fasteners used.*
8   Disconnect the antenna wiring.
9   Remove the mounting bolt and remove the antenna.
10   Installation is the reverse of removal.

15   Instrument panel cluster - removal and installation

Warning: *Some models covered by this manual are equipped with Supplemental Inflatable Restraint (SIR) systems, more commonly known as airbags. Always disable the airbag system before working in the vicinity of any airbag system components to avoid the possibility of accidental deployment of the airbag(s) which could cause personal injury. The yellow wiring harnesses and connectors routed through the console and instrument panel are for this system. Do not use electrical test equipment on any of the airbag system wiring or tamper with it in any way.*

Models through 1996

Refer to illustrations 15.2 and 15.4

1   Detach the cable from the negative battery terminal. **Caution:** *On models equipped with the Theftlock audio system, be sure the lockout feature is turned off before performing any procedure which requires disconnecting the battery.*
2   Remove the instrument panel pad and bezel **(see illustration)**.
3   Remove the steering column bracket and lower the steering column. Lower the tilt wheel to its lowest position and on column shift models place the gear selector lever in the L1 position.
4   Remove the instrument panel cluster **(see illustration)**.
5   Disconnect any switches or controls that will interfere with removal.
6   Installation is the reverse of removal.

1997 through 2003 models

7   Tilt the steering wheel down to the lowest position. **Note:** *If the vehicle is equipped with a column shift lever, place the gear selector in the L1 position.*
8   On Buick models, remove the plastic end caps at the left and right ends of the instrument panel.
9   At the left and right ends of the dash, remove the lower sound insulator panels and the filler panels (short panels at each end that fill the space between the sound insulators and the instrument trim panel). On Grand Prix models, remove the knee bolster panel and the steering column mounting bolts, then lower the steering column.
10   On Buick models, remove the screw at the right end of the dash trim panel (exposed once the filler panel is removed), then release the tab with a screwdriver. Release the trim panel from its clips by gently pulling it away from the dash, working from right to left.
11   On Grand Prix models, pull rearward at the bottom of the instrument cluster trim bezel

15.4 Instrument cluster mounting screws (arrows)

16.5a When measuring the voltage at the rear window defogger grid, wrap a piece of aluminum foil around the probe of the voltmeter and press the foil against the wire with your finger

16.5b To determine if the heating element has broken, check the voltage at the center of each element - if the voltage is 6-volts, the element is unbroken

until the clips are released. Disconnect the fog lamp switch, if equipped.

12   With the trim bezel off (all models), remove the instrument cluster mounting screws. Pull out on the instrument cluster until the electrical connectors can be disconnected. Remove the cluster.

13   Installation is the reverse of removal.

2004 and later models

14   Use a screwdriver wrapped with tape to pry off the bezel of the ignition switch,

15   Pull the center trim panel rearward to expose the lower steering column trim.

16   Remove the cover from the left end of the instrument panel by pulling it straight off.

17   Disconnect the data link connector and allow it to hang.

18   Remove the screws from the lower steering column trim panel and remove the trim panel.

19   Tilt the steering wheel to its lowest position.

20   Pull the instrument trim panel rearward to disengage it from its retainers.

21   Disconnect the wiring from the headlight dimmer switch.

22   Remove the instrument cluster trim panel.

23   Remove the screws from the instrument cluster.

24   Pull the cluster out far enough and disconnect the wiring. Lift the instrument cluster out.

25   Installation is the reverse of removal.

16   Rear window defogger - check and repair

Refer to illustrations 16.5a and 16.5b

1   This option consists of a rear window with a number of horizontal elements baked into the glass surface during the glass forming operation.

2   Small breaks in the element can be successfully repaired without removing the rear window.

Check

3   To test the grids for proper operation, start the engine and turn on the system.

4   Ground one lead of a test light and carefully touch the other lead to each element line.

5   The brilliance of the test light should increase as the lead is moved across the element **(see illustrations)**. If the test light glows brightly at both ends of the lines, check for a loose ground wire. All of the lines should be checked in at least two places.

Repair

Refer to illustration 16.11

6   To repair a break in a line, it is recommended that a repair kit specifically for this purpose be purchased from a dealer parts department. Included in the repair kit will be a decal, a container of silver plastic and hardener, a mixing stick and instructions.

7   To repair a break, first turn off the system and allow it to de-energize for a few minutes.

8   Lightly buff the element area with fine steel wool, then clean it thoroughly with alcohol.

9   Use the decal supplied in the repair kit or apply strips of electrician's tape above and below the area to be repaired. The space between the pieces of tape should be the same width as the existing lines. This can be checked from outside the vehicle. Press the tape tightly against the glass to prevent seepage.

10   Mix the hardener and silver plastic thoroughly.

11   Using the wood spatula, apply the silver plastic mixture between the pieces of tape, overlapping the undamaged area slightly on either end **(see illustration)**.

12   Carefully remove the decal or tape and apply a constant stream of hot air directly to the repaired area. A heat gun set at 500 to

16.11 To use a defogger repair kit, apply masking tape to the inside of the window

700-degrees F is recommended. Hold the gun one inch from the glass for two minutes.

13   If the new element appears off color, tincture of iodine can be used to clean the repair and bring it back to the proper color. This mixture should not remain on the repair for more than 30 seconds.

14   Although the defogger is now fully operational, the repaired area should not be disturbed for at least 24 hours.

17   Windshield wiper module and motor - removal and installation

Models through 1996

Refer to illustrations 17.4, 17.5, 17.7, 17.8a, 17.8b, 17.9, 17.10a, 17.10b and 17.11

1   Detach the cable from the negative terminal of the battery. **Caution:** *On models equipped with the Theftlock audio system, be sure the lockout feature is turned off before performing any procedure which requires disconnecting the battery.*

2   Raise the hood.
3   Disconnect the connector for the windshield washer fluid line at the wiper arms.
4   Pop off the windshield wiper blade cap over the nut and remove the nut **(see illustration)**.
5   Insert a pop rivet or a pin through the holes next to the wiper arm pivots, then grasp the wiper arms and remove them by rocking them back-and-forth, while lifting up **(see illustration)**.
6   On early models, remove the screws from the lower edge of the windshield reveal molding, then lower the hood and remove the molding by lifting it toward the windshield.
7   Remove the engine compartment weatherstrip, then remove the cowl. On early models, the cowl is secured with screws **(see illustration)**. On later models, it's fastened by plastic pushpins. Some early models also have a light switch that has to be disconnected.
8   If the wiper motor will run, rotate the crank arm to the inner Wipe position **(see illustration)**. If the motor will not run, use adjustable pliers to move the arm to the inner Wipe position by engaging the upper jaw against the top edge of the crank arm and the lower jaw against crank arm nut, using it as a

17.4 Lift the protective cap and remove the wiper arm nut

17.5 With a pin or drill bit inserted in the hole at the base, remove the wiper arm by grasping it securely and rocking it back-and-forth while lifting it off the shaft

pivot **(see illustration)**.
9   Unplug the electrical connectors **(see illustration)**.
10   Remove the three screws from the bellcrank housing, then lower the wiper transmission and lift the module from the vehicle **(see illustrations)**.
11   Remove the motor mounting bolts, then

remove the nut that fastens the transmission linkage arm to the motor shaft (crank arm nut), detach the linkage and remove the motor from the module **(see illustration)** :
12   Installation is the reverse of removal.

1997 and later models

Refer to illustration 17.17
13   Refer to Steps 4 through 7 above and remove the cowl cover.
14   Disconnect the electrical connectors from the wiper motor.
15   Remove the wiper linkage bracket mounting bolts.
16   Pull the linkage assembly out from the cowl, then turn it over to access the wiper motor retaining screws.
17   Remove the retaining screws and the wiper motor spindle nut **(see illustration)**. Separate the components. **Note:** *On some models, the wiper crank arm has a socket that snaps off a ball-stud on the motor spindle.*
18   Installation is the reverse of removal.

17.7 Air inlet panel and glass cowl mounting screws (arrows)

17.8a The wiper arm must be in the inner Wipe position when the wiper module assembly is removed

17.8b If the wiper motor won't run, use pliers to rotate the arm to the inner Wipe position

17.9 Unplug the electrical connectors from the wiper motor (arrows)

17.10a Remove the bellcrank housing screws (arrows) and lower the wiper transmission . . .

17.10b . . . then lift the module from the engine compartment

17.11 Remove the wiper motor bolts and the crank arm nut, detach the linkage and remove the motor from the module

18 Horn - replacement

1   Detach the cable from the negative terminal of the battery. **Caution:** *On models equipped with the Theftlock audio system, be sure the lockout feature is turned off before performing any procedure which requires disconnecting the battery.*
2   Open the hood.
3   The horns are located in a variety of places, some are located in the engine compartment in front of the left strut tower behind the air cleaner and battery, some are located at the front of the engine compartment attached to the radiator support below the hood latch and others are located behind the right headlight housing.
4   Locate the horns on particular model.
5   On vehicles with the horns mounted in front of the left strut tower remove the air cleaner assembly, remove the two bolts from the left side engine compartment cross brace, then loosen the remaining bolt and move the brace out of the way. remove the windshield washer reservoir and the battery.

6   On vehicles with the horns mounted at the front of the engine compartment by the hood latch, remove the headlight housing panel or the air deflector panel above the hood latch to access the horns.
7   On vehicles with the horns located

behind the right headlight housing, remove the headlight housing (see Section 10).
8   Remove the horn mounting bracket bolt, lower the horn, unplug the electrical connector and remove the horn.
9   Installation is the reverse of removal.

17.17 On later models, turn the linkage assembly over to access the spindle nut (A) and the wiper motor retaining bolts (B)

19.5 The cruise control module (arrow) is located in the engine compartment on the (driver's side) inner fenderwell - check for damage to the connectors

19 Cruise control system - description and check

Refer to illustration 19.5

1   The cruise control system maintains vehicle speed with an electronic servo motor located in the engine compartment, which is connected to the throttle linkage by a cable. The system consists of the electronic control module, brake switch, control switches, a relay, the vehicle speed sensor and associated wiring. Listed below are some general procedures that may be used to locate common cruise control problems.

2   Locate and check the fuse (see Section 3).

3   Have an assistant operate the brake lights while you check their operation (voltage from the brake light switch deactivates the cruise control).

4   If the brake lights don't come on or don't shut off, correct the problem and retest the cruise control.

5   Inspect the cable linkage between the cruise control module and the throttle linkage. The cruise control module is located on the left (drivers) inner fenderwell of the engine compartment **(see illustration)**.

6   Visually inspect the wires connected to the cruise control actuator and check for damage and broken wires.

7   The cruise control system uses a speed sensing device. The speed sensor is located in the transmission. To test the speed sensor see Chapter 6.

8   Test-drive the vehicle to determine if the cruise control is now working. If it isn't, take it to a dealer service department or an automotive electrical specialist for further diagnosis and repair.

20 Power window system - description and check

Refer to illustration 20.12

1   The power window system operates electric motors, mounted in the doors, which lower and raise the windows. The system consists of the control switches, the motors, regulators, glass mechanisms and associated wiring.

2   The power windows can be lowered and raised from the master control switch by the driver or by remote switches located at the individual windows. Each window has a separate motor that is reversible. The position of the control switch determines the polarity and therefore the direction of operation.

3   The circuit is protected by a fuse and a circuit breaker. Each motor is also equipped with an internal circuit breaker, this prevents one stuck window from disabling the whole system.

4   The power window system will only operate when the ignition switch is ON. In addition, many models have a window lockout switch at the master control switch which, when activated, disables the switches at the rear windows and, sometimes, the switch at the passenger's window also. Always check these items before troubleshooting a window problem.

5   These procedures are general in nature, so if you can't find the problem using them, take the vehicle to a dealer service department or other properly equipped repair facility.

6   If the power windows won't operate, always check the fuse and circuit breaker first.

7   If only the rear windows are inoperative, or if the windows only operate from the master control switch, check the rear window lockout switch for continuity in the unlocked position. Replace it if it doesn't have continuity.

8   Check the wiring between the switches and fuse panel for continuity. Repair the wiring, if necessary.

9   If only one window is inoperative from the master control switch, try the other control switch at the window. **Note:** *This doesn't apply to the drivers door window.*

10   If the same window works from one switch, but not the other, check the switch for continuity.

11   If the switch tests OK, check for a short or open in the circuit between the affected switch and the window motor.

12   If one window is inoperative from both switches, remove the trim panel from the affected door and check for voltage at the switch and at the motor while the switch is operated **(see illustration)**.

13   If voltage is reaching the motor, disconnect the glass from the regulator (see Chapter 11). Move the window up and down by hand while checking for binding and damage. Also check for binding and damage to the regulator. If the regulator is not damaged and the window moves up and down smoothly, replace the motor. If there's binding or damage, lubricate, repair or replace parts, as necessary. **Note:** *The window motor is an integral part of the window regulator assembly. See Chapter 11 for the removal procedures.*

14   If voltage isn't reaching the motor, check the wiring in the circuit for continuity between the switches and motors. You'll need to consult the wiring diagram for the vehicle. If the circuit is equipped with a relay, check that the relay is grounded properly and receiving voltage.

15   Test the windows after you are done to confirm proper repairs.

21 Power door lock system - description and check

The power door lock system operates the door lock actuators mounted in each door. The system consists of the switches, actuators, a

20.12 If no voltage is found at the motor with the switch depressed, check for voltage at the switch

control unit and associated wiring. Diagnosis can usually be limited to simple checks of the wiring connections and actuators for minor faults that can be easily repaired. Since this system uses an electronic control unit, in-depth diagnosis should be left to a dealership service department. The door lock control unit is located behind the instrument panel, to the right of the fuse box.

Power door lock systems are operated by bi-directional solenoids located in the doors. The lock switches have two operating positions: Lock and Unlock. When activated, the switch sends a ground signal to the door lock control unit to lock or unlock the doors. Depending on which way the switch is activated, the control unit reverses polarity to the solenoids, allowing the two sides of the circuit to be used alternately as the feed (positive) and ground side.

Some vehicles may have an anti-theft systems incorporated into the power locks. If you are unable to locate the trouble using the following general Steps, consult your a dealer service department or other qualified repair shop.

1   Always check the circuit protection first. Some vehicles use a combination of circuit breakers and fuses.

2   Operate the door lock switches in both directions (Lock and Unlock) with the engine off. Listen for the click of the solenoids operating.

3   Test the switches for continuity. Replace the switch if there's not continuity in both switch positions.

4   Check the wiring between the switches, control unit and solenoids for continuity. Repair the wiring if there's no continuity.

5   Check for a bad ground at the switches or the control unit.

6   If all but one lock solenoids operate, remove the trim panel from the affected door (see Chapter 11) and check for voltage at the solenoid while the lock switch is operated One of the wires should have voltage in the Lock position; the other should have voltage in the Unlock position.

7   If the inoperative solenoid is receiving voltage, replace the solenoid.

8   If the inoperative solenoid isn't receiving voltage, check for an open or short in the wire between the lock solenoid and the control unit.

Note: *It's common for wires to break in the portion of the harness between the body and door (opening and closing the door fatigues and eventually breaks the wires).*

22 Airbags - general information and precautions

Warning: *Some models covered by this manual are equipped with Supplemental Inflatable Restraint (SIR) systems, more commonly known as airbags. Always disable the airbag system before working in the vicinity of any airbag system components to avoid the possibility of accidental deployment of the airbag(s)*

which could cause personal injury. The yellow wiring harnesses and connectors routed through the console and instrument panel are for this system. Do not use electrical test equipment on any of the airbag system wiring or tamper with it in any way.

Description

1   Some models covered by this manual are equipped with a Supplemental Inflatable Restraint (SIR) system, more commonly known as an airbag system. The SIR system is designed to protect the driver and passenger from serious injury in the event of a head-on or frontal collision.

2   The SIR system consists of an airbag located in the center of the steering wheel, and on some models, another located in the top of the dashboard, above the glove box. 1994 models utilize two impact sensors; one located in the instrument panel and another located just in front of the radiator; an arming sensor located under the center console; and a diagnostic/energy reserve module located at the right end of the instrument panel. On 1996 and later models, the sensors and the diagnostic/energy reserve module have been incorporated into one unit and is located under the center console. 2000 and later models are also equipped with a side-impact airbag located in the left side of the driver's seatback. A side impact sensor is located in the door pillar next to the driver's seat, and a side-impact module is located on the floor under the driver's seat.

Sensors

3   The 1994 system has three separate sensors; two impact sensors and an arming sensor. The sensors are basically pressure sensitive switches that complete an electrical circuit during an impact of sufficient G force. The electrical signal from the crash sensors is sent to the diagnostic module, which then completes circuit and inflates the airbags.

4   On the 1995 and later systems, the sensing circuitry is contained in the sensing diagnostic/energy reserve module. If a frontal crash of sufficient force is detected, the circuitry allows current to flow to the airbags, inflating them. On 2000 and later models, the side impact sensor is located in the driver's door pillar.

Diagnostic/energy reserve module

5   The diagnostic/energy reserve module contains an on-board microprocessor which monitors the operation of the system. It performs a diagnostic check of the system every time the vehicle is started. If the system is operating properly, the AIRBAG warning light will blink on and off seven times. If there is a fault in the system, the light will remain on and the airbag control module will store fault codes indicating the nature of the fault. If the AIRBAG warning light remains on after staring, or comes on while driving, the vehicle should be taken to your dealer immediately for service. The diagnostic/energy reserve module also

contains a back-up power supply to deploy the airbags in the event battery power is lost during a collision.

Operation

6   For the airbag(s) to deploy, an impact of sufficient G force must occur within 30-degrees of the vehicle centerline. When this condition occurs, the circuit to the airbag inflator is closed and the airbag inflates. If the battery is destroyed by the impact, or is too low to power the inflators, a back-up power supply inside the diagnostic/energy reserve module supplies current to the airbags.

Self-diagnosis system

7   A self-diagnosis circuit in the module displays a light when the ignition switch is turned to the On position. If the system is operating normally, the light should go out after seven flashes. If the light doesn't come on, or doesn't go out after seven flashes, or if it comes on while you're driving the vehicle, there's a malfunction in the SIR system. Have it inspected and repaired as soon as possible. Do not attempt to troubleshoot or service the SIR system yourself. Even a small mistake could cause the SIR system to malfunction when you need it. Have a dealer or shop equipped with the proper scan tool diagnose the system.

Servicing components near the SIR system

8   Nevertheless, there are times when you need to remove the steering wheel, radio or service other components on or near the instrument panel. At these times, you'll be working around components and wiring harnesses for the SIR system. SIR system wiring is easy to identify; they're all covered by a bright yellow conduit. Do not unplug the connectors for the SIR system wiring, except to disable the system. And do not use electrical test equipment on the SIR system wiring. *ALWAYS DISABLE THE SIR SYSTEM BEFORE WORKING NEAR THE SIR SYSTEM COMPONENTS OR RELATED WIRING.*

Disabling the SIR system

Refer to illustrations 22.11 and 22.13

9   Turn the steering wheel to the straight-ahead position, place the ignition switch in Lock and remove the key. Remove the airbag fuse from the fuse block (see Section 3). **Note:** *Some models designate the airbag fuse as ARBG#1 while others are designated AIRBAG#1 or SIR.*

10   Unplug the yellow Connector Position Assurance (CPA) connectors at the base of the steering column and under the right side of the instrument panel as described in the following steps.

Driver's side airbag

11   Remove the knee bolster and sound insulator panel below the instrument panel

22.11 The driver's side airbag Connector Position Assurance (CPA) connector is found at the base of the steering column

22.13 The passenger airbag Connector Position Assurance (CPA) connector is located under the instrument panel and is accessible through the glovebox opening

(see Chapter 11) and unplug the yellow Connector Position Assurance (CPA) steering column harness connector **(see illustration)**.

Passenger's side airbag

12   Remove the glove box (see Chapter 11).
13   Unplug the CPA electrical connector from the passenger inflator module under the right side of the dash **(see illustration)**.

Side impact airbag

14   On models with driver-side side-impact airbag, unplug the CPA and disconnect the connector at the side-impact module under the driver's seat. This disables the side-impact airbag.

Enabling the SIR system

15   After you've disabled the airbag and performed the necessary service, plug in the steering column (driver's side), passenger side and side-impact (if equipped) CPA connectors. Reinstall the knee bolster, sound insulator panel and the glove box.
16   Install the airbag fuse.

23   Head-up display (HUD) - general information

Some models use a Head-up Display (HUD) to project information such as vehicle speed and turn signal indicators, as well as battery, engine temperature, high beam and low fuel indicators, toward the front of the car (as seen from the driver's seat).

The system is made up of the HUD unit, which is built into the top of the dash, the HUD dimmer switch on the left side of the instrument panel, and a HUD-specific windshield. On some models a HUD English/metric switch is also used. Troubleshooting of the HUD system is best left to a dealer or other qualified service facility. However, if the HUD display seems dim or unclear, try cleaning the HUD projector window with a soft, clean cloth moistened with glass cleaner. **Caution:** *Do not spray glass cleaner on the HUD unit's projector window as this may cause damage to the HUD components inside. Wipe the HUD window gently, then dry it. Also check to be sure that the windshield area directly in front*

of the HUD unit is clear and unobstructed.

If the windshield on a HUD-equipped car ever needs to be replaced, be sure to replace it with a HUD-specific windshield for optimum HUD performance.

24   Wiring diagrams - general information

Since it isn't possible to include all wiring diagrams for every year covered by this manual, the following diagrams are those that are typical and most commonly needed.

Prior to troubleshooting any circuit, check the fuse and circuit breakers (if equipped) to make sure they're in good condition. Make sure the battery is properly charged and check the cable connections (see Chapter 1).

When checking a circuit, make sure that all connectors are clean, with no broken or loose terminals. When unplugging a connector, do not pull on the wires. Pull only on the connector housings themselves.

1993 and earlier starting and charging systems

1994 and 1995 starting and charging systems

Typical starting and charging system - 1996 models

Typical charging system - 1997 and later models

Typical starting system - 1997 and later models

2.8L engine control system (1 of 2)

2.8L engine control system (2 of 2)

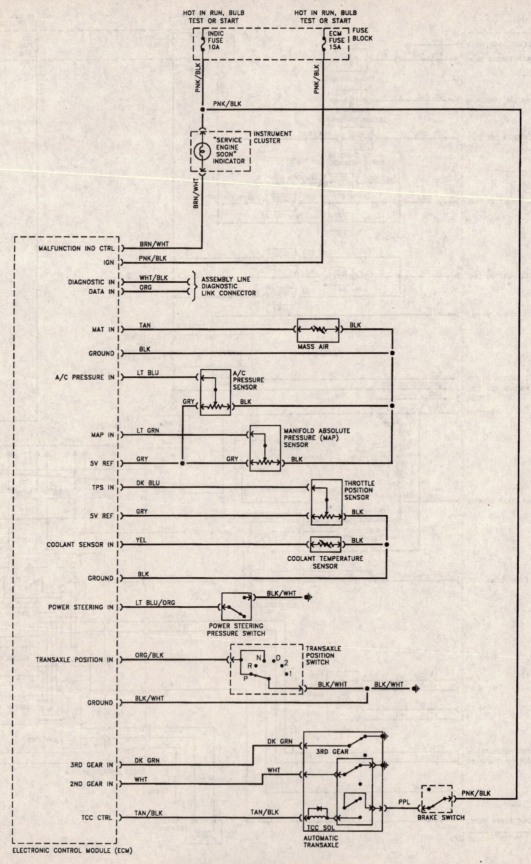

2.3L engine control system (1 of 2)

2.3L engine control system (2 of 2)

1993 and earlier 3.1L (except Generation II) and 3.4L Cutlass Supreme engine control system (1 of 2)

1993 and earlier 3.1L (except Generation II) and 3.4L Cutlass Supreme engine control system (2 of 2)

1993 3.1L Generation II engine control system (1 of 2)

1993 3.1L Generation II engine control system (2 of 2)

1993 and earlier 3.8L engine control system (1 of 3)

1993 and earlier 3.8L engine control system (2 of 3)

1993 and earlier 3.8L engine control system (3 of 3)

1994 and 1995 3100 engine control system (1 of 2)

1994 and 1995 3100 engine control system (2 of 2)

1994 and 1995 3.4L engine control system (1 of 3)

1994 and 1995 3.4L engine control system (2 of 3)

1994 and 1995 3.4L engine control system (3 of 3)

1994 and 1995 3.8L engine control system (1 of 3)

1994 and 1995 3.8L engine control system (2 of 3)

1994 and 1995 3.8L engine control system (3 of 3)

Typical 1996 3100 engine control system (part 1 of 3)

Typical 1996 3100 engine control system (part 2 of 3)

Typical 1996 3100 engine control system (part 3 of 3)

Typical 1996 3.4L and 1997 and later 3100 engine control system (part 1 of 3)

Typical 1996 3.4L and 1997 and later 3100 engine control system (part 2 of 3)

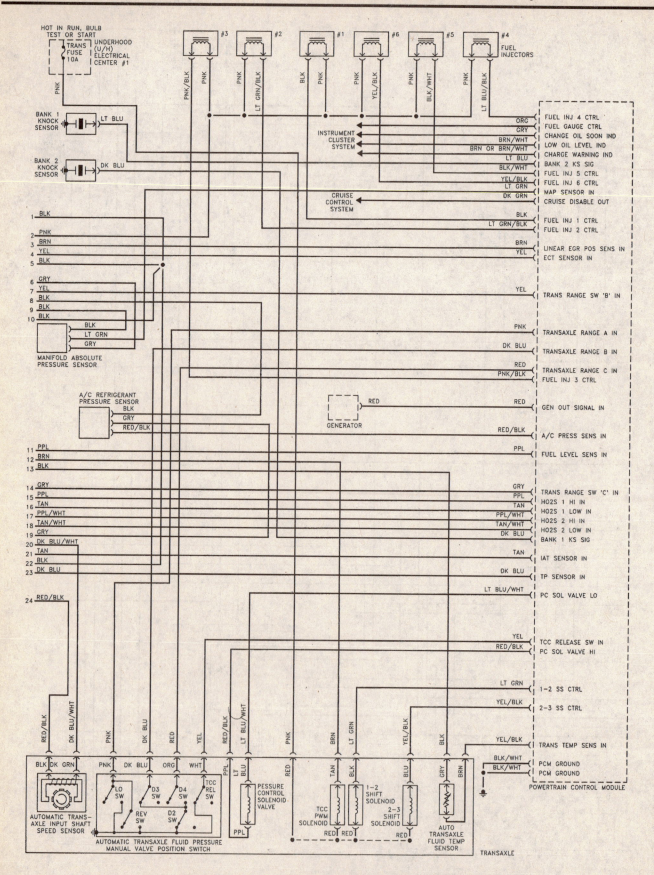

Typical 1996 3.4L and 1997 and later 3100 engine control system (part 3 of 3)

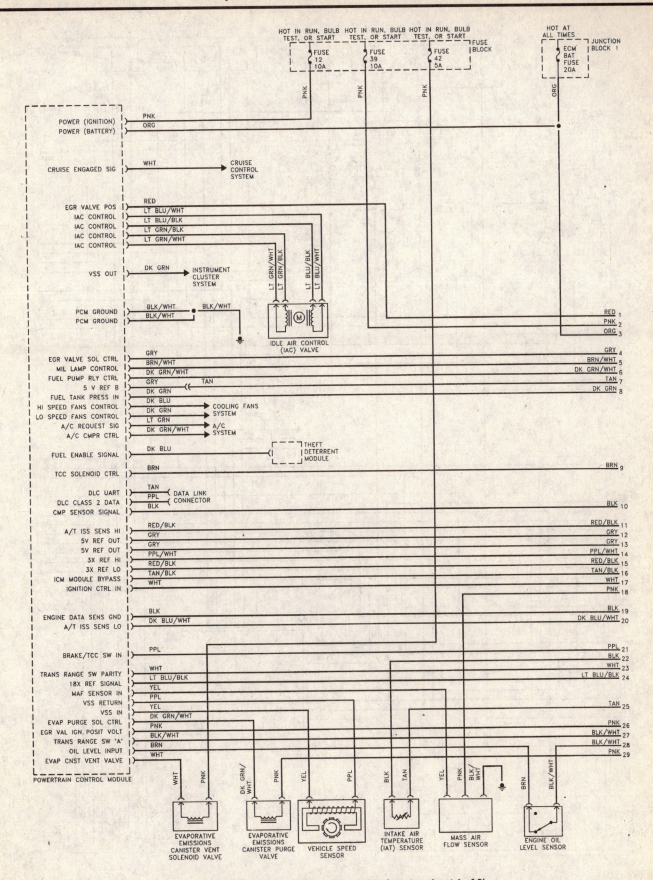

Typical 1996 and later 3800 engine control system (part 1 of 3)

Typical 1996 and later 3800 engine control system (part 2 of 3)

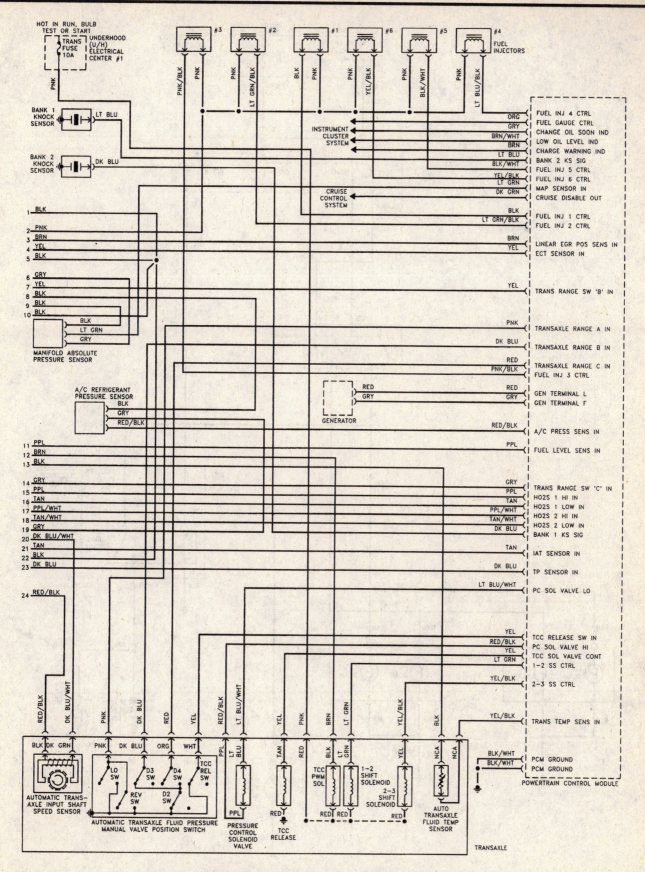

Typical 1996 and later 3800 engine control system (part 3 of 3)

1988 through 1990 headlight circuit

1991 through 1997 headlight circuit

Typical headlight system - 1998 and later models

Typical exterior lights circuit - 1997 and earlier models

Typical exterior light system - 1998 and later models

Power window circuit for 2-door models

Power window circuit for 4-door models

Power window circuit for convertible Cutlass Supreme

Power door lock circuit - 1988 through 1993

Power door lock and keyless entry circuit - 1994 through 1997

Typical power door lock and keyless entry system - 1998 and 1999 models

Typical power door lock and keyless entry system - 2000 and later models

Keyless entry circuit -1991 through 1993

Courtesy lights circuit - 1988 through 1993 (1 of 2)

Courtesy lights circuit - 1988 through 1993 (2 of 2)

Interior lights circuit - 1988 through 1993 (Buick Regal)

Interior lights circuit - 1988 through 1993 (Cutlass Supreme)

Interior lights circuit - 1994 and 1995

Courtesy lights circuit - 1994 through 1997

Typical courtesy light system - 1998 and later models

Chapter 12 Chassis electrical system

12-69

Typical warning light system (models through 1997)

Typical warning light system - 1998 and later models

Cruise control circuit - 1988 through 1993 Cutlass Supreme and Regal (exc. 3.8L)

Cruise control circuit - 1993 3.8L Regal

Typical windshield wiper/washer system - 1998 and later models

Typical windshield wiper/washer circuit

Typical cruise control system - 1998 and later models

Cruise control circuit - 1994 through 1997

Air conditioning circuit - 1988 through 1990

Air conditioning circuit - 1995 models with manual temperature control and 3.8L engines (1 of 2)

Air conditioning circuit - 1995 models with manual temperature control and 3.8L engines (2 of 2)

Air conditioning circuit - 1995 models with manual temperature control and 3.1L/3.4L engines (1 of 2)

Air conditioning circuit - 1995 models with manual temperature control and 3.1L/3.4L engines (2 of 2)

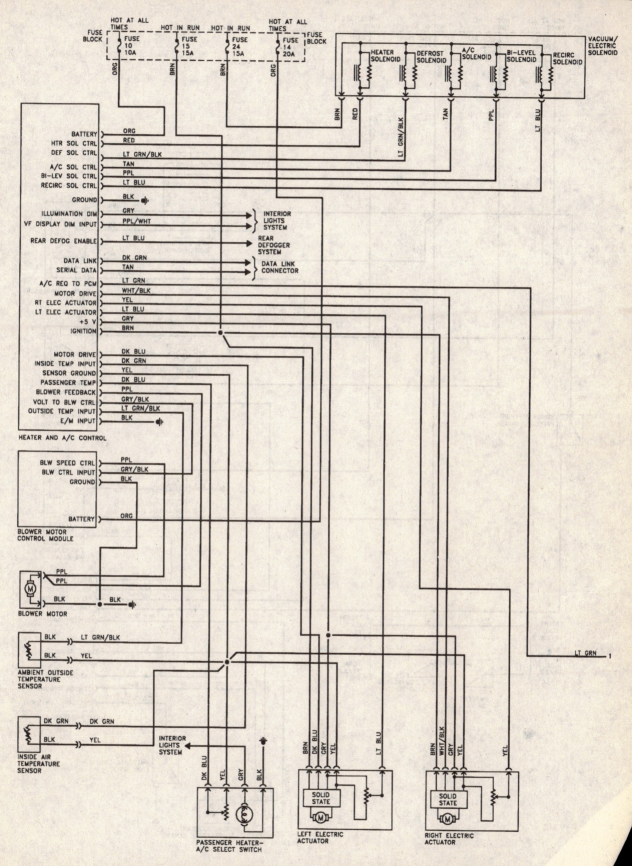

Air conditioning circuit - 1995 models with automatic temperature control (1 of 2)

Air conditioning circuit - 1995 models with automatic temperature control (2 of 2)

Air conditioning circuit - 1991 through 1993 models with manual temperature control

Air conditioning circuit - 1991 through 1993 models with automatic temperature control

Typical heating, air conditioning and cooling system - 1998 and later models (1 of 2)

Typical heating, air conditioning and cooling system - 1998 and later models (2 of 2)

Typical cooling fans circuit

Typical radio circuit

Index

A

About this manual, 0-5
Accelerator cable, removal and installation, 4-14
Air cleaner housing, removal and installation, 4-6
Air conditioning
    accumulator, removal and installation, 3-13
    compressor, removal and installation, 3-14
    condenser, removal and installation, 3-15
    expansion (orifice) tube, removal and installation, 3-15
    system, check and maintenance, 3-11
Air filter and PCV filter replacement, 1-19
Air Injection Reactor (AIR) system, 6-27
Airbags, general information and precautions, 12-17
Alternator, removal and installation, 5-6
Anti-lock Brake System (ABS), general information, 9-19
Antifreeze, general information, 3-2
Automatic transaxle, 7B-1 through 7B-8
    diagnosis, general, 7B-2
    differential seals, replacement, 7B-6
    floor shift control assembly, removal and installation, 7B-5
    fluid and filter change, 1-22
    fluid level check, 1-11
    general information, 7B-2
    mount, check and replacement, 7B-6
    Neutral Start (Starter Safety) switch, replacement
      and adjustment, 7B-3
    park/lock system, removal and installation, 7B-5
    removal and installation, 7B-6
    shift cable, replacement and adjustment, 7B-4
    Throttle valve (TV) cable, replacement and
      adjustment, 7B-3
    Vacuum modulator (4T60-E), check and replacement, 7B-7
    Vehicle Speed Sensor (VSS), removal and installation, 7B-8
Automotive chemicals and lubricants, 0-17

B

Balance shaft (3800), removal, inspection and
    installation, 2H-12
Balljoint, check and replacement, 10-5
Battery
    cables, check and replacement, 5-2
    check and maintenance, 1-12
    emergency jump starting, 0-15
    removal and installation, 5-1
Body, 11-1 through 11-14
    console, removal and installation, 11-13

    door
      handles, removal and installation, 11-10
      lock assembly, removal and installation, 11-9
      lock cylinder, removal and installation, 11-11
      lock striker, removal and installation, 11-11
      removal and installation, 11-11
      trim panel, removal and installation, 11-8
      window glass, removal, installation and adjustment, 11-9
    front fender liner, removal and installation, 11-7
    front fender, removal and installation, 11-7
    hinges and locks, maintenance, 11-3
    hood latch cable, replacement, 11-6
    hood, removal, installation and adjustment, 11-3
    maintenance 11-1
    outside mirror, removal and installation, 11-14
    rear lens assembly, removal and installation, 11-13
    repair
      major damage, 11-3
      minor damage, 11-2
    seat belt check, 11-14
    seats, removal and installation, 11-14
    trunk latch and striker, removal and installation, 11-12
    trunk lid, removal and installation, 11-12
    trunk lock cylinder, removal and installation, 11-12
    upholstery and carpets, maintenance, 11-1
    vinyl trim, maintenance, 11-2
    window regulator, removal and installation, 11-10
    windshield and fixed glass, replacement, 11-3
Booster battery (jump) starting, 0-15
Brake check, 1-18
Brakes, 9-1 through 9-20
    Anti-lock Brake System (ABS), general information, 9-19
    brake light switch, removal, installation and adjustment, 9-19
    disc brake
      caliper, removal, overhaul and installation, 9-6
      pads (front and rear), replacement, 9-2
      inspection, removal and installation, 9-8
    general information, 9-2
    hoses and lines, inspection and replacement, 9-15
    master cylinder, removal, overhaul and installation, 9-12
    parking brake
      adjustment, 9-17
      cables, replacement, 9-17
      shoes, replacement, 9-18
    power brake booster, check, removal and installation, 9-18
    rear brake shoes, replacement, 9-9
    rear wheel cylinder, removal, overhaul and installation, 9-1
    system bleeding, 9-15
Bulb replacement, 12-9
Buying parts, 0-7

C

Camshaft
and lifters, removal and installation, V8 engine, 2G-13
carrier
cover, removal and installation, 3.4 liter V6 engine, 2E-6
removal and installation, 3.4 liter V6 engine, 2E-6
intermediate shaft (3.4L) and balance shaft (3800), removal, inspection and installation, 2H-12
lifters and housing, removal, inspection and installation, 2.3 liter four-cylinder (Quad-4) engine, 2C-8
lifters, sprockets and oil seal, removal, inspection and installation, 3.4 liter V6 engine, 2E-7
timing procedure, 3.4 liter V6 engine, 2E-7
Camshaft and bearings, removal, inspection and installation
2.2 liter four-cylinder engine, 2A-8
2.5 liter four-cylinder engine, 2B-10
Catalytic converter, 6-27
Charging system
check, 5-3
general information and precautions, 5-6
Chassis electrical system, 12-1 through 12-86
airbags, general information and precautions, 12-17
bulb replacement, 12-9
circuit breakers, general information, 12-4
cruise control system, description and check, 12-16
electrical troubleshooting, general information, 12-1
fuses, general information, 12-3
fusible links, general information, 12-4
general information, 12-1
headlight bulb, replacement, 12-8
headlights, adjustment, 12-8
head-up display (HUD), general information, 12-18
horn, replacement, 12-15
ignition switch key lock cylinder, replacement, 12-7
instrument panel cluster, removal and installation, 12-12
power door lock system, description and check, 12-16
power window system, description and check, 12-16
radio and speakers, removal and installation, 12-10
radio antenna, removal and installation, 12-12
rear window defogger, check and repair, 12-13
relays, general information, 12-4
turn signal and hazard flashers, check and replacement, 12-5
turn signal switch assembly, removal and installation, 12-5
windshield wiper module and motor, removal and installation, 12-13
wiring diagrams, general information, 12-18
Chassis lubrication, 1-27
Circuit breakers, general information, 12-4
Clutch
components, removal, inspection and installation, 8-4
description and check, 8-2
hydraulic clutch system, bleeding (1988 and 1991 through 1992 models only), 8-3
se bearing and lever, removal and installation, 8-3
lutch interlock switch, check and replacement, 8-5
riveaxles, 8-1 through 8-10
al and installation, 11-13
al and installation, 10-6
s, 0-18

Coolant reservoir, removal and installation, 3-6
Coolant temperature sending unit or Low Coolant sensor, check and replacement, 3-7
Cooling, heating and air conditioning systems, 3-1 through 3-16
accumulator, removal and installation, 3-13
air conditioning expansion (orifice) tube, removal and installation, 3-15
air conditioning system, check and maintenance, 3-11
antifreeze, general information, 3-2
compressor, removal and installation, 3-14
condenser, removal and installation, 3-15
coolant reservoir, removal and installation, 3-6
coolant temperature sending unit or Low Coolant sensor, check and replacement, 3-7
engine cooling fan, check and replacement, 3-4
general information, 3-2
heater and air conditioner
blower motor, removal and installation, 3-8
control assembly, removal and installation, 3-11
heater core, removal and installation, 3-9
radiator, removal and installation, 3-4
thermostat, check and replacement, 3-3
water pump
check, 3-6
removal and installation, 3-6
Cooling system
check, 1-14
servicing (draining, flushing and refilling), 1-22
Crankshaft, removal and installation, 2H-22
Crankshaft balancer, removal and installation, V8 engine, 2G-9
Crankshaft force balancer, removal and installation, 2.5 liter four-cylinder engine, 2B-11
Crankshaft front oil seal, replacement
2.2 liter four-cylinder engine, 2A-7
2.5 liter four-cylinder engine, 2B-9
2.3 liter four-cylinder (Quad-4) engine, 2C-4
2.8L, 3.1L and 3100 V6 engines, 2D-10
3.4 liter V6 engine, 2E-4
3800 V6 engine, 2F-11
V8 engine, 2G-10
Crankshaft pulley
and vibration damper, removal and installation, 3.4 liter V6 engine, 2E-4
removal and installation
2.2 liter four-cylinder engine, 2A-6
2.5 liter four-cylinder engine, 2B-8
2.3 liter four-cylinder (Quad-4) engine, 2C-4
Crankshaft rear oil seal, replacement, 3800 V6 engine, 2F-15
Cruise control system, description and check, 12-16
Cylinder compression check, 2H-5
Cylinder head, removal and installation
2.2 liter four-cylinder engine, 2A-5
2.5 liter four-cylinder engine, 2B-6
2.3 liter four-cylinder (Quad-4) engine, 2C-11
2.8L, 3.1L and 3100 V6 engines, 2D-7
3.4 liter V6 engine, 2E-9
3800 V6 engine, 2F-9
V8 engine, 2G-8

D

Disc brake
caliper, removal, overhaul and installation, 9-6
pads (front and rear), replacement, 9-2
Door
handles, removal and installation, 11-10
lock assembly, removal and installation, 11-9
lock cylinder, removal and installation, 11-11
lock striker, removal and installation, 11-11
removal and installation, 11-11
trim panel, removal and installation, 11-8
window glass, removal, installation and adjustment, 11-7
Driveaxle boot
check, 1-17
replacement and Constant Velocity (CV) joint overhaul, 8-7
Driveaxles
general information, 8-5
removal and installation, 8-6
Drivebelt check, adjustment and replacement, 1-20
Driveplate, removal and installation
2.5 liter four-cylinder engine, 2B-11
3800 V6 engine, 2F-15
V8 engine, 2G-16

E

Electrical troubleshooting, general information, 12-1
Electronic Spark Control (ESC) system, 6-24
Electronic Spark Timing (EST), 6-24
Emissions control systems, 6-1 through 6-28
Air Injection Reactor (AIR) system, 6-27
catalytic converter, 6-27
Electronic Spark Control (ESC) system, 6-24
Electronic Spark Timing (EST), 6-24
Evaporative Emission Control System (EECS or EVAP), 6-26
Exhaust Gas Recirculation (EGR) system, 6-24
information sensors
general information and testing, 6-17
replacement, 6-20
oxygen sensor, 6-19
Positive Crankcase Ventilation (PCV) system, 6-26
Powertrain Control Module (PCM/ECM), replacement, 6-15
Engine, removal and installation, 2H-8
Engine cooling fan, check and replacement, 3-4
Engine electrical systems, 5-1 through 5-6
alternator, removal and installation, 5-6
battery
cables, check and replacement, 5-1
emergency jump starting, 5-1
removal and installation, 5-1
charging system
check, 5-6
general information and precautions, 5-6
ignition coil and module, removal and installation, 5-5
ignition system, check, 5-2
starter motor, removal and installation, 5-7
starter solenoid, removal and installation, 5-8
starting system, general information and precautions, 5-7
Engine oil and filter change, 1-15

Engine overhaul
disassembly sequence, 2H-12
reassembly sequence, 2H-24
Engine rebuilding alternatives, 2H-7
Engine removal, methods and precautions, 2H-7
Engines
2.2 liter four-cylinder engine, 2A-1 through 2A-10
camshaft and bearings, removal, inspection and installation, 2A-8
crankshaft front oil seal, replacement, 2A-7
crankshaft pulley, removal and installation, 2A-6
cylinder head, removal and installation, 2A-5
engine mounts, check and replacement, 2A-9
exhaust manifold, removal and installation, 2A-4
flywheel/driveplate, removal and installation, 2A-9
hydraulic lifters, removal, inspection and installation, 2A-6
intake manifold, removal and installation, 2A-4
oil pan, removal and installation, 2A-8
oil pump, removal and installation, 2A-9
rear main oil seal, replacement, 2A-9
repair operations possible with the engine in the vehicle, 2A-2
rocker arms and pushrods, removal, inspection and installation, 2A-2
timing chain and sprockets, inspection, removal and installation, 2A-7
timing chain cover, removal and installation, 2A-7
valve cover, removal and installation, 2A-2
valve springs, retainers and seals, replacement, 2A-3
2.5 liter four-cylinder engine, 2B-1 through 2B-12
camshaft and bearings, removal, inspection and installation, 2B-10
crankshaft force balancer, removal and installation, 2B-11
crankshaft front oil seal, replacement, 2B-9
crankshaft pulley, removal and installation, 2B-8
cylinder head, removal and installation, 2B-6
driveplate, removal and installation, 2B-11
engine mounts, check and replacement, 2B-12
exhaust manifold, removal and installation, 2B-5
hydraulic lifters, removal, inspection and installation, 2B-7
intake manifold, removal and installation, 2B-5
oil pan, removal and installation, 2B-10
oil pump, removal and installation, 2B-10
rear main oil seal, replacement, 2B-11
repair operations possible with the engine in the vehicle, 2B-2
rocker arms and pushrods, removal, inspection and installation, 2B-3
timing cover, timing chain, sprockets and tensioner, removal, inspection and installation, 2B-9
valve cover, removal and installation, 2B-2
valve springs, retainers and seals, replacement, 2B-3
2.3 liter four-cylinder (Quad-4) engine, 2C-1 through 2C-16
camshaft, lifters and housing, removal, inspection and installation, 2C-8
crankshaft front oil seal, replacement, 2C-4
crankshaft pulley, removal and installation, 2C-4
cylinder head, removal and installation, 2C-11
exhaust manifold, removal and installation, 2C-3
flywheel, removal and installation, 2C-13
intake manifold, removal and installation, 2C-2

mounts, check and replacement, 2C-14

oil pan, removal and installation, 2C-12

oil pump, removal, inspection and installation, 2C-13

rear main oil seal, replacement, 2C-13

repair operations possible with the engine in the vehicle, 2C-2

timing chain and sprockets, removal, inspection and installation, 2C-5

timing chain housing, removal and installation, 2C-8

valve springs, retainers and seals, replacement, 2C-11

2.8L, 3.1L and 3100 V6 engines, 2D-1 through 2D-12

crankshaft front oil seal, replacement, 2D-10

cylinder heads, removal and installation, 2D-7

exhaust manifolds, removal and installation, 2D-6

flywheel/driveplate, removal and installation, 2D-12

hydraulic lifters, removal, inspection and installation, 2D-8

intake manifold, removal and installation, 2D-5

mounts, check and replacement, 2D-12

oil pan, removal and installation, 2D-11

oil pump, removal and installation, 2D-12

rear main oil seal, replacement, 2D-12

repair operations possible with the engine in the vehicle, 2D-3

rocker arms and pushrods, removal, inspection and installation, 2D-4

timing chain and sprockets, inspection, removal and installation, 2D-10

timing chain cover, removal and installation, 2D-10

valve covers, removal and installation, 2D-3

valve springs, retainers and seals, replacement, 2D-5

vibration damper, removal and installation, 2D-9

3.4 liter V6 engine, 2E-1 through 2E-12

camshaft

carrier cover, removal and installation, 2E-6

carrier, removal and installation, 2E-6

front oil seal, replacement, 2E-4

lifters, sprockets and oil seal, removal, inspection and installation, 2E-7

timing procedure, 2E-7

crankshaft front oil seal, replacement, 2E-4

crankshaft pulley and vibration damper, removal and installation, 2E-4

cylinder head, removal and installation, 2E-9

exhaust manifolds, removal and installation, 2E-3

flywheel/driveplate, removal and installation, 2E-12

intake manifold, removal and installation, 2E-3

intermediate shaft timing belt sprocket and oil seal, removal and installation, 2E-9

mounts, check and replacement, 2E-12

oil pan, removal and installation, 2E-11

oil pump, removal, inspection and installation, 2E-12

rear main oil seal, replacement, 2E-12

repair operations possible with the engine in the vehicle, 2E-2

timing belt

covers, removal and installation, 2E-5

tensioner plate and actuator, removal and installation, 2E-5

tensioner pulley and arm assembly, removal and installation, 2E-6

removal and installation, 2E-5

timing chain

cover, removal and installation, 2E-10

sprockets and tensioner, inspection, removal and installation, 2E-11

valve springs, retainers and seals, replacement, 2E-8

3800 V6 engine, 2F-1 through 2F-16

crankshaft

front oil seal, replacement, 2F-11

rear oil seal, replacement, 2F-15

cylinder heads, removal and installation, 2F-9

driveplate, removal and installation, 2F-15

exhaust manifolds, removal and installation, 2F-8

intake manifold, removal and installation, 2F-6

mount, check and replacement, 2F-15

oil filter adapter and pressure regulator valve, removal and installation, 2F-12

oil pan, removal and installation, 2F-14

oil pump pickup tube and screen assembly, removal and installation, 2F-15

oil pump, removal, inspection and installation, 2F-13

repair operations possible with the engine in the vehicle, 2F-3

rocker arm covers, removal and installation, 2F-3

rocker arms and pushrods, removal, inspection and installation, 2F-4

timing chain and sprockets, removal and installation, 2F-13

timing chain cover, removal and installation, 2F-11

Top Dead Center (TDC) for number one piston, locating, 2F-3

valve lifters, removal, inspection and installation, 2F-7

valve springs, retainers and seals, replacement, 2F-5

vibration damper, removal and installation, 2F-10

V8 engines, 2G-1 through 2G-18

camshaft and lifters, removal and installation, 2G-13

crankshaft

balancer, removal and installation, 2G-9

front oil seal, removal and installation, 2G-10

cylinder heads, removal and installation, 2G-8

driveplate, removal and installation, 2G-16

engine mounts, check and replacement, 2G-16

exhaust manifolds, removal and installation, 2G-8

intake manifold, removal and installation, 2G-7

oil pan, removal and installation, 2G-14

oil pump, removal, inspection and installation, 2G-15

rear main oil seal, replacement, 2G-16

repair operations possible with the engine in the vehicle, 2G-3

rocker arms and pushrods, removal, inspection and installation, 2G-4

timing chain, removal, inspection and installation, 2G-11

Top Dead Center (TDC) for number one piston, locating, 2G-3

valve covers, removal and installation, 2G-4

valve springs, retainers and seals, replacement, 2G-5

General engine overhaul procedures, 2H-1 through 2H-28

camshaft, intermediate shaft (3.4L) and balance shaft (3800), removal, inspection and installation, 2H-12

crankshaft, removal and installation, 2H-22

cylinder compression check, 2H-5

engine, removal and installation, 2H-8

engine overhaul, disassembly sequence, 2H-12

engine overhaul, reassembly sequence, 2H-24
engine rebuilding alternatives, 2H-7
engine removal, methods and precautions, 2H-7
general information, engine overhaul, 2H-3
initial start-up and break-in after overhaul, 2H-24
oil pressure check, 2H-4
pistons and connecting rods, removal and installation, 2H-16
vacuum gauge diagnostic checks, 2H-6
Evaporative Emission Control System (EECS or EVAP), 6-26
Evaporative emissions control system check, 1-24
Exhaust Gas Recirculation (EGR) system, 6-24
Exhaust manifold, removal and installation
2.2 liter four-cylinder engine, 2A-4
2.5 liter four-cylinder engine, 2B-5
2.3 liter four-cylinder (Quad-4) engine, 2C-3
2.8L, 3.1L and 3100 V6 engines, 2D-6
3.4 liter V6 engine, 2E-3
3800 V6 engine, 2F-8
V8 engine, 2G-8
Exhaust system
check, 1-17
servicing, general information, 4-15

F

Floor shift control assembly, removal and installation, automatic transaxle, 7B-5
Fluid level checks, 1-8
automatic transaxle fluid, 1-11
battery electrolyte, 1-9
brake and clutch fluid, 1-9
engine coolant, 1-9
engine oil, 1-8
power steering fluid, 1-12
windshield washer fluid, 1-9
Flywheel/driveplate, removal and installation
2.2 liter four-cylinder engine, 2A-9
2.3 liter four-cylinder (Quad-4) engine, 2C-13
2.8L, 3.1L and 3100 V6 engines, 2D-12
3.4 liter V6 engine, 2E-12
Front fender
liner, removal and installation, 11-7
removal and installation, 11-7
Front stabilizer bar and bushings, removal and installation, 10-5
Front strut and spring assembly, removal, inspection and installation, 10-7
Fuel and exhaust systems, 4-1 through 4-16
accelerator cable, removal and installation, 4-14
air cleaner housing, removal and installation, 4-6
exhaust system servicing, general information, 4-15
fuel filter replacement, 1-21
fuel injection system
check, 4-7
general information, 4-6
fuel pressure relief procedure, 4-2
fuel system check, 1-18
general information, 4-1
lines and fittings, repair and replacement, 4-3
Port Fuel Injection (PFI) and Sequential Fuel Injection (SFI), component removal and installation, 4-9

pump/fuel pressure, testing, 4-2
pump, removal and installation, 4-5
supercharger
general information, 4-16
removal and installation, 4-16
system check, 1-18
tank
cleaning and repair, general information, 4-5
removal and installation, 4-5
Throttle Body Injection (TBI) assembly, removal and installation, 4-7
Throttle Body Injection (TBI), component replacement, 4-8
turbocharger
general information, 4-15
inspection, 4-15
removal and installation, 4-16
Fuel injection system
check, 4-7
general information, 4-7
Fuses, general information, 12-3
Fusible links, general information, 12-4

G

General engine overhaul procedures, 2H-1 through 2H-28
camshaft, intermediate shaft (3.4L) and balance shaft (3800), removal, inspection and installation, 2H-12
crankshaft, removal and installation, 2H-22
cylinder compression check, 2H-5
engine, removal and installation, 2H-8
engine overhaul, disassembly sequence, 2H-12
engine overhaul, reassembly sequence, 2H-24
engine rebuilding alternatives, 2H-7
engine removal, methods and precautions, 2H-7
general information, engine overhaul, 2H-3
initial start-up and break-in after overhaul, 2H-24
oil pressure check, 2H-4
pistons and connecting rods, removal and installation, 2H-16
vacuum gauge diagnostic checks, 2H-6

H

Headlight bulb, replacement, 12-8
Headlights, adjustment, 12-8
Head-up display (HUD), general information, 12-18
Heater and air conditioner
blower motor, removal and installation, 3-8
control assembly, removal and installation, 3-11
Heater core, removal and installation, 3-9
Hinges and locks, maintenance, 11-3
Hood latch cable, replacement, 11-6
Hood, removal, installation and adjustment, 11-3
Horn, replacement, 12-15
Hub and wheel bearing assembly, removal and installation
front, 10-9
rear, 10-11
Hydraulic lifters, removal, inspection and installation
2.2 liter four-cylinder engine, 2A-6
2.5 liter four-cylinder engine, 2B-7
2.8L, 3.1L and 3100 V6 engines, 2D-7

I

Ignition
    coil and module, removal and installation, 5-5
    switch key lock cylinder, replacement, 12-7
    system, check, 5-2
Information sensors
    general information and testing, 6-17
    replacement, 6-20
Initial start-up and break-in after overhaul, 2H-24
Instrument panel cluster, removal and installation, 12-12
Intake manifold, removal and installation
    2.2 liter four-cylinder engine, 2A-4
    2.5 liter four-cylinder engine, 2B-5
    2.3 liter four-cylinder (Quad-4) engine, 2C-2
    2.8L, 3.1L and 3100 V6 engines, 2D-5
    3.4 liter V6 engine, 2E-3
    3800 V6 engine, 2F-6
    V8 engine, 2G-7
Intermediate axleshaft, removal and installation, 8-10
Intermediate shaft (3.4L), removal, inspection and installation, 2H-12
Intermediate shaft timing belt sprocket and oil seal, removal and installation, 3.4 liter V6 engine, 2E-9
Introduction to the Chevrolet Lumina, Chevrolet Monte Carlo, Oldsmobile Cutlass, Buick Regal and Pontiac Grand Prix, 0-5

J

Jacking and towing, 0-16

M

Maintenance schedule, 1-7
Maintenance techniques, tools and working facilities, 0-7
Manifold Absolute Pressure (MAP) sensor, replacement, 6-19
Manifold/Intake Air Temperature (MAT or IAT) sensor, replacement, 6-19
Manual transaxle, 7A-1 through 7A-4
    general information, 7A-2
    lubricant change, 1-22
    lubricant level check, 1-17
    overhaul, general information, 7A-3
    removal and installation, 7A-2
    shift cables, removal and installation, 7A-2
    shift control, removal and installation, 7A-2
    shifter shaft seal, replacement, 7A-2
Master cylinder, removal, overhaul and installation, 9-12
Mounts, engine, check and replacement
    2.2 liter four-cylinder engine, 2A-9
    2.5 liter four-cylinder engine, 2B-12
    2.3 liter four-cylinder (Quad-4) engine, 2C-14
    2.8L, 3.1L and 3100 V6 engines, 2D-12
    3.4 liter V6 engine, 2E-12
    3800 V6 engine, 2F-15
    V8 engine, 2G-16

N

Neutral Start (Starter Safety) switch, replacement and adjustment, 7B-3

O

Oil filter adapter and pressure regulator valve, removal and installation, 3800 V6 engine, 2F-12
Oil pan, removal and installation
    2.2 liter four-cylinder engine, 2A-8
    2.5 liter four-cylinder engine, 2B-10
    2.3 liter four-cylinder (Quad-4) engine, 2C-12
    2.8L, 3.1L and 3100 V6 engines, 2D-11
    3.4 liter V6 engine, 2E-11
    3800 V6 engine, 2F-14
    V8 engine, 2G-14
Oil pressure check, 2H-4
Oil pump pickup tube and screen assembly, removal and installation, 3800 V6 engine, 2F-15
Oil pump, removal, inspection and installation
    2.2 liter four-cylinder engine, 2A-9
    2.5 liter four-cylinder engine, 2B-10
    2.3 liter four-cylinder (Quad-4) engine, 2C-13
    2.8L, 3.1L and 3100 V6 engines, 2D-12
    3.4 liter V6 engine, 2E-12
    3800 V6 engine, 2F-13
    V8 engine, 2G-15
On Board Diagnostic (OBD) system and trouble codes, 6-2
Outside mirror, removal and installation, 11-14
Oxygen sensor, 6-17, 6-20

P

Park/lock system, removal and installation, automatic transaxle, 7B-5
Park/Neutral switch, 6-22
Parking brake
    adjustment, 9-17
    cables, replacement, 9-17
    shoes, replacement, 9-18
Pistons and connecting rods
    connecting rod bearing oil clearance check, 2H-19
    piston ring installation, 2H-17
    removal and installation, 2H-16
Port Fuel Injection (PFI) and Sequential Fuel Injection (SFI), component removal and installation, 4-9
Positive Crankcase Ventilation (PCV) system, 6-26
Positive Crankcase Ventilation (PCV) valve check and replacement, 1-23
Power brake booster, check, removal and installation, 9-18
Power door lock system, description and check, 12-16
Power steering
    fluid level check, 1-12
    pump, removal and installation, 10-15
    system, bleeding, 10-15
Power Steering Pressure Switch, 6-18
Power window system, description and check, 12-16
Powertrain Control Module (PCM/ECM), replacement, 6-15

R

Radiator, removal and installation, 3-4
Radio and speakers, removal and installation, 12-10
Radio antenna, removal and installation, 12-12
Rear lens assembly, removal and installation, 11-13
Rear main oil seal, replacement
    2.2 liter four-cylinder engine, 2A-9
    2.5 liter four-cylinder engine, 2B-11
    2.3 liter four-cylinder (Quad-4) engine, 2C-13
    2.8L, 3.1L and 3100 V6 engines, 2D-12
    3.4 liter V6 engine, 2E-12
    V8 engine, 2G-16
Rear suspension components, removal and installation, 10-12
Relays, general information, 12-4
Repair operations possible with the engine in the vehicle
    2.2 liter four-cylinder engine, 2A-2
    2.5 liter four-cylinder engine, 2B-2
    2.3 liter four-cylinder (Quad-4) engine, 2C-2
    2.8L, 3.1L and 3100 V6 engines, 2D-2
    3.4 liter V6 engine, 2E-3
    3800 V6 engine, 2F-3
    V8 engine, 2G-3
Rocker arm covers, removal and installation, 3800 V6 engine, 2F-3
Rocker arms and pushrods, removal, inspection and installation
    2.2 liter four-cylinder engine, 2A-2
    2.5 liter four-cylinder engine, 2B-3
    2.8L, 3.1L and 3100 V6 engines, 2D-4
    3800 V6 engine, 2F-4
    V8 engine, 2G-4
Rotating the engine, 1-26

S

Safety first!, 0-19
Seat belt check, 1-21, 11-14
Seatback latch check, 1-21
Seats, removal and installation, 11-14
Shift cable
    replacement, removal, installation and adjustment
        automatic transaxle, 7B-4
        manual transaxle, 7A-2
Shifter shaft seal, replacement, manual transaxle, 7A-2
Spare tire and jack check, 1-21
Spark plug
    replacement, 1-24
    wire check and replacement, 1-26
Stabilizer bar, rear, removal and installation, 10-9
Starter motor, removal and installation, 5-8
Starter safety switch check, 1-21
Starter solenoid, removal and installation, 5-8
Starting system, general information and precautions, 5-7
Steering gear
    boots, replacement, 10-15
    removal and installation, 10-14

Steering system
    general information, 10-13
    power steering
        pump, removal and installation, 10-15
        system, bleeding, 10-15
    steering gear
        boots, replacement, 10-15
        removal and installation, 10-14
    steering wheel, removal and installation, 10-16
    wheel alignment, general information, 10-18
    wheel studs, replacement, 10-17
    wheels and tires, general information, 10-17
Strut cartridge, replacement, 10-7
Strut, rear, removal and installation, 10-10
Supercharger
    general information, 4-16
    removal and installation, 4-16
Suspension and steering check, 1-17
Suspension and steering systems, 10-1 through 10-18
Suspension system
    balljoint, check and replacement, 10-5
    control arm, removal and installation, 10-6
    front stabilizer bar and bushings, removal and installation, 10-5
    front strut and spring assembly, removal, inspection and installation, 10-7
    hub and wheel bearing assembly, removal and installation
        front, 10-9
        rear, 10-11
    rear stabilizer bar, removal and installation, 10-9
    rear strut, removal and installation, 10-10
    strut cartridge (1996 and earlier models), replacement, 10-7
    suspension components (rear), removal and installation, 10-12
    tie-rod ends, removal and installation, 10-14
    transverse spring, rear, removal and installation, 10-10

T

Thermostat, check and replacement, 3-3
Throttle Body Injection (TBI)
    assembly, removal and installation, 4-7
    component replacement, 4-8
    mounting bolt torque check (2.5L engine), 1-20
Throttle linkage check, 1-28
Throttle Position Sensor (TPS), replacement, 6-21
Throttle valve (TV) cable, replacement and adjustment, automatic transaxle, 7B-3
Tie-rod ends, removal and installation, 10-14
Timing belt
    covers, removal and installation, 3.4 liter V6 engine, 2E-5
    tensioner plate and actuator, removal and installation, 3.4 liter V6 engine, 2E-5
    tensioner pulley and arm assembly, removal and installation 3.4 liter V6 engine, 2E-6
    inspection, removal and installation, 3.4 liter V6 engine, 2

Timing chain
  and sprockets, inspection, removal and installation
    2.2 liter four-cylinder engine, 2A-7
    2.3 liter four-cylinder (Quad-4) engine, 2C-5
    2.8L, 3.1L and 3100 V6 engines, 2D-10
    3800 V6 engine, 2F-13
    V8 engine, 2G-11
  cover, removal and installation
    2.2 liter four-cylinder engine, 2A-7
    2.8L, 3.1L and 3100 V6 engines, 2D-10
    3.4 liter V6 engine, 2E-10
    3800 V6 engine, 2F-11
  housing, removal and installation, 2.3 liter four-cylinder
    (Quad-4) engine, 2C-8
  sprockets and tensioner, inspection, removal and
    installation, 3.4 liter V6 engine, 2E-11
Timing cover, timing chain, sprockets and tensioner,
removal, inspection and installation, 2.5 liter four-
cylinder engine, 2B-9
Tire and tire pressure checks, 1-10
Tire rotation, 1-17
Top Dead Center (TDC) for number one piston,
locating, 2F-3, 2G-3
Transaxle, automatic, 7B-1 through 7B-8
  diagnosis, general, 7B-2
  differential seals, replacement, automatic transaxle, 7B-6
  floor shift control assembly, removal and installation, 7B-5
  fluid and filter change, 1-22
  fluid level check, 1-11
  general information, 7B-2
  Neutral Start (Starter Safety) switch, replacement and
    adjustment, 7B-3
  park/lock system, removal and installation, 7B-5
  shift cable, replacement and adjustment, 7B-4
  Throttle valve (TV) cable, replacement and adjustment, 7B-3
  Vacuum modulator (4T60-E), check and replacement, 7B-7
  Vehicle Speed Sensor (VSS), removal and installation, 7B-8
Transaxle, manual, 7A-1 through 7A-4
  general information, 7A-2
  lubricant change, 1-22
  lubricant level check, 1-17
  overhaul, general information, 7A-3
  removal and installation, 7A-2
  shift cables, removal and installation, 7A-2
  shift control, removal and installation, 7A-2
  shifter shaft seal, replacement, 7A-2
Transverse spring, rear, removal and installation, 10-10
Troubleshooting, 0-20
Trunk
  latch and striker, removal and installation, 11-12
  lid, removal and installation, 11-12
  lock cylinder, removal and installation, 11-12
Tune-up and routine maintenance, 1-1 through 1-28
Tune-up general information, 1-8
Turbocharger
  general information, 4-15
  inspection, 4-15
  removal and installation, 4-16

Turn signal
  and hazard flashers, check and replacement, 12-5
  switch assembly, removal and installation, 12-5

U

Underhood hose check and replacement, 1-14
Upholstery and carpets, 11-1

V

Vacuum gauge diagnostic checks, 2H-6
Vacuum modulator (4T60-E), check and
replacement, 7B-7
Valve cover, removal and installation
  2.2 liter four-cylinder engine, 2A-2
  2.5 liter four-cylinder engine, 2B-2
  2.8L, 3.1L and 3100 V6 engines, 2D-3
  V8 engine, 2G-4
Valve lifters, removal, inspection and installation, 3800 V6
engine, 2F-7
Valve springs, retainers and seals, replacement
  2.2 liter four-cylinder engine, 2A-3
  2.5 liter four-cylinder engine, 2B-3
  2.3 liter four-cylinder (Quad-4) engine, 2C-11
  2.8L, 3.1L and 3100 V6 engines, 2D-5
  3.4 liter V6 engine, 2E-8
  3800 V6 engine, 2F-5
  V8 engine, 2G-5
Vehicle identification numbers, 0-6
Vehicle Speed Sensor (VSS)
  removal and installation, 7B-8
  replacement, 6-22
Vibration damper, removal and installation
  2.8L, 3.1L and 3100 V6 engines, 2D-9
  3800 V6 engine, 2F-10
Vinyl trim, maintenance, 11-2

W

Water pump
  check, 3-6
  removal and installation, 3-6
Wheel alignment, general information, 10-18
Wheel cylinder, rear, removal, overhaul and
installation, 9-11
Wheel studs, replacement, 10-17
Wheels and tires, general information, 10-17
Window
  defogger, rear, check and repair, 12-13
  regulator, removal and installation, 11-10
  system, power, description and check, 12-16
Windshield and fixed glass, replacement, 11-3
Windshield wiper
  blade inspection and replacement, 1-15
  module and motor, removal and installation, 12-13
Wiring diagrams, general information, 12-18

Haynes Automotive Manuals

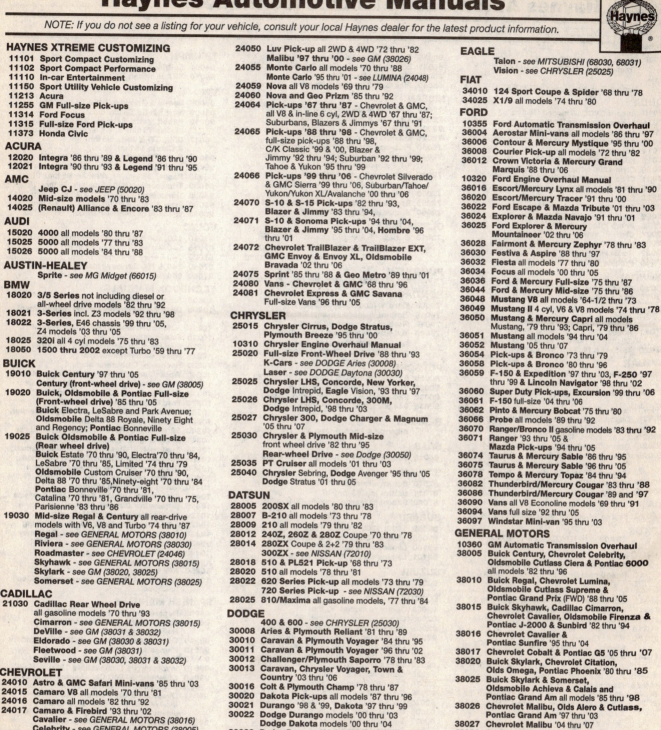

NOTE: If you do not see a listing for your vehicle, consult your local Haynes dealer for the latest product information.

HAYNES XTREME CUSTOMIZING
- **11101** Sport Compact Customizing
- **11102** Sport Compact Performance
- **11110** In-car Entertainment
- **11150** Sport Utility Vehicle Customizing
- **11213** Acura
- **11255** GM Full-size Pick-ups
- **11314** Ford Focus
- **11315** Full-size Ford Pick-ups
- **11373** Honda Civic

ACURA
- **12020** Integra '86 thru '89 & Legend '86 thru '90
- **12021** Integra '90 thru '93 & Legend '91 thru '95

AMC
- Jeep CJ - see JEEP (50020)
- **14020** Mid-size models '70 thru '83
- **14025** (Renault) Alliance & Encore '83 thru '87

AUDI
- **15020** 4000 all models '80 thru '87
- **15025** 5000 all models '77 thru '83
- **15026** 5000 all models '84 thru '88

AUSTIN-HEALEY
- Sprite - see MG Midget (66015)

BMW
- **18020** 3/5 Series not including diesel or all-wheel drive models '82 thru '92
- **18021** 3-Series incl. Z3 models '92 thru '98
- **18022** 3-Series, E46 chassis '99 thru '05, Z4 models '03 thru '05
- **18025** 320i all 4 cyl models '75 thru '83
- **18050** 1500 thru 2002 except Turbo '59 thru '77

BUICK
- **19010** Buick Century '97 thru '05
  - Century (front-wheel drive) - see GM (38005)
- **19020** Buick, Oldsmobile & Pontiac Full-size (Front-wheel drive) '85 thru '05
  - Buick Electra, LeSabre and Park Avenue; Oldsmobile Delta 88 Royale, Ninety Eight and Regency; Pontiac Bonneville
- **19025** Buick Oldsmobile & Pontiac Full-size (Rear wheel drive)
  - Buick Estate '70 thru '90, Electra '70 thru '84, LeSabre '70 thru '85, Limited '74 thru '79
  - Oldsmobile Custom Cruiser '70 thru '90, Delta 88 '70 thru '85, Ninety-eight '70 thru '84
  - Pontiac Bonneville '70 thru '81, Catalina '70 thru '81, Grandville '70 thru '75, Parisienne '83 thru '86
- **19030** Mid-size Regal & Century all rear-drive models with V6, V8 and Turbo '74 thru '87
  - Regal - see GENERAL MOTORS (38010)
  - Riviera - see GENERAL MOTORS (38030)
  - Roadmaster - see CHEVROLET (24046)
  - Skyhawk - see GENERAL MOTORS (38015)
  - Skylark - see GM (38020, 38025)
  - Somerset - see GENERAL MOTORS (38025)

CADILLAC
- **21030** Cadillac Rear Wheel Drive all gasoline models '70 thru '93
  - Cimarron - see GENERAL MOTORS (38015)
  - DeVille - see GM (38031 & 38032)
  - Eldorado - see GM (38030 & 38031)
  - Fleetwood - see GM (38031)
  - Seville - see GM (38030, 38031 & 38032)

CHEVROLET
- **24010** Astro & GMC Safari Mini-vans '85 thru '03
- **24015** Camaro V8 all models '70 thru '81
- **24016** Camaro all models '82 thru '92
- **24017** Camaro & Firebird '93 thru '02
  - Cavalier - see GENERAL MOTORS (38016)
  - Celebrity - see GENERAL MOTORS (38005)
- **24020** Chevelle, Malibu & El Camino '69 thru '87
- **24024** Chevette & Pontiac T1000 '76 thru '87
  - Citation - see GENERAL MOTORS (38020)
- **24027** Colorado & GMC Canyon '04 thru '06
- **24032** Corsica/Beretta all models '87 thru '96
- **24040** Corvette all V8 models '68 thru '82
- **24041** Corvette all models '84 thru '96
- **10305** Chevrolet Engine Overhaul Manual
- **24045** Full-size Sedans Caprice, Impala, Biscayne, Bel Air & Wagons '69 thru '90
- **24046** Impala SS & Caprice and Buick Roadmaster '91 thru '96
  - Impala - see LUMINA (24048)
  - Lumina '90 thru '94 - see GM (38010)
- **24048** Lumina & Monte Carlo '95 thru '05
  - Lumina APV - see GM (38035)

- **24050** Luv Pick-up all 2WD & 4WD '72 thru '82
  - Malibu '97 thru '00 - see GM (38026)
- **24055** Monte Carlo all models '70 thru '88
  - Monte Carlo '95 thru '01 - see LUMINA (24048)
- **24059** Nova all V8 models '69 thru '79
- **24060** Nova and Geo Prizm '85 thru '92
- **24064** Pick-ups '67 thru '87 - Chevrolet & GMC, all V8 & in-line 6 cyl, 2WD & 4WD '67 thru '87; Suburbans, Blazers & Jimmys '67 thru '91
- **24065** Pick-ups '88 thru '98 - Chevrolet & GMC, full-size pick-ups '88 thru '98, C/K Classic '99 & '00, Blazer & Jimmy '92 thru '94; Suburban '92 thru '99; Tahoe & Yukon '95 thru '99
- **24066** Pick-ups '99 thru '06 - Chevrolet Silverado & GMC Sierra '99 thru '06, Suburban/Tahoe/Yukon/Yukon XL/Avalanche '00 thru '06
- **24070** S-10 & S-15 Pick-ups '82 thru '93, Blazer & Jimmy '83 thru '94,
- **24071** S-10 & Sonoma Pick-ups '94 thru '04, Blazer & Jimmy '95 thru '04, Hombre '96 thru '01
- **24072** Chevrolet TrailBlazer & TrailBlazer EXT, GMC Envoy & Envoy XL, Oldsmobile Bravada '02 thru '06
- **24075** Sprint '85 thru '88 & Geo Metro '89 thru '01
- **24080** Vans - Chevrolet & GMC '68 thru '96
- **24081** Chevrolet Express & GMC Savana Full-size Vans '96 thru '05

CHRYSLER
- **25015** Chrysler Cirrus, Dodge Stratus, Plymouth Breeze '95 thru '00
- **10310** Chrysler Engine Overhaul Manual
- **25020** Full-size Front-Wheel Drive '88 thru '93
  - K-Cars - see DODGE Aries (30008)
  - Laser - see DODGE Daytona (30030)
- **25025** Chrysler LHS, Concorde, New Yorker, Dodge Intrepid, Eagle Vision, '93 thru '97
- **25026** Chrysler LHS, Concorde, 300M, Dodge Intrepid, '98 thru '03
- **25027** Chrysler 300, Dodge Charger & Magnum '05 thru '07
- **25030** Chrysler & Plymouth Mid-size front wheel drive '82 thru '95
  - Rear-wheel Drive - see Dodge (30050)
- **25035** PT Cruiser all models '01 thru '03
- **25040** Chrysler Sebring, Dodge Avenger '95 thru '05 Dodge Stratus '01 thru 05

DATSUN
- **28005** 200SX all models '80 thru '83
- **28007** B-210 all models '73 thru '78
- **28009** 210 all models '79 thru '82
- **28012** 240Z, 260Z & 280Z Coupe '70 thru '78
- **28014** 280ZX Coupe & 2+2 '79 thru '83
  - 300ZX - see NISSAN (72010)
- **28018** 510 & PL521 Pick-up '68 thru '73
- **28020** 510 all models '78 thru '81
- **28022** 620 Series Pick-up all models '73 thru '79
  - 720 Series Pick-up - see NISSAN (72030)
- **28025** 810/Maxima all gasoline models, '77 thru '84

DODGE
- 400 & 600 - see CHRYSLER (25030)
- **30008** Aries & Plymouth Reliant '81 thru '89
- **30010** Caravan & Plymouth Voyager '84 thru '95
- **30011** Caravan & Plymouth Voyager '96 thru '02
- **30012** Challenger/Plymouth Saporro '78 thru '83
- **30013** Caravan, Chrysler Voyager, Town & Country '03 thru '06
- **30016** Colt & Plymouth Champ '78 thru '87
- **30020** Dakota Pick-ups all models '87 thru '96
- **30021** Durango '98 & '99, Dakota '97 thru '99
- **30022** Dodge Durango models '00 thru '03 Dodge Dakota models '00 thru '04
- **30023** Dodge Durango '04 thru '06, Dakota '05 and '06
- **30025** Dart, Demon, Plymouth Barracuda, Duster & Valiant 6 cyl models '67 thru '76
- **30030** Daytona & Chrysler Laser '84 thru '89
  - Intrepid - see CHRYSLER (25025, 25026)
- **30034** Neon all models '95 thru '99
- **30035** Omni & Plymouth Horizon '78 thru '90
- **30036** Dodge and Plymouth Neon '00 thru '05
- **30040** Pick-ups all full-size models '74 thru '93
- **30041** Pick-ups all full-size models '94 thru '01
- **30042** Dodge Full-size Pick-ups '02 thru '05
- **30045** Ram 50/D50 Pick-ups & Raider and Plymouth Arrow Pick-ups '79 thru '93
- **30050** Dodge/Plymouth/Chrysler RWD '71 thru '89
- **30055** Shadow & Plymouth Sundance '87 thru '94
- **30060** Spirit & Plymouth Acclaim '89 thru '95
- **30065** Vans - Dodge & Plymouth '71 thru '03

EAGLE
- Talon - see MITSUBISHI (68030, 68031)
- Vision - see CHRYSLER (25025)

FIAT
- **34010** 124 Sport Coupe & Spider '68 thru '78
- **34025** X1/9 all models '74 thru '80

FORD
- **10355** Ford Automatic Transmission Overhaul
- **36004** Aerostar Mini-vans all models '86 thru '97
- **36006** Contour & Mercury Mystique '95 thru '00
- **36008** Courier Pick-up all models '72 thru '82
- **36012** Crown Victoria & Mercury Grand Marquis '88 thru '06
- **10320** Ford Engine Overhaul Manual
- **36016** Escort/Mercury Lynx all models '81 thru '90
- **36020** Escort/Mercury Tracer '91 thru '00
- **36022** Ford Escape & Mazda Tribute '01 thru '03
- **36024** Explorer & Mazda Navajo '91 thru '01
- **36025** Ford Explorer & Mercury Mountaineer '02 thru '06
- **36028** Fairmont & Mercury Zephyr '78 thru '83
- **36030** Festiva & Aspire '88 thru '97
- **36032** Fiesta all models '77 thru '80
- **36034** Focus all models '00 thru '05
- **36036** Ford & Mercury Full-size '75 thru '87
- **36044** Ford & Mercury Mid-size '75 thru '86
- **36048** Mustang V8 all models '64-1/2 thru '73
- **36049** Mustang II 4 cyl, V6 & V8 models '74 thru '78
- **36050** Mustang & Mercury Capri all models Mustang, '79 thru '93; Capri, '79 thru '86
- **36051** Mustang all models '94 thru '04
- **36052** Mustang '05 thru '07
- **36054** Pick-ups & Bronco '73 thru '79
- **36058** Pick-ups & Bronco '80 thru '96
- **36059** F-150 & Expedition '97 thru '03, F-250 '97 thru '99 & Lincoln Navigator '98 thru '02
- **36060** Super Duty Pick-ups, Excursion '99 thru '06
- **36061** F-150 full-size '04 thru '06
- **36062** Pinto & Mercury Bobcat '75 thru '80
- **36066** Probe all models '89 thru '92
- **36070** Ranger/Bronco II gasoline models '83 thru '92
- **36071** Ranger '93 thru '05 & Mazda Pick-ups '94 thru '05
- **36074** Taurus & Mercury Sable '86 thru '95
- **36075** Taurus & Mercury Sable '96 thru '05
- **36078** Tempo & Mercury Topaz '84 thru '94
- **36082** Thunderbird/Mercury Cougar '83 thru '88
- **36086** Thunderbird/Mercury Cougar '89 and '97
- **36090** Vans all V8 Econoline models '69 thru '91
- **36094** Vans full size '92 thru '05
- **36097** Windstar Mini-van '95 thru '03

GENERAL MOTORS
- **10360** GM Automatic Transmission Overhaul
- **38005** Buick Century, Chevrolet Celebrity, Oldsmobile Cutlass Ciera & Pontiac 6000 all models '82 thru '96
- **38010** Buick Regal, Chevrolet Lumina, Oldsmobile Cutlass Supreme & Pontiac Grand Prix (FWD) '88 thru '05
- **38015** Buick Skyhawk, Cadillac Cimarron, Chevrolet Cavalier, Oldsmobile Firenza & Pontiac J-2000 & Sunbird '82 thru '94
- **38016** Chevrolet Cavalier & Pontiac Sunfire '95 thru '04
- **38017** Chevrolet Cobalt & Pontiac G5 '05 thru '07
- **38020** Buick Skylark, Chevrolet Citation, Olds Omega, Pontiac Phoenix '80 thru '85
- **38025** Buick Skylark & Somerset, Oldsmobile Achieva & Calais and Pontiac Grand Am all models '85 thru '98
- **38026** Chevrolet Malibu, Olds Alero & Cutlass, Pontiac Grand Am '97 thru '03
- **38027** Chevrolet Malibu '04 thru '07
- **38030** Cadillac Eldorado '71 thru '85, Seville '80 thru '85, Oldsmobile Toronado '71 thru '85, Buick Riviera '79 thru '85
- **38031** Cadillac Eldorado & Seville '86 thru '91, DeVille '86 thru '93, Fleetwood & Olds Toronado '86 thru '92, Buick Riviera '86 thru '93
- **38032** Cadillac DeVille '94 thru '05 & Seville '92 thru '04
- **38035** Chevrolet Lumina APV, Olds Silhouette & Pontiac Trans Sport all models '90 thru '96
- **38036** Chevrolet Venture, Olds Silhouette, Pontiac Trans Sport & Montana '97 thru '05
  - General Motors Full-size Rear-wheel Drive - see BUICK (19025)

GEO
- Metro - see CHEVROLET Sprint (24075)
- Prizm - '85 thru '92 see CHEVY (24060), '93 thru '02 see TOYOTA Corolla (92036)

(Continued on other side)

Haynes North America, Inc., 861 Lawrence Drive, Newbury Park, CA 91320-1514 • (805) 498-6703

Haynes Automotive Manuals (continued)

NOTE: If you do not see a listing for your vehicle, consult your local Haynes dealer for the latest product information.

40030 Storm all models '90 thru '93
Tracker - see SUZUKI Samurai (90010)

GMC
Vans & Pick-ups - see CHEVROLET

HONDA
42010 Accord CVCC all models '76 thru '83
42011 Accord all models '84 thru '89
42012 Accord all models '90 thru '93
42013 Accord all models '94 thru '97
42014 Accord all models '98 thru '02
42015 Honda Accord models '03 thru '05
42020 Civic 1200 all models '73 thru '79
42021 Civic 1300 & 1500 CVCC '80 thru '83
42022 Civic 1500 CVCC all models '75 thru '79
42023 Civic all models '84 thru '91
42024 Civic & del Sol '92 thru '95
42025 Civic '96 thru '00, CR-V '97 thru '01,
Acura Integra '94 thru '00
42026 Civic '01 thru '04, CR-V '02 thru '04
42035 Honda Odyssey all models '99 thru '04
42037 Honda Pilot '03 thru '07, Acura MDX '01 thru '07
42040 Prelude CVCC all models '79 thru '89

HYUNDAI
43010 Elantra all models '96 thru '01
43015 Excel & Accent all models '86 thru '98

ISUZU
Hombre - see CHEVROLET S-10 (24071)
47017 Rodeo '91 thru '02; Amigo '89 thru '94 and
'98 thru '02; Honda Passport '95 thru '02
47020 Trooper & Pick-up '81 thru '93

JAGUAR
49010 XJ6 all 6 cyl models '68 thru '86
49011 XJ6 all models '88 thru '94
49015 XJ12 & XJS all 12 cyl models '72 thru '85

JEEP
50010 Cherokee, Comanche & Wagoneer Limited
all models '84 thru '01
50020 CJ all models '49 thru '86
50025 Grand Cherokee all models '93 thru '04
50029 Grand Wagoneer & Pick-up '72 thru '91
Grand Wagoneer '84 thru '91, Cherokee &
Wagoneer '72 thru '83, Pick-up '72 thru '88
50030 Wrangler all models '87 thru '03
50035 Liberty '02 thru '04

KIA
54070 Sephia '94 thru '01, Spectra '00 thru '04

LEXUS
ES 300 - see TOYOTA Camry (92007)

LINCOLN
Navigator - see FORD Pick-up (36059)
59010 Rear-Wheel Drive all models '70 thru '05

MAZDA
61010 GLC Hatchback (rear-wheel drive) '77 thru '83
61011 GLC (front-wheel drive) '81 thru '85
61015 323 & Protogé '90 thru '00
61016 MX-5 Miata '90 thru '97
61020 MPV all models '89 thru '94
Navajo - see Ford Explorer (36024)
61030 Pick-ups '72 thru '93
Pick-ups '94 thru '00 - see Ford Ranger (36071)
61035 RX-7 all models '79 thru '85
61036 RX-7 all models '86 thru '91
61040 626 (rear-wheel drive) all models '79 thru '82
61041 626/MX-6 (front-wheel drive) '83 thru '92
61042 626 '93 thru '01, MX-6/Ford Probe
'93 thru '01

MERCEDES-BENZ
63012 123 Series Diesel '76 thru '85
63015 190 Series four-cyl gas models, '84 thru '88
63020 230/250/280 6 cyl sohc models '68 thru '72
63025 280 123 Series gasoline models '77 thru '81
63030 350 & 450 all models '71 thru '80

MERCURY
64200 Villager & Nissan Quest '93 thru '01
All other titles, see FORD Listing.

MGB Roadster & GT Coupe '62 thru '80
MG Midget, Austin Healey Sprite '58 thru '80

...HI
...a, Tredia, Galant, Precis &
...e '83 thru '93

68030 Eclipse, Eagle Talon & Ply. Laser '90 thru '94
68031 Eclipse '95 thru '01, Eagle Talon '95 thru '98
68035 Mitsubishi Galant '94 thru '03
68040 Pick-up '83 thru '96 & Montero '83 thru '93

NISSAN
72010 300ZX all models including Turbo '84 thru '89
72015 Altima all models '93 thru '04
72020 Maxima all models '85 thru '92
72021 Maxima all models '93 thru '04
72030 Pick-ups '80 thru '97 Pathfinder '87 thru '95
72031 Frontier Pick-up '98 thru '04, Xterra '00 thru
'04, Pathfinder '96 thru '04
72040 Pulsar all models '83 thru '86
Quest - see MERCURY Villager (64200)
72050 Sentra all models '82 thru '94
72051 Sentra & 200SX all models '95 thru '04
72060 Stanza all models '82 thru '90

OLDSMOBILE
73015 Cutlass V6 & V8 gas models '74 thru '88
*For other OLDSMOBILE titles, see BUICK,
CHEVROLET or GENERAL MOTORS listing.*

PLYMOUTH
For PLYMOUTH titles, see DODGE listing.

PONTIAC
79008 Fiero all models '84 thru '88
79018 Firebird V8 models except Turbo '70 thru '81
79019 Firebird all models '82 thru '92
79040 Mid-size Rear-wheel Drive '70 thru '87
*For other PONTIAC titles, see BUICK,
CHEVROLET or GENERAL MOTORS listing.*

PORSCHE
80020 911 except Turbo & Carrera 4 '65 thru '89
80025 914 all 4 cyl models '69 thru '76
80030 924 all models including Turbo '76 thru '82
80035 944 all models including Turbo '83 thru '89

RENAULT
Alliance & Encore - see AMC (14020)

SAAB
84010 900 all models including Turbo '79 thru '88

SATURN
87010 Saturn all models '91 thru '02
87011 Saturn Ion '03 thru '07
87020 Saturn all L-series models '00 thru '04

SUBARU
89002 1100, 1300, 1400 & 1600 '71 thru '79
89003 1600 & 1800 2WD & 4WD '80 thru '94
89100 Legacy all models '90 thru '99
89101 Legacy & Forester '00 thru '06

SUZUKI
90010 Samurai/Sidekick & Geo Tracker '86 thru '01

TOYOTA
92005 Camry all models '83 thru '91
92006 Camry all models '92 thru '96
92007 Camry, Avalon, Solara, Lexus ES 300 '97 thru '01
92008 Toyota Camry, Avalon and Solara and
Lexus ES 300/330 all models '02 thru '05
92015 Celica Rear Wheel Drive '71 thru '85
92020 Celica Front Wheel Drive '86 thru '99
92025 Celica Supra all models '79 thru '92
92030 Corolla all models '75 thru '79
92032 Corolla all rear wheel drive models '80 thru '87
92035 Corolla all front wheel drive models '84 thru '92
92036 Corolla & Geo Prizm '93 thru '02
92037 Corolla models '03 thru '05
92040 Corolla Tercel all models '80 thru '82
92045 Corona all models '74 thru '82
92050 Cressida all models '78 thru '82
92055 Land Cruiser FJ40, 43, 45, 55 '68 thru '82
92056 Land Cruiser FJ60, 62, 80, FZJ80 '80 thru '96
92065 MR2 all models '85 thru '87
92070 Pick-up all models '69 thru '78
92075 Pick-up all models '79 thru '95
92076 Tacoma '95 thru '04, 4Runner '96 thru '02,
& T100 '93 thru '98
92078 Tundra '00 thru '05 & Sequoia '01 thru '05
92080 Previa all models '91 thru '95
92081 Prius all models '01 thru '08
92082 RAV4 all models '96 thru '05
92085 Tercel all models '87 thru '94
92090 Toyota Sienna all models '98 thru '02
92095 Highlander & Lexus RX-330 '99 thru '06

TRIUMPH
94007 Spitfire all models '62 thru '81
94010 TR7 all models '75 thru '81

VW
96008 Beetle & Karmann Ghia '54 thru '79
96009 New Beetle '98 thru '05
96016 Rabbit, Jetta, Scirocco & Pick-up gas
models '75 thru '92 & Convertible '80 thru '92
96017 Golf, GTI & Jetta '93 thru '98
& Cabrio '95 thru '98
96018 Golf, GTI, Jetta & Cabrio '99 thru '02
96020 Rabbit, Jetta & Pick-up diesel '77 thru '84
96023 Passat '98 thru '01, Audi A4 '96 thru '01
96030 Transporter 1600 all models '68 thru '79
96035 Transporter 1700, 1800 & 2000 '72 thru '79
96040 Type 3 1500 & 1600 all models '63 thru '73
96045 Vanagon all air-cooled models '80 thru '83

VOLVO
97010 120, 130 Series & 1800 Sports '61 thru '73
97015 140 Series all models '66 thru '74
97020 240 Series all models '76 thru '93
97040 740 & 760 Series all models '82 thru '88
97050 850 Series all models '93 thru '97

TECHBOOK MANUALS
10205 Automotive Computer Codes
10206 OBD-II & Electronic Engine Management
Systems
10210 Automotive Emissions Control Manual
10215 Fuel Injection Manual, 1978 thru 1985
10220 Fuel Injection Manual, 1986 thru 1999
10225 Holley Carburetor Manual
10230 Rochester Carburetor Manual
10240 Weber/Zenith/Stromberg/SU Carburetors
10305 Chevrolet Engine Overhaul Manual
10310 Chrysler Engine Overhaul Manual
10320 Ford Engine Overhaul Manual
10330 GM and Ford Diesel Engine Repair Manual
10333 Building Engine Power Manual
10340 Small Engine Repair Manual, 5 HP & Less
10341 Small Engine Repair Manual, 5.5 - 20 HP
10345 Suspension, Steering & Driveline Manual
10355 Ford Automatic Transmission Overhaul
10360 GM Automatic Transmission Overhaul
10405 Automotive Body Repair & Painting
10410 Automotive Brake Manual
10411 Automotive Anti-lock Brake (ABS) Systems
10415 Automotive Detailing Manual
10420 Automotive Electrical Manual
10425 Automotive Heating & Air Conditioning
10430 Automotive Reference Manual & Dictionary
10435 Automotive Tools Manual
10440 Used Car Buying Guide
10445 Welding Manual
10450 ATV Basics
10452 Scooters, Automatic Transmission 50cc
to 250cc

SPANISH MANUALS
98903 Reparación de Carrocería & Pintura
98904 Carburadores para los modelos
Holley & Rochester
98905 Códigos Automotrices de la Computadora
98910 Frenos Automotriz
98913 Electricidad Automotriz
98915 Inyección de Combustible 1986 al 1999
99040 Chevrolet & GMC Camionetas '67 al '87
Incluye Suburban, Blazer & Jimmy '67 al '91
99041 Chevrolet & GMC Camionetas '88 al '98
Incluye Suburban '92 al '98, Blazer &
Jimmy '92 al '94, Tahoe y Yukon '95 al '98
99042 Chevrolet & GMC Camionetas
Cerradas '68 al '95
99055 Dodge Caravan & Plymouth Voyager '84 al '95
99075 Ford Camionetas y Bronco '80 al '94
99077 Ford Camionetas Cerradas '69 al '91
99088 Ford Modelos de Tamaño Mediano '75 al '86
99091 Ford Taurus & Mercury Sable '86 al '95
99095 GM Modelos de Tamaño Grande '70 al '90
99100 GM Modelos de Tamaño Mediano '70 al '88
99106 Jeep Cherokee, Wagoneer & Comanche
'84 al '00
99110 Nissan Camioneta '80 al '96, Pathfinder '87 al '95
99118 Nissan Sentra '82 al '94
99125 Toyota Camionetas y 4Runner '79 al '95

Over 100 Haynes
motorcycle manuals
also available

10-07